*Studies in Military and Strategic History*

General Editor: **Michael Dockrill**, Professor of Diplomatic History, King's College, London

*Published titles include:*

Nigel John Ashton
EISENHOWER, MACMILLAN AND THE PROBLEM OF NASSER
Anglo-American Relations and Arab Nationalism, 1955–59

Christopher M. Bell
THE ROYAL NAVY, SEAPOWER AND STRATEGY BETWEEN THE WARS

Peter Bell
CHAMBERLAIN, GERMANY AND JAPAN, 1933–34

Antony Best
BRITISH INTELLIGENCE AND THE JAPANESE CHALLENGE IN ASIA, 1914–1941

Philippe Chassaigne and Michael Dockrill (*editors*)
ANGLO-FRENCH RELATIONS, 1898–1998
From Fashoda to Jospin

Michael J. Cohen and Martin Kolinsky (*editors*)
BRITAIN AND THE MIDDLE EAST IN THE 1930s
Security Problems, 1935–39

Paul Cornish
BRITISH MILITARY PLANNING FOR THE DEFENCE OF GERMANY, 1945–50

Michael Dockrill
BRITISH ESTABLISHMENT PERSPECTIVES ON FRANCE, 1936–40

Michael Dockrill and John Fisher
THE PARIS PEACE CONFERENCE, 1919
Peace without Victory?

Robert Frazier
ANGLO-AMERICAN RELATIONS WITH GREECE
The Coming of the Cold War, 1942–47

John P.S. Gearson
HAROLD MACMILLAN AND THE BERLIN WALL CRISIS, 1958–62

John Gooch
ARMY, STATE AND SOCIETY IN ITALY, 1870–1915

G.A.H. Gordon
BRITISH SEA POWER AND PROCUREMENT BETWEEN THE WARS
A Reappraisal of Rearmament

Raffi Gregorian
THE BRITISH ARMY, THE GURKHAS AND COLD WAR STRATEGY IN THE FAR EAST, 1947–1954

Stephen Hartley
THE IRISH QUESTION AS A PROBLEM IN BRITISH FOREIGN POLICY, 1914–18

Brian Holden Reid
J.F.C. FULLER: Military Thinker

Ashley Jackson
WAR AND EMPIRE IN MAURITIUS AND THE INDIAN OCEAN

Stewart Lone
JAPAN'S FIRST MODERN WAR
Army and Society in the Conflict with China, 1894–95

Thomas R. Mockaitis
BRITISH COUNTERINSURGENCY, 1919–60

Bob Moore and Kent Fedorowich
THE BRITISH EMPIRE AND ITS ITALIAN PRISONERS OF WAR, 1940–47

T.R. Moreman
THE ARMY IN INDIA AND THE DEVELOPMENT OF FRONTIER WARFARE, 1849–1947

Kendrick Oliver
KENNEDY, MACMILLAN AND THE NUCLEAR TEST-BAN DEBATE, 1961–63

Elspeth Y. O'Riordan
BRITAIN AND THE RUHR CRISIS

G.D. Sheffield
LEADERSHIP IN THE TRENCHES
Officer–Man Relations, Morale and Discipline in the British Army in the Era of the First World War

Adrian Smith
MICK MANNOCK, FIGHTER PILOT
Myth, Life and Politics

Martin Thomas
THE FRENCH NORTH AFRICAN CRISIS
Colonial Breakdown and Anglo-French Relations, 1945–62

Simon Trew
BRITAIN, MIHAILOVIC AND THE CHETNIKS, 1941–42

Steven Weiss
ALLIES IN CONFLICT
Anglo-American Strategic Negotiations, 1938–44

---

**Studies in Military and Strategic History**
**Series Standing Order ISBN 0–333–71046–0**
*(outside North America only)*

You can receive future titles in this series as they are published by placing a standing order. Please contact your bookseller or, in case of difficulty, write to us at the address below with your name and address, the title of the series and the ISBN quoted above.

Customer Services Department, Macmillan Distribution Ltd, Houndmills, Basingstoke, Hampshire RG21 6XS, England

---

# British Intelligence and the Japanese Challenge in Asia, 1914–1941

Antony Best

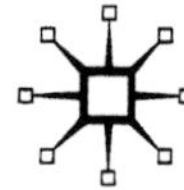



Published by
PALGRAVE MACMILLAN
Houndmills, Basingstoke, Hampshire RG21 6XS and
175 Fifth Avenue, New York, N. Y. 10010
Companies and representatives throughout the world

PALGRAVE MACMILLAN is the global academic imprint of the Palgrave Macmillan division of St. Martin's Press, LLC and of Palgrave Macmillan Ltd. Macmillan® is a registered trademark in the United States, United Kingdom and other countries. Palgrave is a registered trademark in the European Union and other countries.

ISBN-13: 978–0–333–94551–3
ISBN-10: 0–333–94551–4

This book is printed on paper suitable for recycling and made from fully managed and sustained forest sources.

A catalogue record for this book is available from the British Library.

Library of Congress Catalog Card Number: 2002019507

Printed and bound in Great Britain by
CPI Antony Rowe, Chippenham and Eastbourne

*This book is dedicated with all my love to Saho*

# Contents

# List of Maps

# List of Figures and Tables

**Figures**



**Tables**

# Usages and Abbreviations

In this book I have followed the Japanese style of putting the family name first (except in the acknowledgements); Chinese names are given in Wade-Giles as this was the contemporary usage. Formosa has been used in preference to Taiwan. Persia is used for Iran, and Siam for Thailand until these countries changed their names. The following abbreviations appear in the text:

| | |
|---|---|
| AID | Air Intelligence Directorate |
| AMA | Assistant Military Attaché |
| ANA | Assistant Naval Attaché |
| BAT | British-American Tobacco Company |
| BJ | Blue Jacket (the name given to British decrypts of foreign diplomatic correspondence) |
| BSC | British Security Coordination |
| 'C' | Designation for the head of the Secret Service |
| CCP | Chinese Communist Party |
| CER | Chinese Eastern Railway |
| CIB | China Intelligence Bureau |
| CID | Committee of Imperial Defence |
| C-in-C | Commander-in-Chief |
| CMC | Chinese Maritime Customs Service |
| COIC | Combined Operational Intelligence Centre, Australia |
| COIS | Chief of Intelligence Staff at the FECB |
| COS | Chiefs of Staff |
| DCI | Directorate of Criminal Intelligence |
| DCOIS | Deputy Chief of Intelligence Staff at the FECB |
| DIB | Delhi Intelligence Bureau, India |
| DMI | Director of Military Intelligence |
| DMOI | Director of Military Intelligence and Operations |
| DNI | Director of Naval Intelligence |
| DSO | Defence Security Officer |
| ECCI | Executive Committee of the Comintern |
| FEIB | Far East Intelligence Bureau |
| FECB | Far East Combined Bureau |
| FESS | Far Eastern Security Service |
| FMS | Federated Malay States |
| GCCS | Government Code and Cipher School |
| GOC | General Officer Commanding |
| IB | Intelligence Bureau, Shanghai, 1916–20 |

| | |
|---|---|
| IDCEU | Inter-Departmental Committee on Eastern Unrest |
| IGP | Inspector-General of Police |
| IIC | Industrial Intelligence Centre |
| IJA | Imperial Japanese Army |
| IJN | Imperial Japanese Navy |
| JIC | Joint Intelligence Sub-Committee |
| JN-25 | IJN Operational Code from 1939 |
| JNMIB | Joint Naval and Military Intelligence Bureau, Hong Kong |
| JPS | Joint Planning Staff |
| KMT | Kuomintang |
| MBPI | Malayan Bureau of Political Intelligence |
| MCIB | Malayan Combined Intelligence Bureau |
| MCP | Malayan Communist Party |
| MEW | Ministry of Economic Warfare |
| MI1c | Designation for the Secret Service during the Great War |
| MI2c | Section within MID dealing with East Asia |
| MI5 | The Security Service |
| MID | Military Intelligence Directorate |
| MLC | Motorized Landing Craft |
| NCP | Nanyang Communist Party |
| NCO | Non-Commisioned Officer |
| NID | Naval Intelligence Directorate |
| NRA | National Revolutionary Army |
| ODC | Overseas Defence Sub-Committee |
| OM | Oriental Mission (SOE Far East in 1941) |
| PKI | Indonesian Communist Party |
| PNIO | Pacific Naval Intelligence Organization |
| POW | Prisoner of war |
| RAF | Royal Air Force |
| RAN | Royal Australian Navy |
| RDF | Radio Direction-Finding |
| RNZN | Royal New Zealand Navy |
| SAC | Strategic Appreciation Sub-Committee |
| Shaforce | Shanghai Defence Force |
| SIC | Shanghai Intelligence Centre (from 1935) |
| SIGINT | Signals Intelligence |
| SIS | Secret Intelligence Service (Designation for the Secret Service from 1921) |
| SMP | Shanghai Municipal Police |
| SMR | South Manchurian Railway |
| SOE | Special Operations Executive |
| TSR | Trans-Siberian Railway |
| USN | United States Navy |
| WT | Wireless Transmission |
| 'Y' work | Wireless Interception Intelligence |

# Acknowledgements

It is a pleasure to show my appreciation to those who have assisted me in the writing of this book. First I would like to thank the staff at the following institutions for their kind assistance: the Public Record Office; the India Office Library; the Australian War Memorial in Canberra; the Australian National Archives in Canberra and Melbourne (particularly Rosemary Reddick); Birmingham University Library; the Bodleian Library, Oxford; the British Museum Manuscripts Section (particularly Ann Summers for help with the Layton papers); Churchill College, Cambridge; the Imperial War Museum, London; the Liddell Hart Centre for Military Archives, Kings College, London; the Middle East Centre and the Library at St Antony's College, Oxford; the National Maritime Museum, London; Rhodes House Library, Oxford; and Sheffield University Library. I would also like to thank I.D. Goode at the Ministry of Defence, Alan Glennie at the Cabinet Office and the staff of the Foreign Office's Record and Historical Department for declassifying records on my behalf. I am also appreciative to Frank Cass & Company for permission to base Chapter 9 of this book on my article: '"This Probably Over-Valued Military Power": British Intelligence and Whitehall's Perception of Japan, 1939–41', *Intelligence and National Security*, 12 (1997) and to use material from my article 'Intelligence, Diplomacy and the Japanese Threat to British Interests, 1914–41', *Intelligence and National Security*, 17 (2002).

Records from the Public Record Office and the India Office Library appear by permission of the Controller of Her Majesty's Stationery Office. I would like to acknowledge the Trustees of the Liddell Hart Centre for Military Archives for permission to use quotations from the papers in their care; the Trustees of the National Maritime Museum for the Tait papers, the Avon Trustees for the Avon papers; the Department of Documents at the Imperial War Museum and the individual copyright holders for the Grimsdale, Penney, Percival and Vinden papers (every effort has been made to gain permission to use quotations from the Drage, Eady, Godfrey, Maunsell, Pollard, Ross and Ward's papers); and the Director of the Middle East Centre at St. Antony's College for the Lampson papers.

This book has been written and researched in a number of 'homes' and many kind people have provided assistance. Professor Takahiko Tanaka at Hitotsubashi University kindly looked after me during my sabbatical in Tokyo in 1997, and as usual provoked me into deep thinking; he has my profound gratitude. From the summer of 1999 until the spring of 2000 I was given the honour of being invited as a visiting research scholar to the Institute for Research into Humanities (Jinbunken) at Kyoto University and I would like to express my great appreciation to Professor Yuzo Yamamoto and his colleagues for their kindness towards me. In May 2000 I had the chance to visit Australia for research and would like to thank Dr Frank Cain of the Royal Military College and Professor David Horner at Australian National University for their assistance. Words are not enough to thank Joe Straczek of the Naval History Directorate in the Department of Defence in Canberra who steered me towards numerous invaluable documents, who provided guidance on the history of Australian intelligence during the last stages of this book, and who nearly bankrupted me by taking me to all the second-hand bookshops in the city.

Among the many fellow historians who have helped to point me towards interesting sources and to understand the issues raised in this book and their wider ramifications for Anglo-Japanese relations, I would particularly like to thank Lorne Breitenhohlner, Douglas Ford, Peter Lowe, Naoko Shimazu, and lastly Richard Aldrich, who told me that I ought to write a book on this subject. Among historians based in Japan I have benefited from conversations with and advice from Professors Makoto Iokibe, Chihiro Hosoya, Yoichi Kibata, and Ken Ishida, and Associate Professors Masataka Matsuura, Hiroshi Nakanishi, Harumi Goto-Shibata, Kiyoshi Aizawa and Tadashi Kuramatsu. In particular I would like to thank Naoto Kagotani, Shigeru Akita and Kaoru Sugihara who helped to look after me in Kyoto for their stimulating ideas and good companionship. Special thanks go to Joe Maiolo and John Ferris, who were kind enough to read this manuscript for me, to Professor Donald Cameron Watt for his support, and most of all to Professor Ian Nish for all his help and guidance over the years.

I would like to thank Masataka, Ryoko and Kyuma Matsuura for their company in London and Sapporo and I hope to give Kyuma his first English lesson in the near future. Andrew Bell, Tracy Dowson and Tim Pope have as always entertained and kept me sane, and 'Arthur', Sue and Frederick Clarke are simply wonderful friends. Jasper the Dog still insists that walking is the best time to engage in thinking and he may be right. My heartfelt thanks also go to my parents, Philip and Muriel Best, for all their support and particularly my father for doing untold wonders to my tortured prose, and to my parents-in-law, Toru and Midori Matsumoto, who have been so kind to me and tolerant of my struggling attempts to communicate in Japanese. Lastly, my warmest thanks and deepest love go to my wife and fellow historian, Saho Matsumoto-Best, who has done more for me than I could ever record and to whom this book is dedicated.

ANTONY BEST

# 1
# Introduction

Intelligence is a subject that fires the popular imagination. Whether in fact or fiction, stories of agents working undercover against all odds to obtain secret information or engage in sabotage against an enemy make for gripping reading. Moreover, the idea of political leaders cynically using intelligence to outwit their foes and manipulate events to their own ends resonates with all those sceptical of authority. Intelligence is thus accepted by the public as a crucial element in Western political culture, but the reality of what it entails is generally poorly understood. Due to the allure of this secret other world the common image is of intelligence as high drama. At its most extreme this has led to an unwarranted belief in the omnipotence of the intelligence services, which in turn has fostered a tendency to postulate that a number of recent tragedies in history, such as the death of President Kennedy, could be 'explained' if only intelligence documents sealed in ultra-secure government filing cabinets around the world were released into the public domain. There are, of course, many shortcomings in this conspiracy theory approach to intelligence, but the greatest concern for historians is that such accounts serve to trivialize the subject, and to detract from the very real contribution that it can make to our understanding of historical events.

In reality the world of intelligence collection, analysis and use is far from sensational. As Brigadier F.H. Vinden, a military intelligence officer in Malaya in the 1930s, pointed out with a hint of regret in his memoirs, 'Intelligence is not always an affair of spies looking through keyholes or of seduction by charming ladies with big black eyes.'[1] Moreover, in contrast to the delusions of conspiracy theorists, intelligence is far from being the only determinant of state action; it is merely one of the tools used to construct policy, and the information that it produces is invariably judged alongside that available from open sources. Thus when attempting to understand its significance, it is always wise to remember the famous description of intelligence by one diplomat as 'the missing dimension' in history.[2] This phrase has become something of a cliché, but it remains important in part because it reminds us that, although intelligence is an important element in policy, one should never forget that it is but *one* dimension of the policy-making process. The obvious corollary therefore is that one must not be tempted to claim too much for intelligence without running the risk of becoming *ipso facto* one-dimensional.

However, the very nature of intelligence, its role as the state's early warning system, means that its study does illuminate aspects of policy-making and thinking that might otherwise remain opaque. For example, as Wesley Wark and Joe Maiolo have demonstrated in the case of British policy towards Germany in the 1930s, intelligence can be used to identify the moment when a potential threat began to be seen as a serious menace and to explain how an enemy's capabilities and ambitions were perceived.[3] Moreover, as Christopher Andrew and Richard Aldrich have shown, study of the evolution of a state's intelligence apparatus and the rivalries between different organizations can reveal a great deal about a country's strategic priorities.[4]

Intelligence can also be important in a more unexpected way, which is that it can act as an entrée into an even more difficult debate. It seems obvious when studying intelligence and the way in which it is analysed that the raw data is not assessed purely on its merits but read in terms of its relationship to pre-existing assumptions based on culturally derived concepts, such as a belief in the importance of 'national characteristics' and racial hierarchies. Accordingly, the study of intelligence can help to shed light on the sensitive issue of the degree to which such factors help to shape perceptions of potential enemies, and how this then influences policy. This is valuable, for the importance of racial images in international history is notoriously hard to measure, largely because it is not easy to reconstruct the mores of a bygone era in an objective manner. Historical studies of race tend either to be broad in sweep, looking at changing attitudes through the twentieth century as a whole, or to focus on its role under the extraordinary circumstances created by war. The value of looking at race through the prism of intelligence is that it provides a middle ground between these two approaches, for one can focus on a specific case study and follow how a particular racial image and its influence on policy evolved over time.[5]

A good illustration of the way in which research on intelligence can be used to illuminate decision-making and the importance of perception is to study its role in the shaping of British policy and attitudes towards East Asia in the period between 1914 and 1941. Historical analysis of this period has largely concentrated on mapping Britain's gradual alienation from Japan that culminated in the outbreak of the Pacific War in December 1941. However, the sheer volume of primary source material available has meant that the work on these years has tended to cover not the whole period but merely one of three episodes, namely the breakdown of the

Britain's priorities and the problems that it faced in acquiring reliable information. In this field this study will look at the relationship between the various intelligence organizations and government departments and see in what ways the differing priorities of these bureaucratic units had a deleterious effect on the development of the intelligence-gathering apparatus. In particular it will analyse whether the requirements of political/diplomatic intelligence and military intelligence were complimentary or conflicting. Linked to this it will examine the degree to which the faulty handling and dissemination of information by the intelligence users in the Foreign Office and the services contributed to Britain's difficulties.

In addition this volume will investigate the effect of the emergence of threats other than Japan and how these influenced and complicated the development of the British intelligence presence. Accordingly, a substantial part of this book will deal with the British reaction to the emergence of the Comintern as a menace to its interests in the 1920s, and look at how the concentration upon the threat from Bolshevism helped to steer Britain at least temporarily away from its concern with Japan. It will also demonstrate how, during the Great War, the intelligence effort against Germany sparked problems within the Anglo-Japanese alliance which in the long term contributed to its demise.

Another important area of enquiry will be to study the problems generated by the limited resources available to the intelligence organizations and especially the consequences for the gathering of intelligence. In particular a key question is the degree to which British understanding of the region was hamstrung by the difficulty in acquiring intelligence personnel who were proficient in the indigenous languages, most notably Japanese. Historians have too often ignored the difficulties caused by the language-barrier, but quite clearly it is an essential area of investigation for a monograph of this sort. This book will therefore look at how Britain approached the subject of language training, what difficulties arose in this area, and how this more broadly affected the intelligence-gathering effort.

Lastly it is necessary to state what issues this book will not cover. The most obvious point to emphasize is that it will not deal in much detail with day-to-day diplomacy, even though intelligence had a marked effect on such areas as the outcome of the three naval limitation conferences that met in the inter-war period. In addition, for reasons of space, it will not concern itself much with counter-espionage or with those Britons who spied for Japan, such as Frederick Rutland, Herbert Greene and Patrick Heenan.[10] They will have to wait for another day.

## Intelligence organization and sources

Before moving on to to set the scene by looking at British interests at the start of the Great War it is necessary to make a few other introductory remarks. First of all it is important, particularly for the sake of those from an intelligence studies background, to say something about the way in which British intelligence was organized during the Great War and the inter-war period. The key factor to note is that intelligence was not handled in these years by the sort of centralized machinery that evolved during the Second World War and the Cold War, and that accordingly there was not one body at the top of an intelligence pyramid, which disseminated reports to the various departmental customers within Whitehall.

The system that existed prior to 1939 was that the different departments of state received raw intelligence from a variety of sources and then exchanged their assessments (or 'finished all-source intelligence' as it is referred to in intelligence studies parlance) between themselves. No one body was in overall control of this process, but the predominant voice in making policy derived from intelligence was the one organization that contained very few personnel with any intelligence background, the Far East Department of the Foreign Office. The latter's standing rested largely on its function as the guardian of British foreign policy, but was also predicated on the fact that it received a wider and more diverse range of intelligence than any other group, including all diplomatic intercepts and Secret Intelligence Service (SIS) material, most service attaché reports, and many assessments drawn up by the services' intelligence directorates (Figure 1). The result was that the Far Eastern Department provided the most compelling voice in drawing together a consensus in Whitehall on how Japan should be perceived and what policy should be followed.[11] It was only with the strengthening of the Joint Intelligence Sub-Committee (JIC) machinery from 1939 onwards that the flow and use of intelligence became more systematized, thus reducing the Foreign Office's dominance (Figure 2). This point is important because it is only by understanding the lack of central control that one can appreciate many of the resource problems and the inter-departmental rivalries that existed within this period.

It is also important to make a point about intelligence sources. In recent years those interested in intelligence have become accustomed to books making great claims for the contributions made by the highly cerebral world of Signals Intelligence (SIGINT). The result is that the significance of intelligence gathered from human sources has tended to be overlooked except in the most dramatic SIS cases. However, in examining British intelligence in East Asia it is vital to recognize that a great deal of information emanated from the local European communities and occasionally from indigenous sources. Moreover, in order to understand the environment within which the intelligence was collected, and indeed the nature of the British presence in East Asia, it is vital to look at these informants in more detail.

Who, then, were these largely uncelebrated suppliers of intelligence? The answer is that they came from backgrounds that reflected the full range of

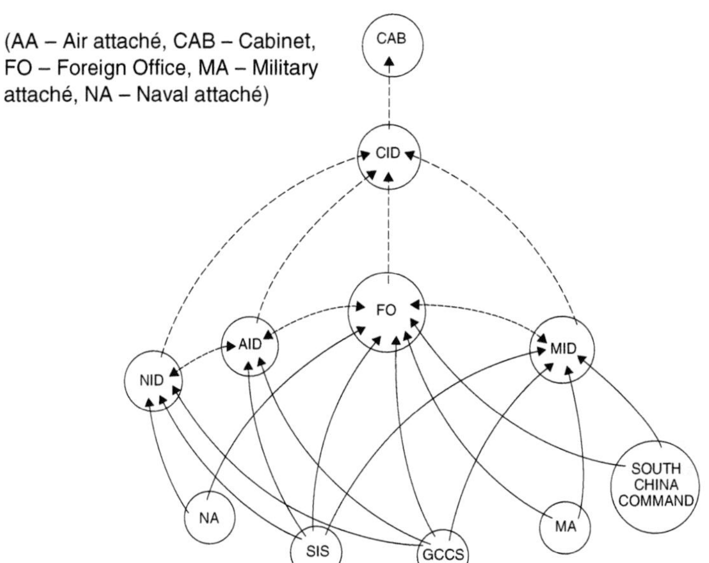


*Figure 1* Intelligence flow into and around Whitehall, 1924

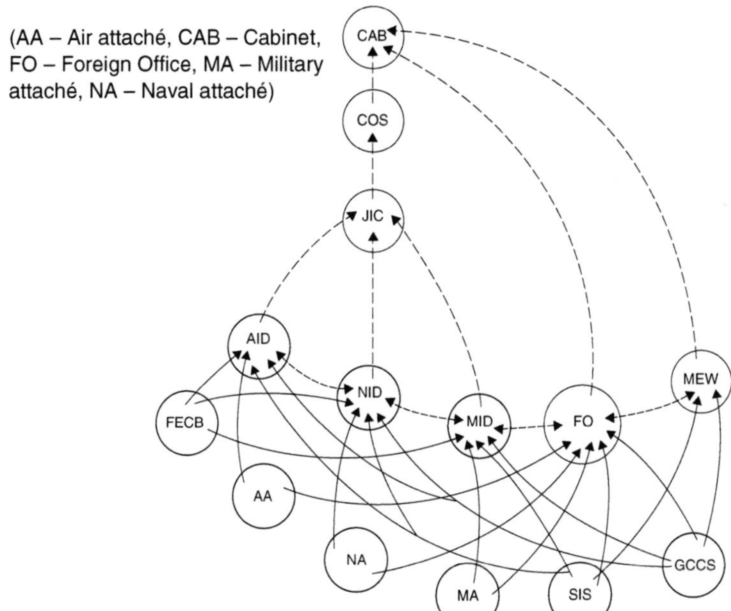


*Figure 2* Intelligence flow into and around Whitehall, 1941

European interests in the East. Those working in intelligence were united in the belief that the best information came from British businessmen. One reason why the latter were seen as extremely valuable was that they travelled widely and visited places not normally frequented by intelligence staff. For example the employees of British-American Tobacco (BAT) were considered useful because the company had interests in the interior in regions such as north China, Manchuria and Mongolia.[12] Businessmen were also considered reliable because their class background and experience of life mirrored that of the officer corps. As one military intelligence officer, Colonel W.F. Blaker, observed in 1928 in a report dealing with the state of British intelligence in the region, 'The type of man who lends a hand is almost invariably a gentleman or the nearest approach to one; he is generally a public school-boy and frequently an ex-officer.'[13] After 1918 the fact that many businessmen had served in the Great War was naturally considered a distinct advantage for, as Blaker noted, this meant that they knew 'something of soldiering and what to look for'.[14] In addition businessmen were considered good sources because the profit motive meant that firms had a great incentive to collect information in order to stay ahead of their rivals. Indeed many of the larger British companies operating in the region maintained what amounted to a private intelligence service, and were willing to share their information with the authorities.[15]

Journalists were another important source of information. Intelligence organizations frequently engaged in a quid pro quo arrangement whereby the news gathered by local British correspondents would be exchanged for private briefings. Certain individual journalists were considered very well informed and thus attracted special attention; in particular it appears that in the 1920s Sir Percival Phillips of *The Times* was close to the intelligence community.[16] Trusted journalists would sometimes be given intelligence assignments if they travelled to areas of special interest. For example, as will be related below, Peter Fleming of *The Times* was presented with a War Office questionnaire before his visit to Manchukuo in 1933–34.[17] The most significant of the links with the press was the one developed with the Reuters representatives in the region, who often allowed intelligence staff prior knowledge of their reports to London.[18] Links were also established with foreign journalists, including a number from Germany. One useful source in the late 1930s was the German Jew, Guenther Stein, who was an expert on the Japanese economy and was later rumoured to be part of the infamous spy-ring led by his fellow German, Richard Sorge.[19]

Linked to the above was the information garnered from visiting regional academic specialists. Such individuals were valuable because they tended to speak and read either Chinese or Japanese and had sources that might otherwise be impossible to reach. Some of the most valuable were those who specialized in studying the outlying areas of the region, such as Mongolia and Sinkiang, as the intelligence that could be gleaned from them would otherwise be unattainable. In addition left-leaning or progressive academics could prove useful in briefing intelligence officers about political radicals. For example, after the American academic Owen Lattimore visited the Chinese Communist Party's (CCP) headquarters at Yenan in the first half of 1937, he met with a British military intelligence officer at Hong Kong who reported his observations to the War Office in London.[20]

Missionaries were another important source of intelligence on the Chinese interior, as they were often the only non-natives living in the remotest areas. During the period of the Great War Findlay Andrew, a missionary at the China Inland Mission at Lanchow in Kansu, provided useful material on Europeans and Japanese travelling into Mongolia and Sinkiang.[21] Surprisingly, considering Britain's religious history, the intelligence services tended to consider information from Catholic missionaries, who were mainly Irish or Italian, to be the most reliable. One reason was that they were seen as more willing than the Protestants to live among the Chinese people. This led to the belief, as Blaker stated, 'that what Roman Catholic missionaries don't know about their surroundings is generally not worth bothering about'. They were also considered to be reliable because their conservative outlook meant that they held 'sound views on political and social questions', which contrasted with the, mostly American, Protestant missionaries, who contained in their ranks 'a certain percentage of cranks full of impracticable, utopian ideas which warp their judgement'.[22]

Useful information was also generated by those European personnel who worked for organs of the Chinese government, such as the Chinese Maritime Customs (CMC) and the postal service. However, as Blaker acknowledged, the number of individuals in such posts who were willing to risk their pensions by engaging in such activities was comparatively small, and probably decreased as the Chinese tightened their grip on these foreign-staffed institutions.[23] In addition, intelligence could be obtained from shady British adventurers, such as Morris 'Two Guns' Cohen, who worked for Chinese warlords, and from some of the German officers who advised Chiang Kai-shek on military matters in the 1930s, notably Captain Walther Stennes.[24]

Unfortunately, very little information exists about how these individuals were handled, but it will be apparent from later chapters that on a number of occasions they supplied very significant intelligence, particularly on events in China. It is also worth noting in this context that, when Britain needed to expand its intelligence resources in Asia in the run-up to the Pacific War, a number of businessmen, journalists and missionaries entered government service. For example, the pre-war head of ICI in China, Valentine Killery, became the leader of the Special Operations Executive (SOE) at Singapore, while Findlay Andrew was engaged in SOE work in China, and Guenther Stein was recommended to the SOE by his friend

Sir Archibald Clark-Kerr, the ambassador to China.[25] The clear implication is that such individuals already had connections in the intelligence world.

## Documentary sources

One final introductory point also unfortunately needs to be made, which is that one must enter a caveat about the primary sources. Despite the fact that recently the British government has become more liberal in releasing documents, any historian writing on intelligence has to use a documentary record that is invariably incomplete. In the case of British intelligence one is still faced with the closure of the files of the SIS, although some of its reports exist in the records of other departments, while the Security Service (MI5) has been only a little more generous. In addition there is the problem that some records were destroyed contemporaneously. At the outbreak of the Pacific War the files of organizations such as the Tokyo embassy and the Far East Combined Bureau (FECB) were burnt in order to deny them to the Japanese. In Britain itself some records were lost in the dark days of 1940; for example, the War Office decided in May to destroy documents over three years old that in *its* judgement did not contain anything valuable from 'an intelligence or historical point of view'.[26] In addition Germany did its bit to deny historians when its bombs destroyed part of the War Office repository during the Blitz.[27] Above and beyond that there is simply the fact that the government cannot for reasons of space keep all records for perpetuity; for example, the records of the Junior JIC and the majority of the War Office's Special Far Eastern Intelligence Summaries have been destroyed.[28]

Even when raw intelligence has survived and been released the problems continue, for in many cases it is difficult to see how policy-makers interpreted this material. For example, the intercepted telegrams of foreign powers (or BJs as they were known) which were circulated around Whitehall by the Government Code and Cypher School (GCCS) have recently become available to researchers. However, there are very few Foreign Office files that indicate how this material was interpreted and thus influenced policy. Hints exist in released Foreign Office documents that comments were made on the BJs and on SIS reports in separate files not entered into the General Correspondence series. However, it transpires that in order to keep knowledge of the intercepts as secret as possible these files were destroyed soon after being compiled.[29] What we have then is but a fragmentary record, which despite all our hopes will never be complete. However, there are enough records in existence to give us some idea of how intelligence influenced policy and policy-makers and to show how, by helping to build up the British image of Japan, it contributed to the process of Anglo-Japanese alienation and eventually to the outbreak of the Pacific War.

# 2
# The British Empire in East Asia in 1914

In 1914 Britain's colonies and interests in East and South-East Asia constituted a vital part of its global portfolio. From the beginning of the nineteenth century its commercial and financial interests had spread throughout the region. In China its substantial economic stake meant that Britain was the dominant foreign presence, with the Hong Kong and Shanghai Bank as the most important foreign financial institution and with major investments in railway construction and shipping. Moreover, Britain's presence was territorial as well as commercial; it possessed the colony of Hong Kong and, although its nationals shared the International Settlement at Shanghai with those from other countries, they held virtually complete sway over the Shanghai Municipal Council. In South-East Asia Britain's interests were concentrated in the Malayan peninsula. Here it directly governed the Straits Settlements, consisting of Singapore, Malacca and Penang, and indirectly ruled over the Federated Malay States (FMS) of Pahang, Perak, Selangor and Negri Sembilan, and the Unfederated Malay States of Johore, Perlis, Kedah, Kelantan, and Trengganu. In addition, it had *de facto* control over northern Borneo consisting of Sarawak, Brunei and the territory controlled by the North Borneo Chartered Company. These territories in South-East Asia were important producers of raw materials such as high-quality rubber, tin and oil, while Singapore was the major entrepôt port in the region. To the south and west of South-East Asia the British Empire had other even more vital interests. To the south lay the White Dominions of Australia and New Zealand. To the west was Britain's most prized possession – India, and under Indian authority lay Burma, the region's leading producer of rice.

In order to defend its interests in East and South-East Asia, Britain maintained a number of military garrisons and naval bases. In north China, as a result of the Treaty of Peking of 1901, Britain and the other major foreign powers had the right to station troops in order to ensure access to the capital. Britain thus maintained an army brigade at Tientsin, which acted as the headquarters of the General Officer Commanding (GOC) North

China, and stationed a legation guard in Peking itself. In addition, it controlled the naval port at Weihaiwei on the northern tip of the Shantung peninsula. Due to its pleasant summer climate this was used as a retreat for the ships on the Royal Navy's China Station from June to September each year. In central China the navy maintained a flotilla of gunboats on the Yangtse and its tributaries which could sail into the interior as far as Chungking, while there were facilities to station troops at Shanghai and Hankow should this prove necessary. In the south, Hong Kong acted as the headquarters for the GOC South China and for the Commander-in-Chief (C-in-C) China Station. There were also British forces in Malaya, with Singapore acting as the headquarters of the GOC Straits Settlements and of

1 East and South-East Asia in 1914

the Royal Navy's local command. Beyond the region lay the vast reservoirs of manpower available to the Indian Army, which had a strength of 155,000 men, and the much smaller armed forces of Australia and New Zealand.

In order to support these forces in their defence of British interests a rudimentary intelligence organization had been established. In 1904 the Admiralty had appointed intelligence officers to head naval reporting centres in Hong Kong and Singapore and had added another at Shanghai in 1913. These officers were given the task of collecting shipping information from local sources such as consuls and reporting it directly to the Naval Intelligence Directorate (NID) in London. The army intelligence effort was concentrated at Tientsin, Hong Kong and Singapore. In Hong Kong the navy and army intelligence officers shared information and together constituted the loosely organized Joint Naval and Military Intelligence Bureau (JNMIB), which was formed in 1911 in response to the need for intelligence during the Chinese revolution.

The work of the intelligence officers was supplemented by that of the service attachés posted to the British embassy at Tokyo and the legation at Peking. The first military attachés were appointed to Tokyo in 1894 and to Peking in 1896. A permanent naval attaché, who was attached to both posts, followed in 1899, although he spent virtually all of his time in Japan. The duties of the attachés consisted of liaising with their hosts, attending manoeuvres, undertaking tours of inspection of serving units, shipyards, arsenals and munitions factories, and producing reports for the head of the diplomatic mission and for their respective intelligence directorates in London. The most important part of their work was providing an assessment of the military effectiveness of their hosts, including an analysis of strategy, tactics, equipment and morale.

Intelligence was also provided by junior officers who had been sent to Japan or China to learn the language. The language officer scheme was first established in Japan in 1903, when four British army officers arrived to receive one year's training in Japanese. Over the next few years this scheme developed apace, with the Indian Army and the Royal Navy also opting to send some of their officers and the practice being expanded to include learning Chinese as well. The idea was to provide a coterie of officers capable of acting as interpreters, who, in the long term, might act as a pool from which to select highly experienced service attachés. It was soon realized in the army that one year was too short a period of study to reach a suitable level of proficiency, leaving officers incapable of anything but the most basic communication. Accordingly, the term of duty was lengthened and by 1911 stood at three years, although the Royal Navy kept to a two-year period. During their stay, the language officers assisted with intelligence through making useful contacts and by assisting the attachés with translation work. Their most valuable contribution, at least on the part of the army officers, was that part of their training consisted of being attached to units and training colleges of the Imperial Japanese Army (IJA). The officers produced lengthy reports on these attachments that contained information that would otherwise be unobtainable from any other source and were highly useful in drawing up a picture of training, equipment and morale. Unfortunately, no such facilities existed for the Royal Navy's officers to be attached to the Imperial Japanese Navy (IJN); only one officer ever received this privilege.[1]

In addition, the diplomatic and consular posts in the region gathered political intelligence from both open and secret sources. The Chinese and Japanese consular services were of particular use because their staff spent virtually all their working lives in the region and were thus immensely experienced and well connected. Their contacts were not limited to the European community, for they underwent rigorous language training and were therefore able to gather information from indigenous sources and the local vernacular press. Their involvement in secret intelligence was, however, limited, as the Foreign Office was loath to let its consuls operate in this field. Moreover, the provision of secret service funds appears to have been haphazard. For example, when in 1914 an informant on seditious Indians in Japan offered information in exchange for money, the ambassador, Sir Conyngham Greene, having no funds available, had to pay him out of his own pocket and then ask to be reimbursed by the Indian government.[2] There is no information to suggest that the position in China was any better.

In Britain's colonies and concessions another useful intelligence source was the local police forces, which kept in close contact with the military, colonial and consular authorities. One particularly useful source was the Shanghai Municipal Police (SMP). This force was, at least in theory, solely responsible to the Municipal Council, but in reality many of its senior figures were British and liaised closely with the British consulate-general and the naval intelligence officer, passing on information about the many undesirable elements who passed through East Asia's most cosmopolitan city.[3]

## The troubled alliance with Japan

Neither these military and naval forces nor the intelligence network were, however, really adequate to defend Britain's interests. The British stake in East Asia lay at the very edge of the Empire, and accordingly always suffered from a lack of resources and difficulties in reinforcement. This position, added to the very obvious threat posed by Russia, led Britain in January 1902 to sign an alliance with Japan, which possessed the largest fleet permanently stationed in the western Pacific. The alliance was renewed in July 1905 and again in July 1911, and proved to be of great benefit, for in 1904–5 the Japanese fought and defeated the Russians, thus reducing the threat from that quarter and allowing the Royal Navy in 1911 to reallocate some of the China squadron ships to the North Sea in order to counter the German menace.[4]

Another useful aspect of the alliance was that it provided a further source of intelligence. In the supplementary military and naval agreements reached between Britain and Japan at the Winchester House conference in July 1902, it was decided that 'all intelligence should be freely exchanged through the channels of the respective British and Japanese naval and military attachés in London and Tokyo' and, in addition, through a Japanese resident military officer who would be stationed in India.[5] This arrangement soon bore fruit. In January 1903 the naval attaché, Captain Troubridge, received from the IJN confidential charts of Korean waters which he then despatched to the C-in-C China and to the Admiralty, and around the same period the Japanese also provided plans of the Russian ports of Port Arthur and Vladivostock.[6] During the Russo-Japanese War, the alliance meant that British military and naval observers were given preferential treatment to those of other countries. This privilege included allowing the naval attaché, Captain Packenham, on Admiral Togo's flagship at the battle of Tsushima, the largest and most decisive naval engagement since Trafalgar. The information garnered from the Japanese military and naval campaigns proved to be of great interest in London, the Committee of Imperial Defence (CID) arranging for the publication of an official history of the Russo-Japanese campaign.[7]

On the surface it might appear that the alliance with Japan was the answer to all of Britain's prayers, for it provided many material advantages, not least the eclipse of the Russian threat. However, beneath the veneer of mutual admiration, it was apparent in the years prior to the outbreak of the Great War that the relationship between Britain and Japan was under strain. The main reason was that the two countries increasingly found their interests clashing over a range of issues, such as Japan's control over south Manchuria, their economic rivalry in the Yangtse valley, Japan's newly won tariff autonomy, and differences over the best political system for post-imperial China. The growing awareness that Japan was itself a rival to British interests meant that the euphoria about the alliance that existed in London in the aftermath of Japan's defeat of Russia began to evaporate, and in its place new negative images of the Japanese emerged.[8]

An important element in the drift towards alienation was the issue of race. In a period when race was considered such a vital element in relations between nations, it was more or less inevitable that mutual miscomprehension and animosity should mar a partnership between two such different racial and cultural entities. It is important to realize in this respect that race was not a simple matter of the British characterizing the Japanese as their racial inferiors and the latter resenting this insult, but that a number of racial images existed. Clearly derogatory views of the Japanese could be found. Among the British trading community, the Japanese were seen as unscrupulous and in military circles the stereotyped image that IJA and IJN officers lacked initiative was already prevalent.[9] However, some contemporary commentators undoubtedly saw Japan in a more positive light, particularly after its victory over Russia. In comparison with other Asian countries, they argued, it had established a rich and vigorous civilization untainted by what was seen as the usual Oriental tendency towards despotism and corruption. Moreover, Japan had shown a laudable ability to modernize, a facet which, as Colin Holmes and Hamish Ion have noted, was seen as having its roots in the discipline of the samurai code of *bushidō*. These supposed qualities meant that at a time when Britain was racked with self-doubt following its tribulations in the Boer War, Japan appeared, to such diverse enthusiasts as Lord Milner and his acolytes, and the Fabians, including famously Sidney and Beatrice Webb, as a guide to the achievement of 'national efficiency'.[10] Indeed, in 1905 one author was so enthused that he compared modern Japan's achievements to those of Ancient Greece and Elizabethan England.[11] Japan was also praised because of the martial spirit of its people. The central place held by military ethics in Japanese life was contrasted with the apparently supine nature of the Chinese, and identified the former as a 'martial race' in much the same way as the northern 'Aryan' tribes of India were singled out for their prowess. To some then, Japan was an Asian power that was qualitatively different from its ill-disciplined neighbours, and thus a worthy ally for Britain. It is also noteworthy in this context that Japan's relative superiority over the other Asiatic races was 'confirmed' by anthropometric research on skull size and motor responses which supposedly showed the Japanese to be more advanced than the more 'primitive' Chinese.[12]

At the same time, however, Japan's relative efficiency as a military state and its clear superiority to other Asian countries meant that there was a thin line between praise and trepidation. The most obvious manifestation of this was the linking of Japan with the idea of the 'Yellow Peril'; that is the fear that the multitudes of Asia might, through sheer force of numbers, turn upon and defeat the 'White' nations. This idea first came to prominence in 1895 when Kaiser Wilhelm II had raised the alarm after the Japanese defeat of China, and received a notable boost when Japan then vanquished the Russians in 1905. The prime concern of those who held to this idea was that as Japan gathered strength it might attempt to provide leadership to the otherwise rudderless masses of Asia, using them as foot soldiers in a challenge to European hegemony. In military terms this idea found expression in the fear of a Chinese army trained and even officered by Japanese. It was widely held at the time that the Chinese soldier was intrinsically of a high quality in terms of both obedience and endurance, but that he lacked leadership as the officer class was irretrievably lost to sloth, incompetence and venality. An infusion of Japanese leadership, it was held, would thus turn the abundant Chinese into a formidable fighting force and pose a serious threat to the West. Another aspect of the 'Yellow Peril' was the danger that, if Japan turned its back on the West and 'rediscovered' its Asian identity, it might seek to support the continent's subject peoples in their struggle for freedom from their European colonial masters. This was of particular concern to Britain because from the 1900s there was a steep rise in political violence in India, and nationalists there openly expressed their admiration of Japan's victory over Russia.[13]

These fears about Japan's potential for leadership in Asia led some commentators to talk of racial war as inevitable and to lament that Britain had ever signed an alliance with a non-white power. Such a combination, it was held, was unnatural on racial grounds and a betrayal of European solidarity; a view epitomized by the journalist B.L. Putnam Weale, who in his book of 1910, *The Conflict of Colour*, argued that '... surely no permanent peace is secured, no racial happiness insured by such unions as the present Anglo-Japanese alliance, which deliberately pits one European state [Britain] against another [Russia] in Asia'.[14] Race was, therefore, important in the period immediately following the Russo-Japanese War because Britain saw the Japanese as the most virile and highly evolved of the Asian races, and thus as the greatest potential threat.

This fear of Japan manifested itself in the political and military spheres in a number of ways. One key concern was that the Japanese community in South-East Asia was preparing the way for conquest. Important in this respect was the development of one of the most pervasive racial stereotypes of the Japanese, the belief that they were naturally over-curious and inclined to indulge in intelligence activities. This distrust of the Japanese arose for a number of reasons. One factor was the propensity of Japanese to engage in areas of employment, such as fishing and photography, which could provide cover for espionage. In addition, the Japanese overseas communities tended to be very insular, and this could easily be interpreted as being deliberately secretive. Once the reputation was established, the idea that all Japanese were intelligence agents quickly became a truism. Some observers were quite rightly sceptical about such a sweeping judgement, but even they sought an explanation for this phenomenon in racial terms. For example, in September 1916 Sir Conyngham Greene argued that the Japanese tendency to eavesdrop arose because an upbringing in houses made of wood and paper naturally encouraged such activity. Thus, he concluded, 'many Japanese are written down as spies and dangerous intriguers all over the world' when in fact they were 'probably harmless, and only following the course of their inherited instincts'.[15]

The growing suspicion of Japan was most evident in one area of great sensitivity – India. With Japan's emergence as the first Asian Great Power in 1905, efforts were made by Indian revolutionaries to interest the Japanese

Pan-Asian lobby, centred around the sinister figure of the veteran nationalist, Tōyama Mitsuru, in their cause. The first evidence that such manoeuvres might work came in 1913 when it transpired that Maulvi Muhammad Baraktullah, a teacher of Urdu at the Tokyo School of Foreign Languages, was using his post to disseminate anti-British propaganda.[16] The Tokyo embassy was so concerned about Baraktullah's activities that it asked the Foreign Office to persuade India to send an intelligence agent to Japan.[17]

At the same time, the Indian Directorate of Criminal Intelligence (DCI) was for its own reasons concerned about Japan's links with Indian revolutionaries. During 1914 Sir Charles Cleveland, the head of the DCI, learned that the Japanese shipping company, Nippon Yusen Kaisha, was engaged in stirring up anti-British feeling and trying to portray Japan as pro-Islam as part of its campaign to win a greater share of the Indian coastal shipping trade.[18] Accordingly, in July 1914 Cleveland requested that a specialist on Japan should be attached to his staff to engage in duties of a 'very secret nature in connection with Japanese community in India', and that the appointment not be publicized.[19] The man chosen was Captain A.M. Cardew of the Royal Engineers, who, as one of his contemporaries noted, was 'a great Japanese scholar' as well as being proficient in Chinese, having studied as a language officer in both Tokyo and Peking. When the inquiry from Tokyo about posting an agent to Japan was received, Cardew had not yet arrived in India. Cleveland therefore postponed making any decision, believing that Cardew should be given time to overhaul intelligence collection on the Japanese in India before dealing with the external situation.[20] He did, however, note that in the future an officer might have to be appointed to keep surveillance on Indians in Japan, particularly as there was now evidence from a Japanese informer linking Baraktullah to a plot to assassinate British officials in Shanghai.[21]

The British suspicion of Japan was also evident in its increasing wariness about exchanging information with the Japanese armed forces. From the start of the alliance the British had been determined that intelligence exchanges should be confined to confidential rather than secret information. Thus when the Japanese military attaché in London had proposed in May 1903 the establishment of 'a joint system of secret service' the offer was politely declined.[22] After 1905 this reluctance to cooperate over exchanging information became even more marked. In September 1909 the Royal Navy decided that in future no information should be given to the Japanese about experimental technology, ships that had not yet been laid down, or changes of tactics until they had been introduced at fleet level.[23] As an Admiralty memorandum of 1918 noted, this gave rise to a position in which:

> Although in theory the Japanese were treated preferentially in regard to the exchange of secret information, in practice little or no confidential

> information as regards material was communicated to them, and we avoided taking advantage of their offers to communicate confidential information of any kind to us.[24]

This secretiveness was, of course, predicated on the belief that the Royal Navy was in a situation where it had little to gain from any exchange as it was technologically so far in advance of the IJN.

However, at the same time Britain's concern about the potential Japanese threat was ameliorated by doubts about whether it would ever be in a position to pose a serious military challenge to British interests. This might seem surprising considering the praise generated by Japan's recent military and naval victories over Russia but, as Philip Towle has noted, following the Russo-Japanese War British observers quickly began to question Japan's martial efficiency and challenge the aura of Japanese invincibility. The only area in which praise was consistently heaped upon Japan was in terms of the morale and patriotism of its troops and officers, for *esprit de corps* was seen as the essential factor that had led the Japanese soldiers to fight without complaint in the wintry wastes of Manchuria. However, the training and equipment of the IJA came in for fierce criticism. This negative image was largely based on observations of the IJA's annual grand manoeuvres, which appeared to demonstrate that it had not understood the lessons of the war, that its officers lacked initiative, and that its staff work was rigid and lacked tactical flexibility. This British perception, as Towle notes, was partly due to differences in approaches to training between the Japanese and British officer corps; the IJA saw manoeuvres as testing staff work, while the British observers came from a background where individual initiative was stressed in such exercises.[25] This difference was important because it was symptomatic of the deep cultural divide between the British and Japanese armed forces. The British officers tended to be recruited from public schools and, as such, had come to laud virtues such as initiative, perseverence and a sense of civic responsibility, seeing these as 'English national characteristics' that underpinned Britain's power and prestige. Coming from such a background, British observers naturally found Japan's excessive communalism and cult of blind obedience alienating. To a degree, these Japanese 'national characteristics' could be viewed as strengths, for they were the basis of the Japanese armed forces' formidable morale, but because they appeared to suffocate initiative, that supposedly vital quality of the good British officer, and to instil rigidity in thinking, they were also deemed to be important weaknesses.[26] The result of this ethnocentric approach was that both the IJA and IJN were viewed as inferior to the British standard and as incapable of catching up due to these racially derived flaws. So pervasive was this view that Japan's supposed weaknesses soon became stereotypes passed from generation to generation.

Moreover, even the deliberate attempt by the Japanese to construct an aura about the singular 'spirit' of their armed forces could backfire, as became evident in the humiliating Siemens scandal of 1913–14. The scandal involved the German armaments firm, Siemens, providing bribes to senior Japanese naval officers in exchange for armaments contracts, news which suggested that the officer class's much vaunted devotion to its duties was the facade rather than the substance. The British service attachés in Tokyo reacted to the scandal with a mixture of shock and derision. For the naval attaché, Captain Brand, the lesson was that 'one can hardly, in the future, be expected to place much value on the honesty and integrity of the [Japanese] Admiralty', and that the whole matter raised questions about how much Japan could be trusted to honour the alliance.[27] The military attaché, Colonel J.A.C. Somerville, concurred in this view, and noted in a report to the War Office that 'if these infernal scoundrels will sell their own country like this, how much more gladly will they sell ours, and any information we may be foolish enough to give them'.[28] Somerville, however, also went further, observing that the case showed that the Navy Ministry was 'one putrid mass of graft and corruption', and that it gave evidence of 'the complete untrustworthiness, where money is concerned, of the whole Japanese race': he even asked rhetorically whether the scandal resulted from the fact that 'they are still too low on the evolutionary ladder'.[29]

The vituperative manner in which Somerville reacted to the Siemens scandal is of interest because both before and afterwards he showed himself to be a keen admirer of the Japanese. He had been one of the earliest of the army's language officers, and had previously recorded his admiration of the 'magnificent fighting spirit' of the IJA and their 'Spartan-like contempt for money'. Later in life, after his retirement from the army in 1925, he became secretary of the Japan Society of London, and in 1936 he asked, after his son's premature death, for his officer's sword to be presented to the IJA regiment to which he had been attached for language duty.[30] That record suggests that Somerville's rough language in 1913 was an aberration caused by the realization that his idealized view of the Japanese officer class had been shattered. As such, this episode hints that one cause of Britain's alienation from Japan in the years before 1914 was that the latter failed to live up to the idealized image that had been created in British minds. Once the 'truth' was revealed, Japan fell from its pinnacle and became once again merely 'Asian', revealing the fine line in racial terms between admiration and contempt.

Clearly, then, in the years before the outbreak of the Great War a dual image of Japan already existed within Britain. On the one hand it feared Japan's expansionism due to the latter's position as the leading Asian state, but on the other doubted its capacity to achieve its ambitions. The result was that there were strains within the alliance, but Britain certainly did not envisage war in the future and India continued to view Russia as its main potential enemy. It is worth noting in this context that there is no evidence from this period that the small cryptographic section attached to the Indian Army's Intelligence Department was attempting to read Japanese diplomatic telegrams, but this section was reading Russian and Chinese ciphers.[31] However, while there was no immediate concern that Japan would turn against Britain, the feeling of suspicion meant that, when mutual confidence was undermined, it did not take much for London to come to the conclusion that Tokyo was harbouring sinister ambitions. These fears would crystallize during the Great War and play an important role in bringing about the termination of the alliance.

# 3
# The Erosion of the Anglo-Japanese Alliance, 1914–21

The Great War in East Asia has not attracted a great deal of scholarly attention. To a large degree this is because the actual hostilities lasted such a short time. The conflict began in the region in August 1914 but by the end of the year a series of victories had placed all the German possessions in the hands of the Entente Powers. In November a Japanese expeditionary corps, with limited assistance from a small British contingent, captured the German lease territory of Kiaochow containing the port of Tsingtao in Shantung province in China, while HMAS *Sydney* forced the surrender of the German cruiser *Emden* at the battle of the Cocos Islands. Then on 8 December the German Pacific naval squadron, after turning Cape Horn, met its end at the battle of the Falkland Islands. In addition, Germany's island colonies in the Pacific were all safely in the hands of Japanese or British Empire forces. These successes, which were a testament to the effectiveness of the Anglo-Japanese alliance, encouraged Whitehall in mid-December to reduce British forces in the region and to rely on the IJN to secure the China Sea. Subsequently, the two China army commands were merged into one with its headquarters at Hong Kong, while the C-in-C China moved his staff to Singapore in order to concentrate with IJN assistance on the threat from German raiders in the Indian Ocean.[1]

However, events over the following four years were to prove that, although Germany had lost its Asian possessions, it still had the power to threaten the British Empire in the east. Operating from the neutral countries in the region, Germany engaged for the rest of the war in a campaign of espionage against British interests, causing unrest particularly in India and China. The result was that the war in East Asia became largely a contest between the British and German intelligence services. This conflict was to have important consequences for the future of Britain's position in Asia. One major effect was that it stimulated the rapid evolution of Britain's regional intelligence-gathering network, thus setting precedents for the inter-war period. Even more significant was that the proliferation of intelligence-gathering played a crucial role in eroding the foundations of the

Anglo-Japanese alliance, for Britain's increased vigilance appeared to reveal that Japan, as well as Germany, was involved in clandestine activities that ran counter to British interests. By the end of the war, Britain's faith in its ally would be severely shaken and the future of the alliance would be in the balance.

## Germany and revolution in India

The first major crisis to disturb East Asia after the eviction of Germany from the region came in January 1915, when the Japanese government of Ōkuma Shigenobu presented its Twenty-One Demands to the Chinese President, Yüan Shih-k'ai. This episode, in which Japan forced Peking to accept a marked extension of its territorial rights and influence in China, led to some disquiet in London at Tokyo's behaviour and fear for the long-term future of British commercial interests.[2] However, despite their later reputation as the first indication of Japan's unquenchable ambitions in Asia, the Demands did not lead to any serious British reaction, such as a reversal of the decision to redeploy its forces. Instead, this crisis was seen merely as an unwelcome distraction from the war. The only British response therefore was to use its diplomatic influence to push for a speedy settlement and, in the aftermath, to press Japan to contribute more wholeheartedly to the vital task of defeating Germany in Europe.

A far more worrying development in the context of the wider war was German-sponsored revolutionary activity among the Indian population in East Asia.[3] The first clear sign of danger came in February 1915, when a mutiny occurred in the ranks of the Indian Fifth Light Infantry regiment as it prepared to leave Singapore for service in the Middle East. This insurrection, which was partly inspired by German prisoners of war (POWs), proved to be a serious affair, and had to be suppressed by a multinational force of British, French, Russian and Japanese military and naval personnel.[4] The mutiny led the newly arrived GOC Straits Settlements, Major-General Dudley Ridout, to conclude that his own intelligence staff needed reinforcing in order to keep an eye upon the activities of disaffected local Indians.

Within the next few weeks the situation worsened, as information from a variety of sources indicated that the Germans were taking advantage of the neutral status of many of the states in the region to encourage Indian sedition. In March reports were received about German activities in Siam, where covert efforts were being made to train and arm an Indian force to invade Burma. The following month the British consul-general in Batavia, W.G. Beckett, reported that members of the substantial German community in the Dutch East Indies were engaged in espionage, and planned to use the islands as a revolutionary centre for Indian unrest.[5] A similar process was evident in China, where the British minister, Sir John Jordan, was increasingly concerned about German efforts to spread sedition among the Sikh population. These activities were particularly disturbing as the Sikhs were the backbone of the SMP and the British Concession police at Hankow. In late June, noting that the matter was too serious to be dealt with by his consular staff, Jordan requested that an official from the Indian DCI be sent to China.[6] In Japan there was some concern about the increasing circulation of revolutionary propaganda, and in April Sir Conyngham Greene ordered the vice-consul at Yokohama, Charles Davidson, to begin his own surveillance of the local Indian population using secret service funds provided by Calcutta.[7]

At first, these outbreaks of German activity appeared to be relatively uncoordinated and thus did not require a centralized response. Soon, however, events suggested that they were part of a larger German plot aimed at delivering a crushing blow to British rule in India. As several historians, including Richard Popperwell and T.G. Fraser, have noted, in the autumn of 1914 Germany and the Indian National Committee in Berlin developed plans to ship a substantial amount of small arms and ammunition from the Pacific coast of the United States to India to be used in an insurrection against the British authorities. This plot foundered due to the incompetence of the participants in America, but not before news of the intended cargo had reached the ears of British intelligence. Not knowing that the plan would sink under its inherent unfeasibility, the British authorities in America and South-East Asia desperately searched for information. These activities were coordinated in Whitehall by an inter-departmental committee consisting of representatives from the Foreign Office, the Colonial Office, the India Office, the Admiralty, and the War Office. In South-East Asia Ridout took the leading role and ran two double agents, Vincent Kraft and 'Oren', who were able to provide vital information on contacts between German intelligence and Indian revolutionaries in Bengal. Armed with this information the DCI in the autumn of 1915 arrested a number of conspirators in Calcutta, thus destroying the Indian end of the operation.[8] However, Britain's problems were not over, for the concerted intelligence-gathering effort revealed further disturbing information. Investigations in Shanghai by the naval intelligence officer, Captain J.W. Seigne, showed that the German consul-general in Shanghai, Knipping, was abusing China's neutrality by attempting to ship arms from the International Settlement for use in the Indian revolution.[9] Further proof of his central role came from confessions made by various suspects arrested at Singapore and from the Admiralty's decrypts of German diplomatic correspondence, in particular letters from Knipping's colleague in Batavia.[10]

## The alliance under pressure

The extent of German support for the Indian revolutionaries was clearly a matter for grave concern, particularly in the light of Britain's decision to keep only skeleton forces in the region. It was therefore logical for Britain to turn to its Japanese ally, to whom it had virtually delegated the security of its interests in the region, for assistance in the counter-espionage campaign against the German menace. Japan, it was believed, could help in a number of ways, such as intercepting ships suspected of carrying seditionaries, arms and propaganda, prohibiting Indian activities in Japan itself, and supporting the Entente's efforts to persuade China to curb Germany's abuse of its neutrality. Unfortunately this call for joint action could not have come at a worse moment, for a number of issues were beginning to strain Anglo-Japanese relations.

The fundamental problem was that Japan appeared to be distinctly tepid in its support for the Entente's war effort. It had refused to commit the IJA to the fighting in Europe, had charged a high price for the munitions it was selling to Russia, and had refused to suppress German commercial interests in Japan. Even more disturbing was that jingoistic Japanese newspapers were openly speculating in the autumn of 1915 that their country might have backed the wrong horse in the European war, and were claiming that Britain had spitefully denied Japan the full fruits of the Twenty-One Demands.[11]

In this unpromising atmosphere it was not surprising that Britain's call for common action against German espionage received a largely negative response. In regard to assistance at sea, where the Royal Navy was greatly overstretched, the IJN proved to be of little help. Much to the frustration of the C-in-C China, Admiral Grant, the IJN ships at Singapore had orders to arrest only Germans on active service, which made them of little use against Indian revolutionaries or intelligence agents masquerading as civilians.[12] In addition Japan proved reluctant to prevent Indians suspected of sedition from travelling in its own merchant ships. It was only when Britain in frustration took matters into its own hands in February 1916 and HMS *Laurentric* intercepted the *Tenyo Maru* and removed nine Indians, that the Japanese decided to refuse passage to Indians without British passports.[13]

In addition, there were problems over the Ōkuma government taking action against Indian revolutionaries residing in Japan. In October 1915 the interrogation of a Bengali arrested in Singapore revealed that an Indian named P.M. Thakur was at that time in Japan. Thakur was of particular interest, because it was suspected that his name was a pseudonym and in reality he was Rash Behari Bose, who in 1911 had been the ringleader of a plot to assassinate the Viceroy of India, Lord Hardinge.[14] Meanwhile, intelligence revealed that another Indian, H.L. Gupta, was soon to arrive in Japan with the express purpose of inspecting the work of the revolutionaries in East Asia, as the Germans were disappointed at the lack of progress.[15] Acting on this information, Greene pressed the Japanese government to detain and deport these individuals, preferably to a British port. The Gaimushō (Japanese Foreign Ministry) promised in early November to comply with this request, but two months later news arrived that Gupta and Bose, having earlier taken refuge in the house of the notorious Tōyama Mitsuru, had now completely disappeared. Unsurprisingly, the reaction in the Foreign Office was one of fury, Sir Beilby Alston of the Far Eastern Department being moved to note that 'the Japanese Govt have certainly not acted as Allies in any sense over this case'.[16]

Even more serious were differences over policy towards China, where Britain's determination to eradicate the German menace came into conflict with Japan's desire to expand its influence. Faced with the evidence of Knipping's activities in Shanghai, the Foreign Office in October 1915 decided that the best way to deal with the situation was to persuade Yüan Shih-k'ai to expel all Germans from China on the grounds that they were infringing its neutrality. This idea met with broad approval from the government in India and from Britain's Entente partners, the Russians being particularly enthusiastic as they had evidence that Knipping was planning to sabotage the Trans-Siberian Railway (TSR).[17] In addition, conditions in China appeared propitious, as Yüan was keen to curry favour with the Entente in order to further his plan to proclaim himself Emperor, and had already indicated his willingness to sell them arms. Therefore, the Entente Powers decided in November 1915 to press China to break off diplomatic relations with Germany, to expel all German nationals, and to begin arms sales, with the explicit hope that this would lead China to enter the war on their side.[18]

Before any overtures could be made to Yüan it was necessary to secure Japanese approval. This proved difficult because Japan, which traditionally distrusted Yüan, had no desire to see him strengthen his authority by either assuming the throne or leading his country into the war. It therefore rejected the Entente's proposal on the spurious grounds that such action might lead pro-German elements in China to initiate a civil war. Even when the Foreign Office presented the Japanese embassy in London with a memorandum detailing the extent of German subterfuge, this failed to sway the Ōkuma government.[19] Further, such was the Japanese opposition to Yüan that from December 1915 it encouraged the provinces of south China to rise up against him, dealing a fatal blow to his political authority.

Japan's hostility towards Yüan cut across the British policy towards China, but its effects went beyond the mere derailing of the attempt to curb German activities, for it also raised new problems. The centre of the campaign to overturn Yüan was Yunnan province, and in order to facilitate its links with the rebels the Japanese strengthened their presence in the provincial capital, Yunnan-fu, by sending an IJA officer to assist its consul. For the Indian government this sudden Japanese interest in Yunnan, which bordered on Burma, led to a wave of panic, for it added substance to the fears that had existed since the pre-war period. Moreover, in 1915 India had already become concerned about what it saw as an increasing Japanese interest in Tibet, and particularly the news that one Japanese traveller had offered to purchase machine guns for the authorities in Lhasa.[20] The Japanese presence in Yunnan thus appeared to fit into a pattern in which Japan was increasing its activities in areas contiguous to India.[21] If this were not enough, Delhi's concern was heightened further by the fact that this interest in Yunnan came to its attention just as it received unsubstantiated reports hinting vaguely at the involvement of Japanese nationals in the Indo-German plots.[22]

Britain's attempt to draw Japan into its counter-espionage campaign thus ended in virtually complete failure, and if anything only compounded the stresses that already existed within the alliance. By early 1916 the strained atmosphere in Anglo-Japanese relations was such that each sensational report bred further suspicion; indeed, the crisis of confidence in the alliance was worse than it had been during the period of the Twenty-One Demands. The effect within Whitehall was to provoke a debate about how to interpret Japan's tardiness and apparent duplicity. This began in April 1916 when A.H. Grant, the Foreign Secretary to the Indian government, produced a lengthy report on the potential threat from Japan. Grant ranged over a variety of issues, noting India's discomfort at Japan's activities in Yunnan and Tibet, and its unwillingness to cooperate in countering the Indo-German plots. In regard to Japanese intelligence-gathering he observed that:

> It is known that Japanese espionage has been actively carried out in India, in Nepal, in Tibet and other neighbouring countries. Up to the present no proof has been obtained of any incitement of the sedition party in India by these agents ... but it is certain that these agents have made and are making a careful study of India's military strength, political questions and commercial possibilities.[23]

In conclusion, Grant stated that India had no wish at that tense time in the war for its fears to be aired publicly, thus straining Anglo-Japanese relations even further, but that it did desire an enhanced intelligence-gathering organization in the region. This report led Sir Arthur Hirtzel, the head of the Political and Secret Department in the India Office, to produce for the Cabinet his own memorandum on the Japanese problem in which he incorporated many of Grant's concerns. At the same time, the General Staff in London prepared its own 'strong indictment of Japan', in which it reiterated the now familiar list of complaints.[24]

Within the Foreign Office a number of views existed. Many officials, including Sir Arthur Nicolson, the outgoing Permanent Under-Secretary, and his successor, the former Viceroy, Lord Hardinge, were as critical of Japan's behaviour as Grant and Hirtzel.[25] Others tried to be more objective. In particular, J.D. Gregory of the Far Eastern Department, who wrote a memorandum in response to the General Staff, noted that, if anything, Japan's behaviour in China had been restrained, for if it had so desired it could already have imposed a Japanese protectorate over the country. Furthermore, he observed that though some Japanese nationals undoubtedly had connections with the Indian revolutionaries there was no evidence of government involvement. Indeed, the government's only crime was its failure, due to its weak domestic position, to curb the excesses of the Japanese press.[26]

This moderate view was corroborated by some of the intelligence information available to the British, which revealed that, while one might argue that Japan was uncooperative and only interested in self-aggrandizement, it was not actively hurting the war effort. For example, intercepted letters from the German diplomats in Asia to Berlin revealed that, apart from the chartering of one Japanese ship to carry arms, there had been no Japanese involvement in the Indian plots in the autumn of 1915. These sources also demonstrated that the effectiveness of the British response to German machinations had led the latter's representatives to become resigned to failure. All that remained for Germany, as Knipping noted in one letter, was to hope that the pro-Indian elements in Japan could be induced to help, but as Captain William 'Blinker' Hall, the Director of Naval Intelligence (DNI), minuted in May 1916, this seemed to be more wishful thinking than anything substantive.[27] This was not for want of trying on Germany's part. On a number of occasions in 1915 and 1916 German diplomats in neutral capitals had approached their Japanese colleagues offering inducements in return for a peace treaty. This included in January and March 1916 offers to transfer its remaining interests in China. The Gaimushō, however, realizing the value of passing on news of these overtures and the firm rejection that they had received, duly informed its allies, thus demonstrating its loyalty to the cause.[28]

After weighing all the evidence, the consensus reached in Whitehall was that Japan was not actively plotting against Britain, but that it did intend to use the war to expand its influence in Asia, and that it would only assist the Entente at a price. Lacking any means of coercing Japan and still needing its assistance, however meagre, Britain had no choice but to reconcile itself to its ally's uncooperative attitude. Thus the correct policy, as the Foreign Secretary, Arthur Balfour, observed in February 1917, was to make the minimum of concessions, to list Japan's misdemeanours for future reference, and to bide time until the war ended and Britain could have a reckoning with its fair-weather ally.[29]

## The evolution of the wartime intelligence network

With little likelihood that Japan would cooperate with Britain against the Indo-German plots, the only option available for the defence of Britain's interests in Asia was to take up the suggestion from India and expand the imperial intelligence shield. From 1916 to 1918 considerable effort was put into this task, the Indian government, the War Office and the Admiralty all adding to their intelligence organizations within the region and the inter-departmental committee in Whitehall providing a degree of coordination. Predictably, the result was that the amount of information available on German and Japanese machinations grew substantially, with further unfortunate ramifications for Anglo-Japanese relations.

The most important initiative in countering the Indo-German plots was the decision to create an Indian DCI office in East Asia. As related above, even before the German plots to ship arms to India were revealed, fears about the loyalty of the Indian population had led to calls for an officer to be sent to the region. The arms plots only heightened this concern, and as early as September 1915 the authorities in India decided to establish an office in Singapore that would be responsible for Indian security throughout the region.[30] The official chosen to fill the post of Indian Intelligence Officer for the Far East was Superintendent David Petrie. Petrie, who later became the head of MI5 during the Second World War, was an experienced police officer in his thirties, who previously had been responsible for the investigation into Bose's attempted assassination of Lord Hardinge. He had already undertaken service in the region in the summer of 1915, giving assistance to Ridout and to Sir Herbert Dering, the minister in Bangkok.[31]

Once Petrie had been appointed the next task was to decide how his office should operate. At first, the Indian government tried to put him in charge of the whole intelligence apparatus in South-East and East Asia. This was successfully resisted by Whitehall, which had already put its faith in Ridout. The result was that it was agreed that Petrie should act primarily as an adviser.[32] The next issue raised was whether Singapore would in fact be the best base for Petrie, considering that the focus of Indo-German activities had now shifted to China and Japan. Events in the summer of 1916 reinforced the impression that Petrie would be more valuable in East Asia, for decrypts of German telegrams and investigations by Davidson in Yokohama indicated that Germany's latest plan was to ship small arms from Japan to Burma via Siam.[33] At the same time, reports from Seigne and Ridout showed that the German community in Shanghai was still endeavouring to sow disorder.[34]

After meeting with Petrie in the summer of 1916, both Greene and Jordan strongly favoured the idea that he should be based at Shanghai. They also supported his plans for controlling the Indo-German menace, which included providing Davidson with agents who could penetrate the Indian community in Japan, and in China appointing a number of intelligence officers to the key ports and using a new Order-in-Council to deport seditious Indians. The inter-departmental committee on Indian sedition agreed to these proposals in October 1916, and to bolster Petrie's efforts recommended that he should be assisted by an inter-departmental intelligence bureau in Shanghai which would 'coordinate the various independent sources of information'.[35]

This latter proposal did not require much work, for an informal intelligence bureau already existed in Shanghai. The impetus for the foundation of this body had come from Captain A. Hilton Johnson, the new second-in-command of the SMP. Hilton Johnson was a former army officer and his appointment in June 1916 had been made on the recommendation of the War Office, if not of the Secret Service itself. His task was to use the detective force of the SMP, which had previously been somewhat uncooperative, to collect intelligence on German and Indian intrigues in China and to report 'privately' to London. Another likely motive for his appointment was that the War Office and the Foreign Office wanted to have a new intelligence representative on the spot as they distrusted Captain Seigne. Ever since 1915 the diplomats in China, including Jordan, had complained about Seigne's alarmist nature, while the latter had in turn resented his reports being 'consistently ridiculed'; there was, therefore, clearly an urgent need for new blood.[36]

Once Hilton Johnson arrived in Shanghai he proposed that an intelligence bureau should be created in order to discuss enemy activities, a move possibly intended to ensure that Seigne's work would be subject to review before being more widely circulated. An Intelligence Bureau (IB) was quickly established with funding from Jordan's secret service account; in addition to Seigne and Hilton Johnson, its members were Herbert Phillips of the consular service, Mr Canning, the GOC China's representative in Shanghai, and Captain Barrett of the SMP.[37] Thus, all that was needed was for Petrie, who was given the rank of vice-consul, to join the extant organization, which he did in March 1917 after spending a few months in India for leave and consultations.[38] Even before Petrie's arrival, the new system of intelligence collaboration in China appeared to work reasonably efficiently, the most significant figure in Petrie's absence being Hilton Johnson. After some initial problems caused by the continuing desire of the head of the SMP, Captain McKuen, to maintain his force's neutrality, Hilton Johnson was put in charge of a special unit of detectives that collected political intelligence, not only within the International Settlement but also further afield in China.[39]

In addition to his role in the development of the intelligence organization in China, Petrie set about creating a region-wide apparatus to report on Indian sedition. This initially caused some difficulties, as the interdepartmental committee in Whitehall was determined that this network should only operate in collaboration with the local diplomatic and consular representatives. The result was a system under which Petrie nominated agents for Japan, Siam, the Dutch East Indies, the Philippines and Hong Kong who were under his general control, but reported from day to day to a local British official. In Japan this meant that the Indian secret service agents reported directly to Davidson in Yokohama, who in turn corresponded with Petrie in Shanghai.[40]

While most of the work of Petrie and the IB was aimed at the Indo-German plots and the German attempts to influence Chinese politics, other initiatives in the expansion of intelligence resources were aimed squarely at the Japanese. One of the most important decisions was to attack Japan's diplomatic ciphers. In March 1916 the Gaimushō requested that its consul in Yunnan be allowed to use the British-owned Bhamo telegram cable to send reports to Tokyo. The Foreign Office immediately saw that by agreeing to this request there was a chance that 'we might obtain some useful hints ... if we asked the I.O. [India Office] to send to their decyphering experts copies of all Japanese telegrams.'[41] The India Office, with its fears about Japan's presence in Yunnan, quickly agreed to this suggestion. The task of translating the telegrams was given in India to Captain Cardew, who by this stage had become the Adviser on Chinese and Japanese affairs in the Foreign and Political Department.[42]

Cardew's work proved useful, for his decrypts revealed that the Japanese were using their cable privileges to allow the rebels in Yunnan to communicate with other Chinese revolutionaries, including the veteran nationalist and leader of the Kuomintang (KMT), Sun Yat-sen. This information confirmed that Japan, in violation of the alliance, was interfering in Chinese domestic politics. On receipt of this news there was some debate whether Britain should confront Japan with this material and call upon it to desist, or whether the telegram facilities should simply be withdrawn. However, both options fell foul of the age-old intelligence dilemma that by acting on intelligence one risks compromising and thus losing the source.[43] Therefore, no direct action was taken, although a decision was made in India in late 1917 to establish a North-East Frontier Intelligence Corps to keep an eye on events in Yunnan.[44]

Cardew's success in reading this traffic led the War Office to ask him to look also at material that was being sent to the Japanese embassy in London.[45] It was, however, a time-consuming procedure to send these intercepts out to India, and therefore in 1917 MI1b, the branch of military intelligence that dealt with signals intelligence, decided that it needed its own Japanese translator. Accordingly, in August 1917 the War Office hired a member of the Japanese consular service, George Sansom, who was given the task of seeking a 'solution of all existing Japanese codes and cyphers'.[46] To what extent Sansom's translations came to influence policy is very difficult to gauge, but the occasional reference in Foreign Office files to information from 'other sources' suggests that it did have its uses.[47]

Another result of the increasing distrust of Japan was that its nationals in Britain became a target of MI5. In January 1917 MI5 informed the Foreign Office that it was unhappy that some Japanese entering Britain were simply giving their address as 'c/o the Japanese Embassy', and suggested that such individuals should be watched. The Foreign Office agreed, noting that the present lack of controls meant that there was nothing to stop a Japanese spy from passing information to the Germans. The following month British ports were ordered to report the arrival of all Asiatics, including Japanese, while Chief Constables were directed to provide information on their movements.[48] Later in the year MI5 went even further, sending an agent to Switzerland as there were reports that a Japanese office in Konstanz was passing British secrets to the Germans.[49] MI5's system of appointing Military Control Officers to handle overseas passport and visa applications was not, however, extended to Japan until very late in the war. It was only in August 1918 that an officer arrived in Tokyo to take up such a post.[50]

The need for vigilance was also apparent in South-East Asia, where the activities of the Japanese naval squadron and of Japanese companies and residents were attracting the attention of the authorities. Sometime in 1917 the Admiralty decided to send out to the C-in-C China's staff an intelligence officer who was fluent in Japanese and could dedicate his time to the translation of anti-British articles and books. The individual chosen was a former language officer in Japan, Staff Paymaster E.P. Jones.[51] In addition, in July 1917 Ridout pressed for the appointment of a Japanese expert of his own to collate and interpret material from intelligence reports and intercepted correspondence. In this case, the man who became 'the secret agent in Singapore with special regard to the Japanese problem' was Frank Ashton-Gwatkin, who had been a consular officer in Japan but had asked to be released for war service. His cover in Singapore was to work as the Assistant Director of the Imports and Exports Office, a job that naturally brought him into close contact with the Japanese community.[52] Ridout's interest in Japan also provoked the head of the Secret Service, Sir Mansfield Cumming or 'C' as he was generally known, to consider sending his own representative to the region. His plans lapsed due to the difficulty of finding appropriate staff, but the concern about Japanese activities led to a consensus in Whitehall that in the post-war period it would be essential to establish a Secret Service presence in the region, for as Ronald Campbell of the Foreign Office noted to Colonel French of MI1a in January 1918:

> The question [of spying on Japan] is of such vast political importance and of such extraordinary delicacy that after the war it should not ... be handled by an intelligence centre, or any other local official body. It must be entirely and absolutely subterranean.[53]

However, in the absence of a formal Secret Service officer, Ashton-Gwatkin proved in the interim to be an admirable replacement.

At the same time, British intelligence sources in Japan itself were further strengthened. One important initiative was the revival of the army's language officer programme, which had lapsed at the start of the war. This came about largely in response to a report in September 1916 that the government in Peking had agreed to appoint one of Japan's leading China specialists as a military adviser to Li Yüan-hung, Yüan's successor as President. This news resurrected the 'Yellow Peril' image of a Chinese army officered by the Japanese, and provoked the British military attaché in Peking to note that such an army 'might become a very formidable instrument for offensive purposes'.[54] This in turn triggered Hirtzel to lament that, due to the lack of officers with East Asian expertise, Britain was in a poor position to counteract the expansion of Japanese influence. The solution, he argued, was to send officers who were unfit for active duty to Japan for language training. This idea appealed to the War Office, which in August 1917 informed the Foreign Office that it had decided to renew language training and that it planned to send Captains R.D. Bennett and Malcolm Kennedy to Japan. Kennedy, who over the next two and a half decades would play an important role in the gathering of intelligence on Japan, had recently been severely wounded in fighting on the Western front, but volunteered for language duty as he did not want to resign his commission.[55]

There was also an expansion in the financing of counter-espionage work in Japan. In January 1918 Greene impressed on the Foreign Office the need for more financial resources in order to fund Davidson's duties. Greene had not until this time been provided with an annual secret service allowance, and he had been forced to meet some of Davidson's expenditure from the embassy's own money, euphemistically referred to as 'Extra Clerk Hire'. He therefore asked for funding to be put on a more formal basis and observed that, as the intelligence gathered now had ramifications for territories other than India, it was unreasonable to expect the Indian government alone to foot the bill. It appears that his request was met.[56]

There was, then, from 1916 until the end of the war, a marked expansion of the intelligence network in Asia. As Popplewell has noted, this proliferation of bodies did not cause any major difficulties or rivalries to develop between the different intelligence organizations. Instead, there tended to be a fluid exchange of information, and even at times of personnel, with the inter-departmental committee in Whitehall providing a sense of central direction, and no serious differences of opinion between the two senior figures in the region, Ridout and Petrie.[57] However, while the process of developing a coherent intelligence presence was remarkably successful, the actual information collected did cause problems, for the wealth of new sources on German and Japanese activities tended to exaggerate the extent of the danger to British interests, which in turn had a detrimental effect on diplomacy and led to disputes between Britain's diplomats and the intelligence community.

## The IB and German plots in China

The problem with the expansion of the intelligence presence in East Asia was that in their enthusiasm the intelligence practitioners sought to identify and pre-empt potential threats without much attention to how their activities might affect wider diplomatic concerns. The problems raised by the increased emphasis on intelligence created particular problems in China. As noted above, by the end of 1916 the IB was fully functional and Hilton Johnson was able to utilize the SMP for work outside the International Settlement. Using this network, he provided important information on the German community in China and its links to the remaining Indian revolutionaries and to the opponents of the Chinese central government. This intelligence proved to be useful, particularly in March 1917 when China broke off diplomatic relations with Germany, for the IB was able to help forestall a German attempt to scuttle its remaining ships at Shanghai thus blocking the entrance to the harbour.[58]

Problems emerged, however, when the IB claimed that the Germans intended to back anti-government forces in an effort to stop China from actually declaring war. The Peking legation, with Alston acting as chargé d'affaires in Jordan's absence, felt that this contention grossly exaggerated Germany's ability to influence events. As far as the legation was concerned whether Germany backed one side or the other did not matter, for its activities were of little consequence compared to the actions of the indigenous political forces. The IB's reports were therefore seen as an unnecessary distraction that diverted attention away from the key issues. Moreover, Alston felt that there was a danger that the IB might go too far, and commit acts that would harm rather than further British interests. Over the following months he therefore regularly complained about the IB's activities and in particular the 'quite astounding inaccuracy of the majority of Seigne's yarns'.[59] In London, 'Blinker' Hall rushed to Seigne's defence, noting that the latter's only problem was the lack of support from 'the local people', who suffered from an 'extremely narrow outlook'.[60] This dispute put the Foreign Office in a difficult position, for it found itself torn between sharing Hall's view that the legation had dangerously neglected the need for good intelligence, and sympathizing with Alston's irritation at Seigne's impetuousness. It therefore sanctioned intelligence-gathering on such matters as Germany's financial links with Sun Yat-sen, while attempting to persuade Hall to restrain Seigne.[61]

This controversy did not precipitate a major crisis, but the disagreements between the legation and the IB were an ominous development. Here one can see in microcosm how the intelligence community was achieving a new prominence arising out of the exigencies of war, and how this was seen by traditional diplomats as an unwarranted intrusion into the world of diplomacy that undercut their authority. The latter's objections were, however, not merely based on sentiment, for, as can be seen in Alston's case, it was genuinely felt that intelligence officers were too prone to believe in the reliability of information gained from secret sources and lacked sufficient understanding of the broad political picture. On the other hand, as can be seen from Hall's comments, the view of the intelligence community was that they were seeing events from the even higher perspective of the worldwide conflict with the Central Powers, and that the diplomats in China displayed an unfortunate parochialism in only seeing how the intelligence pertained to local affairs.

## Japan and the rise of pan-Asianism

The problems that could be created by the existence of an overactive intelligence community were even more evident in the case of Japan. As the German threat receded, the intelligence organizations in Asia increasingly turned their attention to Japan as the major potential threat to British interests. This tendency was clearly noted in a report produced by Petrie at the end of 1916, in which he observed that the European community in the East viewed Japan 'with profound suspicion' because of 'her restless ambition, her arrogance, her desire for aggrandizement and her aggressive spirit'.[62] In regard to the Indian plots, his own area of expertise, Petrie felt there was some cause for concern, noting:

> That the Indian revolutionary party in Japan have received direct and indirect encouragement from the Japanese is, I think, undoubted. They have enjoyed complete immunity and they are encouraged to look up to Japan as the champion of the Asiatic races against the white ...[63]

Here he touched upon the point that, from 1916, was to become central to British concerns about Japan – the rise of pan-Asian sentiment as a factor in Japanese expansionism.

In the first half of the war, Japan's pretensions to regional leadership based upon race had received relatively little attention, even in the context of Japan's interest in Tibet and Yunnan, but a change came about in late 1916 when increasing evidence emerged of close ties between pan-Asianists in Japan and the Indian revolutionary movement. This information reached British circles through a number of sources, the most significant of which was the group of agents Petrie had introduced into Japan to assist Davidson by working undercover within the Indian community. These agents arrived in the autumn of 1916 and soon proved their worth by confirming that 'Thakur', who had escaped deportation in December 1915, was indeed Rash Behari Bose, and that he was still in hiding in Tokyo.[64] Even more disturbing was that they uncovered in Japan a world in which the Indian revolutionaries appeared to be in close contact with an increasingly vociferous pan-Asian lobby that included individuals such as Tōyama, Uchida Ryohei of the Kokuryūkai, and Ōkawa Shūmei, the founder of the Pan-Asian Society. In addition, there was circumstantial evidence that linked these pan-Asianists with important political figures such as the former Prime Minister Ōkuma, and Gotō Shimpei, the Germanophile Home Minister in the new cabinet of Terauchi Masatake. [65]

At the same time, the hope among the Indians that this pan-Asian upsurge would assist their cause was evident from the intercepted telegrams that passed through German diplomatic channels from the leading Indian revolutionary in the United States, Dr Chandra Kanta Chakrabarti, to the Indian National Committee in Berlin. Chakrabarti's correspondence revealed that the Indians had succeeded in placing propaganda in Japanese newspapers and had indeed made approaches to Ōkuma, Gotō and even Terauchi. This source also demonstrated that the Indians had established contact with Sun Yat-sen in China, who himself showed marked pan-Asian tendencies.[66]

Another facet to the rise of pan-Asianism was the presence of various 'suspicious' Japanese individuals in South and South-East Asia. The most prominent of these was Count Otani, who, after resigning in 1914 as the abbot of the Nishi Honganji temple in Kyoto due to financial improprieties, became involved in the proselytizing of Japanese Buddhism in Asia. His journeys included a lengthy stay in India in 1916 and a visit to Singapore and the Dutch East Indies in 1917. The activities of such individuals were a matter of concern because the stress on the shared Buddhist roots of Asian societies had, since the late nineteenth century, become one of the main tenets of pan-Asian and anti-Western thinking in Japan.[67]

For those concerned with the defence of Britain's eastern interests, the growth of pan-Asian sentiment was a deeply unsettling phenomenon, as it hinted that Japan might be willing to offer support to Asian revolutionaries. With Britain's colonies virtually defenceless as long as the war in Europe continued, this was a frightening prospect, and led to an increased sensitivity about intelligence that directly linked the Japanese community to unrest in Asia. Certainly, fragmentary reports indicated that the Japanese in South-East Asia were attempting to build a bridge to the indigenous population. In Malaya, Ridout was unhappy about the tendency of the IJN squadron to fly the flag in a manner designed to impress Japanese power on the Malays.[68] Even more disturbing was the position in the East Indies, where the increasing discontent with Dutch rule led in 1916–17 to a series of revolts in Sumatra. While there was no evidence that Japan was directly linked to these disturbances, investigations by both the Dutch and the British revealed that some Japanese nationals were involved in the distribution of pan-Asian propaganda to the indigenous population. Indeed, so suspicious were the Dutch of Japanese activities that in July 1918 the head of the secret police in Batavia travelled to Singapore to exchange information with Ridout.[69] Watching these activities from London, MI2c, the branch of the Military Intelligence Directorate (MID) that dealt with East Asia, noted in July 1917 that the Japanese, utilizing their 'intricate and highly organized system of secret service', were extending their influence into every corner of the region, and that it was possible that they would be willing to support rebellions against European colonial rule.[70]

Moreover, a spate of reports dealt with the sensitive subject of Japanese land purchases in Malaya, British North Borneo, the Dutch East Indies and the Philippines. To those in the intelligence community it appeared that all too often the Japanese bought plantation land in areas of strategic importance. Japanese landholdings around Singapore, especially in Johore and the Dutch-owned Rhio Islands, attracted the greatest suspicion, for it was feared that in time of war they could be used as bases for espionage activities and observation of British naval movements.[71]

Despite the accumulation of evidence that elements in Japan were actively engaged in pan-Asian plots, this did not lead to any marked change in British policy. In part this was for reasons of expediency, namely that the military and political circumstances of 1917 still dictated caution. The danger posed by the German unrestricted submarine warfare campaign meant that Britain desperately needed more destroyers to cover its shipping lanes, and the obvious source for these vessels was Japan. Thus Britain needed to flatter rather than browbeat Japan, and in February 1917 it agreed to support the latter's claims to the Kiaochow lease in China and the German Pacific islands north of the Equator in return for increased assistance from the IJN in the Indian Ocean and the Mediterranean. Moreover, there was some hope in 1917 that the Japanese might finally be persuaded to send forces to either Europe or the Middle East. Indeed, the importance of wooing the Japanese was such that when one of the former language officers, Major F.S.G. Piggott, proposed that Japan might be induced to be more cooperative by presenting the Emperor with a Field Marshal's baton, this suggestion quickly metamorphosed into the visit to Japan in 1918 by Prince Arthur of Connaught.[72]

Another important restraint on Britain was that it was clear to the more objective observer that much of the intelligence on the pan-Asian threat was based on hearsay. Even a figure such as Petrie, who did believe that there was a real long-term danger, acknowledged that some of the material might be 'a mere mare's nest'.[73] Moreover, even if one took a group such as the Pan-Asian Society seriously, it had to be admitted that there was no clear evidence that the Japanese government was linked with its activities. In fact, there were a number of indications from 1916 onwards that the Terauchi government was inclined to be more cooperative towards Britain than its predecessor. In the spring and summer of 1917 Japan raised few obstacles to China's entry into the war on the side of the Entente, and was willing, although at a price, to allow the IJN to take a greater part in the conflict. This apparent desire to cooperate meant that on a number of occasions British ministers indicated their doubts about Japanese sponsorship of pan-Asianism. For example when, in October 1917, the Far Eastern Department prepared a memorandum on why Japan was unlikely to allow its forces to fight the Turks, Balfour debarred any mention of pan-Asianism on the grounds that there was no evidence that the Terauchi government was influenced by such ideas.[74] This is not to say that there was any great resurgence of confidence in Japan, for it was still widely believed that it was acting in its own selfish interests, but there was, at least in the higher echelons of government, a determination to be objective before deciding that a new 'Great Game' was developing in Asia.

## The Siberian intervention

The delicate problem of how to deal with Japan in the light of the need for its support but distrust of its long-term ambitions, was exemplified by the Siberian crisis of 1918. Following the Bolshevik revolution in Petrograd in November 1917 there was great uncertainty about what would happen in Siberia, where chaotic conditions prevailed. Initially, in December 1917, the Entente's concern focused on the fate of the vast stores of munitions at Vladivostock, but over the coming months this was compounded by the prospect that Germany might obtain access to the region's resources, or even that the large German and Austro-Hungarian POW population in Siberia might seize direct control. The obvious remedy was to sanction the despatch of Japanese forces to Siberia to maintain order and to encourage Tokyo to cooperate with China in seizing control of the Russian-owned Chinese Eastern Railway (CER) in north Manchuria. In the light of Japan's wartime record this was far from a safe option for, as a number of observers commented, there was no guarantee that once the IJA entered these areas it would ever withdraw.[75] Japanese behaviour early in 1918 only added to these fears, for both diplomatic and intelligence sources revealed that the Terauchi government was engaged in a new policy of intervention in China, under which it bolstered the weak government of Tuan Ch'i-jui with loans, advisers and munitions in exchange for economic concessions. Indeed, it was already apparent in the spring of 1918 that Japan was attempting to use the negotiations for a Sino-Japanese military agreement on joint operations in north Manchuria as an excuse to press for Chinese political and economic concessions.[76]

This intelligence about Japan's ambitions towards China suggested that the same fate might await Siberia, and certainly it was clear from various sources that Japan was deeply interested in expanding its political and economic presence around Vladivostock. Noticeably, from the start of the Siberian crisis the Japanese showed a tendency to back those White Russian forces who were willing to make concessions to them, but to oppose those who refused to mortgage their country's future. For example, by the summer of 1918 it was apparent that Japan was willing to support the relatively weak forces of the Cossack leader Ataman Semenov, but not those of Admiral Kolchak, the figure who appealed most to the Entente.[77]

Nevertheless, despite the concern about Japan's intentions, the British government had no doubt that the denial of Siberia to Germany was so important that a Japanese presence was essential. It therefore lobbied hard to achieve this goal, particularly in Washington, where President Woodrow Wilson was by no means convinced of the advisability of Japanese intervention, and its efforts finally bore fruit in August 1918 when a joint American–Japanese expedition was sent to Vladivostock to take charge of the eastern section of the TSR.

Britain thus proved able to put to one side the doubts that it felt about Japan for the sake of furthering the war effort. This might appear to demonstrate that at the grand strategic level the intelligence on Japanese machinations had little real effect, but it is worth noting that this decision to support intervention by the IJA was not made with much enthusiasm. It was rather a case of choosing between the lesser of two evils – anarchy in Siberia or the growth of Japanese influence.

## The post-war era and the Japanese threat

The end of the Great War in November 1918 did not immediately ease the concern about the security of Britain's eastern possessions, for intelligence sources during 1919–21 still indicated that Japan posed a threat. One reason for the continuing sensitivity about Japan was that, as with all conflicts, the formal conclusion of the war did not lead immediately to peace, for in many parts of the world political confusion still reigned. In Asia, China remained mired in the civil strife that had been provoked by its entry into the war, India simmered on the point of rebellion, and in the East Indies the Dutch faced the first coherent indigenous challenge to its authority in the shape of the *Sarekat Islam* party. Complicating the situation further was the collapse of the authority of the Ottoman Sultan and the consequent rise of the pan-Islamic *Khalifat* movement. There were therefore many troubled waters in which Japan might fish.

In this atmosphere continuing evidence of links between Japanese pan-Asianists and revolutionaries from a variety of countries naturally attracted attention. Most notably Japan now appeared to be reaching out to the Muslim world. In Shanghai a number of Japanese were reported to be involved in discussions with Sami Bey, a political emissary from Turkey, and by 1921 there was evidence from Constantinople that the Japanese were sounding out the Kemalists about an anti-Soviet alliance.[78] In addition, sources in the Muslim areas of China, such as the missionary Findlay Andrew, reported coming across parties of Japanese involved in propaganda work, while in the East Indies there were reports that some Japanese were attempting to gain influence over *Sarekat Islam* with the aim of undermining Dutch rule.[79] Islam was not Japan's only focus, for the pan-Asianists also remained in contact with radical groups in India. In late 1918 the Japanese Sanskrit scholar, Professor Kanokoji, visited India; his stay was, however, relatively short, for his attempt to make contact with revolutionary leaders led to his rapid deportation.[80]

Doubts about the Japanese also existed in other areas. One theme that became particularly noticeable after the end of the war was the fear that Japan might develop closer relations with Germany, and that this could in the long term lead to a German–Russian–Japanese combination. In part, this idea appears to have been fostered by rumours circulating in 1919 of a secret wartime German–Japanese convention.[81] In addition, reports from a variety of sources in Europe, including Secret Service agents, indicated that a Japanese intelligence network based in Scandinavia was attempting to establish links in Germany, and that attempts were being made to hire instructors for the IJA and to buy war material.[82]

Another area in which Japanese behaviour attracted attention was Siberia. After the joint intervention of August 1918, British fears of Japan's ambitions were soon confirmed. It was readily apparent from the autumn of 1918 that Japan was concentrating on building up its economic position in eastern Siberia and providing very little assistance to Kolchak. A memorandum by the Foreign Office's Political Intelligence Department in February 1919 noted that recent Secret Service reports from the region demonstrated that Japan's preferred method was to shore up its position by working through minions such as Semenov and General Horvat.[83] Through 1919 Japanese policy did not change to any substantial degree, but its apparent desire for aggrandizement seemed clear in April 1920 when, after Kolchak's collapse and the withdrawal of the other Allied contingents, its forces seized control of north Sakhalin and the Trans-Baikal region between Vladivostock and Chita. The government in Tokyo claimed that this was a reaction to the slaughter of 700 Japanese by the Bolsheviks at Nikolaevsk, but evidence from a variety of other sources suggested that it was a premeditated act.[84]

These indications of a potential Japanese threat continued to fascinate the intelligence fraternity, but over time Whitehall tended to be less convinced that Japan could pose a danger to British interests. The problem for the intelligence services was that, in the calm of relative peace, it was possible to see how far the Japanese menace had been exaggerated over the last few years and how ill-placed it was militarily to challenge Britain in Asia. Thus from 1919 onwards many doubts about the reality of the Japanese threat were voiced, and the wartime intelligence organization began to unravel.

The reassessment of Japan took two forms. One was to look back at its wartime record and try to analyse its activities objectively. This new approach began in late 1918 when the Indian government sought permission to pass a memorandum to Japan detailing its unfriendly activities towards India during the war. Although it was agreed that the memorandum should be handed over, in both the Admiralty and the Foreign Office there were dissenters who felt it was important to draw a line between the activities of Japanese nationals and the role of the government, which had not 'adopted or even patronized a positive policy of intrigue in India'.[85] Building on this sentiment, in October 1919 the Foreign Office put together its own reassessment of Japan's record, which noted that, due to its heightened sensitivity during the war, Britain was 'inclined ... to see in quite innocent activities evidence of all sorts of duplicity', but that there was no reason to believe that the Japanese government had colluded with either Germany or the Indian revolutionaries.[86]

The second element in the post-war reassessment was an increasingly close scrutiny of the contemporary intelligence reports. In particular the idea that Japan would spread its influence through the propagation of pan-Asianism began to be seriously questioned. This reassessment was heavily influenced by a series of reverses to Japanese policy. For example, Japan's savage suppression of an uprising in Korea in the spring of 1919 seriously damaged its pan-Asian credentials. Even more important was that the decision at the Paris peace conference to pass control of the Kiaochow lease to Japan led in turn to the unleashing of the anti-Japanese May Fourth Movement in China and a boycott of Japanese goods that spread even to the Chinese communities in South-East Asia. This had the effect of seriously undermining the efforts of the Japanese government to construct a friendly relationship with the Tuan government and the attempts by Japanese pan-Asianists to build ties with Sun Yat-sen. These two events naturally challenged the credibility of intelligence reports on the pan-Asian threat. Even before the end of the war Sir John Jordan had been sceptical about Japan's ability to appeal to its fellow Asians, and this feeling was now reinforced to the extent that in 1919 he complained about the 'marked anti-Japanese bias' of the reports produced by Ridout's staff at Singapore.[87]

Doubts were also expressed about the ability of the Japanese to exploit Muslim unrest in Asia. In particular, questions were raised about the reports of Japanese penetration of *Sarekat Islam* in the Dutch East Indies. For example, Stephen Gaselee of the Foreign Office, when reading one of Ridout's effusions, observed:

> Can Sarekat Islam and the Japanese *really* ever be Allies ... it all seems to me very remote – Japan can lead a pan-Asiatic movement; but a pan-Islamic movement is a very different affair.[88]

Moreover, a number of correspondents noted that the Japanese were not popular with the indigenous population in the Dutch East Indies. This unpopularity arose from the fact that while on the one hand the Japanese were attempting to undermine Dutch rule by stressing Asian brotherhood, on the other they demanded for reasons of prestige to be treated on equal terms with the Europeans.[89]

Concern also eased about Japanese espionage activities in South-East Asia. In 1918–19 both Jones and Ashton-Gwatkin engaged in detailed studies of the local Japanese community and concluded that the rumours about the Japanese were exaggerated. For example, Jones in one report observed that there were only three hundred Japanese in the whole of the Malay peninsula, that they were 'law-abiding and chiefly anxious to make money', and that the accusations of espionage came largely from 'planters and other Europeans who view the Japanese with considerable distrust and dislike'. Ashton-Gwatkin meanwhile argued that 'Japanese policy during these years of great temptation has shewn itself cautious, short-reaching and faithful in its obligations'.[90] Ridout still begged to differ. In a covering letter to one of Ashton-Gwatkin's memoranda he once again rehearsed the arguments about the suspicious location of Japanese estates, which he averred 'have been selected with peculiar foresight and ingenuity'.[91] His arguments were, however, steadily losing their persuasiveness, with both the civilian authorities in Malaya and the Overseas Defence Sub-Committee (ODC) in London inclined to believe that the threat had been overstated.[92]

The ebbing of concern about Japan's ambitions in Asia was also connected to the slighting assessments of Japanese military capabilities produced during the latter part of the war and in the immediate post-war period. One important source was the reports provided by those naval officers who had worked alongside the IJN squadrons in the Indian Ocean. In contrast to their colleagues in the Mediterranean, who were relatively positive about the IJN, the consensus on the China Station was that the Japanese often hindered operations.[93] To a substantial degree this was due to the language-barrier and the restrictions imposed by Tokyo on the IJN's movements, but the problems were also seen as arising out of the incompetence of Japanese sailors. Early in 1917 Admiral Grant complained to the Admiralty that among the reasons for poor liaison with the IJN was that the Japanese were inept at mastering new technology, in particular radio communication.[94] His predecessor, Admiral Jerram, was similarly jaundiced about the IJN's capabilities. In May 1917 Jerram, who seemed to have cooperated well with the Japanese at the start of the war, was asked by the Admiralty to report on the secret of his success. In his reply the Admiral revealed that in fact he, like Grant, had had great difficulties. Among other complaints, he noted that one of the problems with the Japanese was that 'They are not good ship's husbands: they cannot keep the sea and do their own running repairs as our ships do.'[95] Ironically, of course, the relative backwardness of the IJN was in part a situation deliberately fostered by the

Admiralty, for even during the war it maintained its policy of passing very little information about technological innovations to the Japanese. A memorandum produced in the Admiralty in October 1918 indicated that the IJN had been treated on a par with the Italians, and that Britain had been far more generous in its exchanges with France and United States.[96]

The service attachés in Tokyo were equally scathing in their indictments of Japan's martial abilities. A report by Colonel Somerville in October 1917 on the possibility of using the IJA in Europe noted that its officers had shown little interest in the European campaign, and that as their technology and tactics were woefully outdated the Japanese were in no condition to face the Germans. Moreover, he expressed his doubts about the Japanese soldiers' capacity for withstanding the psychological pressures of trench warfare. Observing that the international standing of the IJA rested largely on the image of the stoical Japanese infantryman in Manchuria in 1904–5, he argued that the effect of a collapse of morale would be disastrous as 'the bubble reputation produced by the Russo-Japanese War would be pricked and his military value would sink to that of the other Oriental fighting races'.[97] His views were shared by the naval attaché, Captain Rymer, who noted in February 1918 that the IJA was at least five years behind the European armies, that the Japanese lacked the 'stamina for an overseas war and that a fraction of the disappointment, reverses and losses which European countries have suffered in this war would bring about a revolution'.[98] Somerville's successor, Brigadier-General C.R. Woodroffe, who had from 1906–8 served as a language officer in Japan, was equally uncomplimentary. Attending the IJA's annual manoeuvres in the autumn of 1919, he noted that the equipment was practically the same as in his previous tour of duty, and that the tendency of Japanese troops to advance in close formation demonstrated that there was no appreciation of the devastating damage that could be inflicted by modern machine guns. In his judgement it would not be until 1926 that Japan would be prepared to fight a modern war.[99]

These negative evaluations were based in part on observation, but they also clearly owed much to the continuing belief in racial stereotypes of the Japanese. The importance of the racial element was particularly evident in regard to Japan's first tentative experiments with military aviation. The general consensus among the British service personnel in Tokyo was that the Japanese were singularly ill-equipped, both on physiological and psychological grounds, to cope with this new form of warfare in the same way that it was held that they made indifferent cavalry. For example, Woodroffe observed in June 1919 that, while it was important for Britain to take a lead in training the nascent IJA air service, it should be recalled that:

> To anyone familiar with the national psychology, it is doubtful whether the Japanese will ever become a first-class Military pilot ... There is always an underlying predisposition to conceit, and consequent carelessness ...

> The Japanese pays little attention to health and habits, and is of a temperament that gets easily "rattled" in the face of emergency. Medical authorities state that his sense of objective balance is poor and that he has hardly any reflex action. His brain works slowly and he lacks mechanical sense.[100]

This sort of judgement was accepted without comment in London, for it merely expressed commonly held truisms.[101]

Within Whitehall these reports depreciating the effectiveness of the armed forces had the effect of reducing the concern about Japanese ambitions. As Sir John Tilley of the Foreign Office noted in June 1919, the circumstances 'do not suggest that Japan will be able to adopt an aggressive policy for some time'.[102] Added to this was evidence from both open and intelligence sources that labour militancy was growing in Japan and that the cult of militarism was losing its attraction.[103] Reports on such subjects led Ashton-Gwatkin, who by 1920 had become a member of the Far Eastern Department of the Foreign Office, to conclude that if such phenomena continued the Japanese menace would naturally subside.[104]

The sense of any immediate threat was also eroded by Britain's ability in London, Malta and India to eavesdrop on Japan's diplomatic communications. At first this task continued to be the responsibility of MI1b, which in February 1919 was able to inform the British representatives in Paris that it had intercepted the instructions to the Japanese delegation to the peace conference.[105] In April 1919 this work was passed to the newly formed GCCS. Around the same time there was also a change in the personnel engaged on Japanese material, Sansom returning to Japan as the assistant commercial counsellor and his place being taken by a newly retired officer from the Japanese consular service, Ernest Hobart-Hampden.[106]

Throughout 1919–21 it became apparent from the diplomatic intercepts that the Japanese were increasingly aware of their relative isolation in the world community and the need to mend fences with Britain and the United States. Among the intercepts received were many stressing Japan's desire to see a renewal of the alliance, the limited nature of its ambitions in Siberia and its growing estrangement from Semenov.[107] In addition, this source revealed that there was nothing particularly sinister about the operations of Japanese intelligence staff in Europe or about the current trend in German–Japanese relations. For example, in November 1919 a GCCS report observed that the telegrams of Captain Yamawaki, a Japanese military commission officer in Poland, contained no 'allusions to any ... intrigue on the part of Japan', while the reports on Germany revealed that the arms sales were limited to small-scale purchases of military equipment.[108]

The degree to which the Japanese threat appeared to be subsiding was reflected in developments in intelligence organization. For example, in India the need to maintain a careful watch on Japanese activities led to further refinements to the British intelligence apparatus. In December 1918 the Indian government decided that Cardew's appointment should be made permanent. In addition, to utilize his skills fully it was agreed that he should travel to China and Japan to improve his language abilities and observe the local conditions, which he proceeded to do, arriving in Japan in December 1919.[109] Moreover, due to the need to have men capable of supplementing Cardew, the Indian Army began in 1918 to despatch officers to Japan for language training.[110] This surge of interest in Japan did not, however, last long. In late 1920 Cardew was forced to take sick leave, and it soon became apparent that he would not be able to remain in India. Initially the Foreign Department tried to arrange a replacement by sending a policeman, Jacobs, to Japan for language training. In November 1921, however, this plan was dropped due to the need for financial retrenchment, and Cardew's post was abolished.[111]

A similar process was evident in Malaya, where in 1919 it was suggested that a special intelligence bureau should be established at Singapore. The originator of this idea was a Colonial Office official, W.H. Lee-Warner, who, after a brief period in MI5, had served from March to October 1918 as the Ministry of Information's representative in the Dutch East Indies.[112] His concern about the range of possible threats to British security in South-East Asia, including Japan and its attempt to link up with the *Khalifat* movement, led him to recommend that a civilian-controlled intelligence bureau be formed at Singapore which would 'run on the lines of the Indian C.I.D. with an eye also on the methods and scope of Dept. MI5 of the War Office'.[113] Within Whitehall this plan met with a positive response from MI5 and the War Office, who both saw the bureau as complementing their plans for an imperial intelligence network. However, in the light of the reappraisal of the nature of the Japanese threat to Malaya and the Treasury's calls for the pruning of expenditure, it stood no chance.[114]

## The death of the alliance

The ebbing away of the fear that Japan posed an immediate threat to British security did not, however, mean that its lacklustre support in the war was forgotten or forgiven, as was evident in the talks about the future of the alliance between 1919 and 1921. Although concern for American and Dominion opinion was clearly the major factor in these discussions, it is undeniable that the intelligence that had been gathered about Japan's dubious activities and ambitions during the war also cast a long shadow. Indeed, despite Lloyd George's attempt at one Cabinet meeting to put matters in context by noting that other apparently friendly powers had engaged in wartime activities 'infinitely worse than anything which had been done by the Japanese', the whole debate about the alliance was couched in terms of whether its renewal would help to restrain Japan in the future and keep it away from a possible alignment with Germany and Russia.[115] The Foreign Secretary, Lord Curzon, who was far from sanguine about the 'insidious and unscrupulous' Japanese, believed that renewal would achieve these aims.[116] This argument also held some appeal to the Admiralty and War Office, who feared that in a period of financial retrenchment Britain could not afford to risk turning Japan into an outright foe.

However, to others this argument did not hold water. Among the diplomats, prominent figures such as Greene, Jordan, Alston, and the new head of the Far Eastern Department, Sir Victor Wellesley, argued against renewal on the grounds that Japan had proved itself to be militaristic and immoral and therefore an unsuitable ally of an upstanding power such as Britain. They suggested that instead Britain should seek an Anglo-Japanese-American declaration on the security of China and the Pacific.[117] In addition, once Canada made clear its objections at the Imperial Conference in June 1921, the Colonial Secretary, Winston Churchill, came out in opposition to the alliance. In a memorandum in July 1921 he argued that Curzon's policy was tantamount to paying Danegeld, and noted caustically that 'Getting Japan to protect you against Japan is like drinking salt water to slake thirst'.[118] To strengthen his argument he sought to prove Japan's perfidy by showing his Cabinet colleagues a secret Japanese map of Gibraltar that had come into the hands of MI5.[119]

Opinion at the highest level was therefore divided between extension and abrogation of the alliance. In this environment, and with only negative reasons for the alliance's retention, it is no surprise that Britain attended the Washington Conference of 1921–22 believing that the best option was for the alliance to be broadened to involve the Americans. This turned out to be close to the eventual outcome, which saw the alliance replaced in February 1922 by a Four-Power Pact of Britain, Japan, the United States and France that would uphold the status quo in the Pacific.

At the same time as the future of the alliance was under debate, Britain also dealt with another issue arising from distrust of Japan: the need for a naval base in Asia to defend British interests and imperial communications. In 1919 the former First Sea Lord, Admiral Lord Jellicoe, visited India and the antipodean Dominions and, impressed by the fear of Japan within the region, argued that Britain should build 'a dock in the Far East that will accommodate our largest ships'.[120] After deliberations in Whitehall, in June 1921 the ODC recommended that a new naval base be constructed at Singapore and that the island be turned into a fortress.[121] The CID duly accepted this proposal at its meeting on 10 June, and noted in passing that 'the most likely war for some time to come would be one between the white and yellow races whose interests lay in the Pacific'. Moreover, in a move that underlined the feeling that Japan could not be trusted, the CID proposed that construction of the base should go ahead whether the alliance was renewed or not.[122]

The Great War therefore had the result of revealing to Britain some unpleasant 'facts' about the Japanese. It might be true to say that the impression left by the war years would have been unsettling even without the intelligence about Japan's more nefarious activities, for the niggardly proffering of assistance, the Twenty-One Demands, and the other encroachments on Chinese sovereignty all contributed to an image of Japan as a selfish power bent on hegemony in East Asia. However, the impact of intelligence was important because it had the effect of continually reinforcing Britain's disquiet, particularly when it appeared to uncover Japanese treachery *vis-à-vis* India. Whether Britain was right to be worried or was too over-sensitive has been a matter of debate among historians. Ian Nish and T.G. Fraser have both inclined towards the latter view, arguing that Britain allowed intelligence phantoms to fog its thinking. On the other hand, Richard Popplewell has sympathized with the intelligence practitioners, stating that their concerns were justified. In the end both these arguments have some validity. The fact is that the British did overestimate the Japanese threat, gave too much credence to unsubstantiated reports, and failed initially to see the distinction between the views of the government in Tokyo and the pan-Asian lobby. However, Britain's extreme sensitivity has to be put in context, for a number of factors meant that they were predisposed to be suspicious. The most important of these was the knowledge that the forces in the region were inadequate to defend British interests. This naturally raised anxiety, which was compounded by the fact that Britain could gain little comfort from asking Japan to protect its interests, as turning to an Asian power to defend its imperial possessions hardly bolstered British racial prestige. Moreover, Japan's behaviour was not reassuring. It was clearly providing the minimum of assistance in the war against Germany, and it was after all Asian, and thus might be tempted to put its Asian identity before its oath of loyalty to Britain. In these circumstances the British sense of insecurity naturally meant that the racial suspicions of Japan that had appeared in the pre-war era came into sharper focus and made the more unpleasant rumours all the easier to believe. The war therefore brought into the cold light of day Britain's racial distrust of Japan, and thus eroded the foundations of the alliance.

However, due to the success of the Washington Conference of 1921–22, with its regulation of foreign relations with China in the Nine Power Treaty and the introduction of naval limitation for capital ships in the Five Power Treaty, Anglo-Japanese relations entered a period of relative calm. Thus Japan's importance as an intelligence target declined, but this was only partly a testament to the efforts of diplomats in both countries: another major reason for this development was that a new and more immediate menace was laying siege to Britain's interests – Bolshevism. For the next decade it was to be the latter that preoccupied British intelligence, and therefore in order to understand the evolution of the organization of British intelligence and the allocation of resources within the region it is necessary to turn to the Communist menace.

# 4
# 'A Cubist Picture': The Soviet Menace in China, 1918–27

Even before the Great War ended in 1918, the potential threat from Bolshevik Russia began to impinge on the consciousness of British intelligence in East Asia and over the next fifteen years, in the guise of the Comintern, it developed into the main challenge to the British stake in the region both in China and in the colonies in South-East Asia. For British interests in China the threat was to become particularly serious, because Bolshevism was able to flourish in that country as it descended into the anarchy of the warlord years, and moreover appealed to Chinese radicals because it provided an ideological rationale for China's plight and their desire to liberate themselves from the shackles of Western imperialism.[1] The Comintern was to prove a difficult foe for Britain to resist, and the struggle against its influence was to reveal many problems with the provision and interpretation of intelligence and to exacerbate the tensions already revealed in the Great War between the diplomats and the intelligence-providers. These tendencies were strikingly revealed in 1927 when a drastic intelligence failure led to the sudden emergence of a threat to British interests in Shanghai and the despatch of a division of British troops to secure the city.

## Post-war intelligence retrenchment in China

The first sighting of a possible Bolshevik in China came in January 1918 when the IB noted the presence of a man named Remisoff in Shanghai.[2] Over the next two years the IB, Petrie's replacement as the DCI officer in Shanghai, Godfrey Denham, and Ridout's organization in Singapore produced a series of ever more dramatic warnings about the Bolshevik menace but, as with the intelligence on Japanese pan-Asianism, these often lacked credibility due to their speculative nature. Such reporting led the traditionally minded diplomats in China and the Foreign Office, who had already expressed doubts about intelligence during the war, to become even more sceptical about the utility of these organizations. For example, when in July

1919 Ridout produced a list of supposed Bolsheviks in East Asia which included a number of Chinese political figures who were clearly not communists, Sir John Jordan commented acidly on the danger 'of labelling distinguished men in other countries as Bolshevists without first consulting those who are in a position to give reliable information'.[3]

As Jordan's comment indicates the fundamental problem, as with the disagreements that had occurred between the Peking legation and the IB in 1917, was that the diplomats felt that the intelligence staff were making judgements about a possible threat without fully understanding the context. In the case of the early reports on Bolshevism the diplomats believed that the IB and Ridout were inferring from the presence of Bolsheviks that a real and immediate threat existed, but without asking how Marxism-Leninism was actually going to appeal to the Chinese or the other nationalities in the region. To the diplomats this was the key point, because their experience of Chinese politics told them that Bolshevism had little chance of gaining a foothold in the region. Thus on a number of occasions Jordan and others noted that, although there was much political unrest in China due to the rise of nationalist sentiment, it was important to differentiate boycotts and strikes from outright Bolshevism.[4]

The doubts about the usefulness of these intelligence reports, combined with the simultaneous eclipse of the Japanese threat, led between 1920 and 1923 to the abolition of those organizations that had been set up during the war. In China the IB's predilection for reporting on all Bolshevik activities no matter how superficial quickly brought about its demise. Observing that the 'ill-digested reports' of the IB led only to confusion, in April 1920 Miles Lampson, the chargé d'affaires in Peking, pressed for its closure and by the end of year it had closed its doors.[5]

The curtailing of the Indian intelligence presence in East Asia soon followed. At first, as the IB declined in importance, Denham's role actually increased as he personally took on the responsibility for collecting intelligence on Bolshevism in China. This redefinition of his work took place late in 1919, when, after a number of abortive attempts to find a suitable candidate, 'C' asked him to act as the Secret Service's 'chief representative in the Far East'.[6] From this point on Denham's reports were widely circulated in Whitehall but with his name replaced by his Secret Service designation 'C/0'.

In April 1920 Denham prepared the first in a series of extensive assessments of the current state of China in which he dramatically proclaimed:

> That Bolshevism is spreading and that it is peculiarly acceptable to the Oriental by its advocacy of race equality and self-determination is undoubted, and that it is a very real danger to the British Empire in Asia is apparent from the bitter anti-English spirit which everywhere seems to be an inherent part of Bolshevik teachings.[7]

In particular, he pointed to the dangers that might arise from contacts between Sun Yat-sen and Bolshevik agents in China and claimed that Sun and those close to him, such as the warlord Ch'en Chiung-ming, had begun to talk openly of their 'admiration of Bolshevism'. Denham could, however, only postulate a few ways in which to counter the Soviet danger, including the interception of propaganda and personal correspondence in Shanghai and stricter control over passports. As far as the Foreign Office was concerned Denham's reports on Bolshevism showed the same weaknesses as those that had previously been circulated by the IB. For example, Lampson, who had returned to London in late 1920, noted of Denham that 'like every special investigator, he exaggerates somewhat', and that 'it is no reflection upon him if I venture the criticism that he takes such men as Sun Yat Sen a little too seriously'.[8] This patronizing analysis of Denham's work was symptomatic of the growing gulf between the intelligence community and the Foreign Office.

In 1921 Denham temporarily moved towards a less alarmist stance, concluding that the Bolshevik hold over China's radicals was in fact comparatively weak because the anarchist movement was too independent to be controlled by an outside force, but in 1922 his position hardened again.[9] The stimulus for this came largely from his growing concern about the situation in Canton, where Sun had established a radical government and was engaging in such disturbing activities as planning a 'northern expedition' to unite the country by force, appointing the avowed Bolshevik, Ch'en Tu-hsui, as his Minister of Propaganda and most important sponsoring a seaman's strike that paralysed the trade of Hong Kong in the winter of 1921–22.

These troubling events did not, however, portend any danger to India, and in March 1922 the Indian government decided for financial reasons to abolish Denham's post.[10] The logical solution to this problem was for the Secret Service, which had now metamorphosed into the SIS, to cover his salary, but in the spring of 1922 it too had to cut its budget for China from the 1921 figure of £1,800 to £1,100, and thus could not step into the breach unless Denham was willing to accept a cut in his pay, which he was not.[11] When this news was forwarded to Peking, the initial response was one of horror for, in the light of recent events at Canton, it was believed that there had to be someone with Denham's qualifications in China who could report on Bolshevik activities. Denham himself encouraged such an assessment, noting to Jordan's successor as minister, Sir Beilby Alston, that if anything the situation called for the establishment of a new intelligence organization in China that would cooperate more fully with the consular staff.[12]

Within a month, however, there was an abrupt change of heart in the Peking legation to a feeling that Denham's services could be dispensed with and that no replacement was necessary. In a letter to the Foreign Office,

Robert Clive, the chargé d'affaires at Peking, noted that while it was useful for someone from India to keep an eye on the Indian community, there was no need for that officer to look at the Bolshevik menace and 'spend money on sub-agents throughout China in order to secure information of a very doubtful value to us from a practical point of view'.[13] This reversal of opinion appears to have arisen for a number of reasons. A key factor was that by the late summer the 'Red tide' of the winter had ebbed away, as Sun's regime in Canton had collapsed leaving him without a power base. In addition, with Alston too ill to continue as minister, those in China who doubted the efficacy of Denham's work came to the fore. In particular, the highly respected if eccentric consul-general at Canton, Sir James Jamieson, made his views clear when he observed somewhat cruelly to Denham that:

> I am filled with profound admiration for the assiduity with which you have collected your bag of communistic societies, but may I be forgiven if I think that many of them consist of the members of the Committee only?[14]

A further nail in Denham's coffin was a resurgence of antagonism in the legation towards the SIS and intelligence in general. This arose largely due to events in Manchuria, where the consul-general in Harbin, Harold Porter, had access to a secret source who provided information on Soviet attempts to regain control over the CER. In order to maximize the utility of this source, in the summer of 1922 the SIS despatched a Russian-speaking representative, Edward Small, to Harbin. To provide him with diplomatic cover he was given a vice-consul's passport, but unfortunately neither the SIS nor the Foreign Office saw fit to consult the Peking legation about this. The result was that the legation was sorely displeased, for it found it embarrassing to have to account for this apparently unwarranted expansion in the consular establishment.[15]

The Foreign Office concurred in the legation's views about Denham, and his services were duly dispensed with in February 1923, after which he moved to a new post as the inspector-general of police (IGP) in Malaya. In hindsight the legation's rejection of Denham was a logical extension of its objections to the activities of Seigne during the First World War. The feeling of those diplomats who specialized in Chinese affairs was that intelligence staff lacked the experience to interpret events in China and that their activities led to unnecessary alarms. They contended that these problems arose because the intelligence staff operated entirely independently from the legation: in other words this was as much a battle for control over policy and for ensuring that the diplomats were the only interpreters of events as it was a conflict over the value of the information. This appears to have been a widespread grievance in the Foreign Office, for when Sir Ronald Macleay arrived in February 1923 to succeed Alston he approved of the suspension of Denham's post on the grounds that he had been faced with a similar intelligence organization in his previous posting in Argentina.[16]

It is probable that the legation discussed the future of intelligence in China in September 1922 with an SIS representative, David Boyle. Boyle was at this point touring the region in order to settle how the SIS should consolidate its operations in the East, which had been largely ad hoc until that point.[17] What was agreed is not clear, but from later evidence it would appear that the mutually acceptable solution was that nominated staff from the consular service should take on the responsibility for political intelligence-gathering and reporting to 'C' in London. That this was the consensus is hinted at by the fact that, in the wake of Denham's departure, two consular officers, Harold Steptoe and Arthur Blackburn, began to take on SIS work, the former being given responsibility for corresponding with India about seditionaries.[18] Steptoe was thirty-two years old in 1923. He had first come to China in 1912 in inauspicious circumstances, having recently collapsed with a nervous breakdown prior to his undergraduate finals at Bristol University. He stayed in China for the next two years recovering his composure and rapidly acquiring Mandarin. In the war he served in East Africa, acting as a liaison officer with the Belgians and attaining the rank of Lieutenant. In 1919, seeking to take advantage of his linguistic ability, he entered the China Consular service.[19] It may be that from the very start he was being trained for intelligence work; in 1929 a Treasury official noted of Steptoe that he had 'a "hush hush" job which has been in existence since after the armistice'.[20] Indeed, it is noticeable that almost immediately on his arrival in China Steptoe's army training and language proficiency led Jordan to send him to Inner and Outer Mongolia to report on the military situation.[21] Blackburn was thirty-six years old and had been a member of the consular service since 1908. During the war he had been engaged in censorship work at Shanghai and had acted as Denham's *locum tenens* in 1920 and thus had some experience of intelligence and counter-espionage.[22]

The general lack of concern about radical activities in China was also apparent in Hong Kong. In March 1922 the Governor, Sir Reginald Stubbs, was sufficiently alarmed about Sun's relations with Moscow at the time of the seamen's strike to ask for reform of the political intelligence presence at Hong Kong. His interest was, however, only transient and apart from persuading the SIS to appoint a representative in Canton brought about no substantive results.[23] The issue of intelligence at Hong Kong then lay dormant until August 1923, when the War Office, concerned about the lack of information on southern China, recommended that a political intelligence bureau should be established in the colony to supplement the JNMIB.[24] This proposal was put to Stubbs, but he provided a lukewarm response, observing that the police already provided adequate information on the situation in Hong Kong and that he doubted whether the colony would be a suitable listening post on China. This effectively killed off the War Office's idea and, after further intermittent debate in Whitehall, the Colonial Office put the issue to one side.[25] Notably around the same time, Stubbs averred to Charles Drage, a young naval officer in Hong Kong and future SIS representative, that '"Intelligence" in the East is somewhat overdone and there is a great deal of eyewash'.[26]

The situation by 1924, therefore, was that the ability to follow events in China had been drastically cut back from its wartime state. All that remained of the previous apparatus was the body that had proved least useful during the war, the JNMIB, whose reporting of political intelligence was notoriously inadequate.[27] The only innovation was the establishment of an untried SIS structure, but this organization was compromised by the fact that, although its representatives were in contact with the local diplomatic posts, its reports were not passed directly to the military and naval authorities and only reached them if forwarded by the intelligence directorates in London.[28] This was clearly an unsatisfactory arrangement, but the SIS was determined to keep its presence as subterranean as possible.

## The emergence of the KMT threat

Despite the continuing doubts of the Peking legation it appears that much of the work of the SIS organization in China after 1922 still concentrated upon the potential Bolshevik threat. This led it to report on such subjects as the political situation surrounding the CER in north Manchuria and the course of the Sino-Soviet negotiations on the opening of diplomatic relations, but the most significant area of study was tracing the growth of ties between the KMT and the Comintern.[29] This work began in March 1923 with a report on an understanding reached in January between Sun Yat-sen and Adolf Joffe, the head of the Soviet diplomatic mission to China, under which the Soviet Union agreed to provide 'moral and financial support' for the KMT in return for the latter's support for Chinese recognition of the Soviet regime.[30] From this point on the SIS representatives produced a series of increasingly detailed reports, particularly once Sun returned to Canton in the spring of 1923. These covered aspects such as the links developing between the CCP and the KMT, the arrival in October 1923 of the Comintern's political adviser to Sun, Mikhail Borodin, the Soviet-influenced centralization of the party machinery, and the tensions that this lurch to the left caused within the party.[31]

One might assume that information of this sort would have been enough to rouse the Peking legation and the Foreign Office from their stupor, but for a number of reasons it made little impact. One factor was that, even though the diplomats now had greater control over the SIS representatives, doubts remained about the accuracy of the latter's reporting. As Foreign

Office officials noted in relation to an SIS report on Korean revolutionaries, this sort of material often constituted nothing more than 'hasty generalization' which 'when subjected to competent criticism' was 'usually found wanting'.[32] Even more important was that there were good political reasons to discount the importance of these developments. One key influence on Foreign Office thinking was the fact that Sun had for his whole career sought foreign backers for his often wholly impractical schemes for uniting China under the KMT, and there was therefore little reason to believe that his new socialist phase was anything more than lip-service to his new patron. Moreover, even if one accepted that the Soviets were radicalizing the KMT, it was not clear that this constituted much of a threat, for at the national level Sun was an insignificant figure compared to northern warlords such as Wu P'ei-fu, who controlled Peking, and Chang Tso-lin who dominated Manchuria. In addition, there was the belief that, as political and military events in north China ultimately dictated the fortunes of the country with Peking as the key prize in any civil conflict, distant Canton could never be more than a regional power-base.[33]

The conviction in the Peking legation and the Foreign Office that Bolshevism and the KMT did not pose a serious threat was held until the autumn of 1924, when a series of events heightened concern about the growing Soviet interest in and influence upon events in China. One disturbing development was that intelligence from Vladivostock, Shanghai and Canton revealed that the Soviet Union had begun arms deliveries to the KMT.[34] This was significant because from May 1919 the Powers, as part of their policy of non-intervention in the ongoing civil war, had embargoed the sale of arms to China. Russia's action thus threatened to tilt the military balance in the KMT's favour. In addition, SIS sources in Europe acquired information that indicated that the Executive Committee of the Comintern (ECCI) had instructed the newly appointed Soviet ambassador in Peking, Lev Karakhan, to 'provide every facility' to the CCP leader, Ch'en Tu-hsui, and that a subsidy of five million roubles had been granted to help organize strikes and acts of industrial sabotage.[35]

These reports had a marked effect, for they arrived at a time of momentous change. In the late summer of 1924 a war broke out in north China between Chang Tso-lin and Wu P'ei-fu. At first it appeared that Wu would triumph, but in October his position was suddenly undermined by the Japanese-sponsored treachery of his subordinate, Feng Yü-hsiang, who launched a coup in Peking. Feng's action precipitated a sudden shift to the left in Chinese politics, for he quickly established a cabinet in Peking and called for a national conference to be held in the capital to which he invited both Chang and Sun.[36]

With rumours circulating that Feng had his own links with Karakhan, the fact that he was bringing Sun back on to the central stage of Chinese politics, thus allowing the KMT to throw off its Cantonese parochialism, appeared deeply ominous to British observers. Sun died of cancer in March 1925 before the conference could meet, but this did not lead to any slackening of concern, for even more disturbing events were soon to follow. On 30 May a detachment of the SMP under a British commander fired upon a crowd of Chinese demonstrators in the International Settlement, killing seven. In response the May Thirtieth Movement, a KMT-sponsored campaign of strikes and boycotts against British commercial interests, began in the Yangtse valley and soon spread to south China. On 22 June a further incident took place, this time in Canton, where British and French guards killed over 100 demonstrators who were marching on the international concession on Shameen Island. This in turn sparked the cessation of trade between Canton and Hong Kong in a sixteen-month long boycott and strike.[37]

In the background, the Soviets whipped up this sudden wave of agitation. British intelligence was by no means blind to their activities thanks to the work of Steptoe, who had just been appointed the SIS representative in the Peking legation, and Blackburn, his counterpart in Shanghai.[38] In June, Steptoe acquired a letter sent by Karakhan to Shanghai that demonstrated that the Bolsheviks were encouraging the strike action. Moreover the arrest of a Russian named Dosser in Hong Kong revealed that he had been sent to organize strike committees in south China.[39] Faced with such information the newly formed Chiefs of Staff (COS) committee in London observed that the Soviets, assisted by their minions in Canton, were fomenting and exploiting the situation in China in order to 'injure vital British interests in a part of the world where they are most vulnerable'.[40]

The events of 1924–25 finally forced both Whitehall and the Peking legation to accept that a potential Bolshevik threat existed to British interests in China. Over the next two exceptionally troubled years this menace remained a constant presence, shaping the formulation of British policy and influencing the evolution of intelligence-gathering in the region. However, the concentration on Soviet activities and goals did not necessarily mean that Britain understood what was happening in China.

This became clearly apparent in 1926–27 when Britain suddenly was faced with the most serious challenge to its interests in China since the Boxer rebellion of 1900. The roots of this crisis lay in the emergence of Chiang Kai-shek, the head of the party's National Revolutionary Army (NRA), as the KMT's most important figure. In July 1926 Chiang launched the Northern Expedition, a military campaign to unite the country under the KMT's rule. His efforts were rapidly successful, and by the autumn the NRA had defeated the army of Wu P'ei-fu, the leading warlord in central China, and had arrived at Hankow in the Yangtse valley. The KMT, now ensconced in the most prosperous area of China, brought its anti-British agitation to the region and in early January 1927 seized the British concessions at Hankow and Kiukiang, and threatened to advance on the greatest commercial prize of all – Shanghai. To Britain, all of this – the dramatic rise of the KMT regime in Canton to national prominence and its ability to challenge British interests in the Yangtse valley – came as a great shock, for its intelligence network in the region had failed entirely to predict such an outcome.

## The Soviets and Feng Yü-hsiang

The intelligence failure of 1926–27 was a very significant event in the evolution of the British intelligence presence in the region in the inter-war period and therefore it is worth examining in some depth the flaws and weaknesses revealed during this fraught period. One of the key problems for Britain was that its political and military intelligence-gathering capabilities were, despite the concern about Canton, still tilted towards acquiring information on north China. This came about partly because of the concentration of personnel in this area, which included the military attaché and the SIS representative at the Peking legation, and the army intelligence officer at Tientsin, but was also due to the continuing tendency to see the capital as the centre of Chinese politics. This, as noted above, had already been a drawback in the 1923–24 period because it meant that the early intelligence on the KMT's links with the Soviets had not been taken sufficiently seriously. From 1925 it was a problem in a different and even more damaging way in that it led Britain to concentrate its attention upon Feng Yü-hsiang, the lesser of the two Bolshevik-sponsored threats, merely because he was competing for control of Peking while the KMT remained isolated in Canton.

The concentration on the menace posed by Soviet support for Feng began in 1925. It arose from two factors. First, that Feng used the May Thirtieth Incident to publicize his nationalist and anti-imperial credentials and thus emerged as a potential threat to British interests: and second, that to strengthen his position *vis-à-vis* his domestic rivals he turned to the Soviets for arms and financial assistance. From Peking it was relatively easy for British intelligence to follow Feng's shift to the left. One important factor was that the military attaché, Colonel G.R.V. Steward, and others in the legation, acquired intelligence from a number of informers, including the BAT agent at Urga [Ulan Bator] on the arms supply that passed from the Soviet Union via Mongolia to Feng's base at Kalgan. These reports also indicated that by September 1925 up to a thousand Russians were assisting Feng as military advisers.[41]

This information was supplemented by an even more significant source, the intelligence that Steptoe was able to acquire from the Soviet embassy. Throughout 1925 to 1927 Steptoe regularly obtained copies of Karakhan's correspondence with Moscow, which from June 1926 were circulated in Whitehall as BJs by the GCCS, and records of meetings of Soviet officials in the embassy.[42] How he acquired this material is not clear, but what is apparent is that this was seen as intelligence of the highest value, for it appeared to reveal step by step the evolution of Soviet policy towards China. Included was confirmation of Steward's information on Soviet arms deliveries to Feng and reports on how Russian money was being distributed in China. Most significant was that it contained evidence of the ebb and flow of Soviet policy. It showed that the Soviets were torn between either backing Feng and the CCP or simply concentrating on fostering anti-imperialism and seeking to expand Soviet influence in potentially easier pastures such as Chinese Central Asia.[43]

The problem with this intelligence was that, as it was derived from the Soviet embassy at Peking, it dealt largely with the responsibilities of that institution, which naturally centred upon the politics of north China and the Soviet relationship with Feng. It did not include much material on the ties with the KMT in the south, and therefore produced a skewed image of Soviet activities. For the unwary interpreter of intelligence in London this was to pose a major problem, as can be seen in a number of memoranda on China produced by Whitehall in 1925–26. For example, in December 1925 the War Office produced a disquieting report on 'The Extension of Soviet Influence in Asia'. Using Steptoe's information and the SIS's ability to acquire ECCI and Politburo reports from Moscow, it noted that the Soviet Union's activities in China were but part of a larger campaign to increase its influence in Asia. It observed that, up to now, Russian efforts within China had centred on utilizing Feng and his supporters, but that these had achieved meagre results and that Karakhan was 'for the time being under a cloud'. Accordingly, the Soviets had recently changed their focus to attempting to gain control over the outlying provinces of China such as Mongolia, Kansu and, most alarmingly, Sinkiang, which bordered on India.[44] The India Office held similar fears and in July 1926 outlined its interpretation of the Soviet threat to Sinkiang in a memorandum for the Inter-departmental Committee on Eastern Unrest (IDCEU).[45] The problem with these reports was that they overstated the nature of the threat described, while at the same time almost entirely ignoring the more disturbing trend of events at Canton. In part, this arose out of a tendency to take Soviet documents at face value rather than realizing, as William Strang of the Far Eastern Department noted, that 'in their discussions the Soviet leaders usually tend to paint a rosier picture of Soviet influence than the facts warrant'.[46] The result of such reports was that in much of Whitehall there was a poor understanding of events in China and only a vague awareness of how the situation might imperil British interests.

Reinforcing the fixation on north China was the belief in most British circles that the forces of Feng and Chang Tso-lin represented the most advanced armies in China. This was, of course, not saying much, for Britain still had nothing but disdain for Chinese warfare, placing China far behind

Japan in terms of its military prowess. The belief in the relative value of Feng's and Chang's armies rested largely on the observations of Steward and his predecessors. Even before his rise to prominence in the autumn of 1924, Feng's army had been viewed as worthy of praise. Its key attributes were that it was reasonably well led and that Feng, as a Christian, had instilled a sense of mission in his troops that differentiated them from the soldiers in other armies, who were little more than mercenaries. The arrival of Russian arms boosted its value even further, so that by 1926 the War Office viewed it as 'the best army in China today'.[47] Chang's army on the other hand had until 1926 the reputation of only fighting well in Manchuria. However, as it emerged as the leading anti-Bolshevik force in north China and developed its artillery and air arm its worth in Steward's eyes began to rise, a judgement that was confirmed when it inflicted a series of defeats on Feng in the summer of 1926. With Chang now in control of Peking, Steward developed a strong relationship with the Manchurian general staff, which further heightened his appreciation.[48] However, this was not necessarily advantageous from the military intelligence perspective, for Steward began to rely too heavily on Chang's staff for information.[49]

## Military intelligence and the Northern Expedition

While Britain concentrated its attention upon the shifting balance of power in the north, major changes were taking place in Canton. The significance of the strengthening of the KMT both militarily and politically was, however, largely missed. This was, of course, partly the result of Britain's obsession with events around Peking, but in addition arose out of the shockingly feeble state of intelligence on Canton.

In the realm of military intelligence, the most important mistake made by British observers was the misguided premise that the KMT did not have the military capability to extend its influence beyond Kwangtung and Kwangsi provinces, for it was this above all that led Britain to view it as solely a regional force. The main culprit was the complacent and parochial general staff at Hong Kong. Confident that there was no threat to the colony's security, it viewed the Cantonese forces with ill-concealed contempt, for example, noting in October 1925 that 'they can be hardly be considered an army, according to modern standards'.[50] Armed with this preconception, Hong Kong failed to recognize the value of the army reforms that Chiang initiated with the assistance of his Comintern advisers, such as the establishment of the Whampoa Military Academy and the introduction of a political commissar system. This was reprehensible, for in 1925–26 it was readily apparent that the NRA was proving victorious against its rivals in a series of campaigns to enlarge the KMT's control over south China.[51] The numbing complacency of Hong Kong was summed up in a letter sent to MI2c in July 1926 in which a local intelligence staff officer noted that 'it is a waste of time, energy and paper to write up lengthy reports on the local Chinese wars or organization, etc. of armies', as most important facts were covered in *The Times*.[52]

This problem might have been alleviated if Colonel Steward had been able to keep a regular watch on events in the south, for he did show some appreciation of the NRA's progress. For example, in March 1925 he visited Whampoa and wrote a favourable report on the training that it was providing to its cadets, and in February 1926 noted the NRA's superiority over other forces in south China.[53] However, stuck as he was in Peking, Steward lacked up-to-date information and therefore failed to see that the NRA also surpassed in quality the forces of Wu P'ei-fu and were easily a match for Chang's army.[54]

Further exacerbating Britain's dilemma was the troubled relationship between the SIS and military intelligence. Following Denham's departure in 1923, the War Office had sought to ensure that the SIS did not become merely an adjunct of the Foreign Office and that it collected items of military importance. In April 1924 this had led it to initiate a new system under which MI2c drew up an annual questionnaire on the subjects that it wished the SIS representatives in the region to investigate.[55] In April 1926 further welcome refinements were introduced, when the Air Ministry agreed to contribute to the questionnaire and the SIS removed the bar on its representatives communicating with the GOCs in Hong Kong and Singapore.[56] However, there is no evidence to suggest that these reforms led the SIS to provide the sort of detailed information that MI2c required on the various Chinese armies, indeed it appears that relations between the SIS representatives and military intelligence remained cool at best.[57]

These shortcomings in military intelligence meant that in the summer of 1926 there was little expectation in either Hong Kong or Peking that a Northern Expedition would succeed or even commence. On 3 July 1926 the South China Command noted scathingly that the new KMT campaign being prepared was 'devoid of military interest and its possibilities are not worth discussing' because it was 'highly improbable that anything of the kind will happen'.[58] Moreover, this constant depreciation of the NRA meant that the Foreign Office and the War Office, lacking any other sources of information, shared in the belief that if it did advance it would meet its 'Waterloo' in the alien environment of the Yangtse valley.[59]

Even when the NRA defeated Wu's forces at Hankow, its achievement was not fully appreciated because British military intelligence on the Yangtse valley was more or less non-existent. This area had always been neglected, because there was no local British garrison, but in the summer of 1926 the problem was exacerbated when the War Office decided to make Hong Kong the headquarters for a South China Command and to re-establish a North China Command at Tientsin.[60] This change had unfortunate consequences, for the boundary between the two Commands was drawn along the Yangtse, which had the effect of dividing responsibility for the collection of intelligence on central China, thus inevitably leading to neglect.[61] Steward was quick to recognize the problem and in July 1926 proposed to the War Office that a centre for the coordination and compilation of intelligence on China should be established at Shanghai. His suggestion was, however, rejected by MI2c, which felt that such an establishment would undermine its own ability to decide how intelligence should be collated and interpreted.[62]

The result was that Britain simply lacked an experienced military intelligence presence in the Yangtse valley, and thus was not able to report on the campaigning. Some civilian observers did exist; for example, both the consul-general at Hankow, Herbert Goffe, and A.H. Williams, an employee of the Canton–Hankow Railway, reported on the NRA's superior morale and organization, but in the absence of accredited intelligence personnel, the dominant voice remained that of the blinkered general staff at Hong Kong. [63] The latter did recognize that the NRA's success showed that it might be better led and trained than it had previously imagined, but it insisted that its victories were most likely the result of the effective use of propaganda and bribery of its opponents.[64]

## Political intelligence and the KMT

Britain's difficulties did not end with the failure to predict the military course of events in China, for there was also much confusion about the KMT's political agenda and lack of knowledge about its key personalities. This ignorance extended to such vital topics as whether Canton was controlled by the KMT government or the Strike Committee that had emerged after June 1925, what influence Borodin exerted, and where Chiang stood politically. The uncertainty surrounding these subjects arose largely from the fact that, especially after the Shameen Island massacre of June 1925, Britain had very few sources of political intelligence on events at Canton. In the wake of the incident, the most obvious source of information, consul-general Jamieson, did not dare to enter the city, and thus lost track of developments. Furthermore, he took the opportunity of his enforced indolence to foster a reputation as 'a public and notorious drunkard', which led both Owen O'Malley, the counsellor at the Peking legation, and Sir Cecil Clementi, the Governor of Hong Kong, to press for his replacement.[65] His successor, John Brenan, managed to improve matters by renewing the dialogue with the KMT leadership and cultivating a number of useful sources, including Sun Yat-sen's former bodyguard, Morris 'Two-Guns' Cohen.[66] In addition, Clementi entered into an occasionally fruitful correspondence with Francis Hayley Bell, the CMC commissioner at Canton, who was able to acquire some privileged information about what was going on within the KMT.[67]

Such sources were, however, no replacement for good secret service work, and this appears to have been noticeably absent in Canton. According to a note written by Steptoe in October 1925 there was still an SIS representative in the city, but no evidence exists to suggest that this source was effective.[68] Another problem was that nothing had ever been done about establishing a political intelligence bureau at Hong Kong that would be able to collate information on the KMT. Indeed, it was not until early 1926 that the Hong Kong police even tried to gather intelligence, employing a White Russian called Koretsky. The latter was initially able to acquire some useful information about the Soviet presence in Canton, but obtained little of value on the KMT itself.[69] The lack of good intelligence in south China was noted in early 1926 by O'Malley, who observed that, in contrast to the riches available to the SIS, 'the Hong Kong dossier is only of interest as showing the poverty of their information'.[70] This view was corroborated by another observer, Superintendent Victor Smith, an Indian police officer who was sent to China from December 1925 to February 1926 to report on the bearing that the Chinese disturbances might have on India. While satisfied with the SIS organizations in Peking and Shanghai, Smith was extremely critical of the lack of any effective intelligence system in Canton, noting in a letter to Petrie, who was now the Director of the Indian DCI, that:

> Nothing has impressed me more in the course of my tour than the general ignorance prevailing regarding Canton, its Kuomintang Government, the actual extent of its subservience to Russian interests and its Strike Committee. There appear to be no inside sources of information, where one might expect to find definite knowledge there is merely speculation and an expression of opinion. This ignorance of affairs Cantonese extends to Hong Kong, Shanghai and Peking equally, but the colonial and insular attitude of Hong Kong in the past seems to be mainly responsible.[71]

Smith's final report included recommendations for reform, but by the end of 1926 these were still being debated and thus the problems remained unresolved.[72]

This intelligence vacuum had dangerous ramifications, for it allowed the various ministries in Whitehall and British authorities in China to interpret the situation in Canton as they saw fit. The general view among the service departments and the Peking legation was that the KMT was entirely under the heel of the Bolsheviks, and a number of policies were recommended to counter the Comintern's influence. These included lifting the ban on British arms sales to China in order to strengthen warlords such as Chang and Wu, actively engaging in anti-Bolshevik propaganda, and applying diplomatic pressure in Moscow. The Foreign Office, drawing on its long-held view that the situation in China had to be seen in its historical and cultural context, took a different view. It believed that the KMT were nationalists first and foremost, rather than mere puppets of the Soviets. Aided by the belief that the KMT, in comparison with its rivals, might be capable of providing good government, this led it in 1926 to speculate about the possibility of winning over the moderates within its ranks.[73]

## Crisis on the Yangtse

The general ignorance about the KMT meant that when the NRA unexpectedly arrived in the Yangtse valley in the autumn of 1926 it was not entirely clear what this portended for Britain. Opinion in Whitehall remained divided between those who feared that China was on the verge of sinking under Russian control and those who viewed the situation more optimistically. Unsurprisingly, the Foreign Office tended towards the latter perspective. It suspected that there would be some disruption, possibly in the form of strikes and boycotts against British commercial interests, but maintained its faith in the possibility of a diplomatic settlement with the KMT. This was predicated on the belief that the nearer the latter came to achieving its goals, the more likely it was to throw over its Bolshevik sponsors. Accordingly, in November 1926 the Foreign Office rejected a proposal from the Secretary of State for War, Sir Laming Worthington-Evans, that a battalion of troops be sent to Shanghai, believing that such a gesture might alienate the Chinese nationalists.[74] On 1 December the Foreign Secretary, Sir Austen Chamberlain, assured the Cabinet that 'he was not disposed to think that the settlements on the Yangtse Kiang were in great danger'.[75] Convinced that only it could put events in China in context, the Foreign Office thus moved ahead with its attempt to demonstrate that Britain was prepared to meet the demands of moderate nationalism. On 26 December it made public its famous 'Christmas Memorandum' in which it announced that Britain was prepared to negotiate about the future of its treaty privileges in China.[76]

Unfortunately for the Foreign Office, the general trend of the intelligence reaching Britain increasingly suggested that its attitude might be too complacent. With the KMT in the ascendant, Moscow was clearly keen to take advantage of the situation, and this was reflected in the SIS material collected in Peking and Moscow. From Steptoe there came news that the Soviets were intent on fomenting anti-British strikes and demonstrations in the Yangtse valley and that Borodin had persuaded the KMT to agree to an alliance with the Soviet Union in return for *de jure* recognition.[77] The intelligence from Moscow included a Politburo decision that the Soviet Union should invite Japan to join a Union of Eastern States, which would include all countries in East Asia as far south as India's neighbour, Tibet.[78] In addition, a document passed to the War Office by the Polish military attaché in London in December 1926 outlined the role of the Revvoensoviet, the

Military Department, in helping to direct Russian policy in China. It made clear the degree of control that the Russians had over the NRA and Feng's forces, noting that they acted as 'the secret guiding force of Chinese military operations'.[79]

Even though this intelligence was mainly political in nature, the War Office was keen to submit these 'reports indicating the policy of the Canton government and showing the extent to which this is inspired and backed up by the Russians' to the CID accompanied by its own memorandum.[80] This placed the Foreign Office in a difficult position, for there was a real danger that the War Office might argue that the intelligence proved that Canton was 'desperately Bolshevik', which would undermine the former's policy of conciliation. The Foreign Office therefore insisted that it alone held responsibility for interpreting political intelligence and thus it would produce the memorandum on Russian activities in China.[81]

The Foreign Office's efforts to hold the line were in the short term doomed to failure, for on 5 January 1927 a Chinese mob seized hold of the British concession at Hankow. This alarming news, allied to the fact that intelligence showed that this agitation was precipitated by the Soviets and that Comintern agitators were now proceeding to Shanghai, undermined at a stroke the Foreign Office's claims about the KMT moderates.[82] To the hardliners in Whitehall, both ministers and officials, these events were ample proof that the KMT was entirely Bolshevik and that the Soviet Union was to all intents and purposes in a state of undeclared war with Britain.[83] Moreover, it appeared that Russia had now chosen Shanghai as the setting for the next blow to British imperialism. Recognizing that the loss of the city would be a disaster for British prestige in Asia, the Cabinet on 17 January put in train plans to send a division of troops, the Shanghai Defence Force (Shaforce), to protect the International Settlement. In the words of the Permanent Under-Secretary at the India Office, Sir Arthur Hirtzel, the stage had now been set for 'the decisive trial of strength between Russia and ourselves'.[84]

Simultaneously, efforts were made at last to improve the quality of military intelligence received from China. This was a matter of urgency because, although no doubts existed about Shaforce's ability to resist a Chinese army, concern was expressed about whether it would arrive in time. The current dearth of military intelligence on the Yangtse valley meant that it was impossible to predict how imminent was the NRA threat to Shanghai, or to assess whether the local warlord, Sun Chuan-fang, would be able to resist its advance. In an effort to rectify this situation, all consuls in China were ordered in late January to report on military movements in their area of jurisdiction and Major Bennett, a military intelligence officer from Hong Kong, was transferred to Shanghai where he was given orders to liaise with the SIS.[85] In addition, on 10 February the Cabinet decided that it was essential that the GOC Shaforce, General Duncan, should establish his own intelligence organization when he arrived at Shanghai later that month. This resulted in the creation of an intelligence bureau under the command of Lieutenant-Colonel Heywood, which began from late February onwards to produce daily situation reports on the Shanghai area and the general trend of the Chinese civil war.[86]

Another intelligence aspect to the despatch of Shaforce, which provides a telling comment on the dangers expected, was the desire to ensure that its troops were not infected by Bolshevik propaganda. This led to the decision that one officer in the intelligence bureau, Captain Shelley, should be designated for defence security duties and allowed to correspond direct with MI5 in London.[87] In addition, as Indian troops were included in Shaforce, the government in Delhi decided to send out a police officer, Inspector G. Halland, to watch for seditious activities among the Indian community in China.[88]

## The 'White Terror' in Shanghai

As the first units of Shaforce arrived in late February the course of events in China began to change once again. The new twist was that, just as the NRA approached Shanghai, a split emerged in the KMT between the left wing of the party and those loyal to Chiang Kai-shek. The divisions were both political and personal, but the fundamental cause was that Chiang was determined to rid the KMT of the malign influence of the CCP and the Comintern advisers. As with the unexpected arrival of the KMT in the Yangtse valley, these developments were both poorly documented and little understood by British intelligence, despite the attempts to rectify its shortcomings.

Evidence that a split was in the offing first appeared in late January 1927 when a BJ of a telegram from the Japanese consul-general in Hankow to the Gaimushō indicated that Chiang was contemplating a break with the Comintern.[89] Over the next two months reports on the tensions within the KMT steadily accumulated from a range of both open and secret sources.[90] Faced with this material, the belief in Whitehall, Hong Kong and the Peking legation was that Soviet omnipotence over the KMT meant that if a struggle for power did take place Chiang would inevitably be the loser. Indeed, so pessimistic was the War Office that in March it warned the CID that Russia had achieved complete domination of China and that a threat was emerging to India and Burma.[91] Just as disturbing was that both BJs and SIS reports showed that the Soviets were attempting to win over Japan by offering an understanding over Manchuria, and were encouraging the Hankow government to do the same.[92]

On 21 March Chiang's forces finally entered the Chinese-owned half of Shanghai, but in a move symbolic of the duality within the KMT, they were greeted by a general strike to celebrate victory called by the powerful

CCP-dominated General Labour Union. A reckoning now appeared imminent. What happened next is only partially clear from the primary sources, but some material suggests that Britain now finally began to take Chiang seriously and attempted to encourage him to shake off the Comintern's shackles. The shift in British policy appears to have been encouraged by reports from both open and secret sources that Chiang had entered into a dialogue with Chang Tso-lin and members of the government in Peking. In the diplomatic field Sir Miles Lampson, the new British minister to China, assisted these overtures, even allowing one of Chiang's contacts, Wang Chang-hui, to send a vital telegram from Shanghai to Peking over the British cable network.[93]

It is also tempting to speculate that Britain intervened in another less direct manner, for on 6 April, with the approval of the Western diplomatic body, the Peking police raided the offices of a number of organizations in the Soviet embassy's compound, including that of the military attaché. Chang Tso-lin had been pressing for such a raid ever since January, but Lampson and the other members of the Diplomatic Body only agreed in early April. Why did this sudden change of heart take place? In attempting to answer this question little light is cast by the Foreign Office documents or by Lampson's voluminous diary. What is noticeable, however, is that on 1 April the Shaforce intelligence bureau received information that Chiang intended to attack the CCP by launching raids in Shanghai and other cities under his control.[94] Moreover, on the following day the Liberal MP Sir Archibald Sinclair, who was close to the SIS, passed on to the virulently anti-Soviet Churchill, then Chancellor of the Exchequer, news that Chiang and Chang were close to an understanding.[95] This may be mere coincidence, or it could possibly indicate that the raid on the Soviet compound was designed in a roundabout way to encourage Chiang to strike. Making the whole matter even murkier is that one of the Foreign Office files on the raid contains a short but tantilizing note added in 1959 that states simply that 'A Mr Steptoe was in charge of the investigation'.[96]

Whether the raid was a signal or not, what is clear is that on 12 April Chiang initiated the 'white terror' by striking with ruthless and bloody efficiency against the CCP in Shanghai, Canton and other cities. Chiang's action and the raid on the Soviet embassy proved to be the turning points in this phase of China's path towards national unification. In the coming months the reverberations of these two acts led to a sharp decline in Soviet influence. In mid-April the Soviets abandoned their embassy and decided to concentrate their efforts on bolstering the Hankow government of Wang Ching-wei in its opposition to Chiang. This proved to be only for the short term, for in July the left-wing of the KMT including Wang, suspicious of the Russians and antagonistic towards the CCP, expelled Borodin and ended the 'United Front', thus paving the way for a rapprochement with Chiang.

Britain took time to adjust to this new situation, for the lack of reliable intelligence on Chinese politics continued to be a major drawback, particularly as Steptoe fell ill at the end of May and had to return to Britain to recuperate.[97] On 21 July Ashton-Gwatkin noted wearily, in a comment that summed up Britain's problems since 1925, that the latest stage in the civil war was 'like a Cubist picture – fragments of familiar objects floating about in murky confusion'.[98] However, while China was not yet at peace, it did appear for the moment that the threat to British interests had eased, for Shanghai had survived the arrival of the KMT.

## Malaya and the KMT

Adding an extra dimension to the crisis in China was the fact that, simultaneously, the Comintern was threatening the European colonial interests in South-East Asia directing propaganda towards both the indigenous and overseas Chinese populations. In the immediate post-war era there had been few signs of Soviet interest in this region, and initially the British authorities in Malaya were as sanguine about Bolshevism as their compatriots in China.[99] By late 1921, however, the rise of labour agitation in the East Indies, where the Dutch Bolshevik Sneevliet had founded a communist party, the PKI, and the fear that the KMT might try to promote agitation among the Chinese population in Malaya, transformed the situation. Encouraged by Denham, who visited Malaya in the autumn of 1921, and by Lee-Warner, who had become the SIS representative in Singapore, the Governor of the Straits Settlements, Sir Laurence Guillemard, established a Malayan Bureau of Political Intelligence (MBPI) under A.S. Jelf.[100]

In its first year of existence the MBPI produced little evidence of Bolshevism in Malaya, but in December 1922 intelligence reports emanating from SIS sources about the Comintern's new 'extremist line' in the East, and the links between Sneevliet and Sun Yat-sen greatly disturbed Guillemard. In a bid for preventive action he called on London to extend to the FMS the ban on KMT lodges introduced in the Straits Settlements in 1914, and asked for Denham, with his secret service experience, to be appointed as the new IGP. After some delay he obtained Denham's services, but for the time being the Colonial Office, with the SIS's approval, rejected a ban on the grounds that it would alienate the KMT at a time when Sun was making overtures to Britain.[101] In late 1924 Guillemard, galvanized by news of Sun's apparent conversion to Bolshevism and by a MBPI report that KMT members in Malaya were beginning to distribute communist propaganda, returned to the offensive and once again called for a ban. This time his efforts proved successful, and in October 1925 a dissolution order against the KMT branches in the FMS took effect.[102]

The situation in the region was now increasingly serious, for there was evidence that the Comintern was turning its attention to supporting the

PKI in the East Indies and the KMT in Malaya. In May 1925 the director of the MPBI warned that the Comintern intended to establish a centre at Singapore to foster revolution in South-East Asia. Over the next months intercepted letters to Malaya from the Indonesian communist, Tan Malaka, suggested that progress was being made and the threat of revolution began to haunt the region.[103] In this atmosphere it was clearly not enough for Britain to take action within its own colonies, and thought therefore turned to collaboration with the other colonial powers in South-East Asia. The difficulty was deciding how formal such cooperation should be. Early in 1925 France and Holland made separate overtures to Britain regarding the sharing of intelligence, which in the Dutch case manifested itself as a request for an exchange of information at the consular level between the East Indies and India.[104] However, neither the Foreign Office nor the Home Office wished to see such a formal arrangement and therefore, after a successful link had been established with the Sûreté in Indo-China, they insisted that liaison only took place between the colonial police forces in the region.[105]

The impending storm broke in November to December 1926, just as the Chinese situation grew more threatening, when a series of abortive PKI uprisings erupted in Java and Sumatra. These proved relatively easy to quell, but the fact that they had taken place was worrying and led the colonial powers to draw even closer together.[106] Encouraged by events in China in early 1927, the unrest spread to Malaya where the left wing of the KMT had gained increasing control over the party, and in March a demonstration outside the police station at Kreta Ayer was fired upon leaving two Chinese dead. The response of the authorities was to initiate raids and arrests which, along with Malaya's own version of the KMT's right – left split, helped temporarily to quieten the situation.[107] Thus, as in China, the tide passed, but left behind a residue of concern and uncertainty about the future.

It was therefore time, by the summer of 1927, for Britain to try to learn the lessons of the recent turbulence in both China and South-East Asia and to ensure that there should be no future intelligence failures. In retrospect, it seems clear that the main lesson should have been that all elements of British intelligence in China had been wholly inadequate both in the paucity of information provided and the naïve conclusions reached and that urgent action needed to be taken to remedy these flaws. To a degree this was the conclusion reached by the War Office which felt that Britain had had a lucky escape. It believed that the recent events demonstrated that its intelligence presence in the region had to be overhauled, particularly as, in its view, the Foreign Office could not be trusted to judge the situation accurately. However, the Foreign Office naturally interpreted the situation differently, for it believed that the eventual positive outcome in China had confirmed the essential soundness of its policy over the previous year and that there was therefore no intrinsic need for large-scale reform of the intelligence organizations. Indeed, it believed that the intelligence-providers and the War Office itself had been too alarmist. Here lay the roots of future disagreement.

This concentration on reform of the apparatus did not, unfortunately, also lead to an awareness of the need for a change in attitudes and, as a result, another important lesson of the recent events in China was quickly forgotten. One of the most significant revelations in retrospect of the Northern Expedition, as Donald Jordan has noted, was that the NRA was significantly better than the warlord armies in terms of equipment, discipline and training.[108] Some contemporary British observers recognized this fact but they were few in number, and thus the orthodoxy remained that the Chinese were militarily incompetent and that all campaigns in China were won through bribery. The general disdain for the Chinese was summed up by two observations by British ministers. In January 1927, as Shaforce prepared to depart, the Secretary of State for India, Lord Birkenhead, stated that British forces should be prepared to use poison gas, noting that it 'ought not be unacceptable to an opium-addicted people'.[109] Then, in July 1927, one of Balfour's final contributions to political debate was to declare at a CID meeting that he 'was impressed by the evidence of everyone he met with local knowledge to the effect that the Chinese forces were beneath contempt'.[110] In the long term, this failure to appreciate the NRA's progress and to understand that warfare in China was changing was to have damaging consequences, for it meant that when the Chinese military acquitted itself reasonably well fighting against Japan in Shanghai in 1932 and 1937 and at Tai'erchwang in 1938, Britain drew the unfortunate lesson that the IJA had performed badly rather than acknowledging that the Chinese had proved a worthy foe.

# 5
# Dealing with the Comintern Threat, 1927–31

The largely accidental victory that Britain attained over communism in China in the spring and summer of 1927 did not lead to any diminution of the threat from the Soviet Union, for over the years down to 1931 a steady stream of intelligence revealed that the Comintern was as active as ever, menacing British interests in China and the European colonial possessions in South-East Asia. Concern about the Comintern's activities was strengthened by the fact that, even though in 1928 the KMT successfully concluded the second wave of the Northern Expedition by vanquishing Chang Tso-lin, and established an internationally recognized Nationalist government at Nanking, this did not bring stability to China. Instead from 1928 to 1931 the country continued to be beset by factionalism and civil war which allowed the Comintern and the CCP to profit from its misery.

In an attempt to deal with the Comintern threat the War Office strove to reform the military intelligence presence in East Asia, but in so doing embroiled itself in a running battle with the Foreign Office. Such was the concern about Russia and the intensity of the debate in Whitehall about how to protect and further British interests that the potential menace posed by Japan was largely forgotten; indeed some officials viewed the Japanese as a welcome bulwark against the spread of Bolshevism in North-East Asia. This phenomenon was to have important consequences, for the concentration on the Soviets meant that, when Japanese expansionism revived in the 1930s, British intelligence would be poorly equipped to deal with this new danger and was therefore slow to react.

## Tentative steps towards reform

The tendency of British intelligence to concentrate almost solely on the threat posed by the Comintern manifested itself as Shaforce reached its destination. Deeply sensitive to the intelligence failure that had led to the hurried despatch of 15,000 men to the other side of the globe, the War Office reflected early in 1927 on how to avoid such a situation in the future. Building on the Cabinet's order of 10 February 1927 for the establishment of an intelligence centre at Shanghai to assist General Duncan, the War Office stated that conditions in the region warranted turning this body into a permanent Far East Intelligence Bureau (FEIB) that would remain even after Shaforce had been withdrawn. This FEIB, it envisaged, would be responsible for the interpretation of military intelligence for the entire region from Singapore to Tokyo, and would collate material from all the intelligence centres in China, including the SIS, as well as receiving reports on the IJA from the military attaché in Tokyo.[1]

Having decided on this solution, in April 1927 the War Office won Treasury approval for the sending out of a new intelligence officer, Colonel W.F. Blaker, to take charge of the existing bureau. Blaker was given extensive powers; the SIS organization in China was put at his disposal, and he had the right to correspond directly with the head of MI5 about the protection of the British forces from 'local contamination by subversive propaganda', and to exchange information with the IJA intelligence centre in Shanghai.[2] In addition to his day-to-day work Blaker was ordered to investigate the potential for a permanent bureau, the War Office clearly hoping that he would use his experience to argue that such a body was indispensable.

While Blaker's instructions were finalized, the War Office sought to prepare the way for its preferred solution by indicating its intentions to the Foreign Office, but the latter responded that it could offer no opinion until it could confer with Steptoe on his arrival in Britain on sick-leave.[3] This was of course not strictly true, for the Foreign Office had a fairly clear idea of its thoughts on this matter. Having fought to limit the SIS's independence early in the 1920s, it was unenthusiastic about the idea of a permanent intelligence bureau in the region that would not be under its own control and which might challenge its central position in the formulation of foreign policy. Moreover, it feared, as Lampson noted, that any such move 'might adversely affect the security of present S.I.S'.[4] Indeed, it is notable that simultaneously the Foreign Office was heading off two other threats in the intelligence field. The first blow was struck against the IDCEU, which in 1927 had become increasingly interested in Chinese affairs. Although having no prior knowledge of China, the IDCEU's secretary, Colonel Smith, took it upon himself to prepare a series of reports that highlighted the apparent threat posed by Soviet ambitions. These highly tendentious memoranda provoked the Foreign Office, with the support of the SIS, into demanding that the IDCEU be wound up. Irritated by the interference of other ministries in foreign affairs, Sir Austen Chamberlain took up the cause and forced the minister responsible for the committee, Lord Birkenhead, to agree to its dissolution.[5] In addition, the Foreign Office delayed any action on the recommendation that Superintendent Smith had made in 1926 that an intelligence organization should be formed at Hong Kong to provide information on south China. The Far Eastern Department, with Steptoe's support, argued that a multiplication of intelligence sources only confused policy-making, and that in any case the idea of an organization that could be influenced by the reactionary authorities in Hong Kong was too awful to contemplate.[6]

## The Chinese Communist threat

As Blaker engaged in his research, more intelligence was gathered on the nature of the past and present Soviet threat in China. Information on the former was supplied by an important new source – the documents captured in Chang Tso-lin's raid on the Soviet military attaché's office in April 1927. From April to December the Peking Metropolitan Police published some documents in pamphlet form and passed on others to the British legation. The impression generated by this information was that Soviet activities had been far more extensive than even alarmists such as Steptoe had imagined. The documents outlined the history of the Comintern's political, military and financial support for the KMT, and described the influence that its advisers had had over the party's evolution and the development of the NRA. It also made clear the extent of Russia's ambitions for the Chinese revolution, and in particular its desire to target Britain and if possible to spark clashes between Chinese demonstrators and the forces of the foreign powers.[7] Most disturbing was that this source revealed something that British intelligence had largely missed – the importance of the CCP in the anti-British movement. In October 1927 Lampson forwarded to the Foreign Office a copy of 'an exceedingly illuminating report' written by the Russians on the history of the CCP. The key claim in this extensive memorandum was that it had been the CCP rather than the KMT that had taken the major role in organizing the strikes and boycotts that had followed the May Thirtieth Incident.[8] This important revelation led Ashton-Gwatkin to note in January 1928 that the legation had done a poor job before May 1925 in informing London 'of the steady growth of this sinister power', and that as a result the Foreign Office had been unaware of the difficulties it was up against in China.[9]

The material seized from the Soviets also revealed the new strategy that the Comintern had recently recommended to the CCP. This consisted of an increased emphasis on linking revolutionary activity to agrarian unrest, thus involving the peasantry in the struggle against imperialism and warlord militarism.[10] However, to British relief, the trend of events in China in the second half of 1927 continued to go against the CCP and its Russian backers. Following the split with the left wing of the KMT in Hankow and Borodin's departure in July, the CCP concentrated on building up its strength in Hunan and trying to recover its position in Kwangtung. In September CCP forces seized control of Swatow but were quickly evicted. In December a Soviet was temporarily established at

Canton, but this was suppressed in a matter of days and with some brutality. The KMT reaction to the Canton coup was to break off diplomatic relations with Russia, forcing all of its consuls to leave the KMT-controlled areas of China, and to strike against the CCP organization in Hankow which it claimed was also planning a revolt.[11]

In the wake of these events, evidence of disillusionment in Comintern circles was rife. In January 1928 information from an SIS agent, ellipitically referred to as the 'usual Japanese source unknown to the Japanese', reported that Karakhan had resigned from the Comintern Commission on Chinese Affairs on the grounds that the scheme for a peasant rebellion was 'quite hopeless'.[12] A few days later, intelligence appeared which indicated that the Comintern had decided to change its policy to one of trying to restore relations with China in the hope that it could once again encourage anti-British activity.[13]

Britain was not, however, tempted to believe that the danger had passed. In February 1928 MI2c observed to the SIS that, despite its recent setbacks, 'The aims of Russia in China require the closest attention', and called particularly for more intelligence on Mongolia and Sinkiang.[14] Indeed, the Comintern was only momentarily subdued, and it did not take long for its interest in Chinese revolution to revive. In the spring of 1928 Steptoe, who had now returned to Peking, reported that Borodin was to be sent back to China to take charge of Comintern activities and in particular to stir up agitation in areas controlled by the KMT. This work was to proceed cautiously while the CCP waited for a suitable opportunity for insurrection to be provided by China's incessant civil wars.[15] Borodin was also active in supporting efforts to create instability in Manchuria. Following Chang Tso-lin's defeat by the KMT in the summer of 1928 and the political confusion following his subsequent death at the hands of Japanese assassins, the Mongolians raided the Burga region in the west of Manchuria and there were reports that the Russian presence at Harbin was being strengthened.[16]

By November 1928 it appeared that the Soviets were preparing to incite trouble in the near future, for in that month Steptoe acquired a series of letters, purportedly from the Comintern bureau at Vladistock to a Soviet representative at Tientsin, which called for revolution in south China in an attempt to divert the foreign powers away from 'the economic & political unrest which has recently arisen in Soviet Russia'.[17] Accordingly, the consuls in China were asked to be on their guard and to report any suspicious activities to the legation, while Lampson took the opportunity to warn the Chinese authorities in Peking.[18] For whatever reason no serious outbreaks occurred, but Soviet machinations continued nonetheless.[19] In the spring of 1929, as tensions rose between the KMT government in Nanking and Feng Yü-hsiang, there were reports that the latter might once again be receiving Soviet support.[20] Meanwhile, SIS sources reported that the Soviets were distributing propaganda designed to get the rank and file of the KMT to demand the return of Wang Ching-wei from exile in the belief that this would bring about a catastrophic split in the party.[21] Clearly the Soviets were waiting their turn, ready to take advantage of the KMT's weakness at the first opportunity.

At the same time this period saw further problems in South-East Asia. By early 1928 there was a recrudescence of activity in Malaya, with leftist propaganda once again in circulation and strikes breaking out. Intelligence soon provided the explanation, which was that, with the encouragement of the CCP, some of the former KMT extremists, largely from the Hailam community in Malaya, had reorganized themselves as the Nanyang (South Seas) Communist Party (NCP).[22] The same period saw communist activities spread into new territories. In 1927 reports came in for the first time from the government in Bangkok indicating that Comintern agents were active in Siam.[23]

Over the next few years the situation remained relatively calm in the Dutch East Indies and Malaya, but it was clear that propaganda material continued to be received from China. Disturbingly, by 1929 there was also evidence that the NCP had realized the need to expand its appeal beyond the Hailams into other Chinese communities and even to the Malays. These tactics did not reap any great success, but it was an unwelcome precedent particularly when the Depression began to hit the Malayan economy.[24] Clearly then, although the Comintern had yet to achieve any notable success in China or South-East Asia, its interest in stirring up anti-imperial, and especially anti-British, agitation could not be ignored. In this environment it was necessary to fine-tune Britain's intelligence apparatus in order to provide early warning of revolutionary outbreaks and hopefully to prevent them from even taking place.

## The Far East Intelligence Bureau

As far as the War Office was concerned the key to containing communism was establishing the FEIB, and in February 1928 it was finally able to take action on this initiative with the arrival of the report drawn up by Blaker. Blaker's recommendations were to prove controversial, for they went beyond the War Office's original remit. What he proposed was that a Hong Kong-based FEIB should consist of representatives from the three services, the Foreign Office, the Colonial Office and India, plus perhaps an officer from Australia, and that it should report on the entire region. This organization would retain responsibility for MI5 functions in the region, maintain close liaison with the SIS, and act as the collation centre for all the intelligence collected in the region including that from attachés. Moreover, he argued that it should have the right to report directly to the CID in London. This organization would cost approximately £18,000 per annum, which was equivalent to the sum needed to maintain a gunboat over the same length of time.[25]

The War Office recognized from the first that Blaker had gone too far. For both Colonel Goldsmith of MI1b and the new officer in overall charge of MI2, Colonel Piggott, the main criticism was that Blaker had stuck too rigidly to the idea of the FEIB serving the entire 'Far East'. To them this seemed too ambitious and likely to stir up suspicion among the other imperial powers. In particular, they were concerned about the idea of the military attaché in Tokyo having links with the FEIB, as this might provoke Japanese suspicions and thus undermine relations with the IJA. They recognized too that Blaker's proposals would be unacceptable to other ministries, and that the Foreign Office would not agree to the FEIB reporting to the CID as this would undermine its authority.[26]

However, there was still a strong feeling that a bureau of some kind was necessary. For example, in February 1928, just before Blaker's report arrived, Lieutenant-Colonel Harrison of MI2c, after lambasting the inadequacy of the military intelligence received from China prior to and during the Northern Expedition, warned that without a bureau Singapore, Hong Kong and Tientsin might retreat again into parochialism. Moreover, he noted that the SIS, although productive, had proved over the last few years to be uncooperative and disdainful of the services' intelligence officers, and that without the bureau it might 'revert to working in corridors made narrower by its wish for insularity'.[27] In the light of such views Piggott and Goldsmith felt that the War Office should propose a slimmed-down version of the FEIB. Accordingly, Piggott recommended that the FEIB should restrict its area of jurisdiction to China, focusing primarily on the Soviet threat, and that it should be established in Tientsin, which would facilitate the exchange of intelligence with the Japanese, French and American military authorities. Meanwhile, Goldsmith emphasized the importance of a cryptographer and a WT station being added in order to intercept foreign military and diplomatic traffic.[28]

The War Office presented its doubts about the feasibility of Blaker's proposals and its own plan to establish a bureau at Tientsin to an inter-services meeting held on 17 April 1928. The Admiralty and Air Ministry supported the new proposal, but made it clear that they would prefer to liaise with such a body rather than attach officers permanently. The only dissenting voice to the whole concept of a bureau came from the head of MI5, Sir Vernon Kell, who proposed that more SIS officers should be appointed instead. This was, however, dismissed as unfeasible by Goldsmith because the SIS could clearly not liaise with the Japanese.[29]

The War Office then arranged for its plans to be put before a full interdepartmental meeting of the interested ministries on 17 July 1928. It was at this meeting that the Foreign Office finally pounced; George Mounsey, the head of the Far Eastern Department, indicated that his superiors were 'disinclined to cooperate' with the FEIB whether its remit be for the 'Far East' generally or just China. Mounsey supported the Foreign Office's position by noting that Blaker's report had been commissioned at a time of great tension, but that now the crisis had passed it was possible to return to the traditional arrangement for collecting information, namely through the consular service in China. The Colonial Office was more enthusiastic, but stated that it would only cooperate if the Foreign Office was involved.[30]

It was now patently clear that Blaker's plans were impractical and that even the War Office's idea of a combined bureau at Tientsin was unacceptable. MI2c therefore decided to change tack. Its new scheme, which surfaced in November 1928, was that on the withdrawal of Shaforce its intelligence section would remain in Shanghai and simply reconstitute itself as a China Intelligence Bureau (CIB). This body would continue to liaise with the SIS, MI5 and other foreign intelligence centres in the city, particularly the Japanese, and also engage in cryptographic work for GCCS.[31] The occasion to put this plan forward formally came in the spring of 1929, when the China Command, including Shaforce, was reunified with its headquarters at Hong Kong and the former military attaché in Peking, Colonel Steward, was nominated to succeed Blaker as the military intelligence chief at Shanghai. The Air Ministry again proved responsive to the War Office's proposals and indicated that its staff officer at Shanghai could be attached to the CIB on Shaforce's departure. The real problem was still persuading the Foreign Office.[32] By the summer of 1929 there was some hope that the latter would not attempt to scupper the CIB, for in May the Far Eastern Department had praised MI2c's recent appreciations of the situation in China, noting that 'They give us exactly what we want in order to form a more or less intelligent idea of what is going on behind the tangle'.[33] The War Office, therefore, submitted its plans to the Foreign Office in June in an optimistic frame of mind, reiterating how close Britain had come to disaster in 1927 and stating how pleased it had been with the results achieved up to now by the intelligence bureau.[34]

Unfortunately, the Foreign Office had already received advanced warning of the War Office's plans in December 1928 through the good offices of the Treasury, and had not liked what it read.[35] It therefore responded in September 1929 in its usual dismissive manner. One complaint that it raised had been suggested by Lampson, namely that the establishment of the CIB at Shanghai might infringe the Nine Power Treaty. In addition, it noted that it was not convinced that the information emanating from Shanghai was as useful as the War Office claimed, observing for example that it had shed very little light on the recent revolt by Feng's forces.[36] The Foreign Office was, however, willing to put forward its own plan, which was that a permanent organization at Shanghai could be established if it was led by an assistant military attaché (AMA) who reported directly to the minister in Peking rather than the War Office. Lampson was agreeable to this proposal, but made the restrictions even tougher by stating that the

AMA's reports should be forwarded to the GOC China and the War Office only if instructed by the minister.[37]

As far as the War Office was concerned this was completely unacceptable, for, as one figure in MI2c noted, the whole point of having the CIB was to make up for the fact that the political forecasts by the Foreign Office 'invariably fail to deliver the goods'.[38] It is thus not surprising that MI2c's response to this proposal was to dismiss it as unworkable and to talk instead about the possibility of decanting the CIB to Hong Kong, where it could act completely independently of Foreign Office interference.[39] Another solution was broached by Steward, who suggested that the CIB could be replaced by appointing a military assistant to the SIS representative in China. This was, however, rejected by MI2c on the grounds that this too would mean that the intelligence collected would be tainted with 'diplomatic atmosphere', which was a telling comment on its perception of the SIS. In the end no immediate remedy was necessary, for the continuing political instability in China meant that Shaforce remained *in situ*, thus postponing the moment of decision. The result was that Steward was able to establish the CIB in Shanghai by default.[40]

While Whitehall prevaricated about his future Steward set to work to make a success of his new post. On arriving in Shanghai he found that Blaker's arrangements were not to his liking, for the latter had used few unpaid informants and had not, in Steward's view, kept up sufficient contacts with British firms or with the local Chinese and French authorities.[41] Steward, therefore, worked to broaden the sources available by touring the region to re-establish contacts and by building ties with his successor as military attaché in Peking, Colonel Badham-Thornhill. In addition, by using his access to SIS telegrams and press reports, particularly from Reuters, he attempted to increase his ability not merely to report on events but also to forecast them.[42]

## Reforming intelligence: SIS and the MBPI

Steward's work was assisted by the fact that by 1929 Shanghai had become the headquarters for the SIS in China. As related earlier, after his travails in the first half of 1927 Steptoe had fallen ill, and was forced to go to Britain to recuperate. He appears to have returned to Peking in March 1928. Evidence of his better health, though not judgement, came soon after when, much to Lampson's exasperation, he decided to motor from Tientsin to Peking at the height of the fighting around the capital in June 1928 and not surprisingly came under fire.[43] Steptoe served in Peking until November, when he passed his duties at the legation to J.A. Barton and transferred to Shanghai. Why this change of venue took place is not recorded, but clearly one factor was that Blackburn had now returned to normal consular duties.[44]

There was some discussion around the time of his transfer about how far-ranging Steptoe's responsibilities should be. Once again, the issue that sparked this debate was the future of the gathering of intelligence on the Indian community in China. Since 1927 this had been in the hands of Inspector Halland of the Indian police, but by late 1928 his two-year tour of duty was drawing to a close. This raised the issue of whether his appointment could be extended, a new officer sent out from India to replace him, or whether Steptoe should step into the breach. Initially Steptoe was willing to undertake this work but feared that the burden would be too great on top of his normal SIS duties. The consul-general in Shanghai agreed, noting that Halland's work was such that 'I can well believe that Steptoe would not be able to carry the extra burden for long'.[45] Fortunately, in January 1929 Halland was appointed for an extra year and subsequently it was arranged that on his departure Blackburn would once again take responsibility for corresponding with the DCI in New Delhi, thus allowing Steptoe to concentrate entirely on his SIS work.[46]

Another issue that casts light on Steptoe's activities was the question of his status within the China consular service. Although he had undertaken SIS duties since the mid-1920s Steptoe was still a consular official receiving his salary from the Foreign Office, with only a special allowance of about £50 per annum paid to him by the SIS for his work on its behalf.[47] However, in 1929 Lampson called for a general reorganization of the consular service on the grounds that, for various reasons, the present establishment could not fill all of the posts. Among other reforms, he proposed that anomalous posts such as Steptoe's should be considered as additional to the normal establishment, a plan which proved acceptable to the Treasury.[48] Two years later, after a further complicated debate about his position, Steptoe was promoted from vice-consul grade two to grade one. This promotion was also deemed extra-establishment because it was accepted by this stage that Steptoe was unlikely to return to normal consular duties. In fact his enthusiasm for SIS work was such that, as one official noted, 'S is most anxious to remain on his present duties even at the risk of missing promotion'.[49]

This period also saw further refinements in the intelligence-gathering apparatus in Malaya. In 1930, following advice from Petrie and Sir Eric Holt-Wilson of MI5, it was decided to abolish the MPBI, which had not been working well in recent years, and to pass its work to the local DCI. In addition, a civilian standing committee was established to advise the Governor on security matters. These new arrangements seem to have been far more satisfactory than the previous cumbersome structure.[50]

## The Communist high tide

The need for more efficient intelligence-gathering about the Comintern was soon confirmed by events, for from late 1929 to 1931 communism appeared to gain new momentum in China and South-East Asia. The alarms began in the autumn of 1929 when fresh reports were received about the possibility of CCP action in the near future.[51] This time the predictions proved accurate, for in the summer of 1930, while the Nanking government found itself in a new war with Feng and his ally Yen Hsi-shan, the CCP advanced from its mountainous retreats in Kiangsi and Hunan, temporarily seizing control of Changsha and menacing Hankow. This action, which demonstrated that the CCP had become a military power in its own right, seemed momentarily to stun the KMT. In its wake both the South China Command and Lampson attempted to put the CCP's offensive into perspective by stating that communism had little inherent appeal to the Chinese people and that most avowed communists were nothing more than bandits.[52] However, this contempt was soon displaced by real concern. In part this was because the NRA's anti-CCP campaigns in 1930–31 failed to make much progress against an enemy whose 'discipline and moral [sic] ... is reported to be as good, if not better than those of the Government forces'.[53] In addition, the British view of the CCP was influenced by the reports of missionaries who attested to their dedication and efficiency. In December 1930 two former captives of the CCP, Fathers Laffan and Linehan, reported to the British consulate-general in Hankow that the Chinese Red Army worked like a machine and that Marxist literature had been much in evidence during their detention. The following year, the Reverend G.W. Shepherd, who ran a mission in Kiangsi, warned that the CCP had learnt to appeal to the peasantry by burning title deeds and redistributing land when they captured villages.[54] This evidence clearly suggested that to dismiss the CCP as mere brigands was grossly to underestimate the threat that they posed. It was also apparent from the sources available to Steptoe that the CCP still maintained close relations with the Comintern, and that the latter was directing its activities.[55]

In addition to the CCP threat there was also concern about continuing reports that the Soviet Union was attempting to stir up dissent in the KMT's ranks, and in particular to re-establish its link with Wang Ching-wei. By 1930 Wang had formed the Reorganization Party in opposition to Chiang. To further his aims he was prepared to form an alliance with the Kwangsi clique in south China and the army that had until 1930 been controlled by Feng in the north. Also, although Wang refused to have anything to do with the CCP, he was not above flirting with Moscow to obtain arms for Feng's former men.[56] In addition, evidence suggested that the Soviets were in contact with other anti-Chiang elements. In May 1931 the French informed the Foreign Office that they had intelligence on secret talks between Eugene Chen and the Russians that had even included discussion of a Sino-Soviet defensive alliance.[57]

Adding to the sense of danger was the fear that the communist parties in South-East Asia were also becoming more active. In 1930 both nationalist and communist disturbances took place in Vietnam. The French were able to suppress these rebellions, but nevertheless they seemed to portend further trouble in the future. In particular, MI2c became worried at the end of 1930 when 'very reliable sources' indicated 'the existence of a measure of co-ordination between the Communist Parties of China and Indo-China'.[58] This was especially disturbing, for at that time the army of Chang Fa-kuei, a general seen as sympathetic to communism, was on the verge of moving into Yunnan, and this obviously raised the prospect that his forces might encourage anti-French sentiments in Tonkin. Such was the level of concern about conditions in South-East Asia that in the autumn the Dutch asked for closer liaison between its police forces and those in Malaya.[59]

As if this were not enough, one other event buttressed the feeling that the Soviet Union was regaining lost ground – the CER crisis of 1929–30. In May 1929 Chang Hsueh-liang, who had succeeded his father Chang Tso-lin as warlord of Manchuria, decided to raid the Soviet consulate-general at Harbin, and in July he seized control of the CER. The Soviet response to this move was to break off all diplomatic relations with China and to demand a return to the status quo, an ultimatum that was backed up by troop movements and the calling up of reservists. At first the Chinese and the foreign powers did not take this threat seriously, believing that Russia's internal problems and the risk of a clash with Japan barred any recourse to coercion.[60] In November 1929 the Red Army corrected this impression by launching a rapid, pulverizing offensive at Manchouli and Chalainor and using its air force to harass Chang's forces as far up the CER as Pokofu. In the face of this assault, Chang quickly sued for peace.[61] This was a significant episode, for it revealed that the Soviet Red Army was far stronger than had previously been imagined and that Russia was prepared to project its power to protect or even expand its interests. This naturally led to concerns about the future of other outlying areas of China, such as Inner Mongolia and Sinkiang. In the spring of 1931 Colonel Badham-Thornhill toured the former and discovered that the Soviets were assiduously disseminating propaganda. Fortunately, however, the average Mongol could not read and instead used 'the paper to wrap up the sour cheese on which he lives during his wanderings'.[62] Despite this setback for Soviet propagandists, the overall impression was still disturbing enough to provoke a Foreign Office official to note that 'The success of Russian imperialism in the Far East is one of the most striking features of recent events there.'[63]

Clearly, Britain had to do its utmost to counter this rise in Soviet influence. An opportunity arose in the summer of 1931 when British intelligence had its greatest single success against the Comintern in East Asia. The official version of this case was that the operation began in May 1931 with the interception by the Singapore police of a letter from Hong Kong, in which the Vietnamese communist Nguyen Ai Quoc told a member of the Malayan Communist Party (MCP), as the NCP had now become, to meet with a visiting Comintern agent, Joseph Ducroux. Ducroux was subsequently put under surveillance, and his intercepted letters revealed that he was in direct contact with Nguyen and with another Comintern agent, Hilaire Noulens, who was living in the International Settlement in Shanghai. Armed with this evidence, in June the British authorities in Singapore and Hong Kong arrested Ducroux and Nguyen respectively, while the SMP apprehended Noulens. Noulens turned out to be a major catch, for he was the representative in Shanghai of the Comintern's Department for International Liaison, handling communications between the ECCI in Moscow, the Far Eastern Bureau of the Comintern, the Pacific section of the Profintern, and the CCP. This meant that he was in charge of the local Comintern and Profintern archives, which proved on capture to be a treasure-trove for British intelligence.[64]

The detention of Noulens might not have been as fortuitous as this official version implies, for an unpublished memoir by one of the CIB's officers, Captain L.F. Field, states that the British had been aware of his presence for at least two years and that he been under surveillance in an attempt to discover what cipher he was using for his correspondence.[65] However, what is clear is that this was a very significant breakthrough, for the material recovered revealed much about the Comintern's present activities in the region; for example, on analyzing Ducroux's coded messages Steptoe discovered that Tan Malaka was due to travel to Burma to discuss collaboration between Burmese communists and the PKI. [66] In addition, the seizure of Noulens's archives was vital because, as an internal history of MI5 later noted, it provided 'unimpeachable documentary evidence' of how a 'highly-developed Communist organization of the illegal type' functioned.[67]

This success did not mean that Britain could rest on its laurels, for, despite this setback, communist activities in South-East Asia and China continued. As early as November 1931 an SIS report revealed that the various organizations that had been hit by the arrests were beginning to revive.[68] Indeed, if anything the Noulens-Ducroux case confirmed the authorities in their belief that the Comintern now constituted the primary threat to Britain's interests in the region. In August 1931 MI2c informed the SIS in its annual submission that it was 'particularly interested at present in the activities of the "Reds" and any spread of communist influence into S.E. Asia'.[69]

By the summer of 1931 British intelligence had thus come to see the Comintern's activities as its priority in both China and South-East Asia. Bitterness had emerged in Whitehall due to the debate about the most efficient way of studying and coping with this threat, and the reform process had still, by 1931, not led to any consensus on the most effective type of organization, but there was no question about the fact that the Comintern was seen as a greater menace than any other potential danger.

However, this raised problems, for the very nature of the Comintern meant that it was seen primarily as a political rather than a military threat. The focus on its activities thus necessarily pushed the SIS and even military intelligence representatives to engage in political reporting and meant that the intelligence presence in the whole region from Malaya to China was weighted towards that approach. This was to ill-prepare Britain for the future, for in the autumn of 1931, while Steptoe travelled back and forth between Shanghai and Singapore unravelling the leads from the Noulens-Ducroux case, a more potent and immediate threat was developing – the re-emergence of Japanese expansionism. Ironically this was a force that was in part provoked by the same fears that actuated the British, for Japan was itself unhappy about the political instability in China and fearful that the Soviet Union might take advantage of this situation. The Japanese reaction, however, in contrast to Britain's, was to deal with the potential Soviet menace by striking out militarily, seizing Manchuria in an effort to protect its interests and to gather the economic resources necessary for a preventative war against Russia. In doing so, it shook the balance of power in East Asia and entered on the road that would lead not to conflict with the Soviet Union, but with Britain and America instead.

# 6
# From 'Weak Power' to Potential Enemy: Japan, 1921–33

From 1921 to the summer of 1931, despite its concentration on the Comintern menace, Britain did not completely ignore the other potential threats in the region, and as a matter of course efforts were made to gain intelligence about Japan's ambitions and capabilities. This was of particular importance to the Royal Navy, which clearly needed intelligence about the strategic and technical innovations of the IJN, as the latter was now the world's third largest fleet and thus a substantial potential threat to imperial defence. However, as over time the Japanese menace to the British Empire appeared to fade, the intelligence resources dedicated to studying the threat began to dwindle. These years, therefore, saw a lack of investment on training in language and intelligence techniques that would have a detrimental effect on the collection and interpretation of information in the 1930s. It was only the Manchurian crisis of 1931–33, and in particular the fighting between Japan and China in Shanghai early in 1932, that again revealed Japan's potential threat to British interests. However, even then the concentration upon the Soviets in the previous years meant not only that Britain lacked the resources to deal with the new circumstances, but also that it took time to adjust to the idea that Japan could be a serious menace to British interests. It was in fact not until 1933 that real efforts would be made to direct intelligence resources against the Japanese and to rectify the problems that had accrued during the years of neglect.

## The Japanese threat subsides

Japanese diplomacy in the 1920s is typically seen as being an interregnum between the expansionism of the 1910s and 1930s, and certainly the view in Britain during these years was that Japan posed much less of a threat than before to the international system. In part, Japan's newly found restraint had its foundations in internal factors, and in particular a series of economic and natural crises, such as the Yokohama earthquake of 1923, which forced retrenchment in military expenditure. In addition, the change in Japanese foreign policy came about as a conscious move towards a more internationalist approach, a development associated with the diplomacy of Shidehara Kijurō, the Foreign Minister between 1924 and 1927 and from 1929 to 1931. This shift was most apparent in Japanese policy towards China, epitomized by Shidehara's stance of non-intervention, which stood in stark contrast to Japan's machinations during the Great War. Although the rigid application of non-intervention led to some tensions with Britain over issues such as the despatch of Shaforce, the overall effect of this change in Japan's approach towards the region was seen in British circles as undoubtedly beneficial.

The easing of concern about Japanese ambitions was reinforced by the diplomatic intelligence available to Whitehall. In the aftermath of the Washington conference, intelligence consistently reiterated that Japan had turned its back on the expansionist policies of the Great War period. The key source that led to this conclusion was the continual stream of translations of intercepted Japanese diplomatic traffic supplied by GCCS, which covered both day-to-day matters and the major conferences of the period.[1]

The intercepts helped to illuminate a number of important changes in Japanese policy, the most substantive of which was Tokyo's general retreat from any flirtation with pan-Asianism. One of the more significant examples was the long-running saga of Persia's attempt to open diplomatic relations with Japan. Negotiations on this issue proved difficult because Persia had been forced to grant extraterritorial rights to the Western powers. Persia's hope in 1922 when it first opened talks with Japan, was that it would not have to grant extraterritoriality to this fellow Asian state, and indeed some Japanese diplomats and pan-Asianists felt that their country could improve its standing in Asia by taking a liberal stance.[2] However, the BJs revealed that, as long as the other Great Powers retained extraterritoriality in Persia, Japan was determined for the sake of its international prestige and its position in China and Siam to be treated in the same manner.[3] As a result, no progress was made in these talks until Britain waived its extraterritorial rights in 1928. Once that obstacle was removed, Japan and Persia exchanged plenipotentaries in 1929. Japan's concern for its own standing, over and above the sensibilities of other Asian states, was also noticeable in its relations with Afghanistan and Turkey. The Afghans proved to be just as ardent suitors of the Japanese as the Persians, lobbying Tokyo to open diplomatic relations continually from 1922. They too found that the Japanese insisted on being treated on the same terms as the Europeans, and it was only in 1928 that a treaty of friendship was signed between the two countries, and even then diplomatic representatives were not exchanged until 1933.[4] In the case of Turkey, a lingering sense of suspicion was engendered when Japan appeared to be deliberately slothful in 1924 in ratifying the Lausanne Treaty that, among other items, ended the Capitulations that granted extraterritoriality to the Great Powers.[5] This Japanese tendency to put its Great Power status first was, of course, gratifying to Britain, which had no desire to see Japan develop strong relations with Asian states that frequently nursed anti-British sentiments.

There was also an improvement in Japanese attitudes towards India. In March 1922 a BJ revealed that the Japanese intended to restrict the numbers of Indians being given visas for Japan to ensure that no incident should mar the forthcoming visit by the Prince of Wales.[6] At the same time it appeared that Bose's support was declining, even though he had been naturalized as a Japanese subject.[7] Of equal significance was the failure of attempts by Japanese pan-Asianists to revive interest in their cause. In August 1926 a pan-Asian conference took place at Nagasaki, but achieved scant results and ended in an altercation between the Japanese and Chinese delegations.[8] Even more heartening was that the Japanese authorities refused to provide a visa to one of the major figures wishing to attend the conference, the Indian radical Mahendra Pratap.[9]

In addition, this period saw a diminution of the concern about Japanese ambitions in South-East Asia. To a large degree this was linked to the reversal of Japan's economic fortunes in the region following the end of the Great War. Rather than purchasing new plantations, Japanese planters in Malaya were now selling land due to the decline in rubber prices, while its fishing fleet in Malayan waters shrank as a number of boats moved to other more lucrative areas. As a result, from 1923 to 1926 the Japanese population in the peninsula fell from 10,000 to 6,000. It was, therefore, difficult to continue with the belief that this community threatened Malaya's security, particularly when compared with the all too apparent menace posed by Bolshevism.[10]

This was not to say that Japan's activities had become completely innocent, for it was readily apparent from BJs and other intelligence sources that it still enthusiastically engaged in espionage. The intercepts, for example, revealed that a steady stream of funds was despatched from Tokyo to Japan's diplomatic and military representatives abroad in order that they might engage in secret service and propaganda work.[11] However, what differentiated the 1920s from the decades around it was that the secret service activities were not directed to encouraging subversion but to acquiring technical intelligence on Western military innovations such as the development of submarines and chemical warfare.[12] In addition, the IJN showed a marked interest in naval aviation, seeking British nationals to work in Japan itself and to act as sources of intelligence in London.[13] MI5 naturally took a keen interest in these matters, but they were an irritation rather than any threat to Anglo-Japanese relations.

## Japan's military backwardness

The military and naval intelligence available to Britain during the 1920s reinforced the belief that Japan had turned its back on expansion, for it gave the impression that the latter had largely ignored the innovations and experiences of the Great War campaigns in Europe. This was most evident in the information about the IJA collected by the military attachés and language officers in Tokyo. At the beginning of the decade the consensus that emerged among British observers of the IJA, including Malcolm Kennedy in his book *The Military Side of Japanese Life*, was that, although technically and tactically backward, its solid morale still made it a 'formidable machine', and that it would not be long before it applied the lessons of the war in Europe.[14] However, for the rest of the 1920s they looked in vain for evidence of the latter conclusion, for years passed without the introduction of technological innovations such as gas, tanks and armoured cars. Even after 1925, when Army Minister General Ugaki Kazunari reduced the IJA's establishment by four divisions in order to concentrate resources on modernization and to reduce the reliance on morale, there was little immediate evidence that progress was being made.[15] For example, in 1928, when the IJA began to replace its obsolete field guns, a report by a language officer from the Royal Artillery noted that little progress had been made with the use of forward or air observation. In addition while the Grand Manoeuvres of 1926 included tanks for the first time, there was no attempt to develop their cooperation with the infantry.[16] Production of poisonous gas appeared from SIS reports to be rudimentary, as was the training of troops in both offensive and defensive chemical warfare.[17]

The modernization process, the military attaché, Lieutenant-Colonel Leslie Hill, observed in his annual report for 1926, was being hampered by a number of factors. In part, it was the result of budgetary pressures and the lack of suitable land for large-scale exercises using tanks and aircraft, but in addition, he pointed his finger at a more fundamental problem, which was that:

> In regard to other minor ways in which improvement might be effected, such as the provision of steel helmets, gas respirators, grenades, etc., the principal obstacle to progress would appear to be the narrow conservatism of the Japanese military mind.[18]

This conservatism was most evident in the IJA's officer training colleges, which were occasionally attended by British language students. In May 1926 Lieutenant George Wards produced a report on his attachment to the Infantry School in Chiba which noted that IJA training was still based on the experiences gained in the Russo-Japanese War rather than the conflict of 1914–18.[19] The result was that the IJA still stressed its superior morale as the foundation of its strength. The wisdom of this approach was clearly open to question, for it could lead to underestimation of potential enemies and inappropriate tactics in the face of modern firepower.[20] Moreover, it appeared that the IJA's approach to training was still doing little to overcome one of its majors flaws, the general lack of initiative, particularly on the part of its NCOs.[21]

All of these criticisms made their way into the new *Handbook of the Japanese Army* produced by MI2c in June 1928 for general distribution to the British military. This volume observed that the IJA still relied on its superior morale, the use of enveloping tactics, and the timely arrival of reserves when it took the offensive, but that the use of tanks and modern artillery was not appreciated. The IJA's attitude, it surmised, was that:

> Modernization is realized as a necessity for competing with the armies of other first-class powers, but the Japanese accept it only half-heartedly for they evidently do not visualize fighting against armies that are highly technical.[22]

In other words, MI2c believed that current IJA doctrine demonstrated that it had no intention of fighting Britain and that it was being trained and equipped only to fight in North-East Asia against the Chinese or the Russians.[23]

Similar criticisms were aimed at the IJN, which on paper appeared formidable. As the naval attaché from 1922 to 1924, Captain Ragnar Colvin, noted shortly after arriving in Japan, it was 'an efficient weapon of war which in the hands of a leader of imagination might yield great results'.[24] In particular it benefited from its possession of two modern battleships, *Nagato* and *Mutsu*, that were the equal of anything afloat. In 1924 Colvin's successor, Captain Guy Royle, was allowed on board *Mutsu* and recorded in an interestingly worded backhanded compliment that 'It was remarkable to think that this magnificent ship had been built and armed entirely by the Japanese.'[25] However, here too doubts existed about the IJN's willingness to apply the lessons of the Great War. For example, Colvin noted in 1923 that Japan was not doing enough to defend its surface vessels against attacks by submarines or mines, and that there was too much reliance on capital ships. He also felt that the IJN lacked initiative, which he in part ascribed to the fact that the officers did not spend enough time at sea.[26] Another perceived failure was its technological backwardness, a problem that British observers stated would get worse over time as the Royal Navy's decision not to share information with the IJN after the end of the alliance took effect.[27]

The area of greatest interest was the IJN's efforts to create a naval air arm. In this area Japan, at least in the early 1920s, received considerable assistance from Britain in the shape of an unofficial mission led by the aviator, the Master of Sempill. Sempill, whose task was to run a training school for IJN pilots at Kasumigaura, arrived in Japan in April 1921 and stayed until the end of 1922. During this period he kept in contact with the British embassy and seemed to be fairly pleased with the progress that his wards had made. His main criticisms were not of the pilots but of the IJN high command, which had no coherent air policy and refused to take his advice about aircraft design.[28] Another member of the mission, Flight Officer

R. Vaughan-Fowler, confirmed Sempill's impression of the IJN pilots. They were, he noted in 1924, 'slow thinking' and lacked mechanical sense, but were brave and enthusiastic and had the makings of good airmen.[29] Following Sempill's departure it was inevitably felt in British circles that standards had dropped back, but in 1927 the naval attaché, Captain Cloudsley Robinson, noted that the available evidence indicated that, although Japanese pilots could probably not compete in combat with the British, 'the Service is progressive and efficient'.[30]

This qualified praise of the IJN air service was not extended to its IJA equivalent. It was clear to the RAF language officers who served in Japan from 1920 onwards that the IJA was putting much effort into aviation but appeared to be achieving little. In 1926 and 1927 respectively Flight-Lieutenants Longinotto and Chappell produced devastating assessments of the IJA air arm after attachment to aviation schools. Both observed that the IJA pilots were poor and that in particular they were inept at formation flying.[31] Further evidence of the IJA's relative backwardness came when the press in Japan reported on a combined services bombing exercise in which the IJN pilots performed impressively but their IJA counterparts missed the target with all eighteen bombs dropped.[32] Adding to Japan's problems was that its early attempts at aircraft design proved unsuccessful. In 1928 trials were held for a new IJA fighter, but the three Japanese models put forward all failed to meet the criteria, leading Ashton-Gwatkin to observe 'This miserable fiasco shows how weak the Japanese air arm still is, and tends to show that the Japanese are still far behind the West in technical matters.'[33]

These assessments of Japan's military power continued, of course, to be strongly influenced by racial truisms about the Japanese. The most prevalent was the persistence of the belief that the Japanese as a race suffered from 'slow mental adaptability', which accounted for the oft-cited 'lack of initiative' shown by IJA and IJN officers, and the perception that they were not mechanically minded; traits which in turn helped to explain the delays in the modernization process.[34] The tendency to come to such a conclusion was still rooted in ethnocentrism. This was clearly apparent in a report on the IJN produced in 1927 by Captain Royle. He noted that the Japanese character was marked by an unnatural degree of 'self-control' and 'complete suppression of one's real feelings', which led to a marked inclination towards obedience and a highly developed fighting spirit. This was in its way laudable, but fell short of British values:

> Our training aims at developing character and personality. Enterprise and initiative are more admired than blind obedience – good comradeship between officers and men is a sina qua non. Habits of quick thinking and alertness are essential. These are some of the qualities which the Japanese as a nation have not yet developed.[35]

The Japanese failure to inculcate these 'qualities' was in part put down to the fact that its training was too narrowly focused on academic subjects, and some observers noted that alertness, initiative and camaraderie would be improved by more emphasis on that great panacea of the English public schools, outdoor team sports. For example, Longinotto noted in 1926 that the lack of recreation activities had 'to no small degree an adverse effect on a Japanese pilot's skill in handling a machine'.[36]

Racial thinking thus contributed to the intelligence image of Japan by stressing that there were both physiological and cultural explanations for the more obvious Japanese traits whether positive, such as high morale and fighting spirit, or negative, such as the lack of initiative. Overall, it reinforced the idea that Japan was backward by emphasizing its inclination towards rigidity of thinking and suggested that the Japanese would find it temperamentally difficult to shake themselves free from their innate conservatism. As such, racial difference continued to act as a comfort to the British, who could relax in the ethnocentric knowledge that they were physically and culturally superior.[37]

## Japan as neither enemy nor ally

The general impression created in Whitehall by the assessments of Japan's foreign policy and military capabilities was that it had now decided to become a good neighbour and that it was, as Sir Charles Eliot, the ambassador to Tokyo, noted in 1924, 'a weak rather than a strong Power'.[38] There was, however, some resistance to this assumption among the service ministries, who wished to use the image of a belligerent Japan in the annual campaign to extract funding from the Treasury. Concerned about what it saw as the potential danger posed by the IJN, the Admiralty from 1924 to 1927 insisted that the construction of the Singapore naval base and the building of modern cruisers be expedited in the interests of imperial security. Then in 1928 the War Office sought to win approval for a permanent expansion of its garrison in China on the grounds that this would deter any future Japanese attack on British interests in the region.[39] Without sufficient intelligence to back up their claims, and in the Royal Navy's case its possessing a very substantial quantitative and qualitative advantage over the IJN and no other potential enemy to worry about, these rather transparent manoeuvres were easily defeated. The Chancellor of the Exchequer, Winston Churchill, while willing to allow some spending on cruisers, rejected the idea that Britain was in 'mortal peril' due to the possibility of a Japanese attack.[40] In this he had the support of Sir Austen Chamberlain, who persuaded the CID in 1925 to accept the formula that no war should be expected for at least ten years, thus laying the basis for the 'ten years rule' that was to influence defence spending until 1932.[41] Two years later Chamberlain went so far as to state that 'I think it common ground to those who have studied Japanese policy that never was Japan in recent times more pacifist – I will even say so pacifist – as she is at present time'.[42] The War Office's bid was subject to even greater derision, with the Permanent Secretary at the Treasury, Sir Warren Fisher, noting that 'I had hoped that the "Japanese Menace" had died of its own inherent folly'.[43]

The Treasury was indeed wise to distrust the motives of the War Office, for in truth the latter was probably the most Japanophile department of state in the 1920s. The War Office's benevolent view of Japan arose in part from the lack of any apparent Japanese threat, but was also due to evidence that it might be a partner in the struggle against Bolshevism. The first signal that the IJA was willing to cooperate against the Comintern by sharing intelligence came in July 1925, when it asked the military attaché in Tokyo, Colonel Piggott, if the British could confirm that the Soviets were providing assistance to the May Thirtieth Movement. This overture was, however, rejected by the legation in Peking for fear that what Japan really wished to acquire was information about the state of the SIS in China.[44] Despite this setback, in July 1926 the IJA tried again by offering to pass MI2c a general staff paper on the 'Red Menace' in Manchuria.[45] The War Office response was enthusiastic for, as MI2c noted to Piggott, 'both Japan and ourselves are strongly anti-Bolshevik and ... our interests in this respect are therefore identical'.[46] Accordingly, a regular exchange of intelligence was developed, with the IJA providing information on Russian arms deliveries to Feng Yü-hsiang in north China and Russia's efforts to increase its influence in border regions such as Mongolia.[47]

Encouraged by these overtures and by hints from the IJA that, but for Shidehara, it would have willingly cooperated in the defence of Shanghai in 1927, the War Office was keen to extend Anglo-Japanese ties. Early in 1928 it was this attitude that led the ardent Japanophile Colonel Piggott, as the officer in charge of MI2, to reject the idea that the FEIB should gather intelligence on Japan and to propose instead collaboration with Japanese intelligence. The War Office even speculated at this time that the best way to deter Soviet expansionism in China and Afghanistan was for Britain to renew its alliance with Japan, an idea rejected by Hill in Tokyo who noted that the Japanese would ask for a stiff quid pro quo for defending British interests, such as use of the Singapore naval base and access to British technological innovations.[48] The desire for cooperation proved, however, to be only transitory. In 1929 the intelligence exchange was brought to an end due to the feeling that the IJA was not particularly useful, but it is still a remarkable testament to the perceived commonality of interests in the 1920s that it was ever initiated in the first place.[49]

## Creating intelligence deficiencies

In the strained financial climate of the mid-1920s, the perception that the Japanese could be trusted unfortunately reinforced the already existing trend towards retrenchment in the provision of intelligence about Japan. This was evident particularly in respect of the gathering of covert intelligence on Japan by the SIS. In December 1922, when discussing the plans to build a naval base at Singapore, the CID accepted a call from the First Lord of the Admiralty, Leo Amery, for a strengthening of the SIS in the 'Far East' so that early warning could be provided of any Japanese attack.[50] This led to the idea that a fully effective organization to gather intelligence on Japan should be ready by 1928, and that once operational it should be able to report within twenty-four hours of any threat developing. However, by 1925 the convenient assumption by the CID that there would be no war with Japan for ten years whittled away the *raison d'être* for the SIS network, and the matter appears to have been left in abeyance.[51]

Information was still collected on Japan by the SIS, for MI2c asked for intelligence on a variety of subjects in its annual submission, especially Japan's progress with mechanized and gas warfare, but no major organization was established on the lines developed in China.[52] In 1928 the SIS tried to address this issue itself, asking what work Whitehall wanted it to undertake in Japan while noting to its customers that to set up an intelligence organization in 'this very difficult country' would take considerable time and expenditure.[53] Its overture met with little enthusiasm. In particular it failed to receive any backing from the War Office, as Piggott was adamant that an SIS organization in Japan was unnecessary. In February 1928 he recorded that he had told the SIS that:

> military intelligence was best left to above-board methods. The position of trust and confidence built up during the days of the Alliance, and continued since 1922 by successive Military Attaches and language officers, was a far more valuable potential source of information than anything which could possibly be obtained by S.I.S.[54]

The result was that the SIS organization in Japan remained moribund and continued to be in that state when Japan emerged four years later as a threat to the British Empire. This was a grave problem, for already the Japanese armed forces were becoming extremely secretive. In particular, the naval attachés found that their visits to both IJN and private dockyards were strictly policed and that from the mid-1920s they were not allowed to board IJN vessels.[55]

Financial stringency had an effect on other aspects of intelligence-gathering. For the Air Ministry it acted as an obstacle to the appointment of an air attaché to the Tokyo embassy. In 1920 the Treasury sanctioned an Air Ministry scheme to send one officer per year to learn Japanese, as this would provide a pool of experienced officers who could act in the future as air attachés.[56] With Japan taking an increasing interest in aviation after the Sempill mission, the Air Ministry decided in 1923 that it must have its own attaché in Tokyo, as this would reduce its reliance on the military and naval representatives, who had little knowledge of contemporary aviation developments. However, this scheme fell through when the Yokohama earthquake wrecked the embassy compound.[57] There the matter rested until 1926, when the Air Ministry broached the idea once again due to the inadequacy of the information on the IJN's air arm. As the RAF's language officers were still too junior to be attachés, the Air Ministry asked the Treasury if it would agree to a senior officer being trained in Japanese. It met with a flat refusal and after that rebuff decided that its priority was to gain Treasury approval for an air attaché in Prague instead.[58] Financial pressures also prevented the appointment of an AMA to the Tokyo embassy, even though both Piggott and Hill felt such a post was essential. In 1929 the War Office told the Foreign Office that for reasons of economy neither it nor India could spare any officers.[59] The Admiralty, in contrast, was more fortunate, for in 1927 its proposal for a Japanese-speaking assistant naval attaché (ANA) to be posted to Tokyo was accepted. Its application had more weight, for up to that point no naval attaché had ever possessed Japanese language. This was because only officers with the rank of Captain could be appointed as attachés and no interpreter had yet risen to such an exalted rank. As there was, however, an urgent need to have a Japanese linguist in Tokyo the appointment of an ANA was the logical option.[60]

Difficulties also emerged over the despatch of language officers to Japan. In the wake of the Great War there was much interest in the Empire in the need for officers and civil servants to learn Japanese and in 1921 twenty men took language examinations in Tokyo. Apart from the usual British service personnel, the men sent to Japan included a large number of Indian Army officers, officials from the colonial administrations in Hong Kong and Singapore, and a small contingent of officers from the Australian Army and the Royal Australian Navy (RAN).[61] From 1921 onwards a major problem appeared in that the high rate of inflation in Japan meant that the allowance provided to language officers was inadequate to meet their everyday needs. In the case of some officers from India, this meant that they were forced to give up their studies, as they had no way of supporting themselves.[62] In late 1922 the War Office was able to persuade the Treasury to raise the allowance, but even then it remained inadequate, with the result that only unmarried officers could be sent to Japan for training. Worse still, with the collapse of Japanese prices following the Yokohama earthquake the Treasury promptly demanded a cut in the allowance. With no Japanese danger in sight the War Office had to acquiesce, but warned in passing that it was 'finding it increasingly difficult to secure officers ... for the study of the language in Japan', where officers complained that even the old post-1922 allowance had been inadequate.[63]

The Royal Navy's language officer programme was similarly affected. After allowing the training of Japanese language interpreters to fall into abeyance during the war, in 1919 the Admiralty was keen to revive and expand its training programme, for which it received the Treasury's blessing.[64] The result was that in the early 1920s ten officers underwent language training in Japan. However, problems soon emerged over the duration of the training and the question of allowances. In 1925 an Admiralty committee on foreign languages recommended that training should be extended to three years, that the allowances paid to qualified interpreters should be continual whether the officer was on the China Station or not, and that they should be drastically increased from their current level of 2/6 and 1/- per day for fully and partly qualified interpreters respectively to 5/- and 2/6.[65] The Treasury agreed to the extension of training and the continual allowances, but did not endorse the full daily payments, allowing only a rise to 4/- and 2/- respectively.[66] The Admiralty felt that this was still insufficient, but due to the severe pressure from the Treasury was forced to concur.[67]

The result of these financial pressures was that the inducements to study Japanese proved too small to guarantee a regular flow of language officers to Japan, or to keep fully trained interpreters within the services. It is important to note in this context that language training was already indirectly discouraged by the perception that over-specialization could act as a bar to promotion, the cutting back of allowances thus undermined one of the few privileges that accrued to interpreters. Between 1921 and 1929 sixty-one officers from the British and Australian armed forces underwent language training; of these eight failed to qualify as interpreters, four retired almost immediately on completion of their tour of duty, and four died, including Longinotto (see Table 1). The attrition rate, therefore, cut quite severely into the idea of establishing a large pool of experts.

## Naval signals intelligence and Japan

The lack of sufficient interpreters was particularly important for the Admiralty, for it affected its capacity to develop a vital new source of intelligence on the IJN – SIGINT. From the early 1920s the Admiralty was keen to transpose to the Eastern theatre the wireless interception or 'Y' techniques that it had developed during the war against the German fleet. In 1924 when a naval section was added to the GCCS the former intelligence officer on the China Station, Paymaster-Commander E.P. Jones, was appointed as its Japanese specialist.[68] Simultaneously, work began at Hong Kong to intercept and decipher IJN radio communications and identify call signs and chains of command. At first the achievements on the China station were limited, but the success rate improved in 1925 when Paymaster-Lieutenant Eric Nave of the RAN took charge of the 'Y' activities. Nave had begun to learn Japanese in 1918, and by 1920 had made such progress that the RAN had thought it worthwhile to send him

*Table 1* Language officers sent to Japan, 1917–29

| Date | Name | Service | Remarks |
|---|---|---|---|
| 1917 | Capt. R. Bennett | BA | |
| | Capt. M. Kennedy | BA | Retired 1922, GCCS |
| 1918 | Lt. A. Withers | BA | Died 1921 |
| | Capt. C. Langhorne | IA | Retired |
| | Flt.-Lt. L. Wanless O'Gowan | RAF | Retired |
| 1919 | Capt. G. Alms | BA | Japanese wife |
| | Capt. K. Morgan | IA | Retired, Singapore SB |
| 1920 | Major D. Hill | BA | Retired |
| | Major J. Lecky | IA | Retired |
| | Capt. R.W. Russell | IA | Retired |
| | Major Y. Smith | IA | Failed LO examination |
| | Major R. Woodward | IA | Retired |
| | Lt. R. Boucher | RN | Failed LO examination |
| | Lt. R. Leeds | RN | 'Y' Intelligence HK |
| | Pay.-Lt. Cmdr H. Shaw | RN | GCCS, FECB |
| | Lt. D. Tufnell | RN | NA Tokyo 1938–41 |
| | Lt. J. Broadbent | AA | Singapore 1941 |
| | Lt. G. Capes | AA | Died 1938? |
| 1921 | Capt. E. Saunders | BA | Retired |
| | Major R. Smith | BA | |
| | Capt. Ferguson | IA | Did not finish studies |
| | Capt. T. Fuge | IA | Did not finish studies |
| | Capt. D. Whitworth | IA | Did not finish studies |
| | Pay.-Lt. Capell | RN | Did not finish studies |
| | Lt. R. Chichester | RN | GCCS |
| | Pay.-Lt. E. Nave | RAN | GCCS, FECB |
| 1922 | Lt. C. Delamain | BA | MI2, Intelligence Tientsin |
| | Capt. B. Mullaly | IA | MA Tokyo 1939–41 |
| | Lt. J. Eccles | RN | GCCS |
| | Lt. W. Keith | RN | GCCS, FECB |
| | Lt. S. Lushington | RN | GCCS |
| | Pay.-Lt. Cmdr H. Thompson | RN | |
| | Flt.-Lt. W. Bryant | RAF | AA Tokyo 1937–41 |
| 1923 | Capt. I. MacPherson | BA | |
| | Lt. N. Toft | BA | Died 1924 |
| | Capt. B. Dicker | IA | |
| | Capt. G. Wards | IA | Intelligence Tientsin, AMA Tokyo 1937–40, MA Tokyo 1941 |
| | Flt.-Lt. E. Longinotto | RAF | Died 1926 |
| 1924 | Lt. A. Boyce | BA | Retired after LO duties |
| | Lt. S. Hunt | BA | Liaison Shanghai, 1938 |
| | R. Ball | RAN civilian | Some intelligence work |
| 1925 | Lt. W. Humpherson | BA | Retired |
| | Capt. J. Ridley | BA | |
| | Lt. B. Stockton | BA | Died 1928 |
| | Capt. G. Oxley Brennan | IA | |

*Table 1* Language officers sent to Japan 1917–29 (continued)

| Date | Name | Service | Remarks |
|---|---|---|---|
| | Capt. A. Millar | IA | Did not finish studies |
| | Flt.-Lt. R. Chappell | RAF | AA Tokyo 1935–38, FECB |
| 1926 | Capt. P. Gwyn | IA | SIB |
| | Capt. K. Himatsinjhi | IA | AMA Tokyo 1941 |
| | Lt. G. Windeyer | RN | 'Y' Intelligence HK |
| 1927 | Capt. A. Ferguson | BA | SIB, FECB |
| | Lt. E. Colegrave | RN | GCCS, FECB |
| 1928 | Capt. E. Ainger | BA | SIB |
| | Major W. Craig | BA | |
| | Eng.-Cmdr Evington | RN | ANA Tokyo 1930–33 |
| | Flt.-Lt. L. Nixon | RAF | Did not finish studies |
| | Pay.-Lt. McLaughlin | RAN | Some intelligence work |
| 1929 | Lt. R. Walker | BA | |
| | Capt. D. Hutchings | IA | |
| | Capt. F. Steed | IA | |

BA British army, IA Indian army, AA Australian army

as a language officer to Japan, where he studied for the next two years. Nave proved not just to be a good linguist, but also to possess a great aptitude for 'Y' work.[69]

The change in personnel at Hong Kong coincided with a drive by the Admiralty to expand its intelligence work against foreign navies, including the IJN. In late 1925 an Admiralty report on 'Special Intelligence' noted that very little work had been done on deciphering the operational radio communications of the Japanese fleet and urged that this situation be rectified. In addition, it suggested that work should be done in China to ascertain whether in time of war it would be feasible to use 'a ship as a combined intercepting and decrypting centre', as it was felt that Hong Kong was too remote from Japan. In January 1926 orders were sent out to the China Station to expedite 'Y' work against the IJN and to experiment with interception at sea. Instructions, therefore, were given requiring all ships, including those from the RAN, to carry out wireless interception when in the vicinity of IJN craft.[70]

The progress that had already been made at Hong Kong meant that the China Station was in a good position to provide the information that the NID required, and by July 1926 it was able to report that considerable progress had been made on the interception of naval codes and in understanding the structure of the IJN's chain of command.[71] So impressive was this work that in December 1926 the Admiralty noted, in browbeating the

C-in-Cs North Atlantic and West Indies for their lack of progress against foreign navies, that:

> Over 1,000 Japanese W/T messages are being intercepted per month and in addition to interception a large amount of information has been collected concerning the Japanese naval W/T organization. Lines of traffic have been observed, methods of procedure, call signs and many signals elucidated and at the same time a number of previously unknown stations have been identified.[72]

As expected, the information from East Asia revealed that interception was poor at Hong Kong, which reinforced the belief that in wartime a ship should carry out the interception work. Accordingly, in December the Admiralty insisted at a meeting with the GCCS that, as it was impractical for the latter's staff in London to decrypt IJN material in time of war, the best idea was to use a large passenger ship as both an interception and a decryption centre. It was also proposed that work should begin on the establishment of radio direction-finding (RDF) stations at Hong Kong and Shanghai.[73]

These proposals raised one major difficulty, which was that the Admiralty lacked the necessary staff to run this intelligence station. The dearth of sufficient interpreters became clear in the autumn of 1926 when Jones's successor at the GCCS, Paymaster Lieutenant-Commander Shaw, found that he could not cope with the sudden flood of intercepts arriving from Nave, and was forced to request an additional interpreter to assist him.[74] A decision was therefore taken at the Admiralty-GCCS meeting to request that funds be provided for the training of six interpreters as Japanese cryptographers. The head of the SIS, Admiral Sir Hugh 'Quex' Sinclair, in his capacity as the overall controller of the GCCS, was prepared to agree to this proposal, but the problem remained that for the long term not enough officers were learning Japanese.[75] These difficulties became even more apparent in the late 1920s. In 1928 Nave, who was by this time working in GCCS's naval section, broke the IJN's nine-letter general purpose '43' code. However, it was difficult to make much of this breakthrough, as the Admiralty could only afford to provide funding for one interpreter to work in the GCCS on Japanese material, and his main priority was the Japanese naval attaché traffic.[76] In his reports for 1929 and 1930 the head of the GCCS's naval section, Captain W.F. Clarke, complained bitterly about this shortcoming, noting in particular that Nave's work on Japanese telegrams during the London Naval Conference was hindered by the fact that he had no assistant.[77] Work had thus begun in the new crucial area of SIGINT but it was continually hindered by the lack of financial and personnel resources available.

## The Manchurian triangle

The situation by the end of the 1920s was therefore that Japan no longer appeared to be a threatening power, but was rather a partner in international politics. This discrediting of the idea of a Japanese menace had unfortunate consequences for British seapower, for it meant that the Admiralty could not use this 'danger' as a justification to ward off further naval limitation. The result was that in 1930 it was in no position to resist the moves by the Labour government of Ramsay MacDonald at the London Naval Conference to bring the Royal Navy down to fifty cruisers and to continue the moratorium on the construction of capital ships established at the Washington Conference of 1921/22, both initiatives that jeopardized imperial defence. Ironically, in the same period there were hints of trouble ahead, for it was clear that Japan was finding it difficult to maintain its policy of non-intervention in China in the face of its fear of Soviet ambitions in the region and Nanking's provocations. This restlessness did not necessarily threaten Britain's own interests, indeed as noted above the War Office saw Japan as a useful bulwark against Bolshevism, but the situation did require careful attention.

The first clear sign that Japan might be on the verge of pursuing a more active defence of its stake in North-East Asia came with the death of Chang Tso-lin outside Mukden in June 1928. At first, British knowledge about the incident was limited to Japanese sources which reported that the bomb that had destroyed Chang's train was of Russian origin.[78] Over the following months the situation remained hazy, and in October MI2c affirmed that the most likely protagonist was the Soviet Union, even though no firm evidence could be found to support such a conclusion. However, in 1929 a detailed investigation by the Tokyo embassy suggested a different conclusion, namely that the assassination had been carried out by elements within the Japanese military in south Manchuria, the Kwantung Army. As one Foreign Office official noted, this was 'almost incredible' news, and accordingly it was decided for the sake of Anglo-Japanese relations that the report should not be distributed to other departments.[79]

This discreet attitude was symptomatic of the sympathy felt in Whitehall with the problems Japan faced in North-East Asia. This sentiment manifested itself again in the spring of 1929, when the War Office studied the question of the proper reaction to any future Japanese expansionism in Manchuria, and concluded that it was better for Japan to expand there than for it to be tempted to go south. Indeed, the report went so far as to claim that such an outcome would be advantageous to Britain because a strong Japanese presence would act as a 'powerful barrier against the extension of Soviet influence in the Far East and the Pacific'.[80] At this stage, therefore, Russia was still considered to be the prime menace to British interests.

In the latter half of 1929 and into 1930, tensions in Manchuria continued to escalate in the light of the CER incident in the north and Sino-Japanese railway disputes in the south. Early in 1931 the Foreign Office received intelligence that indicated that the Japanese government was becoming weary of the continual erosion of its treaty rights and that it was devising 'appropriate measures of self-protection'.[81] In June, this information was supplemented by a paper that came into the possession of Badham-Thornhill which outlined 'the military arrangements the Japanese have in hand towards taking over Manchuria' and noted that extensive stores had been built up to support such an offensive.[82] These signs of potential Japanese belligerence did not mean, however, that Britain believed that Japan had any overarching plans for domination of East Asia outside Manchuria. Notably in July 1931, when the SIS acquired a copy of the infamous 'Tanaka memorial', both the Foreign Office and Colonel Simson, the military attaché in Tokyo, felt that the overwrought ambitions for war with Russia and America outlined in the document indicated that it was not genuine.[83]

As Whitehall weighed this evidence, further signs accrued that Sino-Japanese relations were coming to a dangerous pass. By the end of August intelligence from SIS sources and the CIB suggested that the patience of the Kwantung Army was about to be exhausted. On 8 September Steward, after visiting Manchuria, reported that it was 'Now only a question of time and occurence of suitable "incident" before Japanese will be forced to assert themselves'.[84] The storm finally broke on 18 September when a bomb exploded on the Japanese-run South Manchurian Railway (SMR) just outside Mukden. The Kwantung Army claimed disingenuously that the bomb had been planted by the Chinese, and used the incident as an excuse to seize Mukden and other towns in the railway zone and to expand further into south Manchuria. Despite the warning signs that had preceded the incident, both the Foreign Office and War Office were not inclined to question Japan's version of events, and showed some sympathy for its actions. Indeed, the DMOI, General Bartholomew, went as far as to state on 22 September that 'I am glad there are some people left who kick back when their nationals are ill-treated or even murdered', while the *War Office Monthly Intelligence Summary* for September argued that the fighting might help to bring the Chinese to their senses in talks with the other foreign powers.[85]

It was not long, though, before intelligence arrived that suggested that the Mukden incident was a premeditated act of violence by the Kwantung Army. On 21 September Lampson argued that the timing of Japanese movements when the incident took place proved that the IJA had placed the bomb on the SMR. For example, the Kwantung Army's General Staff, he observed, had arrived in Mukden from Dairen at 3 a.m. on 19 September, just five hours after the explosion, which indicated that they must have started their journey before the bomb had gone off! Moreover, Japanese gunboats had been able to arrive at Newchwang on the morning of

19 September.[86] This view was supported by Badham-Thornhill, who noted on 22 September that the artillery used for bombarding the Chinese barracks in Mukden had been specially brought from Korea, and by the C-in-C China, Admiral Sir Howard Kelly, who concluded on 1 October that the Japanese account of events was 'trying to strain the credulity of the Powers a little too high'.[87]

What in retrospect seems to be explosive information that proved Japanese duplicity did not change Whitehall's view of events. As far as the War Office was concerned, Japanese aggression in Manchuria did not pose any threat to British interests, rather it strengthened Japan's ability to contain Russia and therefore should be viewed with equanimity. Indeed, the danger, as it saw the situation, was not that Japanese expansionism endangered Britain but that pro-League opinion could damage relations with Japan, which might 'have the most far-reaching and disastrous effect upon the future security of our interests in the Far East'.[88] The Foreign Office felt similarly, and decided when forwarding one of Badham-Thornhill's reports to the Secretary-General of the League, to expunge all references to Japan's actions being premeditated, on the grounds that such an accusation would make the League's efforts to restore peace more rather than less difficult.[89] This inconvenient intelligence was thus put to one side, nominally in the name of peace but in reality because Britain still had at this stage more sympathy for Japan than China.

Over the coming months, as the fighting in Manchuria spread to Tsitsihar in the north and Chinchow in the south-west, Britain's attitude remained pro-Japanese, but intelligence suggested that two disturbing trends were emerging. The first was that the government in Tokyo seemed unable to control the Kwantung Army, and the second that, while the Gaimushō followed a policy of conciliation at the League, its actions behind the scenes in China were considerably more selfish. Both traits were present in BJ.044941 in November 1931, in which Shidehara noted that he had tactfully told rather than ordered the Kwantung Army to avoid provoking any incidents with the Soviet Union in its Tsitsihar operation, and that he favoured an unobtrusive consolidation of Japan's position in Manchuria.[90] Even more worrying was that intelligence from both BJs and SIS sources in December indicated that in the talks between Chang Hsueh-liang and the Japanese Minister to China, Shigemitsu Mamoru, concerning Japan's request that Chang's forces withdraw from Chinchow, the latter had threatened that non-compliance would mean that the former 'was in danger of losing everything'.[91]

## The Shanghai crisis

Britain's complacency about the consequences of the fighting did not last long, for in late January 1932 the conflict spread to Shanghai, the seat of its commercial power. As has been related elsewhere, its concern for its interests now led Britain to take a more substantial role in the diplomatic efforts to end hostilities, which is often contrasted with its lethargy over Manchuria.[92] The talks that took place under largely British auspices in Shanghai were an unrewarding, gruelling affair and the Foreign Office's frustration cannot have been helped by the fact that Japan's truculent negotiating stance was revealed day-by-day in the BJs that flooded into Whitehall from GCCS. Indeed, on one occasion in March 1932 the Permanent Under-Secretary at the Foreign Office, Sir Robert Vansittart, noted forlornly to a Cabinet committee that he had 'reliable information' that the latest Japanese proposals would prove unacceptable.[93]

Britain's close attention to the events in Shanghai was not, however, generated solely by its desire to mediate, for it also had an interest in studying the fighting to see what lessons it offered for its strategic interests in the region. The conflict in Shanghai provided the first opportunity Britain had to assess Japan's martial progress since observers had witnessed the IJA's performance in the Siberian intervention. Typically, the assessment reached in 1932 noted both reassuring and disturbing facets about Japan's armed forces. The most common conclusion reached by British observers was that both the IJN marines and the IJA performed poorly against the Chinese Nineteenth Route Army. On 9 February the CIB lambasted the marines' landing party as 'manifestly unsuited to land warfare', a judgement concurred in by Captain John Godfrey, who observed in his diary that in their assault on the Woosung forts they had 'seemed to have learnt nothing from the 1914–1918 war ... and committed every mistake we made at the Dardanelles'.[94] The IJA, meanwhile, was criticized by Badham-Thornhill for the 'quite unjustifiable risks' it was taking in its strategy, which would be heavily punished if it were fighting a modern Western force.[95] These observations thus supported the image generated by the attachés and language officers in the 1920s that the Japanese had singularly failed to learn the lessons of the Great War.

This poor impression was balanced by a distinctly disturbing event, for the IJA was able in February 1932 to send an expeditionary force of three divisions to Shanghai without any prior warning. This operation was kept secret from the British, not because Japanese codes were unreadable, but through the maintenance of complete radio silence and the lack of any disruption to normal ocean traffic. This demonstrated for the first time a very worrying Japanese strength – its ability to undertake large-scale combined operations without providing any forewarning to its adversaries.[96] To the British, whose defences in East and South-East Asia lay woefully incomplete, Japan's apparent ability to launch an assault out of the blue against Hong Kong or Singapore came as a great shock, and led to calls for a change in defence planning. In late February the COS warned the CID that:

> One of the most disquieting features of recent events is the suddenness with which Japan took action and the success with which her intentions were concealed ... If Japan were ever to prepare for operations of wider scope it must be assumed that these preparations would be concealed with equal care and her blows delivered with equal suddenness.[97]

Accordingly, the COS called for and the Cabinet agreed to the abrogation of the ten-year rule and to work on the Singapore naval base being expedited.[98]

This decision did not mean that Britain now accepted that Japan was likely to attack in the near future, and did not completely reverse the indulgent attitude it had initially taken towards Japanese actions in Manchuria. In making the case for abrogation the COS were careful to stress that 'we have no reason to impute aggressive intentions to Japan'.[99] The problem was thus not Japan *per se* but rather the lack of British preparedness and the need to rectify this, so that in the abstract contingency of Britain having to take action on behalf of the League of Nations it could stand its ground more effectively. Indeed, there continued to be a great deal of resistance within Britain to the idea that Japan should be viewed as hostile. In both the War Office and the Admiralty Japan was still seen as a useful barrier to the main threat to British interests, the Soviet Union. On 4 February 1932 MI2c's annual questionnaire for the SIS, despite Manchuria and the rise of tensions in Shanghai, stressed that its priorities were the same as the previous year, in other words the main target was the Comintern.[100] Undoubtedly, the Deputy Director of Military Intelligence and Operations, Brigadier Temperler, spoke for many when he stated in September 1932 that 'our material interests lie in allowing Japan to develop Manchuria both to her own advantage and as a bulwark against communism'.[101] Moreover, Britain was still concerned about Chinese communism, and the presence of British troops in the International Settlement in Shanghai continued to be justified by reference to the threat posed by CCP-sponsored agitation.[102]

## The Japanese threat revives

Throughout 1933 the perception that Japan did not really constitute anything but a theoretical menace to British interests was severely eroded. The most obvious cause of concern was the continuing fighting in China. As the League of Nations Assembly voted in February to accept the report produced by the Lytton mission on the fighting in Manchuria, the IJA launched an offensive to seize the province of Jehol and then advanced south of the Great Wall, thus threatening Peking and Tientsin. This was highly disturbing, for although Manchuria could be viewed as a region that had a long history of autonomy, this was not the case in north China where Japanese aggression could only be seen as territorial aggrandizement.

In addition to the general fears, the intelligence on the crisis pointed to a number of disturbing trends. Once again there was evidence that the Gaimushō was prepared to use military pressure to bring about its own ends. On 11 and 14 March BJs revealed that the Gaimushō had ordered its minister to China, Ariyoshi Akira, to stress to the Chinese leadership that any counteroffensive could lead to a Japanese strike against Peking.[103] In addition, SIS reports indicated that the disunity displayed by the Chinese could have worrying ramifications for British interests. It became clear that Chiang Kai-shek was not willing to fight even to save Peking, and that some of his followers, such as Huang Fu, were all too willing to compromise with the Japanese.[104]

Moreover, intelligence in the early months of 1933 appeared to demonstrate that Japan was not satiated by its conquest of Manchuria but entertained larger if still indistinct ambitions, looking with hostility towards its northern neighbour, the Soviet Union, and once again becoming active in the colonies of South-East Asia. The evidence of a deepening rift between Japan and the Soviet Union caused some concern in Whitehall, for it raised the danger of an all-out war breaking out in the region with unforeseeable consequences for Britain. Already in June 1932 MI2c had produced a memorandum about the security of Manchuria which predicted that Soviet-Japanese competition over control of the CER might lead to war, although this was not thought to be imminent because the railway network on the Manchurian side of the border was too primitive to support a large-scale Japanese military campaign.[105] By the end of 1932 the situation looked more serious. In December Sir Francis Lindley, the ambassador in Tokyo, reported that the consensus among the military attachés was that Japan was preparing for war against the Soviet Union.[106] The effect of this news on Whitehall was to bring home to policy-makers that Manchuria might not be an end in itself, but rather an attempt to improve Japan's position *vis-à-vis* Russia in preparation for what the Japanese believed to be an inevitable war. This, as the DNI, Admiral Gerald Dickens, noted, demonstrated that 'the Far Eastern situation ... might easily and rapidly become dangerous for ourselves'.[107]

This assessment was confirmed by the evidence that was reaching Whitehall about Japanese rearmament. From a variety of sources, both official and clandestine, it became obvious by the start of 1933 that both the IJA and IJN had begun large-scale rearmament programmes. In the IJA's case this was linked to an announcement by Army Minister General Araki on 28 December 1932 that a major reorganization was to take place in order to modernize the Army following its lapses at Shanghai. The new measures included more training in mechanized warfare, an expansion of the officer class, and the provision of new equipment.[108] In the coming months it was apparent that the process of producing new munitions was already under way, with Japanese arsenals working at full capacity.[109] Linked to this it was evident that Japan was engaged upon a determined effort to stockpile imported raw materials. In 1933 the newly formed Industrial Intelligence Centre (IIC) produced a number of reports on the Japanese economy for the CID's Advisory Committee on Trade Questions in Time of War. In March 1933 it noted that Japan was purchasing unusually large amounts of nickel and copper, and that it might already possess a year's supply of raw cotton, wool and coke in order to nullify the effect of any economic blockade.[110] A further report in October 1933 on Japanese industry observed that Japan was engaged in an assiduous effort to locate mineral resources within its empire, and that the production for military use of materials such as glycerine, tin plate and chemicals had increased dramatically.[111]

Beyond the concern about Russo-Japanese rivalry and the long-term prospects for rearmament, an even more disturbing factor for Britain was the awareness of renewed Japanese activities in South-East Asia. Concern began to be expressed in February 1933, when the COS received an intelligence report outlining a Japanese plan devised during the Shanghai crisis for an offensive against Singapore by one IJA division supported by light artillery.[112] Perhaps more than any other, this report galvanized Whitehall into once again looking at Japan with suspicion, for here was evidence that it saw Britain as an obstacle to its ambitions. In March a detailed memorandum on the activities of Japanese fishermen around the coast of Malaya showed that the suspicions of the Malayan Command had been reawakened.[113] Evidence from Japan itself suggested that recent events had led to a revival of interest in pan-Asianism. In March 1933 Lindley reported from Tokyo that a Great Asia Society had been formed, and that its inaugural meeting had attracted such luminaries as Araki, his predecessor, General Minami, the former C-in-C of the Kwantung Army, General Honjo, former Foreign Minister Yoshizawa, and the former Chief of the Naval Staff, Admiral Kato, and that one of the coming men of Japanese political life, Konoe Fumimaro, had agreed to act as its president.[114] Even more worrying was that this surge of interest led to a revival in the fortunes of both Rash Behari Bose and Mahendra Pratap, who once again found a responsive audience for their anti-British propaganda.[115] In addition, there was renewed evidence of links between the Japanese and nationalist groups in the East Indies, with Mohammed Hatta, in particular, engaging in pan-Asian rhetoric. In June 1933 the Dutch authorities in Batavia communicated their fears about pan-Asianism to a visiting SIS representative, which in turn led the Admiralty to observe that this trend required attention 'as India may be involved'.[116]

The intelligence gathered in 1933 on Japanese ambitions in China and South-East Asia and its preparations for war, possibly with the Soviet Union, obviously gave great cause for concern. It demonstrated that the Japanese aggression in Manchuria and Shanghai was not necessarily a temporary phenomenon, and raised the image of future conflicts in East Asia that might well have unfortunate ramifications for the British stake in the region. It thus re-emphasized the need for greater defence readiness and an expansion of Britain's intelligence-gathering apparatus. The result was that in October 1933 the COS in their annual report for the CID recommended that Britain should urgently attend to its defence deficiencies in the East. Meanwhile, MI2c provided a new order of priority for the SIS in East Asia with Japan heading the list above the Soviet Union.[117]

# 7
# 'The Situation in the Far East Has Changed Completely', 1933–37

The resurgence in 1933 of the Japanese threat to British interests in Asia could not have come at a worse time, for it coincided with the emergence of a revisionist and rapidly rearming Germany in Europe. This, and the split with Fascist Italy over the Ethiopian crisis in 1935, meant that Britain was faced with a 'strategic nightmare', in which there was the possibility that it might find itself at war simultaneously with three Great Powers. In this situation the need for good intelligence on East Asia became more important than ever. This period, therefore, saw a major reform and expansion of Britain's intelligence-gathering operations as the priority shifted from acquiring information on the Comintern to measuring Japan's potential for war.

The intelligence gathered was used to assess the extent of the threat posed by Japanese intentions and capabilities and to decide whether the threat was best met through resistance or appeasement. As such, the study of intelligence in this period sheds light on the current historiographical controversy between British and Japanese scholars about these years. The former describe British policy in East Asia as one of drift, neither resisting nor appeasing Japan but relying instead on a cautious 'wait and see' attitude.[1] In contrast the latter, including such scholars as Hosoya Chihiro and Kibata Yoichi, tend to concentrate on British overtures towards Japan, and assert that on occasions the policy bordered on appeasement. Britain's supine approach to East Asian issues, they contend, was based on its fear of Japanese military predominance in the region allied to awareness of its own fragile hold over its Asian colonies.[2] Analysis of Britain's evolving intelligence image of Japan during this period and the way that it influenced policy is clearly relevant to this debate, for it can be used to see which description of British policy is closer to the truth.

## Addressing intelligence deficiencies

In order to understand the effect that intelligence had on British policy from 1933 to 1937 it is necessary to begin with a review of the evolution of the intelligence organizations during this period, for once again this had a marked effect on the material provided to Whitehall. In the aftermath of the Manchurian crisis and the scare about the security of South-East Asia in 1933, it was obvious to those involved in intelligence that Britain's resources in the region required considerable improvement. The response of the services to the growing perception of a Japanese threat was twofold: first, they sought to improve and reform their own intelligence-gathering networks in the region, and second, they belatedly recognized the need to move towards a pooling of resources and information. The structure of intelligence-gathering thus underwent major reform.

While these aims were laudable their actual execution proved difficult, particularly the acquisition of better intelligence from Japan itself, for it was one thing to want more intelligence but quite another to acquire it. From 1933 the Japanese Empire became more secretive than ever and restrictions on the activities of foreigners, whether diplomatic staff or private individuals, escalated markedly. For example, many new areas of strategic importance were declared off-limits, the police regularly tailed foreigners and on occasions arrests were made. Even the task of gathering intelligence from open sources was increasingly difficult, as Japanese official publications, including the annual breakdown of government expenditure, steadily became less informative.

Another important obstacle to the gathering of intelligence was the Depression, for it had unfortunate repercussions on the services' language officer programmes. As pressure for cuts was exerted in Whitehall and New Delhi, the sending of officers for three years training in Japanese was an obvious target. By 1930 India had decided to stop sending officers; Australia followed suit and the British services seem in the early 1930s to have lowered their quotas.[3] Moreover, the problems were compounded by the fact that fluctuations in currency levels again adversely affected the value of the language allowance, thus making such training an unattractive option for young officers.[4] The result was that in the 1930s the language officer system fell into neglect and there were not enough interpreters to fill all the relevant posts, with obvious consequences for intelligence-gathering.

Despite this unpromising environment, it was essential that the services improve their intelligence-gathering on Japan. For the Air Ministry this meant bringing a decade's prevarication to an end and finally appointing air attachés to both Peking and Tokyo. The decision to appoint the former was taken on the grounds that the recent fighting in China provided a good platform for judging the air capabilities of both combatants, and received sanction from the Treasury in 1933.[5] The Air Ministry then decided to free itself even further from reliance on the other services by pushing, in April 1934, for an air attaché in Tokyo, explaining to the Treasury that this was necessary in order 'to improve our very limited knowledge of Japanese aviation'.[6] The Treasury again proved to be forthcoming and in January 1935 Squadron Leader R.W. Chappell, who had been a language officer in 1926–27, arrived in Japan to take up the post.[7] However, once in Japan Chappell found that the security-conscious Japanese worked doggedly to restrict his activities, refusing him permission to visit Formosa and to view air defence manoeuvres over Tokyo.[8] The amount of extra information generated was therefore fairly minimal.

For MI2c the main priority was the collection of material on the IJA's reform programme, but here too major difficulties existed due to Japan's secretiveness. From 1932 the IJA put restrictions on all military attachés in Tokyo, for example barring them from seeing any exercises except the IJA's annual manoeuvres. The latter continued to be of limited use for, as the GOC Malaya, Major-General William Dobbie, who attended in 1936, noted, they were primarily a public spectacle and thus resembled 'an item in the Aldershot Tattoo (representing some mediæval battle) rather than modern war'.[9] Another problem was that although the IJA still allowed the remaining British language officers to be attached to its schools and units, their activities were increasingly constrained and thus they could glean relatively little about the reforms.[10] Recognizing the difficulties faced by the military attaché, as early as March 1933 MI2c in its annual submission asked the SIS to assist in gathering intelligence about the IJA's reorganization, including the introduction of new weapons. Unfortunately, the SIS proved unable to provide much useful information as its organization in Japan was still woefully inadequate. In January 1934 MI2c was forced to inform the SIS that its requirements had not changed from the previous year's questionnaire as 'we have received comparatively little of the information therein asked for'.[11]

Faced with these problems, other possibilities were looked at. One option was to increase the role of the consular service. In January 1934 the embassy in Tokyo circulated a note to all holders of consular posts asking them 'to intimate to British subjects that their Consul is the proper recipient for information', although with the proviso that individuals were not to be encouraged to engage in actual espionage.[12] However, with Japanese police surveillance of all foreigners becoming ever more severe this was hardly a feasible policy. Another proposal put forward in 1936 was to get the military attaché to extend his activities and generate his own secret reservoir of information. This too failed, for it met an immovable obstacle in the shape of Piggott, by then a Major-General, who was just starting his second term as military attaché. Piggott, who was appointed in the belief that his presence would be proof of Britain's lack of animosity against Japan, returned to his 'second home' hoping that he could bring about a miraculous political rapprochement. Unfortunately, this exacerbated his natural disinclination, already evident in 1928, to acquire intelligence about Japan through covert means, and thus when asked by the DMOI in

*Table 2* Language officers sent to Japan, 1930–39

| Date | Name | Service | Remarks |
|---|---|---|---|
| 1930 | Capt. J. Randall | BA | |
| | Lt. C. Boxer | BA | Intelligence HK |
| | Lt. N. Barham | RN | GCCS, FECB |
| | Lt. M. Burnett | RN | GCCS, FECB |
| | Pay.-Lt.Cmdr R. Thatcher | RN | GCCS, FECB |
| 1932 | Lt. J. Chapman | BA | MI2 |
| | Flt.-Lt. A. Warburton | RAF | FECB, AA China 1940–41 |
| 1933 | Lt. P. Marr Johnson | BA | GCCS, FECB |
| | Lt. C. Holmes | RN | FECB |
| | Pay.-Lt. J. MacIntyre | RN | FECB |
| | Flt.-Lt. W. Kennedy | RAF | |
| 1934 | Pay.-Lt. A. Merry | RN | FECB, Liaison Melbourne |
| 1935 | Lt. T.H. Winterborn | BA | MI2c |
| | Flt.-Lt. H. Bennett | RAF | FECB |
| 1936 | Lt. F. Piggott | BA | Invalided 1938 |
| | Flt.-Lt. T.Parselle | RAF | Liaison Hankow |
| 1937 | Capt. P. Parker | BA | Liaison Tientsin, AMA Tokyo 1941 |
| | Lt. P. Pender-Cudlip | BA | Liaison Shanghai, FECB |
| 1938 | Major Stables | IA | |
| | Lt. B. Thunder | IA | |
| | Flt.-Lt. R. Barclay | RAF | |
| 1939 | Capt. Close | BA | Studies not completed |
| | Lt. J. Ridsdale | BA | Studies not completed, MI2 |
| | Lt. Thomas | BA | Studies not completed |

June 1936 to produce secret reports he refused, stating that he did not want to risk prejudicing his efforts.[13] Indeed, Piggott's appointment led to a general decline in the overall standard of reporting, as his obsession with his 'mission' led him to concentrate on political matters to the detriment of observations on the IJA's worth as a fighting force. Thus, despite its efforts to improve intelligence-gathering in Japan, the War Office by 1937 was as badly off as ever.

As the dominant arm in any war against Japan, the Admiralty faced the greatest task in improving its intelligence-gathering apparatus. As with the other services, it suffered from the problems raised by the restrictions on the activities of attachés. Japanese secrecy was such that, as Commander George Ross, the ANA from 1933 to 1936, noted in his memoirs, cameras were not allowed at naval reviews where, in any case, IJN deck equipment was invariably covered by tarpaulin. In addition, the tours of inspection granted to the naval attaché, Captain Guy Vivian, were so devoid of content that in 1936 he asked the Admiralty to withdraw goodwill from his Japanese counterpart in London.[14] The situation was not helped by the fact that the naval attachés still spoke no Japanese.[15] The obvious remedy was to rely upon the ANAs, but interpreters were so scarce that even this post could not be filled by trained Japanese linguists, and the Treasury proved reluctant to cover language tuition fees while they were at their posts.[16] The intelligence collected through the attachés thus remained unsatisfactory.

Budgetary concerns also figured in what the DNI, Admiral Gerald Dickens, considered to be the most pressing need, the expansion of SIGINT capability. This required a number of reforms. One of the most important was the need for more cryptographers. In July 1933 the Admiralty asked for and received money from the Treasury to fund a scheme to train five officers over three years to become Japanese interpreters.[17] Having achieved this, Dickens then pushed for a special cryptographer's allowance to be established on the grounds that the officers who worked on SIGINT were sacrificing promotion because of their over-specialization, and thus had to be adequately compensated. On being warned in October 1933 that this might be unacceptable, Dickens responded in frustration:

> Economy has to be considered, but so have the following most important points:
> (a) The situation in the Far East has changed completely and has left our intelligence arrangements high and dry.
> (b) Unless we have a good deal of Japanese wireless our intelligence will be quite inadequate, and we may find ourselves critically at fault.[18]

He need not have worried, for here too the Treasury eventually acquiesced and an Order in Council was issued in June 1934 which meant that by the end of the year all seven officers trained in Japanese cryptography were receiving an extra 2/6 per day for their services.[19]

As well as increasing the pool of officers available, the Admiralty also sought to make its SIGINT capabilities more extensive and efficient. As early as February 1932 the DNI noted that the 'Y' organization on Stonecutters Island in Hong Kong should be supplemented by a cryptographical unit.[20] In order to win funding for this scheme, the NID decided early in 1933 to collaborate with the GCCS in an intensive three-month watch on Japanese WT activity in East Asia with the intention of showing the potential wealth of information available. The plan involved using HMS *Medway* as a picket-ship off China to gather information on Japanese consular, military, and mandated islands traffic; naval traffic was excluded as this material was already being gathered at Stonecutters Island.[21] The watch began in June 1933 and continued into the autumn. By far the greatest amount of material gathered was consular, but there was also much valuable IJA traffic from Manchuria and some from the mandates. The result of the watch was that by the beginning of 1934 the GCCS had broken the consular code and there was some progress with the IJA material.[22] Admiral Dickens was greatly encouraged by this success, and pushed ahead with the idea of establishing a permanent cryptographic unit at Stonecutters, which finally became operational in April 1934.[23]

The NID also revived its ideas for the development of a regional RDF capability. It was noted in a memorandum in March 1933 that during the Shanghai crisis many of the IJN's movements had taken place without prior warning because Britain could not read the IJN's ciphers. The proposed solution was that, in addition to the enhanced WT interception, a number of RDF stations should be established in places such as Shanghai, Hong Kong, Sandakan, Kuching, Darwin and Singapore in order to give complete coverage of the west Pacific.[24] The problem, as ever, was one of finance. To introduce such a system and man it effectively would cost the Admiralty money it did not have and which the Treasury was probably unwilling to provide. In order to prove that the stations were necessary, the Admiralty had to demonstrate their potential worth, so in the autumn of 1934 HMS *Cornwall* kept watch on IJN manoeuvres off the Shantung peninsula in order to show how RDF readings along with WT interception could be used to plot naval movements. The exercise proved to be a notable success, and included the added bonus that it revealed valuable information about the IJN's own WT work.[25] The potential of this work having been demonstrated, an RDF station was opened at Stonecutters and trials began at Kranji in Singapore to see whether it would be a suitable location.

In addition to the attempts by the Admiralty to expand its 'Y' capability, the GCCS also increased its ability to provide decrypts of Japanese cable and wireless traffic. Using its links with the cable companies, it arranged for the Japanese traffic to be passed over more rapidly than ever before. Moreover, in 1934 the GCCS was able to add to its sources by breaking the new machine cipher used by Japan's naval attachés and the top-level diplomatic cipher, which was encrypted on the recently introduced Type A machine. These successes increased the amount of high-grade material available to the GCCS and necessitated an increase in staff. In 1935 the GCCS decided to employ four extra specialists on the 'Far East', consisting of a former China consul, Tours, and three retired military officers, Colonel J.W. Marsden, Captain Malcolm Kennedy and N.K. Roscoe.[26]

## The foundation of the Far East Combined Bureau

The effort to improve the capabilities of the individual services was but one small part of the picture. Concerned by the possibility that Britain faced war with Japan, the Admiralty in the autumn of 1933 decided to engage in a major reorganization of its entire system of intelligence in East Asia and the Pacific. In order to understand the issues involved, it arranged for the Deputy Director of Naval Intelligence, Captain W.E.C. Tait, to travel out to East Asia to study all facets of intelligence-gathering. This move met with the approval of the War Office, which hoped that his mission might pave the way towards an 'inter-service intelligence organization' which would eliminate duplication of information and provide a quicker and more efficient service than had existed previously.[27]

Tait arrived on the China Station in December 1933. The following month he attended a staff conference at Singapore with representatives from the China and East Indies Stations and Australia. The conference agreed that liaison in intelligence matters was poor and that Tait should make detailed proposals for reform.[28] Tait then travelled to Shanghai, where he met Steptoe to discuss SIS matters, before writing his report in Hong Kong in March 1934.[29] His recommendations rested on the assumption that 'British interests in Eastern Asia can only be menaced seriously by one Power, Japan' and that the latter had 'the power and may have the will to strike a sudden and most serious blow at British interests and possessions in the Far East [with] little or no warning ...'.[30] His main proposal was that, in the light of the above, the area of probable hostilities should be seen as a whole for intelligence purposes. This meant that the intelligence centres at Colombo, Singapore, Melbourne, Auckland, Hong Kong, Shanghai and Ottawa should in time of war form a Pacific Naval Intelligence Organization (PNIO), which would report directly both to the Admiralty and to the C-in-C China. In order to collate the vast amount of information that would flow from the PNIO to the C-in-C China at a time of imminent or actual hostilities, Tait recommended that a permanent Chief of Intelligence Staff (COIS) with the rank of Captain should be appointed to the China Station where he would head an onshore naval intelligence centre.[31]

Tait affirmed that Hong Kong was the most suitable site for this centre in time of peace. Shanghai was considered to be too precarious and Singapore too distant, but Hong Kong was the Station's winter base, it had excellent communications, it already possessed the 'Y' facilities at Stonecutters Island and, unlike Shanghai, it was British territory. Tait also touched on the issue, originally raised in Blaker's report in 1928, of establishing a regional inter-service intelligence centre. Following Whitehall's example in 1928, he rejected the idea of a body that would include Foreign and Colonial Office officials as well as representatives from India and the Dominions. However, influenced by the War Office and Steward, he recognized the need for greater liaison between the services than had occurred hitherto, and recommended that the Admiralty should discuss with the War Office and the Air Ministry the establishment of a 'Main Intelligence Centre' at Hong Kong. Another important element in his report was that he proposed an expansion of WT interception and argued that a combined services 'Y' section should be established at Stonecutters Island.[32]

Tait's report was discussed in Whitehall by a number of inter-service committees that notably did not include any representatives from the Foreign Office; indeed there is no evidence to suggest that the latter was consulted at any stage, which perhaps was a response to its obstructive behaviour in 1928–29. The result of the services' deliberations was that in 1934 orders were issued for the establishment of both the PNIO and a combined intelligence bureau under the general leadership of the COIS, while the Co-ordination of Interception Committee concurred on the idea that a combined cryptographic unit should be established on Stonecutters Island. Thus in April 1935 the Far Eastern Combined Bureau (FECB) at Hong Kong opened under the command of Captain John Waller, with Paymaster Commander Harry Shaw as the head of the 'Y' section. The leading army representative was Colonel Steward, who was transferred from Shanghai, although he left two of his officers behind in the city in order to maintain a Shanghai Intelligence Centre (SIC) that would report on military affairs in central China. An RAF officer, Wing Commander Bishop, followed in July, and in early August Commander Ian MacDonald RAN was posted as the Deputy Chief of Intelligence Staff (DCOIS).[33]

As with all new organizations, the FECB had its teething troubles. The difficulties that arose were due largely to the entirely foreseeable problem of how to ensure that a Navy-dominated combined bureau could adequately meet the intelligence needs of the other services. Disputes arose over a variety of issues, but always came back to the problem that the COIS ran the FECB primarily to provide information for the C-in-C China and the Admiralty.[34] In particular, there were concerns that the Navy monopolized information from SIGINT. In early 1937 MI2c noted in frustration that at present only the COIS was allowed to summarize and comment upon 'Y' material, and that the War Office and Air Ministry had not received some important information. This led to new arrangements being put in place, although disgruntled letters continued to circulate.[35]

It was not only the other services that complained about the Navy's handling of the 'Y' section, for Shaw also felt aggrieved. He believed that Waller did not understand cryptography and therefore failed to appreciate the intelligence that he collected. Moreover, he was frustrated that his requests for more resources were often turned down.[36] In hindsight his complaints were justified, but it is important to note that one of the reasons Waller was reluctant to allocate more resources was that he was not convinced that the current results of the 'Y' section warranted the extra expenditure. As a post-war report noted, the problem was that:

> the cryptic Japanese 'signalese' ... was not material which answered the Intelligence queries of peace-time about Japan's fixed defences, and the organization, material and efficiency of the Japanese Navy. It was difficult to visualise what this traffic, of so little use in peace, would mean directly war broke out.[37]

In other words, although the IJN's naval codes were being read it was not easy in peacetime to use this material to predict Japan's future actions or capabilities, and therefore Shaw's requests remained a fairly low priority.

However, the decision to appoint an officer to the position of COIS did have its advantages in that it was now clear that this officer was in charge of liaison within the region, which allowed for greater coordination of the intelligence effort. This was particularly apparent in cooperation with the RAN, which was greatly assisted by the appointment of MacDonald as Waller's deputy.[38] Tait had informed the RAN delegation at the Singapore conference of 1934 of the importance of Australia's concentrating upon gathering intelligence about the Japanese Mandates, including the use of WT interception to identify call signs and chains of command. Once Waller took up his post at the FECB he reiterated this request, and asked for RAN intelligence to be forwarded directly to Hong Kong. The RAN duly delivered riches, which included the SIGINT material gathered by a former RAN telegraphist, H.J. Barnes, who was now in charge of the radio station on the island of Nauru and listened into IJN wireless communications originating in the Mandates in his spare time. There is also evidence that the RAN put Waller in contact with a potential agent called Fox who, as a P & O employee at Kobe, was in a position to provide information about the Mandates, although whether in the end he provided intelligence is not clear.[39] However, there was a limit to Australian utility for, as with Britain, financial stringency meant that money was unavailable for the training of telegraphists and that the few Japanese-speaking officers in the RAN had not been trained in cryptography.[40]

## Reforming the SIS in East Asia

Tait's visit to East Asia led not only to the formation of the FECB, but also to reform of the SIS presence in the region. That changes were necessary can be clearly seen since, as noted above, the SIS proved unable in 1933–34 to meet the War Office's request for military intelligence on Japan. The problem that the SIS faced was not, however, just the inherent difficulty of penetrating Japan's security shield; it is clear that it was also constrained by the inadequacy of its representatives in the region. In particular, it appears that many in the region were increasingly disappointed with Steptoe's performance.

Steptoe seems to have had a number of failings. One was an inability to filter the intelligence that reached him. For example, it is noticeable that both Lampson and his successor in China, Sir Alexander Cadogan, recorded in their diaries a sense of being unimpressed by his reports, or as Lampson put it in January 1933, 'Steptoe looked in, as usual full of "definite" information.'[41] Another problem was his notorious lack of discretion. In his memoirs Commander Ross records that on his voyage out to Japan in 1933 he was on the same ship as 'a remarkable little Englishman', who seemed to be conspicuously knowledgeable and an inveterate name-dropper. Ross became suspicious until, in 'strict confidence', Steptoe revealed his identity. Ross also records that an American girl told him of meeting Steptoe dressed in the uniform of an honorary Portuguese consul at a reception in Hong Kong, and that she had 'unaware of this ... stepped up to him and said "Mr Steptoe, at last I know what the uniform of the British Secret Service looks like"'.[42] Further corroboration comes from Sir Frederick Dreyer, the C-in-C China from 1933–36, who observed in April 1934 that:

> 'C.X.' [Steptoe] is in the habit of talking too much. He is anxious to impress everyone in the Far East with his importance; in fact he behaves in a manner which I should imagine was the exact opposite from that which one would wish secret service agents to adopt.[43]

Even more serious were Steptoe's flawed use of sources and his unwillingness to cooperate with other intelligence personnel in the region. These weaknesses were outlined by Steward in his valedictory report in March 1935 on the CIB, in which he criticized Steptoe for not developing sufficient underground sources, stating that he had 'no penetration whatever into Chinese military circles'.[44] He also observed that Steptoe relied far too much on European agents 'most of whom are so to speak club members and in more daily contact with the enquirer than with the subjects of enquiry'. This was a serious error, because such individuals lacked 'penetration' and because it was obvious that in time of war, agents of European origin 'would cease to function automatically by virtue of counter-espionage'. In addition, Steward strongly deprecated Steptoe's reluctance to liaise with the CIB, noting that in the future there should be 'insistence on local S.I.S. working in collaboration with Bureau not in competition'.[45]

In his report on the SIS Tait recorded the same faults, and recommended that inter-service cooperation be improved, that Steptoe's appointment be reconsidered, and that a second SIS representative, designated 'CY', be based in Hong Kong with responsibility for the collection of intelligence from the Japanese Empire. These recommendations were supported by Dreyer, who recorded in a covering letter that he had 'completely lost all confidence in "CX"', and that Lampson and General Borrett, the GOC China, felt similarly.[46] However, Tait's proposals were only partly taken up by the SIS, for though it was agreed that a second regional officer would be useful, Steptoe managed to retain his position.[47] One explanation for this might be that, despite his shortcomings in the military sphere, the SIS appreciated Steptoe for his ability to acquire information on the byzantine machinations of Chinese politics.[48] In addition, it is probable that Steptoe's experience in working against Soviet and Comintern activities was still considered to be of value, for the Bolshevik menace had not gone away. Indeed, in this period Steptoe was still closely involved with the SMP's efforts to clamp down on the CCP in Shanghai.[49] His worth is also attested to by the fact that in 1936 Steptoe himself asked to be relieved after a further bout of ill health, but was apparently persuaded to stay on.[50]

Despite the failure to remove Steptoe, Tait's recommendations did lead to the appointment of 'CY'. The man chosen was Commander Charles Drage, who had been on the China Station in the mid-1920s.[51] Drage took up his post in mid-1935, and soon gained plaudits from the local commanders and the War Office for his willingness to cooperate with other intelligence bodies. As Lieutenant-Colonel Gordon Grimsdale, the officer in charge of MI2c, noted '... in contradistinction to the complete lack of it on the part of CX, this collaboration is a pleasant change and gives hope of some ultimate result from CY's labours'.[52] Moreover, Drage impressed MI2c by rapidly establishing an agent network in Formosa, which as early as 1936 was supplying information on this vital but previously virgin territory.[53]

## Assessing Japan's readiness for war

Britain's reform of its intelligence apparatus in East Asia between 1933 and 1937 thus saw some important changes, with greater resources directed towards the region and increased coordination between the services, particularly with the establishment of the FECB and its 'Y' section. The increasing sophistication of the intelligence structure and the expansion of the SIGINT capability meant that more information than ever before was generated about Japan's intentions and its actions in China. The problem, however, was that, although these reforms improved British intelligence in the region as a whole, they largely failed to dent the wall of secrecy surrounding Japanese rearmament. This in turn meant that on one of the key issues facing British intelligence, the assessment of Japan's military capability, it was still difficult to obtain reliable information.

One key difficulty was assessing whether the IJA's reform programme was being implemented effectively and whether it would be able to hold its own against a modern European army. Japanese security arrangements meant that this task was not easy; the information about its reorganization tended to be fragmentary both in regard to its new equipment and its changes in training and tactical doctrine. However, despite the obstacles to acquiring accurate intelligence, from 1933 to 1935 the military attaché, Colonel E.A.H. James, and the language officers were able to provide some useful information. James's view was that the IJA was aware of its backwardness and determined to catch up. As early as 1935 he indicated that the reorganization was more advanced than commonly imagined, noting that the grand manoeuvres in the autumn of 1934 had included far more mechanized units than before, including tanks. Moreover, he dismissed the assumption that the Japanese were naturally inclined to be technologically backward, arguing that in the future their designs would equal those of Britain.[54] This relatively positive assessment was reinforced by language officers such as Lieutenant Charles Boxer and Lieutenant J. Chapman, who after attachment to IJA units reported on the substantial changes being made in tactical doctrine.[55]

These advances were balanced by evidence that the old faults, such as the lack of tactical flair among junior officers, still existed. For example, in January 1937 an instructor from the Quetta Staff College in India visited the IJA equivalent at Ushigomi but was not impressed by what he saw of Japanese officer training, noting:

> It is difficult to avoid the conclusion that the ... output must be a sealed super private soldier, whose tendency will be to go with the crowd rather than to lead, and who will always defer a decision which involves individual responsibility.[56]

In addition, doubts were raised about the IJA's ability to introduce reforms in the specialized branches of the military. A report by a language officer, Lieutenant P. Marr Johnson, on an attachment to an artillery unit in 1936 and 1937 noted that the IJA was slow at deployment and too wedded to set-piece exercises.[57] These criticisms revealed that it would take a long time before training in the new tactics and equipment was complete. Even traditional enthusiasts for the IJA, such as Malcolm Kennedy, recognized the problems the IJA faced. In 1935 Kennedy wrote a book, *The Problem of Japan*, calling for an Anglo-Japanese rapprochement, and in it dealt briefly with the IJA's present condition. Although he praised it for its ability at planning and its high morale, and warned of the need not to judge it by its performance at Shanghai in 1932, he still accepted that it was behind Western armies in both equipment and training in modern warfare.[58]

Based on this mixed evidence, the general impression that developed in the War Office was that, although the IJA had finally decided to enter the modern era and learn the lessons of the Great War, its efforts at reform were fitful. Part of the problem in appreciating the IJA's progress was that, contrary to an assertion by John Ferris, MI2 in this period was not dominated by Japanese specialists. The two Colonels who served in these years, Hastings Ismay and L.E. Dennys, both lacked oriental languages as did Grimsdale as the officer in charge of MI2c and his successor Major C.R. Major. The only Japanese experts in MI2c were former language officers of the rank of Captain who had just returned from their three-year tour of duty in Japan and had little background in formal intelligence work.[59] This relative lack of expertise, particularly among the senior officers, fostered a conservative view of the IJA. For example it is notable that the lectures given by representatives from MI2 at the Imperial Defence College in 1935–36 still emphasized the IJA's relative backwardness, and the care-worn clichés of the past twenty years were aired for another generation. For example, Grimsdale's précis of his notes for a lecture in February 1935 included the following criticisms 'technical training behind European armies', 'Staff work good until something goes wrong' and that old favourite 'Absence of recreation or games'.[60] In the same tradition the War Office's Monthly Intelligence Summary series contained reports that tended to accentuate the IJA's problems rather than its virtues. When, in October 1936, the IJA official gazette reported the opening of a Japanese tank school, it was noted that this growing interest in mechanization was but a belated response to the Red Army's superiority in this arm, while in June 1937 much was made of the fact that an imperial ordinance had recently lowered the physical standards for recruits.[61] The general view held by the War Office was summed up in the assessment of the IJA's reorganization process that it submitted to the Minister of Defence Co-ordination, Sir Thomas Inskip, in February 1937:

> It is safe to assume that the Japanese Army is much better equipped than it was ... at Shanghai in 1932; but it does not yet compare with first-class

*Table 3* MI2 officers, 1931–41

| Date | Name | Service | Language qualification |
|---|---|---|---|
| **MI2 Colonels** | | | |
| 1930–33 | Col. G. Dawnay | BA | None |
| 1933–36 | Col. H. Ismay | IA | None |
| 1936–39 | Col. L. Dennys | IA | None |
| 1939–40 | Col. Hammond | IA | None |
| **MI2c Staff** | | | |
| 1930–34 | Lt.-Col. E. Miles | BA | None |
| 1930–33 | Capt. C. Major | BA | None |
| 1930–31 | Capt. C. Delamain | BA | Japanese |
| 1932 | Capt. A. Ferguson | BA | Japanese |
| 1933–34 | Capt. S. Hunt | BA | Japanese |
| 1934–36 | Lt.-Col. G. Grimsdale | BA | None |
| 1934–37 | Major L. Field | BA | Chinese |
| 1935–36 | Capt. C. Boxer | BA | Japanese |
| 1936–40 | Major C. Major | BA | None |
| 1937–38 | Major A. Little | BA | None |
| | Capt. D. Stansby | BA | Cantonese |
| 1937–41 | Capt. J. Chapman | BA | Japanese |
| 1939 | Capt. J. Palmer | BA | None |
| 1939 | Capt. R. Dewar-Durie | BA | Chinese |
| 1939–40 | Capt. T. Winterborn | BA | Japanese |
| 1940–41 | Lt.-Col. L. Field | BA | Chinese |
| 1940–41 | Lt.-Col. D. MacKenzie | BA | None |
| 1940–41 | Capt. J. Ridsdale | BA | Japanese |

> standards or even with the Russian standard as regards provision of modern weapons or training in their use.[62]

The IJA was thus judged to have improved but not to a level that meant it could pose a serious menace to a European Great Power.

Information on the Japanese air services during this period was just as incomplete. However, despite the problems posed by the very limited rights of inspection in Japan, the Air Intelligence Directorate (AID) did receive some reports from Chappell and his language officers. Most were critical; in particular the army air service was berated for its apparently poor standards of maintenance and for the obsolescence of its aircraft. Flight-Lieutenant Kellett, who was attached to the IJA for eight months in 1936-37 to advise on technical matters, was particularly waspish, observing that pilots had little idea of how to maintain aircraft as all repairs were done by mechanics in station workshops.[63] Not all observers, however, were so sanguine. One language officer, Flight-Lieutenant Warburton, was relatively impressed by the IJA, and noted in two reports that, although it was not up to the RAF's standards, its officers and men had high morale and that it was not as backward in efficiency and equipment as generally imagined. However, when forwarding the second of these two reports to the ambassador Chappell qualified Warburton's conclusions, noting that Japan lacked both sufficient men and aircraft to weather a long war.[64] In London the AID generally accepted the critical impressions it received from Tokyo, believing that Japanese aircraft continued to lag behind those in the West and that the Japanese aircraft industry was too small to sustain a war.[65]

Of all the Japanese services it was, ironically, the supposedly Anglophile IJN that remained the most obscure from the intelligence point of view. From open sources it was known that the IJN was undergoing an extensive expansion and modernization which included the refitting of all of its nine battleships, the construction of new capital ships and the expansion of its air service, but little was known about the details of this programme. Between 1933 and 1937 neither the naval attaché nor the C-in-C China was allowed to inspect any of the modernized vessels. The nearest that anyone came was when Vivian's successor, Captain Bernard Rawlings, attended a naval review in 1936, an experience that led him to observe that the manoeuvring of the IJN ships was unimpressive and that the cluttered appearance 'of the control portion of the ship indicates a pathetic trust in the instrument because it is an instrument'.[66] In addition, although some rumours about the expansion of slipways at dockyards suggested that Japan's new capital ships would be about 50,000 tons, no firm intelligence was gathered about their displacement or armament.[67] Neither was much information available about new weaponry, although Commander Ross claims in his memoirs that he was informed during a visit to the Taura torpedo school about the development of the 24-inch 'Long Lance' torpedo, only for the NID to state that such a large weapon could never be fitted on the deck of a destroyer.[68]

What the Admiralty thought about the IJN's capabilities is not entirely clear, for in the light of the acrimonious debates about defence spending that began in Whitehall in 1934 it paid to exaggerate the extent of the danger in order to strengthen the case for higher naval expenditure; a tendency noted by the War Office.[69] It does appear, however, that, like the War Office, the Admiralty was prone to relying on well-honed clichés that denigrated the Japanese. Infamous in this respect is the report on the 'Efficiency of the Japanese Navy' produced by Vivian in February 1935. In it Vivian, while praising certain aspects of the IJN such as its patriotism and the quality of its staff work, noted that the Japanese, due to their 'peculiarly slow brains', tended to become overspecialized, that they were unable to innovate to meet a crisis, and that they were technologically backward. This led him to the conclusion that the world's third largest navy was of the '2nd class', and that it probably was not even aware of its own deficiencies.[70] When these opinions reached the Admiralty they met with a broadly favourable reception. In particular, there was agreement with Vivian's assessment of Japanese 'national characteristics', and especially the inability to cope with unexpected events. The President of the Royal Naval College at Greenwich and former naval attaché to Japan, Rear-Admiral Ragnor Colvin, produced a report based on evidence from the Russo-Japanese War that supported this conclusion. In addition, he noted from more recent times that:

> The Shanghai operations ... bear out the lessons of the Russo-Japanese war in that the initial planning was elaborate and that an unexpected check led to some demoralisation in the command, and revealed the Japanese lack of adaptability in facing a situation not previously studied.[71]

Influenced by Vivian's report the new C-in-C China from 1936, Admiral Sir Charles Little, came to the conclusion that the British probably overrated the IJN, and that the completion of the Singapore base and renewed naval building would deter 'these slow witted but fantastically gallant Japanese'.[72] Moreover, this optimistic assessment was supported by the conclusion that, in any war with Britain, the IJN was unlikely to extend its offensive operations south of Hong Kong due to its fear of an attack by the United States Navy (USN) on Japan's home waters.[73]

Behind this belittling of Japanese capabilities by all three of the services rested a continuing belief in Britain's innate racial superiority to the Japanese. A notable example of the prevalence of this attitude, and the desire to stereotype the Japanese by reference to their 'national characteristics', can be seen in the NID's naval intelligence reports on foreign countries. In 1932 the NID asked the Foreign Office to provide the political sections of these reports, which were to be divided into three parts; an assessment of general aims, a catalogue of treaty and alliance commitments, and a description of national characteristics.[74] So concrete was the Japanese stereotype that when the Foreign Office asked its embassies and legations to provide the third parts of the reports, it used Japan as a template, noting:

> For instance, it is characteristic of the average Japanese to work well and efficiently along a carefully thought-out and pre-arranged plan ... but inability to improvise and adjust themselves to unexpected situations tends to handicap them should that plan be upset by their opponent taking the initiative.[75]

In 1936 the Tokyo embassy was asked to revise its political section; perhaps afraid to disappoint, it reassuringly produced a report that reiterated this perception of Japan.[76] Interestingly, this contrasted with the practice of the newly established British embassy in Nanking and the legation in Bangkok, both of which went against the grain in 1936 by challenging the idea of 'national characteristics'. In the Chinese case, the recent military successes of the KMT against the CCP and the good practices inculcated by the German military advisory group in China led the embassy to suggest that the assessment of the Chinese military as worthless should be revised.[77] Sir Josiah Crosby in Bangkok filled in his 'national characteristics' section with a potted history of recent Siamese politics and did not allude to any supposed ethnic failings or strengths at all, simply noting that the Siamese were Buddhists.[78] Thus, static ethnocentric values were being challenged, but, unfortunately, this does not seem to have affected assessments of Japan where racial views continued to hamper Britain's understanding of the Japanese military reforms and contributed in an important way to the sense of complacency that permeated Whitehall.

As well as criticism of Japan's military potential, doubts were expressed about its economy's ability to support a long campaign. Although from 1933 it had been clear that Japan recognized the need to increase its production of munitions and stockpile raw materials in order to secure itself against blockade, there were signs that these policies had not worked. At first it was assumed that Japan's efforts to stockpile raw materials had been successful, and that by 1935 it had built up a year's supply. However, in 1936 the IIC reported that Japan had only been able to stockpile reserves for two to three months of industrial production. This was a serious problem, for it implied that Japan, despite its strenuous efforts to achieve self-sufficiency, would still have to rely in wartime on foreign countries for materials such as nitrates, iron ore and non-ferrous metals.[79] Moreover, it appeared that Japan might find it difficult during wartime to fund its purchases of raw materials from overseas. Evidence collected by the Tokyo embassy certainly suggested that in a war Japan would be forced to cut back on its exports, and thus would have to rely on its scant gold and foreign currency reserves to finance its purchases of raw materials. The Treasury had some doubts about whether this was true, but the services and the IIC included this assessment in their calculations.[80]

The position in regard to industrial mobilization was also judged to be unsatisfactory. One major criticism was that Japan still suffered from a lack of sufficient skilled workers.[81] It was also felt that it significantly lagged behind the West in technological innovation due to its tendency to copy Western designs rather than engaging in original research, and that it would suffer markedly if it was unable to import precision machine tools from Europe and the United States.[82] Moreover, it was apparent in early 1937 that the drive for rearmament was beginning to face internal opposition due to its adverse effects on government finances. In January 1937 the Diet rejected the budget for 1937–38 causing the fall of the Hirota government, while the efforts by the IJA and the Ministry of Commerce and Industry to introduce controls over the economy ran into opposition from the private sector.[83]

## The threat to British interests

Given that British intelligence propagated this less than flattering image of Japan during the mid-1930s, it seems logical to ask why the latter was still considered to be a danger. The answer to this is essentially that, looked at from the Olympian heights of grand strategy, Japan posed a threat because it was part of the global menace to the British Empire. Although it was not thought likely that Japan would prevail in a prolonged bilateral conflict, there was a real danger that if Britain's prime enemy, Germany, forced a war in Europe the Japanese would take advantage of the situation and evict the British from East Asia. The danger was compounded by the fact that Britain's focus on Germany meant that it concentrated on rearmament in Europe and consequently had to leave its defences in Asia in a general state of disrepair. Although work was expedited in order to complete the Singapore naval base by 1938, there was little attempt to fortify Hong Kong and the RAF presence in the region remained weak. Thus, even though there were reservations about Japanese capabilities, it was accepted that if a European war broke out Japan could do a great deal of damage to Britain's largely undefended interests. After all, while one might question Japan's military efficiency, it was undeniable that its nine battleships and large standing army made it the dominant force in the region. [84] Indeed, the view in British naval circles was that the Royal Navy could not rely on its qualitative superiority alone in any engagement with the IJN but that it would need a quantitative advantage as well in order to exploit fully the latter's shortcomings.[85]

Another factor that provoked concern was the fear that Japan's success in 1932 in bringing its divisions to Shanghai without any warning meant that it might be able to launch a surprise attack on Hong Kong or Singapore. This possibility was studied in 1936 when the newly formed Joint Intelligence Sub-Committee (JIC), consisting of representatives from the three service intelligence directorates, put together its contribution to an assessment of Far Eastern defence issues. All three services were united in warning that, due to the inadequacy of the SIS's intelligence-gathering and the likelihood that any Japanese expeditionary force would maintain radio silence, no guarantee could be given of preparations being made, particularly around Formosa and the Pescadores.[86] Fear of such an attack was heightened by the belief that, if faced with international resistance to its expansion, Japan might lash out without warning as it had done at the start of its war with Russia in 1904.[87]

With these considerations in mind, the other priority for British intelligence in this period was to assess Japan's future intentions. What Britain needed to know was whether Japan would now merely concentrate on consolidating its position in North-East Asia or seek to expand further, and, if the latter, whom this would threaten, the Soviet Union, China, or Britain and the other Western states. Intelligence on this subject was of the greatest importance, for it clearly had a significant role to play in the debate over whether Britain should seek to resist or appease Japan.

## Japan, Pan-Asianism and South-East Asia

In 1933 Britain's fears of Japan had become concrete due to the perception that the latter, with its high-handed diplomacy towards the Dutch East Indies and the revival of pan-Asianism, was once again becoming a threat to South-East Asia. Assessing Japanese intentions towards this region was therefore key to any judgement of how far it had belligerent intentions towards Britain, particular attention being paid to analysing the effects of its propaganda and assessing the strategic implications of its commercial ventures.

From the autumn of 1933 until 1937 the general assessment from both open and covert sources was that the potential threat of the summer of 1933 had largely failed to materialize. In particular, it appeared that the feared revival of pan-Asian activity posed little threat. A number of gatherings were held in the Japanese Empire in 1934, such as the third Pan-Asiatic conference in Dairen and the Pan-Pacific Young Buddhist Association meeting in Tokyo, but they proved to be of little significance. For example, the Dairen conference, which was organized by Mahendra Pratap, included a few Indian delegates but none from the Dutch East Indies or the Philippines, and the Chinese who attended remained anonymous, for fear of victimization by their own people, an act that starkly revealed the inherent weakness of any Japanese-sponsored Pan-Asian movement. The failure of this movement to catch fire became even clearer in subsequent years; in 1935 no congresses took place and in 1936 the fourth Pan-Asiatic Conference was stillborn.[88]

Linked to this, it appeared from observation of Indians in Japan that, although many were anti-British, they did not pose any danger. In April 1934 the government in New Delhi, concerned about pan-Asianism, asked for an investigation into the Indian community. The general response of the consuls in Japan was that, although it was difficult to gain much information on covert activities, there was no reason to believe that the community was heavily involved in stirring up anti-British feeling.[89]

Within South-East Asia it seemed clear that pan-Asian rhetoric had failed to stir up anti-Western agitation. On a number of occasions the Dutch indicated to Foreign Office officials that they were satisfied that pan-Asian ideas had made little impact on the indigenous population; for example, Japan's propaganda had persuaded very few to learn Japanese.[90] It also appeared that the Japanese effort to strengthen its relations with Siam, in which much stress was put on their shared Asian identity, was not having any great effect. While the Japanese attempted to curry favour by such moves as inviting military personnel, students and Buddhist priests to visit Japan, and showing their respect for and interest in Siam by appointing naval and military attachés to their legation, there was little evidence that the Siamese were moving away from neutrality towards the Japanese camp. By the end of 1936 Sir Josiah Crosby, the British minister in Bangkok, could detect no sign of an increase in Japanese influence.[91]

Although it appeared that Japan was experiencing problems in broadening its appeal to the indigenous population of South-East Asia, it did, however, seem to be using its new economic power to improve its strategic position in areas such as the Portuguese Empire. Intelligence sources revealed in 1935 that it was attempting to acquire commercial interests in both Macao and East Timor. Macao was of particular concern to the British because Japan's plans to establish a presence in that territory could lead to a threat to Hong Kong's security. Such was the importance of the issue that in March 1935 the Cabinet discussed Japan's secret plan to purchase a waterworks in Macao, and shortly afterwards a successful counterbid was made by a British company.[92] In the Dutch East Indies it was quite clear that the authorities were suspicious of Japanese activities such as fishing in territorial waters and the purchasing of concessions in underdeveloped areas such as Dutch New Guinea. However, there was no evidence that the Japanese economic presence was actively undermining Dutch rule or coercing Batavia into making concessions that would impair Britain's security.[93] Whitehall could therefore afford to remain close to the Dutch, and give advice on the appropriate defences for the East Indies, while avoiding any formal exchange of military intelligence which might denote a defence commitment.[94]

The fact that no overt threat appeared to exist towards the region did not mean that Japanese activities were seen as innocent. In a return to the atmosphere of the Great War, it was widely suspected that the Japanese trading community was involved in espionage activities. In particular, though the evidence was far from conclusive, the Japanese fishing fleet was frequently accused of surreptitiously surveying coastlines, particularly in west Malaya and the Tenasserim Archipelago, in order to pinpoint landing sites and possible harbours.[95] Such was the level of suspicion that the Viceroy of India, Lord Linlithgow, after hearing rumours of Japanese activities around Mergui on the Burmese coast, called for a CID assessment of the threat to Burma and the Bay of Bengal.[96] Indeed, not all of the reports of Japanese subterfuge were mere rumour. In 1934 police investigations and the breaking of the Japanese consular code revealed the existence of an IJN spy-ring in Singapore collecting information on the naval base. In December 1934 two undercover IJN officers were arrested and another suspect, a businessman called Nishimura, committed suicide in British custody.[97]

Faced with such security problems, there was clearly a need for Malaya to reorientate itself away from its former single-minded pursuit of the MCP in order to deal with the Japanese menace. In October 1934 the Straits Settlements asked for a Japanese-speaking officer to be appointed to Special Branch, which resulted after some delay in the appointment of Major K.S. Morgan from the Indian Army, who had studied Japanese in the early 1920s.[98] The service commands in Malaya also felt that they had to improve their own counter-intelligence apparatus, and in 1935 the Malayan Combined Intelligence Bureau (MCIB) was established at Fort Canning.[99] Furthermore, MI5 in November 1935 appointed a Defence Security Officer (DSO), Commander Hopkinson, to Malaya, although he was shortly replaced by Clementi's former contact in the CMC, Hayley Bell.[100]

The same period saw similar improvements at Hong Kong, where there had also been problems with Japanese activities, such as IJN ships arriving without prior notification and 'tourists' blatantly gazing at the port through binoculars.[101] The threat was not as serious as at Singapore because Hong Kong had not been fortified, but as Whitehall's attitude towards the fortification of the colony began to change in 1935 so did the need for increased security. In September of that year, Hong Kong asked for and received permission to establish a Japanese special branch of its CID, and this was followed in 1937 by MI5's appointment of a DSO.[102]

The position in South-East Asia, therefore, was that tensions declined from their peak in 1933 and it did not look as if a Japanese advance was imminent. The most that had to be countered was a return to the kind of Japanese espionage that had been common at the end of the Great War, which caused concern but not panic. The threat to the region thus did not play a significant role in strategic terms, arguing for neither appeasement nor deterrence of Japan.

## Assessing the likelihood of the 'inevitable war'

Japan's lack of activity in South-East Asia did not, however, mean that it had retreated into its shell; instead it concentrated on its strategic rivalry with the Soviet Union and the expansion of its influence in China. As noted in the previous chapter, in 1933 Russia and Japan entered into an acrimonious war of words. Over the next few years, as tensions escalated on the Siberian–Manchurian border, it became a truism in international politics that war between these two countries was inevitable. For a variety of reasons this turned out to be a false prophecy, but the depth of Japanese–Soviet antagonism had a profound effect on East Asian international relations.

The irony is that from 1933 to 1935 many in Whitehall assumed that Japan's fascination with the menace from the north would benefit British interests by turning Tokyo away from any desire for southward expansion. This view first appeared in late 1933, when senior diplomats in the Foreign Office questioned the argument put forward in the COS's annual 'Review of Imperial Defence' that Japan posed a greater menace to the Empire than Germany. Coming at a time of rising friction in Russo-Japanese relations, officials such as Vansittart argued that this assessment was wrong, for as long as the tension on the Manchurian–Siberian border remained high Japan was in no position to challenge Britain.[103]

Over the coming months this conviction became stronger, particularly as evidence from both open and intelligence sources indicated that what was developing on the border was not an imminent conflict but rather a prolonged war of nerves. For example, the Tokyo embassy noted in January 1934 that many obstacles barred the path to a Russo-Japanese war: the Manchurian railway system was still too primitive to support a large-scale offensive, Japan lacked allies, and there was strong domestic opposition to such an adventure.[104] Moreover, an intercept, BJ.054588, from November 1933 revealed that a recent Five Ministers Conference in Japan had decided to 'avoid at this juncture a clash with the Soviets' in order to concentrate on the development of Manchukuo.[105] Armed with this evidence, Vansittart concluded in early 1934 that a permanent military stalemate on the Manchurian–Siberian border would benefit Britain, for as long as Japan and Russia remained fixated on each other, but without the means to begin a war, neither would be free to threaten British interests.[106]

The emergence of this cold war in North-East Asia was doubly useful, for it also provided a tool with which Vansittart could resist the pressure from the Treasury in 1934 for a diplomatic rapprochement with Japan. The Treasury was convinced, for financial and strategic reasons, that the poten-

2 China and Manchukuo in 1939

tial Japanese threat to British interests had to be ameliorated through the granting of concessions, but the Foreign Office disagreed. It feared that such a policy would wantonly offend China and the United States, and believed that Japan was in any case unappeasable, for the intercepts around this time demonstrated that it sought nothing less than to have a veto over the activities of the Western powers in China.[107] Vansittart used the existence of the Russo-Japanese tension to argue that the threat was not as immediate as the Treasury implied, and that any attempt to placate the Japanese might only encourage Tokyo to believe that it had Britain's tacit approval to attack Russia. This would be bad policy, for in terms of the global balance of power, if the Soviets were threatened in the east they were less likely to assist with the containment of Germany in Europe.[108] The increasing seriousness of the Russo-Japanese rivalry also had an effect on thinking in the Admiralty and the War Office. Both recognized that, as long as Japan saw Russia as the chief threat to its security, it was not likely to turn on Britain: thus although they pushed for friendly relations with Japan while Britain built up its defences, they recognized that the Japanese did not pose an immediate danger.[109] This meant in turn that the Treasury was not able to win the services' support for a policy of one-sided concessions to Japan.

Throughout 1934 and into 1935 the intelligence available to the War Office supported the estimate that the stalemate in the north could continue almost indefinitely and, by showing that Japan was not ready for war with Russia, implied that it would not fight Britain either.[110] One important source was the BJs, which throughout 1934 indicated that the Japanese were not prepared for war and that they were aware that Russia's defensive preparations were outstripping their own efforts.[111] Moreover, the War Office put a great deal of work into predicting whether war might break out, and in particular attempted to collect information on conditions within Manchuria itself. In January 1934 MI2c, in its annual submission to the SIS, stressed the importance of gathering intelligence on the Kwantung Army's strength and the progress of railway construction.[112] They were also not averse to asking trusted British visitors to Manchuria to gather information for them. As noted earlier, in 1934 the journalist Peter Fleming toured the region armed with a questionnaire prepared by MI2c asking for information about the extension of the railways in north Manchuria, the numbers and dispositions of Japanese tanks and aircraft, and the present situation in Inner Mongolia.

The intelligence gathered by MI2c confirmed that a Japanese attack was unlikely. One reason was that it was quite clear that the Russians were rapidly strengthening their position in the region by increasing the size of the Red Army in Siberia and double-tracking the TSR as far as Chita.[113] At the same time, Japan's own attempt to bolster its position was running into difficulties. A report by Major Ferguson of the SIC, who toured Manchuria in July 1935, stands as a good illustration of the range of problems that Japan faced. Ferguson observed in his report that the Japanese had so far been unable to pacify Manchuria, that banditry was widespread, and that as many as 10,000 communist guerrillas were still providing resistance. Moreover, he noted that, although the Japanese were engaged in a number of railway projects in north Manchuria, this did not mean that they had solved their communications difficulties, for some of the railway construction had been undertaken too hastily. For example, in the case of the Harbin–Lafa line the railway appeared to suffer from poor ballast and weak bridges. These discoveries led him to conclude that 'there is little likelihood of an outbreak of hostilities before the autumn of 1936 and probably some years later'.[114]

Another important factor was that MI2c's own investigation into the likely course of a Japanese campaign against the Maritime Provinces revealed many difficulties. It was clear that the IJA could only afford to launch an attack against Blagoveschensk and Vladivostock if it had first secured its flank by moving into the Khingan mountain range in western Manchuria. Yet the communications in the latter region were so poor that it would take three months for the IJA to build up a sufficient concentration of troops, meaning that the Russians would have plenty of warning of any impending offensive.[115] In addition, the problems with Japan's arms build-up and the apparent slow pace of IJA re-equipment and reorganization, as mentioned above, suggested that it was not likely to be ready for war in the immediate future.

Intelligence upon Japan's rivalry with the Soviet Union thus came to play a prominent role in 1934–35 in the British assessment of the former's strategic position. Both within and outside Whitehall it was accepted that Japan saw Russia as its main enemy, thus logically reducing the threat to Britain. In addition, the fact that Japan did not strike against Siberia appeared to indicate that, despite its rearmament and aggressive rhetoric, it was not yet ready for war. Unfortunately, the importance of this factor in undermining the Treasury's case for appeasement of Japan has largely been overlooked both by British and Japanese scholars, and yet it clearly was an important aspect in the contemporary debate. Moreover, as Canadian historians, such as Brian McKercher, Greg Kennedy and Simon Bourette-Knowles, have argued, it was a factor that influenced the Foreign Office's attitude towards Britain's global crisis. By showing that Japan was preoccupied with the Russian menace, it demonstrated that British diplomacy and rearmament should be directed towards the European situation and that Britain should not do anything in East Asia that might prevent Russia acting as a balance to Germany in Europe.[116] However, whether Britain was wise to take comfort from Japan's Russian obsession is a moot point, for it soon transpired that Vansittart's sanguine belief, that British interests would best be served by Russo-Japanese tensions remaining high but without war breaking out, proved to be fundamentally flawed.

## The strategic consequences of the Soviet–Japanese rivalry

The problem with Vansittart's calculation was that, despite its pretensions about judging events from the grand imperial perspective, it wrongly assumed that the 'staring match' between Japan and Russia would remain anchored to a distant corner of Asia. From late 1934 onwards, however, Soviet–Japanese rivalry began, like a contagion, to spread from the desolate border between Manchuria and Siberia to infect other areas of East Asia. One stimulus for this was that both parties feared that control over Mongolia by the other would allow them to be outflanked, thus weakening their strategic position. This naturally led to competition for domination over Mongolia, the Japanese encouraging Inner Mongolian autonomy and the Soviets increasing their influence over Outer Mongolia. In addition, the IJA's interest in economic autarky led it to believe that the resources of north China would have to be utilized in any conflict with the Soviets, and thus it sought control over this region by encouraging an autonomy movement. The Soviet Union responded to this threat by backing the establishment of a new united front in China directed against the Japanese and hinting to Nanking of its willingness to provide support should war with Japan break out. The result, therefore, was that in 1935–36 Soviet-Japanese competition was transferred to China and began to spiral out of control.

This sudden and unexpected escalation in the geographical scope of the Soviet–Japanese rivalry caused serious problems for Britain, for anything that might exacerbate tensions between China and Japan was clearly unwelcome. Britain was able to follow the deteriorating situation in China through the diplomatic utterances of Nanking and Tokyo, but its fear about the trend of events was reinforced by BJs and SIS reports which revealed some disturbing strands that open sources left opaque. For example, information from the SIS reinforced the impression that the IJA was steadily becoming more extreme and provided evidence of its deep distrust of Chiang Kai-shek and its desire to treat China as three separate units – north, central and south, while BJs indicated that the government was finding it difficult to restrain the military.[117] In the early summer of 1935, when the Japanese demanded that the KMT should withdraw from Hopei and Chahar provinces in north China, BJs revealed that these demands had come not through diplomatic channels but through the IJA garrison at Tientsin, and, moreover, that the Gaimushō's objections had been ignored.[118] The impression generated, as Colonel Henry Pownall of the CID Secretariat noted in his diary, was that the 'military party seems to be completely in charge of affairs'.[119] Another area in which intelligence proved important, was confirming in 1936 that the Chinese government, outraged by the north China autonomy movement and spurred on by the Soviets, had decided to cast aside its previous acquiescence to Japanese demands and begin to resist. Here too the SIS proved useful, reporting on the mood within Nanking and, to a degree, on the preparations for war, although typically Steptoe stinted on the latter, noting on one occasion, to MI2c's horror, that the details were of 'too military and technical a nature to be included'.[120] Utilizing such information in the summer of 1936, MI2c predicted that war might break out as the result of '"face-saving" resistance on the part of the Chinese' and that 'the initial clash may arise out of any trifling incident, and may occur almost anywhere in China'.[121] Britain was thus faced with a deteriorating situation in East Asia, over which it had very little control.

Moreover, Japan's antagonism towards the Soviet Union did not have ramifications in China alone, for it also affected other aspects of its foreign policy, once again with potentially detrimental consequences for Britain. One area of activity was that Japan sought improved relations with the independent states in Asia in order to strengthen its position *vis-à-vis* the Soviet Union, in particular concentrating on countries such as Persia and Afghanistan. In 1934 it appointed a military attaché to its legation in Tehran, and following this, according to SIS sources, talks opened in Tokyo about Persian recognition of Manchukuo, Japanese arms sales to Persia and even the possibility of a military alliance.[122] The documents obtained by the SIS referred to these talks being only part of a broader effort by Japan to construct an anti-Soviet bloc in Asia that would also include Afghanistan and Turkey. British intelligence about Japanese relations with Afghanistan certainly supported this possibility, for within two years of their exchange of diplomatic representatives in 1933 it was discovered that Japan was offering to sell arms to the Afghans.[123] It was also clear, from both open and intelligence sources, that as early as 1934 Japan saw sponsorship of Islam as a way of proving the sincerity of its friendship. In December 1934 the Japanese gave permission for a mosque to be built in Kobe and started to employ Muslims as propagandists in Asia.[124] This naturally raised the possibility that Japan might try to appeal to all Muslim states and not just those bordering on Russia. However, whether Japan could turn this campaign into anything substantial was a moot point, for it had no real affiliation with the Islamic world and its predatory trade policy in the Middle East caused resentment.[125]

The most significant move, however, was that, in an effort to threaten the Soviet Union with the possibility of war on two fronts, Japan sought to build strong relations with Germany. The rapprochement began in 1934 with a trade agreement between Germany and Manchukuo, but the most significant turning point came in March 1935 when the Germans renounced all claims to the Japanese mandates in the Pacific.[126] After this territorial issue had been settled there was a rapid move towards the exchange of technical information between the IJN and the Reichsmarine, which Britain was able to follow due to the GCCS's ability to read the Japanese naval attaché cipher.[127] Unfortunately, the GCCS had not broken the military attaché's cipher, and therefore the conversations that took place in 1935–36 between the military attaché in Berlin, General Ōshima Hiroshi, and Hitler's foreign policy 'expert', Joachim von Ribbentrop, went largely unnoticed until the negotiations were transferred to more traditional diplomatic channels in the summer of 1936. However, from August

Whitehall was able to follow the progress of the talks that finally led to the signing of the German–Japanese Anti-Comintern Pact in Berlin on 25 November 1936.[128]

With both open and intelligence sources demonstrating that Japan was moving into more dangerous waters, both strategically and diplomatically, the effect in London was to bring the COS more into line with the views of the Treasury. By early 1937 they were adamant that recent events demonstrated that the time had come for at least a temporary rapprochement with Japan in order to allow Britain to concentrate on the European threat.[129] However, the Foreign Office, while accepting that an easing of tensions would be beneficial, was still not prepared either to enter into talks precipitously or to make serious concessions to Japan. This apparent sangfroid arose partly from its own reading of the intelligence on Japanese diplomacy. One important revelation based on the GCCS's reading of the Japanese telegrams exchanged between Tokyo and Berlin was that the Anti-Comintern Pact contained little of substance.[130] Equally significant was that BJs in the spring of 1937 showed that the new Hayashi government in Japan was genuinely desirous to ameliorate tensions with both China and Britain. This implied that Britain did not need to woo Japan with concessions, but could contemplate the opening of talks which would genuinely attempt to resolve the many pending issues in Anglo-Japanese relations without infringing Chinese sovereignty.

At the same time, however, it was clear that civil–military relations in Japan were far from stable. Early in the summer of 1937 a report received from a European source in Shanghai included apparently verbatim quotations from two speeches that the Chief of the IJA General Staff, Prince Kanin, had made to his senior generals in April, one of which took place in the Emperor's presence. In both, Kanin lambasted the civil authorities for forcing the IJA to abandon expansion in China and for criticizing the Pact with Germany, and stated that the parliamentary system might have to be abolished. As Major C.R., Major of MI2c noted, the implication was that 'the Army ... appears to be prepared to go to almost any lengths to implement their policy and are well on the way to a fresh attempt to dominate the life of the nation'.[131]

Intelligence thus continued to offer conflicting signals about the extent of the Japanese threat and therefore did not give any clear guidance to the debate in the first half of 1937 about whether it was necessary to appease Japan. However, even if it had been possible to present a more coherent image it would have been in vain, for on 7 July 1937 a small incident of the type that MI2c had warned could lead to a full-scale Sino-Japanese conflict took place at Lukouchiao outside Peking, and rapidly escalated into war, thus totally changing the picture.

The period from 1933–37, therefore, saw intelligence play a significant and complicated role in the debate about the policy Britain should follow in

East Asia. On the one hand, by providing information about Japanese ambitions and the growing links with Germany, it stressed the incompatibility of interests between Britain and Japan and the potential for a clash. This suggested to some policy-makers that a policy of appeasement might be necessary if Britain wished for stability in Asia in order to concentrate upon Europe. On the other hand, however, it balanced these fears with a more reassuring assessment of events. For example, by demonstrating the extent of Japan's obsession with Russia, intelligence gave the impression that Tokyo might be too bogged down in North-East Asia to pose a threat to British interests and possessions. Analysis of its military and economic power also qualified the extent of the threat, raising important doubts about its military efficiency and capacity for conquest. Moreover, ethnocentrism naturally played an important part in the adoption of unflattering conclusions about Japan.

This intelligence about Japan's strategic concerns and its relative weakness undermined the drive for an appeasement policy, for it implied that the Japanese could be deterred from aggression against British interests with a modicum of force. Armed with this analysis it was possible for Britain, though discomforted, to live with its inability to defend its Asian colonies, for the Japanese threat could for much of the time be rationalized away. Intelligence thus helped to provoke the debate in Whitehall about whether or not to appease Japan, but simultaneously nullified the likelihood that a new policy would emerge. It is, therefore, possible to conclude in regard to the historiographical debate about this period that Japanese historians such as Hosoya and Kibata have overrated the degree to which Britain saw Japan as a threat and have mistaken drift for appeasement.

It is also possible to come to some tentative conclusions about the importance of this intelligence for British foreign policy as a whole. It can be argued that, by stressing the limitations on Japanese power, intelligence underlined the idea that Japan would only emerge as a threat once a European war had broken out. For policy-makers, such as Vansittart, this confirmed that the main menace that Britain had to contend with was Germany. Thus Europe became the focus of British diplomacy and the prime influence on rearmament, for if peace could be maintained in Europe then Japan would be unlikely to challenge the might of the Royal Navy.

# 8
# The Sino-Japanese War, 1937–40

From a strategic perspective it might seem that the outbreak of war between Japan and China in the summer of 1937 should have been a matter of relief to Britain. After all, Japan's involvement in a major conflict was, at least in the short term, likely to reduce the immediate threat to British interests. Moreover, the fact that Japan was fighting in a foreign land meant that its armed forces were forced to emerge from their veil of secrecy, thus allowing British intelligence more opportunities to assess Japanese military capabilities and calculate their potential worth in any conflict with a Great Power. In reality, however, the matter was not so simple, for the hostilities between these two countries inherently posed a threat to the British stake in Shanghai and Hong Kong. Britain, therefore, could not afford to stand aloof from the war and treat it merely as an interesting military laboratory.

With Britain forced to take a position due to its regional interests, the basis of its policy was to prevent Japan securing economic and military predominance over China. It therefore sought to temper Japanese expansion through support for China in the hope that this would lead to a compromise peace, but the difficulty was to judge what level of assistance Britain could give the latter without turning Japan into its inveterate enemy. In these circumstances, the task of the intelligence-providers was to help Whitehall to decide how far it could afford to tilt towards the Chinese in order to contain the Japanese. As in the period between 1933 and 1937, this role required intelligence to supply a careful analysis of Japan's military and economic capabilities, which meant not only judging the effectiveness of its war effort but also calculating whether Japan could, if provoked, strike against British territories in the region even while the Chinese conflict was still in progress. In addition, it meant analysing Japan's foreign policy, and particularly its attempt to strengthen its ties with Germany and Italy and its continuing efforts to subvert the Western presence in South-East Asia.

## Acquiring intelligence on the Sino-Japanese War

For Britain, one of the most important aspects of the Sino-Japanese War was that it provided a welcome opportunity to assess how successful Japan had been in the modernization programme it had begun in 1933. British intelligence, therefore, sought to collect information upon all aspects of Japan's performance for signs of its strengths and weaknesses and its use of technological and tactical innovations. As before, however, the ability to collect this material was shaped by the intelligence resources available and, in view of past problems about recruiting personnel and obtaining sanction for expenditure from the Treasury, this naturally caused problems.

The acquisition of intelligence naturally involved the existing sources in China, most notably the embassy's military and air attachés, the FECB in Hong Kong and the SIC at Shanghai. From the start of hostilities the last two organizations produced detailed twice-monthly reports on events in China. Their intelligence came from a variety of sources, including close scrutiny of the press, the reports of consular and SIS personnel, and the decrypts of both diplomatic and naval telegrams derived from Shaw's 'Y' section. Another important source was information acquired directly from the Chinese military, which began to reach Britain in March 1938 when an AMA, Major Robert Scott, was appointed to Hankow in order to liaise with the Chinese authorities.[1] In 1939 the Chinese general staff established its own liaison group in Hong Kong, which also passed on information.[2] Naturally, care had to be taken with Chinese official sources. One danger was that if Japan became aware of these contacts it might have adverse political consequences. Another was that the information had to be treated with due scepticism in the knowledge that China had much to gain from passing on negative images of Japan that would encourage more open British support for its cause.

A useful way of balancing these Chinese reports was to acquire information from the German military advisers in China. For example, in February 1938 the head of the German mission, General Alexander von Falkenhausen, provided Captain Charles Boxer of the FECB with a generally critical analysis of the IJA.[3] When some of the advisers opted to remain, even after Hitler ordered the mission to leave in the spring of 1938, these contacts grew even closer, particularly with Captain Walther Stennes of Chiang Kai-shek's staff. As Colonel Grimsdale, who became the senior military representative at the FECB in March 1939, noted in his unpublished memoirs, Stennes 'gave us much good advice and not a little valuable information, both about Germany and Japan'.[4] Some private sources were also available, including once again Morris Cohen, who was close to Charles Drage of the SIS and to the military wing of the FECB. Both Drage's post-war biography of Cohen and Grimsdale's memoirs note that this colourful figure, with his 'remarkable sources of information', proved to be an important contact. Indeed, Drage recounts that Cohen, on one memorably noxious occasion, even provided him with an example of a Japanese gas shell.[5]

As well as collecting second-hand information, it was possible until late 1939 for intelligence staff in China to undertake tours of the front to observe the fighting at first hand. In August 1937, for example, Colonel Valentine Burkhardt, the then head of the FECB's military section, witnessed the first Japanese amphibious landings of the war at Taku and Tangku in the Gulf of Peking.[6] These tours could, however, prove to be a precarious business. In the summer of 1939 the military attaché to China, Lieutenant-Colonel C.R. Spear, visited north China in order to report on the CCP's resistance against the Japanese, and on the IJA itself. Unfortunately, when the IJA denied him the identity certificate that he needed to cross into Japanese-occupied territory, Spear continued his mission regardless and was subsequently interned when he crossed the Japanese lines seventy miles south-west of Peking. He remained in Japanese custody for the next four months and became the centre of a minor diplomatic incident. The result of this irresponsible bungling was that, in future, movements were more restricted, with negative consequences for military intelligence.[7]

The main problem for the intelligence personnel in China was that there were simply too few of them to provide adequate coverage. The fact that Grimsdale replaced Burkhardt at the FECB was symptomatic of the difficulties faced, for the former, despite his long period of service in MI2c, did not have any oriental language and was, on his own admission, appointed because no other officers of suitable rank and qualifications were available.[8] It is notable too that when Major Scott died of illness in January 1939 no replacement could be found and his post lay vacant until the spring of 1940, and that similar problems hampered the appointment in 1939 of a Japanese-speaking liaison officer at Tientsin.[9] Such was the personnel shortage that once language officers qualified as interpreters they were immediately pressed into intelligence and liaison duties. Another key problem, which was identified by Colonel H.G. Eady of MO2 on a visit to Hong Kong in January 1939, was that the military intelligence personnel tended to be isolated from the upper echelons of the British community in East Asia and particularly the taipans of British firms in China, who possessed much useful information. This was, as Eady noted, 'purely a matter of social activities', arising out of the lack of honours given to intelligence staff which inhibited them from mixing at the highest levels of society.[10]

The situation might have been eased had it been possible to gain useful information from Japan itself, but here too there were difficulties. Apart from the continuing Japanese obsession with secrecy, the main obstacle was Piggott. Even after the start of the war Piggott insisted that his priority was the largely political task of rebuilding relations with the upper echelons of the IJA, and that he would do nothing that might compromise his efforts. As early as August 1937 Colonel L.E. Dennys of MI2 complained that Piggott's interpretation of his duties meant that MI2c was receiving virtually no military intelligence from Tokyo. As it was not possible to remove him without antagonizing the Japanese, Dennys argued that the best solution was to appoint an AMA.[11] The man chosen was Major George Wards of the Indian Army, who had been a language officer between 1923 and 1927. Wards arrived in Tokyo to take up his appointment in November 1937.

The arrival of an assistant did not, however, change Piggott's stance towards intelligence-gathering, as he still maintained that an attaché should have 'a complete divorce from anything to do with Secret Service or espionage'. Piggott stressed that, as reports on 'identifications, movements of troops and tactical methods' could only be obtained by illicit methods, he would concentrate instead on assessing 'the various sensational stories, and propaganda, which have currency at such times as the present'.[12] Piggott, therefore, continued to frustrate the collection of military intelligence on Japan. In contrast, Wards proved to be valuable asset, as he was hardworking and astute, but his worth was constrained by Japanese restrictions; for example, during a visit to Shanghai in December 1937 he was allowed to see relatively little and could not even give a breakdown of the IJA order of battle.[13]

Despite the tense relations between Britain and Japan during this period, there was one valuable resource that still reported on the IJA, the language officers from both the British and Indian Armies, whose numbers revived a little in this period (see Table 3). In this field at least Piggott proved his worth, for he lobbied for more officers to be sent to Japan and his good relations with the Japanese meant that language officers could still be attached to IJA units. The reports on these attachments, while necessarily limited in scope, were useful, and the mere fact that the production line for Japanese-speaking officers continued to operate was extremely important, for such men were essential for intelligence duties.

If Piggott lacked good intelligence on the IJA the naval and air attachés were in an even less satisfactory position. Both now found their visits more restricted than ever. In 1938 the new air attaché Group Captain W. Bryant was allowed to see only one IJA airfield and none run by the IJN, and was even barred from inspecting the civilian facilities at Haneda.[14] The Admiralty, meanwhile, attempted to improve its intelligence in 1939 by appointing for the first time a Japanese linguist, Captain D.N.C. Tufnell. However, it does not appear that this decision made much difference, for Tufnell remained as much in the dark about the IJN's activities as his predecessors.

## The SIS and special intelligence

The problems in collecting intelligence from open sources obviously meant that the SIS's role became even more important. The available evidence indicates, however, that many of the problems that had been evident at the time of Tait's visit in 1934 still existed, including Steptoe's propensity to advertise his presence to one and all. In 1938 Wing-Commander Wigglesworth of the AID visited British posts in East Asia only to be asked by civilians:

> if I knew 'Steptoe'. No, who is he. Oh he's the head of the secret service organization at Shanghai – he's the 'arch-spy' – everyone in China knows who and what 'Steptoe' is![15]

In addition, within Japan itself the tight security regime continued to hamper intelligence-gathering. When Wigglesworth visited Tokyo in 1938 he was not able to meet the local SIS representative for fear of being tailed.[16]

A more serious difficulty was that the SIS still proved wanting in the gathering of military intelligence. In February 1938 MI2c's annual submission to the SIS emphasized that it was almost entirely reliant on secret sources for information as the material from open channels was so limited. It produced an extensive list of subjects about which it desired intelligence, ranging from the order of battle, to the organization of a variety of IJA units from infantry regiments to engineers and transport sections, and to details about the distribution and types of weapons.[17] However, when the SIS asked MI2c in February 1940 to comment on its performance, the response was generally critical. While accepting 'the difficulties that confront S.I.S. in the Far East – particularly as regards Japan' and praising the intelligence from Formosa, MI2c noted in reference to China that 'it is not unfair to say that military information is meagre and of doubtful reliability'. As an example it cited the case of a Japanese staff map that had recently been sent to London and which turned out to be in reality a Chinese edition first published in 1915! Moreover, it observed that it deprecated the use of adjectives such as 'large' and 'small' to describe the size of units, for far more definite intelligence was clearly required.[18]

To be fair, it is worth noting that the task faced by the SIS representatives in the region was enormous, for they not only had to report on Japanese matters but also on China and the Soviet Union. For example, Steptoe was given the task of collecting intelligence on Soviet support of the KMT and, in particular, the activities of the Russian 'volunteer' pilots who arrived in Hankow in 1938.[19] This was important work, for there was concern that Russia was using the war to build up its influence in China, which meant

that even if the latter survived the Japanese onslaught, the outcome might still be detrimental to British interests. In the light of this it is tempting to conclude that a large part of the SIS's problem was that it simply lacked the necessary resources to cope with its responsibilities.

In contrast, Shaw's section at the FECB proved to be an abundant source of reliable intelligence. SIGINT could not offer much information about Japanese capabilities, but through the reading of IJN and consular ciphers did provide warning of forthcoming operations and intelligence on how Japan viewed its relations with Britain and the other Powers.[20] The only problem was that this section continued to be dominated by naval personnel and therefore concentrated on IJN material to the detriment of the needs of the other services. An attempt had been made to rectify this from early 1937 when a 'Y' team was established in the British concession at Tientsin to intercept IJA traffic, but its results were meagre and soon after the start of the China war it was withdrawn for safety reasons to Hong Kong. The work continued, but despite the fact that the head of the GCCS's military section, Captain John Tiltman, visited in 1937 and in 1939, it achieved only slow progress.[21]

While SIGINT could prove useful, reliance on it as a source contained an obvious danger, namely that there was no guarantee that newly issued ciphers would be readable. By the end of the 1930s the introduction by Japan of increasingly sophisticated enciphering machines made decryption a real problem. In May 1939 the IJN replaced its existing operational cipher with the far more advanced JN-25, thus removing one of the key means of predicting Japan's future intentions.[22] The same problem dogged the GCCS's interception of high-grade Japanese diplomatic and attaché traffic, which provided essential information on subjects such as Japan's alliance talks with Germany and Italy. In January 1938 a change to the most important of the naval attaché ciphers rendered it unreadable, and from February 1939 the highest grade Japanese diplomatic telegrams evaded Britain's prying eyes when the major embassies began to use the newly introduced Machine B (the 'Purple' machine).[23] These were major setbacks with both strategic and political implications. A concerted effort was made by Britain to regain its 'sight', but in the interim it was denied the chance to spy on Japan's most sensitive communications unless they were repeated to an embassy or legation that only possessed Machine A.

## Japan at war: navy and air

Using the material from the above sources, Whitehall attempted to arrive at an assessment of Japan's performance in China and the threat it could pose to British interests. All three of the intelligence directorates had an interest in the conflict, but their degree of concern and the amount of material they circulated varied.

Probably the branch that was least directly concerned was the NID, which produced a weekly diary of East Asian events and included some material in its monthly summary, but went into less detail than the other services. The NID's treatment of the war reflected the IJN's limited role in the conflict, which consisted mainly of blockade duties, assisting with combined operations and using the bombers of the naval air service against land targets. Observation of these activities clearly could not provide much information about the IJN's ability to engage in large-scale fleet actions or the capabilities of its new ships, but the war was seen as giving some idea of its value. Captain Rawlings observed in his annual report for 1938 that what was known of the IJN's actions in China confirmed the impression that it lacked initiative. In particular, he noted that in the Hankow campaign in the autumn of 1938 the IJN was overcautious about using its ships on the Yangtse, and observed that, if this was reflected at fleet level, the idea built up in the wake of Vivian's 1935 report about the IJN being 'vulnerable to surprise moves on the part of the enemy' might be true.[24] Such comments can only have strengthened the Admiralty's belief in the IJN's relative backwardness, a judgement summed up in the June 1939 assessment that if the IJN fought an offensive war within British-dominated waters it would stand at only 80 per cent of the efficiency of the Royal Navy.[25]

While the IJN's qualities as a fighting force were undervalued another of its activities earned the warmest praise, for the war in China confirmed what had been apparent at Shanghai in 1932 – Japan's skill at combined operations. In this field one observer, whose views were circulated by MI2c in June 1938, judged the Japanese to be 'the most expert in the world', noting their skill in 'preliminary planning and detailed tactical administrative arrangements during the landing'.[26] One of the secrets of their success was the development of a variety of well-designed motorized landing craft (MLC). Both the MID and the NID were unaware that these vessels existed before they first made an appearance in August 1937, but the fact that they were superior to British landing craft was quickly appreciated and information on their specifications rapidly circulated.[27]

Of the many landings that Japan attempted, the most impressive was considered to be that at Hangchow Bay on 5 November 1937, a manoeuvre that outflanked the Chinese defensive positions at Shanghai and paved the way for the advance on Nanking. This landing was significant for two reasons. First, the forces mobilized were moved from north China and Japan in the utmost secrecy, meaning that the operation could be launched without any prior warning.[28] Second, the landing took place at a time of year when stormy weather conditions made such operations very dangerous, particularly as Hangchow Bay was very shallow, with strong crosscurrents – and at low tide there were extensive mudflats, which meant that the transports had to stay a long way from the shore. The Japanese had not only risked landing at such an unprepossessing spot, but had disembarked no less than 40,000 men who advanced inland at a rapid rate. This clearly indicated 'a high degree of organization and staff work' and constituted 'a military operation of a very high order'.[29]

However, this praise came over time to be tempered with the circumspection that was typical when dealing with Japan. In 1940 the C-in-C China produced a memorandum on Japanese combined operations in which he praised their meticulous planning, but he also noted that these landings had taken place only in China and had not been used in a war with a Great Power. This left the possibility that if Japan faced a well-prepared force 'a surprise stroke might well throw the whole machine out of gear'.[30] Thus, even when the British were assessing Japan's greatest achievement, it seems that their ethnocentricism compromised their critical faculties.

Of greater significance than the naval aspects of the Sino-Japanese War was the opportunity to assess the efficiency of the Japanese air forces. In air warfare the situation in China was very favourable to Japan because it possessed virtually complete air superiority against an enemy that lacked any kind of anti-aircraft defences. Japanese pilots could thus be used extensively for ground support, in which they acted as another branch of the artillery. The general consensus reached about the Japanese performance was that they had acquitted themselves reasonably well, that the war had proved to be a useful training ground, and that Japan was not far behind the other Great Powers. In some respects the Japanese did come in for criticism. For example, it was observed that Japanese pilots were prone to be overexcited under stress, and that they tended not to press home their advantage. This could be seen in the fact that, despite vastly outnumbering the Chinese aircraft, the Japanese never managed completely to destroy them or their airfields, nor were they ever used to turn one of China's orderly retreats into a rout.[31]

An area of particular interest was Japan's ability at strategic bombing, especially in regard to attacks on railways. From as early as the autumn of 1937 Japan realized it needed to destroy the railways around Canton which were acting as major conduits of munitions to central China. The Japanese air forces were therefore ordered to accomplish this. The subsequent campaign met with a marked lack of success. One report received by MI2c noted that from October 1937 to January 1938 eighty-one low-level raids had been made on the Chinese section of the Kowloon-Canton Railway, but that over this period traffic had only been suspended for an aggregate of seven and a half days. The ineffectiveness of the Japanese pilots appeared to be due to poor aiming of bombs and a lack of coordination in attacks on specific targets.[32] In addition, it was not until August 1938 that the Japanese appeared to realize that, if the damage was to have any lasting effect, it was necessary to attack the very efficient Chinese labour gangs that were responsible for repairs.[33]

The general consensus on the quality of Japanese aircraft was that they continued to be inferior to those in the West. For example, the War Office, in its *Handbook on the Imperial Japanese Army,* noted that the performance of the IJA's aircraft tended 'to lag behind those of the best European or American types... a state of affairs which seems likely to continue for some years'.[34] The IJN's aircraft, however, came in for some praise, the Type-97 single-seat fighter introduced in 1937 receiving particular acclaim from the air attaché in Tokyo.[35] In theory, the relative efficiency of Japanese aircraft should have been revealed in the clashes that took place with Russian volunteer pilots in China and during the large-scale incidents between Japan and the Soviet Union at Changkufeng in July–August 1938 and Nomonhan in the summer of 1939, but these engagements produced a mixed picture. The dogfights in China led the air attaché in Chungking, Wing Commander Kerby, to believe that Soviet aircraft were probably superior, and that Japan 'cannot be considered a first-class air power'.[36] In contrast, accounts of the Russo-Japanese fighting in North-East Asia displayed a different picture, particularly at Nomonhan where early reports suggested that Japanese aircraft were better than the Russian models.[37]

The image constructed of the Japanese air forces was therefore relatively positive, and certainly more favourable than that prior to the China war. However, this assessment was not widely disseminated, for the AID continued to pay little attention to Japan in its *RAF Monthly Confidential Intelligence Summary,* which only infrequently mentioned events in China.[38] To a degree this was compensated for by the JIC's decision in July 1938 to sanction a series of memoranda comparing air warfare in the conflicts in Spain and China, but these documents, although thorough and perceptive, had much more restricted circulation than the monthly summaries.[39] The result was that RAF field commanders and other interested parties were largely denied up-to-date information about the war in China, and thus continued to hold anachronistic, racially tinged views about Japanese capabilities.

## Japan at war: the IJA

By far the greatest effort to study the Sino-Japanese conflict was made by the War Office, which circulated its conclusions very effectively in the *War Office Monthly Intelligence Summary* series and in the revised *Handbook on the Imperial Japanese Army* that it produced in 1939. MI2c produced an ambivalent view of the fighting in China, partly because the peculiar nature of the campaign meant that it was not easy to draw clear lessons. The main difficulty was that from an early stage the IJA clearly gained the upper hand over the Chinese, which was hardly surprising considering its superior training and vast material advantage in aircraft, artillery and tanks. This meant that MI2c was faced with the problem that the war did not necessarily provide an accurate image of the IJA's abilities. Consequently, MI2c was wary about reaching solid conclusions. For example, in the *Handbook* it noted that, although some general observations could be made, 'specific instances of the employment of troops may not be entirely typical and, in general, the conclusions that may be drawn from these operations should be treated with some reserve'.[40] That, of course, was all very well as an analytical caveat, but whether officers in the field took note of it is a moot point, particularly considering the extant image of the IJA.

Even with this reservation in mind, MI2c felt that in a number of areas the IJA had performed very well. As might be predicted from its training and past history, the IJA's tactics largely depended upon rapid offensive strikes, often using enveloping movements to outflank the Chinese and thus force them into a retreat. In these attacks the discipline and hardiness of the Japanese soldier were clearly revealed, and on a number of occasions MI2c drew attention in the monthly summaries to the IJA's ability to cover ground very rapidly. For example, the March 1938 summary noted that in a recent offensive in Honan and Shansi IJA units had been able to advance eight miles per day in the face of a Chinese force almost three times their size.[41] MI2c also noted that the IJA had quickly moved away from its traditional reliance on 'Banzai' attacks by massed groups of infantry and had begun to utilize artillery and tanks in close support. Another aspect judged to be excellent was the use of engineers who were skilled in repairing damage to lines of communication.[42]

Despite these laudable features, in other areas of modern warfare the IJA still appeared to be well behind Western thinking and practice. This was evident both from events in China and from the reports of the British army language officers in Japan. One area of doubt concerned the ability of Japanese artillery units. In China the IJA used its artillery comparatively close to the Chinese lines, and proved to be reasonably effective, but this was only done because the Chinese lacked any counter-battery capability, and thus raised questions about this practice's feasibility against a more materially advanced opponent. The training and equipment of the IJA artillery units, as observed by the language officers, also left something to be desired. Among the criticisms made were that the Japanese tended to be 'slow' in firing and overcautious in their handling of high explosive, that the 70cm mortar for the infantry was ineffective, and that generally the two-year period of service for conscripts was too short for them to be properly trained.[43] IJA tactics were also criticized. It was noted that at the start of the war its flanking movements had often not been broad enough to allow for the successful envelopment of Chinese units, and that it had proved to be too cautious in pursuit.[44] A language officer attached in 1938 to an IJA regiment that had recently returned from Shanghai noted that in training soldiers relied too much on close-quarter fighting, that machine-guns positioned on the flank were hardly ever used to support an attack, and that Japanese defensive positions were ill-thought out with no clearly defined fields of fire.[45]

Drawing on these observations, MI2c arrived at a formula in 1939 to describe the IJA's worth which it then repeated at frequent intervals. Its assessment was that:

> The Japanese Army is an efficient fighting machine, although it is not yet up to the standard of the best European Armies. It is, however, trained for operations in Eastern Asia where it has inherent and obvious advantages over an opponent.[46]

Although in retrospect this formula appears prescient, its carefully chosen words were not taken to heart outside MI2c. This was chiefly because this cautious judgement was contradicted in the wider world by the occasional reverses that Japan suffered in the war against China, and by MI2c's own references to the IJA's weak points.

To understand the popular image of Japan generated by the war it is important to remember that for most British observers the Chinese were considered to be an unmartial race, whose civil conflicts were settled by bribery and treachery, and that the progress made by the KMT around the time of the Northern Expedition and the recent influence of the German military mission had not been widely appreciated. This sense of contempt continued during the war with Japan: the most colourful outburst came in October 1938 when Chinese forces in Canton collapsed in front of a Japanese assault, which led the SIC to note, 'It has always been suspected that the Cantonese were largely piss and wind, but it had perhaps not been realized how wet and gaseous they really were.'[47] The Japanese, in contrast, were thought to be at the top of the racial hierarchy in Asia and therefore, though unable to defeat a first-class Western power, to be capable of achieving relatively easy victory over any fellow Asians. Yet despite this the Chinese proved capable of inflicting a series of setbacks on the IJA. This suggested that the latter could not defeat 'the least military minded race in Asia', which in turn stressed their inability ever to challenge Britain's might.[48]

The setbacks began with the fighting around Shanghai in August 1937, when the IJA was surprised by the degree of Chinese resistance and failed to make headway until the amphibious landing at Hangchow Bay in November. Significantly, as in 1932, the IJA's relatively poor performance at Shanghai was visible to ordinary British serving officers and to the media, and, accordingly, many took away the impression that the IJA had been found wanting without making any allowances for the extraordinary conditions of the campaign. For example, one naval officer, Commander Sidney Armstrong of HMS *Danae*, noted in a lecture to his crew on 20 November 1937 that, despite the IJA's vast superiority in firepower, the

Chinese had held 'doggedly to their positions' and when finally forced to retreat had done so in good order. This led him to the judgement that 'the Chinaman was, man for man, a better fighter than the Japanese'.[49] This denigration of the IJA appears to have been common in Shanghai. For example, when visiting the city in December 1937 Major Wards noted to his consternation the number of foreign observers who believed 'that the Japanese Army as a fighting force cannot be considered a first-class Army and that in so far as land warfare is concerned, we need not really feel any anxiety in the event of war with Japan'.[50]

The Shanghai campaign thus created a dangerous complacency among the British forces that proved difficult to modify. The IJA cemented this image in the coming months through the wanton cruelty that its poorly trained garrison troops inflicted on the Chinese in Shanghai, in full view of the British units manning the perimeter of the International Settlement. As the local force commander in Shanghai, Major-General Telfer-Smollet, commented, it was not surprising that in the face of such 'extreme and unmitigated brutality' the ordinary British regimental officer and soldier should form 'a poor opinion of the Japanese Army'.[51] News of the massacre that took place at Nanking in December 1937 also eroded Japan's reputation. In January 1938 Admiral Little reported back to the Admiralty that:

> During the past thirty years we have, perhaps, allowed ourselves to be unduly impressed with the strides made by Japan towards the attainment of a 'Western' civilization. The façade of Japan is imposing, but behind it stands a barbarous Eastern nation, with all the qualities and limitations of purely Oriental culture.[52]

The implication was clear; as Japan engaged in a sadistic war in China it reverted to its Asian identity and thus became less worthy of respect or fear.

Equally important in the construction of this negative image of Japan was that in April 1938 the IJA suffered a substantial defeat at the battle of Tai'erchwang in Shantung province. The IJA soon regained its poise and brought its offensive in the region to a successful conclusion, but it was the memory of the setback that remained in Western minds. Tai'erchwang was particularly important because it helped to create the image of Japan as being bogged down in China. For example, in May 1938 Linlithgow noted to Lord Zetland, the Secretary of State for India, that while six months previously the Japanese menace had caused concern, Japan was now 'regarded as being so deeply involved in China that an immediate threat to India is less likely'.[53] It is hardly surprising, therefore, to see that in his post-war memoirs, Grimsdale lamented that 'the almost universal under-estimation of the Japanese armed forces' was the result of the press stories of 'Chinese prowess and Japanese ineptitude' at Tai'erchwang.[54]

The complacency induced by the apparently lacklustre IJA performance spread widely among the British military in the region. For example, in March 1939 one visitor to Singapore found that the authorities there saw Japan as expansionist, but that its efforts in China were denigrated and that it was held that 'their troops are so bad that they could not put up a good show against any well trained forces'.[55] This scepticism about the IJA was reinforced by the fact that reverses in military operations in China continued intermittently in 1939 and 1940. In May 1939 a Japanese offensive against Siangyang failed with relatively heavy casualties. MI2c noted that this was not due to any 'particular tactical skill on the part of the Chinese' but to poor Japanese planning.[56] A further setback occurred in October 1939 when an offensive on Changsha failed to achieve its objective. Then in January 1940, although initially successful, the IJA's campaign to seize the area around Nanning in an effort to prevent supplies reaching China from Tonkin was soon bogged down.[57] In addition, the initially vague reports that reached Whitehall about the fighting at Nomonhan in 1939 suggested that the Red Army had inflicted a substantial reverse on the IJA.[58]

From Tokyo, Piggott and Wards attempted to redress the balance in favour of a more positive assessment of the IJA. Following the fall of Canton and Hankow in October 1938 they stressed that campaigning in China had come effectively to an end, that the IJA had settled down to garrison duties, and that Japan could therefore afford to fight another war if pressed. To this they added that the IJA had apparently acquitted itself well in the fighting with the Soviet Red Army at Changkufeng.[59] The effectiveness of these warnings was diluted by a number of factors. First, despite Piggott's passionate Japanophilia his writings on the IJA lacked depth or insight. Indeed, while he wrote reams about its inherent friendliness towards Britain his assessment of it as a fighting force often rested on old clichés such as its lack of tactical initiative.[60] Second, their faith in the IJA's relative standing was undermined by the defeats that it apparently suffered in China and at Nomonhan, which suggested that it was not in fact ready to fight a war against a first-class power. Third, their belief that the IJA was engaged merely in garrison duties was contradicted in 1939 and 1940 by reports on the relative effectiveness of Chinese guerrilla warfare, most notably by the CCP in north China.[61] In January 1940, drawing on Nomonhan and the effects of the guerrilla war, Piggott's successor, Colonel Bernard Mullaly, revised his predecessor's assessment of the IJA's position, noting in the embassy's annual report:

> The outlook for the Japanese Army in 1940 cannot ... be regarded as bright, and, in spite of its efforts and impressive gains, it has not yet succeeded in writing 'finis' to the war in China, nor does there appear to be any real prospect of its being able to do so in the coming year.[62]

By 1940 therefore there were few voices that indulged in unadulterated praise of the IJA.

The general impression of the IJA from the first years of the Sino-Japanese War was thus ambivalent. On the one hand, MI2c attempted to create in the monthly summaries and the new *Handbook* a balanced image of the IJA, emphasizing both its strengths, such as its bold execution of the offensive, and its weaknesses, such as its relative backwardness in mechanized warfare. In addition, it frequently reiterated that the war in China, due to its peculiar nature, did not necessarily reflect the IJA's true worth. On the other hand, the view that developed among senior military and naval personnel in the region was that events in China had finally and definitively revealed that the IJA's supposed invincibility based on its performance in 1904–5 was, as long suspected, nothing more than a myth. This perspective also seems to have existed in Whitehall itself, particularly in the Far Eastern Department of the Foreign Office. It is easy to assume that this view was merely the residue of the racially charged perceptions of the IJA described in the previous chapters, and that those who perceived it in this way consciously rejected the more balanced judgements of MI2c. This is not entirely true, for, if anything, MI2c inadvertently reinforced this image through its use of ambivalent language and its tendency to find the IJA still wanting in comparison to the British Army. In particular, by stressing Japan's lack of technical innovation, MI2c emphasized that, although the IJA was the most capable army in Asia, it was backward compared to a first-class European power such as Britain. This approach unfortunately underlined the perception that Japan could be treated as an 'Asian power' and thus did nothing to challenge the existing preconceptions about Japanese inferiority.

## The Japanese economy in crisis?

It was also important for Britain to assess Japan's economic strength in the light of its war with China. As noted in the previous chapter, even in the mid-1930s Whitehall had doubted whether the Japanese economy was healthy enough to sustain a long military campaign, and on the eve of the war this impression was reinforced by the publication of Freda Utley's book *Japan's Feet of Clay*, which provided a detailed study of Japanese economic vulnerability.[63] The events of 1937–40 suggested that this was a correct assessment.

One of Japan's main problems, as previously predicted, was that its move towards wartime production presented it with a conundrum – how to purchase the raw material imports necessary to produce munitions at a time when its trade balance was moving precipitously into the red. As early as the autumn of 1937 the Tokyo embassy reported that Japan's overseas liquid assets were exhausted and that it was selling gold to pay for its imports, an impression confirmed by the German economic specialist on Japan, Guenther Stein, in the journal *Pacific Affairs*.[64] In 1938 the situation deteriorated further, and by the autumn a number of experts were predicting that, although the war effort had not yet been hindered by the trade deficit, Japan might run out of gold in 1939 unless there was severe domestic retrenchment which could in turn have consequences for its domestic stability.[65] This prophecy was, however, not completely fulfilled, for though the Japanese government was forced to introduce greater state controls over wages and prices there was no backlash.[66] This was of course disappointing, but the fact that Japan was in such serious financial difficulties was taken nevertheless to indicate that it would be averse to any further military adventures.

The other prediction made in the mid-1930s about the Japanese economy's limitations – its weakness at industrial mobilization – also proved to have some substance. One of its major problems, as far as Britain could gauge, was that Japan's productivity was undermined by the lack of skilled labour and of domestically produced precision instruments, particularly in regard to the manufacture of aircraft.[67] By 1938 the aircraft industry had with state assistance been put on a wartime footing and increased production to 4,000 frames per annum, but it was questionable whether it was capable of expanding still further considering the lack of skilled mechanics.[68]

In regard to the extremely secretive world of naval construction, there was some disagreement about whether Japan was expanding steadily or precipitously. As Wesley Wark has noted, some senior figures in the Admiralty tended to arrive at exaggerated figures of Japan's intentions, putting too much faith in unreliable secret sources in Japan.[69] However, their views were contradicted by more trustworthy guides. For example, in March 1939 Tufnell noted that it was likely that the IJN hoped to produce under its third and fourth replenishment plans six new battleships, but that these could only be completed by 1945 as Japan had only two dockyards large enough to produce such craft.[70] Moreover, when the First Sea Lord, Admiral Sir Dudley Pound, assured the First Lord of the Admiralty, Winston Churchill, in February 1940 that the Japanese could be building as many as five battleships, this was contradicted by Desmond Morton, the head of the intelligence section at the Ministry of Economic Warfare (MEW). Using his own sources on Japanese steel and ferro-alloy production, Morton argued that it was hard to see how Japan could carry out any programme as large as that envisaged by the Admiralty.[71] Morton's figures did not convince Pound but were persuasive to Churchill, with his great interest and experience in war production, who took away from this incident a deep scepticism of the reliability of the NID on Japanese matters.[72]

Overall, the image generated by Japan's economic difficulties reinforced the general impression that the strain imposed by the war made it unlikely that Japan could afford further military adventures or risk alienating the other Great Powers. As the Foreign Office, in an effort to impress the Thais, observed to Crosby in June 1939, Japan was 'already functioning at approximately the maximum capacity for war purposes and ... despite great efforts this capacity is being only slowly increased'.[73]

## Japan's alliance with the Axis and the possibility of sanctions

Adding to the impression of Japan's relative weakness was evidence that the authorities in Tokyo were themselves aware that their country could not afford to become involved in further international complications as long as the conflict in China continued. One important indicator of Japanese caution was that it appeared to be careful to ensure that its campaigning in China was not too provocative. This was apparent from the information that the FECB acquired through SIGINT about the IJN's operations on the Chinese coast, as this source revealed Japan's sensitivity about the effect that the fighting in China might have on the Anglo-Saxon Powers. For example, in December 1937 the FECB discovered that, following the diplomatic ructions caused by the Japanese shelling of USS *Panay* and HMS *Ladybird*, the Imperial Headquarters cancelled a large-scale landing at Canton 'owing to the international situation'. Even when Japan finally seized Canton in October 1938 its forces were ordered to avoid any incidents involving British interests.[74] A similar impression was generated by intelligence that revealed Japan's willingness in August 1938 to accept a diplomatic solution to the fighting with the Soviet Union at Changkufeng on the Russian–Korean border. This, too, seemed to indicate that it recognized its own limitations.[75]

An even more important source that pointed to the same conclusion was the intelligence received in the autumn and winter of 1938–39 on the Triple Alliance talks between Japan, Germany and Italy. From the autumn of 1937 it was apparent from the BJs that Japan was attempting to use its links with the Axis powers as a way of pressing Britain not to support China. This became evident for the first time when in November 1937, after six months of negotiations between Tokyo, Rome and Berlin, Italy acceded to the Anti-Comintern Pact. For Japan, as the intercepts distributed by the GCCS clearly demonstrated, the value of this development was that it might help to 'rectify the British attitude' towards the China incident.[76] The Japanese shift towards the Axis did not end there, for in the spring of 1938 BJs revealed that Ribbentrop and Ōshima had begun tentative talks about an anti-Soviet military alliance, even though this was against the Gaimushō's wishes. By the autumn of 1938, with Ōshima's elevation to ambassador to Berlin and the appointment of Shiratori Toshio to Rome, these negotiations became official.[77]

At first glance, it might be thought that the mere knowledge of the existence of such talks would have pushed Britain firmly towards a policy of appeasement, for they threatened to make the 'strategic nightmare' an established fact. In reality the negotiations did the opposite, because the information derived from BJs tellingly revealed that the Japanese government felt unable to take an overtly anti-Western stance. The crucial moment came in January 1939, when Germany and Italy pressed Japan to agree to an alliance that would be directed against any third power rather than only the Soviet Union as had first been intended. The Japanese response to this was to assert to its ambassadors in Berlin and Rome that its position differed significantly from its prospective alliance partners in that its economy relied on access to British and American markets, and that it therefore could not afford to alienate these Powers. For the Foreign Office this was an important revelation and the Foreign Secretary, Lord Halifax, quickly passed on this information to his Cabinet colleagues.[78] Further evidence of Japan's disquiet emerged in the same year just before and after the start of the war in Europe. In July 1939 BJs demonstrated Japan's concern about the American decision to abrogate its commercial treaty and in September revealed its fear that the war effort against Germany would require Britain and France to monopolize their imperial resources, thus restricting Japan's access to trade.[79] Here, apparently, was Japan's weakness and the explanation for its relative caution in its dealings with the West.

For Britain, this intelligence about Japan's fear of being embroiled in a war with a Great Power and its concern about its vulnerability to sanctions was of great significance. It demonstrated that Japan was too preoccupied with its own problems to contemplate an attack against British interests and that it was merely bluffing when it threatened retaliation against Britain for not following a policy of strict neutrality in the Sino-Japanese War. Accordingly, it followed that Britain could afford to give some support to China without provoking a violent response. Indeed, it is noticeable that Britain extended its first major currency loan to China shortly after the GCCS circulated the BJ revealing Japan's belief that it could not afford to alienate the Western powers. In addition, the revelation of the extent of Japanese economic vulnerability led to some debate in Whitehall about whether Britain could afford to go further and introduce economic sanctions against Japan. The Far Eastern Department of the Foreign Office was keen to exploit Japan's concerns in this way, but initially in 1939 it failed to persuade the other ministries who were convinced that such action would be too provocative. However, by the summer of 1940 its argument that Japan could be controlled by the intelligent use of sanctions began to win adherents, thus paving the way for the policy of economic warfare that began later that year.[80]

## Intelligence and the defence of Malaya

The immediate effect of the British perception of Japanese weakness based on the latter's military performance in China, its financial difficulties, and its apparent innate cautiousness can most clearly be seen in the debates about the defence of Malaya from 1937 to the summer of 1940. To the GOC Malaya, Major-General William Dobbie, and his Chief of Staff, Colonel Arthur Percival, the war in China had grave implications for Malaya, particularly as shortly before its opening intelligence had been received about the latest Japanese operational plans for an attack on Singapore.[81] Their greatest concern, stimulated by the news of events at Hangchow Bay in November 1937, was Japan's prowess at combined operations and particularly the superior nature of its equipment, for the fact that the Japanese MLCs were armoured meant that they could only be disabled by the use of shore-based artillery, which Malaya lacked in sufficient numbers.[82] Moreover, their fears were stimulated further by the unwelcome news in the autumn of 1937 that, contrary to previous belief, it was possible, if dangerous, to land troops on the east coast of Malaya in the monsoon season between November and February. This conclusion was reached when it was discovered that Chinese coolies were often smuggled by ship into east Malaya under the cover of the monsoon to avoid detection. It was also observed that visibility was so poor in this season that the chances of air reconnaissance providing advance warning of a landing would be much reduced.[83] This revelation, combined with Japan's obvious willingness to engage in combined operations in perilous conditions, meant that those credited with the defence of Singapore now had to wrestle with the possibility that an assault on Malaya could come at any time of the year.

Dobbie's response to the apparent threat to the region was to call for the allocation of more resources, including tanks, to improve the beach defences in Singapore and the east coast of Malaya.[84] The War Office, armed with its intelligence image of the war in China, refused to meet this request, arguing that while Japan's skill at combined operations was undoubted it was already too drained and overstretched to contemplate an attack elsewhere.[85] The Governor of Singapore, Sir Shenton Thomas, who was equally concerned about the situation in Malaya, took a different tack to Dobbie, pressing instead for a stronger air and naval presence on the grounds that the best way to defend the colony was to attack any expeditionary force at sea. His ideas were similarly dismissed on the grounds that the Japanese were too preoccupied with China to descend on Malaya, and that in any case a landing on the east coast would not be as easy as he imagined.[86]

Symptomatic of Whitehall's misplaced optimism was a meeting of the ODC that took place in March 1940. Faced with another of Thomas's calls for reinforcements, Nigel Ronald of the Foreign Office's General Department reminded his colleagues that the threat to Singapore was 'extremely remote' because 'Japan had already been at war for three years and was not in a position to embark on adventures against distant fortresses'.[87] On receiving the ODC minutes Dobbie's disgruntled successor, Lieutenant-General Lionel Bond, reminded the War Office that the east coast of Malaya could be used for landings throughout the year and that the IJA had an extremely impressive record at combined operations. He met with the usual complacent response, Major Steel of the Directorate of Military Operations and Plans dismissing his praise for the IJA with the glib assertion that 'the Japanese ability to maintain [combined operations] forces ... against European troops and aircraft is questionable'.[88] The fact that the whole basis of the request was that British forces did not exist in sufficient numbers seems to have escaped Steel's notice.

Much the same reasoning was used early in 1939 when the Admiralty rejected a proposal from the Foreign Office and the senior British diplomatic and colonial representatives that a fleet should be permanently stationed at Singapore. Despite the fact that Britain's numerical supremacy in capital ships was at its most slender in 1939 due to the ongoing modernization process, the Admiralty felt that the immediate threat to Britain's interests lay not from the world's third largest fleet but from Italy and Germany. Japan, it was argued, would only attack if Britain were to be distracted by a European war, and even then, as the First Lord of the Admiralty, Lord Stanhope, observed, 'Japan's efforts in China afford a clue to the difficulties she would have to face.'[89] Moreover, the Admiralty even began to postulate during the deliberations of the CID's Strategic Appreciation Sub-Committee (SAC) that Japan might not be able to take advantage of a European war for fear of the United States. These views found some support in the Foreign Office, which noted in a political review for SAC that the military and economic strain caused by its present commitments meant Japan would 'be reluctant to embark on a policy of adventure outside China at this time'.[90]

The beginning of the war in Europe in the autumn of 1939 did not lead to any major change in British assumptions. In both September and December 1939 the COS produced memoranda for the War Cabinet arguing that there was no sign of imminent peace in East Asia and that continuation of the China conflict was vital for British interests. Indeed, the COS argued that 'so long as Japan has this commitment in China, she is unable to concentrate upon us, and the continued drain on her economic resources must react on her capacity to wage war in the future against a major power'.[91] Thus the formula that Japan could only be a danger to British interests in Asia in the case of a European war began to change, for the Japanese were now judged to be hopelessly distracted and thus unlikely to take advantage of Britain's weakness. Therefore, all Britain had to do to safeguard its interests was to avoid needless provocation of Japan, to improve its relations with Washington, and avoid disaster in Europe.

## Japan and South-East Asia

The belief that no immediate military threat existed did not mean, however, that the British could afford to be sanguine about Japan's increasing hostility, for in the global crisis of the late 1930s the Japanese could still do much to embarrass Britain in its empire. From 1937 Japan's machinations against Western interests and its efforts to attain influence in Asia steadily escalated. These activities raised the possibility of two potential dangers: first, that Japan might be laying the foundations for an eventual drive southwards through the acquisition of intelligence and the cultivation of indigenous peoples, and, second, that Japan, in the event of a European war, might be able to provide covert assistance to the Axis Powers by furthering their cause in Asia.

The most worrying theatre was, as ever, South-East Asia. The degree of paranoia in this region was such that, as early as the autumn of 1937, the Dutch were reporting the presence of Japanese submarines off Singapore.[92] The British dismissed this as alarmism, but before too long a palpable threat emerged when, in 1939, Japan rapidly gained strategic dominance over the South China Sea by occupying Hainan in February and the Spratly Islands a month later. Through this process Japan completed its encirclement of Hong Kong and crept ever closer to Singapore.[93]

At the same time, there was a recrudescence of Japanese intelligence-gathering and propaganda dissemination that affected all of the territories in the region. At first, the British were ill-prepared to deal with this threat, as a review of police information in August 1937 revealed that the refusal of the Malayan Special Branch's Japan expert, Major Morgan, to liaise with the MCIB or the DSO, Hailey Bell, was hindering the effective countering of Japanese espionage. This led Dobbie to force through reforms of the current procedures, and within a few months the situation was considerably improved.[94] Armed with this more effective counter-intelligence apparatus, the services and the police within the British colonies were able through BJs and Special Branch sources to follow the espionage and propaganda activities of both the Japanese consulate-general at Singapore and the consulate at Rangoon. The intelligence revealed a marked escalation in these fields, particularly in propaganda designed to weaken the hold of the KMT over the Chinese community.[95] In Rangoon, intelligence even suggested that the local consul had become involved in Burmese internal politics, and that his agents were connected to the communal violence that swept the city in the autumn of 1938.[96] Moreover, information collected from the summer of 1939 onwards by Crosby in Bangkok suggested that Burmese nationalists were in touch with the Japanese legation there and were plotting to smuggle arms into Burma.[97]

The obvious response to these activities was to improve surveillance and to deport those engaged in the most glaring infringements. In the first six months of 1938 four suspected spies were deported from Malaya, and in 1939 action was taken against a further three, including the leader of the fishing fleet.[98] Following a visit to the colony by Sir Eric Holt-Wilson of MI5, new restrictions were introduced on Japanese nationals, such as the withdrawal of fishing licences and a reduction in the number of visas issued.[99] The result of the new policy was evident from the intercepted telegrams to and from Singapore, which revealed the intense Japanese irritation at these restrictions. In a testament to the success of British harassment, the Japanese finally decided in November 1939 to shift their intelligence headquarters in South-East Asia from Singapore to Bangkok.[100]

The British concern about Japanese activities was not limited to its own colonies, for it was also sensitive about the possibility that Japan might acquire influence in Thailand (as Siam became in 1939) and subvert the position of the other Western colonial powers. One area of concern, particularly for Dobbie, was that Japan might try to woo Thailand in order to obtain the use of its airfields, which it could then use to provide air cover for a Japanese landing in the vicinity of Singapore.[101] The evidence from Thailand certainly suggested that Japanese activities were increasing, particularly in regard to propaganda and winning over the Thai elite through invitations to visit or study in Japan. Rumours occasionally circulated that the Japanese had persuaded the Thais to agree to a military compact, but no firm evidence was ever produced to substantiate these claims. What was clear, however, was that in the face of this Japanese pressure, Thailand's friendship could not be taken for granted.[102]

Japanese activities in other parts of the region also bred suspicion. From 1937 onwards there was a steady increase in the number of intelligence reports on the strategic implications of Japan's commercial activities. In October 1937 it was noted that two Japanese commercial concerns had begun to operate in Celebes, which raised the possibility that the island might provide a stepping stone for a Japanese southern advance from Formosa towards Timor and Australia.[103] Portuguese Timor was itself a matter of grave concern, for in mid-1937 it had been revealed that the Nanyo Kohatsu Kaisha (South Seas Development Company) was seeking to purchase a concession in the territory to prospect for oil. So weak and underdeveloped was this colony that it was feared that an injection of Japanese capital would be enough to bring it under Tokyo's de facto control.[104] As in the case of Macao, Britain therefore sought to remedy the situation by sponsoring a rival Australian bid for the concession. Over the next few years tortuous negotiations with Lisbon held the Japanese in check, but they never resolved the issue completely, and Britain's diet of BJs made sure that its anxiety never abated.[105]

Another notable development was the revival in 1938–39 of the dissemination of Japanese pan-Asian and pro-Islamic propaganda in the Dutch East Indies. This material, which apparently was distributed from Japan's consulates, was of better quality than that produced in 1933 because it dealt directly with the concerns of the Chinese and Indonesian communities rather than engaging in ideological verbiage.[106] The Dutch were clearly concerned about its possible effect, and the FECB certainly found it dangerous, noting that, while it might seem facile from a European perspective, it had appeal to 'an unsentimental and ill-educated Asiatic with an undercurrent of dislike for all Europeans'.[107]

## Japan, Asia and Islam

The appearance of pan-Asian and pro-Islamic propaganda in the Dutch East Indies from 1938 was not an isolated event, for this period saw a general upsurge in Japan's effort to win the support of both the independent states in Asia and those peoples living under colonial rule. One key interest for Japan was simply that it wanted to ensure that it had a broad degree of sympathy and support in Asia and thus isolate the Chinese. In order to achieve this it used a number of devices, such as stressing its hostility towards the Soviet Union and offering military supplies. Most importantly, it attempted to reaffirm its sympathy for the Muslim faith by inviting dignitaries from the Islamic world to the opening of mosques in Kobe and Tokyo in 1938 and 1939 respectively, and raising the legal status of Islam in Japan.[108] These efforts were not particularly successful. In the case of Afghanistan, it was evident from BJs as early as 1937 that the Japanese had compromised their position. This was due to the dubious activities of their military attaché, Miyazawa, who had recruited agents to spy in the Pamirs and support the independence movement in Bokhara, and in so doing aroused Soviet and British suspicions of the Afghans. Naturally unamused by these amateurish shenanigans, the Afghans demanded Miyazawa's recall, leading to a period of frosty relations.[109] Japan also failed in its attempt to woo Turkey, which was suspicious of the former's ambitions in Sinkiang and still smarted from Tokyo's uncooperative behaviour over the abolition of the Capitulations in the 1920s.[110]

Another motive for interest in the Islamic world was that Japan, afraid of its overreliance on the United States and the Dutch East Indies for oil, wanted to find alternative sources of supply. This led to an attempt in 1938–39 to open relations with Saudi Arabia with the aim of acquiring an oil concession on the Persian Gulf. This overture also met with little success, for all Japan gained in the end was Saudi approval in November 1939 for a consulate in Jedda.[111] This meagre achievement was mirrored in Iran (formerly Persia) and Iraq, where all Japan had to show for its efforts by the end of 1939 was respectively a friendship treaty and the opening of diplomatic relations.[112]

The relative failure of Japan's Middle Eastern diplomacy did not mean that Britain could afford to ignore its endeavours, for Whitehall was under no delusion about Japan's intention to sow anti-British sentiment.[113] Indeed, Britain used the intelligence it received in a deliberate attempt to sabotage Japan's efforts. When BJs revealed in April 1938 that Japan's frustration with Afghanistan had led it to establish contacts with the ex-King Amanullah, this information was promptly sent to the British minister to Kabul for the information of the Afghan government. At the same time the British minister in Jedda was supplied with intelligence on Japanese activities in the Hejaz.[114] A particularly pleasing episode came in August 1938 when the Gaimushō sought without Turkish permission to hold a conference of its Middle Eastern diplomats in Istanbul. On learning of this plan the British tipped off the Turks, with the result that the Japanese were forced to decamp in bad grace to Beirut.[115]

Another unwelcome aspect of Japan's Asian policy was that it was once again showing an interest in India. From 1938 the Delhi Intelligence Bureau (DIB), the latest manifestation of the Indian DCI, recorded a rise in the espionage and propaganda activities of Japanese consuls and company employees.[116] These grew more serious over time, particularly once the war in Europe had begun, as it became apparent that Japan was engaged in a serious effort to collect military and naval intelligence.[117] Even more perturbing was the fact that the Japanese were keen to make contact with leading figures in the Indian National Congress. Most dangerous from the British perspective was the attempt from the end of 1938 to build a bridge to the radical president of the Indian National Congress, Subhas Chandra Bose, which culminated in June 1940 with a meeting between Bose and a senior Gaimushō official, Ōhashi Chuichi.[118]

## Broadening the intelligence net

As long as relations with Japan remained relatively calm it was difficult for Britain to counter this growth in intelligence and propaganda activities, but they did provoke a reassessment of Britain's counter-espionage capability. In the spring of 1938 Sir John Ewart, the DIB's director, made a tour of East and South-East Asia in order to discuss the need for better liaison with the PNIO area. This led to the appointment of a new deputy director of the DIB who would spend much of his time outside India visiting those British colonies in Asia and Africa with significant Indian communities.[119] In Malaya, the major initiative was the establishment in December 1939 of a new counter-espionage section, the Far East Security Service (FESS). This was part of the FECB, which had in August transferred from Hong Kong to Singapore in the interests of security. FESS had the task of pooling information from a variety of sources, including consuls, for the use of the local DSO.[120] After its transfer to Singapore the FECB also added an Operational Intelligence Centre in order to help it keep track of the IJN's movements. This unit was to utilize information from a number of sources, such as intercepts of IJN ciphers and the fruits of the newly established RDF system, in order to provide intelligence as promptly as possible.[121]

The increasingly high-profile role taken by the FECB, particularly in establishing the FESS, meant that its presence was more highly advertised than before and that its existence finally became known to the Foreign Office. The latter had received intelligence from the FECB ever since its inception, but there is no evidence to show that it understood where exactly this information was coming from. The 'cat emerged from the bag' in January 1940 when a puzzled and agitated Sir Josiah Crosby requested clarification from the Foreign Office after the FECB, 'of which I had not previously heard', asked him for assistance.[122] On receiving this request the Far Eastern Department was equally baffled, possessing no records referring to any such organization, and therefore had to seek enlightenment from the Admiralty, which duly provided a detailed description of the activities undertaken by the FECB.[123]

Japan's flirtation with the Axis, and the fact that it might strike in the East while Britain was tied down in a European war, also forced Whitehall to realize that it could not afford to rely entirely on its own intelligence resources. The need to acquire as much intelligence as practically possible and to interest potential allies in Britain's security meant that cooperation with other countries became increasingly important.

In South-East Asia the two main potential sources of information were the Dutch and French authorities. As noted in previous chapters, the relationship with the Dutch had always been fairly close, and as soon as the China war began, intelligence contacts regarding the movement and activities of the Japanese in South-East Asia were strengthened. From 1938 a number of British officials visited Java, including Ewart, Colonel Molesworth, the DMOI India, and Captain F.H. Vinden, the military representative on the MCIB. To reciprocate, in March 1939 the Adviser on Far Eastern Affairs in Batavia, Lovink, visited Singapore to consult with the Malayan authorities.[124] This cooperation, however, remained solely concerned with the exchange of security intelligence and did not extend to SIGINT, even though the Dutch strongly hinted both in London and in Batavia that they were reading Japanese naval and diplomatic ciphers. One can only assume that Britain's caution was dictated by the desire not to commit itself irrevocably to the defence of the Dutch East Indies or to advertise its own SIGINT capability.[125] This cautious attitude was reinforced by the outbreak of the war in Europe. In May 1940 the Dutch told Malaya Command that they wished for greater liaison with Singapore, but the JIC in London felt that, due to the pro-Nazi sympathies of some in the Dutch bureaucracy and armed forces, this request should be treated with care, and that Britain should accept Dutch information but do little to reciprocate.[126]

The situation in regard to the French authorities was that intelligence collaboration began in earnest after a joint defence conference held in

Singapore in June 1939. From this point on, there were frequent exchanges of military intelligence and of information relevant to counter-espionage in both South-East Asia and Europe, with the SIS exchanging information with its French counterpart, the Deuxième Bureau.[127] The only problem was that the French information was neither particularly extensive nor reliable. As Colonel Grimsdale noted after visiting Hanoi in April 1940 to meet his opposite number, Colonel Maupin, the information provided by the authorities in Indo-China was of doubtful utility, as their consuls were not used as intelligence providers and the French could read only the Japanese consular cipher and none of the military material.[128]

If the Dutch and French were seen as useful providers of extra intelligence, the relationships with the Dominions and the United States were seen in slightly different terms. Again there was a desire to gain more information, but in addition intelligence cooperation with the English-speaking world took on more of a political hue, becoming a weapon designed to assure the Dominions of Britain's interest in imperial solidarity, and to emphasize to the United States the global implications of the Japanese threat.

The period from 1937 onwards saw a further expansion of collaboration with the Dominions, but the most notable developments came around the start of the European War. From the summer of 1939 the GCCS encouraged New Zealand and Canada to assist in the gathering of Japanese SIGINT, particularly the WT traffic between Japan and the Americas, thus adding to the pool of intelligence available.[129] There was also an increase in cooperation between Britain and Australia. From September 1939 Australia received for the first time summaries of Japanese BJs relevant to its interests. It was also asked to cooperate with FESS.[130] Another important step forward was that finally during 1939–40 Australia's RDF stations at Canberra, Darwin and Perth became operational, thus significantly increasing the FECB's ability to track Japanese shipping. Information was therefore shared to a greater degree than ever before, but at the same time Australia continued to be treated as a Dominion rather than an independent country. When in 1940 it sought advice about establishing its own cryptographic section, London turned the idea down, saying that there was no point in replicating the existing British capabilities. While there may have been some truth in this advice it is hard to believe that the political value of Australia's reliance on Britain for intelligence was inconsequential.[131]

The most important intelligence relationship of all was, as one might expect, that with the United States. The tentative cooperation developed between the British and American navies in regard to war plans as a result of the visit of Captain Ingersoll to London in January 1938 and the reciprocal visit by Commander Hampton to Washington in June 1939 is already well known.[132] This was, however, merely one element in the story. From early in the Sino-Japanese War, information was pooled between the local

British and American commanders. For example, in December 1937 it was Admiral Harry Yarnell, the commander of the USN's Asiatic Fleet, who provided Admiral Little with information about the possibility of a Japanese landing at Canton. The United States also forwarded intelligence about Japan's Canton operations in October 1938. This time the information was passed on in Washington, indeed the USN's Chief of Naval Operations informed the British ambassador, Sir Ronald Lindsay, that his orders to relay this material had come from the 'highest authority'.[133]

Even more significant was the cooperation that developed in the field of diplomatic intelligence. This began in November 1937 when Secretary of State Cordell Hull passed to Lindsay an American translation of the secret protocol attached to the Anti-Comintern Pact, which had clearly been derived from its reading of Machine A. However, this version contained some important inaccuracies, which left the Foreign Office in a quandary about whether or not to bring this to Washington's attention. After some deliberation the decision was taken to inform the State Department's Far Eastern expert, Stanley Hornbeck, who was in London at the time, of the gist of the protocol but not its actual text, thus keeping him in the dark about the source.[134] A similar episode took place in early 1939 in relation to the Triple Alliance talks. Once again the Foreign Office took it upon itself to forward information from BJs in order to correct the State Department's information.[135] Although progress in this area was cut short soon afterwards by Japan's introduction of its new Machine B cipher, a basis for collaboration had thus been established which would prove useful in coming years.

The intelligence that Britain collected between the summer of 1937 and the summer of 1940 thus had an important effect on how it viewed the potential Japanese threat. Perhaps surprisingly, considering Britain's dire strategic position, the intelligence prognosis that emerged from observation of the war in China was relatively optimistic. This was because that conflict created a perception that Japan was as much constrained by circumstance as Britain itself. Japan was viewed as being bogged down in China, as having still failed to develop modern armed forces capable of fighting against a first-class European power, and as doubtful of its own ability to take on the West. The fear occasionally expressed before 1937 that Japan might commit some kind of 'wild dog' act and attack the West in the same way that it had sprung war on Russia in 1904 was thus forgotten. Instead, Japan, based on its record during the China conflict, was viewed as a cautious and calculating power that was well aware of its own weakness. In addition, linked to this belief in Japanese cautiousness, was the perception that Japan was increasingly susceptible to sanctions as the China war steadily drained its economic resources and that Tokyo was perturbed about this itself. Moreover, despite some shift in attitude in intelligence circles, these views tended to be underpinned among the majority of policy-makers by a continuing reliance on ethnocentric views of the Japanese armed forces that depreciated their worth and exaggerated every fault. The result was that, though Britain's strategic fortunes ebbed and flowed, a consensus began to emerge in Whitehall that the Japanese threat to British interests was founded mainly on bluff. It therefore followed that Britain could afford to take a tougher line towards Japan and provide support to the Chinese, particularly if it was able to keep in step with the United States, without it leading to war. From here it was but a short step to the policies pursued in 1941.

# 9

# The Immediate Origins of the Pacific War

From the start of the Sino-Japanese War in July 1937 until the end of the 'phoney' war in Europe in the spring of 1940, Anglo-Japanese relations somehow survived the tensions caused by the conflicts in the two continents: but from the summer of 1940, as the wars in Asia and Europe became more and more intertwined, Britain and Japan drifted into a state of confrontation. Indeed, relations became so strained that in a 'war-scare' in February 1941 Britain believed that Japan was on the verge of launching an offensive against its territories in South-East Asia. Accordingly, Britain attempted to contain the Japanese menace by strengthening its ties with the other Powers which were opposed to Japan's ambitions, building up its military forces in the region, and initiating with the like-minded states a policy of economic warfare against the Japanese. The intelligence received in this period played a significant role in Britain's decision to opt for a policy of deterrence rather than appeasement, but in addition, the belief that Japan could be contained was the logical result of the image that intelligence had helped to construct over the previous twenty-five years.

## Towards Greater East Asia

The slide towards Anglo-Japanese confrontation began in June 1940 when Japan, impressed by the rapid German victories in Scandinavia and Western Europe and captivated by the prospect of a power vacuum in South-East Asia, began to set its sights on the construction of the Greater East Asian Co-Prosperity Sphere. Over the following months Japanese policy became far more assertive; it exerted pressure on the Dutch East Indies for greater access to raw materials, occupied bases in northern Indo-China, and offered itself as a mediator in the Thai–French border dispute that broke out in the autumn. All these activities were open attempts to increase its influence, but the image of a newly expansionist Japan was supplemented by disturbing intelligence reports that revealed an escalation in

Japanese espionage and propaganda and efforts to coerce the weaker powers in Asia.

The dramatic rise in intelligence-gathering by Japanese consular staff, touring officers, businessmen and journalists could be followed through BJs. These revealed a number of particularly objectionable cases. One of the most infamous was the tour of the northern coast of Borneo by the Japanese consul at Sandakan in October 1940, which allowed him to report to Tokyo full details of the region's oil wells and to propose that their seizure should be the priority in any offensive operations.[1] In addition, the Special Branch in Singapore discovered in September 1940 that two Japanese consular officials were engaged in military intelligence and the dissemination of pro-Wang Ching-wei propaganda.[2] It was clear too that this tendency was likely to get worse rather than better. In December 1940 a number of sources revealed that Japan had sent agents with linguistic abilities to a number of posts in Asia, including India and Burma, and the following month the Gaimushō sent a list of intelligence priorities to Japanese consulates.[3]

Even more disturbing were the indications that Japan's new stridently pan-Asian rhetoric and its coercion of the smaller colonial powers were beginning to bear fruit. BJs circulated in December 1940 showed that the Thai Prime Minister, Luang Pibul Songgram, had been persuaded to collab-

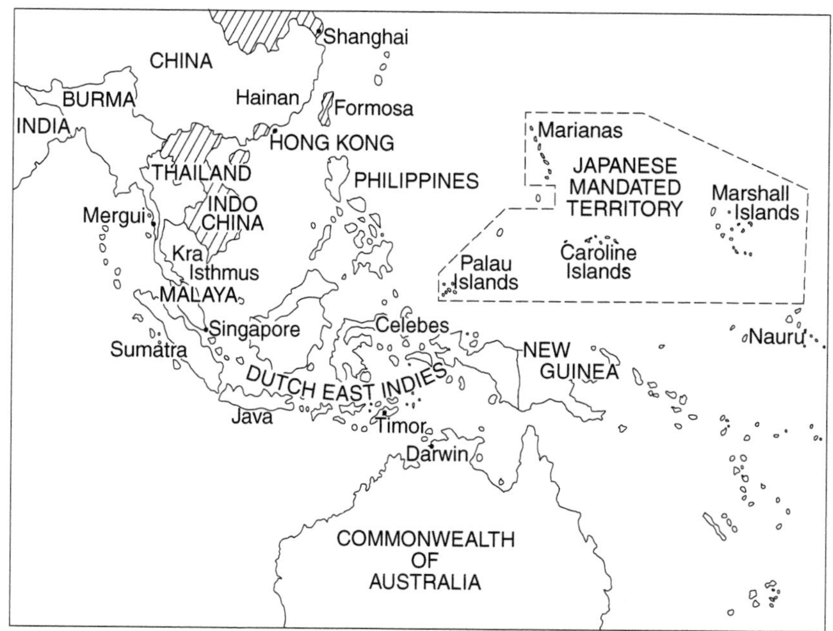


3 South-East Asia in 1941

orate with Japan's 'New Order' in return for support for Thai territorial claims on Cambodia, and that he might be prepared to sign a military agreement. This was deeply worrying, for it was obvious that if Japan acquired military bases in Thailand this would seriously compromise the security of Malaya and Burma.[4] Moreover, BJs and information from the Dutch showed that Japanese pressure on Portugal had begun to pay dividends. Throughout 1940 the Japanese raised tensions over Macao in an effort to coerce the Portuguese government to give them more facilities in East Timor, and by November they were rewarded with the news that they could now open an air service to Dili. This too was a success for Japan that could have unfortunate consequences for British interests because Timor could be used as a base from which to disturb communications with Australia.[5]

The disturbing interplay of material from open sources and intelligence reached its height in February 1941, when the start of the Japanese-sponsored armistice talks between France and Thailand coincided with a stream of alarming intelligence reports emanating from both South-East Asia and the Japanese embassy in London. Faced with these 'straws in the wind', Britain convinced itself that war was imminent and engaged in a propaganda campaign designed to deter Japanese aggression. In reality, its fears were mere phantoms, but its recourse to panic was symptomatic of the times.[6]

Britain was thus faced with a concerted Japanese effort to gain a firm hold over South-East Asia. This, of course, had been one of Whitehall's great fears ever since the recrudescence of Japanese pan-Asianism in 1933, but in the years preceding 1940 it had always been more mirage than reality. Now it was finally coming to pass, and at a time when Britain more than ever needed the abundant raw materials supplied by the region. Britain therefore had to defend its interests by strengthening its forces in the region and curbing Japanese espionage and propaganda.

## The Tripartite Pact and the Middle East

If Japan had concentrated merely on expansion in South-East Asia that would in itself have been a menace to Britain, but in fact the Japanese threat went much further. The most significant episode in Japanese diplomacy in the latter half of 1940 was its signing of the Tripartite Pact with Germany and Italy on 27 September. The Pact has often been treated as merely an exercise in diplomacy that failed to have any dramatic strategic effect: in reality, however, its influence was profound.

Even before the Pact was signed, Japan had been supplying Germany with scarce raw materials via the TSR, but once the two countries became allies this trade escalated markedly. Economic intelligence from British consuls and commercial agents in Latin America showed that Japan was purchasing on Berlin's behalf a number of materials vital to the German war economy such as rubber, iodine, nickel, copper and wolfram. Moreover, in South-East Asia the threatening Japanese attitude towards the Dutch East Indies and the increased hold that it possessed over Indo-China and Thailand raised the prospect that Germany might be able to draw on the rich resources of this region as well.[7]

Just as disturbing was that BJs revealed that this collaboration also extended into such areas as intelligence-exchange between the Tripartite Powers and cooperation to support anti-British regimes in the Middle East. The most famous example of German–Japanese intelligence collaboration is the *Automedon* incident. The *Automedon* was a British merchant ship that was boarded in November 1940 by the crew of a German raider, who were able to seize from the ship's safe a copy of a Chiefs of Staff report on the inadequate nature of British defences in Malaya. This information was promptly passed to the authorities in Tokyo, and there has been speculation that it might have played a significant role in Japanese planning in 1941.[8] Just as important, however, was the intelligence that was passing in the other direction.

Japan's major contribution to the Axis in the intelligence field was the information that it, as a neutral, could collect in one of the chief war zones in the fight against Britain, namely Egypt. Ever since the Ethiopian War in 1935 Britain had known through BJs that the Japanese consulate in Port Said maintained a close watch on shipping movements in the Suez Canal. The authorities in Egypt did not initially take this spying very seriously, for the Japanese personnel did not seem to be particularly efficient. Indeed, Brigadier R.J. Maunsell, the wartime head of Security Intelligence Middle East, noted in his memoirs that in 1939 a Japanese official who had filmed facilities in Palestine had had his camera seized and its contents were then replaced by 'a rather horrible, locally made, "blue" movie' before it was handed back to him.[9] However, in 1940 the levity ended, for from May it became apparent in BJs from Port Said, Cairo and Alexandria that the Japanese were collecting detailed military and naval intelligence on the situation in Egypt and passing it on to the Italians.[10] Once the Tripartite Pact was signed these activities dramatically increased. In October the GCCS intercepted a telegram stating that there was to be a complete intelligence exchange with the Axis.[11] In accordance with this order the Japanese minister in Cairo established a system for passing intelligence through both telegrams and diplomatic bags to the Japanese embassy in Ankara, from where it was forwarded to Rome for the Italians.[12]

Other Japanese posts in the Middle East, such as Beirut and Baghdad, also passed on military intelligence. For example, in August 1940 Desmond Morton, who was the intelligence adviser to the Prime Minister, Winston Churchill, brought to the latter's notice BJ.082965 from Beirut to Tokyo that contained detailed figures about the number of British aircraft at

Haifa.[13] In Baghdad an even more disturbing side to Japanese collaboration with the Axis emerged. From October 1940 it became clear from BJs and SIS reports that the Japanese legation in Baghdad was becoming an advocate of Tripartite support for pan-Arabism as epitomized by the staunchly Anglophobe Iraqi Prime Minister, Rashid Ali Gailani.[14] Linked to this were reports that the Japanese were engaged in talks about arms sales to Iraq, and that these weapons might be used to help the Grand Mufti of Jerusalem stir up a revolt in Palestine.[15] At first these Japanese efforts came to nothing, for in the winter of 1941 the British were able to displace Rashid Ali. However, in April 1941 he returned to power and immediately sought German and Italian protection from British intervention. In the Iraqi crisis of April to June 1941 the Japanese continued to play a sinister role. Its legation collected military intelligence for the Axis, provided a courier link between Baghdad and the German legation in Tehran, and advised Rashid Ali on the production of anti-British propaganda.[16] Even when Rashid Ali fell from power following the British invasion of Iraq, Japan's nefarious activities in the Middle East did not end. In September 1941, after Britain and the Soviet Union had invaded Iran in order to expel the German and Italian communities, an Italian BJ revealed to Churchill's fury that the Grand Mufti had obtained sanctuary in the Japanese legation in Tehran before escaping to Italy.[17]

The lesson of these activities in South-East Asia and the Middle East was that Japan had unquestionably become Britain's implacable enemy and was doing all that it could, short of war, to undermine the British cause against the Axis. Thus in Whitehall the Tripartite Pact was not seen as merely a vague declaration of intent, but as the guiding light of Japanese foreign policy. Britain therefore had to treat Japan as a hostile power, but the question was how much of a danger did it pose. Would it enter the war against Britain at the earliest opportunity, or bide its time and wait for the latter to be on the verge of surrender in Europe? Would it be fatally weakened if subjected to sanctions, or strike out before they took full effect? Would a mixture of limited reinforcements and bluff be adequate as a deterrent? The task of intelligence was to answer these questions, for this information necessarily influenced the shape of Britain's containment policy.

## Could Japan attack?

The chief question in deciding policy was whether Japan was actually capable of launching a military offensive against British interests in South-East Asia. The task of assessing whether this was possible or likely involved detailed study of Japan's economic and military resources and further efforts to measure the effect of the war in China. The economic aspect was of great significance, for the Foreign Office had presumed in 1939 that this was Japan's Achilles heel and that the latter's fear of sanctions would deter it from reacting adversely to Western pressure. From the summer of 1940 Britain could no longer be so certain of this assessment, for it did not appear that Japan's commitments in China would necessarily stop it from launching hostilities elsewhere. Moreover, there was a danger that too severe a policy of sanctions may only provoke Japan into launching an offensive against largely undefended South-East Asia in order to seize the region's raw materials.[18] The economic logic of Japan's situation was thus just as likely to lead to expansion as restraint.

However, an advance could only take place if Japan had sufficient naval and military forces. Unfortunately, here too there was evidence that the conflict in China would not necessarily hold Japan back. After all, the IJN was not heavily involved in China and therefore was free to pursue operations elsewhere, while it appeared that the IJA was large enough to cope with fighting in another theatre. In a report in July 1940 the JIC concluded that, even if the China war did not cease, Japan could still attack British possessions with the Combined Fleet, an IJA force of up to six divisions, and an airforce of 432 land-based and 284 carrier-borne aircraft. This assessment was confirmed by a further JIC report in January 1941 and an FECB assessment of June 1941.[19]

The nature of the Japanese threat did not only rest on the size of the forces available, for Britain also had to reckon with the possibility that Japan might strike with little prior warning. Given that the IJN had a record of maintaining radio silence before large-scale operations, the only sure way of learning of the formation of an expeditionary force was through visual observation. However, with the restrictions that existed on the attachés and consuls in Japan, and the ineffectiveness of the SIS, it was likely that the first warning Britain would have of impending danger would be by air and sea reconnaissance from Hong Kong or Singapore. In September 1940 the JIC was forced to conclude that a direct attack on Malaya could take place within twenty-one days of Japanese mobilization and that Britain could only expect five days' warning. Worse threatened if the IJN gained control of Cam Ranh Bay in south Indo-China, for the assembly of a fleet at a location so close to Singapore would reduce the period to three days.[20]

The awareness that Japan had sufficient resources to attack did not, however, mean that Britain was reduced to defeatism, for the intelligence on the war in China and the image of the Japanese constructed over the previous decades still tempered Britain's sense of concern. Perceptions of the IJA were dominated, of course, by the fact that it still was unable to win the war in China. By 1940 the impression generated by this failure was compounded by intelligence that suggested that the lack of a clear victory was beginning to have a dispiriting effect on Japan's soldiers. Reports on declining Japanese morale had reached the War Office from quite early on in the China conflict, but had originally been given little credence.[21] By

October 1940, however, the War Office was sufficiently convinced to mention in one of its daily intelligence summaries that the attitude of recently captured Japanese POWs demonstrated that morale had 'shown a steady deterioration during the last two years of comparatively static warfare'. The following month it noted that the IJA troops who had just been withdrawn from Kwangsi were in a poor mental and physical condition.[22] Over the next few months further evidence emerged; for example, in January and May 1941 SIS sources in China produced reports on the circulation of anti-war literature among IJA units.[23] This was a subject of the greatest importance for, despite the IJA's failure to modernize, it had always been taken as given that its morale was second to none. If, however, the ordinary IJA soldier was losing the will to fight, it suggested that Japan could be in deep trouble.

Further corroboration of the problems faced by the IJA emerged in accounts of its recent clashes with the Soviet and French armies. During 1940 a number of reports were received and distributed by the intelligence directorates in Whitehall about the dramatic defeat that Japan had suffered at Nomonhan. In November 1940 the War Office noted in an annex to one of its weekly intelligence commentaries that, despite some successes, the battle had revealed that the IJA did not perform well against tanks, and that infantry/artillery liaison was poor.[24] The NID put it even more bluntly, telling the readers of its own weekly intelligence report that the Red Army had inflicted defeat 'on some of Japan's best troops'.[25] Moreover, it was noted that when the IJA had made a limited incursion into north Indo-China in September 1940, one regiment of the Foreign Legion and one of Tonkinese troops had inflicted losses on the Japanese.[26]

Doubts still existed too about the capability of the IJA and IJN air services. As with the IJA, extra information reinforced the assessment that had already been made from the war in China. One new feature was that 1940–41 saw Japan develop a long-range strategic bombing capability. The British were reasonably impressed by the endurance of the Japanese bombers and crews, but there was no evidence that the bombing itself had achieved any notable results.[27] Further, it was observed in Malaya Command that, in the few circumstances when they had met with determined anti-aircraft fire, the Japanese pilots had been forced to go to high altitudes with further deleterious consequences for their bombing accuracy.[28] In addition, the new intelligence on the battle of Nomonhan reversed the good impression generated in the initial reports and showed that the IJA air service had suffered 'considerable losses' against the Russians who constituted the first proper resistance it had ever met.[29]

Another important caveat about Japanese capabilities was that it was still held that a sizeable proportion of Japanese aircraft were, by Western standards, obsolete. This impression was in part based on the events in China and at Nomonhan, but also came from other sources. In August 1940 the

AID noted with interest that an American company had beaten Mitsubishi when tendering for sales to a Latin American country, which hinted at 'Japan's continued weakness in aircraft design'. This view was corroborated in October 1940 when the AID learnt that a RAF-trained member of a Thai delegation to Japan had received 'a very poor impression of the performance of the Japanese aircraft' when he had visited the IJN base at Yokosuka. This was thought to be particularly significant as it was possible that he might have seen the latest types of Japanese naval aircraft, including the Type 99 bomber, and that he was therefore including these within his criticism.

What is perhaps most disturbing is that even when the AID had information that put Japan into a good light it does not seem to have made much impact. For example, in late 1940 and into 1941 some useful intelligence was received about the superior combat performance of the Mitsubishi Type-O 'Zero' single-seat fighter. Information about it first came into British hands in October 1940 when Chiang's Air Adviser, Claire Chennault, passed details of its specifications and performance to the Air Liaison Officer at Hong Kong.[30] Further intelligence arrived in the spring of 1941 when the Chinese handed reports to the air attaché at Chungking, Wing-Commander Warburton, about a dog-fight that had taken place at Chengtu between twelve Type-Os and thirty-one Chinese-piloted I-15-3s. In this battle four Type-Os had been shot down for the loss of twelve I-15-3s. However, instead of treating this as confirmation of the efficiency of Japan's new fighter, both Warburton and the AID dwelled on the incident from the perspective of the poor training and combat performance of the Chinese pilots.[31]

Based on the above, the tendency within British circles was to depreciate the ability of the Japanese air forces to a greater degree than in the first years of the Sino-Japanese conflict. The common description, reiterated time and again in Whitehall in 1941, was that 'the operational value of the Japanese is less than that of the Italians'.[32] Some doubts about this assessment did exist; for example, in September 1941 the RAN's DNI, Commander Rupert Long, noted that he had recently received information that suggested that 'Japan is much stronger in the air than we had thought'.[33] Such reports did not, however, overturn the existing consensus.

The doubts about Japanese capabilities also extended to the IJN. The common assumption in Whitehall was that, despite its clear naval superiority in East Asian waters, the IJN would at the start of a war only use a small part of its fleet to provide cover for expeditionary forces in South-East Asia, while the majority of its ships remained in home waters to protect Japan from the USN. The only other offensive action it could contemplate was to send a few heavy cruisers to harass British trade in the Indian Ocean and communications with Australia. This perception was fed by the belief, as the JIC noted in May 1941, that the IJN had 'a fine tradition' but 'little experience of modern warfare'.[34] There was no awareness that the IJN had taken on board the lessons learnt during the Scandinavian campaign and the air attack on Taranto about the effectiveness of air power against naval forces. Nor was there any recognition of the technological and tactical advances made by the IJN, such as the development of the oxygen-propelled 24-inch torpedo or its skill at night-fighting.[35]

It is important to note that these examples of Japan's shortcomings were given fairly broad distribution, thus demonstrating that Whitehall gave credence to these reports. This is not to say that departments such as MI2c turned their back on the careful judgements that had been arrived at in 1938, but to stress again that the intelligence circulated had the effect of compromising these judgements by putting greater emphasis on Japan's weaknesses rather than its strengths. This dangerous tendency to qualify judgements on Japanese capabilities was also evident in material produced by the FECB in Singapore. Recently, the FECB has come in for some praise for its judgements because of the discovery by Peter Elphick of what appears to be one of its few surviving pamphlets from 1941 on the IJA. Elphick argues that this document demonstrated a prescient understanding of the qualities that the IJA would display in the Malayan campaign, but that its conclusions were ignored by the upper echelons.[36] Certainly there is much in the pamphlet that reflects the favourable conclusions that MI2c had reached about the China campaign, such as the skill of IJA envelopment movements, its ability at combined operations, and the high quality of its reconnaissance work and battlefield intelligence. However, the document also mirrored MI2c's work in that it contained the fatal qualification that the observation of IJA tactics was based on its campaigning in China 'against an inferior enemy' and that:

> The exaggerated idea of their prowess gained as a result of their victorious advance through China may lead the Japanese officers and men to feel that similar tactics to those employed on that occasion may succeed against other enemies. This may lead to large initial losses in a future war. There is, however, evidence that such a danger is well realised by senior commanders and staff officers.[37]

By any standard, this was hardly a clear, crisp assessment and, in an environment in which the ethnocentric belief in British superiority and Japanese inferiority was common, it was hardly likely to concentrate the minds of officers on the dangers that awaited them. The head of the military wing of the FECB, Colonel Grimsdale, affirmed in his unpublished memoirs that he had 'tried hard to make people realise the stark fact that we were up against a first class army, well armed, well trained and fanatically brave', but this document does not fully substantiate his claim.[38]

## Exercises in wishful thinking

Beyond these doubts about the relative value of the Japanese armed forces was an even more significant assumption, that even though Japan desired control of South-East Asia it was essentially a cautious state which would act only if assured of victory. For example, in December 1940 Lieutenant-General Haining, the Vice-Chief of the Imperial General Staff, noted:

> I feel their ability to carry offensive operations into the South of the Pacific, involving a naval convoying, is unlikely. Though tactically rash, I think the Japanese are strategically cautious and the problems which such operations would entail on top of their present dis-organization or economic situation would ... be sufficient to decide against sea-borne expeditions, into areas where they might come up against hostile shipping.[39]

It was also assumed that the Japanese were aware of their weaknesses. In January 1941 the newly appointed C-in-C Far East, Air Chief Marshal Sir Robert Brooke-Popham, affirmed that the fact that the Japanese had never made a seaborne landing or engaged in bombing against concerted opposition would 'have no small effect on their possible courses of action'.[40]

Churchill, too, believed that Japan was inherently cautious and that, as such, a Japanese attack was likely only under very specific circumstances; he noted to the War Cabinet's Defence Committee in May 1941, 'The Japanese would behave like the Italians. They would enter the war when they thought that we are on the point of defeat, so that they could gather the spoils without danger to themselves.'[41] The most probable scenario was thought to be that a Japanese offensive on Singapore would be timed to coincide with a German invasion of Britain. Indeed, this was one of the reasons behind the February 'war-scare', for Japan's forward movements at that time coincided with the arrival of reports that indicated that a German landing might be attempted in the spring.[42]

Britain's image of Japan was also shaped by its own exercises in ethnocentric confidence-building. To a number of British observers it was taken as read that Japan would not be so foolish as to confront a country as powerful as Britain. In December 1940 Esler Dening of the Far Eastern Department noted in response to a report from Mullaly deprecating the IJA that 'Japan has never seen battle against a first-class power – and probably wouldn't like it if she did.'[43] Lord Linlithgow took a similar view when observing to Leo Amery, the Secretary of State for India, in February 1941 that:

> I should like to think that the Japanese military machine, which has not had to stand up to a major military opponent since 1905, and which

> then was dealing with an opponent which one would hardly regard as of first quality in Far Eastern waters, may, like our friends, the Italians, prove a little less invincible when the time comes than it looks on paper.[44]

The most blatant case of this whistling in the dark arose in Malaya during the visit made in April 1941 by Wards prior to his appointment as military attaché to Tokyo. During his time in Singapore, Wards was invited by Lieutenant-General Bond to address his staff on the subject of the IJA. In his talk Wards attempted to dispel the complacency of Malaya Command by overturning many of the clichés that hindered assessment. As he recalled later, his efforts were in vain, for as soon as he ended his lecture Bond contradicted his praise of the IJA, saying 'What Wards has told you is merely his own opinion and is not in any way a correct appreciation of the situation.' A flabbergasted Wards was then told behind closed doors by Bond that this had been necessary because 'We must not discourage the chaps; we must keep their spirits up.'[45]

Furthermore, it is evident that the FECB indulged in this kind of false optimism. In June 1941 it produced a report entitled *Japan at the Cross Roads*, which assessed Japan's prospects in the aftermath of the signing of the Russo-Japanese Neutrality Pact in April. It observed that Japan had recently strengthened its position *vis-à-vis* South-East Asia and that it had the necessary forces to launch an attack. However, this pessimistic assessment was then qualified by references to Japan's war-weariness, its poor economic condition and its fear of America. These last factors, the FECB affirmed, showed that 'it looks as if Japan has left it too late'. The report then changed tack again, warning that Japanese fanaticism might nevertheless lead it to go to war. But before that thought had sunk in, it too was softened by the reflection that, unless Britain suffered a serious reverse in the Middle East, Japan 'may be expected to continue to sit on the fence, making the maximum nuisance of herself, without actually provoking it'.[46] Ambivalence had apparently become a British speciality.

## Intelligence and containment

The perception of Japan held by Whitehall and the British authorities in Asia was thus one of an opportunistic power torn between ambition and caution. On the one hand, it was clearly understood that, if Japan entered the war without triggering an American response, it could cause great inconvenience to Britain by endangering the supply of vital raw materials and threatening to cut communications with the antipodean Dominions. On the other hand, Japan's perceived weaknesses meant that there was a feeling that it could be deterred if Britain kept its nerve. Accordingly, from the autumn of 1940 British policy, under the influence of this intelligence image of Japan as a cautious power, was to undermine the Japanese position by slowly reinforcing Malaya, tightening economic sanctions and disseminating propaganda designed to erode Japan's faith in Germany. In addition, Britain sought to strengthen its ties with the United States and the other countries with interests in the region, and to encourage them to resist Japan. The policy was thus one of containment, designed to gain time and to weaken Japan, and in which negotiation with Tokyo had no role to play except if it furthered these ends.

Intelligence undoubtedly influenced Britain's decision to adopt this policy, and it continued to be important thereafter. One key attribute of intelligence was that it was an asset that Britain could trade with the other powers in the region in its effort to build up an anti-Japanese front. Intelligence collaboration with the other powers could benefit Britain in at least three ways; more intelligence would become available, the powers concerned could pool their resources to break Japanese codes and ciphers, and Britain could use the provision of intelligence to the other states as a tool to encourage their resistance to Japan. There were, however, also disadvantages, which meant that Britain had to proceed cautiously. To provide intelligence to others was to risk leaks and the compromising of Britain's intelligence sources, and there was the danger that, just as Britain sought to influence others by providing a selective flow of information, the same thing could happen in reverse.

The two states with which Britain had to take the greatest care were China and France. The Chinese still clearly had much to gain from exaggerating reports of Japanese military ineptitude and speculating wildly about Japan's intentions. There were, too, serious doubts about Chinese security, which arose in part because the intercepts of the telegrams sent by the Japanese consulate-general in Hong Kong to Tokyo revealed the scale of the intelligence gathered by Japan's agents in Chungking and Shanghai, even occasionally including paraphrases of Chinese telegrams.[47] As MI2c noted in October 1941, 'It must be assumed that anything discussed with the Chinese is likely to get to the Japanese.'[48] Despite this, there were efforts from the autumn of 1940 to get closer to the Chinese. In particular, the danger posed by the prospect of a sudden Japanese swoop on Malaya meant that it was necessary to cooperate with the Chinese to improve intelligence-gathering in the ports of south China. Accordingly, in October 1940 Major Boxer, the chief military intelligence officer in Hong Kong, travelled to Chungking for discussions with the head of Chinese military intelligence, Yang Hsuan-cheng. These discussions led to an agreement that the Chinese would smuggle radio sets into Canton, Bocca Tigris and Hainan in order to decipher traffic on IJA troop concentrations, and by the spring of 1941 this organization was providing a stream of information which was to prove valuable during the Japanese move into south Indo-China in July and in the build-up of October and November.[49]

The French were perhaps even more of a problem. While France had been an ally against Germany, cooperation in East Asia had been advantageous, but once the Vichy regime made peace with Germany it became a hazardous business. The authorities in Indo-China were keen to have an unofficial relationship with British intelligence and the latter, with the Foreign Office's approval, reciprocated due to the desperate need for information about Japanese activities in the South China Sea. Thus, information from French agents, or AX sources as they were known, continued to be passed to the SIS representative in Singapore after June 1940.[50] The problem was that the information tended to be weighted to support French interests, and, in particular, provided questionable material on subjects such as Japan's assistance to Thailand and its demands for French concessions. This was realized by MI2c which, in a report to the SIS on 3 February 1941, noted of the situation in Indo-China that:

> Most of your reports are from AX and Chinese Intelligence sources, neither of which are, in our experience, reliable. In many cases it is clear that they put out information in order to propagandize a particular point for their own ends.

A more useful source of information on Chinese and French intelligence was available to Britain – its ability to read the diplomatic telegrams of both countries. In the case of France, the GCCS was able to read all but the 'more confidential diplomatic ciphers', and thus could get an idea of French information on such subjects as Japanese troop concentrations.[51] Chinese telegrams were deciphered with relative ease and they too provided useful intelligence, most notably from the consul in Penang, who clearly ran an extensive spy network in Malaya and Thailand.[52]

A more significant intelligence relationship existed with the Dutch. In late autumn 1940 the British began to overcome their fear of possible Dutch collaboration with Germany and moved towards more open ties. In January 1941 Colonel Verkuyl, the chief special intelligence officer at Bandung, visited Singapore and informed the new COIS, Captain K.L. Harkness, that his staff could read some Japanese consular and diplomatic ciphers and had undertaken research on JN-25 and other IJN traffic.[53] This was an important revelation, and encouraged the British to agree to a fuller exchange of information than at first contemplated. In order to facilitate this link naval liaison officers were exchanged between Singapore and Batavia, and soon this practice was extended to Dutch–Australian relations.

In addition to cooperation in the field of special intelligence there was increased counter-espionage collaboration between the British and Dutch authorities. The most notable case came in March 1941 when the Dutch arrested an IJA officer, Major Hashida, who had just made an extensive tour of Australia. Among Hashida's possessions were a number of sketchbooks from his Australian jaunt that made it clear that he had engaged in the gathering of military intelligence and the improvement of espionage capabilities. The Dutch duly handed this material to the British and Australian liaison officers and then deported Hashida to Japan.[54]

Dutch information generally proved to be of moderate value, but Britain remained keen on the exchange of intelligence because the mere fact that the cooperation existed was seen as bolstering Dutch resistance.[55] Moreover, Britain could explicitly use the relationship to pass on to the Dutch material that would encourage it to take a tough line towards Japan. For example, in November 1940 the British passed on information about the poor morale of the IJA troops being withdrawn from Kwangsi, with the hope that this would communicate to the Dutch that 'You're on a good wicket, but don't play it too hard'.[56] With the closer ties that existed after January 1941 this manipulation was extended, and reports on the Japanese negotiating stance in the economic talks at Batavia were handed over in the hope that this would stiffen Dutch resolve.[57]

As in the case of France and China, Britain was not content merely to share intelligence with the Dutch, for it also spied on them. From March 1941 the number of BJs of Dutch material circulated by the GCCS rapidly increased. Britain also appears to have engaged in espionage against the Dutch legation in Washington. From the summer of 1941 a number of Dutch dispatches came into the hands of British Security Co-ordination (BSC), the SIS network in the United States controlled by William Stephenson. This material included a report by Lovink to the Dutch authorities in London about a Japanese spy called Ono, a memorandum by the Governor of the East Indies on Japanese penetration, and the transcript of a conversation between the Dutch and the American military authorities in Washington.[58]

## Anglo–US–Australian intelligence cooperation

The cooperation which Britain established with the Dutch was helpful in a limited way and had the advantage that it could help to reinforce the latter's morale, but it was still a minor affair compared to liaison with the most significant obstacle to Japanese ambitions – the United States. Here, too, there was a marked expansion in intelligence collaboration. The situation began to change in the late summer of 1940, when an American military delegation arrived in London to discuss the standardization of arms. On 31 August the leading American army representative, Brigadier-General Strong, informed the Chiefs of Staff that the United States was prepared to exchange intelligence with Britain and that it was close to breaking the Machine B or 'Purple' cipher.[59] Britain jumped at the offer, for the latter was a major breakthrough which GCCS did not have the resources to achieve due to the priority given to German ciphers. By November 1940, with 'Purple' completely broken, the British embassy in Washington forwarded selected intercepts to the Foreign Office with the prefix 'FIXIT' added to denote the source.[60] This channel was supplemented in February by extra material which the War Department, without the knowledge of the State Department, decided to supply to the British military attaché in Washington; this material was referred to as 'MASS'.[61] In addition, as talks with American representatives made progress in the autumn of 1940, the United States agreed to send a cryptographic mission to Britain which would bring a 'Purple' machine for GCCS. This mission duly arrived on 6 February 1941, and nine days later, at the height of the February warscare, the British 'Purple' machine became active.[62]

In addition to the cooperation over 'Purple' there was slow progress over Japanese naval traffic. In November 1940 the DCOIS, Commander Wisden, visited Manila to discuss the exchange of intelligence with the USN's Asiatic Fleet, but discovered that the Americans lagged a long way behind the British in naval intelligence and had a poor WT and RDF capability. This made the question of collaboration difficult, for Britain was keen to get hold of American secrets but unenthusiastic about the idea of passing on its own superior knowledge.[63] However, with the arrival of the American mission in Britain in February 1941 it was clear that the British could not afford to remain aloof, and on 10 February the Admiralty ordered the C-in-C China, Admiral Sir Geoffrey Layton, to begin a 'full exchange of special intelligence material and methods'.[64] Simultaneously, further talks between USN staff and the FECB revealed that there were advantages to be gained by a pooling of resources in the attack upon the IJN's operational code JN-25. Ever since September 1939 the FECB had worked hard to break JN-25, and had made some progress, but in December 1940 there was a temporary setback when a new codebook (JN-25B) was introduced. This meant that there was a new incentive to work with the Americans to break this vital code. The result was that from February 1941 the FECB collaborated with the American special intelligence section at Cavite Bay in the Philippines in a concerted effort to break JN-25B, again with an exchange of officers to ease liaison.[65]

Further advances in intelligence cooperation were made in the next few months. In March the British agreed to an American proposal that the two countries should collaborate in attacking IJA codes and ciphers, and handed to the American observer at Singapore a copy of the IJA transport code and what the FECB had of the army airforce cipher.[66] In June the American military attaché in London, Brigadier-General Lee, proposed a further extension in the exchange of intelligence by asking the British to agree to go beyond a sharing of information about SIGINT and to begin cooperation between military representatives all over East Asia. The JIC in London responded with some enthusiasm and enlarged upon Lee's proposal with a request that Britain should receive information from the

American consulate in Vladivostock and that the agreement should include naval as well as military intelligence. Orders were duly sent to Layton and Brooke-Popham, although in them it was noted that information from SIS and Special Operations Executive (SOE) sources should be treated with discretion.[67] The same scheme was recommended to Australia in September 1941.[68] A further sign of the improving ties came with the decision in August 1941 to stop research into IJA traffic at the FECB and send its expert on this subject, Lieutenant Geoffrey Stevens, to Washington to work with the War Department.[69] However, despite these efforts, problems still remained in a relationship that was tinged with mutual suspicion and marred by American inter-service rivalries. Notably, in November 1941 the naval representative on Britain's JIC Washington, Captain Edward Hastings, announced that he felt it necessary to visit Honolulu in December to put intelligence relations 'on a more satisfactory basis', while Stevens arrived in the same month to find his work affected by the ill feeling that existed between the War and Navy Departments.[70]

Britain did not rely simply on its willingness to cooperate to win Washington over; it also tried to influence American thinking by the judicious forwarding of intelligence information that showed the Japanese or Germans in the worst possible light. During the February war-scare, Britain passed on material acquired from the telephone-tapping of the Japanese embassy and the Thai legation to the Americans in a deliberate attempt to create a crisis atmosphere.[71] In addition, Churchill sometimes ordered BJs to be sent directly to Roosevelt. For example, when, in August 1941 in BJ.094723, the Japanese ambassador to Berlin, Lieutenant-General Ōshima Hiroshi, informed Tokyo that he had been informed that Germany would support Japan if the latter found itself at war with the United States, the Prime Minister ordered that the President should be informed.[72]

America did not, however, always reciprocate. One problem that bedevilled Anglo-American relations was that Washington does not appear to have passed on in the FIXIT or MASS material any telegrams referring to the talks that were taking place between the Japanese ambassador, Admiral Nomura Kichisaburō, and Secretary of State Hull. Britain, therefore, had to turn to its own sources to find out what was happening. Some information was generated by reading Japanese traffic to Rome and Berlin and the telegrams despatched by the Italian ambassador in Tokyo, Indelli, but this intelligence was fragmentary and led Britain to fear that the Americans might be duped or that they might sell out British interests. The dangers were demonstrated in a well-known incident in May 1941 when the British ambassador to Washington, Lord Halifax, warned Hull about the dangers posed by talking to the Japanese but met with a poisonous rebuff. It transpires that this misjudged British overture was the result of reading Matsuoka's latest proposals in one of Indelli's telegrams.[73]

The other significant British intelligence relationship was with the Dominions. Britain's interest was naturally to utilize the resources of the Dominions to expand the intelligence net. It therefore encouraged Canada, Australia and New Zealand to develop cryptographic capabilities that would supplement rather than compete with Britain's own efforts. This could cause problems. In the summer of 1941 Britain discovered that Canada was attempting to improve its capabilities by hiring the notorious Herbert Yardley, the American codebreaker who in 1931 had revealed in his book *The Black Chamber* that the United States had read Japan's codes during the Washington conference of 1921–2. Britain persuaded Canada that this would be neither wise nor tactful.[74]

The most important Dominion in the field of intelligence was Australia, and in 1940–41 efforts were made to integrate its work even further with that undertaken at the FECB. One of the key reasons for this was that by 1940 it was clear that Eric Nave, who had been assigned to the FECB's cryptographic section in 1937, was no longer able to serve in the tropics for health reasons. Accordingly, he had been sent to Melbourne for recuperation but, as his talents could not afford to be wasted, this raised the question of what work he could do in Australia that would assist the FECB. In January 1941 the outgoing COIS, Captain Wylie, visited Melbourne to discuss, among other subjects, SIGINT collaboration. The outcome was that the RAN increased the scale of its RDF and WT work, particularly in relation to the Japanese Mandates, and that there was mutual agreement that a special intelligence section under Nave should look at naval, diplomatic and consular traffic.[75] Shortly after, a small group of Australian professors who had been working for the Australian Army in Sydney were relocated to Melbourne and formed a cryptographic organization under Nave. Over the next few months this group began to produce useful material on the IJN traffic used in the Mandates, and assisted Singapore by taking charge of the decryption of diplomatic and consular telegrams to and from Australia.[76]

The Admiralty also worked with the RAN and the Royal New Zealand Navy (RNZN) to increase the flow of naval intelligence passing through the region. As noted above, this included encouraging Dutch–Australian cooperation but, in addition, the RAN and RNZN exchanged liaison officers with Washington, and an RNZN officer was stationed in San Francisco.[77] Cooperation over intelligence also emerged at the political level, for in August 1941 Australia decided to send a diplomatic representative, V.G. Bowden, to Singapore on the grounds that it had become the region's clearing house for the exchange of intelligence.[78]

Britain's efforts had, therefore, led by the end of 1941 to the construction of an extensive intelligence network in South-East Asia and the Pacific designed to facilitate the rapid transmission of information on Japan's military moves and intentions. Moreover, it was a network that acted as a symbol of the united resolve to resist any further Japanese expansion.

## Reforming British intelligence in South-East Asia

In addition to the policy of collaboration with other powers, British intelligence sought to further the containment of Japan by reorganizing its own operations within the region, and by initiating an aggressive policy of propaganda and other measures against Japan. An important area of activity was improving the FECB. On the naval side, the most important reform in 1940 was the introduction of a 'W' section which dealt with the intelligence generated by WT call-signs and RDF work. As Commander Jack Newman, the RAN's Director of Signals Communications, noted in May 1941, this section's work was invaluable for it could generate intelligence even when the IJN's codes and ciphers proved impervious to penetration.[79] Meanwhile, the 'Y' section was expanded and continued its exhaustive investigation of JN-25B. The army and air sections, however, continued to suffer from a lack of resources, and in April 1941 Brooke-Popham asked Whitehall for both to be expanded. He was particularly concerned about the air section, which lacked sufficient staff to digest the ample material it was receiving. The Air Ministry's response was to send out Group Captain Chappell, the former air attaché in Japan, to the FECB's air section and to double as air attaché to Bangkok. Whether the FECB proved effective in the provision of intelligence is a matter of debate. In November 1940 the Australian Assistant Chief of Naval Staff, Captain Joseph Burnett, noted after a visit to a conference in Singapore that the FECB's staff were inadequately trained and did not forward 'sufficient "hot" intelligence to outlying authorities'.[80] A year later Long, the Australian DNI, came to much the same conclusion, noting that the FECB staff involved in the 'routine work of receiving, assimilating and distributing information' were of poor quality.[81] The Chancellor of the Duchy of Lancaster, Alfred Duff Cooper, who was visiting Singapore in the autumn of 1941, took away a different impression, viewing the FECB as impressive in its efficiency though lacking a civilian branch that would add weight to its judgements.[82]

The most obvious priority in reforming British intelligence was to revamp the moribund SIS network. By the autumn of 1940 it was clear that the existing structure was becoming a liability, particularly in the face of the need for forewarning about the formation of a Japanese expeditionary force for operations in South-East Asia. In August 1940 the outgoing C-in-C China, Admiral Sir Percy Noble, forwarded to the DNI, Rear-Admiral John Godfrey, a blistering report by Captain Wylie on the local SIS representatives, which noted that the SIS was not working, largely because the information generated was poor and the representatives refused to cooperate with each other. As this document has been heavily censored it is not possible to say who was doing what to whom, but it can be inferred that the major problem was the competitive relationship between Steptoe and Drage, the latter now transferred to Singapore. So great was this sense of competition that one of the SIS representatives had attempted to 'break the connection between French Secret Service and our Military Intelligence, in order to provide the link himself'. To remedy these problems Wylie proposed that the network be reformed with a head at Singapore who would control the activities of the others, but stipulated that this figure should not be chosen from the existing officers. Surprisingly, considering the way it had ignored such complaints in the past, the SIS proved receptive to this criticism and asked Noble to recommend a new head 'preferably big business man or possibly Armed Force Officers, age about 40'.[83]

Wylie's criticisms were backed up in January 1941 by a similar protest from Brooke-Popham, who demanded immediate action. The SIS responded by sending out an experienced officer to investigate the problems, namely Godfrey Denham, its former representative in Shanghai, who since retiring as the Malayan IGP had worked for Anglo-Dutch Plantations Ltd, a rubber company in Java. Denham arrived in Singapore to begin his mission in February 1941 and completed his report in May. His conclusions were that the personalities involved, the lack of training and central control, and the erosion of trust in the SIS by the services had brought it to its current sorry state, and recommended that a regional coordinator be appointed to restore confidence.[84] As Denham was already on the scene he was handed the poisoned chalice. Over the next six months he exerted himself to improve the situation, but was too late on the scene to have much impact.[85]

The other major intelligence innovation was the decision to establish an SOE organization at Singapore, which was known as the Oriental Mission (OM). Its head, Valentine Killery, arrived in Singapore in May and promptly set about establishing networks in Thailand and Indo-China that would engage in espionage if Japan went to war, while the OM's military wing under Major Gavin provided training in irregular warfare to soldiers and officers from a number of different nationalities. The OM's efforts to create an efficient organization were, however, hampered by a lack of experience in such matters and, as with Denham, the fact that so little time was left.[86]

## Keeping Japan in check

The one area in which SOE did make an impact was in black propaganda, one of the few weapons in Britain's containment arsenal. In the autumn of 1939 Britain had established a Far Eastern Bureau in Hong Kong to run propaganda in East Asia. Its work was to explain Britain's war effort by open methods, using the printed media and broadcasting, but the arrival of SOE at Singapore opened up the prospect of engaging in the dissemination of 'rumours' and other more nefarious types of propaganda that would 'bear no trace of British origin'.[87] This held some attraction, for as early as

October 1940 the Junior JIC had pointed to the importance of using covert propaganda to divide Japan and Germany. Moreover, when Japan appeared to back away from confrontation in the February 'war-scare', the British believed mistakenly that this retreat was partly the result of its skilful use of rumours, such as the story planted in the British and Australian press that a Royal Navy squadron was sailing for Singapore. It was therefore concluded that Japan was particularly susceptible to this kind of weapon.[88] The OM was thus given the task of beginning a campaign of 'whispers' against Japan designed to heighten suspicions of Germany, create fears about the Russians, and emphasize the impossibility of winning a war against the combined might of the Anglo-Saxon powers.[89] Sir George Sansom was drafted in to advise the OM on such matters.

In the summer of 1941 the propaganda campaign against Japan began to hit its stride. When BJs revealed in June that the Japanese intended to occupy south Indo-China in the near future this news was, on the recommendation of the COS and the JIC, leaked to the British press, although not in such a way that it might compromise the BJ source.[90] As at the time of the February 'war-scare', the idea was that a media campaign would overawe the Japanese and force them to consider the consequences of their actions. In addition, moves were made to circulate black propaganda in cooperation with the Americans. In July 1941 a series of articles was published in the *New York Post* on the subject of German 'fifth column' activities in Japan under the byline of the veteran American journalist C.N. Spinks. After the initial publication and syndication of these articles they were collected together in pamphlet form and, with the cooperation of an American official referred to as G50,000, 800,000 copies of a Japanese translation were distributed in Hawaii in the name of the 'Society of Patriotic Japanese Living Abroad'. Further copies were sent to prominent figures in Japan such as the Prime Minister, Konoe Fumimaro, and the Home Minister, Hiranuma Kiichiro, who had recently survived an assassination attempt by a 'pro-German' fanatic.[91]

This campaign was considered initially to be a success, for evidence soon emerged of a Japanese crackdown on all foreign propaganda in Japan, including in October the arrest of a journalist named Richard Sorge. However, this was a false dawn, for Sorge was arrested as a Soviet spy rather than for any machinations on Germany's behalf, and it soon transpired that the Japanese call to the belligerents to end their propaganda activities was not meant to apply to the Axis.[92] In retrospect, it seems that the propaganda campaign had little decisive effect.

Another major plank of British policy was steadily to reduce Japan's capacity to collect intelligence on its own and the Axis's behalf. In the Middle East action began to be taken in the autumn of 1940, shortly after the discovery that the Japanese were passing intelligence from Egypt to the Axis Powers. The first move was to get the censorship authorities in Egypt to delay the transmission of Japanese telegrams by ninety-six hours in order to render any intelligence as worthless as possible. This practice was then extended to other key points such as Bombay, Colombo, Mombasa and Singapore.[93] It was soon clear that even this was not enough, for the Japanese turned to the use of couriers from Cairo to Ankara as a way of outflanking the censorship. The final straw came in February 1941, when the Japanese consul at Port Said, Tada Shigeru, was caught photographing ships that had been sunk by Italian mines in the Suez Canal.[94] Following this, the British took a series of measures to clamp down on the Japanese presence in Egypt. Tada was deported and the Port Said consulate was closed down, Japanese agents, including one Briton, were arrested, further visas for couriers were denied, and the Egyptian authorities were persuaded to withdraw all Japanese cipher telegram and diplomatic bag facilities.[95] This last measure had first been suggested in the autumn of 1940, but had been rejected initially as too provocative and also as denying the British the chance to plant false information on the Japanese. The C-in-C Mediterranean, Admiral Sir Andrew Cunningham, was keen on the latter ploy, and had used it to his advantage in the preparations for the battle of Cape Matapan against the Italian fleet, but by April 1941 the Japanese breaches of British security were so serious that the cipher loophole had to be plugged.[96] As one might expect, the British also took similar action in Iraq and Iran. Following the fall of Rashid Ali, Japanese cipher facilities in Baghdad were removed in August, and, in addition, the Japanese minister who had done so much to help Rashid Ali was declared *persona non grata* and forced to withdraw.[97] In Tehran pressure on the Iranian authorities led to the withdrawal of facilities in late September.[98]

In South-East Asia and India the main weapon against Japanese espionage apart from the delaying of telegrams was surveillance and arrest of those engaged in suspicious activities. In Malaya, Burma and India the period from August 1940 saw a sharp escalation in the number of detentions of Japanese, both officials and businessmen, and their indigenous agents.[99] In part this came about in response to the wave of arrests of British subjects that had taken place in Japan and Korea in July and August 1940, which had culminated in the death in custody of the Reuters correspondent in Tokyo, Melville Cox.[100] In addition, legislation was introduced to prohibit Japanese access to places of military importance such as oilfields and fortifications, and in the case of Burma, the whole of the Federated Shan States.[101]

By July 1941 India was convinced that much more needed to be done and pressed, along with Burma, for Japanese cipher privileges and immunity from censorship to be withdrawn and the consulates eventually closed down.[102] As these were controversial proposals that could provoke Japanese retaliation, they were put up to the War Cabinet's Far Eastern Committee, which in turn asked the JIC for advice about the implications of such moves.[103] The JIC found itself in two minds, for although it could understand the necessity for tough action in India and Burma, it feared that if Japan retaliated by closing the British consulates in the Japanese Empire and occupied China, particularly Shanghai, 'the effect on our intelligence reporting system would be grave'. However, it was not convinced that Japan would take action against the Shanghai consulate-general unless British action seemed disproportionately harsh. It therefore decided that it could sanction the withdrawal of facilities in India, but thought it better not to extend this action to Burma.[104] This caution regarding Burma continued until the outbreak of war, and led to similar decisions about Japanese telegrams from Colombo, Cape Town and, most importantly, Singapore.[105]

## The height of complacency

The belief that propaganda and the gradual curtailment of its diplomatic privileges could be effective weapons against Japan was symptomatic of Britain's increasing sense of confidence about events in East Asia during 1941. The growth of this optimism was a slow process which had its origins in the apparently successful outcome of the February 'war-scare'. From that point on, the ever closer military ties between Britain, the United States, and the Dutch, and the tightening economic noose around Japan suggested that, as long as Britain kept in step with the United States, the 'cautious' Japanese could be deterred from a direct attack on British possessions. Moreover, the steady flow of reinforcements to Malaya showed that Britain itself was redressing the military balance.

This confidence was not seriously jolted even in July 1941 when Japan moved its forces into south Indo-China, although this obviously increased the threat that could be posed to Malaya by bringing the northern part of the peninsula into the range of Japanese land-based aircraft. In part, Britain remained calm because, as the Foreign Secretary, Anthony Eden, noted to the War Cabinet, the tough American response to the Japanese move into Indo-China suggested that it could be relied upon to come to Britain's aid.[106] Moreover, although there were fears for Thai security in the aftermath of the occupation of south Indo-China, it appeared that the more serious trend in IJA movements was towards Manchuria for a possible attack on the Soviet Union following the German unleashing of Operation Barbarossa in June.

The intelligence coming into Whitehall in the late summer of 1941 tended to reinforce British confidence. The BJs intercepted in this period appeared to demonstrate that the Konoe government was confused about the direction it should take in foreign policy: whether to continue the southward advance, strike northwards against the Soviet Union, or attempt to solve its problems through negotiations with the United States. In particular, Japan, despite the IJA's preparations in Manchuria, seemed to be unable to decide whether or not to attack Russia, and it was clear that this was causing stress within the Tripartite Pact. In August and September a number of intercepts suggested that a chill had entered German–Japanese relations, and that the former were suspicious of the Hull-Nomura talks.[107]

A further reason for optimism came from the awareness that Japan was receiving information on the improvements that had been made to the British military position in Malaya. In September 1941 a series of BJs revealed that the Japanese consul-general in Singapore was reporting to Tokyo information on the improvements made to the island's anti-aircraft defences and on defence cooperation with the Dutch.[108] Then in October the same official lamented in BJ.096628 that Britain had constructed 'a secret intelligence network through which an ant could not creep', and that the authorities seemed to be far more confident about Malaya's defences.[109]

In Singapore this intelligence gave sustenance to British complacency. Despite its drive to persuade London to send out more aircraft as a matter of urgency, the new consensus that emerged in Singapore from August 1941 was that the Japanese would only attack Malaya after invading the Kra Isthmus in Thailand.[110] This view was formalized in September in a tactical appreciation by the GOC Malaya, Lieutenant-General Percival, which argued that a direct attack on Malaya 'would be contrary to the traditional Japanese method of a cautious step-by-step progress with limited objectives'.[111] Important to this argument was the perception that most Japanese aircraft had too short a range to launch attacks on Malaya from Indo-China, and that, therefore, the Japanese would need to seize control of airfields in Thailand prior to any offensive against the British possessions.[112] This in turn had the unfortunate effect of encouraging forward deployment of the RAF's limited resources in north Malaya and inadequate preparations for the denial of those airfields close to the Thai border. In addition, there was a reversion to the idea that the monsoon in the Gulf of Thailand might benefit the British. In September, Brooke-Popham informed Whitehall that a recent reconnaissance of south Thailand had demonstrated that during the rainy season, from November to February, the isthmus became waterlogged and therefore virtually impassable to tanks and armoured cars. This suggested that during that period 'a comparatively small force could hold this front'.[113] The misplaced confidence began to permeate British briefings. In October, Layton informed the new Australian minister to Chungking that he was confident of getting a three-week warning of any Japanese attack and noted that in any case, 'The Japanese are undoubtedly cautious, and proceed by gradual steps.'[114] Brooke-Popham made a similarly complacent impression the same month when he met the Australian Advisory War Council in Canberra, assuring them that the aerodromes in Indo-China lacked the capacity to support an attack on Malaya, which was in any case defended by 'superior' Brewster Buffalo fighter aircraft.[115]

In London, too, complacency was rife. Both Eden and Churchill subscribed to the idea that Japan was hesitating about what action it would take next, and were convinced that the front that was developing against it was acting as a deterrent. In October they decided to send the capital ships, HMS *Prince of Wales* and HMS *Repulse* to Singapore, believing that the arrival of this squadron would, as Eden put it, help the Japanese 'to understand their isolation'.[116] This was largely a matter of propaganda, a point underlined by the fact that, at the same time, Churchill rejected dispatching Hurricane fighter aircraft to Malaya, a move that would have made a real difference to its defence, preferring instead to send them to Russia. Churchill also wrestled with the need to find a replacement for Brooke-Popham, who had been criticized for being too old and out of touch. In October he decided to appoint Lieutenant-General Bernard Paget to the job, but soon changed his mind as he felt he could not spare such a talented individual for 'this extended supervisory job'.[117] A recent returnee from Malaya, Air Vice-Marshal Babington, was deeply disturbed by the attitude in Whitehall, and noted to Brooke-Popham that Churchill believed there would be three months warning of war and that the COS were manipulating expected Japanese air strength into 'altogether too convenient' figures.[118]

## Stumbling into war

By late October, clear signs emerged that a further Japanese move was imminent and that the IJN Combined Fleet was readying itself for action. In September it had returned to home waters and started its annual reorganization, two months before this procedure was usually carried out; within a month it was fully mobilized. The available intelligence did not, however, make prediction easy, for while in late October it appeared that four of the IJN's aircraft carriers were congregating off Formosa, by 11 November they had apparently merged back into the Combined Fleet in home waters.[119] The military intelligence was equally confusing. A considerable IJA build-up in south China and Tonkin in late October momentarily convinced London, Washington and Chungking that a Japanese offensive against Kunming, the Chinese terminus of the Burma Road, was imminent. This fear soon lifted, for in early November a steady shift of forces from Hanoi to Saigon took place. However, the relocation of Japan's forces once again raised the question of what its intentions were.[120]

Although we now know that these forces were being prepared primarily for an assault on Malaya, this was not how the matter was read in November 1941; instead the *idée fixe* was that the immediate target of Japanese aggression would be Thailand. This, of course, conveniently reflected the ideas in Percival's tactical appreciation in September, and demonstrated that the stereotypical idea that Japanese strategy was influenced by an innate sense of caution remained ever present. The intelligence received by Singapore and Whitehall was interpreted with this belief in mind. The evidence to support the idea of a Japanese attack on Thailand came from both BJs and SIS sources. In mid-November the SIS, using intelligence from French sources in Indo-China, reported that the build-up of men and aircraft was aimed at an assault on Thailand to take place within the next fortnight.[121] BJs confirmed this information. On 14 November GCCS circulated a French telegram from Hanoi to Vichy in which the Governor, Admiral Decoux, speculated that the Japanese might be preparing for an attack on Thailand.[122] Two days later a BJ from the Gaimushō to the Japanese ambassador in Vichy asked the French to allow the IJA greater freedom to operate south of the Red River, a move interpreted by the War Office as increasing 'the evidence in support of a movement against Thailand'.[123] During the next few days, further information reinforced this idea, and the impression that the Thais were next on the menu was sealed on 26 November when the American consul in Hanoi reported that the French had information that the attack would take place on 1 December.[124]

Over the same period, BJs also indicated an intensification of Japanese interest in Malaya. On 25 September the consul-general at Singapore had reported to Tokyo that although the quality of RAF pilots in Malaya was good their equipment and logistical support was poor. This subject was clearly of interest to the Japanese authorities, for they asked for more air intelligence on 22 October. A reply came two days later in which the consul-general recorded, just over a week after Brooke-Popham's assurances to the Australians, that the Buffalo's capabilities need 'cause no concern in the day of battle'.[125] Another disturbing sign came at around the same time when the ambassador to Thailand asked for Japanese fishermen from the east coast of Malaya to be sent to Bangkok to report in detail 'on the state of the surf'.[126] Furthermore, it was clear from BJs that the Japanese had recruited a number of Malays, referred to as the Young Men's Malaya League or *Kame* organization, to assist in espionage, propaganda work and the policing of Japanese-occupied areas.[127] Other BJs in late November suggested that Japan expected to break with the Western powers in the coming weeks. On 25 November two separate intercepts contained references to the possibility of a severing of diplomatic relations, one of which was the infamous 'Winds' message which noted that, if Japanese relations with Britain were about to be severed, the words '*Nishi no kaze hare*' would be used in a radio weather-broadcast.[128]

This information obviously raised the prospect of a Japanese attack on Malaya sometime in the near future, but it was still not believed in Whitehall that such an offensive was imminent. On 28 November the JIC, in its summary and interpretation of the latest intelligence, still affirmed that Japan's first move would be an attack on Thailand alone. Drawing on the consensus that the Kra Isthmus would be waterlogged and that the Japanese needed Thai airfields before any attack on Malaya the JIC insisted that:

> After successful operations in Thailand the Japanese would need time to improve lines of communications and for extending and equipping aerodromes of the Kra Isthmus, before they attempted an advance on Malaya. This period would last two or three months and might last longer if weather conditions were unfavourable.[129]

Obviously, this assessment could change if the IJN's aircraft carriers entered the Gulf of Thailand to provide close air cover for an attack on Malaya, but there was no evidence in late November that this was likely. The best intelligence available to the Admiralty, from both their own and American sources, suggested that the majority of the IJN Combined Fleet was still in Japanese home waters and the area around Formosa except for the Fourth Fleet in the Mandates, which contained two aircraft carriers.[130] The intelligence was thus taken to suggest that the current deployment of Japan's forces was intended for another incremental advance, this time into Thailand, rather than a Japanese offensive against Britain and possibly the United States.

It was only slowly that hints came of Japan's true intentions. On 1 December all IJN call-signs were changed for the second time in a month, an event that led Australia's Combined Operational Intelligence Centre to note that 'it can be assumed that this change is made in preparation for an offensive'.[131] Then on 2 December a telegram from the Gaimushō to Ōshima warned of the possibility of an 'armed collision' with Britain and the United States. Even here, however, the GCCS's translation of the Japanese allowed for some ambiguity, for it did not make clear whether Japan intended to attack these countries or whether it envisaged that there would be an armed Anglo-American response to its next incremental advance.[132] On 4 December a new version of JN-25 was introduced, another sign that the IJN intended to keep its activities secret.[133] It was not until 6 December that events became clearer. On that day a Japanese convoy was spotted in the Gulf of Thailand, and BJs revealed that the embassies in London and Washington had been ordered to destroy their cipher machines; it was only then that the Inter-departmental Committee to Coordinate Departmental action in the Event of War with Japan observed that 'recent Japanese moves ... suggested the imminence of attack'.[134] It was still not apparent, however, whether this force intended to attack Thailand alone, and debates raged in Whitehall about the possibility that a British pre-emptive offensive into the Kra Isthmus or attack on the convoy at sea might alienate the United States. Finally, in the afternoon of

7 December (GMT) Hong Kong picked up a Japanese broadcast that used the fatal words '*Nishi no kaze hare*'; the simultaneous attacks at Kota Bharu in Malaya and Songkhla in Thailand followed shortly afterwards.[135] The Japanese offensive did not therefore follow British expectations, for the attack on the Isthmus was combined with an assault on Malaya itself. With no period of grace in which to fine-tune its defences, the British were quickly forced to retreat. Most disastrously, as a dire consequence of the failure to read Japanese strategy correctly, Britain, with its airforces too close to the Thai border, rapidly lost air superiority, for the Japanese not only destroyed the British aircraft but seized control of the airfields in northern Malaya.

The war that began on 7 December (GMT) was not, however, only a Malayan affair, for it also involved Japanese attacks on the United States at Hawaii and the Philippines. These too seem to have come as a surprise to the British, despite the reference in BJs to Japanese relations with both London *and* Washington being in crisis, and a sense of shock is recorded in a number of contemporary documents. However, it has been claimed recently by Richard Aldrich that in the final days before war, Britain might have expressed its concern to Washington about the security of Pearl Harbor through a secret SIS channel. This argument rests on the memoirs and reminiscences of some of the protagonists in London and Washington, but no documentary evidence supports this assertion.[136] The problem is that the records of a number of key organizations no longer exist. If the minutes of the Junior JIC and the JIC Washington, and the telegrams sent by the JIC to Malaya in early December, had survived, or access were to be given to SIS papers, it may be that these would confirm or negate this story.

One tantalizing document from the Australian archives does demonstrate, however, that Britain was aware of the Japanese interest in Hawaii, although not necessarily that it was forewarned of the coming attack. On 14 November 1941, the Australian legation in Washington forwarded to the Department of External Affairs in Canberra some 'reports on Japanese activities in the Pacific area, particularly in the Sandwich Islands'; the latter being the original name given to Hawaii by Captain Cook.[137] The reason for this subterfuge in referring to Hawaii was that these reports had come from the BSC in New York, who appear to have received their information from an unnamed American source. On forwarding this material to the Australian legation, the BSC explicitly warned that 'it is essential that there should be no communication with the F.B.I. concerning this matter', which suggests that this source was far from official.[138] Unfortunately, only the covering letter to these reports exists, so it is not possible to say what they contained or how they were interpreted, but clearly if the BSC had this information it would have been sent to the SIS in London and would have led to concern there about the security of Hawaii. Moreover, this information must surely have been available to Washington if it came from an

American source. It is possible that this report was linked to the mysterious case of the double-agent, Dusko Popov or 'Tricycle', who was asked by the Abwehr to collect information about Hawaii, but this is mere speculation.[139] This document, therefore, does not confirm Aldrich's contention, it merely adds another exasperating twist to the tale, and one that will not be fully explained until the SIS records enter the public domain.

What is clear, however, is that the policy of deterrence that Britain had followed in 1940–41 had ended in miserable failure. Despite the very public arrival of reinforcements in Malaya, the development of a propaganda campaign designed to confront Japan with the awesome economic power of the Anglo-Saxon powers, and the construction of a united front against Japan which included the coordination of sanctions and a degree of defence planning, war had not been averted. There were many reasons for this failure, but a fundamental one was that the deterrence policy had been based on an unrealistic intelligence assessment of Japanese power. Believing that Japan was weak and was only too aware of its weakness, Britain felt that it was possible to pursue a containment policy in partnership with like-minded states that would involve a tough, uncompromising negotiating stance with only minimal forces to back it up. It is sometimes asked whether better intelligence would have made any difference for, in the light of its commitments in Europe and the Middle East, Britain could never have freed adequate forces to defend Singapore, but this is to see only the military side of the intelligence picture. The crucial point about the role of intelligence in 1941 was that its influence went beyond military matters, and that the image that it constructed of Japan was part of the very foundations of British policy and woven into every decision made. The obvious corollary is that a more enlightened intelligence image of Japan might have led to a less confrontational, more flexible policy being implemented, and that in that case war might have been averted. However, this is to enter into the wild alternative universe of counterfactual history, and is not in the end as important as understanding why the intelligence failure of 1941 took place.

# 10
# 'The Jap is Good': Epilogue and Conclusions

The war that broke out on 7 December GMT with the Japanese landing at Kota Bharu was clearly not the conflict that the British had been contemplating, for Japan entered the fray with a force and efficiency that surprised virtually all in Whitehall and Singapore. The sense of shock was ably summed up by Sir Shenton Thomas who, in a letter to the Colonial Office on 17 December, noted, 'The Jap is good. In the air and on land he has already done things which we didn't expect.'[1] Meanwhile, one official in the AID, following the sinking of HMS *Prince of Wales* and HMS *Repulse*, noted with a fine sense of understatement that 'Events in the Far East suggest that Japanese naval aircraft may be worthy of closer study than has yet been undertaken.'[2]

In the wake of the attack, the post-mortem on Britain's failure to predict the intensity of the Japanese assault saw many criticisms of the intelligence-providers by senior figures both in London and Malaya. Indeed, one of the few things that the commanders in Malaya could agree upon, while they exchanged accusations amongst themselves, was that the FECB and the SIS had provided them with poor intelligence on Japanese intentions and capabilities. For example, Lieutenant-General Percival noted in his official report that a briefing in October 1941 by a senior figure from the FECB had 'painted a very indecisive picture of the Japanese intentions'. Moreover, he observed that, although the IJA's skill at combined operations and its high morale had been appreciated, other assets such as its ability at night-fighting and the efficiency of its air forces had been underestimated.[3] Similar points were made by Lieutenant-General Heath, Air Vice-Marshal Maltby and Brooke-Popham.[4] In particular, emphasis was put on the poor quality of air intelligence, a facet also noted by *The Times* journalist and sometime intelligence operative, Ian Morrison, in his 1942 account of the Malayan campaign.[5] The general consensus, therefore, was that the SIS had failed to deliver any intelligence of value and that the FECB had not worked properly as a combined bureau.[6]

Grimsdale, as the head of the military section of the FECB, rejected these criticisms. In a letter to Ismay in March 1942 he observed that the headquarters staff had 'never believed us and always called us 'alarmists' when we told them how many divisions or aeroplanes the Japs could use'.[7] In his unpublished memoirs he went even further, claiming that 'the lack of warning, scale, method and nature of attack, were all pretty well accurately forecast'. Moreover, he insisted that his section had given a correct assessment of the military worth of the IJA, but that British ethnocentrism had proved too strong to be dislodged:

> The tradition that a British soldier is worth 2 or 3 of any other army, irrespective of how they are armed, dies very hard. However good the information supplied by the 'I' [intelligence] staff may be, it is useless unless the Commander and his 'operations' staff take it to heart and act on it.[8]

A number of historians, such as Peter Elphick and Richard Aldrich, have taken a similar view, arguing that British intelligence in Singapore presented a reasonably accurate picture of Japanese capabilities and intentions, but that their warnings were ignored.[9] Certainly there is some reason to believe that this was the case. For example, it is notable that in his official report Brooke-Popham stated that he had been badly advised by military intelligence about the possibility of a Japanese landing on the east coast of Malaya in the monsoon, the mobility of the IJA, and the skill of its engineers.[10] These, however, were all qualities that MI2c had repeatedly emphasized in its reports, and certainly the FECB's pamphlet on the IJA had been clear about its speed in the offensive. The failure by senior figures to take into account what intelligence had been provided can therefore be said to have been a major problem. Also *post facto* evidence suggests that the intelligence collected by the FECB was poorly disseminated in Malaya by both the air and army general staffs. Brigadier Stewart of the Argyll & Sutherland Highlanders observed to the official historian of the campaign, Major-General Kirby, that he had received 'no clear indication of the Jap efficiency relative to our own, or their tactics'.[11] Another witness observed after the war that what intelligence did exist on the 'Zero' fighter was kept in the Air headquarters and not passed down to individual units due to a lack of junior intelligence staff.[12] Thus, one could say that the intelligence officers should not be criticized for the fact that others failed to disseminate their conclusions.

However, the story does not end there, for contemporary accounts by junior intelligence officers also criticized the workings of the intelligence organizations in Malaya. For example, one officer who joined the FECB in August 1941, Lieutenant-Commander E. Sandwith, noted in retrospect that relations between the 'Y' section and the rest of the FECB were poor, that RDF bearings were frequently unreliable, and that the bureau's monthly reports contained too little information.[13] Arthur Cooper, a former member of the FECB's air section, also found it wanting. In 1949 he informed Nigel de Grey of the GCCS that good intelligence had been obtained from the correspondence of the leading Japanese agent in the Singapore consulate-general. However, this material had been so 'meticulously translated with all flowers of speech' that the information was not taken seriously. Cooper also indicated that Shaw's section 'made no attempt to elucidate ... or indicate the implications' of the material it generated, an accusation that de Grey from previous experience was willing to accept.[14] Poor handling and dissemination of intelligence was thus something of which the FECB itself was guilty.

Another area of contention aired after the event, and more recently in the search for an explanation of the Malayan debacle, has been the lack of an effective counter-espionage system.[15] This is considered to be significant because the Japanese gained immeasurably from the lax pre-war security that allowed Japan's agents to roam the length and breadth of the peninsula collecting intelligence. Certainly some contemporary observers believed that there had been serious problems in this area; for example, A.H. Dickinson, the IGP at the time war broke out, stated in 1945 that internal security had been poor because the position of the DSO had never been made strong enough.[16] Accordingly, it has been argued that the authorities in Malaya should have done more to control the Japanese population, including the consular staff, perhaps even introducing internment before hostilities had begun. The problems with this argument are twofold: first, that Britain did not contemplate an attack, and second, that any action against Japanese nationals or diplomatic staff would have led to reprisals. It might be said that the latter was a risk worth taking, but one needs to remember that reprisals would not merely have had disturbing humanitarian consequences for British subjects in the Japanese Empire and occupied China, but also have led to a drying up of intelligence from these areas, which would in turn compromise Singapore's security.[17] Britain's options in this area were simply not as broad as the critics argue.

The picture that emerges of Malaya in 1941 is therefore one in which the FECB did not speak with a clear enough voice to an audience that was already profoundly deaf. Conditions in London were not that different. Again, it has been argued that the problem in Whitehall lay with the upper echelons and not the intelligence community, and it is easy to find quotations to support such a conclusion, most obviously from the pen of Churchill himself. Indeed, so pervasive was the complacency that it is easy to believe, as was claimed later, that the reaction of the Secretary of State for War, David Margesson, to news of the Japanese attack on Malaya was to state that 'The Japanese can only be rated in the fifth class and this has been amply demonstrated in the fighting against the Chinese during the past years. What have they done against the Chinese – nothing!?'[18]

While the complacency of the senior figures is undeniable, it is more difficult to decide whether this was solely due to wilful ignorance or also the result of sub-standard briefings and assessments by the intelligence professionals. In defence of the intelligence analysts, Aldrich has argued that the JIC worked well in 1941, producing a series of reports that provided a reasonable prediction of the timing, strength and strategy used by the Japanese, and uses contemporary assessments, such as an MID review from January 1942 and a post-war report by NID historians, to support his assertion.[19] However, this claim is open to question. For example, the conclusion of the MID review cited by Aldrich does note that generally the intelligence was sound, but it also refers in the main text to the underestimation of Japanese air power in 1941 and to the final JIC paper of 28 November 1941 as being a 'a rather long and woolly paper' which had failed to predict 'that move into Thailand was concerned with attack on Malaya'.[20] One can either interpret the reluctance to include such statements in the conclusion as a sign that these failures were deemed to be relatively insignificant or that the review was primarily intended as an exercise in self-justification. Other contemporary accounts also cast doubt on the JIC's sagacity. In January 1942 an aggrieved Churchill demanded to know who had informed him that the Kra Isthmus would be too waterlogged to allow for a rapid advance southwards until the spring. This led the War Office to trawl through the JIC memoranda for 1941, and after this exercise one official was moved to observe to the COS secretariat that, though not guilty in regard Churchill's complaint, 'the [JIC] Sub-Committee were certainly a long way out in many of their prognostications'.[21]

Even more damning was the report produced in the winter of 1946 by the Joint Planning Staff (JPS) in response to the question of whether a public inquiry should be held into the military events that had led to the ignominious surrender of Singapore in February 1942. In a spirit befitting the bureaucratic tradition, the JPS noted that for a whole raft of reasons the British people should not be allowed to learn why their country had suffered such an appalling defeat. An inquiry, it was explained, would only provoke calls for investigations into other military reverses, might strain relations with the United States, the Dominions and India, lead to inter-service friction, damage the prestige of the Colonial Service in Malaya and raise questions about Churchill's war leadership. Moreover, the report observed that an inquiry was unacceptable because it would also necessitate some discussion of intelligence methods, which 'are and should remain secret'.[22] Clearly, intelligence could not be kept out of any inquiry for, as the annexe to the report observed, it had played an unfortunate role in Britain's defeat in that 'our intelligence appreciations of the timing, strength and quality of the Japanese attack were gravely at fault'.[23] In the annexe the JPS elaborated on the intelligence mistakes that had been made, noting that Japanese capabilities, particularly in the air, had been grossly underestimated. Moreover, among its comments it too singled out the final JIC report of 28 November 1941, in which it had been asserted that a Japanese attack on Malaya could only follow two to three months after the seizure of the Kra Isthmus.

The fact of the matter is that in 1941 both the intelligence-providers and customers were at fault. Put bluntly, the British simply never imagined that the Japanese would have the temerity to launch a frontal assault on the Empire and thus, days from disaster, they whistled into the wind, imagining the storm would somehow hit Thailand instead. Despite the tone of the post-war mud-slinging it is, however, important to realize that many of the reasons for the intelligence failure lay not with the contemporary problems of 1941, but deeper in the past. As Brooke-Popham noted wearily in 1946 when confronted with the question of why intelligence about the Zero fighter was not better handled, 'what we lacked was a good secret service established years before'.[24]

In assessing the long-term causes of the intelligence failure of 1941 and the problems with assessment in the inter-war period three key themes emerge. These are, first, the continual lack of resources available for intelligence; second, the damage caused by the various rivalries that existed between the intelligence-providers themselves and with and between their customers; and, third, the problems caused by the influence of racial thinking and ethnocentrism.

The allocation of resources was always a severe problem for those who held the responsibility for British security in East Asia, the most distant part of the Empire. From the failure to provide adequate resources to establish an SIS organization in Japan to the underfunding of Shaw's section at the FECB, it is clear that lack of money hampered intelligence-gathering. This was a serious problem, for this was a region in which it was not in any case easy to acquire intelligence due to the strict security measures taken by the Japanese and the high visibility of Caucasians. The most important consequence of this frugality was the effect it had on the services' language officer scheme. Throughout the inter-war period, the services fought a long-running battle to improve the pay and conditions of those officers who had often sacrificed promotion to become language experts. Some victories were achieved, but overall the low allowances granted by the Treasury had a debilitating effect. In 1938, Piggott reported to the War Office that thirty-four British and Indian army language officers had been trained since the end of the Great War, but that at the time of writing only sixteen were still on the active list. Moreover, he observed that of the thirty-four only three had been sent to the Military Staff Colleges at Camberley and Quetta.[25]

Clearly, Britain could afford neither this haemorrhaging of its already scarce experts on Japan nor this under-utilization of those who remained.

The result was that Britain lacked suitable officers for general staff posts where knowledge of Japanese would be useful, thus leading to non-linguists, such as Grimsdale, being posted to head MI2c and the military wing of the FECB. In addition, it meant that too few interpreters were available for training in cryptography, which held back the work of the GCCS and the FECB. One can, therefore, sympathize with Grimsdale when he lamented to Ismay in March 1942 about '... those who refused to allow us to spend more than a few hundreds of pounds on training language officers and building up a proper "I" staff'.[26]

Further exacerbating this problem, Britain did not concentrate on one enemy, Japan, but found its attention diverted at different times by Germany, Indian seditionaries, and the Comintern. This could have unfortunate results, for different foes not only require different languages to be learnt but also a different kind of intelligence approach. For example, the shift from the Comintern to Japan meant a change from focusing on largely political to predominantly military intelligence, and it is difficult not to come away with the conclusion that Harold Steptoe was well suited to the struggle against the former but found it difficult to adjust when the latter became Britain's priority.

Linked to the above is the second major problem that Britain faced in acquiring information in East Asia – the rivalries that bedevilled the effective collection and interpretation of intelligence. These rivalries were sometimes personal, such as that between Steptoe and Drage in the late 1930s, but the most damaging were those that developed at an institutional level. The most obvious difficulty was that generated by the Foreign Office's antagonism towards what it perceived as any attempt by another department to construct an alternative channel of political reporting on events in East Asia. This led it to push for the abolition of the IB in 1920 and of Denham's post in 1923, to take over supervision of the SIS's activities in 1922, and to oppose the establishment of the FEIB and the CIB in 1928–29. The result of this obstructive policy was that Britain took a long time to construct a regional combined intelligence bureau, an organization that had a very important role to play at such a distance from London. Only established in 1935, the FECB was still overcoming its teething problems as the Japanese menace lengthened its stride. Moreover, it is possible to speculate that when forming the FECB the services deliberately circumvented the Foreign Office in order to deny it a veto, and that this may explain why no diplomatic staff were assigned to the bureau and, thus, why the political context of intelligence was often missed or poorly understood.

The divide between military and diplomatic intelligence also had another important consequence, which was that the diplomats' control over the SIS meant that the latter concentrated on political matters to the detriment of military intelligence. Indeed, one of the most consistent complaints of the intelligence directorates in the 1930s was that the SIS representatives in the region were not providing adequate information about military subjects. Despite this, the situation did not improve and the leading culprits, namely Steptoe, were not replaced; one can only speculate that this was because the Foreign Office, judging the situation from its own needs, refused to accept these criticisms.

Rivalries also appear to have had some damaging effects on British intelligence collaboration with other Powers. A number of historians have noted that the Anglo-American exchanges in 1941 were fraught with difficulties due to the mutual suspicions that existed, even though these were caused largely by disagreements about intelligence in the Atlantic theatre rather than the Pacific.[27] How far these affected the assessment of Japan's intentions and capabilities is difficult to quantify, but the fact that British officials in Washington stated as late as November 1941 that the reasons for American discontent must be urgently addressed suggests that the consequences were serious. One might also note the grudging attitude that Britain took towards intelligence cooperation with the Dutch and the Australians. In particular, the British appear to have done little to encourage the growth of the Australian intelligence community in the inter-war period when such sponsorship might have aided the RAN in its struggle for funding.

It could be said, however, that even if all of the problems listed above were solved, one overriding fatal flaw would still have hampered the British assessment of the strategic threat to its interests in East Asia – race. Following John Ferris's example, it is necessary here to differentiate between the views of the professional observers of Japan and the wider audience.[28] At the professional level, it appears that as time passed there was a shift in the way that race impinged upon assessment. From the Great War until the mid-1930s, experts working under the influence of ethnocentrism tended to believe in the existence of stereotyped Japanese 'national characteristics'. This focus on 'national characteristics' had both advantages and disadvantages. It did mean that observers were willing to praise certain aspects of the Japanese military, notably its morale and meticulous staff work, but unfortunately it also encouraged the sort of generalization in which Japan was compared with an idealized view of what the British services were capable of achieving. This meant that, even when Japan made progress in the use of aircraft or tanks, its performance was undervalued because it was measured against the superior technical and strategic standards deemed to exist in Europe. Ironically, the criticisms made of the Japanese have a remarkably similar ring to those that David French has described when looking at British assessments of Germany in the same period; the same attention paid to over-rigid staff work, the lack of initiative in battle and allegedly outmoded tactical doctrine.[29] That British forces might not rise to the exalted heights expected of them seems never to have crossed anyone's mind, nor was a serious assessment made of whether

Britain would be able to fight a modern, fully mechanized war in the underdeveloped territories of East and South-East Asia.

However, while still to a degree influenced by these ideas, the intelligence professionals did attempt, particularly after the start of the Sino-Japanese War, to provide a balanced and even objective judgement of the performance of the Japanese military, and this is epitomized by MI2c's contributions to the *Monthly Intelligence Summary* series. However, the problem was that these assessments were often too judicious for their own good and written as if the reader shared the same objectivity as the writer. As such, they did nothing to acknowledge or even challenge the racial perceptions of Japan. The result was that MI2c's guidance was ambivalent; stating that the IJA was not a first-class army but that it was a formidable opponent in Asia did not make it clear whether the latter caveat only applied to a war with other Asian countries or to all states, including Britain.

This of course reveals the fundamental problem that the intelligence-providers faced, which was that although their own views of the Japanese may be becoming more sophisticated this was not necessarily true of their customers. Particularly within Asia itself, it appears that the British community held to the idea of an Asian racial hierarchy with Japan at its apex and China lingering towards the bottom. Japan's privileged status was based on the fact that it was an ancient yet still virile culture which had managed to adopt a patina of Western-derived sophistication; it was thus half of the East and half of the West. Its grip on this position was, however, tenuous, and when it suffered defeats at the hand of the Chinese and engaged in barbarous acts such as the Rape of Nanking, it was viewed as slipping back into Asianism. Respect for Japan was thus always a fragile entity. Indeed, the irony is that just as MI2c constructed its balanced assessment of the IJA from 1937 onwards, the view of Japan held by most British observers in Asia was becoming less rather than more complimentary. The failure of MI2c and the FECB to challenge or even address racially derived thinking was therefore a significant failing. Moreover, the intelligence providers faced the problem that to construct a new positive interpretation of Japanese capabilities was to contradict the image of Japan that they had helped to construct since before the Great War. This was by no means an easy task for that mental picture of Japan had become the orthodoxy and could not be changed overnight.

British intelligence on Japan was thus prone to serious flaws but despite this it played a crucial part in the shaping of attitudes towards Japan from 1914 and 1941, for it influenced policy from day to day and at a broader level helped to construct Whitehall's image of Japanese intentions and capabilities. The intelligence image of Japan was one of a country whose interests were at heart inimical to those of Britain but which lacked the means to challenge the latter's interests. Thus, Japan was seen as desiring paramount influence in China and as being tempted to pose as a liberator to the subject peoples of South-East and South Asia, but it was not believed to be capable of achieving these goals unless Britain's attention was distracted elsewhere. Underlining Japan's shortcomings was what was seen as its innate conservatism, a trait recognizable in its failure to learn the tactical lessons of the Great War and its sloth in adopting new military technologies. This image of Japan reached its maturity in the 1920s when, in contrast to the living model of 'national efficiency' that it had briefly become in the 1900s, it metamorphosed into Sir Charles Eliot's 'weak power'.

In the 1930s, despite Japan's militancy in foreign affairs and its obvious efforts at rearmament, this image persisted once Britain had passed through a brief period of panic in 1933. Indeed, as Wesley Wark has noted, intelligence on Japanese capabilities in this decade was used to construct a 'suitable Japan', which was unlikely to attack British interests in Asia even if these remained largely undefended.[30] Moreover, factors such as Japan's economic difficulties and the tense stalemate on the Manchurian–Siberian border were seen as guarantees that in the end it posed a paper rather than a real threat. This intelligence image played a key role in British policy, for it argued against both the rapid British reinforcement of its garrison in Asia and the temptation to appease Japan. The Sino-Japanese War and the isolated clashes with the Soviet Union in 1938–39 had the effect of merely confirming this assessment of Japan. Thus Britain felt no need in 1941 to panic about the Japanese threat, for if it were carefully handled there was every reason to think that Japan could be deterred.

Study of the role of intelligence therefore illuminates the evolution of British diplomacy towards and strategic thinking about Japan. Moreover, perhaps more than any other area of policy-making, it acts as a window on the changing racial images of Japan held by the British in this period and illustrates an aspect of Anglo-Japanese relations that has been obscure for too long. Thus it forcefully reminds us that, when studying this period, we must immerse ourselves in the mores of the era and not force our own preconceptions on the actors.

The three key themes emphasized in this study – resources, rivalries and race – are of course not factors limited to British intelligence in East Asia, as the reference to David French's recent work on British perceptions of the German army makes clear. Indeed, the most obvious parallel is with the state of American intelligence on the eve of the attack on Pearl Harbor. Despite the efforts of the conspiracy theorists to prove that President Roosevelt had prior knowledge of the Japanese assault, the evidence available suggests that the United States faced similar dilemmas to the British. Here, too, there was a failure to distribute resources in an effective manner, with the result that there was no American secret service in existence and that too few staff were involved in breaking JN-25B, the only code that could have revealed Japan's intentions. In addition, as noted in the previous chapter, the military and naval intelligence offices in Washington were barely on speaking terms, and thus the intelligence drive against Japan was poorly coordinated; a tendency most notable in the bizarre way in which the services handled the distribution of decrypts from the 'purple' machine. Lastly, as John Dower has made clear, the United States suffered in its attempts to measure Japan's military efficiency from similar racial delusions to the British; for example, sharing the idea that the Japanese for physiological reasons made poor pilots.[31] The result of these failings, as with the British, was that Washington believed that a policy of containment would suffice to deal with the Japanese and that its forces were not prepared for the reality of war with Japan. Indeed, one might go as far as to say that some in the United States have never come to terms with the fact that Japan proved to be America's equal, for is not the entire notion that Roosevelt must have known that the attack on Pearl Harbor was coming itself implicitly racist? After all it seems to imply that Japan could only have 'surprised' America if the latter was complicit in the attack.

The themes emphasized in this book are thus ones that have a general application to the study of intelligence. In regard to race, this study demonstrates how important it is for intelligence historians to take into account the prejudices of the providers and the customers, and not to imagine that this gilded community is somehow immune from the factors that warp perception. Ethnocentrism, as Ken Booth has argued, is an issue that cannot be ignored when dealing with threat assessment, but in talk about organizational problems and flows of information, this basic fact can all too easily be forgotten.[32] In addition, the history of British intelligence and the Japanese threat points to another general factor that is too often neglected, which is that to understand the way in which intelligence is provided and utilized one has to look at the problems posed by the existence of seemingly mundane linguistic and financial obstacles. To measure the significance of intelligence thus involves more than looking at events of high drama or dealing with the political struggles between intelligence organizations: it requires analysis of abstract concepts such as race and administrative minutiae, such as how many officers can understand foreign languages. Only by using such a comprehensive approach can the full impact of the 'missing dimension' finally be felt, thus enriching our knowledge of episodes in recent history that have previously remained opaque and adding a new, more nuanced dimension to traditional diplomatic history.

# Notes

*Additional abbreviations used in the footnotes*

| | |
|---|---|
| A Dept | American Department (FO) |
| AA | Air attaché |
| ACNS | Assistant Chief of Naval Staff, RAN |
| AI2 | AID section dealing with East Asia |
| AM | Air Ministry |
| BL | British Library |
| BO | Burma Office |
| BUL | Birmingham University Library |
| C Dept | Central Department (FO) |
| CCC | Churchill College, Cambridge |
| CGS | Chief of the General Staff |
| CIGS | Chief of the Imperial General Staff |
| CNS | Chief of Naval Staff, RAN |
| CO | Colonial Office |
| DCAS | Deputy Chief of Air Staff |
| DDMOI | Deputy Director of Military Operations and Intelligence |
| DSC | Director of Signal Communications, RAN |
| DSD | Director of Signals Division, Admiralty |
| Egypt Dept | Egyptian Department (FO) |
| FE Dept | Far Eastern Department (FO) |
| FP Dept | Foreign and Political Department, India |
| FO | Foreign Office |
| FSL | First Sea Lord |
| HK | Hong Kong |
| IA | Indian army |
| IO | India Office |
| IOLR | India Office Library and Records |
| IPI | Indian Political Intelligence (IO) |
| IWM | Imperial War Museum |
| JNA | Japanese naval attaché |
| LHCMA | Liddell Hart Centre for Military Archives, Kings College, London |
| LO | Language Officer |
| MA | Military attaché |
| MECSA | Middle East Centre, St Antony's College, Oxford |
| Mil Dept | Military Department (IO) |
| N Dept | Northern Department (FO) |
| NA | Naval attaché |
| NAA | National Archives of Australia |
| News Dept | News Department (FO) |
| NMM | National Maritime Museum |
| no. | Denotes correspondence sent by dispatch |
| OAG | Officer Administering the Government |
| PCO | Passport Control Officer |

| | |
|---|---|
| PID | Political Intelligence Department (FO) |
| PJ Dept | Public and Justice Department (IO) |
| PS Dept | Political and Secret Department (IO) |
| RHL | Rhodes House Library, Oxford |
| SFEIS | Special Far Eastern Intelligence Summary |
| T | Treasury |
| tel. | Denotes correspondence by telegram |
| WO | War Office |

Unless stated at the start of the footnote all archival material comes from the Public Record Office in London. All BJs are of Japanese material unless otherwise indicated.

## 1 Introduction

1 Vinden papers, IWM, memoirs -'By Chance, A Soldier', p. 75.
2 C. Andrew and D. Dilks, 'Introduction' in C. Andrew and D. Dilks (eds), *The Missing Dimension: Governments and Intelligence Communities in the Twentieth Century* (London: Macmillan, 1984), p. 1.
3 W. Wark, *The Ultimate Enemy: British Intelligence and Nazi Germany, 1933–1939* (London: I.B. Tauris, 1985), and J.A. Maiolo, *The Royal Navy and Nazi Germany, 1933–39: A Study in Appeasement and the Origins of the Second World War* (Basingstoke: Macmillan, 1998).
4 C. Andrew, *Secret Service: The Making of the British Intelligence Community* (London: Heinemann, 1985), and R.J. Aldrich, *Britain and the Intelligence War against Japan, 1941–45: The Politics of Secret Service* (Cambridge: Cambridge University Press, 2000).
5 Broad studies of race and international relations include K. Booth, *Strategy and Ethnocentrism* (London: Croom Helm, 1979), F. Furedi, *The Silent War: Imperialism and the Changing Perception of Race* (London: Pluto Press, 1998), and P.G. Lauren, *Power and Prejudice: The Politics and Diplomacy of Racial Discrimination* (Boulder: Westview Press, 1988). For a more specific study of racial images during wartime see J.W. Dower, *War Without Mercy: Race and Power in the Pacific War* (London: Faber and Faber, 1986).
6 The one book that does cover virtually the whole period is W.R. Louis, *British Strategy in the Far East, 1919–1939* (Oxford: Clarendon, 1971). On the end of the alliance see I.H. Nish, *Alliance in Decline: A Study in Anglo-Japanese Relations, 1908–23* (London: Athlone, 1972); on the Manchurian crisis see C. Thorne, *The Limits of Foreign Policy: The West, the League and the Far Eastern Crisis of 1931–1933* (London: Hamish Hamilton, 1972) and I.H. Nish, *Japan's Struggle with Internationalism: Japan, China and the League of Nations, 1931–33* (London: Kegan Paul, 1993); and on the origins of the Pacific War, see B.A. Lee, *Britain and the Sino-Japanese War, 1937–1939* (Stanford: Stanford University Press, 1973), P. Lowe, *Great Britain and the Origins of the Pacific War: A Study of British Policy in East Asia, 1937–1941* (Oxford: Clarendon, 1977), C. Thorne, *Allies of a Kind: The United States, Britain and the War against Japan, 1941–1945* (Oxford: Oxford University Press, 1978), A. Best, *Britain, Japan and Pearl Harbor: Avoiding War in East Asia, 1936–41* (London: Routledge, 1995), and N. Tarling, *Britain, Southeast Asia and the Onset of the Pacific War* (Cambridge: Cambridge University Press, 1996). Essays on Anglo-Japanese relations in this period can be found in I.H. Nish, (ed.), *Anglo-Japanese Alienation, 1919–1952* (Cambridge: Cambridge

University Press, 1982), I.H. Nish and Y. Kibata (eds), *The History of Anglo-Japanese Relations: The Political and Diplomatic Dimension*, Vols 1 and 2 (Basingstoke: Macmillan, 2000), and S. Akita and N. Kagotani (eds), *1930 – nendai Ajia kokusai chitsujo* [The International Order of Asia in the 1930s] (Hiroshima: Keisui–sha, 2001).

7 J. Ferris, '"Worthy of Some Better Enemy?" The British Estimate of the Imperial Japanese Army 1919–41 and the Fall of Singapore', *Canadian Journal of History*, 28 (1993), 223–56, P. Lowe, 'Great Britain's Assessment of Japan Before the Outbreak of the Pacific War', in E.R. May (ed.), *Knowing One's Enemy. Intelligence Assessment before the Two World Wars* (Princeton: Princeton University Press, 1984), W. Wark, 'In Search of a Suitable Japan: British Naval Intelligence in the Pacific before the Second World War', *Intelligence and National Security*, 1 (1986), 189–211, and Aldrich, op. cit. See also A. Best, 'Constructing an Image: British Intelligence and Whitehall's Perception of Japan, 1931–39,' *Intelligence and National Security*, 11 (1996), 403–23, and idem, '"This Probably Over-Valued Military Power": British Intelligence and Whitehall's Perception of Japan, 1939–41', *Intelligence and National Security*, 12 (1997), 67–94. Useful but less academic studies are also available; see P. Elphick, *The Far Eastern File: The Intelligence War in the Far East, 1930–1945* (London: Hodder and Stoughton, 1997), and M. Smith, *The Emperor's Codes: Bletchley Park and the Breaking of Japan's Secret Ciphers* (London: Bantam Press, 2000).

8 C. Thorne, 'Racial Aspects of the Far Eastern War of 1941–1945', *Proceedings of the British Academy*, 66 (1980), 329–77.

9 R. Bickers, *Britain in China: Community, Culture and Colonialism, 1900–1949* (Manchester: Manchester University Press, 1999), pp. 27–31 and 71–73.

10 On Rutland and Greene see Elphick, op. cit., pp. 44–7; for Heenan see P. Elphick and M. Smith, *Odd Man Out: The Story of the Singapore Traitor* (London: Hodder and Stoughton, 1993).

11 For definitions and analysis of all-source and finished intelligence see M. Herman, *Intelligence Power in Peace and War* (Cambridge: Cambridge University Press, 1996), pp. 61–112.

12 See FO228/2926 Fraser (Shanghai) to Jordan (Peking) 20 March 1918 no.146 and England (BAT) to Phillips (Shanghai) 1 April 1918.

13 WO106/5393 'Report on Military Intelligence in the Far East With Proposals for the Organization of a Far Eastern Intelligence Bureau', Blaker (FEIB) memorandum 16 January 1928.

14 Ibid.

15 WO106/6143 'Notes on the Organization of the Intelligence Service in China', Miles (MI2c) undated [November 1933?]

16 WO106/5393 'Report on Military Intelligence in the Far East With Proposals for the Organization of a Far Eastern Intelligence Bureau', Blaker memorandum 16 January 1928.

17 WO106/5392 'Questionnaire for Mr Fleming', unattributed and undated [MI2 note,1933?].

18 WO106/5255 Steward (CIB) to GOC HK 25 July 1929.

19 FO371/19354 F6595/246/23 Sansom (Tokyo) to Orde (FE Dept) 17 July 1935.

20 WO106/5371 Burkhardt (FECB) note 6 July 1937.

21 IOLR L/PS/11/139 Lampson (Peking) to Langley (FO) 30 June 1918.

22 WO106/5393 'Report on Military Intelligence in the Far East With Proposals for the Organization of a Far Eastern Intelligence Bureau', Blaker memorandum 16 January 1928.

23 Ibid.
24 See C. Drage, *The Life and Times of General Two-Gun Cohen* (New York: Funk and Wagnalls, 1954) and idem, *The Amiable Prussian* (London: Blond, 1958).
25 For Killery and Andrew see Aldrich, op. cit., pp. 103 and 282 respectively. For Stein see FO371/27804 F2578/275/61 Clark Kerr (HK) to Eden 7 April 1941 no.5 Tour.
26 IOLR L/WS/1/194 Hammond (MI2) to Roberts (IAGS) 30 May 1940 no.DO/21.
27 MOD to author 25 November 1997.
28 Ibid., and Cabinet Office to author 11 July 1997 and 17 September 1997.
29 FO to author 21 December 1998.

## 2 The British Empire in East Asia in 1914

1 A good description of the language officer scheme in Japan is contained in F.S.G. Piggott, *Broken Thread: An Autobiography* (Aldershot: Gale &Polden, 1950), pp. 24–84.
2 FO371/2013 22472/4826/23 Greene (Tokyo) to Langley (FO) 23 April 1914.
3 On the SMP see R. Bickers, 'Who Were the Shanghai Municipal Police, and Why Were They There? The British Recruits of 1919', in R. Bickers and C. Henriot (eds), *New Frontiers: Imperialism's New Communities in East Asia, 1842–1953* (Manchester: Manchester University Press, 2000), pp. 170–91.
4 The two seminal works on the alliance are I.H. Nish, *The Anglo-Japanese Alliance: The Diplomacy of Two Island Empires, 1894–1907* (London: Athlone, 1966) and idem, *Alliance in Decline: A Study in Anglo-Japanese Relations, 1908–23* (London: Athlone, 1972). On the second renewal of the alliance see also P. Lowe, *Britain and Japan, 1911–15: A Study of British Far Eastern Policy* (London: Macmillan, 1969).
5 WO106/46 Winchester House conference minutes 7 July 1902.
6 ADM116/1231B Troubridge (NA Tokyo) to Admiralty 26 January 1903. On the Port Arthur and Vladivostock information see HD3/124 Trotter (WO) to Sanderman (FO) 19 May 1903.
7 See P. Towle, 'British Naval and Military Observers of the Russo-Japanese War', in J. Hoare (ed.), *Britain and Japan: Biographical Portraits,* Vol. III (Richmond: Japan Library, 1999), pp. 165–6.
8 Nish, *Alliance in Decline*, pp. 99–105, and Lowe, op. cit., pp. 17–31.
9 For the racial image of Japanese businessmen, see J.-P. Lehmann, *The Image of Japan From Feudal Isolation to World Power, 1850–1905* (London: George Allen and Unwin, 1978), pp. 134–8, and on the military see P. Charrier, 'The Evolution of a Stereotype: The Royal Navy and the Japanese "Martial Type", 1900–1945', *War and Society*, 19 (2001), 23–46.
10 See C. Holmes and H. Ion, 'Bushidō and the Samurai: Images in British Public Opinion, 1894–1914', *Modern Asian Studies*, 14 (1980), 309–29.
11 M.J.E. McCarthy, *The Coming Power, 1898–1905* (London: Hodder and Stoughton, 1905), pp. 382–3.
12 R. Kowner, '"Lighter Than Yellow, But Not Enough": Western Discourse on the Japanese "Race", 1854-1904', *Historical Journal*, 43 (2000), 103–31.
13 See, for example, G. Lynch, *The Path of Empire* (London: Duckworth, 1903), pp. 91–105, and A.Wellesley Kipling, 'The Yellow Peril', *National Defence*, Whitsun 1912, 50–66. Surprisingly there is no book-length study of the 'Yellow Peril' phenomenon.

14 B.L. Putnam Weale, *The Conflict of Colour* (London: Macmillan, 1910), p. 225.
15 FO371/2647 222589/83924/23 Greene to Grey 26 September 1916 no.485.
16 See Lowe, op. cit., p. 290.
17 FO371/2013 22472/4826/23 Greene to Langley 23 April 1914.
18 FO371/1947 29475/25071/10 Wheeler (Secretary to Indian Govt) to Chief Secretary Bengal 4 June 1914.
19 IOLR L/MIL/7/16123 Viceroy to IO 7 July 1914 and Stuart (WO) to Barrow (Mil. Dept) 13 July 1914.
20 For the assessment of Cardew see FO262/1261 Davidson (Yokohama) minute undated [August 1916].
21 FO371/2013 42066/4826/23 Cleveland (DCI India) to Ferrer (PJ Dept) 28 July 1914, and IOLR IOR.POS.7147 *Plot Connected with the Seditious Movement in India, to Poison British Officials in Shanghai* ... HDA: August 1914, nos 7–16.
22 HD3/124 Trotter to Sanderman 19 May 1903.
23 ADM116/1231C 'Interchange of Information', Admiralty memorandum September 1909.
24 ADM1/8541/280 'Conference on the Rules for Supplying Secret Information to Allied and Neutral Representatives', Admiralty note undated [October 1918].
25 P. Towle, 'British Estimates of Japanese Military Power', in idem, (ed.), *Estimating Foreign Military Power* (London: Croom Helm, 1982), pp. 125–8.
26 See S. Collini, 'The Idea of "Character" in Victorian Political Thought', *Transactions of the Royal Historical Society*, 35 (1985), 29–50, and D. French, *Raising Churchill's Army: The British Army and the War Against Germany, 1919–1945* (Oxford: Oxford University Press, 2000), pp. 49–50.
27 Langley papers, FO800/31, Brand (NA Tokyo) to Oliver (DNI) 28 November 1913.
28 WO106/5553 Somerville (MA Tokyo) to Yates (WO) 29 November 1913.
29 Ibid.
30 On Somerville, see Towle, 'British Estimates of Japanese Military Power', p. 128, and Piggott, op. cit., p. 38 and pp. 273–6.
31 See J. Ferris, 'Before "Room 40": The British Empire and Signals Intelligence, 1898–1914', *Journal of Strategic Studies*, 12 (1989), 438–42.

## 3 The Erosion of the Anglo-Japanese Alliance, 1914–21

1 WO106/669 WO to GOC S.China 11 December 1914 tel.2414, and GOC S.China to WO 30 December 1914 tel.156, and ADM137/179 Jerram (C-in-C China) to Admiralty 15 January 1915 tel. 19.
2 F. Dickinson, *War and National Reinvention: Japan in the Great War, 1914–1919* (Cambridge, Mass.: Harvard University Press, 1999), Chapter 3, P. Lowe, *Britain and Japan, 1911–15: A Study of British Far Eastern Policy* (London: Macmillan, 1969), pp. 220–66, and I.H. Nish, *Alliance in Decline: A Study in Anglo-Japanese Relations, 1908–23* (London: Athlone, 1972).
3 R. Popplewell, *Intelligence and Imperial Defence: British Intelligence and the Defence of the Indian Empire, 1904–1924* (London: Frank Cass, 1995), pp. 287–9.
4 R.W.E. Harper and H. Miller, *Singapore Mutiny* (Singapore: Oxford University Press, 1984).
5 FO371/2495 59339/281/45 IO to FO 12 May 1915. See also T.G. Fraser, 'Germany and Indian Revolution, 1914–18', *Journal of Contemporary History*, 12 (1977), 267–8.

6 FO371/2332 117013/60715/10 Jordan (Peking) to Grey 30 June 1915 no.158.
7 FO371/2495 77951/281/45 Davidson (Yokohama) to Home Dept, India 26 April 1915.
8 Fraser, op. cit., pp. 255–66 and Popplewell, op. cit., pp. 201–39 and p. 263–4.
9 FO371/2340 168591/161367/10 Shuckburgh (IO) to Alston (FE Dept) 10 November 1915.
10 ADM125/63 Grant (C-in-C China) to Admiralty 14 October 1915 no.1, and CO273/435 MO6 report 4 December 1915.
11 Dickinson, op. cit., pp. 117–9.
12 ADM125/63 Grant to Admiralty 9 November 1915 no.2 and Grant to Admiralty 9 March 1916 no.17.
13 Nish op. cit., p. 185.
14 WO106/1412 Ridout (GOC Straits) to WO 5 October 1915 tel.517.
15 FO371/2496 170278/281/45 Grey to Spring-Rice (Washington) 10 December 1915 tel.512.
16 FO371/2784 31444/211/45 Greene to Grey 5 January 1916, and Alston minute 19 February 1916. See also T.G. Fraser, 'India in Anglo-Japanese Relations during the First World War', *History*, 209 (1978), 367–73.
17 FO371/2340 161476/161367/10 Langley (FO) minute 27 October 1915, and 168591/161367/10 Shuckburgh to Alston 10 November 1915, and FO371/2342 192831/192831/10 Buchanan (Petrograd) to Grey 16 December 1915 tel.1888. This episode is also described in P. Lowe, 'Great Britain, Japan and the Fall of Yuan Shih-k'ai, 1915–1916', *Historical Journal*, XIII (1970), 706–20.
18 FO371/2340 168694/167912/10 Grey to Greene (Tokyo) 12 November 1915 tel.334.
19 FO371/2341 174748/167912/10 Grey to Greene 20 November 1915 tel.348, FO371/2340 201833/161367/10 Alston minute 28 December 1915, and FO371/2647 50/50/10 Greene to Grey 31 December 1915 tel.551.
20 IOLR L/PS/11/104 Viceroy to IO 24 March 1916 P.1087.
21 FO371/2645 78504/49/10 IO to FO 25 April 1916 P.1469A.
22 ADM125/63 Grant to Admiralty 2 December 1915 no.3.
23 IOLR L/PS/10/578 Grant (FP Dept) to Hirtzel (PS Dept) 14 April 1916.
24 Fraser, 'India in Anglo-Japanese Relations', pp. 374–5.
25 FO371/2693 92535/83294/23 Nicolson (PUS FO) minute 22 May 1916 and FO371/2646 171550/49/10 Hardinge (PUS FO) minute undated [August 1916].
26 CAB37/148/12 Gregory (FE Dept) memorandum 19 May 1916.
27 ADM223/667 Bangkok to Berlin (German) 2 January circulated 2 May 1916, and Shanghai to Berlin (German) 26 February circulated 8 May 1916, and ADM137/371 Hall (DNI) minute 27 May 1916.
28 FO371/2653 20344/20344/10 Grey to Bertie (Paris) 27 January 1916 no.88, and 22074/20344/10 Grey to Greene 3 February 1916 tel.40, and FO371/2691 45021/31446/23 Howard (Stockholm) to Grey 1 March 1916 no.52.
29 FO371/2693 263898/83924/23 Balfour to Greene 13 February 1917 no.25.
30 FO371/2332 156086/60715/10 Alston minute 17 October 1915.
31 Popperwell, op. cit., pp. 80–1.
32 FO371/2785 42617/211/45 Viceroy to IO 24 February 1916 tel.P718, 45386/211/45 WO to IO 7 March 1916, and 58512/211/45 IO to Viceroy 23 March 1916.
33 FO371/2786 85175/211/45 Ridout to WO 3 May 1916 tel.844, FO228/2702 Ridout to Jordan 23 May 1916, ADM125/63 Grant to Admiralty 27 July 1916 no.37, and FO371/2789 190668/211/45 Greene to Grey 7 August 1916 no.377.

34 ADM125/63 Grant to Admiralty 11 May 1916 no. 26, and 15 June 1916 no. 31. For the TSR plot see ADM125/64 Seigne (Naval Staff Officer, Shanghai) report 19 August 1916.
35 FO228/2702 Greene to Fraser (Shanghai) 12 July 1916 unnumbered telegram, and Jordan to Grey 12 September 1916 tel.249, and FO371/2789 196450/211/45 Grey to Fraser 6 October 1916.
36 Jerram papers, NMM, JRM/16/5 Jordan to Jerram 12 April 1915, and Hall papers, CCC, HALL6/3, 'Notes on Work of Naval Intelligence Centre, Shanghai', Seigne undated memorandum [1918?]. See also Popperwell, op. cit., pp. 269–70.
37 FO371/2789 200623/211/45 Fraser to Grey 8 October 1916 tel.137, ADM137/1220 Seigne to Admiralty 16 November 1916, and ADM137/1433 'Briefing for Admiral Tudor, 1917', Rayment (NID) 1 June 1917.
38 FO371/3065 50010/1220/45 Ridout to WO 3 March 1917 tel.1234.
39 See Popperwell, op. cit., p. 271.
40 Ibid, pp. 265–8.
41 FO371/2648 51639/865/10 Lyons (FE Dept) minute undated [March 1916].
42 IOLR P/CONF/64 H(A): March 1921, *Question of the Regularisation of the Position and the Pay Drawn by Major A.M. Cardew*, no.185–95.
43 FO371/2648 164152/856/10 Shuckburgh to Gregory 19 August 1916, and Langley minute undated [August 1916], and 173564/856/10 FO to WO 31 October 1916. Cardew's involvement is mentioned in FO371/2915 26392/26392/10 Hirtzel to Gregory 31 January 1917.
44 IOLR L/MIL/7/7819 Army Dept India to Military Secretary IO 8 September 1917.
45 IOLR L/PS/8/78 Viceroy to IO 5 March 1917.
46 FO369/939 160262/160262/223 WO to FO 15 August 1917, and HW3/35 'Nominal Role of MI1B', unattributed note 2 August 1919.
47 See for example FO371/3285 78179/6/W38 Hardinge minute undated [May 1918].
48 FO371/2951 20083/20083/23 Bonar (MI5) to Langley 24 January 1917, and Langley minute undated, FO372/1065 30390/596/350 MI5E note to all ports 6 February 1917, and FO372/1066 44020/596/350 MI5 circular to chief constables undated [February 1917?]
49 FO371/2955 229313/229313/23 French (MI1a) to Campbell (FO) undated [December 1917?]. For the office in Konstanz see diary entry 13 December 1917 in B. Thomson, *The Scene Changes* (New York: Doubleday, 1937), p. 396.
50 FO372/1142 170122/16227/323 Greene to Balfour 21 August 1918 no.308.
51 ADM125/66 Tudor (C-in-C China) to Admiralty 15 November 1917 no.104, and FO371/3235 13827/13827/23 WO to FO 21 January 1918.
52 FO262/1310 Ridout to Greene 2 July 1917 CRSS.11360, FO371/3069 217765/1220/45 Greene to Langley 5 October 1917, and FO262/1419 Ridout to Greene 3 March 1919.
53 FO369/1171 104197/86366/223 Campbell to French (MI1a) 8 January 1918. See also A. Judd, *The Quest for C: Sir Mansfield Cumming and the Making of the British Secret Service* (London: HarperCollins, 1999), p. 423 and Popplewell, op. cit., p. 326.
54 FO371/2658 206574/175521/10 Robertson (MA Peking) 13 September 1916, and IOLR L/PS/11/109 P.3598 Jarrow (PS Dept) minute 27 October 1916.
55 IOLR L/PS/11/109 P.3598/16 Hirtzel minute 26 October 1916, L/MIL/7/7326 IO to WO 7 November 1916, and FO371/2949 153979/8828/23 WO to FO

4 August 1917. See also M. Kennedy, *The Military Side of Japanese Life* (London: Constable, 1924).

56 FO371/3423 58914/327/45 Greene to Balfour 14 January 1918 and Macleay (FE Dept) minute 5 April 1918.

57 See Popplewell, op. cit., pp. 274–6.

58 FO371/2910 55607/5752/10 Alston (Peking) to Balfour 14 March 1917 tel.176.

59 FO371/2917 107941/71852/10 Alston to Gregory 12 April 1917.

60 FO371/2917 107941/71852/10 Hall note 11 October 1917.

61 FO371/2911 120155/5752/10 Lyons minute 23 May 1917.

62 FO371/3065 63504/1220/45 'Notes on a Recent Tour in the Far East', Petrie (DCI India, Shanghai) 4 December 1916.

63 Ibid.

64 FO371/3065 40716/1220/45 Greene to Balfour 15 January 1917 no.31.

65 See, for example, FO371/3064 31152/1220/45 Greene to Grey 7 December 1916 no.638 and 31161/1220/45 Greene to Balfour 18 December 1916 no.662. See also Popperwell, op. cit., pp. 278–80.

66 See the intercepts in ADM223/667, in particular no.589B Washington to Berlin 21 September circulated 24 October 1916 and A.535 Washington to Berlin 15 November circulated 22 December 1916.

67 For Otani, see IOLR L/PS/11/108 P.3009 Grant to Hirtzel 29 June 1916 no.DO.109, and FO228/3211 'Secret Abstracts of Intelligence', General Staff Singapore report November 1917.

68 FO371/2694 246628/202440/23 Ridout to WO 2 November 1916 CRSS.10136.

69 FO371/2691 264948/31466/23 Greene to Grey 18 November 1916 no.601 and Macleay minute 20 February 1917, and IOLR L/PS/10/630 Dunn (Batavia) to Balfour 20 July 1918 no.134.

70 WO106/869 'Japanese Policy and Aspirations in Asia and the Pacific', MI2c memorandum 14 July 1917.

71 See C-C Ong, *Operation Matador: Britain's War Plans Against the Japanese, 1918–1941* (Singapore: Times Academic Press, 1997), pp. 4–5.

72 See FO371/3064 3178/1220/45 'Indian sedition in Japan', FO memorandum undated [February 1917?], FO371/2693 263898/83294/23 Balfour to Greene 13 February 1917 no.1, and WO106/5553 Piggott note 11 September 1917. For further details see Nish, op. cit., pp. 242–8.

73 IOLR L/PS/10/578 Petrie to Cleveland (DCI) 16 May 1918.

74 FO371/2951 123198/31166/23 Viceroy to IO 4 May 1917, and FO371/2955 186492/168031/23 Macleay minute 5 October 1917.

75 WO106/5724 'Note on the Japanese Attitude towards the Situation at Vladivostock', MI2c report 8 January 1918.

76 FO228/2968 'China and Japan', unattributed note [MI1c?] 14 April 1918, and 'Disclosure of Terms of New Secret Treaty Between China and Japan', anonymous note 19 April 1918.

77 FO371/3286 115256/6/W38 Jordan to Balfour 27 June 1918 tel.541.

78 FO228/2950 Denham (DCI India, Shanghai) to Jordan 14 June 1919 no.225, and FO371/6707 F3105/3105/23 'Japan and Turkey', SIS report 10 May 1921 no.200.

79 IOLR L/PS/11/155 Jordan to Curzon 18 June 1919 no.281, FO395/299 001552/0099/N50 Rushton (Batavia) to Gaselee (News Dept) 18 February 1919, and CO273/504 DNI to FO 16 April 1920.

80 See Popplewell, op. cit., p. 282.

81 FO371/3816 132165/951/23 Kennard (Rome) to Oliphant (FO) 18 September 1919.

82 FO371/2820 47207/47207/23 Sinclair (DNI) to FO 24 March 1919, and FO371/3821 94243/94243/23 CX072699/R/SW/D22 SIS Stockholm report 12 June 1919.
83 FO608/204 611/2/1-1265 'Japanese Activity in Siberia and Recognition of the Omsk Government,' PID memorandum 18 February 1919.
84 HW12/6 BJ.001630 London to Paris/Rome 11 March circulated 15 March 1920 and ADM1/8581/24 Sinclair minute 27 June 1920.
85 FO371/4242 2519/117/45 Sinclair to FO 1 January 1919 and Tilley (FO) minute 10 January 1919.
86 FO371/3816 148769/1634/23 'Japan's General Foreign Policy', FO memorandum 22 October 1919.
87 FO371/3191 214187/214187/10 Jordan to Langley 29 May 1918, and FO228/3211 Jordan to Jamieson (Canton) 28 March 1919.
88 FO371/4244 87816/117/45 Gaselee minute 18 June 1919.
89 FO371/4244 81438/117/45 Ridout to WO 1 April 1919 CRSS.13976 and FO371/4557 A547/39/45 Dunn to Curzon 14 January 1920 no. 10.
90 FO371/3235 167556/13287/23 MI1a to Sperling (FO) 4 October 1918 and FO262/1419 'The Japanese in the South Seas: A Historical Sketch', Ashton-Gwatkin (Singapore) report undated [March 1919].
91 FO371/3235 11883/117/45 Ridout to WO 20 November 1918 CRSS.13519.
92 CO537/890 James (Singapore) to Milner 16 December 1919 and CAB5/3 CID123-C 'Acquisition by Japanese Subjects of Properties in the Vicinity of Singapore', ODC memorandum 23 March 1920.
93 Godfrey papers, IWM, Memoirs, vol.II.
94 ADM137/1433 Grant to Admiralty 5 January 1917 no.6/505.
95 ADM137/1634 Jerram to Hall 19 May 1917.
96 ADM1/8541/280 'Conference on the Rules for Supply of Secret Information to Allied and Neutral Representatives', Admiralty note undated [October 1918?].
97 FO371/2954 216188/120436/23 Somerville (MA Tokyo) memorandum 2 October 1917.
98 FO371/3233 46022/397/23 'Japan at War 1914–191-', Rymer (NA Tokyo) memorandum 8 February 1918.
99 FO371/3823 177951/177951/23 Woodroffe (MA Tokyo) memorandum 16 December 1919 no.XC.
100 FO371/3819 32925/32925/23 Woodroffe memorandum 30 June 1919 no.XLIV.
101 FO371/3233 58948/734/23 Bridgeman (FE Dept) minute 4 April 1918, WO32/5317 'The Defence of Hong Kong', WO memorandum undated [January 1920], and FO371/6693 F4649/421/23 Eliot (Tokyo) to Curzon 3 November 1921 no.609.
102 FO371/3821 90416/90416/23 Tilley minute 20 June 1919.
103 FO371/3823 154403/154403/23 'General Situation in Japan' SIS report 6 October 1919 CX080977.PC/1293 and FO371/5364 F1164/1164/23 Woodroffe memorandum 1 May 1920.
104 FO371/2358 F304/199/23 Ashton-Gwatkin (FE Dept) memorandum 23 March 1920.
105 CO532/139 CO2719/19 FO memorandum undated [January 1919] and FO371/3819 22242/19701/23 Sperling (A Dept) minute 11 February 1919.
106 See the files FO371/4383 PID601/601 and HW3/35.
107 HW12/9 BJ.002645 London to Paris 25 May circulated 28 May 1920, HW12/10 BJ.002798 Tokyo to Paris 25 May circulated 10 June 1920, and HW12/21 BJ.006237 Paris to London 23 April circulated 27 April 1921.

108 HW12/2 BJ.000341 'Captain Yamawaki' 29 November 1919 and HW12/8 002133 London to Paris 6 April circulated 14 April 1920.
109 IOLR P/10648 FP(A):June 1919, *Appointment of Major A.M. Cardew, R.E., as Adviser to Government for Far Eastern Questions*, nos. 1–4, and FO262/1419 Viceroy to IO 2 September 1919.
110 See the files IOLR L/MIL/7/7326 and 7329.
111 See the files IOLR L/PS/11/197 P.2264/21, and P/11082 FP(B) Establishment papers March–August 1921.
112 FO369/1695 K6/6/229 Grindle (CO) to FO 31 December 1920.
113 CO537/889 'Need for Establishment of a "Special Intelligence Bureau" ("SIB") i.e. a "C.I.D." and Contre Espionage Office at Singapore', Lee-Warner (Malayan Civil Service) memorandum 14 July 1919.
114 CO323/838 Kell (MI5) to Haldane Porter (Home Office) 29 August 1919 SF1001/1/Gen/4, and IOLR L/MIL/7/7817 DMI to IO 2 January 1920.
115 CAB23/25 43(21) Cabinet meeting 30 May 1921.
116 CAB2/3 CID 134th meeting 14 December 1920.
117 FO371/6672 F1169/63/23 'Report of the Anglo-Japanese Alliance Committee' FO memorandum 14 January 1921.
118 For the Cabinet memorandum of 4 July 1921, see M. Gilbert (ed.), *Winston S. Churchill*, Vol. III: *Companion*, Part III (London: Heinemann, 1977), p. 1540.
119 Chartwell papers, CCC, CHAR22/6, Churchill note [undated] and Sinclair (CO) minute 31 July 1921.
120 Jellicoe papers, BL, Add.Mss.49045, Jellicoe to Long 2 May 1919, and 'Naval Mission to India and the Dominions, 1919–20', Jellicoe memorandum 3 February 1920.
121 CAB5/4 CID143–C 'Singapore: Development of as Naval Base', ODC memorandum 7 June 1921.
122 CAB2/3 CID 140th meeting 10 June 1921 and CAB5/4 CID144–C 'Strategic Situation in the Event of the Anglo-Japanese Alliance Being Determined', CID memorandum 17 June 1921.

## 4 'A Cubist Picture: The Soviet Menace in China, 1918–27

1 A. Pantsov, *The Bolsheviks and the Chinese Revolution 1919–1927* (Richmond: Curzon, 2000), pp. 41–52.
2 FO228/3214 SIB report 24 January 1918.
3 FO371/3702 139969/139969/10 Jordan (Peking) to Curzon 22 August 1919 no.384.
4 FO228/2986 Jordan to Balfour 26 April 1919 no.173, FO371/3702 182048/139969/10 Jordan to Curzon 17 January 1920 no.26, and FO371/3550 F1845/175/10 Alston (Peking) to Curzon 4 June 1920.
5 FO228/3214 Lampson (Peking) minute 7 April 1920, and Fraser (Shanghai) to Lampson 17 April 1920. The last IB monthly summary was produced in October 1920.
6 A. Judd, *The Quest for C: Sir Mansfield Cumming and the Making of the British Secret Service* (London: HarperCollins, 1999), p. 423.
7 FO371/5341 F2551/1110/10 'Memorandum Respecting Bolshevism in the Far East', Denham (SIS Shanghai) report 7 April 1920.
8 Ibid, Lampson (FE Dept) 1 December 1920.
9 FO371/6602 F4310/34/10 'Bolshevism and Chinese Communism and Anarchism in the Far East', Denham report undated [August 1921?].

10 FO228/3092 Dumbell (IO) to FO 18 March 1922.
11 Fisher papers, CAB127/356 'Secret Service Expenditure', WO memorandum 1 June 1921, and Committee on Secret Service 3rd meeting 27 March 1922. On Denham's pay, see FO228/3140 Macleay (Peking) minute 24 February 1923.
12 FO228/3092 Alston to Curzon 8 June 1922 tel.197, and Denham to Alston 27 June 1922, and FO228/3140 Alston to Curzon 10 July 1922 no. 404.
13 FO371/8040 F3215/2646/10 Clive (Peking) to Wellesley (FO) 23 August 1922.
14 FO228/3140 Jamieson (Canton) to Denham 2 August 1922.
15 FO228/3140 Clive to Wellesley 23 August 1922.
16 FO228/3140 Macleay minute 24 February 1923.
17 CO537/753 Morton (SIS) to Beckett (CO) 31 March 1922 no.CX7823, and CO273/516 Boyle (SIS) to Sinclair (CO) 19 June 1922 no.CX10.460/Prod. Boyle's presence in Peking is noted in FO371/8219 N8835/8835/38 Alston to Curzon 25 September 1922 tel.292.
18 FO371/9204 F2122/93/10 Barton (Shanghai) to Macleay 5 April 1923.
19 FO369/1292 2630/2630/250 Wellesley to Civil Service Commission 17 January 1919.
20 T162/613 E6279/2 Wright (T) minute 1 July 1929.
21 FO371/3701 128747/124334/10 Jordan to Curzon 26 July 1919 no.352.
22 CO323/837 Cubitt (WO) to CO 28 February 1920 and IOLR IOR.POS.8955 *Deputation of Mr. G.C. Denham ... for Secret Service Work in Ireland*, HDA, August 1920 nos 382–91.
23 CO129/474 Stubbs (HK) to CO 11 March 1922, and CO537/753 Beckett minute 5 April 1922.
24 CO537/757 WO to CO 30 August 1923.
25 CO129/497 Clutterbuck (CO) minute 6 July 1926.
26 Drage papers, IWM, reel 2, vol. 3, diary 15 October 1923.
27 See for example FO228/3211 Teichman (Peking) minute 26 October 1923.
28 WO106/5258 'Instructions for Colonel Blaker', Charles (DMOI) note 24 May 1927.
29 FO371/9207 F2974/211/10 SIS to Ashton-Gwatkin (FE Dept) 5 October 1923 CX11157 and FO371/10282 F1186/445/10 SIS report 14 April 1924.
30 FO371/9216 F902/650/10 'Joffe's Activities in Shanghai', SIS report 24 March 1923 no.1117.
31 FO371/9224 F1683/274/61 CX11717 'The Kuomintang', SIS report 1 June 1923 and F2770/274/61 CX11361 'The Split in the Kuomintang', SIS report 24 July 1923, and FO371/10279 F1074/387/10 CX11361 'Report on the KMT During 1923', SIS report 18 March 1924.
32 FO371/9227 F2296/154/23 CX9274 SIS report 27 July 1923 and F3662/154/23 Collier and Newton (FE Dept) minutes 28 and 29 December 1923.
33 FO371/10279 F2390/387/10 'The Kuomintang', Mills (FE Dept) note 5 August 1924, and FO228/3005 Teichman minute 27 September 1924.
34 FO371/10242 F4407/15/10 Macleay to Chamberlain 30 October 1924 no.670, and FO371/10915 F1253/1/10 Macleay to Chamberlain 18 February 1925 no.105.
35 FO228/3140 Blackburn (SIS Shanghai) undated memorandum in Pratt (Shanghai) to Macleay 4 December 1924 no.171, and CAB21/286 'Evidence of Bolshevik Activity in the Far East', Chamberlain memorandum 25 June 1925.
36 A. Waldron, *From War to Nationalism: China's Turning Point, 1924–1925* (Cambridge: Cambridge University Press, 1995), passim.

37 E.S.K. Fung, *The Diplomacy of Imperial Retreat: Britain's South China Policy, 1924–1931* (Oxford: Oxford University Press, 1991), pp. 40–54.
38 FO228/3092 Steptoe (SIS Peking) minute 16 October 1925.
39 FO371/10942 F2191/194/10 Palareit (Peking) to Chamberlain 11 June 1925 tel.119, and F2306/194/10 'C' to Bland (FO) 15 June 1925 C/622, and FO371/10944 F2812/194/10 F2812/194/10 Palareit to Chamberlain 2 July 1925 tel.192.
40 CAB4/13 CID617-B (revised) 'Situation in China', COS memorandum 25 June 1925.
41 FO228/3011 Vereker (Peking) minute 30 April 1925, and FO228/3456 Steward (MA Peking) to Palareit 15 September 1925 no.XXIV.
42 The first BJ based on Steptoe's work is HW12/85 BJ.023649 Moscow to Peking 1 June circulated 26 August 1926.
43 FO228/3456 Steptoe minute 28 October 1925, and CAB4/15 CID724-B 'The Communist Movement: Review of the Period November 1925–July 1926', Hankey note 11 October 1926.
44 CAB4/14 CID655-B 'The Extension of Soviet Influence in Asia', Worthington-Evans memorandum 15 December 1925.
45 AIR5/485 EU4 'Situation in China With Special Reference to Russian Activities', Smith (IO) memorandum 23 July 1926.
46 FO371/11775 N32/3/38 Strang (FE Dept) minute 13 January 1926. See also on the IDCEU memorandum, FO371/11678 F3448/307/10 Dobinson (FE Dept) minute 23 August 1926.
47 FO371/9181 F1424/12/10 Macleay to Curzon 24 March 1923 no.189, FO371/11687 F1266/1266/10 Macleay to Chamberlain 5 February 1926 no.97, and FO371/11680 F2756/394/10 Wagstaff (MI2c) to Mounsey (FE Dept) 6 July 1926.
48 FO371/11687 F2615/1266/10 Steward to Macleay 26 April 1926 no.X, and FO228/3155 Steward to Macleay 21 July 1926 no.XVI.
49 Lampson papers, MECSA, diary 22 August 1928.
50 WO32/5351 GOC HK to WO 3 October 1925.
51 For the NRA, see D. Jordan, *The Northern Expedition: China's National Revolution of 1926–28* (Honolulu: Hawaii University Press, 1976), pp. 287–95.
52 WO106/5267 Roberts (HK) to MI2c 9 July 1926.
53 FO371/10955 F2193/2193/10 Palareit to Chamberlain 6 April 1925 no.228, and FO371/11624 F1510/1/10 Steward to Macleay 3 February 1926 no.XI.
54 FO228/3154 Steward minute 24 May 1926, and FO228/3019 Steward to O'Malley (Peking) 19 November 1926 no.XXIII.
55 WO106/5392 MI2c questionnaire April 1924.
56 WO106/5392 Menzies (SIS) to Wagstaff (MI2c) 9 April 1926, and Wagstaff minute 22 April 1926.
57 WO106/5258 Harrison (MI2c) note February 1928.
58 FO228/3212 *China Command Intelligence Diary, June 1926*, IG533/16. See also FO228/3155 Brenan (Canton) to Macleay 26 July 1926 no.97, and FO228/3018 Vereker minute 19 September 1926.
59 FO371/11658 F2625/10/10 Mounsey minute 29 June 1926, F3457/10/10 Stark Toller (FE Dept) and Ashton-Gwatkin minutes 24 August 1926, and WO106/5393 'Extracts From General Staff Appreciations of the Situation in China 1926/1927', WO note undated [1928?].
60 FO371/11680 F2756/394/10 Wagstaff to Mounsey (FE Dept) 6 July 1926.

61 WO106/5393 'Collection of Military Intelligence in China Prior to Despatch of Shanghai Defence Force, 1927', WO memorandum undated [1928?].
62 WO106/5255 Steward to Harrison 30 July 1926, and Wagstaff minute 23 September 1926.
63 FO228/3018 Goffe (Hankow) to Macleay 30 August 1926 no.110, and FO228/3019 Williams (Canton–Hankow Railway) to Hubbard 23 September 1926.
64 FO228/3212 *China Command Intelligence Diary September 1926* and *China Command Intelligence Diary November 1926*.
65 FO228/3152 O'Malley (Peking) to Strang 10 February 1926.
66 Clementi papers, RHL, box 2, file 1, Brenan to Clementi (HK) 21 April 1926.
67 Clementi papers, RHL, box 2, file 2, Hayley Bell to Clementi 31 May 1926.
68 FO228/3092 Steptoe minute 16 October 1925.
69 CO129/492 Korestky to King (DCI, HK) 16 January 1926.
70 O'Malley papers, St Antony's College, Oxford, file 6, O'Malley to Strang 22 February 1926.
71 CO129/497 Smith (Officer on Special Duty) to Petrie (DCI India) 22 February 1926.
72 CO129/497 CO to FO 16 July 1926, and Clementi papers, RHL, box 4, file 4, Clementi to Brenan 9 December 1926.
73 See Fung, op. cit., pp. 90–6.
74 FO371/11697 F4934/4934/10 Worthington-Evans to Chamberlain 18 November 1926, and Pratt (FE Dept) minute 19 November 1926.
75 CAB23/53 61(26) Cabinet meeting 1 December 1926.
76 Fung, op. cit., pp. 99–104.
77 FO371/11662 F5314/10/10 Widdows (WO) FO 6 December 1926, and FO371/11775 N1851/3/38 'Bolshevik Hostility in China', N Dept memorandum 9 December 1926.
78 FO371/11706 F5467/648/23 Mounsey (FE Dept) to Tilley (Tokyo) 13 December 1926 no.420.
79 WO32/2521 Widdows to FO 17 December 1926.
80 FO371/11662 F5334/10/10 Charles (DMOI) to Bland 27 November 1926, and F5314/10/10 Widdows to FO 6 December 1926.
81 FO371/11662 F5334/10/10 Ashton Gwatkin minute 30 November 1926, and F5314/10/10 Mounsey to WO 21 December 1926.
82 On Hankow see FO228/3157 Vereker undated minute [January 1927]. For Shanghai see ADM1/8712/154 Admiralty to C-in-C China 5 January 1927.
83 See, for example, Chamberlain papers, FO800/260, Joynston-Hicks to Chamberlain 7 January 1927.
84 Chamberlain papers, FO800/260, Hirtzel (PUS IO) to Chamberlain 17 January 1927. For the Cabinet decision see CAB23/54 1(27) Cabinet meeting 17 January 1927.
85 FO371/12438 F618/87/10 Chamberlain to Lampson (Peking) 22 January 1927 tel.63, and FO371/12466 F823/823/10 Chamberlain to Barton 27 January 1927 tel.15.
86 CAB23/54 9(27) Cabinet meeting 10 February 1927, and FO371/12438 F1737/97/10 WO to Duncan (GOC Shaforce) 22 February 1927 tel.93158.
87 WO106/5258 'Security Instructions for Chief Military Intelligence Officer, China, April 1927', Holt-Wilson (MI5) note 29 April 1927.
88 Clementi papers, RHL, box 6, file 3, CO to Clementi 24 February 1927.
89 HW12/90 BJ.025230 Hankow to Tokyo 13 January circulated 24 January 1927.

90 FO371/12401 F1282/2/10 Lampson to Chamberlain 9 February 1927 tel.270, FO228/3451 Steptoe minute 9 February 1927, FO371/12401 F1416/2/10 Tilley to Chamberlain 14 February 1927 tel.86, and Pratt (FE Dept) minute 14 February 1927.
91 CAB4/16 CID782-B 'Soviet Activities in Central and Eastern Asia', Worthington-Evans memorandum 15 March 1927. For estimates of Chiang's chances see FO371/12439 F2891/87/10 Lampson to Chamberlain 28 March 1927 tel.544, FO228/3161 Connor Greene (Peking) minute 31 March 1927, and FO228/3212 *China Command Intelligence Diary March 1927*.
92 FO228/3405 Steptoe minute undated [2 February 1927?], and FO371/12403 F2666/2/10 Strang minute 25 March 1927.
93 FO228/3021 Barton (Shanghai) to Lampson 29 March 1927 tel.131, and Lampson to Barton 4 April 1927 tel.418.
94 This information is referred to in WO191/2 Shaforce to WO 13 April 1927 D.5138.
95 Chartwell papers, CCC, CHAR2/151 Sinclair to Churchill 2 April 1927.
96 FO371/12500 F4647/3241/10 Security Dept minute June 1959.
97 FO228/3577 Connor Greene minute 12 June 1927.
98 FO371/12483 F6319/1530/10 Ashton-Gwatkin minute 21 July 1927.
99 Milner papers, Bodleian Library Oxford, File 387, Guillemard (Singapore) to Thornton (CO) 3 June 1920, and FO395/327 P876/68/150 Guillemard to Milner 20 June 1920.
100 CO537/904 Guillemard to Churchill 18 October 1921. On Lee-Warner and the SIS, see FO369/1695 K6/6/229 Bland minute 19 February 1921.
101 CO537/907 Guillemard to Devonshire 6 December 1922, Lee-Warner (SIS Singapore) to SIS 13 December 1922, and Devonshire to Guillemard 24 February 1923. On Denham see CO273/524 Guillemard to Devonshire 15 December 1922 and Beckett minute 23 January 1923.
102 CO273/526 Guillemard to Thomas 21 October 1924, and CO537/925 MBPI report 30 September 1924, no.21.
103 CO537/934 MBPI report 1 July 1925 no.31, and FO371/11698 F82/82/61 Crosby (Batavia) to Chamberlain 28 November 1925 no.150.
104 FO371/11010 N1161/29/38 Wellesley minute 27 February 1925, and F0371/11084 W5157/156/29 Fock (Governor NEI) to Irwin (Viceroy India) 6 March 1925.
105 IOLR L/PJ/12/249 Ferard (PJ Dept) to FO 1 December 1926.
106 FO371/12696 W4489/171/29 Crosby to Chamberlain 14 April 1927 no.47.
107 CO273/535/11 MBPI April and May 1927 nos 48 and 49.
108 Jordan, op. cit., pp. 287–95.
109 Irwin papers, IOLR, Mss.Eur.C152/3 Birkenhead to Irwin 27 January 1927.
110 CAB2/5 CID 229th meeting 14 July 1927.

## 5 Dealing with the Comintern Threat, 1927–31

1 WO106/5258 'The Necessity for a Permanent Intelligence Bureau in the Far East', [undated, 1927] and 'Instructions for Colonel Blaker', Charles (DMOI) note 24 May 1927.
2 WO106/5258 'Instructions for Colonel Blaker', Charles note 24 May 1927, and 'Security Instructions for Chief Military Intelligence Officer, China, April 1927', Holt-Wilson (MI5) 29 April 1927.

3 FO371/12439 F4549/87/10 Harrison (MI2c) to Ashton-Gwatkin (FE Dept) 11 May 1927, and FO371/12507 F5316/5315/10 Ashton-Gwatkin minute undated [June 1927].
4 FO371/12439 F4549/87/10 Lampson (Shanghai) to Chamberlain 26 May 1927 tel.185, and FO371/12507 F5316/5315/10 Ashton-Gwatkin minute undated [June 1927].
5 J. Fisher, 'The Interdepartmental Committee on Eastern Unrest and British Responses to Bolshevik and Other Intrigues Against the Empire During the 1920s', *Journal of Asian History*, 34/1 (2000), pp. 26–31.
6 FO371/12511 F6764/6764/10 Strang (FE Dept) minute 17 August 1927, and Bland (FO) minute 13 January 1928.
7 FO371/12501 F5518/3241/10 Lampson (Peking) to Chamberlain 2 May 1927 no. 453.
8 FO371/12502 F9497/3241/10 Lampson to Chamberlain 28 October 1927 no.1187.
9 FO371/12502 F9497/3241/10 Ashton-Gwatkin minute 5 January 1928.
10 FO371/12501 F6820/3241/10 Lampson to Chamberlain 17 June 1927 no. 629.
11 WO191/7 Intelligence Summary no.45 Heywood (FEIB) 23 December 1927.
12 WO106/5809 Special Far Eastern Intelligence Summary (SFEIS) 2 January 1928 no.51.
13 WO106/6090 SFEIS 17 January 1928 no.53.
14 WO106/5394 'Principal Military and Aerial Intelligence Requirements in the Far East', MI2c memorandum February 1928.
15 WO106/6090 CX[delete] 'Soviet Activities in China: Possible Return of Borodin', SIS report 8 March 1928, and CX[delete] 'Borodin's Movements', SIS report 11 June 1928.
16 FO228/3903 Grant Jones (Harbin) to Lampson 15 September 1928 no.101 and Steptoe (SIS Peking) minute 21 September 1928, and Tours (Mukden) to Lampson 2 November 1928 no.74, and Steptoe minute 6 November 1928.
17 FO228/3776 Steptoe draft despatch undated [November 1928], and FO371/13931 F708/302/10 Acheson (FP Dept) to IO 16 January 1929 no.D.O.F.7–x/29.
18 Lampson papers, MECSA, diary 22 January 1929.
19 WO106/6090 SFEIS 9 April 1929 no.88.
20 FO228/3968 Clementi (HK) to Amery 5 April 1929, and FO371/13889 F2814/3/10 Toller (FE Dept) minute 6 June 1929.
21 WO208/181 SFEIS 4 February 1929 no.85.
22 FO371/13243 F5518/154/61 MBPI August 1928 no.63.
23 FO371/12536 F5572/2987/40 Waterlow (Bangkok) to Chamberlain 10 May 1927, and F9572/2987/40 Stafford (Passport Office) minute 16 December 1927.
24 CO273/564/10 Onraet (DCI Singapore) to Fairburn (IGP Singapore) 1 April 1930, and CO273/561/15 'The Kuomintang and Opposed Societies in Malaya July to September 1930', Jordan (Chinese Secretariat FMS) 13 September 1930.
25 WO106/5393 'Report on Military Intelligence in the Far East with Proposals for the Organization of a Far Eastern Intelligence Bureau', Blaker report 16 January 1928.
26 WO106/5393 Piggott (MI2) note 3 April 1928, and Goldsmith (MI1b) note 5 April 1928.
27 WO106/5258 Harrison note February 1928.
28 WO106/5393 Piggott note 3 April 1928, and Goldsmith note 5 April 1928.
29 WO106/5393 Inter-service meeting minutes 17 April 1928.
30 WO106/5393 Inter-Departmental meeting minutes 17 July 1928.

31 FO371/13207 F7072/121/10 Creedy (WO) to Fisher (PUS T) 30 November 1928, and WO106/5255 'Instructions for Colonel Steward' [undated, March 1929]
32 WO106/5265 ADOI to Charles 9 August 1929.
33 WO106/5267 Toller to Rawson (MI2c) 28 May 1929.
34 FO371/13925 F3258/156/10 WO to FO 29 June 1929.
35 FO371/13207 F7072/121/10 Fisher to Tyrrell (PUS FO) 24 December 1928 and Mounsey to Lampson 30 January 1929.
36 FO371/13925 F3258/156/10 Toller minute 2 July 1929.
37 FO371/13925 F3258/156/10 Henderson to Lampson 17 August 1929, and F4363/156/10 Lampson to Henderson 26 August 1929 tel.694, and WO106/5267 Mounsey to Piggott 22 August 1929, and Mounsey/Piggott conversation 3 September 1929.
38 WO106/5267 unattributed and undated note [August 1929].
39 WO106/5267 'The Future of the China Intelligence Bureau', MI2c memorandum 13 September 1929.
40 WO106/5267 Miles note 19 February 1930, and Goldsmith to Steward (CIB) 20 February 1930.
41 WO106/5265 Steward (CIB) to Rawson 1 June 1929.
42 WO106/5265 Steward to WO 30 July 1930 no.D.O.7, and Steward to GOC China 30 August 1929.
43 Lampson papers, MECSA, diary 7 June 1928.
44 FO369/2189 K4490/1171/210 Kelsey (Consular Dept, FO) minute 25 April 1931
45 FO228/3738 Garstin (Shanghai) to Lampson 6 December 1928.
46 FO228/3729 Ferard to FO 2 January 1929, and Garstin to Lampson 13 November 1929 tel.280.
47 FO369/2189 K4490/1171/210 Kelsey minute 22 July 1931.
48 FO369/2074 K6502/1811/210 Lampson to Chamberlain 3 May 1929 no.668.
49 FO369/2189 K4490/1171/210 Kelsey minute undated [May 1931].
50 WO32/5628 Passfield to Clementi (Singapore) 3 June 1930, GSO3 Malaya to MI2c 10 July 1930, and GSO3 Malaya to MI2c 23 April 1931.
51 FO371/13925 F5743/156/10 Wellesley minute 1 November 1929.
52 FO228/4307 *Hong Kong Intelligence Summary July 1930*, and FO371/14741 F5764/2956/10 Lampson to Henderson 3 August 1930 no.1115.
53 FO371/15473 F6046/69/10 Lampson to Reading 27 August 1931 no.1262.
54 FO371/15475 F972/88/10 Russell Brown (Hankow) to Lampson 17 December 1930 no.130, and FO371/15476 F4426/88/10 Martin (Foochow) to Lampson 19 June 1931 no.41.
55 FO676/77 Steptoe (SIS Shanghai) memorandum 15 February 1931.
56 WO208/181 SFEIS 9 February 1931 no.112.
57 FO371/15484 F2534/278/10 Cambon/Wellesley conversation 5 May 1931.
58 WO106/5764 China Intelligence Summary December 1930 no.20.
59 CO273/564/10 Clementi to Passfield 5 September 1930.
60 FO371/13932 F3638/328/10 MI2c weekly summary 18 July 1929.
61 FO228/4344 Badham-Thornhill (MA Peking) to Lampson 14 January 1930 no.1.
62 FO371/15488 F5396/1006/10 *WO Monthly Intelligence Summary September 1931*.
63 FO371/15488 F3055/1006/10 Mackillop (FE Dept) minute 5 June 1931.
64 WO106/5814 'Secret History of the Case of Joseph Ducroux', Onraet report 25 June 1931. See also F. Wakeman, *Policing Shanghai, 1927–1937* (Berkeley: University of California Press, 1995), pp. 147–51.
65 Field papers, IWM, memoirs 'That's the Way It Was', pp. 37–41.

66 WO106/5814 'Secret History of the Case of Joseph Ducroux', Onraet report 25 June 1931.
67 KV4/1 'The Security Service: Its Problems and Organizational Adjustments', Curry (MI5) report March 1946.
68 WO106/5815 SFEIS 16 December 1931 no.119.
69 WO208/506A Major (MI2c) to MI1c 18 August 1931.

## 6 From 'Weak Power' to Potential Enemy: Japan, 1921–33

1 HW3/32 Denniston (GCCS) memorandum 31 October 1944.
2 FO371/10127 E3745/76/34 Ashton-Gwatkin (FE Dept) minute 5 May 1924, and HW12/78 BJ.022281 Constantinople to Tokyo 18 January circulated 29 January 1926.
3 See, for example, HW12/34 BJ.010314 Tokyo to Rome 5 May circulated 26 May 1922, and HW12/84 Tokyo to Constantinople 5 July circulated 8 July 1926.
4 HW12/31 BJ.009840 Berlin to Kabul (Afghan) 3 February circulated 8 February 1922, HW12/72 BJ.020860 Tokyo to London 27 June circulated 9 July 1925, and HW12/105 BJ.030581 London to Tokyo 4 April circulated 18 April 1928.
5 HW12/58 BJ.016633 Constantinople to Tokyo 16 May circulated 21 May 1924.
6 HW12/32 BJ.009674 Tokyo to London 25 February circulated 1 March 1922.
7 IOLR L/PJ/12/163 Palareit (Tokyo) to FP Department India 17 June 1923.
8 FO371/11701 F3272/3162/61 Tilley (Tokyo) to Chamberlain 11 August 1926 tel.98.
9 CO273/534/20 MBPI report July 1926 no.40.
10 CO537/933 MBPI report, May 1925 no.30, and CAB53/12 COS-50 'Japanese Interests in Malaya with Specific Regard to Singapore', Milne (CIGS) memorandum 29 September 1926.
11 WO106/6095 'The Japanese Intelligence System', MI2c draft memorandum 23 June 1928.
12 HW12/43 BJ.012632 IJN Tokyo to JNA Berlin 2 February circulated 20 February 1923, WO106/5392 Bacon (MI5B) note 30 July 1926.
13 See, for example, my treatment of the case of Squadron Leader Frederick Rutland in 'Intelligence, Diplomacy and the Japanese Threat to British Interests, 1914–41', *Intelligence and National Security*, 17 (2002) 87–102.
14 FO371/6680 F201/201/23 Woodroffe (MA Tokyo) to Eliot (Tokyo) 10 December 1920 no.MA172, FO371/6681 F4646/201/23 Kennedy (MI2c) to Phipps (FO) 12 January 1922, and M. Kennedy, *The Military Side of Japanese Life* (London: Constable, 1924), pp. 33–6.
15 On the IJA reforms see L.A. Humphreys, *The Way of the Heavenly Sword: The Japanese Army in the 1920s* (Stanford: Stanford University Press, 1995), pp. 77–107.
16 FO262/1697 Hill to Tilley 6 July 1928 no.23, and AIR5/755 Japan: Intelligence Summary no.11 MI2c report 31 March 1927.
17 WO188/798 *WO Monthly Intelligence Summary October 1926*, and CX10216/17433 'Japan: Study of Status of Chemical Warfare in the Japanese Army', SIS report 16 June 1927.
18 FO371/12159 F2622/208/23 Hill (MA Tokyo) to Tilley 23 February 1927 no.7.
19 FO371/11704 F2472/141/23 Hill to Tilley 21 May 1926 no.14.
20 FO371/6681 F4646/201/23 Marsden (MA Tokyo) to Eliot 27 October 1921 no.MA159, and WO106/5494 Hill to Dormer (Tokyo) 29 March 1928 no.9.

21 FO371/9229 F3214/155/23 Piggott (MA Tokyo) to Palareit 17 September 1923 no.XLII, and FO371/10311 Piggott to Palareit 19 February 1924 no.XIV.
22 IOLR L/MIL/17/20/23 *Handbook of the Japanese Army, 1928*, WO publication 25 June 1928.
23 See also J. Ferris, '"Worthy of Some Better Enemy?" The British Estimate of the Imperial Japanese Army 1919–41 and the Fall of Singapore', *Canadian Journal of History*, 28 (1993), 233–4.
24 FO262/1566 Colvin (NA Tokyo) to Eliot 19 May 1922 no.12.
25 FO262/1619 Royle (NA Tokyo) to Eliot 11 December 1924 no.16.
26 FO371/9233 F1325/1325/23 Eliot to Curzon 26 March 1923 no.188, and FO371/10309 F1016/268/23 Colvin to Palareit 18 February 1924 no.3.
27 FO371/12523 F2623/1797/23 Royle to Tilley 23 February 1927 no.1. See also P. Charrier, 'The Evolution of a Stereotype: The Royal Navy and the Japanese "Martial Type", 1900–1945', *War and Society*, 19 (2001), 33.
28 FO371/8051 F2109/2109/23 Marriot (NA Tokyo) to Eliot 9 January 1922 no.1, and FO371/8050 F1065/1065/23 Eliot to Curzon 6 February 1922 no.69. See also J. Ferris, 'A British "Unofficial" Aviation Mission and Japanese Naval Developments, 1919–1929', *Journal of Strategic Studies*, 5 (1982), 416–39.
29 AIR5/358 'Japan & Japanese Aviation', Vaughan-Fowler memorandum February 1924.
30 AIR5/754 Robinson to Domvile (DNI) 12 December 1927.
31 AIR5/756 Hill to Tilley 27 May 1926 no.16, and Hill to Tilley 8 August 1927 no.28.
32 AIR5/755 Japan: Intelligence Summary no.8 MI2 report 30 November 1926.
33 FO371/13250 F6054/3771/23 Hill to Dormer 26 September 1928 no.29, and Ashton-Gwatkin minute 9 November 1928.
34 FO371/12519 F2069/208/23 Johnstone (FE Dept) minute 9 March 1927.
35 FO371/12523 F2623/1797/23 Royle to Tilley 23 February 1927 no.1.
36 AIR5/756 Hill to Tilley 27 May 1926 no.16. See also FO371/10962 F1457/172/23 Mullaly (IA LO) report 20 March 1925.
37 Charrier, op. cit., 28–32.
38 FO371/10961 F28/28/23 Eliot to Chamberlain 14 November 1924.
39 CAB4/17 CID-900B 'Imperial Defence Policy', COS memorandum 25 June 1928.
40 See J. Ferris, '"It is Our Business in the Navy to Command the Seas": The Last Decade of British Maritime Supremacy, 1919–1929', in K. Neilson and G. Kennedy (eds), *Far Flung Lines: Studies in Imperial Defence in Honour of Donald Mackenzie Schurman* (London: Frank Cass, 1997), pp. 136–40, and C.M. Bell, *The Royal Navy, Seapower and Strategy between the Wars* (Basingstoke: Macmillan, 2000), pp. 18–25.
41 CAB2/4 CID 198th meeting 30 March 1925, and CAB23/53 CM50(26) 3 August 1926.
42 CAB27/355 NP(27) 2nd meeting 18 November 1927.
43 T161/819 S.33566 Fisher (PUS T) 17 September 1928.
44 FO228/3143 Eliot to Palareit 2 July 1925 tel.51, and Garstin (Peking) minute 5 July 1925
45 WO106/5134 Harrison (MI2c) minute 29 July 1926.
46 WO106/5134 MI2c to Piggott (Tokyo) 6 August 1926.
47 See, for example, WO106/5134 'Soviet–Russian Relations with Feng', IJA memorandum 29 September 1926
48 WO106/129 'The Desirability, from a Military Point of View, of Reviving the Alliance With Japan', MO1a memorandum 1 February 1928.

49 WO106/5134 Beaumont-Nesbitt (DMOI) minute 29 March 1940.
50 CAB2/3 CID 168th meeting 14 December 1922.
51 FO371/10958 F4637/9/61 Flint (Admiralty) to WO 1 September 1925, and Cubitt (WO) to ODC Secretary 17 September 1925.
52 WO106/5392 'Principal Military and Aerial Intelligence Requirements Regarding the Far East', MI2 memorandum 11 June 1926, and WO106/5394 'Principal Military and Aerial Intelligence Requirements Regarding the Far East', MI2 memorandum February 1928.
53 Fisher papers, CAB127/371, 'Memorandum on Secret Service Funds', 'C' report 9 October 1935.
54 WO106/129 Piggott (MI2) note 9 February 1928.
55 FO371/11708 F5021/1991/23 Royle to Tilley 5 October 1926 no.11, and FO371/17158 F3835/820/23 Vivian (NA Tokyo) to Snow (Tokyo) 1 May 1933 no.4.
56 T162/278 E17439/1 Barstow (T) to AM 13 July 1920.
57 AIR2/302 420765 Webster (AM) to FO 25 April 1923, and Newton (FE Dept) to Webster 12 May 1923.
58 AIR2/302 525717 Carmichael (AID) to DCAS 20 October 1926, T162/278 E17439/1 Slater (AM) to Fraser (Treasury) 3 November 1926, and Fraser to Slater 8 November 1926, and AIR2/302 525717 Newall (DCAS) minute 16 February 1929.
59 FO262/1716 WO to FO 6 June 1929.
60 T162/973 E.18739 Wright (T) minute 21 March 1934.
61 On the Colonial Office officials see CO273/521 James (OAG Singapore) to Devonshire 25 January 1923 no.55. For the Australian contingent see the files NAA A981/4 JAP28 on the army and NAA MP472/1 5/18/8652 on the RAN.
62 IOLR L/MIL/7/7329 Piggott (MA Tokyo) to CGS India 8 March 1922 no.LO3/10.
63 T162/278 E.17439/1 WO to Treasury 28 May 1925.
64 T162/972 E.17426/1 Anderson (Admiralty) to Treasury 29 November 1919, and Barstow (T) to Anderson 31 December 1919.
65 ADM116/2351 Walker (Admiralty) to Treasury 3 November 1925.
66 T162/972 E17426/2 Perry (T) to Admiralty 25 September 1926.
67 ADM116/2351 Admiralty to Treasury 14 November 1927.
68 HW3/1 'GC+CS (Naval Section) 1919–1941', Clarke notes undated.
69 ADM116/6324 Walker to C-in-C China 26 June 1925. On Nave's early career see M. Smith, *The Emperor's Codes: Bletchley Park and the Breaking of Japan's Secret Ciphers* (London: Bantam Press, 2000), pp. 21–7.
70 ADM116/6320 Flint (Admiralty) to C-in-C China 13 January 1926.
71 ADM116/6320 'WT Procedure "Y"', C-in-C China memorandum 1 July 1926.
72 ADM116/6320 Walker to C-in-Cs North Atlantic and West Indies 16 December 1926.
73 ADM178/63 Fisher (DNI) report 4 December 1926.
74 ADM1/8714/173 Fisher minute 10 November 1926.
75 ADM178/63 Fisher report 4 December 1926, and 'C' to DNI 21 December 1926 C/2306, and ADM1/8717/213 Hotham (DNI) 26 January 1927.
76 Nave memoirs, p. 219.
77 HW3/1 'Naval Section, 1928', Clarke (GCCS) report undated, and HW3/1 'Naval section, 1929' Clarke report 27 February 1930.
78 FO371/13168 F2892/7/10 Dormer to Cushendun 6 June 1928 tel.129.
79 WO106/5750 'The Death of Chang Tso-lin', MI2c note 19 October 1928, and FO371/13889 F2022/3/10 Tilley to Chamberlain 23 March 1929 no.113, and Wellesley minute 29 April 1929.

80 WO106/5493 Dawnay memorandum 22 October 1931.
81 FO371/15445 F757/10/10 Wellesley to Lampson (Peking) and Snow 28 January 1931.
82 FO371/15488 F4706/1391/10 Badham-Thornhill (MA Peking) to Lampson 30 June 1931 no.XIV.
83 FO371/15446 F4250/10/10 Woolcombe (SIS) to Mackillop (FE Dept) 27 July 1931 no.CX1124, Mackillop to Woolcombe 29 July 1931, and Woolcombe to Mackillop 14 August 1931.
84 WO208/4942 Intelligence Shanghai to GOC Hong Kong 8 September 1931. See also WO106/5492 Dawnay (MI2) to Bartholomew (DMOI) 10 September 1931, which refers to evidence in the Special Far Eastern Intelligence Summary of 31 August [not found].
85 WO106/5492 Bartholomew minute 22 September 1931, and FO371/15488 F5396/1006/10 *WO Monthly Intelligence Summary September 1931*.
86 FO371/15489 F5118/1391/10 Lampson to Reading 21 September 1931 tel.375. See also Lampson papers, MECSA, diary 19 September 1931.
87 FO371/15489 F5177/1391/10 Badham-Thornhill to WO 22 September 1931 tel.107, and ADM125/69 Kelly (C-in-C China) to Admiralty 1 October 1931 no.7.
88 WO106/5493 Dawnay memorandum 22 October 1931.
89 FO371/15490 F5410/1391/10 Charles (FE Dept) minute 7 October 1931, and FO371/15491 F5502/1391/10 Orde (FE Dept) minute 9 October 1931.
90 HW12/149 BJ.044941 Tokyo to Paris 13 November circulated 18 November 1931.
91 HW12/150 BJ.045342 Peking to Tokyo 5 December circulated 17 December 1931. See also WO106/5562 SFEIS 26 January 1932 no.120.
92 See C. Thorne, *The Limits of Foreign Policy: The West, the League and the Far Eastern Crisis of 1931–1933* (London: Hamish Hamilton, 1972), pp. 204–72, and I.H. Nish, *Japan's Struggle with Internationalism: Japan, China and the League of Nations, 1931–33* (London: Kegan Paul, 1993), pp. 90–106.
93 CAB27/482 CJC(32) 5th meeting 8 March 1932.
94 Pollard papers, IWM, 'Intelligence Summary', CIB report 9 February 1932, and Godfrey papers, IWM, memoirs vol.III, diary 9 February 1932.
95 Lampson papers, MECSA, diary 22 February and 5 March 1932.
96 ADM1/24708 WO note 30 May 1932, and CAB56/2 JIC-7 'Far Eastern Appreciation', DDMOI report undated [August 1936].
97 CAB53/22 COS-295 'Imperial Defence Policy', COS memorandum 23 February 1932.
98 CAB23/70 19(32) 23 March 1932.
99 CAB53/22 COS-295 'Imperial Defence Policy', COS memorandum 23 February 1932.
100 WO208/506A MI2c to MI1c 4 Feb. 1932.
101 WO106/5397 Temperler (DDMOI) to Bartholomew 23 September 1932.
102 Penney papers, LHCMA, 2/2, 'The Situation in and around the International Settlement of Shanghai', Foreign Garrison Commanders memorandum 9 March 1932, and FO371/16212 F7392/310/10 Ingram (Peking) to Simon 17 August 1932 no.1060.
103 HW12/165 BJ.051682 Tokyo to Peking 9 March circulated 11 March 1933, and BJ.051721 Tokyo to Peking 10 March circulated 14 March 1933.
104 WO106/5569 CX11737/45 'Correspondence Between Chiang Kai-shek and Ho Ying-chin', SIS report 21 April 1933, and CX11737/55 'Sino-Japanese Relations', SIS report 15 May 1933.

105 WO106/5495 'The Situation at the End of May 1932; the Present Policy and Military Position of Japan in Relation Thereto; and the Likelihood of Hostilities Developing Between Japan and the USSR', Miles (MI2c) 8 June 1932.
106 FO371/17152 F154/154/23 Lindley (Tokyo) to Simon 9 December 1932 tel.660.
107 ADM116/3116 Dickens minute 10 March 1933. See also FO371/17149 F747/11/23 Wellesley minute 7 February 1933, and F2615/11/23 Lindley to Simon 24 March 1933.
108 FO371/17149 F762/11/23 James (MA Tokyo) to Lindley 19 January 1933 no.1.
109 FO371/17149 F747/11/23 Lindley to Simon 5 January 1933 no.8.
110 CAB47/4 ATB-95 'Japan: Purchase of War Stores and Raw Materials', FCI Committee report 1 March 1933.
111 CAB47/4 ATB-98 'Japan: Recent Reports on the Development of Industry', IIC report 19 October 1933.
112 CAB53/4 COS 107th meeting 28 February 1933 and 108th meeting 27 March 1933, and CAB53/23 COS-305 'The Situation in the Far East', COS report 31 March 1933.
113 WO106/5594 Grant Taylor (Malaya Command) to Miles 8 March 1933 DO.83.
114 FO371/17166 F2302/1652/23 Lindley to Simon 7 March 1933 no.144.
115 IOLR L/PJ/12/163 DIB Weekly Report 31 August 1933 no.34.
116 ADM116/3116 CX10508/99 'Japanese Activities in the South Seas', SIS report 12 September 1933, and DCNS minute 27 September 1933. For Hatta's activities, see FO371/14707 W9005/663/29 Fitzmaurice (Batavia) to Simon 27 June 1933 no.77.
117 CAB4/22 CID1113-B 'Annual Review of Imperial Defence', COS 12 October 1933, and WO106/5392 'Order of Priority of MI2 Countries from S.S. Point of View', MI2c note undated [1933].

## 7 'The Situation in the Far East Has Changed Completely', 1933–37

1 A. Trotter, *Britain and East Asia, 1933–1937* (Cambridge: Cambridge University Press, 1975), I.H. Nish, 'Japan in Britain's View of the International System', in I.H. Nish (ed.), *Anglo-Japanese Alienation, 1919–1952* (Cambridge: Cambridge University Press, 1982), and A. Best, 'The Road to Anglo-Japanese Confrontation, 1931–41', in I. Nish and Y. Kibata (eds), *The History of Anglo-Japanese Relations: The Political and Diplomatic Dimension, Vol.2 1931–2000* (Basingstoke: Macmillan, 2000).
2 See, for example, in Japanese, C. Hosoya, '1934-nen no Nichi-Ei fukashin kyotei mondai, [The Problem in 1934 of the Anglo-Japanese Non-Aggression Pact], *Kokusai Seiji* [International Politics], 58 (1977), 69–85, Y. Kibata, 'Risu-Rosu shisetsudan to Ei-Chu kankei' [The Leith-Ross Mission and Anglo-Chinese Relations] in Y. Nozawa (ed.), *Chukogu no heisei kaikaku to kokusai kankei* [The Chinese Currency Reform and International Relations], (Tokyo: Tokyo University Press, 1981), and idem, 'Igirisu teikoku no henyo to higashi Ajia' [East Asia and the Changing Nature of the British Empire], in S. Akita and N. Kagotani (eds), *1930-nendai Ajia kokusai chitujo* [The International Order of Asia in the 1930s] (Hiroshima: Keisui-sha, 2001), pp. 261–82. For English language essays, see C. Hosoya, 'Britain and the US in Japan's View of the International System, 1919–37' in I.H. Nish (ed.), *Anglo-Japanese Alienation, 1919–1952* (Cambridge: Cambridge University Press, 1982), and Y. Kibata,

'Anglo-Japanese Relations from the Manchurian Incident to Pearl Harbor: Missed Opportunities?', in I.H. Nish and Y. Kibata (eds), *The History of Anglo-Japanese Relations: The Political and Diplomatic Dimension,* Vol.2: *1931–2000* (Basingstoke: Macmillan, 2000). A useful English-language review of the Japanese arguments can be found in S. Akita, 'British Informal Empire in East Asia, 1880–1939: A Japanese Perspective', in R.E. Dumett (ed.), *Gentlemanly Capitalism and British Imperialism: The New Debate on Empire* (Longman, London, 1999).

3 F.S.G. Piggott, *Broken Thread* (Aldershot: Gale & Polden, 1950), p. 250.

4 IOLR L/MIL/7/7328 James (MA Tokyo) to WO 9 November 1932.

5 AIR2/871 Harries (AID) minute 17 September 1932, and Treasury to AM 20 June 1933.

6 AIR2/302 DCAS minute 9 February 1934.

7 AIR2/302 Treasury to AM 22 May 1934, and FO371/18192 F4051/1780/23 Calder (AM) to Norton (FO) 3 July 1934.

8 FO371/19348 F5352/28/23 Chappell (AA Tokyo) to Clive (Tokyo) 17 July 1935 no.15, and F5633/28/23 Clive to Hoare 30 August 1935 tel.229.

9 WO287/231 *WO Monthly Intelligence Summary, January 1937.*

10 FO371/17149 F1653/11/23 James to Lindley (Tokyo) 4 February 1933 no.3, WO106/5510 James to DMOI 3 December 1935 no.344, and WO106/5494 Edwards (Quetta) report undated [1937].

11 WO106/5392 'Principal Military and Air Intelligence Requirements', MI2 report 25 April 1933, and WO208/506A Grimsdale (MI2c) to MI1c 24 January 1934. On the SIS in Japan see Fisher papers, CAB127/371, 'Memorandum on Secret Service Funds', SIS report 9 October 1935.

12 FO371/18187 F1215/719/23 Crowe (Tokyo) to Consuls 25 January 1934.

13 WO208/1214 Piggott (MA Tokyo) to Haining (DMOI) 29 June 1936.

14 Ross papers, IWM, memoirs, p. 218, and ADM178/178 'Difficulties Encountered by the Naval Attaché in Tokyo in Visits to Naval and Industrial Establishments', Vivian (NA Tokyo) report 6 April 1936.

15 CAB56/1 JIC 1st meeting 7 July 1936. For IJN criticism of Vivian see HW12/203 BJ.065186 IJN Tokyo to JNA London 26 May circulated 28 May 1936.

16 T162/973 E.18739 Treasury to Admiralty 29 March 1934, and Medrow (Admiralty) to Wright (T) 29 October 1934.

17 T162/972 E17426/3 Admiralty to Treasury 4 July 1933.

18 ADM116/3114 Dickens (DNI) minute 26 October 1933.

19 See the file ADM116/3114.

20 ADM116/6324 DNI note 18 February 1932.

21 ADM116/6324 DDNI/DSD/GCCS conference 5 January 1933, and Admiralty to Dreyer (C-in-C China) 30 January 1933.

22 ADM116/6324 Dreyer to Admiralty 13 September 1933 tel.1547/02508, and Admiralty to Dreyer 20 February 1934.

23 ADM116/6324 Dickens to Dreyer 27 September 1933, and Dreyer to Admiralty 7 April 1934 tel.336/02508.

24 ADM116/6323 'D/F in the Event of War in the Far East', DSD memorandum 6 March 1933.

25 ADM116/6323 NID0825/34 Wilson (HMS *Cornwall*) to Dreyer 8 October 1934.

26 See M. Smith, *The Emperor's Codes: Bletchley Park and the Breaking of Japan's Secret Ciphers* (London: Bantam Press, 2000), pp. 34–5 and 42–7.

27 WO106/5393 'Organization of General Staff Intelligence', MI2c memorandum 21 November 1933.

28 ADM116/3121 'Report of the Singapore Conference, 1934', Dreyer report 29 January 1934.
29 Cadogan papers, CCC, ACAD1/2, diary 24 February 1934, and ADM125/72 'China General Letter no.14', Dreyer report 7 May 1934.
30 Tait Papers, NMM, TAI/8, 'Digest of the Report on Intelligence by Captain W.E.C. Tait...', Dickens memorandum undated [1934].
31 WO106/6143 'Chapter IV: Establishment of a Main Intelligence Centre and Co-operation with Other Services', Tait report undated [1934]. The original title for the organization was the Pacific Naval Intelligence Service (PNIS), but this title was dropped presumably because of its phallic connotations.
32 ADM116/6324 'Chapter III: Interception and Cryptography', Tait report undated [1934].
33 WO106/6143 'Report of the Inter-Service Committee on Intelligence Organization in the Far East', undated [1934], and ADM223/297 'HMS Anderson and Special Intelligence in the Far East', Barrett (Admiralty) memorandum undated.
34 See, for example, AIR20/374 'Notes on the Tour of R.A.F. and Combined Intelligence Organizations in the Far East', Wigglesworth (AI2) 30 June 1938.
35 WO106/6143 'Note on Procedure for Dealing with Intercepts at Hong Kong', MI2c memo undated [1937].
36 HW4/25 'History of the "Far East Combined Bureau"', Shaw report undated.
37 ADM/223 'HMS Anderson and Special Intelligence in the Far East', Barrett memorandum undated.
38 NAA A5954/69 ACNS to Defence Minister 3 April 1935, and MP1049/5 2021/8/198 'Report, 1935', unattributed 13 January 1936 S.C.2021/5/185.
39 On Barnes see NAA MP1049/9 1997/5/196 Cresswell (Assistant DSC) to Walter (Assistant DNI Melbourne) 26 February 1936. For Fox see NAA M1049/5 1877/13/213 Walter to Waller (COIS) 21 May 1935 no.02200.
40 NAA MP1185/8 2002/2/260 'Procedure "Y" (Japanese Section)', Newman (DSC) memorandum 27 March 1936, and MP1185/8 1997/5/305 ACNS to DSC 15 May 1936.
41 Lampson papers, MECSA, diary, 30 January 1933, and Cadogan papers, CCC, ACAD1/3, diary 20 November 1935.
42 Ross papers, IWM, memoirs pp. 208–9.
43 Tait Papers, NMM, TAI/8, Dreyer to Admiralty 19 April 1934 no.610/02501.
44 WO106/6143 Grimsdale minute 24 April 1935.
45 WO106/6143 Steward (CIB) memorandum 19 March 1935.
46 Tait Papers, NMM, TAI/8, Dreyer to Admiralty 19 April 1934 no.610/02501.
47 WO106/6143 Grimsdale minute 24 April 1935.
48 Tait Papers, NMM, TAI/8, Dreyer to Admiralty 19 April 1934 no.610/02501.
49 F. Wakeman, *Policing Shanghai, 1927–1937* (Berkeley: University of California Press, 1995), p. 221.
50 The Foreign Office index for 1936 notes this episode under the heading Steptoe, H.N. with a reference to the file K833/210, this material has not, however, been placed in FO369.
51 ADM116/2349 NID6486/23 NID note 26 June 1923. On Drage see also P. Elphick, *The Far Eastern File: The Intelligence War in the Far East, 1930–1945* (London: Hodder & Stoughton, 1997), pp. 83–4.
52 WO106/5354 Grimsdale note 19 August 1935.
53 WO208/506A MI2c to MI1c 5 February 1936.

54 FO371/19358 F1470/445/23 James to Clive 18 January 1935 no.3, and F1770/445/23 James to Clive 20 February 1935.
55 FO371/17149 F1562/11/23 James to Lindley 19 January 1933 no.2, and FO371/19358 F2625/445/23 James to Clive 7 March 1935 no.7.
56 WO106/5494 Edwards report undated [1937].
57 FO371/21037 F1244/228/23 Piggott to Clive 15 January 1937 no.2.
58 M. Kennedy, *The Problem of Japan* (London: Nisbet, 1935), pp. 235–7.
59 J. Ferris, '"Worthy of Some Better Enemy?" The British Estimate of the Imperial Japanese Army 1919–41 and the Fall of Singapore', *Canadian Journal of History*, 28 (1993), 229–30.
60 Percival Papers, IWM, file 41, 'The Japanese Army', Grimsdale lecture 6 February 1935.
61 WO287/229 *WO Monthly Intelligence Summary, October 1936*, and WO287/236 *WO Monthly Intelligence Summary, May 1937*.
62 WO106/5643 MI2c report for Minister for Defence Co-ordination 1 February 1937.
63 FO371/21037 F2849/225/23 Chappell to Clive 14 April 1937 no.4.
64 FO371/18187 F4442/719/23 James to Lindley 6 June 1934 no.12, and FO371/19348 F1118/28/23 Chappell to Clive 21 January 1935 no.1.
65 AIR8/210 *RAF Confidential Intelligence Summary July 1936*, and WO32/4189 AM to WO 9 March 1937 no.S.38919/S6.
66 FO371/20290 F7402/2849/23 Rawlings (NA Tokyo) to Clive 6 November 1936 no.10.
67 FO371/20645 A328/6/45 Rawlings to Clive 9 December 1936 no.12.
68 Ross papers, IWM, memoirs p. 237.
69 See, for example, WO106/5501 'Appreciation on British policy towards Japan', DNI memorandum September 1934 and Grimsdale minute 8 October 1934, and Trotter, op. cit., pp. 89–92.
70 ADM116/3862 'Efficiency of the Japanese Navy', Vivian report 18 February 1935. See also W. Wark, 'In Search of a Suitable Japan: British Naval Intelligence in the Pacific Before the Second World War', *Intelligence and National Security*, 1 (1986), 194–6.
71 ADM116/3862 Colvin (Royal Naval College, Greenwich) to Admiralty 18 September 1936.
72 ADM116/3862 Little to Admiralty 18 September 1936 no.1358/01515.
73 Chatfield papers, NMM, CHT/4/4, Chatfield (FSL) to Dreyer 2 February 1934, and Dickens papers, LHCMA, 'Japan and Sea Power', Dickens lecture 15 May 1935.
74 FO371/17312 W228/228/50 Dickens to Vansittart (PUS FO) 21 October 1932.
75 FO371/20448 W18855/27/50 Congdon (NID) to Campbell (Egypt. Dept) December 1936.
76 FO371/20448 W15695/27/50 Clive to Eden 21 October 1936 no.553.
77 FO371/20448 W14300/27/50 Howe (Peking) to Eden 1 September 1936 no.943.
78 FO371/20448 W7321/27/50 Crosby (Bangkok) to Eden 20 June 1936 no.246.
79 WO106/5660 James to Dill 2 May 1935 no.131, and FO371/20282 F8070/136/23 ICF-448 'General Survey of Japanese Material Resources and Industry in Their Bearing Upon National War Potential', IIC report 29 December 1936, and ICF-177 'Japan: Iron Supplies', IIC report 30 January 1937.
80 Ibid, and FO371/21033 F4512/111/23 Dodds (Tokyo) to Eden 1 July 1937 no.347E.

81 AIR5/1154 Morton (IIC) to Medhurst (AID) 5 July 1935 no.ICF/426.
82 FO371/20282 F8070/136/23 ICF-448 'General Survey of Japanese Material Resources and Industry in Their Bearing Upon National War Potential', IIC report 29 December 1936.
83 FO371/21034 F2857/142/23 Clive to Eden 22 April 1937 no.229E, and CAB48/5 FCI-103 'Organization for Industrial Mobilization in Foreign Countries' 25 June 1937.
84 See, for example, CAB53/25 COS403 'Strategic Position in the Far East With Particular Reference to Hong Kong', Montgomery–Massingberd (CIGS) memorandum 16 September 1935.
85 See C.M. Bell, *The Royal Navy, Seapower and Strategy between the Wars* (Basingstoke: Macmillan, 2000), pp. 63–5.
86 CAB56/2 JIC13 'Far Eastern Appreciation', JIC report 7 October 1936.
87 CAB55/8 JP158 'Strategical Review', JPC memorandum 3 July 1936.
88 FO371/18185 F1763/612/23 Lindley to Simon 1 March 1934 no.125, and F6382/612/23 Clive to Simon 26 September 1934 no.512, and IOLR L/PS/12/103 Clive to Eden 4 November 1936 no.572.
89 IOLR L/PJ/12/480 Stephens (Information Dept India) to MacGregor (Information Dept IO) 9 April 1934, L/PJ/12/366 DIB weekly report 17 November 1934 no.45, and FO371/18185 F7156/612/23 Allen (FE Dept) minute 11 December 1934.
90 FO371/18185 F3762/612/23 Fitzmaurice to Simon 14 May 1934 no.74, FO371/19353 F149/149/23 Orde/Mouw conversation 4 January 1935, and FO371/20504 W500/4/29 Walsh (Batavia) to Eden 7 January 1936 no.3.
91 FO371/21051 F163/159/40 Crosby to Eden 11 December 1936 no.499. See also R. Aldrich, *The Key to the South: Britain, the United States and Thailand during the Approach of the Pacific War, 1929–1942* (Kuala Lumpur: Oxford University Press, 1993), pp. 123–32.
92 CAB23/81 17(35) Cabinet meeting 27 March 1935.
93 CAB53/24 COS380 'Japanese Designs on the Netherlands East Indies', FO memorandum 16 February 1935.
94 FO371/20504 W6771/252/29 Eden/ Colijn talk 21 July 1936.
95 Linlithgow papers, IOLR, Mss.Eur.F125/60, 'Note by the Intelligence Bureau on Japanese Activities in Burma', Ewart (DIB) 5 June 1936.
96 Linlithgow papers, IOLR, F125/3, Linlithgow to Zetland 25 May 1936, no.7 appendix.
97 WO106/5504 'Japanese Espionage', Kirkby (Singapore) report undated [December 1934].
98 FO371/18165 F6505/6505/61 Caldecott (Singapore) to CO 12 September 1934, CO273/604/11 CO to Thomas (Singapore) 24 January 1935, and Caldecott to Indian Government 15 November 1935. See also NAA A981/4 JAP185 PART 3 'Nippon Southward Advance', Wynne (SB Singapore) 31 December 1934.
99 AIR2/1349 Bladon (Singapore) to AM 3 January 1935 no.S/47/10/Air.
100 FO371/21042 F2642/969/23 Little (C-in-China) to Dickens 25 March 1936. On Hayley Bell see Elphick, op. cit., pp. 115–17.
101 WO106/5617 Borrett to Dill 19 September 1935 HKIR no.9.
102 FO371/19366 F6062/6062/10 CO to FO 20 September 1935, and KV4/1 'The Security Service: Its Problems and Organizational Adjustments', Curry (MI5) report March 1946.
103 FO371/17338 W11987/11987/50 Leeper (News Dept.) minute 26 October 1933, and Vansittart minute 30 November 1933.

104 FO371/17149 F8023/35/23 Snow (Tokyo) to Simon 24 November 1933 no.654, and WO106/5499 Vivian to DNI 19 January 1934.

105 HW12/173 BJ.054588 Tokyo to London 25 October circulated 3 November 1933.

106 FO371/18176 F823/316/23 Vansittart minute 22 February 1934.

107 See A. Best, *Britain, Japan and Pearl Harbor: Avoiding War in East Asia, 1936–41* (London: Routledge, 1995), pp. 9–10.

108 N. Chamberlain papers, BUL, NC2/23a, diary 9 October 1934. See also S. Bourette-Knowles, 'The Global Micawber: Sir Robert Vansittart, the Treasury and the Global Balance of Power, 1933–35', *Diplomacy and Statecraft,* 5 (1995) 91–121.

109 Chatfield papers, NMM, CHT/4/4, Chatfield (FSL) to Dreyer 2 February 1934, ADM116/3471 Dickens minute 8 May 1934, and WO106/5501 Dill (DMOI) to Dickens 9 October 1934.

110 M. Kennedy, 'Russo-Japanese Friction', *Nineteenth Century and After,* October 1934, pp. 380–90.

111 HW12/180 BJ.057218 Tokyo to Moscow etc. 18 June circulated 20 June 1935.

112 WO208/506A 'Military Intelligence Requirements in the Far East', Grimsdale minute 24 January 1934.

113 WO106/5499 Ismay minute 7 September 1934. See also CAB127/7 'The Far East', Ismay lecture undated [1936?].

114 WO106/5282 'Report of Tour in Manchuria', Ferguson (SIB) note 15 August 1935.

115 WO106/5499 'Appreciation of the Probable Plans of Operations and Initial Deployment in a Russo-Japanese War', WO memorandum undated [October 1935]. See also the file WO106/5138 for correspondence between MI2 and the Quartermaster-General's Department in the autumn of 1934, and T.J. Betts, 'The Strategy of Another Russo-Japanese War', *Foreign Affairs,* July 1934, pp. 593–603.

116 On Britain, Japan and the global balance of power see B. McKercher, *Transition of Power: Britain's Loss of Global Pre-eminence to the United States, 1930–1945* (Cambridge: Cambridge University Press, 1999), pp. 186–215, G. Kennedy, '1935: A Snapshot of British Imperial Defence in the Far East', in K. Neilson and G. Kennedy (eds), *Far Flung Lines: Studies in Imperial Defence in Honour of Donald Mackenzie Schurman* (London: Frank Cass, 1997), pp. 190–215, and S. Bourette-Knowles, op. cit., passim.

117 WO106/6097 CX1124/68 'Sino-Japanese Relations', SIS report 1 August 1935, and CX[delete]/75 'Sino-Japanese Relations', SIS report 26 August 1935.

118 HW12/192 BJ.060798 Peking to Tokyo 30 May circulated 4 June 1935.

119 Pownall papers, LHCMA, Box 1, diary, 11 June 1935.

120 WO106/6248 CX1124/19' 'Question of Chinese Resistance to Japanese Encroachment', SIS report 3 March 1936, and WO106/6097 CX1124/35 'Conversations Between the Japanese Ambassador and the Chinese Minister for Foreign Affairs', SIS report 9 April 1936.

121 WO106/5629 'Appreciation of the Probable Course of a Sino-Japanese War', MI2c memorandum June 1936. See also Best, op. cit., pp. 25–6.

122 FO371/17889 E1140/47/34 Howe (Tehran) to Simon 1 February 1934 no.54, and WO106/5588 CX [delete] 95 & 96 'Japanese-Persian Relations', SIS reports 13 December and 21 December 1934.

123 HW12/188 BJ.059405 Kabul to Bombay 27 December 1934 circulated 6 February 1935, and FO371/19240 N2186/134/97 'Japanese–Afghan Relations', Burrows (N.Dept) memorandum 30 April 1935.

124 IOLR L/PJ/12/480 DIB weekly report 15 December 1934 no.49.
125 See H. Shimizu, *Anglo-Japanese Trade Rivalry in the Middle East in the Inter-War Period* (London: St Antony's Middle East Monographs, 1986), passim.
126 FO371/18187 F2994/720/23 Allen memorandum 22 May 1934, and FO371/19362 F2720/1870/23 Bush (NID) to Allen 16 April 1935.
127 See, for example, HW12/193 BJ.061200 Tokyo to JNA Berlin 4 July circulated 17 July 1935, and WO106/5530 'German-Japanese Relations', MI2c memorandum 19 August 1935.
128 FO371/20285 F674/303/23 Lawford (C.Dept) memorandum 24 January 1936, and 'C' to Lawford 29 January 1936 C/315.
129 CAB24/268 CP73(37) 'Review of Imperial Defence', Inskip memorandum 26 February 1937, Chatfield Papers, NMM, CHT3/1, Chatfield (FSL) note 5 January 1937, and WO106/130 Deverell (CIGS) note 2 February 1937.
130 FO371/20285 F7223/303/23 Eden minute 29 November 1936, FO371/20286 F7504/303/23 Ronald (FE Dept) minute 4 December 1936, and WO106/5606 Major (MI2c) note 8 December 1936.
131 WO106/6098 CX[delete]/939 'Japan – Military Policy', SIS report 10 June 1937, and Major minute 6 July 1937.

## 8 The Sino-Japanese War, 1937–40

1 WO208/230 WO to Bartholomew (GOC HK) 14 July 1938 tel.51561.
2 FO371/23537 F12392/12392/10 Hayter (Chungking) to Halifax 18 December 1939 tel.209.
3 FO371/22111 F217/106/10 Gage (Hankow) to Eden 5 January 1938 tel.80, and WO208/1445 'Report on Military Information Obtained at Hankow', Boxer (FECB) report 5 February 1938.
4 See Grimsdale papers, IWM, memoirs – 'Thunder in the East', p. 17. See also C. Drage, *The Amiable Prussian* (London: Blond, 1958), p. 12.
5 Grimsdale memoirs, pp. 18–19, and C. Drage, *The Life and Times of General Two-Gun Cohen* (New York: Funk & Wagnalis, 1954), pp. 264–7.
6 WO106/5354 Burkhardt (FECB) to Dennys (MI2) 3 September 1937 no. HKIR.18/37.
7 For Spear, see the file WO208/289. For the restrictions on the movement of intelligence officers see Grimsdale IWM, memoirs – 'Thunder in the East', p. 19.
8 Grimsdale papers, IWM, memoirs – 'Thunder in the East', p. 11.
9 For the AMA replacement see FO371/24696 F24696/709/10 Greenway (Chungking) to Halifax 15 February 1940 tel.143. On Tientsin see FO371/23475 F6884/166/10 WO to FO 5 July 1939.
10 Eady papers, IWM, 'Tour of Defended Ports Abroad, 1939', Eady report undated [1939].
11 WO106/5584 Dennys to Haining (DMOI) 10 August 1937.
12 WO106/5584 Haining to Piggott (MA Tokyo) 20 October 1937, and WO208/1214 Piggott to Craigie (Tokyo) 18 November 1937 no. 29.
13 Wards papers, IWM, Shanghai report 1937 file, Wards (AMA Tokyo) report 15 December 1937.
14 FO371/23570 F2162/2162/23 Bryant (AA Tokyo) to Craigie 30 January 1939.
15 AIR20/374 'Notes on the Tour of R.A.F. and Combined Intelligence Organizations in the Far East', Wigglesworth (AI2) 30 June 1938.
16 Ibid.

17 WO208/506A 'Japan: Principal Military Intelligence Requirements', MI2c note 25 February 1938.
18 WO208/506A 'Japan' and 'China' Major (MI2c) notes 7 February 1940.
19 AIR20/374 'Notes on the Tour of R.A.F. and Combined Intelligence Organizations in the Far East', Wigglesworth 30 June 1938.
20 Ibid.
21 HW3/102 'The Japanese War', de Grey (GCCS) memorandum undated.
22 ADM223/297 'Japanese Cyphers – Notes', Barham (NID) report 18 July 1942.
23 For the JNA cypher see HW12/227 GCCS note on BJ.071423 Tokyo to JNA London 26 May circulated 31 May 1938.
24 FO371/23570 F2031/2031/23 Craigie to Halifax 1 January 1939 no. 1.
25 CAB53/50 COS931 'Situation in the Far East', COS report 24 June 1939. See C.M. Bell, *The Royal Navy, Seapower and Strategy between the Wars* (Basingstoke: Macmillan, 2000), p. 65.
26 WO287/67 *WO Monthly Intelligence Summary June 1938*, p. 23.
27 WO287/240 *WO Monthly Intelligence Summary September 1937*, pp. 266–7, and WO287/63 *WO Monthly Intelligence Summary February 1938*, pp. 164–5.
28 WO287/242 *WO Monthly Intelligence Summary November 1937*, p. 10–11.
29 ADM116/3895 'Far East Weekly Diary no. 2', NID report 9 November 1937, and WO287/63 *WO Monthly Intelligence Summary February 1938*, p. 122.
30 NAA AWM124 4/361 'Japanese Combined Operations', Noble (C-in-C China) memorandum 1940.
31 CAB56/4 JIC89 'Spain and China: Intelligence Regarding Air Warfare', JIC report 10 June 1939, WO287/89 *Notes on the Japanese Army, 1939*, and WO208/857 'Appreciation of the Sino-Japanese Military Situation at the Present Time With Particular Reference to the Air Situation', AI2 report 1 December 1939.
32 WO287/65 *WO Monthly Intelligence Summary April 1938*, pp. 217–8.
33 WO287/70 *WO Monthly Intelligence Summary September 1938*, p. 145.
34 WO287/89 *Notes on the Japanese Army, 1939*.
35 ADM1/9588 'Japanese Naval Air Service: Annual Report 1938', Bryant report undated.
36 AIR2/3558 'Air Operations During Sino-Japanese Hostilities', Kerby (AA Shanghai) report undated, and AIR22/70 Air Ministry Weekly Intelligence Summary 30 May 1940 no. 39.
37 WO287/103 *WO Monthly Intelligence Summary August 1939*.
38 The only detailed RAF narrative on the war in China up to the end of 1939 was in AIR8/252 *RAF Monthly Intelligence Summary June 1939*.
39 CAB56/1 JIC 18th meeting 8 July 1938.
40 WO287/89 *Notes on the Japanese Army, 1939*.
41 WO287/64 *WO Monthly Intelligence Summary March 1938*, p. 178.
42 WO287/89 *Notes on the Japanese Army, 1939*.
43 WO287/234 *WO Monthly Intelligence Summary March 1937*, pp. 213–18, and WO287/89 *Notes on the Japanese Army, 1939*.
44 WO287/89 *Notes on the Japanese Army, 1939*, pp. 279–81.
45 WO287/71 *WO Monthly Intelligence Summary October 1938*, pp. 209–16.
46 WO287/99 *WO Monthly Intelligence Summary April 1939*, p. 191.
47 WO106/5365 Shanghai Intelligence Report 28 October 1938 no. 43 part 1.
48 FO371/23560 F875/456/23 Rawlings (NA Tokyo) to Craigie 29 December 1938 no. 5.
49 Armstrong papers, LHCMA, 'China, 1937' Armstrong (HMS *Danae*) lecture 20 November 1937.

50 Wards papers, IWM, Shanghai report 1937 file, Wards report 15 December 1937.
51 WO32/4347 'The Shanghai Emergency 1 February–31 December 1938', Telfer-Smollet (GOC Shanghai) despatch 1 February 1939.
52 ADM116/3683 Little (C-in-C China) to Admiralty 19 January 1938 no. 100/2301.
53 Linlithgow papers, IOLR. Mss.Eur.F125/5, Linlithgow to Zetland 24 May 1938.
54 Grimsdale IWM, memoirs – 'Thunder in the East', p. 10.
55 FO371/23456 F3233/687/61 Fitzmaurice (Batavia) to Ronald (FE Dept) 7 March 1939.
56 WO287/101 *WO Monthly Intelligence Summary June 1939*.
57 On Changsha, see WO208/2256 WO Weekly Intelligence Commentary 12 October 1939 no. 8. On Nanning, see WO208/264 'Nanning Operations', MI2c memorandum 2 April 1940.
58 WO208/2268 WO Daily Intelligence Summary 15 September 1939 no. 17.
59 FO371/23570 Craigie to Halifax 1 January 1939 no. 1, WO106/5684 Piggott to Craigie 25 March 1939 no. 15, and FO371/23564 F8684/538/23 Piggott to Craigie 29 June 1939 no. 27.
60 See, for example, FO371/22178 F9015/11/23 Piggott to Craigie 26 July 1938 no. 19.
61 WO208/276 'Report of Trip Through Guerrilla Regions in N. China', Bapwood (Chinese Industrial Cooperatives) report 21 January 1940.
62 FO371/24743 F2417/2417/23 Craigie to Halifax 1 January 1940 no. 1.
63 F. Utley, *Japan's Feet of Clay* (London: Faber & Faber, 1937). See also the talk at Chatham House by a former language officer, E. Ainger, 'An Impression of the Far East', *International Affairs*, May 1937.
64 FO371/21035 F10365/142/23 Craigie to Eden 1 November 1937 no. 554E, FO371/21034 F11315/111/23 Craigie to Eden 21 December 1937 tel.857, and G. Stein, 'Japanese State Finance', *Pacific Affairs*, December 1937.
65 FO371/22183 F10642/103/23 'Japan – The Financial Position as Regards Foreign Trade, September 1938', IIC report 1 October 1938, and F11370/103/23 Craigie to Halifax 8 October 1938 no. 781E.
66 FO371/23558 F13020/232/23 Craigie to Halifax 27 December 1939 tel.1693.
67 FO371/22178 F13885/11/23 Rawlings to Craigie 1 December 1938 no. 4.
68 AIR8/252 *RAF Confidential Intelligence Summary November 1938*, and *RAF Confidential Intelligence Summary December 1938*.
69 Wark, op. cit., pp. 202–6.
70 FO371/23563 F3600/535/23 Craigie to Halifax 14 March 1939 no. 193.
71 ADM116/5757 Morton (MEW) to Seal (Admiralty) 13 February 1940, and ADM1/10318 Morton to Seal 16 February 1940.
72 ADM205/5 Churchill to Alexander 15 September 1940 M.96.
73 FO371/23595 F4802/1860/40 Halifax to Crosby (Bangkok) 7 June 1939 no. 99.
74 HW12/222 BJ.070222 FECB to Admiralty 22 December 1937, and IOLR L/PO/5/36 DO to Dominions 12 October 1938 no. 381.
75 WO208/847 Ronald minute 23 August 1938.
76 FO371/21028 F10344/26/23 Thomas (FE Dept) minute 2 November 1937.
77 See A. Best, *Britain, Japan and Pearl Harbor: Avoiding War in East Asia, 1936–41* (London: Routledge, 1995), pp. 64–5.
78 HW12/235 BJ.073458 Tokyo to Berlin 9 January circulated 26 January, IOLR L/WS/1/72 Dennys to Henderson (IAHQ) 2 February 1939, and FO371/22944 C2029/421/62 Ronald minute 14 February 1938.

79 HW12/242 BJ.075422 Washington to Tokyo 2 August circulated 14 August 1939, and HW12/243 BJ.076006 FECB to Admiralty 19 September 1939.
80 Best, op. cit., pp. 74–86 and 112–20.
81 ADM223/495 NID.0487/37 CX37300 'Japan – War Plans Against Hong Kong and Singapore', SIS report 25 May 1937.
82 WO32/9366 Dobbie (GOC Malaya) to WO 27 January 1938 CRMC.33523/G. See also C-C Ong, *Operation Matador: Britain's War Plans Against the Japanese, 1918–1941* (Singapore: Times Academic Press, 1997), pp. 69–76.
83 WO106/2441 Dobbie to Haining 2 October 1937.
84 WO32/9366 Dobbie to WO 27 January 1938.
85 WO32/4188 WO to Dobbie 7 March 1938, and WO106/2430 Pownall to Dobbie 11 March 1938.
86 CO323/1592/31 Thomas (Singapore) to MacDonald 22 November 1938, and Gent (CO) minute 12 December 1938, and WO32/9366 Thomas to CO 27 January 1940.
87 CAB94/1 ODC (40) 2nd meeting 8 March 1940.
88 WO106/2440 Bond (GOC Malaya) to WO 13 April 1940, and Steel (MO2) to Dewing (DMOP) 5 May 1940.
89 ADM1/9909 Stanhope minute 27 March 1939.
90 See the comments of Backhouse and Stanhope in CAB16/209 SAC 2nd meeting 13 March 1939, and SAC–16 Annex 'Political Review for SAC', FO memorandum 17 April 1939.
91 CAB66/1 WP(39)56 'Sino-Japanese Hostilities', COS memorandum 28 September 1939, and CAB66/4 WP(39)152 'The Present Sino-Japanese Military Situation, December 1939', COS memorandum 9 December 1939.
92 FO371/21026 F11722/1326/61 Fitzmaurice to Dobbie 24 November 1937.
93 Best, op. cit., pp. 67–8.
94 Percival papers, IWM, file 39 'Organization for the Security of the Fortress', Percival memorandum undated [October 1937], WO106/2441 Dobbie to Haining 5 January 1938, and CO273/656/7 Fitzmaurice to Ronald 7 March 1939.
95 See the monthly Burma Defence Bureau reports in IOLR M/5/47.
96 Linlithgow papers, IOLR, F125/6, Linlithgow to Zetland 23 November 1938 no. 46, and IOLR M/6/43 Seymour (Rangoon) to BO 6 January 1939 no. 3D(C)39.
97 IOLR M/5/79 'Report of a Conspiracy to Smuggle Arms into Burma from Thailand', BO memorandum undated [1940].
98 See the files CO273/644/12 and CO273/656/7.
99 FO371/22174 F8450/532/61 Inter-departmental meeting minutes 5 August 1938.
100 HW12/239 BJ.074657 Singapore to Tokyo 17 March circulated 17 May 1939, and IOLR L/PJ/12/506 'Weekly Survey of Activities of Germans, Italians and Japanese in India', DIB report 30 November 1939 no. 28
101 WO32/4188 Dobbie to WO 16 November 1937. See also Percival papers, File 39 'Deductions From Japanese Appreciation of the Attack on the Fortress of Singapore', Percival (COS Singapore) note undated [November 1937].
102 FO371/22215 F3594/2113/40 Crosby to Halifax 3 March 1938 no. 90, and FO371/23595 F4802/1860/40 Halifax to Crosby 7 June 1939 no. 99.
103 FO371/21023 F9373/39/61 Fitzmaurice to Eden 30 October 1937 no. 176E.
104 FO371/21041 F3648/615/23 Fitzmaurice to Eden 17 June 1937 no. 84E.
105 See, for example, HW12/237 BJ.073843 GCCS summary circulated 2 March 1939, and FO371/23541 F2710/179/61 Grasset (GOC HK) to WO 17 March 1939 tel.4940.

106 FO371/23456 F687/687/61 Fitzmaurice to Halifax 27 December 1938 no. 346.
107 NAA SP195/3 P3/3 'Intelligence Summary: Propaganda', FECB report 22 May 1940.
108 FO371/21826 E2631/784/91 Craigie to Halifax 7 May 1938 tel.574, and HW12/239 BJ.074598 Tokyo to Cairo 1 April circulated 9 May 1939.
109 FO371/21071 N5630/5630/97 McCann (Kabul) to Eden 5 November 1937 no. 114, and HW12/221 BJ.070015 Kabul to Tokyo 17 September circulated 30 November 1937.
110 FO371/20868 E7255/7255/44 Loraine (Angora) to Eden 27 November 1937 no. 711.
111 FO371/23274 E2828/2828/25 Bullard (Jedda) to Halifax 13 April 1939, IOLR L/WS/1/72 Cawthorn (MI2a) to Stuart (IAGS) 27 April 1939 no. DO/26, and HW12/246 BJ.077137 Mecca to London (Saudi) 29 November circulated 3 December 1939.
112 FO371/23265 E7044/7044/34 Seymour (Tehran) to Halifax 19 October 1939 tel.158, and HW12/246 BJ.077379 London to Ambassadors in Europe 1 December circulated 5 December 1939.
113 FO371/23274 E2828/2828/25 Ronald minute 20 April 1939.
114 FO371/22257 N1716/1716/97 Collier (N.Dept) to Fraser-Tytler (Kabul) and Bullard 5 April 1938.
115 FO371/21839 E4972/3966/65 Loraine to Halifax 19 August 1938 tel.12 saving.
116 IOLR L/PJ/12/505 'The Activities of Foreign Agents in India', DIB note undated [August 1938?].
117 IOLR L/PJ/12/507 'Weekly Survey of Activities of Germans, Italians and Japanese in India – 18 May 1940', DIB report no. 19.
118 IOLR L/PJ/12/158 'Weekly report', DIB 3 December 1938, HW12/238 BJ.074344 Calcutta to Tokyo 31 March circulated 18 April 1939, and IOLR L/PJ/12/217 'Subhas Bose's Japanese Connections', IPI note 22 October 1940.
119 IOLR L/PJ/12/613 'Proposal for Making Provision for Co-operation Between the Central Intelligence Bureau and the Intelligence Organizations of British Possessions to the West and East of India', Ewart (DIB) memorandum 21 November 1938.
120 NAA A816/1 25/301/30 Eden to Menzies 11 May 1940 no. 116.
121 See the file ADM223/482.
122 FO371/24715 F914/914/61 Crosby to Howe (FE Dept) 12 January 1940.
123 FO371/24715 F914/914/61 Ashley Clarke (FE Dept) minute 27 February 1940, and F2933/914/61 Admiralty to FO 23 April 1940 no. M/NID.01369/40.
124 IOLR L/PJ/12/613 Ewart to Dibdin (IO) 27 June 1938, L/WS/1/72 Stuart to Dennys 30 March 1939, FO371/23533 F10938/10938/61 Lambert (Batavia) to Halifax 18 September 1939 no. 201, and Vinden memoirs. For Lovink's visit see CO273/656/7 Thomas to MacDonald 12 April 1939. See also H.T. Bussemake, 'Paradise in Peril: The Netherlands, Great Britain, and the Defence of the Netherlands East Indies', *Journal of Southeast Asian Studies*, 31 (2000), 121–3.
125 See the file ADM1/27120.
126 CAB81/87 JIC(40) 41st meeting 6 June 1940.
127 FO371/23573 F9024/5733/23 Wright (Paris) to Ronald 14 August 1939, and WO208/264 Grimsdale (FECB) to DMI 24 January 1940 no. IB/2263.
128 WO208/506B 'Tour of Indo-China, China and Burma', Grimsdale report 1 June 1940 no. IB/2322.
129 HW14/1 Denniston (GCCS) to DSD Admiralty 12 October 1939, and Japanese Diplomatic Section note 12 October 1939.

130 NAA A1606/1 E12/1 PART 1 Stirling (London) to External Affairs 10 September 1939 tel.466, and MP1185/8 1937/2/159 COIS to Long (DNI Melbourne) 1 March 1940 no. 184/069.
131 NAA A816 42/302/18 Menzies to Eden 11 April 1940 no. N8/1, and Cranborne to Menzies 15 October 1940.
132 See I. Hamill, *The Strategic Illusion. The Singapore Strategy and the Defence of Australia and New Zealand* (Singapore: Singapore University Press, 1981), pp. 303–4.
133 ADM116/3693 Little to Admiralty 9 December 1937 tel.2222/8, and FO371/22044 F10055/2/10 Lindsay (Washington) to Halifax 21 September 1938 tel.350.
134 FO371/21028 F10616/26/23 Lindsay to Eden 30 November 1937 tels.437 and 438, and 'C' to Norton (FO) 6 December 1937 C/1803.
135 FO371/22944 C1500/421/62 Halifax to Mallet 4 February 1939 tel., and C1612/421/62 Ronald to Mallet (Washington) 16 February 1939.

## 9 The Immediate Origins of the Pacific War

1 HW12/257 BJ.084532 Sandakan to Tokyo 13 October circulated 24 October 1940, and HW12/259 BJ.086335 Sandakan to Tokyo 20 October circulated 21 December 1940.
2 CO323/1831/23 Jones (OAG Singapore) to Moyne 12 February 1941.
3 HW12/259 BJ.086159 Tokyo to Singapore etc. 11 May circulated 15 December 1940, IOLR L/PJ/12/508 'Weekly Survey of Germans, Italians and Japanese in India', DIB report 21 December 1940, and WO208/892 COIS to DNI no. 0826Z/23 23 January 1941.
4 HW12/259 BJ.086052 and BJ.086080 Bangkok to Tokyo 28 November 1940 circulated 12 and 13 December 1940 respectively.
5 FO371/24705 F1388/7/61 Henniker-Major (FE Dept) minute 28 February 1940, and FO371/25040 W8831/182/87 DO to Menzies 31 August 1940 tel.311, and W12124/182/87 Butler minute 27 November 1940.
6 A. Best, 'Straws in the Wind: Britain and the February 1941 War Scare in East Asia', *Diplomacy & Statecraft*, 5 (1994), 642–65
7 A. Best, *Britain, Japan and Pearl Harbor: Avoiding War in East Asia, 1936–41* (London: Routledge, 1995), pp. 134–5.
8 See S. Hatano and S. Asada, 'The Japanese Decision to Move South, 1939–41', in R. Boyce and E.M. Robertson (eds), *Paths to War: New Essays on the Origins of the Second World War* (Basingstoke: Macmillan, 1989), pp. 393–4.
9 Maunsell papers, IWM, memoirs – 'Security Intelligence in the Middle East 1914–1934 and 1934–1944', p. 24.
10 IOLR L/PJ/12/507 'Weekly Survey of Germans, Italians and Japanese in India', DIB report 31 May 1940, and Lampson papers, MECSA, diary 21 August 1940.
11 HW12/257 BJ.084690 Tokyo to Berlin etc. 26 October circulated 28 October 1940.
12 HW12/258 BJ.085704 Port Said to Tokyo 20 November circulated 30 November 1940.
13 PREM7/7 Morton to Churchill 28 August 1940.
14 HW12/257 BJ.084658 Baghdad to Tehran 21 October circulated 28 October 1940, and WO208/4558 CX37892/198 'The Japanese, the Axis and the Iraqis', SIS report 30 October 1940.

15 HW12/259 BJ.085828 Baghdad to Tehran 26 October circulated 4 December 1940, and WO208/4558 WO to MICE 5 December 1940 tel.71672.
16 FO371/27042A E2683/44/65 Fraser Tytler (Kabul) to Eden 27 May 1941 tel. 168, PREM3/238/7 Eden to Churchill PM/41/55 27 June 1941, and FO624/23/239 Cornwallis (Baghdad) to Eden 10 July 1941 tel.751.
17 HW12/268 BJ.095844 Rome to Tokyo [Italian] 20 September circulated 25 September 1941, and FO371/27221 E6054/3326/34 Churchill to Eden 25 September 1941.
18 FO371/24735 F3267/205/23 Economic report for June 1940 [unattributed].
19 CAB81/98 JIC(40)205 'Appreciation of the Future Policy for the Conduct of the War', JIC memorandum 30 July 1940, CAB81/99 JIC(41)11 ' Sea, Land and Air Forces Which Japan Might Make Available for an Attack on Malaya', JIC memorandum 6 January 1941, and WO208/902 *Japan at the Cross Roads*, FECB report 5 June 1941 no. 1824.
20 CAB81/98 JIC(40)272 'Time Required for the Japanese to Stage an Attack Against Malaya', JIC memorandum 7 September 1940, and JIC(40)335 'Period of Warning of an Attack on Singapore', WO memorandum 23 October 1940.
21 WO106/5571 CX[delete] 'Japan – Morale', SIS report 9 January 1940, and Winterborn (MI2c) minute 12 January 1940.
22 WO208/2772 WO Daily Intelligence Summary 28 October 1940 no. 421, and WO208/2258 WO Weekly Intelligence Commentary 21 November 1940 no. 66. See also AIR23/1970 'Japanese Army – Minor Tactics', MCIB memorandum undated no. IB/2032.
23 WO106/5571 CX[delete]/709 'Anti–War Propaganda Among Japanese Troops', SIS report 29 January 1941, and CX[delete]/105 'Anti-War Propaganda Among Japanese Troops', SIS report 10 May 1941.
24 WO208/2258 WO Weekly Intelligence Commentary 7 November 1940 no. 64.
25 ADM223/147 NID Weekly Intelligence Report 19 July 1940 no. 19.
26 WO208/2772 WO Daily Intelligence Summary 6 October 1940 no. 399, and AIR22/73 AID Weekly Intelligence Summary 10 October 1940 no. 58.
27 IOLR L/WS/1/517 Indian-Malayan defence conference 1st meeting 27 January 1941, and AIR22/74 AID Weekly Intelligence Summary 10 April 1941 no. 84.
28 Layton papers, BL, Add.Mss.74797, 'Tactical Appreciation in Accordance with COS Telegram no. 2', unattributed October 1940.
29 AIR22/73 AID Weekly Intelligence Summary 4 December 1940 no. 66.
30 AIR40/1453 ALO HK Intelligence Summary 29 October 1940 no. 30.
31 AIR22/74 AID Weekly Intelligence Summary 17 April 1941 no. 85, and AIR40/1448 Warburton (AA Chungking) to DAI 22 April 1941 no. 19.
32 AIR22/73 AID Weekly Intelligence Summary 6 February 1941 no. 75, and CAB81/101 JIC(41)155 'Future Strategy of Japan', Shoosmith (JIC Secretariat) note 17 April 1941.
33 NAA MP1587/1/181i Long (DNI Melbourne) to Gray (Army Intelligence Melbourne) 5 September 1941.
34 CAB81/102 JIC(41)175 (Revise) 'Future Strategy of Japan', JIC memorandum 1 May 1941. For assessments of Japanese strategy see CAB69/2 DO12(41) Defence Operations Committee meeting 9 April 1941.
35 See T.G. Mahnken, 'Gazing at the Sun: The Office of Naval Intelligence and Japanese Naval Innovation, 1918–1941', *Intelligence and National Security*, 11 (1996), 431–8.

36 P. Elphick, *The Far Eastern File: The Intelligence War in the Far East, 1930–1945* (London: Hodder & Stoughton, 1997), pp. 158–9 and 166–7. Elphick's interpretation is repeated in R. Aldrich, *Britain and the Intelligence War Against Japan, 1941–45: The Politics of Secret Service* (Cambridge: Cambridge University Press, 2000), p. 62. A more circumspect view of the FECB's military wing is taken in J. Ferris, '"Worthy of Some Better Enemy?" The British Estimate of the Imperial Japanese Army 1919–41 and the Fall of Singapore', *Canadian Journal of History*, 28 (1993), 247–9.
37 IOLR L/MIL/17/20/24 'Japanese Army Memorandum', General Staff Malaya with Modifications by General Staff India report March 1941.
38 Grimsdale papers, IWM, memoirs – 'Thunder in the East', p. 45.
39 WO208/1225 Haining (VCIGS) note undated [December 1940].
40 Brooke-Popham papers, LHCMA, 6/3/3, Brooke-Popham (C-in-C FE) to Street (PUS AM) 15 January 1941.
41 CAB69/2 DO30(41) Defence Operations Committee meeting 15 May 1941.
42 CAB66/15 WP(41)34 'Implications of a Japanese Southward Move', COS memorandum 15 February 1941.
43 FO371/24742 F5525/961/23 Dening (FE Dept) minute 29 December 1940.
44 Linlithgow papers, IOLR, Mss.Eur.F125/10 Linlithgow to Amery 12 February 1941 no. 7.
45 Wards papers, IWM, general file, Wards to Kirby 15 January 1952.
46 WO208/902 *Japan at the Cross Roads*, FECB report 5 June 1941 no. 1824.
47 See, for example, HW12/262 BJ.088317 HK to Tokyo 13 February circulated 4 March 1941, and HW12/263 BJ.089427 HK to Tokyo 5 March circulated 4 April 1941.
48 WO208/876 'Comments by HM Ambassador Tokyo on C-in-C Far East', MI2c note undated [October 1941].
49 WO208/2049A 'Visit to Chungking', Boxer (Army Intelligence HK) report 14 October 1940. On the Chinese WT sets see also M. Yu, 'Chinese Codebreakers, 1927–45', in D. Alvarez (ed.), *Allied and Axis Signals Intelligence in World War II*, (London: Frank Cass, 1999), pp. 208–9.
50 FO371/24710 F4969/193/61 Field (MI2) to Gage (FE Dept) 31 October 1940, and Gage minute 31 October 1940. For an early AX report see IOLR M/5/47 CX37502/117 'Japanese Plans in the South', SIS report 25 October 1940.
51 HW14/14 Earnshaw Smith (GCCS) to Travis (GCCS) 4 April 1941, and HW12/264 BJ.090442 Hanoi to Singapore [French] 27 April circulated 1 May 1941.
52 See, for example, HW12/263 BJ.089955 Penang to Chungking [Chinese] 14 April circulated 19 April 1941.
53 ADM199/1477 COIS to Admiralty 14 January 1941 tel.1101Z/14, and Layton (C-in-C China) to Admiralty 18 February 1941 tel.0344Z/18.
54 NAA A981/4 JAP145 Walsh (Batavia) to Harkness (COIS) 19 March 1941, and Secretary External Affairs to Secretary Army 17 July 1941.
55 HW14/18 COIS to DNI 5 August 1941 tel.01107Z/5.
56 FO371/24722 F5341/3654/61 WO to Ismay 21 November 1940.
57 ADM199/1477 COIS to DNI 20 March 1941 tel.0348Z/20, and Admiralty to COIS 13 April 1941 tel.1744/13.
58 NAA A3300/194 Ellis (PCO NY) to Casey (Washington) 17 May 1941 and Ellis to Heydon (Washington) 20 June 1941, and A3300/197A BSC to Casey 23 October 1941.

59 CAB81/98 JIC(40)263 'Exchange of Information with the United States Authorities', (Annex A) Edwards (JIC Secretariat) note 1 September 1940.
60 ADM223/479 Cavendish-Bentinck (JIC) minute 22 November 1940. One of the first telegrams is FO371/24717 F4987/2729/61 Butler (Washington) to Halifax 1 November 1940 tel.2512 FIXIT.
61 FO850/5 Y909/13/651 Cadogan (PUS FO) minute 28 February 1941.
62 HW14/12 ACOS (?) to DNI 6 February 1941 tel.1605/6. The first British 'Purple' telegram was probably HW12/261 BJ.087736 Rome to Tokyo 10 January circulated 15 February 1941.
63 Layton papers, BM, Add.Mss 74797, Wisden (DCOIS) to Wylie (COIS) 27 November 1940, and ADM199/1477 Layton to Admiralty 19 December 1940 tel.0357Z/19.
64 ADM199/1477 Admiralty to Layton 10 February 1941 tel.1656/10.
65 See M. Smith, *The Emperor's Codes: Bletchley Park and the Breaking of Japan's Secret Ciphers* (London: Bantam Press, 2000), pp. 78–9.
66 ADM199/1477 COIS to Admiralty 14 March 1941 tel.0828Z/14, and Admiralty to COIS 22 March 1941 tel.1819/22.
67 CAB81/102 JIC(41)241 'Cooperation with the USA in Intelligence Matters in the Far East', Capel Dunn (JIC Secretariat) 2 June 1941, and CAB81/88 JIC(41) 16th meeting 10 June 1941.
68 NAA A981/4 FAR22 Cranborne to Fadden 2 September 1941 tel.610.
69 WO208/2049A WO to Brooke-Popham (C-in-C FE) 22 August 1941 tel.85606.
70 Shedden papers, NAA, A5954/69 559/10 NA Washington to Royle (CNS) 26 November 1941 tel.1025, and HW14/22 Hastings (JIC Washington) to Denniston (GCCS) 11 November 1941.
71 Best, *Britain, Japan and Pearl Harbor*, p. 146.
72 HW1/25 Churchill to 'C' 24 August 1941.
73 HW12/264 BJ.091101 Tokyo to Rome (Italian) 12 May circulated 17 May 1941. On this incident see Best, *Britain, Japan and Pearl Harbor*, pp. 168–9.
74 S. Budiansky, *Battle of Wits: The Complete Story of Codebreaking in World War II* (London: Viking, 2000), p. 210.
75 NAA MP1185/8 1945/2/6 Conference in Naval Board Room minutes 4 January 1941, MP1185/8 2021/5/529 Nave (SIB) to Newman (DSC) 12 March 1941.
76 ADM223/496 Long to Harkness 30 July 1941 no. NID43/81.
77 See, for example, NAA AWM124/4/132 Casey to External Affairs 19 April 1941 tel.TROPICAL 2, AWM124/4/137 Rangi (RNZN Liaison Officer Washington) to Fraser 19 August 1941 tel.ARCTIC 12.
78 NAA A3300/178 External Affairs to Casey 27 August 1941 tel.735.
79 NAA MP1185/8 1937/2/415 Newman to Nave 19 March 1941.
80 'Report on Singapore Conference', ACNS 8 November 1940 (copy held by Naval History Directorate Canberra).
81 NAA AWM124/4/292 Long to Kennedy (RAN Liaison Officer Batavia) 27 October 1941.
82 Norwich papers, CCC, DUFC3/7, diary 13 September 1941, and Sansom papers, St Antony's Oxford, file 8, 'British Administration in the Far East', Duff Cooper report 29 October 1941.
83 ADM223/496 'S.I.S. in the Far East', Wylie report 15 July 1940, and Godfrey to Noble (C-in-C China) undated draft telegram [autumn 1940].
84 See R. Aldrich, 'Britain's Secret Intelligence Service in Asia during the Second World War', *Modern Asian Studies*, 32 (1998), 187–9. For Denham's arrival in Singapore see Thomas papers, RHL, box 1, diary 19 February 1941.

85 Norwich papers, CCC, DUFC3/7 diary 15 September 1941, and Brooke-Popham papers, LHCMA, V/9/5/2, 'Notes on the Far East', Brooke-Popham memorandum 12 March 1942.
86 On SOE see Aldrich, *Britain and the Intelligence War against Japan*, pp. 103–12.
87 FO371/27773 F119/54/61 Eden to Clark Kerr (Chungking) 27 March 1941 tel.324.
88 Best, *Britain, Japan and Pearl Harbor*, pp. 141–2 and 147.
89 FO898/266 Inter-departmental meeting on propaganda 4 March 1941.
90 CAB121/748 Hollis (COS Secretariat) to Cadogan 25 June 1941, and Eden papers, FO954/6/445 FE/41/20 Sterndale Bennett (FE Dept) minute 16 July 1941.
91 FO898/267 'Political Warfare Against Japan', PID report April 1942. It can safely be presumed that G.50,000 referred to Colonel William Donovan.
92 FO371/27903 F12185/27/23 Eden to Craigie (Tokyo) 16 November 1941 tel.1528 INDIV.
93 FO371/25132 W10389/66/49 Halifax to Lampson (Cairo) 26 September 1940 tel.1006, and W11067/66/49 Admiralty to C-in-Cs Mediterranean, E. Indies and China 26 October 1940 tel.1750/26.
94 FO371/27438 J226/37/16 Lampson to Eden 10 February 1941 tel.272.
95 On the cipher facilities see FO371/27466 J1160/418/16 Lampson to Eden 26 April 1941 tel.1125, on the other actions see FO371/27469 J2716/418/16 'Enemy Espionage in Egypt Since the Outbreak of War', Kirk (GSO Egypt) memorandum 12 July 1941.
96 Budiansky, op. cit., p. 184.
97 FO371/27108 E5186/2933/93 Cornwallis to Eden 28 August 1941 tel.988.
98 FO371/27214 E5612/3326/34 Eden to Bullard (Tehran) 13 September 1941 tel.725.
99 See, for example, IOLR M/3/1013 Dorman-Smith to BO, 19 November 1940 tel.1069, CO323/1831/23 Jones to Moyne 12 February 1941, and IOLR L/PJ/12/508 'Weekly Survey of Activities of Foreigners in India', DIB report 5 April 1941.
100 Best, *Britain, Japan and Pearl Harbor*, pp. 123–4.
101 ADM1/10856 Lloyd to Alexander 29 October 1940, and IOLR M/3/896 Dorman-Smith to BO 5 February 1941 tel.87.
102 WO208/1221 External Affairs India to Amery 25 July 1941 tel.3775, and IOLR M/3/818 Dorman-Smith to BO 26 July 1941 tel.584.
103 CAB96/2 FE(41) 28th meeting 31 July 1941.
104 CAB81/88 JIC(41) 24th meeting 8 August 1941.
105 IOLR L/PS/12/2749 Sterndale-Bennett to Gent (CO) 29 October 1941, M/3/818 Ashley Clarke (FE Dept) to Johnston (BO) 10 November 1941, and FO371/29251 W13410/7726/58 Godfrey (DNI) to Cavendish-Bentinck, 13 November 1941 no. P.1021.
106 CAB66/17 WP(41)172 'Japanese Plans in Indo-China', Eden memorandum 20 July 1941.
107 Best, *Britain, Japan and Pearl Harbor*, p. 171.
108 ADM223/321 NID Special Intelligence Summary 23 September 1941 no. 341.
109 HW1/146 BJ.096628 Singapore to Tokyo 9 October circulated 17 October 1941.
110 CAB121/761 Brooke-Popham to WO 20 August 1941 tel.359/4.
111 AIR23/3575 'Tactical Appreciation as to the Strength of the Military Forces Required in Malaya', Percival (GOC Malaya) memorandum 16 September 1941.
112 AIR22/75 AID Weekly Intelligence Summary 21 August 1941 no. 101.

113 WO208/908 Brooke-Popham to WO 3 September 1941 tel.492/4.
114 NAA A663/066/1/602 Eggleston (Chungking) to External Affairs 19 October 1941 no. 4.
115 Shedden papers, NAA, A5954/554/1 Advisory War Council meeting 16 October 1941.
116 Avon papers, BUL, AP20/1/21, diary 12 September 1941. See also Best, *Britain, Japan and Pearl Harbor*, pp. 175-7.
117 CAB121/191 Churchill to Ismay 28 October 1941.
118 Brooke-Popham papers, LHCMA, 6/11/1 Babington to Brooke-Popham 1 August 1941, and 6/11/2 Babington to Brooke-Popham 15 September 1941.
119 NAA MP1587/1/775f COIC Daily Summary 29 October 1941 no. 132 and 13 November 1941 no. 142.
120 CAB66/19 WP(41)259 'Weekly Resumé', Cabinet Office memorandum 6 November 1941.
121 AIR40/2618 CX37065/153 'Japanese in Indochina and Thailand', SIS report 11 November 1941, and CX37400/240 'Japan-Thailand', SIS report 15 November 1941.
122 HW12/270 BJ.097693 Hanoi to Vichy (French) 9 November circulated 14 November 1941.
123 ADM223/321 NID Special Intelligence Summary 16 November 1941 no. 404.
124 FO371/27767 F12823/9/61 Meiklereid (Saigon) to Eden 26 November 1941 tel.226.
125 HW12/269 BJ.096465 Singapore to Tokyo 25 September circulated 12 October 1941 and BJ.097036 Tokyo to Singapore 22 October circulated 28 October 1941, and HW12/270 BJ.097201 Singapore to Tokyo 24 October circulated 1 November 1941.
126 HW12/269 BJ.097037 Bangkok to Singapore 23 October circulated 28 October 1941.
127 HW12/270 BJ.097610 Bangkok to Singapore 6 November circulated 12 November, and HW1/235 BJ.097924 Singapore to Tokyo 8 November circulated 20 November 1941.
128 HW12/270 BJ.098127 Tokyo to London 19 November circulated 25 November 1941, and HW1/259 BJ.098152 Tokyo to Berlin 20 November circulated 25 November 1941. The former is the 'Winds' message which appears from the HW1 files not to have been shown to Churchill.
129 CAB81/105 JIC(41)449 'Possible Japanese Action', JIC report 28 November 1941.
130 ADM199/1477 BAD Washington to DNI tel.2225/26R, 26 November 1941, and NAA MP1587/1/775f COIC Daily Summary of Operational Intelligence 4 December 1941 no. DS/156.
131 NAA MP1587/1/775f COIC Daily Summary of Operational Intelligence 3 December 1941 no. DS/155.
132 HW1/288 BJ.098452 Tokyo to Berlin 30 November circulated 2 December 1941.
133 HW4/25 'History of the "Far East Combined Bureau"', Shaw report undated.
134 For the order to destroy ciphers see HW1/12 BJ.098603 Tokyo to London 2 December circulated 6 December 1941. On the ad hoc committee see CAB107/3 JWB(41) 4th meeting 6 December 1941.
135 ADM199/1472A Young (HK) to CO 8 December 1941.
136 Aldrich, *Britain and the Intelligence War Against Japan*, pp. 86–8.
137 NAA A3300/7/197A Macmillan (Washington) to External Affairs 14 November 1941 no. 363/41.

138 NAA A3300/7/197A Ellis to Casey 21 October 1941.

139 See B. Bruce-Briggs, 'Another Ride on Tricycle', *Intelligence and National Security*, 7 (1992), 77–100, and J.W.H. Chapman, 'Tricycle Recycled: Collaboration Among the Secret Intelligence Services of the Axis States, 1940–41', *Intelligence and National Security*, 7 (1992), 168–99.

## 10 'The Jap is Good': Epilogue and Conclusions

1 CO967/76 Thomas (Singapore) to Parkinson (CO) 17 December 1941.

2 AIR40/35 'Japan: Preliminary Report on T97/1.T97/2 Torpedo Bombers and T.99 Navy Dive Bomber', AI2c 13 December 1941.

3 Percival papers, IWM, file 71, 'Despatch on Operations in Malaya', Percival report March 1946.

4 Brooke-Popham papers, LHCMA, 6/8/8, Brooke-Popham comments on Maltby report 18 November 1946, and Heath papers, RHL, Mss.Ind.Ocn.S117, 'The Malayan Campaign, November 1941–February 1942', Heath report 1942.

5 I. Morrison, *Malayan Postscript* (London: Faber & Faber, 1942), p. 87.

6 Brooke-Popham papers, LHCMA, V/9/5/2, 'Notes on the Far East', Brooke-Popham report 12 March 1942, Layton papers, BL, Add.Mss.74806 Admiralty to Layton 4 June 1947, and Thomas papers, RH, box 2, file 5, 'Comments on General Percival's Despatch', Thomas notes 1948.

7 Ismay papers, LHCMA, 4/14/1 Grimsdale to Ismay 8 March 1942.

8 Grimsdale papers, IWM, memoirs – 'Thunder in the East', p. 111.

9 P. Elphick, *The Far Eastern File: The Intelligence War in the Far East, 1930–1945* (London: Hodder & Stoughton, 1997) pp. 165–70, and R.J. Aldrich, *Britain and the Intelligence War Against Japan, 1941–45: The Politics of Secret Service* (Cambridge: Cambridge University Press, 2000), pp. 60–5.

10 Brooke-Popham papers, LHCMA, V/9/5/2, 'Notes on the Far East', Brooke-Popham report 12 March 1942.

11 CAB101/156 Stewart to Kirby 23 January 1955.

12 CAB101/160 Marchbank to Maltby 21 September 1954. See also S.W. Kirby *et al.*, *The War Against Japan: Vol. 1: The Loss of Singapore* (London: HMSO, 1957), p. 240.

13 ADM223/495 'The Loss of Singapore and its Lessons for NID', Barrett (NID) report undated [1947?].

14 HW4/30 'Mr Arthur Cooper', de Grey (GCCS) report 11 November 1949.

15 P. Elphick, *Singapore: The Pregnable Fortress, A Study in Deception, Discord and Desertion* (London: Hodder & Stoughton, 1995), pp. 115–42, and Aldrich, op. cit., pp. 38–43.

16 Dickinson papers, IWM, 'Organizations in Malaya Concerned in the Period September 1939–February 1942 with Political Intelligence and Security', Dickinson memorandum 12 January 1946.

17 CAB81/88 JIC(41) 24th meeting 8 August 1941.

18 Percival papers, IWM, file 43, Morgan to Percival 4 February 1949.

19 Aldrich, op. cit., pp. 52–9. The documents he refers to are WO208/871 'Comment on DMI's Minutes', undated [January 1942], and ADM223/494 'JIC Appreciations in 1941 of Japanese Intentions', NID report undated.

20 WO208/871 'Comment on DMI's Minutes', undated [January 1942].

21 CAB121/761 Churchill to Ismay no. D4/2, 19 January 1942, and CAB121/748 DiD [?] to Hollis (COS Secretariat) 19 January 1942.

22 CAB119/208 JP(46)29 Final 'Malayan Campaign – Public Inquiry', JPS report 5 March 1946.
23 Ibid.
24 Brooke-Popham papers, LHCMA, 6/8/8, Brooke-Popham note on Maltby (AM) report 18 November 1946. See also A.E. Percival, *The War in Malaya* (London, Eyre & Spottiswode, 1949), p. 72.
25 WO208/1214 Piggott to DMOI 19 August 1938 no. 173.
26 Ismay papers, LHCMA, 4/14/1, Grimsdale to Ismay 8 March 1942.
27 See especially B. Smith, *The Ultra-Magic Deals and the Most Secret Special Relationship, 1940–1946* (Shrewsbury: Airlife, 1993), pp. 65–97.
28 J. Ferris,'"Worthy of Some Better Enemy?", The British Estimate of the Imperial Japanese Army 1919–41 and the Fall of Singapore', *Canadian Journal of History*, 28 (1993), 223–56.
29 D. French, *Raising Churchill's Army: The British Army and the War Against Germany, 1919–1945* (Oxford: Oxford University Press, 2000), passim.
30 W. Wark, 'In Search of a Suitable Japan: British Naval Intelligence in the Pacific Before the Second World War', *Intelligence and National Security*, 1 (1986), 189–211.
31 S. Budiansky, *Battle of Wits: The Complete Story of Codebreaking in World War II* (London: Viking, 2000), pp. 215–7, C. Andrew, *For the President's Eyes Only: Secret Intelligence and the American Presidency From Washington to Bush* (London: HarperCollins, 1995), pp. 103–22, and J.W. Dower, *War Without Mercy: Race and Power in the Pacific War* (London: Faber & Faber, 1986), pp. 108–11.
32 K. Booth, *Strategy and Ethnocentrism* (London: Croom Helm, 1979).

# Bibliography

## Primary sources

### Government documents

*Britain*


*India Office Library, St Pancras*
L/MIL/7 Military Department: Military Collections
L/MIL/17 Military Department Library: Far East Collection
L/PJ/12 Public and Judicial Department: Separate Papers
L/PS/8 Political and Secret Department: Secret Service and Intelligence Papers
L/PS/10 Political and Secret Department: Separate Papers
L/PS/11 Political and Secret Department Papers, 1911–30
L/PS/12 Political External Papers, 1931–41
L/WS/1 War Staff Papers
M/3 Burma Office: Annual Files
M/5 Burma Office: Private and Intelligence Files
M/6 Burma Office: Collections
M/8 Burma Office: Miscellaneous Papers
P/ India Office Proceedings Files

*Public Record Office, Kew*
ADM1 Admiralty Secretariat Papers
ADM116 Admiralty Secretariat Cases
ADM125 China Station
ADM137 War of 1914–18, Official History Cases
ADM178 Admiralty Papers and Cases, Supplementary Series
ADM199 War of 1939–45, War History Cases
ADM205 First Sea Lord
ADM223 Naval Intelligence Division
AIR2 Air Ministry Registered Files
AIR5 Air Historical Branch, Series II
AIR8 Chief of the Air Staff
AIR9 Directorate of Plans
AIR20 Air Ministry Unregistered Papers
AIR22 Intelligence Summaries
AIR23 RAF Overseas Commands
AIR40 Directorate of Air Intelligence
CAB2 CID Minutes
CAB4 CID Memoranda Series B
CAB5 CID Memoranda Series C
CAB16 CID Sub-Committees
CAB21 Cabinet Secretariat
CAB23 Cabinet Minutes
CAB24 Cabinet Memoranda

CAB27 Cabinet Committees
CAB47 Advisory Committee on Trade Questions in Time of War (ATB Committee)
CAB48 Sub-Committee on Industrial Intelligence in Foreign Countries
CAB53 Chiefs of Staff Committee
CAB55 Joint Planning Sub-Committee
CAB56 Joint Intelligence Sub-Committee
CAB65 War Cabinet Minutes
CAB66 War Cabinet Memoranda (WP Series)
CAB69 War Cabinet Defence Committee
CAB79 Wartime Chiefs of Staff Committee Minutes
CAB80 Wartime Chiefs of Staff Committee Memoranda
CAB81 Wartime Joint Intelligence Sub-Committee
CAB84 Wartime Joint Planning Sub-Committee
CAB94 Wartime Overseas Defence Committee
CAB96 Far Eastern Committee
CAB101 Official War Histories: Military Series
CAB104 Cabinet Secretariat Supplementary Registered Papers
CAB107 Co-ordination of Departmental Action in the Event of War With Japan Committee
CAB119 Joint Planning Staff
CAB120 Wartime Ministry of Defence
CAB121 Special Secret Information Centre
CAB122 Joint Staff Mission, Washington
CO129 Hong Kong Correspondence
CO273 Straits Settlements Correspondence
CO323 Colonial Office General Department
CO532 Dominions Correspondence
CO537 General Department, Secret Series
CO717 Federated Malay States Correspondence
CO967 Private Office
CO968 Colonial Office Defence Department
DO35 Dominions Office General Correspondence
FO115 Washington Embassy
FO228 Peking Legation
FO262 Tokyo Embassy
FO366 Chief Clerk's Department
FO368 Commercial Department
FO369 Consular Department
FO371 Foreign Office General Correspondence
FO372 Treaty Department
FO395 Press Department
FO608 Peace Conference 1919
FO624 Baghdad Legation
FO676 Nanking, Shanghai and Chungking Embassy
FO837 Industrial Intelligence Centre and Ministry of Economic Warfare
FO850 Communications Department
FO898 Political Intelligence Department
HD3 Foreign Office Permanent Under-Secretary's Office
HO45 Home Office General Correspondence
HO283 Defence Regulations 18B Advisory Committee
HS1 Special Operations Executive (Far East)

HW1 Signals Intelligence for the Prime Minister, 1941
HW3 GCCS inter-war
HW4 FECB papers
HW7 Room 40 papers
HW12 GCCS: BJ series
HW14 GCCS Second World War
HW37 GCCS Messages for the Director
KV1 MI5 First World War
KV2 MI5 Personal Files
KV4 MI5 Second World War
PREM1 Prime Minister's Office to 1940
PREM3 Prime Minister's Office from 1940
T160 Finance Division
T161 Supply Division
T162 Establishment Division
WO32 Registered Papers
WO106 Directorate of Military Operations and Intelligence
WO154 First World War: War Diaries
WO172 War of 1939–45, Command War Diaries
WO188 Chemical Warfare files
WO190 MI3 Appreciations for the General Staff
WO191 Peacetime War Diaries
WO193 Wartime Directorate of Military Operations
WO208 Wartime Directorate of Military Intelligence
WO287 Directorate of Military Intelligence 'B' Series

*Australia*

*Australian War Memorial, Canberra*
AWM51 Security Classified Records
AWM54 Second World War Written Records
AWM113 Military History Records
AWM124 Naval History Collection

*National Archives of Australia, Canberra*
A663 Defence Department, General Unclassified Files
A816 Defence Department, General Classified Files
A981 External Affairs Department
A1606 Prime Minister's Department General Papers
A1608 Prime Minister's Department Correspondence
A2684 Advisory War Council Minutes
A2937 External Affairs Liaison Officer London Files
A3300 Washington Legation Files
A8911 Commonwealth Investigation Service
SP109/3 Information Department

*National Archives of Australia, Melbourne*
B197 Defence Department Secret and Confidential Reports
MP472 Navy Office Secretariat
MP729/6 Army Secret Correspondence
MP729/7 Army Classified Correspondence

MP1049/5 Navy Classified General Correspondence
MP1049/9 Navy Secret Correspondence
MP1185/8 Navy Secret and Confidential Correspondence
MP1587/1 Naval Historical Records

### Private papers

*Australian War Memorial, Canberra*
Sir Earle Page (AWM92)

*Birmingham University Library*
Lord Avon (Anthony Eden)
Neville Chamberlain

*Bodleian Library, Oxford*
Lord Inverchapel (Sir Archibald Clark Kerr)
Lord Milner
Lord Simon

*British Library, London*
Lord Jellicoe
Admiral Sir Geoffrey Layton

*Churchill College, Cambridge*
Sir Alexander Cadogan
Sir Winston Churchill
Admiral Sir Frederick Dreyer
Admiral W.R. Hall
Sir Hughe Knatchbull Hugessen
Lord Norwich (Alfred Duff Cooper)
Lord Strang

*Imperial War Museum, London*
Major-General R.H. Dewing
Commander Charles Drage
Colonel H.G. Eady
Brigadier L.F. Field
Admiral Sir John Godfrey
Major-General G.E. Grimsdale
Brigadier R.J. Maunsell
Lieutenant-Colonel P. Pender-Cudlip
Lieutenant-General A.E. Percival
Major-General F.S.G. Piggott
Major A.R.E. Pollard
Rear-Admiral G.C. Ross
Brigadier F.H. Vinden
Colonel G.T. Wards

*India Office Library, London*
Lord Irwin
Lord Linlithgow

Sir Frederick Whyte
Lord Zetland

*Liddell Hart Centre for Military Archives, Kings College, London*
Lord Alanbrooke
Commander Sidney Armstrong
Air Chief Marshal Sir Robert Brooke-Popham
General Sir Francis Davidson
Commander Graham De Chair
Admiral Gerald Dickens
Major J.M.L. Gavin
Lord Ismay
Major-General Sir William Penney
Lieutenant-General Henry Pownall
C.A. Vlieland

*Middle East Centre, St Antony's College, Oxford*
Lord Killearn (Miles Lampson)

*National Archives of Australia, Canberra*
Sir Frederick Shedden (A5954)

*National Maritime Museum*
Lord Chatfield
Admiral Sir Thomas Jerram
Admiral Sir Howard Kelly
Admiral W.E.C. Tait

*Public Record Office, Kew*
Sir Austen Chamberlain (FO800)
Sir Warren Fisher (CAB127)
Sir Edward Grey (FO800)
Lord Hankey (CAB63, CAB127)
Lord Ismay (CAB127)
Sir John Jordan (FO350)
Sir Walter Langley (FO800)
Ramsay MacDonald (PRO30/69)
Sir Desmond Morton (PREM7)

*Rhodes House Library, Oxford*
Sir Cecil Clementi
Lieutenant-General Sir Lewis Heath
D.A. Somerville
Sir Miles Shenton Thomas

*St Antony's College, Oxford*
Owen O'Malley
Sir George Sansom

*Sheffield University Library*
Captain Malcolm Kennedy

*Trinity College, Cambridge*
Lord Butler

*Privately held*
Commander Eric Nave (in possession of Professor David Horner)

## Published documents and diaries


Barnes J. and Nicholson J. (eds), *The Leo Amery Diaries,* Volume 1: *1896–1929* (Hutchinson, London, 1980)

Bond, B. (ed.), *Chief of Staff: The Diaries of Lieutenant-General Sir Henry Pownall,* 2 vols (Leo Cooper, London, 1972 and 1975)

Chapman, J.W.M. (ed.), *The Price of Admiralty: The War Diary of the German Naval Attaché in Japan, 1939–1943,* Vols.1–4 (University of Sussex Press, Lewes, 1982, 1984, 1989)

Dilks, D. (ed.), *The Diaries of Sir Alexander Cadogan, 1938–1945* (Cassell, London, 1971)

*Documents on Australian Foreign Policy 1937–1949,* Volumes IV and V (Australian Government Publishing Service, Canberra, 1980–2)

*Documents on British Foreign Policy 1919–1939,* 1st, 2nd and 3rd Series (HMSO, London, 1955–84)

Gilbert, M. (ed.), *Winston S. Churchill,* Vol. III: *Companion, Part III* (Heinemann, London, 1977)

Gilbert, M. (ed.), *Winston S. Churchill, Vol.V: Companion, Part 1* (Heinemann, London, 1979)

Halpern, P. (ed.), *The Keyes Papers: Selections from the Private and Official Correspondence of Admiral of the Fleet Baron Keyes of Zeebrugge,* Vol.II: *1919–1938* (Navy Records Society, Aldershot, 1980)

Harvey, J. (ed.), *The Diplomatic Diaries of Oliver Harvey, 1937–1940* (Collins, London, 1970)

Harvey, J. (ed.), *The War Diaries of Oliver Harvey, 1941–1945* (Collins, London, 1978)

Ike, N. (ed.), *Japan's Decision for War: Records of the 1941 Policy Conferences* (Stanford University Press, Stanford, 1967)

*The Magic Background to Pearl Harbor,* Vols 1–8 (Dept of Defense, Washington DC, 1977)

Pimlott, B. (ed.), *The Second World War Diary of Hugh Dalton, 1940–45* (Jonathan Cape, London, 1986)

Pimlott, B. (ed.), *The Political Diary of Hugh Dalton, 1918–40, 1945–60* (Jonathan Cape, London, 1986)

Ranft, B.M. (ed.), *The Beatty Papers: Selections from the Private and Official Correspondence and Papers of Admiral of the Fleet Earl Beatty,* Vol.II: *1916–1927* (Naval Records Society, Aldershot, 1993)

Self, R. (ed.), *The Austen Chamberlain Diary Letters* (Cambridge University Press, Cambridge, 1995)

Taylor, A.J.P. (ed.), *W.P. Crozier: Off the Record: Political Interviews, 1933–1943* (Hutchinson, London, 1973)

Yapp, M.E. (ed.), *Politics and Diplomacy in Egypt: The Diaries of Sir Miles Lampson, 1935–37* (Oxford University Press, Oxford, 1997)

K. Young, *The Diaries of Sir Robert Bruce-Lockhart,* 2 vols (Macmillan, London, 1972 and 1980)

## Selected secondary sources

### Contemporary books, articles, memoirs, official histories

Ainger, E., 'An Impression of the Far East', *International Affairs*, May 1937.
Betts, T.J., 'The Strategy of Another Russo-Japanese War', *Foreign Affairs*, July 1934.
Chamberlain, W.H., *Japan Over Asia* (London: Duckworth, 1938)
Chapman, F. Spencer, *The Jungle is Neutral* (London; Chatto & Windus, 1949)
Colvin, R., *Memoirs* (Durley: Wintershill Publications, 1992)
Craigie, R., *Behind the Japanese Mask* (London: Hutchinson, 1946)
Drage, C., *The Life and Times of General Two-Gun Cohen* (New York: Funk & Wagnalls, 1954)
Drage, C., *The Amiable Prussian* (London: Blond, 1958)
Kennedy, M., *The Military Side of Japanese Life* (London: Constable, 1924)
Kennedy, M., *Some Aspects of Japan and Her Defence Forces* (London: Kegan Paul, 1928)
Kennedy, M., *The Changing Fabric of Japan* (London: Constable, 1930)
Kennedy, M., 'Russo-Japanese Friction', *Nineteenth Century and After*, October 1934.
Kennedy, M., *The Problem of Japan* (London: Nisbet, 1935)
Kennedy, M., *The Estrangement of Great Britain and Japan, 1917–1935* (Manchester: Manchester University Press, 1969)
Kipling, A.Wellesley , 'The Yellow Peril', *National Defence*, Whitsun 1912.
Kirby, S.W. *et al.*, *The War Against Japan:* Volume I: *The Loss of Singapore* (London: HMSO, 1957)
Layton, E. Pineau, R. and Costello, J. *'And I Was There': Pearl Harbor and Midway, Breaking the Secrets* (New York: William Morrow, 1985)
Lynch, G., *The Path of Empire* (London: Duckworth, 1903)
McCarthy, M.J.E., *The Coming Power, 1898–1905* (London: Hodder & Stoughton, 1905)
Morris, J., *Traveller from Tokyo* (London: Penguin, 1946)
Morrison, I., *Malayan Postscript* (London: Faber & Faber, 1942)
Percival, A.E., *The War in Malaya* (London: Eyre & Spottiswode, 1949)
Piggott, F.S.G., *Broken Thread: An Autobiography* (Aldershot: Gale & Polden, 1950)
Puttnam Weale, B.L., *The Conflict of Colour: Being a Detailed Examination of Racial Problems throughout the World with Special Reference to the English-Speaking Peoples* (London: Macmillan, 1910)
Robertson, E., *The Japanese File: Pre-War Japanese Penetration in Southeast Asia* (Singapore: Heinemann, 1979)
Sempill, Colonel The Master of, 'The British Aviation Mission in Japan', *Transactions and Proceedings of the Japan Society*, 1925.
Stead, A., *Great Japan: A Study in National Efficiency* (London: Bodley Head, n.d.)
Timperley, H.J., *Japanese Terror in China* (Calcutta: Thacker, Spink & Co., 1938)
Utley, F, *Japan's Feet of Clay* (London: Faber & Faber, 1937)
Vespa, A., *Secret Agent of Japan* (London: Gollancz, 1938)

### Books

Akita, S. and Kagotani, N. (eds) *1930-nendai Ajia kokusai chitsujo* [The International Order of Asia in the 1930s] (Hiroshima: Keisui-sha, 2001)
Allen, L., *Singapore, 1941–1942* (London: Davis-Poynter, 1977)

Aldrich, R.J., *The Key to the South: Britain, the United States and Thailand during the Approach of the Pacific War, 1929–1942* (Kuala Lumpur: Oxford University Press, 1993)

Aldrich, R.J., *Britain and the Intelligence War Against Japan, 1941–45: The Politics of Secret Service* (Cambridge: Cambridge University Press, 2000)

Alvarez, D. (ed.), *Allied and Axis Signals Intelligence in World War II* (London: Frank Cass, 1999)

Andrew, C. and Dilks, D. (eds), *The Missing Dimension: Governments and Intelligence Communities in the Twentieth Century* (London: Macmillan, 1984)

Andrew, C., *Secret Service: The Making of the British Intelligence Community* (London: Heinemann, 1985)

Andrew, C., *For the President's Eyes Only: Secret Intelligence and the American Presidency From Washington to Bush* (London: HarperCollins, 1995)

Ball, D. and Horner, D., *Breaking the Codes: Australia's KGB Network, 1944–1950* (St Leonards: Allen Unwin, 1998)

Barnhart, M., *Japan Prepares for Total War: The Search for Economic Security, 1919–1941* (Ithaca: Cornell University Press, 1987)

Bell, C.M., *The Royal Navy, Seapower and Strategy between the Wars* (Basingstoke: Macmillan, 2000)

Bell, P., *Chamberlain, Germany and Japan, 1933–4* (Basingstoke: Macmillan, 1996)

Best, A.M., *Britain, Japan and Pearl Harbor: Avoiding War in East Asia, 1936–41* (London: Routledge, 1995)

Bickers, R., *Britain in China: Community, Culture and Colonialism, 1900–1949* (Manchester: Manchester University Press, 1999)

Booth, K., *Strategy and Ethnocentrism* (London: Croom Helm, 1979)

Boyd, C., *Hitler's Japanese Confidant: General Oshima Hiroshi and MAGIC* (Lawrence: University of Kansas Press, 1993)

Brown, A.C., *'C': The Secret Life of Sir Stewart Menzies, Spymaster to Winston Churchill* (New York: Macmillan, 1987)

Budiansky, S., *Battle of Wits: The Complete Story of Codebreaking in World War II* (London: Viking, 2000)

Chi, H.S., *Nationalist China at War: Military Defeats and Political Collapse, 1937–1945* (Ann Arbor: Michigan University Press, 1982)

Clausen, H. and Lee, B., *Pearl Harbor, Final Judgement* (London: Leo Cooper, 1993)

Connaughton, R., *The War of the Rising Sun and the Tumbling Bear: A Military History of the Russo-Japanese War, 1904–5* (London: Routledge, 1988)

Conroy, H. and Wray H. (eds), *Pearl Harbor Re-examined: Prologue to the Pacific War* (Honolulu: University of Hawaii Press, 1990)

Cowman, I., *Dominion or Decline: Anglo-American Naval Relations in the Pacific, 1937–1941* (Oxford: Berg, 1996)

Coox, A., *The Anatomy of a Small War: The Soviet-Japanese Struggle for Changkunfeng/Khasan* (London: Greenwood Press, 1977)

Coox, A., *Nomonhan: Japan Against Russia, 1939* (Stanford: Stanford University Press, 1985)

Crowley, J.B., *Japan's Quest for Autonomy: National Security and Foreign Policy, 1930–1938* (Princeton: Princeton University Press, 1966)

Dickinson, F., *War and National Reinvention: Japan in the Great War, 1914–1919* (Cambridge, Mass.: Harvard University Press, 1999)

Dockrill, M. and McKercher, B. (eds), *Diplomacy and World Power: Studies in British Foreign Policy, 1890–1950* (Cambridge: Cambridge University Press, 1996)

Dockrill, S. (ed.,), *From Pearl Harbor to Hiroshima: The Second World War in Asia and the Pacific, 1941–45 (*Basingstoke: Macmillan, 1994)
Dower, J.W., *War Without Mercy: Race and Power in the Pacific War* (London: Faber & Faber, 1986)
Drea, E., *In the Service of the Emperor: Essays on the Imperial Japanese Army* (Lincoln: University of Nebraska Press, 1998)
Elphick, P., *Singapore: The Pregnable Fortress, A Study in Deception, Discord and Desertion* (London: Hodder & Stoughton, 1995)
Elphick, P., *The Far Eastern File: The Intelligence War in the Far East, 1930–1945* (London: Hodder & Stoughton, 1997)
Elphick, P. and Smith, M., *Odd Man Out: The Story of the Singapore Traitor* (London: Hodder and Stoughton, 1993)
Endicott, S., *Diplomacy and Enterprise: British China Policy, 1933–1937* (Manchester: Manchester University Press, 1975)
Evans, D.C. and Peattie M., *Kaigun: Strategy, Tactics, and Technology in the Imperial Japanese Navy, 1887–1941* (Annapolis: Naval Institute Press, 1997)
Fergusson, T.G., *British Military Intelligence, 1870–1914: The Development of a Modern Intelligence Organization* (London: Arms & Armour Press, 1984)
Ferris, J., *Men, Money and Diplomacy: The Evolution of British Strategic Policy, 1919–26* (Ithaca: Cornell University Press, 1989)
French, D., *Raising Churchill's Army: The British Army and the War against Germany, 1919–1945* (Oxford: Oxford University Press, 2000)
Furedi, F., *The Silent War: Imperialism and the Changing Perception of Race* (London: Pluto Press, 1998)
Fung, E.S.K., *The Diplomacy of Imperial Retreat: Britain's South China Policy, 1924–1931 (*Oxford: Oxford University Press, 1991)
Garver, J.W., *Chinese–Soviet Relations, 1937–1945: The Diplomacy of Chinese Nationalism (*New York: Oxford University Press, 1988)
Gilchrist, A., *Malaya, 1941* (London: Robert Hale, 1992)
Goto-Shibata, H., *Japan and Britain in Shanghai, 1925–31* (Basingstoke: St Antony's/ Macmillan, 1995)
Haggie, P., *Britannia at Bay: The Defence of the British Empire Against Japan, 1931–1941 (*Oxford: Clarendon, 1981)
Hamill, I., *The Strategic Illusion: The Singapore Strategy and the Defence of Australia and New Zealand* (Singapore: Singapore University Press, 1981)
Handel, M., *War, Strategy and Intelligence* (London: Frank Cass, 1989)
Harper, R.W.E. and Miller, H., *Singapore Mutiny* (Singapore: Oxford University Press, 1984)
Haslam, J., *The Soviet Union and the Threat from the East, 1933–1941* (Basingstoke: Macmillan, 1992)
Heinrichs, W.H., *Threshold of War: Franklin D. Roosevelt and American Entry into World War II* (New York: Oxford University Press, 1988).
Herman, M., *Intelligence Power in Peace and War* (Cambridge: Royal Institute of International Agyui/Cambridge University Press, 1996)
Hoare, J.E. (ed.), *Britain and Japan: Biographical Portraits,* Vol. III (Richmond: Japan Library, 1999)
Horner, D., *High Command: Australia and Allied Strategy, 1939–1945* (Sydney: Allen & Unwin, 1982)
Humphreys, L.A., *The Way of the Heavenly Sword: The Japanese Army in the 1920s* (Stanford: Stanford University Press, 1995)

Iriye, A., *After Imperialism: The Search for a New Order in the Far East, 1921–1931* (Cambridge, Mass.: Harvard University Press, 1965)

Iriye, A., *The Origins of the Second World War in Asia and the Pacific* (London: Longman, 1987)

Jordan, D., *The Northern Expedition: China's National Revolution of 1926–28* (Honolulu: Hawaii University Press, 1976)

Judd, A., *The Quest for C: Sir Mansfield Cumming and the Founding of the British Secret Service* (London: HarperCollins, 1999)

Kirby, S.W., *Singapore: The Chain of Disaster* (London: Cassell, 1971)

Komatsu, K., *Origins of the Pacific War and the Importance of 'Magic'* (Richmond: Japan Library, 1999)

Lauren, P.G., *Power and Prejudice: The Politics and Diplomacy of Racial Discrimination* (Boulder: Westview Press, 1988)

Lee, B.A., *Britain and the Sino-Japanese War, 1937–1939* (Stanford: Stanford University Press, 1973)

Lehmann, J.-P., *The Image of Japan: From Feudal Isolation to World Power, 1850–1905* (London: George Allen & Unwin, 1978)

Louis, W.R., *British Strategy in the Far East, 1919–1939* (Oxford: Clarendon, 1971)

Lowe, P., *Great Britain and Japan, 1911–1915: A Study of British Far Eastern Policy* (London: Macmillan, 1969)

Lowe, P., *Great Britain and the Origins of the Pacific War: A Study of British Policy in East Asia, 1937–1941* (Oxford: Clarendon, 1977)

McKercher, B., *Transition of Power: Britain's Loss of Global Pre-eminence to the United States, 1930–1945* (Cambridge: Cambridge University Press, 1999)

Maiolo, J., *The Royal Navy and Nazi Germany, 1933–39: A Study in Appeasement and the Origins of the Second World War* (Basingstoke: Macmillan, 1998)

Malik, K., *The Meaning of Race: Race, History and Culture in Western Society* (Basingstoke: Macmillan, 1996)

Marder, A.J., *Old Friends, New Enemies: The Royal Navy and the Imperial Japanese Navy, Strategic Missions, 1936–1941* (Oxford: Oxford University Press, 1981)

May, E.R. (ed.), *Knowing One's Enemy: Intelligence Assessment Before the Two World Wars* (Princeton: Princeton University Press, 1984)

Meaney, N., *Fears and Phobias: E.L. Piesse and the Problem of Japan* (Canberra: National Library of Australia, 1996)

Neilson, K. and Kennedy, G. (eds), *Far Flung Lines: Studies in Imperial Defence in Honour of Donald Mackenzie Schurman* (London: Frank Cass, 1997)

Nish, I.H., *The Anglo-Japanese Alliance: The Diplomacy of Two Island Empires, 1894–1907* (London: Athlone, 1966)

Nish, I.H., *Alliance in Decline: A Study in Anglo-Japanese Relations, 1908–23* (London: Athlone, 1972)

Nish, I.H. (ed.), *Anglo-Japanese Alienation, 1919–1952* (Cambridge: Cambridge University Press, 1982)

Nish, I.H., *Japan's Struggle with Internationalism: Japan, China and the League of Nations, 1931–33* (London: Kegan Paul, 1993)

Nish, I.H., and Kibata, Y. (eds), *The History of Anglo-Japanese Relations: The Political and Diplomatic Dimension,* 2 vols (Basingstoke: Macmillan, 2000)

Nozawa, Y. (ed.), *Chukogu no heisei kaikaku to kokusai kankei* [The Chinese Currency Reform and International Relations] (Tokyo: Tokyo University Press, 1981)

Omissi, D., *The Sepoy and the Raj: The Indian Army, 1860–1914* (Basingstoke: Macmillan, 1994)

Ong, C.-C., *Operation Matador: Britain's War Plans Against the Japanese, 1918–1941* (Singapore: Times Academic Press, 1997)

Pantsov, A., *The Bolsheviks and the Chinese Revolution 1919–1927* (Richmond: Curzon, 2000)

Popplewell, R.J., *Intelligence and Imperial Defence: British Intelligence and the Defence of the Indian Empire, 1904–1924* (London: Frank Cass, 1995)

Pritchard, R.J., *Far Eastern Influences upon British Strategy Toward the Great Powers, 1937–1939* (New York: Garland, 1987)

Reynolds, E.B., *Thailand and Japan's Southern Advance, 1940–45* (New York: St Martin's, 1994)

Rich, P., *Race and Empire in British Politics* (Cambridge: Cambridge University Press, 1986)

Rusbridger, J. and Nave, E., *Betrayal at Pearl Harbor: How Churchill Lured Roosevelt into War* (London: Michael O'Mara, 1991)

Sato, K., *Japan and Britain at the Crossroads, 1939–1941. A Study in the Dilemmas of Japanese Diplomacy* (Tokyo: Senshu University Press, 1986)

Shimazu, N., *Japan, Race and Equality: The Racial Equality Proposal of 1919* (London: Routledge, 1998)

Shimizu, H., *Anglo-Japanese Trade Rivalry in the Middle East in the Inter-war Period* (London: St Antony's Middle East Monographs, 1986)

Smith, B., *The Ultra-Magic Deals and the Most Secret Special Relationship, 1940–1946* (Shrewsbury: Airlife, 1993)

Smith, M., *The Emperor's Codes: Bletchley Park and the Breaking of Japan's Secret Ciphers* (London: Bantam Press, 2000)

Stinnet, R.B., *Day of Deceit: The Truth About F.D.R. and Pearl Harbor* (New York: Free Press, 1999)

Sun, Y-L., *China and the Origins of the Pacific War, 1931–1941* (New York: St Martin's, 1993)

Tarling, N., *Britain, Southeast Asia and the Onset of the Pacific War* (Cambridge: Cambridge University Press, 1996)

Thorne, C., *The Limits of Foreign Policy: The West, the League and the Far Eastern Crisis of 1931–1933* (London: Hamish Hamilton, 1972)

Thorne, C., *Allies of a Kind: The United States, Britain and the War against Japan, 1941–1945* (Oxford: Oxford University Press, 1978)

Thorne, C., *The Issue of War: The State, Society and the Far Eastern Conflict of 1941–1945* (London: Hamish Hamilton, 1985)

Towle, P. (ed.), *Estimating Foreign Military Power* (London: Croom Helm, 1982)

Trotter, A., *Britain and East Asia, 1933–1937* (Cambridge: Cambridge University Press, 1975)

Utley, J.G., *Going to War with Japan, 1937–1941* (Knoxville: University of Tennessee Press, 1985)

Wakeman, F., *Policing Shanghai 1927–1937* (Berkeley: University of California Press, 1995)

Waldron, A., *From War to Nationalism: China's Turning Point, 1924–1925* (Cambridge: Cambridge University Press, 1995)

Wark, W., *The Ultimate Enemy: British Intelligence and Nazi Germany, 1933–1939* (London: I.B. Tauris, 1985)

Wasserstein, B., *Secret War in Shanghai: Treachery, Subversion and Collaboration in the Second War* (London: Profile, 1998)

Wilbur, C.M., *The Nationalist Revolution in China, 1923–1928* (Cambridge: Cambridge University Press, 1983)

Wilbur, C.M. and How, J.H-Y., *Missionaries of Revolution: Soviet Advisers and Nationalist China, 1920–1927* (Cambridge, Mass.: Harvard University Press, 1989)

Winter, B., *The Intrigue Master: Commander Long and Naval Intelligence in Australia, 1913–1945* (Brisbane: Boolarong Press, 1995)

Wohlstetter, R., *Pearl Harbor: Warning and Decision* (Stanford: Stanford University Press, 1962)

Yong, C.F. and McKenna, R.B., *The Kuomintang Movement in British Malaya, 1912–1949* (Singapore: Singapore University Press, 1990)

## Articles and essays

Aldrich, R.J., '"Conspiracy or Confusion?" Churchill, Roosevelt and Pearl Harbor', *Intelligence and National Security*, 7 (1993), 335–46.

Aldrich, R.J., 'Britain's Secret Intelligence Service in Asia During the Second World War', *Modern Asian Studies*, 32 (1998), 179–217.

Barnhart, M., 'Japanese Intelligence Before the Second World War: "Best Case" Analysis', in May, E.R. (ed.), *Knowing One's Enemy: Intelligence Assessment before the Two World Wars* (Princeton: Princeton University Press, 1984)

Bell, C.M., 'The "Singapore Strategy" and the Deterrence of Japan: Winston Churchill, the Admiralty and the Dispatch of Force Z', *English Historical Review*, CXIV (2001), 608–34.

Bennett, G., 'British Policy in the Far East 1933–1936: Treasury and Foreign Office', *Modern Asian Studies*, 26 (1992), 545–68.

Best, A., 'Straws in the Wind: Britain and the February 1941 War Scare in East Asia', *Diplomacy and Statecraft*, 5 (1994), 642–65.

Best, A., 'Constructing an Image: British Intelligence and Whitehall's Perception of Japan, 1931–39,' *Intelligence and National Security*, 11 (1996), 403–23.

Best, A., '"This Probably Over-Valued Military Power": British Intelligence and Whitehall's Perception of Japan, 1939–41', *Intelligence and National Security*, 12 (1997), 67–94.

Best, A., 'The Road to Anglo-Japanese Confrontation, 1931–41', in I.H. Nish and Y. Kibata (eds), *The History of Anglo-Japanese Relations: The Political and Diplomatic Dimension*, Vol. 2: *1931–2000* (Basingstoke: Macmillan, 2000)

Best, A., 'Intelligence, Diplomacy and the Japanese Threat to British Interests, 1914–41', *Intelligence and National Security*, 17 (2002) 87–102.

Bickers, R., 'Who Were the Shanghai Municipal Police, and Why Were They There? The British Recruits of 1919', in Bickers, R. and Henriot C. (eds), *New Frontiers: Imperialism's New Communities in East Asia, 1842–1953* (Manchester: Manchester University Press, 2000)

Bourette-Knowles, S., 'The Global Micawber: Sir Robert Vansittart, the Treasury and the Global Balance of Power, 1933–35, *Diplomacy and Statecraft*, 6 (1995), 111-121.

Boyd, C., 'Significance of MAGIC and the Japanese Ambassador in Berlin: The Formative Months before Pearl Harbor', *Intelligence and National Security*, 2 (1987), 150–69.

Bruce-Briggs, B., 'Another Ride on Tricycle', Intelligence and National Security, 7 (1992), 77–100.

Budiansky, S., 'Too Late for Pearl Harbor', *US Naval Institute Proceedings* (1999), 47–51.

Bussemake, H.T., 'Paradise in Peril: The Netherlands, Great Britain, and the Defence of the Netherlands East Indies', *Journal of Southeast Asian Studies*, 31 (2000), 115–36.

Chapman, J.W.H., 'Commander Ross R.N. and the Ending of Anglo-Japanese Friendship, 1933–1936', in I.H. Nish (ed.), *Anglo-Japanese Naval Relations* (LSE STICERD International Studies Series, 1985)

Chapman, J.W.H., 'Japanese Intelligence, 1919–1945: A Suitable Case for Treatment', in C. Andrew and J. Noakes (eds), *Intelligence and International Relations, 1900–1945* (Exeter: Exeter University Publications, 1987)

Chapman, J.W.H., 'Pearl Harbor: The Anglo-Australian Dimension', *Intelligence and National Security*, 4 (1989), 451–60.

Chapman, J.W.H., 'Signals Intelligence Collaboration among the Tripartite Pact States on the Eve of Pearl Harbor', *Japan Forum*, 3 (1991), 231–56.

Chapman, J.W.H., 'Tricycle Recycled: Collaboration among the Secret Intelligence Services of the Axis States, 1940–41', *Intelligence and National Security*, 7 (1992), 168–99.

Charrier, P., 'The Evolution of a Stereotype: The Royal Navy and the Japanese "Martial Type", 1900–1945', *War and Society*, 19 (2001), 23–46.

Collini, S., 'The Idea of "Character" in Victorian Political Thought,' *Transactions of the Royal Historical Society*, 35 (1985), 29–50.

Doerr, P.W., 'The Changkufeng/Lake Khasan Incident of 1938: British Intelligence on Soviet and Japanese Military Performance', *Intelligence and National Security*, 5 (1990), 184–99.

Drea, E.J., 'Reading Each Other's Mail: Japanese Communications Intelligence, 1920–1941', *Journal of Military History*, 55 (1991), 185–206.

Ferris, J., 'A British "Unofficial" Aviation Mission and Japanese Naval Developments, 1919–1929', *Journal of Strategic Studies*, 5 (1982), 416–39.

Ferris, J., 'Whitehall's Black Chamber: British Cryptology and the Government Code and Cypher School', *Intelligence and National Security*, 2 (1987), 54–91.

Ferris, J., 'The British Army and Signals Intelligence in the Field during the First World War', *Intelligence and National Security*, 3 (1988), 23–48.

Ferris, J., 'From Broadway House to Bletchley Park: The Diary of Captain Malcolm Kennedy, 1934–1946', *Intelligence and National Security*, 4 (1989), 421–50.

Ferris, J., 'Before "Room 40": The British Empire and Signals Intelligence, 1898–1914', *Journal of Strategic Studies*, 12 (1989), 431–57.

Ferris, J., '"Worthy of Some Better Enemy?" The British Estimate of the Imperial Japanese Army 1919–41 and the Fall of Singapore', *Canadian Journal of History*, 28 (1993), 223–56.

Ferris, J., '"Indulged in All Too Little"? Vansittart, Intelligence and Appeasement', *Diplomacy and Statecraft*, 6 (1995), 122–75.

Ferris, J., '"It is Our Business in the Navy to Command the Seas": The Last Decade of British Maritime Supremacy, 1919–1929', in Neilson, K. and Kennedy, G. (eds), *Far Flung Lines: Studies in Imperial Defence in Honour of Donald Mackenzie Schurman* (London: Frank Cass, 1997)

Fisher, J., '"Backing the Wrong Horse": Japan in British Middle East Policy 1914–18', *Journal of Strategic Studies*, 21 (1998), 60–74.

Fisher, J., 'The Interdepartmental Committee on Eastern Unrest and British Responses to Bolshevik and Other Intrigues Against the Empire during the 1920s', *Journal of Asian History*, 34 (2000), 1–34.

Foster, A.L., 'Secret Police Cooperation and the Roots of Anti-Communism in Southeast Asia', *Journal of American–East Asian Relations*, 4 (1995), 331–50.

Fraser, T.G., 'Germany and Indian Revolution, 1914–18', *Journal of Contemporary History*, 12 (1977), 255–72.

Fraser, T.G., 'India in Anglo–Japanese Relations During the First World War', *History*, 209 (1978), 366–82.

Gobert, W., 'The Origins of Australian Diplomatic Intelligence in Asia, 1933–1941', *Canberra Papers on Strategy and Defence* (1992).

Goto-Shibata, H., 'Anglo-Japanese Cooperation in China in the 1920s', in Nish, I.H. and Y. Kibata (eds), *The History of Anglo-Japanese Relations: The Political and Diplomatic Dimension,* Vol. 1: *1600–1930* (Basingstoke: Macmillan, 2000).

Harris, R., 'The "Magic" Leak of 1941 and Japanese–American Relations', *Pacific Historical Review*, 50 (1981), 76–95.

Harvey, A.D., 'Army Air Force and Navy Air Force: Japanese Aviation and the Opening Phase of the War in the Far East', *War in History*, 6 (1999), 174–204.

Hatano, S. and Asada, S., 'The Japanese Decision to Move South, 1939–41', in R. Boyce and E.M. Robertson (eds), *Paths to War: New Essays on the Origins of the Second World War* (Basingstoke: Macmillan, 1989)

Holmes, C. and Ion, A.H., 'Bushidō and the Samurai: Images in British Public Opinion, 1894–1914', *Modern Asian Studies*, 14 (1980), 309–29.

Hosoya, C., '1934-nen no Nichi-Ei fukashin kyotei mondai' [The Problem of the Anglo-Japanese Non-Aggression Pact in 1934], *Kokusai Seiji* [International Politics], (1977), 69–85.

Hosoya, C., 'Britain and the US in Japan's View of the International System, 1919–37', in Nish, I.H. (ed.), *Anglo–Japanese Alienation, 1919–1952* (Cambridge: Cambridge University Press, 1982)

Inoue, T., '1934-nen no Nihon no fukashin kyōtei kōso to Ei-Bei no taiō' [Anglo-American Responses to Japan's Envisioned Non-Aggression Pact in 1934], *Kindai Nihon Kenkyu* [Journal of Modern Japanese Studies], 11 (1989), 93–119.

Ion, A.H., 'Japan Watchers: 1903–1931', in Howes, J.F. (ed.), *Nitobe Inazo: Japan's Bridge Across the Pacific* (Boulder: Westview, 1995)

Kahn, D., 'The Intelligence Failure of Pearl Harbor', *Foreign Affairs*, 70 (1991–2), 138–52.

Kaiser, D., '"Conspiracy or Cock-up?" Pearl Harbor Revisited', *Intelligence and National Security*, 9 (1994), 354–72.

Kennedy, G., '1935: A Snapshot of British Imperial Defence in the Far East', in Neilson, K & Kennedy, G. (eds), *Far Flung Lines: Studies in Imperial Defence in Honour of Donald Mackenzie Schurman* (London: Frank Cass, 1997)

Kibata, Y., 'Risu-Rosu shisetsudan to Ei-Chu kankei' [The Leith-Ross Mission and Anglo-Chinese Relations], in Y. Nozawa (ed.), *Chukogu no heisei kaikaku to kokusai kankei* [The Chinese Currency Reform and International Relations] (Tokyo: Tokyo University Press, 1981)

Kibata, Y., 'Anglo-Japanese Relations From the Manchurian Incident to Pearl Harbor: Missed Opportunities?', in I.H. Nish and Y. Kibata (eds), *The History of Anglo-Japanese Relations: The Political and Diplomatic Dimension,* Vol. 2, *1931–2000* (Basingstoke: Macmillan, 2000)

Kibata, Y., 'Igirisu teikoku no henyō to higashi Ajia' [East Asia and the Changing Nature of the British Empire], in S. Akita and N. Kagotani (eds), *1930–nendai Ajia kokusai chitsujo* [The International Order of Asia in the 1930s] (Hiroshima: Keisui–sha, 2001)

Kowner, R., '"Lighter Than Yellow", But Not Enough: Western Discourse on the Japanese "Race", 1854–1904', *Historical Journal*, 43 (2000), 103–31.

Litten, F.S., 'The Noulens Affair', *China Quarterly*, 138 (1994), 492–512.

Lowe, P., 'Great Britain, Japan and the Fall of Yuan Shih-k'ai, 1915–1916', *Historical Journal*, XIII (1970), 706–20.

Lowe, P., 'Great Britain's Assessment of Japan before the Outbreak of the Pacific War', in May, E.R. (ed.), *Knowing One's Enemy: Intelligence Assessment before the Two World Wars (*Princeton University Press, Princeton, 1984)

Louis, W.R., 'The Road to Singapore: British Imperialism in the Far East, 1932–41', in W.J. Mommsen and L. Kettenacker (eds), *The Fascist Challenge and the Policy of Appeasement* (London: Allen & Unwin, 1983).

McKercher, B., '"A Sane and Sensible Policy": Austen Chamberlain, Japan, and the Naval Balance of Power in the Pacific Ocean', *Canadian Journal of History*, 21 (1985), 187–213

McKercher, B., 'Old Diplomacy and New: The Foreign Office and Foreign Policy, 1919–1939', in M. Dockrill and B. McKercher (eds), *Diplomacy and World Power: Studies in British Foreign Policy, 1890–1950* (Cambridge: Cambridge University Press, 1996)

Mahnken, T.G., 'Gazing at the Sun: The Office of Naval Intelligence and Japanese Naval Innovation, 1918–1941', *Intelligence and National Security*, 11 (1996), 424–41.

Neilson, K., '"That Difficult and Dangerous Enterprise": British Military Thinking and the Russo-Japanese War', *War and Society*, 9 (1991), 17–37.

Nish, I.H., 'Echoes of Alliance, 1920–30' in I.H. Nish and Y. Kibata (eds), *The History of Anglo-Japanese Relations: The Political and Diplomatic Dimension,* Vol. 1: *1600–1930* (Basingstoke: Macmillan, 2000)

Sakai, T., '"Ei-Bei kenkyu" to "Nichi-Chu teikei"' [Cooperation with the West or Collaboration with China: An Interpretative Essay on Early Showa Diplomacy], *Kindai Nihon Kenkyu* [Journal of Modern Japanese Studies], 11 (1989), 61–92.

Sissons, D.C.S., 'More on Pearl Harbor', *Intelligence and National Security*, 9 (1994), 373–9.

Tarling, N., '"A Vital British Interest": Britain, Japan and the Security of the Netherlands India in the Inter-War Period', *Journal of Southeast Asian Studies*, 9 (1978), 180–218.

Thorne, C., 'Racial Aspects of the Far Eastern War of 1941–1945', *Proceedings of the British Academy*, 66 (1980), 329–77.

Towle, P., 'British Naval and Military Observers of the Russo-Japanese War', in J.E. Hoare (ed.), *Britain and Japan: Biographical Portraits,* Vol. III (Richmond: Japan Library, 1999)

Walton, R.D., 'Feeling for the Jugular: Japanese Espionage at Newcastle, 1919–1926', *Australian Journal of Politics and History*, 32 (1986), 20–38.

Wark, W., 'In Search of a Suitable Japan: British Naval Intelligence in the Pacific Before the Second World War', *Intelligence and National Security*, 1 (1986), 189–211.

Yu, M., 'Chinese Codebreakers, 1927–45', in D. Alvarez (ed.), *Allied and Axis Signals Intelligence in World War II* (London: Frank Cass, 1999)

# Index

KU-781-352

RUSSIA
SWEDEN
FINLAND
NORWAY
ESTONIA
LATVIA
LITHUANIA
GREAT BRITAIN
DENMARK
IRELAND
NETH.
POLAND
BELARUS
GERMANY
BELGIUM
LUX.
CZECH
UKRAINE
SLOVAKIA
LIECH.
FRANCE
HUNGARY
MOLD.
ITALY
BULGARIA
GEORGIA
ARM.
AZER.
SPAIN
GREECE
TURKEY
KAZAKHSTAN
MONGOLIA
UZBEKISTAN
KYRGYZSTAN
TURKMENISTAN
TAJIKISTAN
N. KOREA
S. KOREA
JAPAN
CHINA
MALTA
TUNISIA
CYPRUS
SYRIA
LEB.
ISRAEL
IRAQ
IRAN
JORDAN
AFGHANISTAN
MOROCCO
ALGERIA
LIBYA
EGYPT
KUWAIT
SAUDI ARABIA
BAHRAIN
UNITED ARAB EMIR.
OMAN
PAKISTAN
NEPAL
BHUTAN
BANGLADESH
INDIA
MYANMAR (BURMA)
VIETNAM
LAOS
TAIWAN
PACIFIC OCEAN
MALI
NIGER
CHAD
SUDAN
ERITREA
YEMEN
DJIBOUTI
THAILAND
CAMBODIA
PHILIPPINES
BURKINA FASO
BENIN
GUINEA
IVORY COAST
LIBERIA
NIGERIA
CENTRAL AFRICAN REP.
ETHIOPIA
SRI LANKA
BRUNEI
MALAYSIA
GHANA
TOGO
CAMEROON
SOMALIA
UGANDA
EQUATORIAL GUINEA
GABON
CONGO
ZAIRE
RWANDA
BURUNDI
KENYA
TANZANIA
SEYCHELLES
INDIAN OCEAN
INDONESIA
PAPUA NEW GUINEA
CABINDA (ANGOLA)
COMOROS
ANGOLA
ZAMBIA
MALAWI
MOZAMBIQUE
NAMIBIA
ZIMBABWE
BOTSWANA
MADAGASCAR
MAURITIUS
REUNION (FRANCE)
SWAZILAND
SOUTH AFRICA
LESOTHO
AUSTRALIA

# MARKETING

FIFTH EDITION

# MARKETING

FIFTH EDITION

**WILLIAM G. ZIKMUND**
*Oklahoma State University*

**MICHAEL D'AMICO**
*University of Akron*

**WEST PUBLISHING COMPANY**
*Minneapolis/St.Paul ■ New York ■ Los Angeles ■ San Francisco*

PRODUCTION CREDITS
*Copyeditor* Beverly Peavler
*Interior Design* Roslyn M. Stendahl
*Page Layout* DeNee Reiton Skipper
*Photo Researcher* Eva Tucholka
*Artwork* Randy Miyake
*Composition* Parkwood Composition
*Indexer* Terry Casey
*Cover Image* Richard Mackson/Sports Illustrated/© Time Inc.

WEST'S COMMITMENT TO THE ENVIRONMENT

In 1906, West Publishing Company began recycling materials left over from the production of books. This began a tradition of efficient and responsible use of resources. Today, up to 95 percent of our legal books and 70 percent of our college and school texts are printed on recycled, acid-free stock. West also recycles nearly 22 million pounds of scrap paper annually—the equivalent of 181,717 trees. Since the 1960s, West has devised ways to capture and recycle waste inks, solvents, oils, and vapors created in the printing process. We also recycle plastics of all kinds, wood, glass, corrugated cardboard, and batteries, and have eliminated the use of Styrofoam book packaging. We at West are proud of the longevity and the scope of our commitment to the environment.

Production, Prepress, Printing and Binding by West Publishing Company.

British Library Cataloguing-in-Publication Data. A catalogue record for this book is available from the British Library.


610 Opperman Drive
P.O. Box 64526
St. Paul, MN 55164-0526



Printed in the United States of America

03 02 01 00 99 98 97 96 8 7 6 5 4 3 2 1 0

Library of Congress Cataloging-in-Publication Data

Zikmund, William G.
Marketing / William G. Zikmund, Michael d'Amico. — 5th ed.
p. cm.
Includes index.
ISBN 0-314-06214-9 (Student Edition)
ISBN 0-314-07170-9 (Annotated Instructor's Edition)
1. Marketing. I. d'Amico, Michael. II. Title.
HF5415.Z54 1996
658.8—dc20 95-23375
CIP

*To Tobin and Noah Zikmund*
*Kathy and Alyse d'Amico*

# Brief Contents

# Contents

## CHAPTER 6 Consumer Behavior: Decision-Making Processes and Sociocultural Forces 170



## CHAPTER 7 Business Markets and Organizational Buying 204

SHISEIDO
食事、おしゃべり、キス、着がえ。
落ちない、つかない、パーフェクトルージュ
Perfect Rouge
レシェンテ
Perfect Rouge

AQUATRED

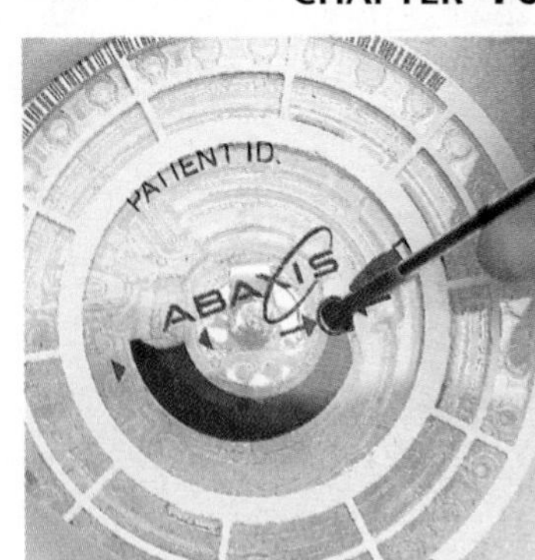
PATIENT ID.
ABAXIS

# MARKETING

FIFTH EDITION

# PART ONE

# Introduction

THE NATURE OF MARKETING

MARKETING MANAGEMENT: STRATEGY AND ETHICAL BEHAVIOR

ENVIRONMENTAL FORCES IN A DIVERSE WORLD:
THE MACROENVIRONMENT

THE MICROENVIRONMENT IN AN ERA OF GLOBAL COMPETITION

There is only one boss—the customer. And he can fire everybody in the company from the chairman on down, simply by spending his money somewhere else.

Sam Walton

CHAPTER

# 1 The Nature of Marketing

## LEARNING OBJECTIVES

After you have studied this chapter, you will be able to:

1. Understand how marketing affects our daily lives.
2. Define *marketing* and discuss marketing in its broadened sense.
3. Identify the elements of the marketing mix.
4. Understand that marketers must contend with external environmental forces.
5. Explain the marketing concept.
6. Explain total quality management.
7. Recognize the contribution of marketing to the economy and our way of life.
8. Define the societal marketing concept.

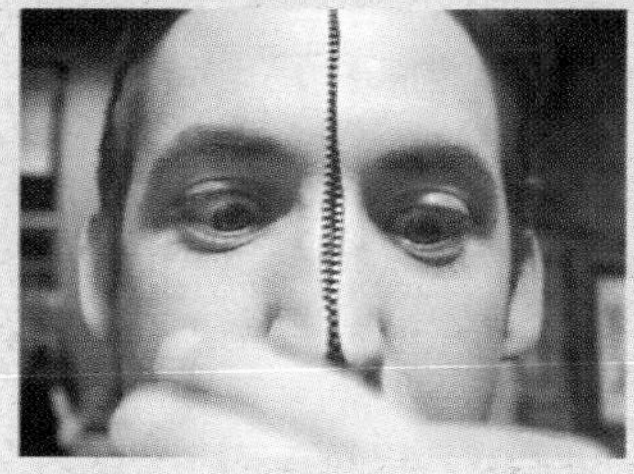

The television commercial opens with a fish-eyed security-camera's eye view of a convenience store and a strung-out young man in the cold cereal aisle. Looking furtively over his shoulder, he takes boxes of Cheerios, Wheaties, and Trix to checkout, where a cashier laughingly says, "Trix? Trix are for kids."

The edgy customer tosses the money at her and flees. Back at his apartment, he triple locks himself inside and tosses the Wheaties and Cheerios to the floor. The kitchen table awaits with an empty bowl and an open carton of milk. "Finally," he gasps, "after all these years of 'Trix are for kids! Trix are for kids!' Well, today. . . they're for rabbits! Hah hah hah hah!"

Thanks to computer animation, the guy has reached back and unzipped his face. What we now realize was a remarkable costume is peeled away to reveal a familiar cartoon character: the Trix rabbit himself.

Cackling with glee, rabbit takes the carton and begins to pour milk onto the cereal he has been waiting 30 years to eat, but—to his horror and frustration—only a few drops dribble out. Then comes the title card and the voice of an announcer saying: "Got milk?"

The commercial is a recent entry in a marketing campaign created by the advertising agency of Goodby, Silverstein & Partners and sponsored by the California Fluid Milk Processor Advisory Board. An earlier commercial in the series featured an Aaron Burr–obsessed history buff who blows a chance at radio-quiz riches because his mouth is full of peanut butter when he has to answer who shot Alexander Hamilton. The point in both advertisements is clear: you'd better have milk around!

Before the "Got milk" series debuted in November 1993, reminding consumers of milk's health and nutritional benefits, there had been an uninteresting belaboring of obvious ideas—like "Milk does a body good"—that accompanied a steady decline in per capita milk consumption.

The "got milk" message defied conventional dairy-marketing wisdom by positioning milk not as a life essential but as a lifestyle essential—something you need to have on hand, if only to go with the foods you need to have it on hand for. The consequence of this marketing effort has been a sharp increase in sales and the first leveling off of per capita milk consumption in years.

Why do people drink milk? What role does advertising play in increasing the consumption of milk? How important is the price of the product? Are all brands of milk thought of as the same? What do supermarkets and organizations like the California Fluid Milk Processor Advisory Board do that motivate consumers to buy? Is being socially responsible an important concern for a marketing organization? The answers to questions like these lie in the field of marketing, the subject of this book.

Chapter 1 begins by developing a definition of *marketing*. It then discusses the components of the marketing mix and the environment in which marketing must operate. The marketing concept, which is central to all effective marketing, is described next. Finally, the chapter discusses the role of marketing in society and as an academic discipline.

**ALTERNATIVE EXAMPLE**

Ticketless travel or electronic ticketing by airlines like Southwest, Western Pacific, and ValuJet benefit both the customer and the company. Ticketless travel makes it simpler and faster to board an airplane. Passengers also benefit because they don't have to worry about remembering or losing their tickets. Airlines save millions of dollars by eliminating hundreds of accounting positions necessary to track tickets. (SOURCE: M. Wilke, "Nix to Tix," *Advertising Age*, August 14, 1995, p. 1).

## Marketing Affects Our Daily Lives

Perhaps you have thought of some answers to the questions we asked in the introduction. After all, you have visited shopping centers, examined retail displays, compared prices, dealt with salespeople, and evaluated and purchased a wide range of products. If you think about it, as customers, we all play a part in the marketing system, so we all know something about marketing. We all recognize brand names and corporate logos. Television advertising has been an irritant and a source of pleasure to us all.

Some aspects of marketing are, of course, more widely known than others. The brand names shown in Exhibit 1–1 are probably quite familiar to you. The brand names in Exhibit 1–2 are probably not; they identify corporations most consumers seldom encounter directly. These companies buy goods and services in order to produce other goods and services, thus performing important marketing activities "behind the scenes." Although most of us deal regularly with retailers and sales clerks, we less frequently encounter wholesalers, industrial sales representatives, and advertising agents. Indeed, there are many aspects of marketing that many people have never considered systematically. Most people do not fully understand marketing's place in society or how marketing activities should be managed. To fully understand marketing, we must first know what it is and what it includes.

**EXHIBIT 1–1** You Already Know Something about Marketing

**EXHIBIT 1–2**

Many Companies Engaged in Marketing Operate "Behind the Scenes"

## Marketing—What Is It?

As we will see, there are several ways to consider the subject of marketing, so there are a number of ways to define the term itself. Because for most people marketing has a business connotation, it is best to begin by discussing marketing from a business perspective.

Marketing, as the term implies, is focused on the marketplace. (In fact, for shoppers of past generations, the word *marketing* meant going to a store or market to buy groceries.) A businessperson who is asked the question "What is marketing?" might answer that marketing is selling, or advertising, or retailing. But notice that these are marketing activities, not definitions of marketing as a whole.

At the broadest level, the function of marketing activities is to bring buyers and sellers together. At the beach, the thirsty sunbather seeks the Pepsi stand owner. The owner is, in turn, interested in selling soft drinks to satisfy the customer's thirst. The owner's marketing activities, such as locating the stand at the beach and advertising the price on a sign, help bring buyer and seller together. The owner's goal is to consummate a sale to satisfy a customer. This, of course, is a simple example. A more sophisticated situation requires more complex marketing activities.

POINT TO EMPHASIZE

The heavy demand for Power Rangers might lead to the conclusion that they need no marketing, but that is not the case. The firm may need to allocate products among distributors and to communicate well with them in order to maintain good relationships.

Suppose you were the marketing vice-president of Bandai America, a company in Cerritos, California, that markets the Mighty Morphin Power Ranger toys. The company's headquarters are in Japan, and most of Bandai's toys are produced in Asia and Mexico. Thus, production—which is an important business activity but not a marketing activity—is not directly under your control. Instead, your marketing activities might be identified as product planning, determining prices, advertising, selling, distributing products to consumers, and servicing the products after sales have been made. And even this extensive list is not complete.

A full understanding of marketing requires recognition of the fact that product development activities and product modifications are planned in response to the public's changing needs and wants. A major marketing activity, then, is paying continuous attention to customers' needs, identifying and interpreting those needs *before* other steps, including production, are undertaken. Although most marketing activities are intended to direct the flow of goods and services from producer to consumer, the marketing process begins with customer analysis even before the product is manufactured.

ALTERNATIVE EXAMPLE

*Elle* magazine was launched in the United States in 1985 as a very French, very visual magazine, but it languished until Amy Gross was named editorial director in 1993. Putting more content into the magazine by adding a health column, movie reviews, and other features improved the magazine's appeal to the modern American woman. Gone were traditional sections such as food. In 1994, *Elle* passed *Harper's Bazaar* to become the number-two magazine in its category. By recognizing that women need more information, *Elle* better serves its market and consequently sells more magazines. SOURCE: June Weir, "*Elle* Fashions Climb into No. 2 Slot." *Advertising Age,* March 6, 1995, p. S12.

Consider again Bandai's Mighty Morphin Power Ranger toys. These action figures are toy replicas of the multi-ethnic characters on television's popular *Mighty Morphin Power Rangers* show. The program features six teen-age characters who, armed with power derived from prehistoric animals, do battle against evil forces and robot vehicles to save the earth.[1] (See Exhibit 1–3.)

Before the Power Rangers, Bandai's main business—creating toys from popular Japanese movie and television characters—had been very successful in Japan but had failed abroad. Popular Japanese toys such as Ultraman, a metallic superhero with laser-beam eyes, were "too foreign" for the U.S. market.[2] In essence, Bandai had failed to mount the marketing efforts needed to adapt its toys to American markets.

However, with the support of Japanese moviemaker Toei Company, California producer Saban Entertainment, and Fox Children's Network, Bandai was able to make the long-running Japanese *Jyu Rangah* (Power Ranger) television series and toys work for U.S. viewers.

Based on American needs, Bandai made some changes in the Japanese models. It toned down the violence of the television program for the U.S. audience, portraying the off-duty Rangers as normal kids who shoot baskets, mall-hop, and do aerobics when they aren't battling evil space aliens. And it added a moral at the end of each show. Bandai also "Americanized" the toys, making the unmasked characters look

EXHIBIT 1–3 The Mighty Morphin Power Rangers

American and giving more focus to the female part of the team. It did, however, stay faithful to the toys' original technical intricacy—ensuring, for example that the index finger moves to hold a laser gun—because both Japanese and American children like such features.

By discussing the new product idea with Americans before beginning to manufacture the toys, Bandai marketers developed a better understanding of the differing needs of Japanese and American children. Thus, Bandai's American operation does not merely manufacture toys; it interprets the U.S. market's needs. Today, Power Rangers can be found adorning all sorts of products. The distinctive images of Billy the Blue Ranger, Jason the Red Ranger, Trini the Yellow Ranger, Zak the Black Ranger, Kimberly the Pink Ranger, and Tommy the Green Ranger are popping up on underwear, T-shirts, bottles of bubble bath, jigsaw puzzles, stickers, coloring books, paper plates, and wastebaskets.

## Not-for-Profit Organizations Are Marketers Too!

"Perform a death-defying act—eat less saturated fat." The American Heart Association offered this admonition in an advertisement, yet the Heart Association does not seek to make a profit, nor does it charge a price for most services. Is the American Heart Association engaging in marketing? Are your university, church, and local police department marketers? If we take a broadened perspective of marketing, the answer is unquestionably "Yes."

**EXHIBIT 1–4** A Broader Perspective of Marketing Includes Not-for-Profit Organizations

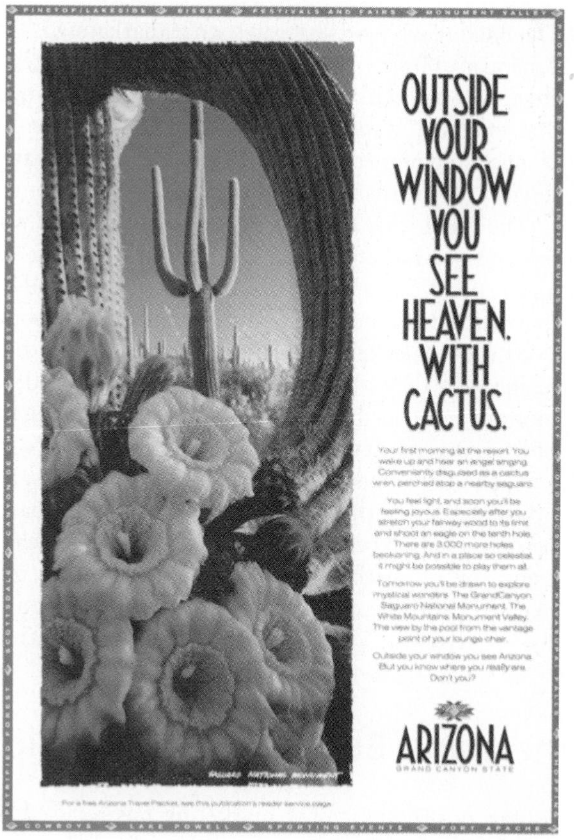


**EXCHANGE PROCESS**
The interchange of something of value between two or more parties.

DISCUSSION CONSIDERATION
Do individuals engage in marketing? Ask students whether they are engaging in marketing when they try to make friends, meet potential dates, and interview for jobs. Do professors market courses? If these efforts of students and professors aren't marketing, then what are they?

If the concept of marketing is broadened to include not-for-profit organizations, then the primary emphasis of marketing involves an **exchange process** requiring that two or more parties exchange, or trade, something of value.[3] An economic transfer of goods or services in exchange for a price expressed in monetary terms is the most frequently analyzed marketing exchange. However, exchanges also occur in a politician's campaign, a zoo's fund-raising drive, or an antismoking group's program. When a donation is made to the Partnership for a Drug Free America, to a zoo, to a political campaign, or to an antismoking effort, something is given and something is received—even though the "something received" may be intangible, such as a feeling of goodwill or a sense of satisfaction. In each situation, there has been a transaction either between an individual and a group or between two individuals. The characteristic common to these situations is the set of activities necessary to bring about exchange relationships. Additional examples include the offering of a vote or a volunteer effort in exchange for a candidate's pledge to work hard for his or her constituents; the donation of blood to help the sick and injured; and time spent working for a United Way campaign, where the reward is a sense of satisfaction. All these activities may be viewed from a marketing perspective when they are planned to bring about an exchange.[4] (See Exhibit 1–4.)

## A Definition of Marketing

**MARKETING**
The process of planning and executing the conception, pricing, promotion, and distribution of ideas, goods, and services to create exchanges that will satisfy individual and organizational objectives.

**DISCUSSION CONSIDERATION**
The term *effective* means meeting the institution's or individual's goals. For profit-oriented firms, this means making enough profits. What does it mean for nonprofit organizations? That enough people are aware of the American Heart Association? That enough people attend church? For nonprofits, measuring effectiveness is difficult.

The Bandai example illustrates what marketing is like in a well-managed business. The American Heart Association example illustrates that not-for-profit organizations engage in marketing. Thinking about these examples should help you to understand that effective marketing consists of a consumer-oriented mix of business activities planned and implemented by a marketer to facilitate the exchange or transfer of goods, services, or ideas so that both parties profit in some way.

The American Marketing Association's definition of marketing embodies these principles: **Marketing** is the process of planning and executing the conception, pricing, promotion, and distribution of ideas, goods, and services to create exchanges that will satisfy individual and organizational objectives.[5]

Effective marketing requires the conception and development of goods, services, or ideas so they may be brought to market and purchased by buyers. Pricing, promotion, and distribution of these goods, services, or ideas facilitate the basic function of bringing marketers (suppliers) together with consumers (buyers).

Each party must gain something; revenues satisfy the marketer's objectives, and products satisfy the consumer's needs.[6] Each party contributes something of value because each expects to be satisfied by the exchange. Effective marketing involves using the resources of the entire organization to facilitate exchanges between the marketer and the customer so that both parties are satisfied.

## Keeping Customers and Building Relationships

So far, our discussion of marketing has focused on the idea of creating exchanges. Said somewhat differently, we have talked about getting customers; but keeping customers is equally important. Marketers want customers for life. Effective marketers

An old business adage says, "It costs six times as much to get a new customer as it does to keep an old customer." Although the figures may change from industry to industry, the point remains valid. Cost-effective marketers should work to retain customers by managing their relationships with those customers.

**RELATIONSHIP MARKETING**
Marketing activities aimed at building long-term relationships with parties that contribute to the company's success, especially customers. Also called *relationship management.*

work to build long-term relationships with their customers. The term **relationship marketing** (or relationship management) is used to communicate the idea that a major goal of marketing is to build long-term relationships with the parties who contribute to the company's success.

Once an exchange is made, effective marketing stresses managing the relationships that will bring about additional exchanges. Effective marketers view making a sale not as the end of a process but as the start of the organization's relationship with a customer. Satisfied customers will return to a company that has treated them well if they need to repurchase the same product in the future. If they need a related item, satisfied customers know the first place to look.

In summary, marketers strive to initiate exchanges and build relationships. More simply, you can think about marketing as an activity involved in *getting* and *keeping* customers. It is the marketer's job to use the resources of the entire organization to create, interpret, and maintain the relationship between the company and the customer.[7]

## What Is a Market?

**MARKET**
A group of potential customers that may want the product offered and that have the resources, the willingness, and the ability to purchase it.

The root word in the term *marketing* is *market.*[8] A **market** is a group of potential customers for a particular product who are willing and able to spend money or exchange other resources to obtain the product. The term *market* can be somewhat confusing, because it has been used to designate buildings (the Fulton Fish Market), places (the Greater Houston Metropolitan Market), institutions (the stock market), and stores (the supermarket), as well as many other things. But each usage—even the name of a building in which trading is carried out—suggests people or groups with purchasing power who are willing to exchange their resources for something else. It will become clear as you read this book that the nature of the market is a primary concern of marketing decision makers.

FedEx knows that keeping existing customers is just as important as getting new ones. So it strives to build lasting relationships with customers by providing the assurance that if a package "absolutely, positively has to be there overnight," it will. Friendly personnel and computer software for shipping and tracking packages also contribute to customer satisfaction.

## The Marketing Mix

**MARKETING MIX**
The specific combination of interrelated and interdependent marketing activities in which an organization engages to meet its objectives.

**FOUR Ps OF MARKETING**
The basic elements of the marketing mix: product, place (distribution), promotion and price. Also called the *controllable variables* of marketing, because they can be controlled and manipulated by the marketer.

Our definition of marketing indicates that marketing includes many interrelated and interdependent activities meant to encourage exchange. The term **marketing mix** describes the result of management's efforts to creatively combine these activities.[9] Faced with a wide choice of product features, messages, prices, distribution methods, and other marketing variables, the marketing manager must select and combine ingredients to create a marketing mix that will achieve organizational objectives.

The marketing mix may have many facets, but its elements can be placed in four basic categories: product, place (distribution), promotion, and price. These are commonly referred to as the **four Ps of marketing** or—since they can be influenced by managers—as the **controllable variables** of marketing.[10] Because virtually every possible marketing activity can be placed in one of these categories, the four Ps constitute a framework that can be used to develop plans for marketing efforts. Preparing a marketing strategy requires considering each major mix area and making decisions about the development of substrategies within each era.

### The First Element—Product

**PRODUCT**
A good, service, or idea that offers a bundle of tangible and intangible attributes to satisfy consumers.

**POINT TO EMPHASIZE**
The four marketing mix elements are what marketers can *control.* They cannot change other factors that affect marketing, such as competition, economic pressures such as inflation, and consumer trends. Part of controlling the four elements is keeping them consistent. Product and price should match—a low-quality product will have a low price, for example. It may be sold in discount/lower-priced outlets with little promotion.

**DISCUSSION CONSIDERATION**
Like most companies, Binney and Smith has defined its product line very broadly so as not to restrict thinking about the product line. How might the Bandai Corporation, makers of Mighty Morphin Power Rangers, define its product/service?

The term **product** refers to what the business or nonprofit organization offers to its prospective customers or clients. The offering may be a tangible good, such as a car; a service, such as an airline trip; or an intangible idea, such as the importance of parents' reading to their children.

Because customers often expect more from an organization than a simple, tangible product, the task of marketing management is to provide a complete offering—a "total product"—that includes not only the basic good or service but also the "extras" that go with it. The core product of a city bus line may be rides or transportation, for example, but its total product offering should include courteous service, on-time performance, and assistance in finding appropriate bus routes. The chairman of Binney and Smith, marketers of Crayola Crayons, once said, "We are no longer just a crayon company. We are in the business of providing assorted products that are fun to use and inspire creative self-expression."[11] This effective marketer realizes what a product is. One of Xerox Corporation's products is a copying machine plus repair service, supplies, advice, and other customer services that extend beyond the initial sale. Xerox's product definition allows the company to realize that the sale is not the end of the marketing process.

The product the customer receives in the exchange process is the result of a number of product strategy decisions. Developing and planning a product involve making sure that it has the characteristics and features customers want. Selecting a brand name, designing a package, developing appropriate warranties and service plans, and other product decisions are also concerned with developing the "right" product. Product strategies are addressed in Chapters 9–11.

As we will see, product strategies must take into consideration the other three elements of the marketing mix. Price, distribution, and promotion enhance the attraction of the product offering.

### The Second Element—Place

**PLACE (DISTRIBUTION)**
An element of the marketing mix involving all aspects of getting products to the consumer in the right location at the right time.

Determining how goods get to the customer, how quickly, and in what condition involves **place,** or **distribution,** strategy. Transportation, storage, materials handling, and the like are physical distribution activities. Selecting wholesalers, retailers, and other types of distributors is also a place activity.

The examples so far have shown that every organization engages in marketing. Every organization, however, does not have the resources or ability to manage all the

A product is what is offered to customers. A rock concert by Pearl Jam is not a tangible good, but it is a product nonetheless. Developing a product, even a concert, requires that it have the characteristics and features the customer wants. Every product, whether it is a good, a service, or an idea, requires marketing. Some organizations are effective marketers; others are not.

activities required in the distribution process. Thus, organizations may concentrate on activities in which they have a unique advantage. Wholesalers, retailers, and various other specialists have developed to allow for such specialization and to make the distribution process more efficient. For example, the Pepsi-Cola Corporation, which specializes in the production and promotion of soft drinks, finds it efficient to utilize independent bottlers and retailers to distribute its products to the ultimate consumer.

**CHANNEL OF DISTRIBUTION**
The complete sequence of marketing organizations involved in bringing a product from the producer to the consumer. The channel of distribution often includes such intermediaries as wholesalers and retailers.

POINT TO EMPHASIZE
Channels of distribution are constantly changing. For example, catalog companies and television shopping have exploded, which means a lower share of potential sales for wholesalers and retailers. And now catalogs are appearing on the Internet, causing the growth of traditional catalog sales to decline. Each challenger firm may in turn become a victim.

A **channel of distribution** is the complete sequence of marketing organizations involved in bringing a product from the producer to the consumer. Its purpose is to make possible transfer of ownership and/or possession of the product. Exhibit 1–5 illustrates a basic channel of distribution consisting of the manufacturer, the wholesaler, the retailer, and the ultimate consumer. Each of these four parties engages in a transaction that involves movement of the physical good and/or a transfer of title (ownership) of that product.

Some definitions are in order:

**Manufacturer** An organization that recognizes a consumer need and produces a product from raw materials, component parts, or labor to satisfy that need.

**Wholesaler** An organization that serves as an intermediary between manufacturer and retailer to facilitate the transfer of products or the exchange of title to those products, or an organization that sells to manufacturers or institutions that resell the product (perhaps in another form). Exhibit 1–5 shows the type of wholesaler that sells to retailers. Wholesalers neither produce nor consume the finished product.

**Retailer** An organization that sells products it has obtained from a manufacturer or wholesaler to the ultimate consumer. Retailers neither produce nor consume the product.

**Ultimate consumer** An individual who buys or uses a product for personal consumption.

The actual path that a product or title takes may be simpler or much more complex than the one illustrated in Exhibit 1–5. For example, a manufacturer may sell

**EXHIBIT 1–5**

Who Is Involved in a Basic Channel of Distribution?

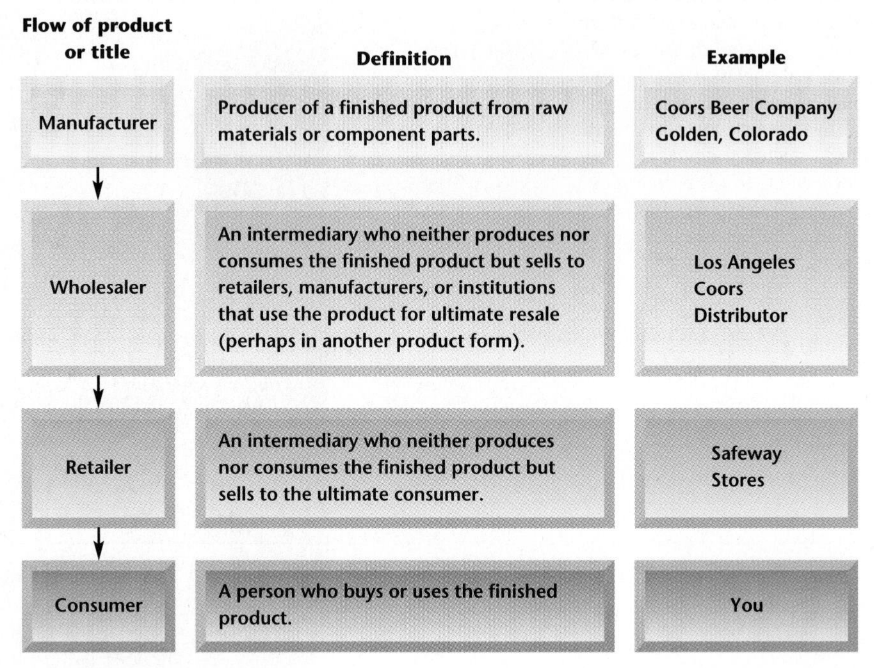

| Flow of product or title | Definition | Example |
|---|---|---|
| Manufacturer | Producer of a finished product from raw materials or component parts. | Coors Beer Company Golden, Colorado |
| Wholesaler | An intermediary who neither produces nor consumes the finished product but sells to retailers, manufacturers, or institutions that use the product for ultimate resale (perhaps in another product form). | Los Angeles Coors Distributor |
| Retailer | An intermediary who neither produces nor consumes the finished product but sells to the ultimate consumer. | Safeway Stores |
| Consumer | A person who buys or uses the finished product. | You |

ALTERNATIVE EXAMPLE

Because Greet Street sells upscale, unusual greeting cards, its products are not suitable for mass marketing, as Hallmark's cards are. Instead, Greet Street sells on the Internet—a new means of distributing products. Buyers browse Greet Street's offerings on America Online and on a World Wide Web home page, where they find more variety than they would in a store. They order electronically, and the cards are shipped directly to them. SOURCE: Kate Fitzgerald, "Alternative Cards Try Alternative Marketing," *Advertising Age*, February 20, 1995, p. 13.

**INDUSTRIAL BUYER**

An organization that purchases a product to use in the production of another good or service or in the operation of its business.

directly to an industrial buyer. The term **industrial buyer** refers to an organization, such as an automobile manufacturer, that purchases a product (such as steel) that it will use to produce another good or service or a product (such as a computer) that it will use in operating its business. Various distribution systems are explained in Chapters 12–14.

**FACILITATOR**

A specialist, such as a trucking company, that aids the flow of products through a channel of distribution but is not a member of the channel.

Excluded from the channel of distribution are numerous specialists that perform specific facilitating activities for manufacturers, wholesalers, or retailers—for example, the airline or the railway that transports the product from Boston to Philadelphia or the advertising agency on Madison Avenue that creates the advertising message and selects the appropriate media. These specialists, or **facilitators,** are hired because they can more efficiently or more effectively perform a certain marketing activity for an organization in a basic marketing channel. However, they are not among the organizations included in our definition of *channel of distribution.*[12]

DISCUSSION CONSIDERATION

If channels of distribution change to better meet the needs of consumers, why have catalog, television, and Internet sales grown? What consumer needs do these intermediaries meet better than regular retailers? What, if anything, could retailers do to retain sales going to catalog and television shopping?

It is important to realize that distribution mixes vary widely even among companies selling directly competitive products. For example, Avon and Amway use sales representatives selling directly to consumers as their primary source of distribution, while Gillette and Colgate-Palmolive, selling similar goods, deal with many wholesalers and retailers in their distribution systems.

## The Third Element—Promotion

**PROMOTION**

The element of the marketing mix that includes all forms of marketing communications.

Marketers need to communicate with consumers. **Promotion** is the means by which marketers "talk to" existing customers and potential buyers. Promotion may convey a message about the organization, a product, or some other element of the marketing mix, such as the new low price being offered during a sale period.

To illustrate the value of promotional efforts in a marketing mix, think about Energizer batteries. You probably can envision one of the television commercials featuring the pink mechanical Energizer bunny in some hilarious situation. Perhaps you

ALTERNATIVE EXAMPLE
In the 1990s, McDonald's advertising has mostly promoted combination meals and lower-priced burgers. According to a senior vice president, these ads weren't memorable and emphasized short-run goals—getting today's sales. McDonald's wanted ads with more charm that would emphasize a better relationship with the consumer. Hence, McDonald's new ads use slogans—such as "Have you had your break today?"—that resonate with the fast-food company's most successful slogan, "You deserve a break today," from the 1970s. SOURCE: Kevin Goldman, "McDonald's Mixes Past with New Slogan," *Wall Street Journal,* February 17, 1995, p. B4.

recall the tireless, drum-playing bunny in a cartoon setting being chased by Wile E. Coyote. Or perhaps you remember the spoof of the Star Wars movies, in which Darth Vader attempts to silence the bunny's drum with his light saber only to discover that it won't work because he has used an inferior product from Energizer's rival, the Super Volt battery company. However, from the marketer's point of view, the most important thing for you to remember is that Energizer "keeps going, and going, and going." Energizer's promotion accomplishes its task; it communicates a message about its long-lasting battery to consumers.

Advertising, personal selling, publicity, and sales promotion are all forms of promotion. While each offers unique benefits, all are forms of communication that inform, remind, or persuade. For example, advertising that tells us "Always Coca-Cola" or "Always the Real Thing—Coca-Cola" reminds us of our experiences with a familiar cola. An IBM sales representative delivers a personal message that explains how a computer network will help an organization and then attempts to persuade the company to purchase the product. The essence of all promotion is communication aimed at informing, reminding, or persuading potential buyers.

Different firms emphasize different forms of promotional communication. Some firms advertise heavily, for example, while others advertise hardly at all. A firm's particular combination of communication tools is its promotional mix. The topic of promotion is addressed in greater detail in Chapters 15–18.

## The Fourth Element—Price

PRICE
The amount of money or other consideration—that is, something of value—given in exchange for a product.

The amount of money, or sometimes goods or services, given in exchange for something is its **price.** In other words, price is what is exchanged for the product. Just as the customer buys a product with cash, so a company "buys" the customer's cash with the product. In not-for-profit situations, price may be expressed in terms of volunteered time or effort, votes, or donations.

Marketers must determine the best price for their products. To do so, they must ascertain a product's value, or what it is worth to consumers. Once the value of a product is established, the marketer knows what price to charge. However, because consumers' evaluations of a product's worth change over time, prices are subject to rapid change.

Promotion is a marketer's means of communication. Marketers promote their goods and services in many different ways. Advertising that uses interactive media, such as America Online, is growing in popularity.

**EXHIBIT 1–6** Elements of the Marketing Mix—Creative Examples

| MARKETING MIX ELEMENT | COMPANY OR ORGANIZATION | EXAMPLE |
|---|---|---|
| | ***Product*** | |
| Product development | Ford Motor Company | Ecostar electric vans |
| | American Home Products Corp. | Choles Trac, kit for testing cholesterol levels at home |
| Product modification | Procter & Gamble | Old Spice after-shave reformulation eliminates alcohol by using a new technology called "cooling sensates" |
| | Disney | DisneyWorld's Tomorrowland is remodeled and modernized |
| Branding | 3M Company | Scotch brand cellophane tape |
| | National Multiple Sclerosis Society | MS—as in "Help fight MS" |
| Trademark | Michelin | Tire Man |
| Warranty | Sears | "If any Craftsman hand tool ever fails to give complete satisfaction, Sears will replace it free" |
| | ***Distribution*** | |
| Channel of distribution | Hoover Vacuum | Ships directly to Wal-Mart |
| | U.S. Postal Service | Sells stamps by mail order, in vending machines, and at post offices |
| Physical distribution | West Educational Publishing | Uses FedEx to transport rush orders |
| | ***Promotion*** | |
| Advertising | Australia Office of Tourism | "Australia—come and say g'day" |
| | The Advertising Council | "Remember, only you can prevent forest fires" |
| Personal selling | Girl Scouts | Door-to-door cookie sales |
| | Hitachi | Sales representatives sell fiber optic communication systems to business organizations |
| Sales promotion | Bloomingdale's | Irish heritage celebrated with exhibits of Irish homes and country cottages in 14 stores |
| | Metropolitan Life Insurance | Gives away "Let's Go Mets" T-shirts at New York Mets baseball games |
| Publicity | The Cranberries (band) | Appear on the David Letterman show |
| | ***Price*** | |
| Price strategy | Absolut Country of Sweden Vodka | Expensive |
| | AT & T System | "True Savings" |
| | Southwestern Bell | "The Works"—12 best-selling services offered together at a price 45% lower than what a customer would pay if the services were ordered separately |

**POINT TO EMPHASIZE**

The consumer's perception is not independent of marketing. Activities such as promotion, branding, and packaging create images and add value. Well-known (promoted) brand names usually cost more. For example, Benetton T-shirts sell for more than T-shirts at Sears.

According to economists, prices are always "on trial." Pricing strategies and decisions require establishing appropriate prices and carefully monitoring the competitive marketplace. Price is discussed in Chapter 19 and 20.

## The Art of Blending the Elements

A manager selecting a marketing mix may be likened to a chef preparing a meal. Each realizes that there is no "one best way" to mix ingredients. Different combinations

ment. This involves anticipating environmental changes that will affect the organization. Correct environmental assessment makes marketing decisions more successful.

LEARNING OBJECTIVE **5** *Explain the marketing concept.*

The marketing concept is a philosophy of business and a set of objectives for organizations to pursue. According to this concept, organizations can succeed by focusing on consumers' wants and needs, long-term profitability, and an integrated marketing effort. Product orientation and sales orientation are less effective alternative philosophies.

LEARNING OBJECTIVE **6** *Explain total quality management.*

Total quality management is a management process that focuses on integrating the idea of customer-driven quality throughout the organization. Under total quality management, all employees strive for continuous quality improvement.

LEARNING OBJECTIVE **7** *Recognize the contribution of marketing to the economy and our way of life.*

Marketing delivers a standard of living to society. The aggregate of all organizations' marketing activities, especially transportation and distribution activity, affect a society's economic well-being. The efficiency of the system for moving goods from producers to consumers is an important factor determining a country's quality of life.

LEARNING OBJECTIVE **8** *Define the societal marketing concept.*

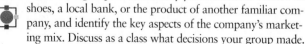

The societal marketing concept, which can be in perfect harmony with the marketing concept, stresses the need for marketers to consider the collective needs of society as well as individual consumer desires and the organization's need for profits. It recognizes that every consumer, as a member of society, has both long-term and short-term needs.

## Key Terms

exchange process (p. 9)
marketing (p. 10)
relationship marketing (p. 11)
market (p. 11)
marketing mix (p. 12)
four Ps of marketing (p. 12)
controllable variable (p. 12)
product (p. 12)
place (distribution) (p. 12)
channel of distribution (p. 13)
manufacturer (p. 13)
wholesaler (p. 13)
retailer (p. 13)
ultimate consumer (p. 13)
industrial buyer (p. 14)
facilitator (p. 14)
promotion (p. 14)
price (p. 15)
uncontrollable variable (p. 17)
production orientation (p. 19)
sales orientation (p. 19)
marketing concept (p. 20)
market orientation (p. 22)
total quality management (TQM) (p. 23)
macromarketing (p. 24)
societal marketing concept (p. 24)

## Questions for Discussion

1. Think about what you did this morning. In what ways did marketing affect your activities?
2. Define *marketing* in your own words.
3. If marketing activities involve exchange, what isn't a marketing activity?
4. Do lawyers, accountants, doctors, and dentists need marketing?
5. Why is relationship marketing important?
6. Identify some goods, services, or ideas that are marketed by not-for-profit organizations—organizations that are not traditional businesses.
7. What are the elements of the marketing mix?
8. Describe the marketing mixes used by these organizations:
   a. McDonald's.
   b. Your local zoo.
   c. An anti–air pollution group.
   d. The Xerox Corporation.
9. The marketing concept is profit-oriented. What kinds of profit does it stress? How does this apply to nonprofit organizations?
10. What organizations in your college town have not yet adopted the marketing concept?
11. How might a firm such as Pillsbury conduct its business as (a) a product-oriented, (b) a sales-oriented, and (c) a marketing-oriented company?
12. Given the existence of the marketing concept, why do so many products fail? Why are consumer groups still displeased with many products and companies?
13. How can an organization's management prove that it has adopted the marketing concept?
14. A zoo designer says she begins work by asking, "In what sort of landscape would I want to observe this animal?" Discuss this approach to design in terms of the marketing concept.
15. Can a small business embrace the marketing concept philosophy as discussed in this chapter?
16. What role does marketing play in society?
17. What is the societal marketing concept?
18. Form small groups as directed by your instructor. Select Nike shoes, a local bank, or the product of another familiar company, and identify the key aspects of the company's marketing mix. Discuss as a class what decisions your group made.

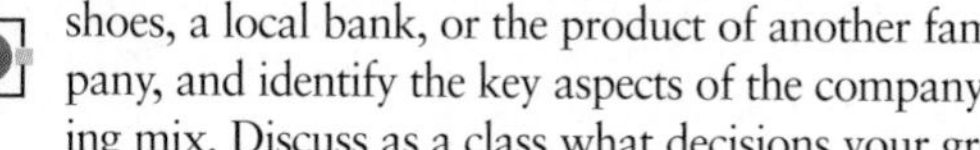

**ETHICS IN PRACTICE**

## *What's Ahead*

We discuss ethical issues in Chapter 2. An Ethics in Practice section at the end of each of the remaining chapters incorporates an Ethics Exercise and Take-a-Stand Questions. This feature gives you the chance to think about your own ethical principles and how they would apply in specific situations.

VIDEO CASE 1–1

## Garden Botanika

Twenty years ago, a young, environmentally conscious woman in the United Kingdom got the idea of creating and marketing "natural" cosmetics and skin care products free from animal fat. The original products were sold in cheap, reusable bottles with handwritten labels. Over time, the business grew and ultimately became The Body Shop International, an innovator in the manufacturing and retailing of natural and colorful shampoos, lotions, soaps, and cosmetics. Customers who shopped at the Body Shop not only bought products that were not tested on animals but also carried home the products in biodegradable plastic bags. They didn't balk at paying premium prices, either. They felt socially responsible buying from the Body Shop, because part of the company's profits went to fund environmental campaigns such as saving Amazon rain forests. During the 1980s and 1990s, the Body Shop expanded beyond the United Kingdom and now has more than 700 shops around the world. While the Body Shop has always marketed environmentally sound products, one thing the Body Shop has never featured are low prices. And as any classical economist will tell you, high prices invite competition.

The co-founders of Garden Botanika, Jeff Brotman and Mike Luce, were among those who saw opportunities in the natural cosmetics market. It all began in 1989, when Luce, Garden Botanika's current president, started searching for a new retailing idea to develop when he was at Eddie Bauer. The Bauer company was up for sale, and Luce decided it was time to leave. At one point, Luce approached Brotman, then and still Costco Wholesale's chairman, to see if Brotman's Jeffrey Michael stores might be for sale. Brotman wasn't interested in selling the clothing store chain, but he was interested in starting a mall-based natural cosmetics chain along the lines of the Body Shop. Several months later, Brotman and Luce teamed up to start Garden Botanika.

The company's products, like those of the Body Shop, are natural cosmetics, but they are less expensive. Garden Botanika appeals to working women in their 30s and 40s who have bought cosmetics in department stores but are seeking less expensive alternatives. These customers, surveys show, want a nicer atmosphere and more service than drugstores or discounters provide. So Garden Botanika gives it to them. The 1,200-square-foot Garden Botanika store in the Bellevue Square mall in Seattle, Washington, reflects the company's basic store design. Bright and airy, the design features lots of glass, white shelving filled with richly colored cosmetics, and customer-friendly touches, such as a small sink where shoppers can test and remove cosmetics. Garden Botanika does not do a great deal of advertising. Its promotional efforts stress in-store customer service.

Arlee Jensen, the company's vice president for merchandising and product development, estimates that Garden Botanika faces more than two dozen competitors in the bath-and-body-shop industry. Among the competitors, besides the Body Shop, are The Limited's Bath and Body Works, H2O Plus, Bare Essentials, and Nature's Elements.

### QUESTIONS

1. What do consumers really want from a shampoo and the store that sells it?
2. Describe Garden Botanika's marketing mix. How does it differ from that of the Body Shop?
3. Has the company adopted the marketing concept?
4. How important is the price of a product?
5. What does a company like Garden Botanika do that motivates shoppers to buy?

CASE 1–2

## Timberland

An advertisement for Timberland, The New England Shoemaker, proclaims: "Give racism the boot." Another urges consumers to "Mess with Mother Nature." The more you get involved with Mother Nature, the company says, the better off you will be. And Timberland builds boots, shoes, and clothing to let you mess with nature whether in a rugged wilderness or an urban jungle. "With Timberland gear, you and Mother Nature don't just coexist on this planet. You're true friends."

This contemporary, socially responsive advertising, combined with environmentally conscious, down-to-earth products and other imaginative marketing maneuvers, have helped turn the Timberland Company into a huge success. However, not very long ago—during the late 1980s and early 1990s—the Timberland Company had major problems. Inventories piled up, while retailers expressed anger about missed shipments and merchandise that didn't get into their stores on time. Timberland's venture into outdoorsy apparel stalled when consumers shunned its high price. And in an era when global business was becoming imperative, the Hampton, New Hampshire, company was little known outside of the Northeastern United States. What was it that turned Timberland around?

For one thing, a favorable fashion shift enhanced Timberland's prosperity. Hiking boots with a casual, outdoorsy look—a look that Timberland cultivated—became trendy. Although Timberland's classic waterproof boot had traditionally been strong with under-40 males, the new fashion craze embraced all ages and both sexes. Diverse groups ranging from suburban professionals to inner-city youth found Timberland the hottest boots to buy. Jill Swid, the 24-year-old fashion editor of *Spin* magazine, said, "Some of my friends are even wearing them with sun dresses." While the winds of fashion change were certainly welcome at Timberland, the company's marketing success was not due to good fortune alone.

The family-owned company began its turnaround in 1991 when Sidney Swartz gave his 33-year-old son Jeff Swartz, who had studied business at Dartmouth College's Amos Truck School, day-to-day control over marketing and other company operations. His first task was to tighten operations. By slashing the number of products nearly in half and filling orders promptly, Swartz reduced inventory. That helped Timberland cut costs and allowed the company to trim some of its high prices. For example, to capitalize on the shift toward more casual office dress among whitecollar workers, the company cut the price of its waterproof Weatherbuck casual men's dress shoes from $135 to $99. The price reduction more than doubled sales.

Timberland had always measured productivity by the size of each delivery, so department-store orders were given priority over those from small retailers. As Swartz began to realize that small retail "boutiques" were an increasingly important share of business, the company changed its marketing strategy. It began by scheduling two or more shipments a week to each customer instead of one big delivery. The company developed an optical scanner system that automatically tracks inventory and creates shipping bills. This system handles small orders as efficiently as big ones.

Another part of the marketing strategy was to open new Timberland outlets. There are now more than a hundred Timberland departments, or "concept shops," in Nordstrom's, Macy's, and other U.S. retail stores. And the company does not focus on the United States alone; it operates in 45 countries, and international business accounts for 40 percent of its sales.

### QUESTIONS

1. From what you know about Timberland, what is its marketing mix?
2. Who are Timberland's customers? What do Timberland's customers get in exchange for the price they pay for shoes?
3. How important is price in the purchase of a Timberland shoe?
4. How important is advertising in the purchase of a Timberland shoe?
5. How can Timberland implement the marketing concept?

VIDEO CASE 1–3

## Texas Department of Transportation

Over the last few decades, the population of Texas has grown at an unprecedented rate. And the state's litter problem—especially the careless disposal of beverage containers—has grown with the population. By 1985, the cost of collecting litter along the state's highways amounted to more than $20 million.

The Texas Department of Transportation determined that a marketing effort to educate the people of Texas about the detrimental effects of littering was in order. It believed that every citizen needed to be reminded or persuaded not to litter. Furthermore, it wanted to encourage citizens to become active in the antilitter effort. In 1985, it was decided that a full-blown public education program should be established. Researching public opinion about litter, sponsoring antilitter and cleanup programs, creating antilitter materials, and advertising in the mass media were among the many possibilities. The Department decided to run a series of creative ads to educate the public.

### QUESTIONS

1. Can a state agency such as the Texas Department of Transportation implement the marketing concept? Who are its consumers? What benefits does it seek?
2. What is the product being marketed by the Texas Department of Transportation? What is exchanged between the department and its consumers?
3. What type of antilitter and cleanup programs should the department develop?
4. Identify and evaluate each element of the Texas Department of Transportation's marketing mix. In particular, what promotional efforts would you expect from the department?

VIDEO COHESION CASE

## Minnesota Twins

This section includes seven cases dealing with various marketing issues facing the Minnesota Twins. The cases are interrelated, but each can stand alone. The cases are supplemented with several videos that help tie the issues and concepts together to portray a cohesive picture of how an organization deals with planning, implementing, and controlling all aspects of marketing strategy.

CHAPTER

# 2

# Marketing Management: Strategy and Ethical Behavior

LEARNING OBJECTIVES

After you have studied this chapter, you will be able to:

1. Differentiate between marketing strategy and marketing tactics.
2. Discuss the role of marketing planning at the corporate level, at the strategic business unit level, and at the operational level of management.
3. Understand the concept of the organizational mission.
4. Understand the nature of a competitive advantage.
5. Understand the importance of total quality management strategies in product differentiation.
6. Discuss demarketing.
7. Explain the market/product matrix.
8. Describe marketing objectives and marketing plans.
9. Identify the stages in the strategic marketing process.
10. Explain what positioning involves.
11. Understand the nature of marketing ethics and socially responsible behavior.

What is now the nation's number-one bookseller was born in 1971, when Barnes & Noble's founder and chief executive, Leonard Riggio, bought a single stagnant Manhattan store. Today it's a 937-store chain. Why? Credit two profound insights into what consumers really want and creative development of marketing strategies based on that understanding.

Insight 1: "Shopping is a form of entertainment," as Riggio phrases it. Consumers aren't corporate purchasing managers, single-mindedly seeking specific commodities at the best possible price. To consumers, shopping is a social activity. They do it to mingle with others in a prosperous-feeling crowd, to see what's new, to enjoy the theatrical dazzle of the display, to treat themselves to something interesting or unexpected.

So Riggio developed a marketing strategy emphasizing stores designed to give customers a pleasant shopping experience. In 1989, he began to perfect the strategy: a high-visibility, upscale, usually suburban location to draw the crowds where they live; enough woody, traditional, soft-colored library atmosphere to please the book lovers; enough sophisticated modern architecture and graphics, sweeping vistas, and stylish displays to satisfy fans of the theater of consumption. And for everyone, plenty of welcoming public space, where they can meet other people and feel at home in a refined environment. Approachable employees complete the welcoming scene; they're intentionally nothing like the snooty booksellers that boss Riggio—short, sad-faced, and unassuming—found intimidating when he was young.

People at Riggio's superstores settle in at his many heavy chairs and tables to browse through piles of books; they fill the cafes he's put into the superstores to increase the festivity; they hang out in their chosen sections to pick up like-minded lovers of sports and fitness, high-toned fiction, New Age emoting, or gay and lesbian studies. Consumers attend the readings and signings he puts on; they bring their kids to his puppet shows and story hours; they read the accolades to his stores in newspapers and lifestyle magazines, captivated by something new and hot. Riggio makes sure they always have clean bathrooms, too, so they don't have to leave in a hurry. "If I get you for two hours, I've got you." he says. "I don't need more books; I need more people." As one company executive sums it up: "The feel-good part of the store, the quality-of-life contribution, is a big part of the success."

A second pillar underlying the marketing strategy is the insight that books are no different from other consumer products. Says Riggio: "People have the mistaken notion that the thing you do with books is read them. They think all a book is about is information." Wrong. Maybe 5 percent of what gets printed gets read, and those who read most are also the biggest accumulators of unread volumes. People buy books for what the purchase says about them—their taste, their cultivation, their trendiness. Their aim, says Riggio, is to connect themselves, or those to whom they give books as gifts, with all the other refined owners of Edgar Allan Poe collections or sensitive owners of Virginia Woolf collections.

The consequence is that, if you try, you can sell books as consumer products, with enticing displays, flashy posters, an emphasis on the glamour of the book as an object and the fashionableness of the best seller and the trendy author. Riggio has found he can even wrap his customer in the glamour, by sending him or her out with shopping bags sporting his trademark high-style sketches of famous authors. "It's amazing," says Riggio, "how people almost wear the bag that they take from the store."

Barnes & Noble built itself around a marketing strategy that differentiated it from its competitors. As this example illustrates, developing a marketing strategy is crucial to an organization's success. Marketing strategy is the subject of this chapter.

The chapter begins by discussing the activities of marketing managers and defining *marketing strategy.* Next, it discusses planning at various levels in the organization, giving special attention to the organizational mission and to planning for marketing at the strategic business unit level. It then addresses the challenges managers face during each stage in the strategic marketing process. A discussion of execution and control follows the material on marketing planning. Finally, the chapter introduces the topic of ethics and social responsibility in marketing, an important and pervasive topic that will be discussed throughout the book.

## Marketing Management

Organizations, whether charities, universities, or giant global businesses like the Microsoft Corporation, must have managers. Managers develop rules, principles, and ways of thinking and acting that can be of use in attaining the organization's goals and objectives.

Corporate managers, or top managers, are the executives responsible for the entire organization. Every aspect of the organization's operations—production, finance, personnel, marketing—depends on their plans for the organization's long-term future. Top managers, with titles such as chief executive officer (CEO) and executive vice president, provide strategic direction for the organization. They realize that advertising, pricing, distribution, and personal selling are marketing activities—not marketing. Top managers recognize that at the corporate level, marketing is a business philosophy rather than a series of activities. Top managers see marketing as a process that may require the resources of the entire organization. An important part of their job is to ensure that all business functions work together to achieve marketing success.

Marketing managers who work at the middle levels of the organization are responsible for the management of marketing efforts in the organization's business units and major departments.

**MARKETING MANAGEMENT**
The process of planning, executing, and controlling marketing activities to attain marketing goals and objectives effectively and efficiently.

**Marketing management** is the process of planning, executing, and controlling marketing activities to attain marketing goals and objectives effectively and efficiently. Of course, the time, effort, and resources associated with Johnson & Johnson's introduction of a new flavor of dental floss differ from the time, effort, and resources associated with Microsoft's development of computer software that understands normal spoken language, a project that Microsoft has been working on for years. Yet in both cases, success depends on planning, execution, and control. These are the basic functions of management at every level.

Managers in today's dynamic and rapidly changing business world confront extraordinary challenges that were rarely encountered before the 1980s. Today's marketing manager must be flexible and versatile to deal with changes that come more quickly and are more dramatic, complex, and unpredictable than ever before.[1]

Because marketing managers must deal with change, the marketing management process is a continuous one: Planning, execution, and control are ongoing and repetitive activities.[2] A major aspect of dealing with change is the development of appropriate strategies.

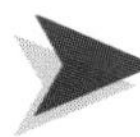

## What Is a Marketing Strategy?

Marketers, like admirals and generals, must develop strategies calculated to help them attain the objectives they seek. The military planner's endeavors can end more disastrously than those of business people, but the loss of the means to make a living, the closing of a factory, and the "defeat" of a product in the marketplace are serious matters indeed to the investors, executives, and workers involved. Many executives have noticed similarities between military strategy and marketing strategy. Therefore a number of military terms—*strategy, tactics, campaigns, maneuvers,* and so on—have been adopted by businesspeople, just as they have been by football coaches, to relate their organizational activities to those of competitors.

**MARKETING STRATEGY**
A plan identifying what marketing goals and objectives will be pursued and how they will be achieved in the time available.

Because of its widespread usage, the term *strategy* has been defined in many different ways.[3] For our purposes, a specific definition is appropriate: A **marketing strategy** consists of a plan identifying what basic goals and objectives will be pursued and how they will be achieved in the time available. A strategy entails commitment to certain courses of action and allocation of the resources necessary to achieve the identified goals.

**TACTICS**
Specific actions intended to implement strategies.

The armed forces describe *strategy* as what generals do and *tactics* as what lower officers, such as captains and lieutenants, do. This description rightly suggests that tactics are less comprehensive in scope than strategies. **Tactics** are specific actions intended to implement strategy. Therefore, tactics are most closely associated with the execution of plans.

McDonald's basic strategy, for example, is to have clean family-type restaurants that offer friendly service, high-quality food, and good value. Offering Happy Meals for children at reasonable prices is a tactic used to implement this strategy. It encourages consumers to bring their families to McDonald's because high-quality children's

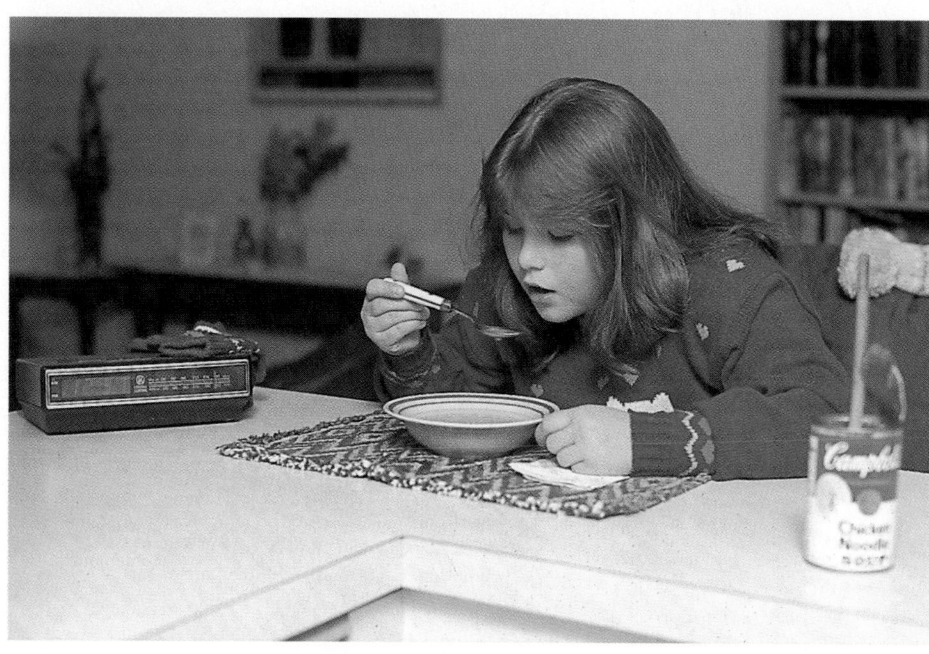

The Campbell Soup Company is very creative at the tactical level. For example, Campbell tracks all major storms moving across the United States during the winter months. The information gathered allows Campbell to advertise "hot soup for cold weather" on the radio the day before, the day of, and the day after a storm.

POINT TO EMPHASIZE
Marketing concepts are meant to be applied in many situations. What is your strategy for finding a starting career position? Can you state your goals, your plan to achieve them, and a realistic time frame?

meals are a good value there. Providing pamphlets explaining that "your fork" is the only thing that is not nutritious in a Chunky Chicken Salad is another specific action that helps convey the idea that McDonald's offers an assortment of high-quality food for the entire family. McDonald's uses many tactics like these to implement its "quality, service, cleanliness, and value" strategy.

## Planning—Designing a Framework for the Future

Recall that the basic functions of management are planning, execution, and control. In the next part of the chapter, we focus on planning.

PLANNING
The process of envisioning the future, establishing goals and objectives, and designing organizational and marketing strategies and tactics to be implemented in the future.

**Planning** is the process of envisioning the future, establishing goals and objectives, and designing organizational and marketing strategies and tactics to be implemented in the future. The planning process consists of analyzing perceived opportunities and selecting those courses of action that will help achieve the organization's objectives in the most efficient manner. Marketing managers plan what future activities will be implemented, when they will be performed, and who will be responsible for them.

DISCUSSION CONSIDERATION
Balancing a consumer orientation with society's long-term best interests requires consumers to make trade-offs. As a consumer, are you willing to pay higher prices for products that are environmentally safe—a "green fee?" For example, disposable diapers would have a green tax because of their effect on landfills, and nonreturnable packages might require a green tax and thus cost more than less convenient but more environmentally friendly products.

The purpose of planning is to go beyond diagnosis of the present and attempt to predict the future by devising a means to adjust to an ever-changing environment before problems develop. Planning helps an organization to shape its own destiny by anticipating changes in the marketplace rather than merely reacting to those changes. For example, an organization that anticipates changes in the public's and legislators' attitudes toward the need for recyclable packaging may plan to convert to environmentally "friendly" packaging before laws require this action. Planning allows the manager to follow the maxim "Act! Don't react." In short, planning involves deciding in advance.

Planning goes on at various organizational levels. For simplicity's sake, we will say that there are three such levels: top management, middle management, and operational, or first-line, management. These levels are shown in Exhibit 2–1.

STRATEGIC PLANNING
Long-term planning dealing with the organization's primary goals and objectives. Also called *corporate strategic planning.*

**Strategic planning,** or long-term planning dealing with an organization's primary goals and objectives, occurs at the top management levels. As we move from top management to middle management, determining long-term goals and planning strategies for the entire organization becomes a less time-consuming part of the job,

**EXHIBIT 2–1** Three Levels of Administration

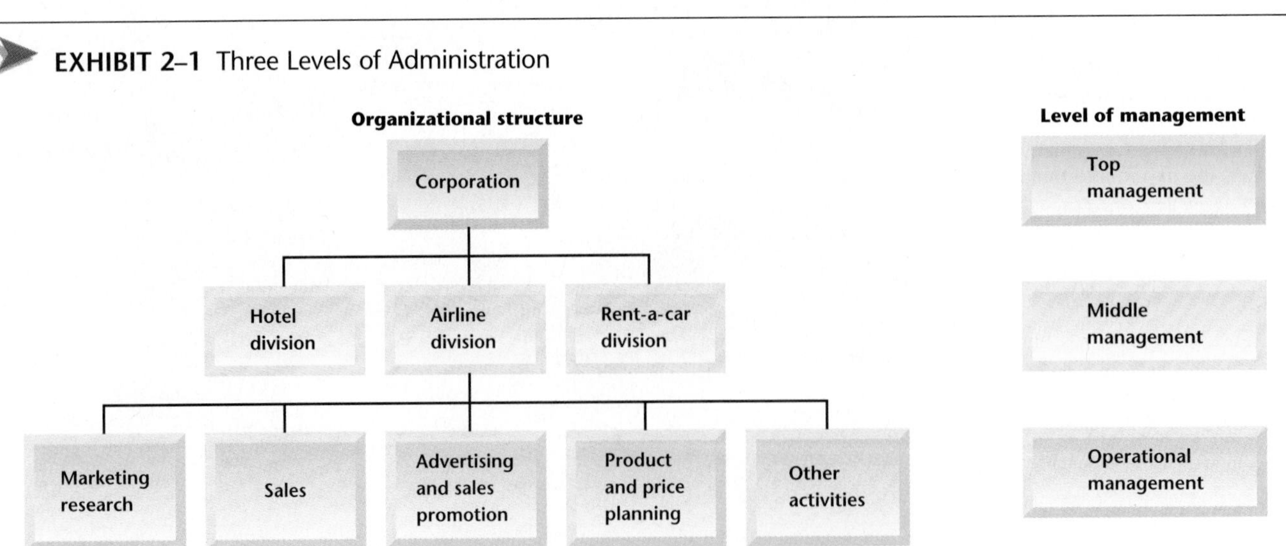

The adage "Act! Don't react" advises companies to anticipate change. Today, U.S. companies cannot do business with Cuba. However, companies like Gerber Products envision a time when the embargo will be lifted. In the meantime, Gerber donates its products to humanitarian groups that send aid to Cuba. This gesture of goodwill, which creates brand awareness and product knowledge, will pay dividends when the Cuban market reopens.

while planning strategy and tactics for business units (such as divisions) and specific products becomes a more important job dimension. In the realm of marketing, middle managers are responsible for planning the marketing mix strategy, allocating resources, and coordinating the activities of operational managers. At the level of operational management, **operational planning,** which concerns day-to-day functional activities, becomes dominant. Thus, while a vice president of marketing (a top-level manager) spends most of his or her time planning new products and strategy modifications for entire product lines, a sales manager (an operational manager) concentrates on supervising and motivating the sales force. Exhibit 2–2 shows how the focus of planning and basic strategic and tactical questions vary at the three major levels of the organization.

**OPERATIONAL PLANNING**
Planning that focuses on day-to-day functional activities, such as supervision of the sales force.

## EXHIBIT 2–2

A Manager's Level in the Organization Dictates the Focus of Planning

| Level of management | Focus of planning | Basic marketing questions |
|---|---|---|
| Top management | Corporate plans | What is our organizational mission? How do we organize our business? |
| Middle management | Strategic business unit (e.g., division or product) | What is our competitive strategy for growth? What is our competitive advantage? |
| Operational management | Operational plans for tactical execution | How can we best support the competitive strategy? What are our schedules for weekly operations? |

# Top Management Makes Corporate Strategic Plans

As noted, strategic planning is the responsibility of top management and pertains to long-term planning for the organization as a whole. It is the process of determining the organization's primary goals and developing a comprehensive organizational framework for accomplishing them. Answering questions such as "What business are we in?" and "How do we organize our business?" determines the organization's strategies for long-term growth. All organizations, not just major corporations, should engage in strategic planning to determine the organization's direction.

**STRATEGIC CORPORATE GOAL**
Broad organizational goal related to the long-term future. The organization's primary strategic corporate goal is identified in its organizational mission statement.

**Strategic corporate goals** are broad statements about what the organization wants to accomplish in its long-term future. The organization's mission statement identifies its primary strategic corporate goal.

## Defining the Organizational Mission

**ORGANIZATIONAL MISSION**
A statement of company purpose. It explains why the organization exists and what it hopes to accomplish.

Top managers decide the organizational or corporate mission. It is a strategic decision that influences all other marketing strategies. An **organizational mission** is a statement of company purpose. It explains why the organization exists and what it hopes to accomplish. It provides direction for the entire organization.

For example, when the Ford Motor Company was founded in 1903, Henry Ford had a clear understanding that cars need not be only for the rich—that the average American family needed economical transportation in the form of a low-priced car. Ford also had the insight to know that he could use product standardization and assembly-line technology to accomplish this mission. Modern marketers should strive to have an equally clear sense of each aspect of the business domain in which they operate.

The mission statement of The Limited, Inc., provides an example of a comprehensive mission statement:

> Our commitment is to offer the absolute best customer shopping experience anywhere—the best store—the best merchandise—the best merchandise presentation—the best customer service—the best of everything that a customer sees and experiences. To achieve this goal:
>
> We must maintain a restless, bold and daring business spirit noted for innovation and cutting-edge style;
>
> We must maintain a management culture which is action-oriented, always flexible and never bureaucratic;
>
> We must be tough-minded, disciplined, demanding, self-critical and yet supportive of each other, our team, and our suppliers;
>
> We must seek and retain Associates with an unquestioned reputation for integrity and respect for all people: customers, suppliers, shareholders and fellow Associates;
>
> We must continue to make risk acceptable by rewarding the risk-taker who succeeds—that goes without saying—and not penalizing the one who fails;
>
> And we must utilize our capacity to set qualitative and quantitative standards for our industry.
>
> We are determined to surpass all standards for excellence in retailing by thinking—and thinking small. By staying close to our customer and remaining agile, we will continue as a major force in retailing.[4]

**POINT TO EMPHASIZE**
How would you define the corporate mission of the local charitable organization devoted to distributing food to homeless people? Is it important for nonprofit organizations to define a mission?

**ALTERNATIVE EXAMPLE**
Al Nachom, president of 1-800-GIFT-LINE/SUPERFLORA, says "My interest is not . . . to sell flowers. . . . I don't care what I sell to customers. My goal is to satisfy customers." SUPERFLORA sells to people who don't have time to shop for gifts and get them gift-wrapped and mailed; so they rely on SUPERFLORA to take care of those tasks for them. SUPERFLORA has moved from the brink of bankruptcy to having 16,500 gift and floral affiliates that deliver more than 250,000 gift options a year. SOURCE: Kelly Shermach, "His Goal: Satisfy Customers, Don't Sell to Them," *Marketing News,* March 13, 1995, p. 6.

Product success, industry leadership, and even the organization's survival depend on satisfying the consumer. When a company defines the broad nature of its business, it must take a consumer-oriented perspective. It must avoid short-sighted, narrow-minded thinking that will lead it to define its purpose from a product/production orientation rather than a consumer orientation. Thus, Motorola defines itself as being in the wireless communication business, not just as a maker of cellular phones or

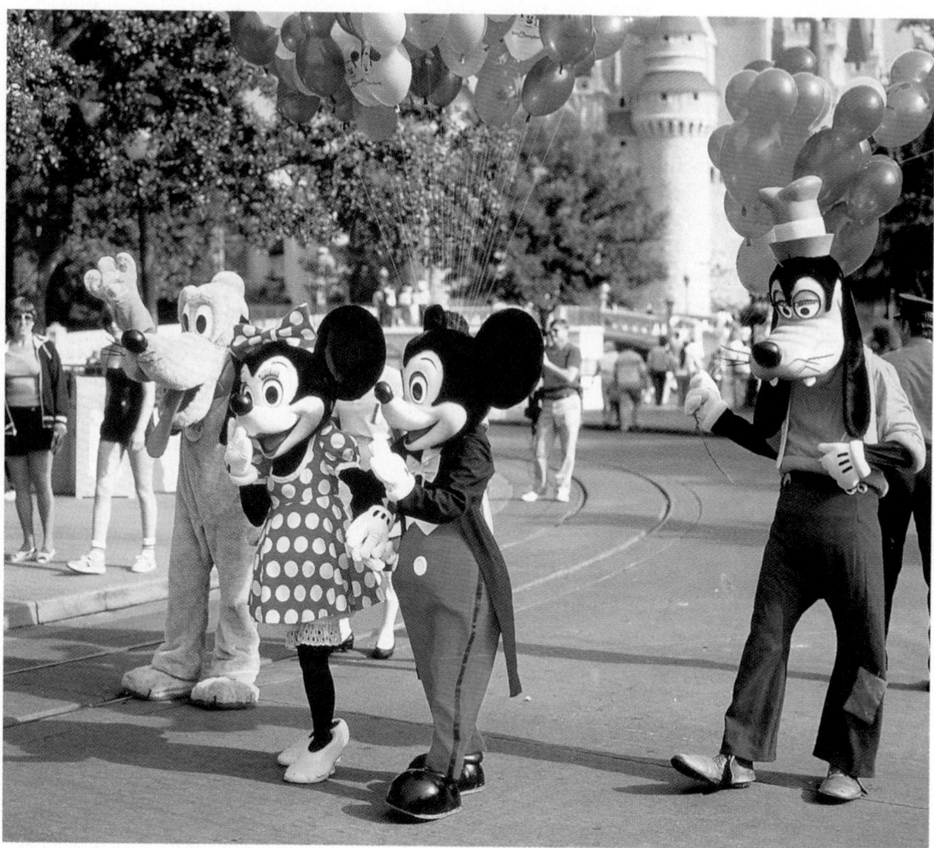

Disney says it is in the business of "Using our imagination to bring happiness to millions." It understands that the broad nature of its business goes beyond animation and movies. It entertains people in movie theaters, in its theme parks, and in their homes. Disney as a marketer of happiness is not marketing-myopic.

pagers (beepers). Companies that make movies, like Disney, should see themselves as being in the entertainment business rather than the movie business. A firm's failure to define its purpose from a broad consumer orientation is referred to as **marketing myopia.**[5]

**MARKETING MYOPIA**
Failure to define organizational purpose from a broad consumer orientation.

## Establishing Strategic Business Units

The organizational mission and other strategic corporate goals, once established, provide a framework for determining what organizational structure is most appropriate to the organization's marketing efforts. For a company that markets only a single product or service, the organization will be relatively simple. However, many organizations—like General Electric—operate a diverse set of businesses. General Electric's businesses, for example, range from the marketing of light bulbs to the marketing of aircraft engines. In the medium-sized and large organizations that engage in diverse businesses, establishing strategic business units is another aspect of corporate-level planning.

**STRATEGIC BUSINESS UNIT (SBU)**
A distinct unit, such as a company, division, department, or product line, of the overall parent organization with a specific marketing focus and a manager who has the authority and responsibility for managing all unit functions.

A **strategic business unit** (SBU) is a distinct unit, such as a company, division, department, or product line, of the overall parent organization with a specific market focus and a manager who has the authority and responsibility for managing all unit functions. For example, a bank may have a real estate division, a commercial division, and a trust division, as well as a retail division, which offers traditional banking services for the general public.

The logic that underlies the concept of the strategic business unit is best understood through example. Consider these statements: Procter & Gamble does not compete against Kimberly-Clark, and Dow Chemical does not compete against Union

ALTERNATIVE EXAMPLE
Cadbury-Schweppes and Dr Pepper/Seven Up have recently merged. The union enhances Dr Pepper's competitive position abroad, where Cadbury has a stronger market position and channels of distribution. Cadbury will be able to take advantage of Dr Pepper's distribution channels in the United States. As a result of the union, Cadbury–Dr Pepper is the third largest company in the soft drink market. As an executive in a competing firm said, "Now, all our competitors are under one roof." SOURCE: Jeanne Whalen, "Cadbury–Dr Pepper Merger Deemed Mutually Beneficial," *Advertising Age,* January 30, 1995, p. 33.

Carbide. Competition isn't carried on at the corporate level but at the individual business-unit level. Thus, Procter & Gamble's Pampers compete against Luvs disposable diapers, a Kimberly-Clark product. Dow might compete with Union Carbide for certain types of chemical customers but not others. Acknowledgment of this simple reality has led top managers to identify separate manageable units or autonomous profit centers within their organizations so that performance can be monitored at the level of individual business activities rather than at the overall corporate level only.

The idea is that each SBU operates as a "company within a company." The SBU is organized around a cluster of organizational offerings that share some common element, such as an industry, customer needs, target market, or technology. It has control over its own marketing strategy, and its sales revenues may be distinguished from those of other SBUs in the organization. It can thus be evaluated individually and its performance measured against that of specific external competitors. This evaluation provides the basis for allocating resources.

## Middle Managers Plan Strategies for SBUs

Top managers are responsible for the entire organization. They assign the responsibility for planning business-unit strategy and marketing strategy for individual products to middle managers. Corporate-level planning does, however, strongly influence the marketing planning activities of middle managers. Corporate-level strategies outline broad principles that are expected to cascade down through the organization. Exhibit 2–3 depicts how corporate strategies influence marketing strategies at the business-unit level and at the operational level.

COMPETITIVE ADVANTAGE
Superiority to or favorable difference from competitors along some dimension important to the market.

### Business-Unit Stratgegies for Competitive Advantage

One of the most common business-unit goals is to establish and maintain a **competitive advantage**—to be superior to or favorably different from competitors in a way

EXHIBIT 2–3
Corporate Strategy Filters Down to Other Levels

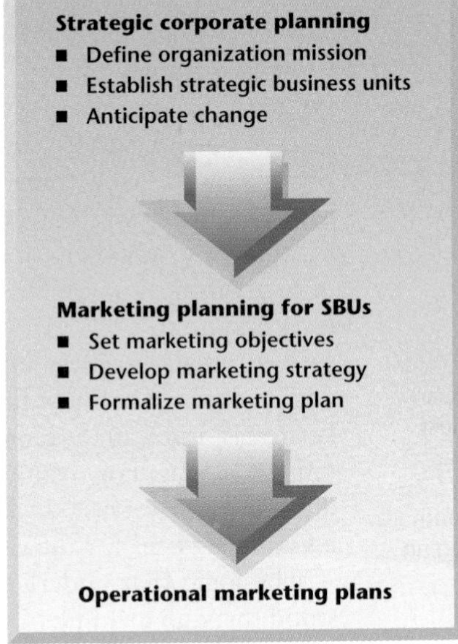

**DIVERSIFICATION**
The strategy of marketing new products to a new market.

Marketing new products to a new set of customers is called **diversification.** When Sega Corporation felt a need to diversify outside its video-game operations, it created two high-tech, virtual-reality theme parks in Japan. Its expansion into North America with simulator rides that are part video game and part 3D movie is a major diversification effort for Sega.

A company that diversifies expands into an entirely new business. Often the company's marketing research staff and its engineering research and development staff are instrumental in identifying market opportunities and product ideas for diversification. An alternative approach is the acquisition of new products by merger with or purchase from other companies. Nestlé used this strategy when it purchased Alpo Petfoods from the Pillsbury Company division of London-based Grand Met.

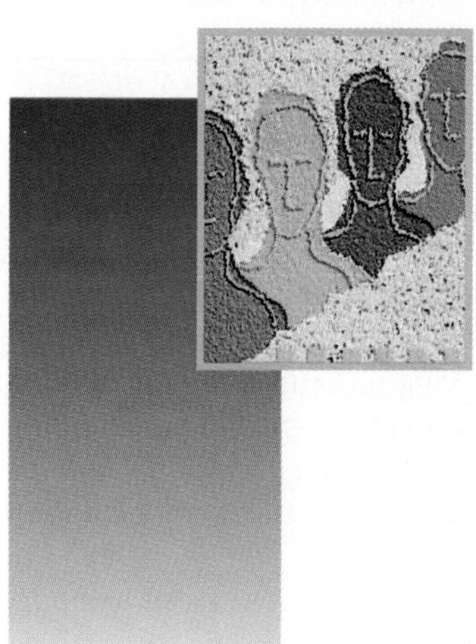

### FOCUS ON RELATIONSHIPS

*Apple, IBM, and Motorola*

For years, the personal computer buying decision was simple—a clear product choice between an Apple Macintosh and an IBM or IBM-compatible PC. Most buyers opted for the IBM-compatible PCs that used Intel Corporation's computer chips and ran Microsoft Corporation's MS-DOS or Windows operating system software. The prevalence of the IBM clones helped Microsoft and Intel flourish and grow into giant global companies. Meanwhile, Apple and IBM were not doing as well. So Apple and IBM formed an alliance with Motorola, the supplier of Apple's computer chips, to develop a new product—the PowerPC. PowerPC delivers more power than Intel's potent Pentium chip at half the price. The partners, in an alliance that would have been unthinkable 10 years ago, are betting that their collaboration will put Apple and IBM back into leadership of the personal computing industry. ■

## The Strategic Marketing Process

**STRATEGIC MARKETING PROCESS**
The entire sequence of managerial and operational activities required to create and sustain effective and efficient marketing strategies.

Marketing managers engage in many diverse activities, ranging from formulating strategy to evaluating whether existing strategies are effective and efficient. The term **strategic marketing process** refers to the entire sequence of managerial and operational activities required to create and sustain effective and efficient marketing strategies.

There are six major stages in the strategic marketing process:

1. Identifying and evaluating opportunities.
2. Analyzing market segments and selecting target markets.
3. Planning a market position and developing a marketing mix strategy.
4. Preparing a formal marketing plan.
5. Executing the plan.
6. Controlling efforts and evaluating the results.

As Exhibit 2–5 shows, the first four stages involve planning activities to develop a marketing strategy that will satisfy customers' needs and meet the goals and objectives of the organization. The latter two stages involve execution and control to make the plan work.

The various activities involved in developing marketing strategy may be carried out by a number of people over varying time periods, and the actual sequence of decisions may differ among organizations. Nevertheless, each stage is crucial to effective strategy development.

**EXHIBIT 2–5**

The Six Stages of the Strategic Marketing Process

**PLANNING STAGES**
- **Identifying and evaluating opportunities.**
- **Analyzing market segments and selecting target markets.**
- **Planning a market position and developing a marketing mix strategy.**
- **Preparing a formal marketing plan.**

↓

- **Executing the plan.**

↓

- **Controlling efforts and evaluating the results.**

## Stage 1: Identifying and Evaluating Opportunities

The powerful and ever-changing impact of environmental factors presents opportunities and threats to every organization. *Opportunities* occur when environmental conditions favor an organization's attaining or improving a competitive advantage. *Threats* occur when environmental conditions signal potential problems that may jeopardize an organization's competitive position. The marketer must be able to accurately "read" the environment and any changes in it and to translate the analysis of trends into marketing opportunities.

ALTERNATIVE EXAMPLE
Kodak recently realized that for decades it had been missing a market opportunity. Lots of consumers have photographs that they might like to copy or enlarge, but they've lost the negatives. Today, they can take the pictures to a CopyPrint Station and make copies and enlargements themselves! The cost? Enlargements are $10, compared with $7 normally, so the product appears to be a good deal. Shops that add the CopyPrint Station usually quadruple their enlargement business. SOURCE: Mark Maremont, "The Times of Your Life—As Many Times as You Want," *Business Week,* January 30, 1995, p. 68.

An environmental change may be interpreted as a threat or an opportunity, depending on the nature of an organization's or strategic business unit's competitive position. Declining per-capita coffee consumption is clearly an unfavorable trend and an environmental threat to coffee marketers. The marketers of soft drinks, however, will see this trend as an opportunity to increase consumption of cola in the morning to sell more of their products.

Effective managers analyze threatening situations and foresee problems that may result. They then adapt their strategies in hopes of turning threats into opportunities. For example, noticing a threat—declining coffee consumption—Mr. Coffee created an opportunity by developing an appliance for brewing iced tea.

**SITUATION ANALYSIS**
The interpretation of environmental attributes and change in light of the organization's ability to capitalize on potential opportunities.

**Situation analysis** is the diagnostic activity of interpreting environmental conditions and changes in light of the organization's ability to capitalize on potential opportunities and ward off problems. Kodak is a company that recognizes that timing can be crucial to marketing success. Situational analysis ascertained that the environmental threats and opportunities facing the company changed dramatically between the late 1980s and the mid-1990s. Kodak altered its strategy to fit with changing times. Its success is described in the accompanying Competitive Strategy feature.

**ENVIRONMENTAL SCANNING**
All information gathering designed to detect changes in their initial stage of development.

Situation analysis requires both environmental scanning and environmental monitoring. **Environmental scanning** includes all information gathering designed to detect indications of changes that may be in their initial stages of development. For example, in 1994, as a result of scanning the environment, marketers of lingerie and brassieres learned that women considered the new push-up Wonderbra very fashionable. Maidenform and other competitors, betting that curves and cleavage were coming back in fashion, introduced push-up bras and body enhancers with names like It Really Works, The Super Uplift, Bodysationals, Her Secrets, and It Must Be Magic.

**ENVIRONMENTAL MONITORING**
Tracking of certain phenomena, such as sales data and population statistics; to observe whether any meaningful trends are emerging.

**Environmental monitoring** involves tracking certain phenomena, such as sales data and population statistics, to observe whether any meaningful trends are emerg-

**EXHIBIT 2–7**

Planning, Execution, and Control Are Interrelated

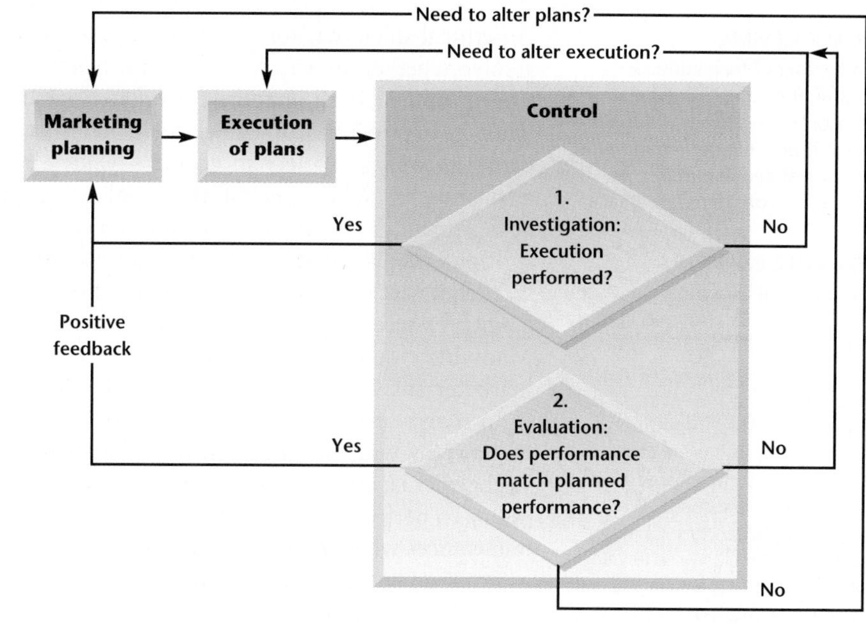


**SOCIAL RESPONSIBILITY**
The ethical consequences of a person's or an organization's acts as they might affect the interests of others.

Society clearly expects marketers to obey the law, but a socially responsible organization has a responsibility broader than legal responsibility. **Social responsibility** refers to the ethical consequences of a person's or an organization's acts as they might affect the interests of others.[13] Every marketing manager makes decisions that have ethical implications.

## The Nature of Ethics

**MARKETING ETHICS**
The principles that guide an organization's conduct and the values it expects to express in certain situations.

**MORAL BEHAVIOR**
In regard to marketers, how well an individual's or organization's marketing activity exhibits the ethical values to which the individual or organization subscribes.

**NORM**
A social principle identifying what action is right or wrong in a given situation.

*Ethics* involves values about right and wrong conduct. **Marketing ethics** involves the principles that guide an organization's conduct and the values it expects to express in certain situations.[14] **Moral behavior** in the marketing context reflects how well an individual's or an organization's marketing activity exhibits these ethical values.

Ethical principles reflect the cultural values and norms of a society. **Norms** suggest what ought to be done under given circumstances. They indicate approval or disapproval, what is good or bad. Many norms in Western society are based in the Judeo-Christian ethic. Being truthful is good. Being fair—doing unto others as you would have them do unto you—meets with approval. Other norms have a utilitarian base.[15] They may arise from a concern about the consequences of one's actions: "You ought to obey product safety laws, or you may go to jail." They may also arise from expectations about how society should function: "It is good that a company's shareholders receive its profits, because profits are the shareholders' reward for investment and risk taking."

Some ethical principles for personal conduct dictated by broad norms have direct counterparts in marketing actions. Being truthful, a societal norm, and avoiding deceptive, untruthful advertising are closely linked. Where such clear-cut links exist, the expected moral behavior is relatively clear. Some actions, such as murdering a competitor, are so noticebly linked to norms that they would be morally indefensible in all circumstances although morally accepted behavior may be clear-cut in many circumstances, in others, determining what is ethical is a complicated matter open to debate.

## Resolving Ethical Dilemmas

**ETHICAL DILEMMA**
In the context of marketing, a predicament in which a marketer must resolve whether an action, although it benefits the organization, the individual decision maker, or both, may be considered unethical.

An **ethical dilemma,** for a marketer, is a predicament in which the marketer must resolve whether an action, although it benefits the organization, the individual decision maker, or both, may be considered unethical.[16] An ethical dilemma may arise when two principles or values are in conflict. It may be that a corporation president—as well as society in general—values both high profits and a pollution-free environment. When one of these values or preferences in any way inhibits the achievement of the other, the businessperson is faced with an ethical dilemma.

ALTERNATIVE EXAMPLE
In China as well as some other Asian nations, brands are not protected by law. Hence, local firms can copy American brands and sell them on the local market at lower prices. An example is Chrysler Corporation's discovery that a Chinese factory located near its Jeep operation was turning out Jeep knockoffs. When Chrysler complained, the Chinese response was, "Well, we're developing an auto industry, and you should help us." To Westerners, copying brands is highly unethical, but in many Asian countries, it's just good business. SOURCE: Amy Borrus, "Eyeball to Eyeball with China," *Business Week,* February 20, 1995, pp. 32–33.

Problems also arise when others do not share the principles or values that guide a marketer's actions. Consider these questions: Is it wrong to pay a bribe in a foreign country where bribery is a standard business practice? Should MTV avoid airing a Madonna video if its sexual overtones offend certain viewers but not others? How a marketer answers these questions involves resolving ethical dilemmas.

In many situations, individuals agree on principles or values but have no fixed measure by which to judge actions. An engineer can calculate exactly how strong a steel girder is, and a chemist can usually offer the right formulation of chemicals necessary to perform a task, but the business executive often cannot be so precise. Even in instances where specific laws would seem to guide action, the laws and their application may be subject to debate. Although marketers and other businesspeople often pride themselves on their rational problem-solving abilities, the lack of permanent, objective ethical standards for all situations continues to trouble the person seeking the ethical course of action in business.

Thus, there rarely is an absolute consensus on what should be done when ethical behavior is discussed. Different people, and even a single person, can evaluate a question from several different perspectives. For example, the belief that smoking is injurious to health has led to regulations that restrict smoking in airplanes and other public places and bar cigarette commercials from radio and television. Yet to some, this is a controversial matter. Of course, good health is important, but what about the smoker's freedom of choice?

POINT TO EMPHASIZE
Most students and professors agree that an important value in education is academic honesty. What is your understanding of the standards used to judge honesty on tests, written papers, and computer assignments? Are you aware of others who judge similar actions differently?

In general, when marketing decision makers encounter ethical dilemmas, they consider the impact of the organization's actions and operate in a way that balances the organization's short-term profit needs with society's long-term needs. For example, a cookie marketer, such as Keebler, knows that people buy cookies because they taste good. It also knows certain inexpensive cooking oils that enhance taste are not as low in saturated fat as other, more expensive ingredients. The company may conduct extensive research to reformulate the cookies by changing to more healthful ingredients while maintaining good taste.

More specifically, marketers must ask what is ethical in a particular situation. They must establish the facts in the situation and determine if their plans are compatible with the organization's ethical values. They must determine at what point certain marketing practices become ethically questionable. Is it ethical for a sales representative to pay for a purchasing agent's lunch? To give the purchasing agent a gift on his or her birthday?[17] To arrange for an expense-free vacation for the agent if the sales representative's company gets a big contract?

To help marketers act in a socially responsible manner, President John F. Kennedy outlined the consumer's basic rights: the right to be informed, the right to safety, the right to choose, and the right to be heard. Since Kennedy's pronouncement, others have argued that consumers have other rights, such as the right to privacy and the right to a clean and healthy environment. Arguments have been made that children have special rights because they have not developed mature reasoning powers.

**CODE OF CONDUCT**
A statement establishing a company's or a professional organization's guidelines with regard to ethical principles and acceptable behavior.

Rights like these are embodied in organizations' and associations' codes of conduct. A **code of conduct** establishes a company's or a professional organization's guidelines with regard to its ethical principles and what behavior it considers proper. The American Marketing Association's Code of Ethics appears in Exhibit 2–8.

CHAPTER

# 3

# Environmental Forces in a Diverse World: The Macroenvironment

## LEARNING OBJECTIVES

After you have studied this chapter, you will be able to:

1. Describe the domestic and foreign environments in which marketers operate and their effects on organizations.
2. Understand that social values and beliefs are important cultural forces.
3. Explain how demographic trends, such as changes that have occurred in the American family, influence marketers.
4. Explain the various ways in which economic conditions influence marketers.
5. Appreciate how the three levels of U.S. law and the laws of other nations can influence marketing activity.
6. Explain how the various elements of the marketing environment interact.

Late on a weekend night, students line up to get into one of the University of Michigan's hottest new night spots, the courtyard at Angell Hall. It contains 320 gleaming personal computers, wired up to networks all over campus—and the world. Students flock here to write love notes, send letters to their parents, turn in homework to professors, post classified ads, catch up on campus news, talk about Rousseau and Locke on a special bulletin board for members of a political science class (more than 25 percent of all classes have their own discussion boards), and look one another up in an electronic phone directory (complete, in some cases, with such personal details as "male, blond, nice guy").

Computer networks and information technology are transforming life at the University of Michigan, as well as at other campuses across the country. No longer merely a tool for nerds and wonks, they have become a pervasive cultural and social force for everybody. The Angell Hall courtyard offers a glimpse of a revolution that is just on the horizon. Right now, perhaps 10 percent of Americans use a personal computer to communicate (compared with nearly 100 percent of University of Michigan undergraduates). But signs abound that the e-mail culture is finally entering the mainstream.

These days, nearly 40 percent of personal computers have a modem, the device that lets you send messages from one computer to another via a phone line. The biggest e-mail network of all, an anarchic sprawl called the Internet, is suddenly a feverish trend. Formerly a hangout for heavy-duty hackers at computer companies and universities, it's now the toast of national magazine articles and media barons. Rupert Murdoch's empire is buying a little company that offers a link into the Internet. A big television company, Continental Cablevision, Inc., is figuring out a way to patch the Internet into a home's cable line. The first waves of advertisers are hungrily circling around the network. *Au courant* tycoons flash business cards with an Internet address (the one with the funny "@" glyph in the middle) next to their phone and fax numbers.

All these players smell big money in consumer personal computer networks, and with good reason. Already an estimated 15 million people in 50 countries use the Internet. With traffic rising as much as 15 percent a month, Internet boosters call it the fastest-growing telecommunications system ever built, surpassing even the telephone network in its prime.

Like so many social revolutions, this one has its roots on campuses—at the Angell Hall courtyard and other college computer rooms like it. Colleges began widely offering e-mail during the past decade, first within their own campus walls, and then via the Internet with links to other campuses and companies around the world. It was free and intensely addictive. Students graduated and took the habit with them out into the real world, colonizing thousands of new workplaces and families.

ALTERNATIVE EXAMPLE

In 1995, McDonald's launched McFamily on American Online, a service which offers entertainment and family advice. It also includes a catalog of McDonald's merchandise. McFamily is also on the Microsoft Network and it may expand to the World Wide Web. McDonald's uses McFamily to collect customer names, addresses, and other data. SOURCE: Jeanne Whalen and Keith Kelly, "Mickey, McD Hop Online," *Advertising Age*, August 28, 1995, p. 34.

Information technology, computer networks, and the Internet are powerful environmental forces that will dramatically change the nature of marketing in the next decade. This chapter discusses marketing's environment. It begins by explaining the differences between the domestic and foreign environments and the macro- and microenvironments. It then examines the various components of the macroenvironment: physical environment, sociocultural forces, demographic forces, economic forces, science and technology, and politics and laws.

## A World Perspective for the 21st Century

POINT TO EMPHASIZE
Products can mean services, too. The United States exports products, such as fast-food restaurants (McDonald's, Kentucky Fried Chicken), that are services. Information services, such as computer networks and scanner data gathering and analysis (IRI, A. C. Nielsen), are services, too.

You may drive a Toyota, Mazda, or Mercedes automobile. You may fill your tank at a Shell service station with gasoline refined from crude oil from Nigeria or Venezuela. You may sign the credit slip with a Bic pen. Each of these products comes from a non-U.S. company and is made available in the United States as a result of international marketing. Today, we live in a global village. It is difficult to speak of matters that do not influence or are not themselves influenced by other areas of the world. Jet age transportation, satellite television networks, computer modems, e-mail, and other electronic technologies are reshaping and restructuring the patterns of business. The world is getting smaller, and the external environment is taking on a more global character.

**DOMESTIC ENVIRONMENT**
The environment in an organization's home country.

**FOREIGN ENVIRONMENT**
The environment outside an organization's home country.

Some organizations that market products only in their home countries are influenced solely by environmental forces operating in the **domestic environment.** However, in today's global economy, most corporations must anticipate and respond to opportunities and threats in **foreign environments** as well. (See Exhibit 3–1.) It may be easier to envision a large multinational corporation like Xerox or Honda being influenced by forces from both the domestic and foreign environments than to understand how uncontrollable foreign forces affect the marketing activities of, say, a small local electronics retailer. Yet both large and small organizations—indeed, the entire economy—can be influenced by forces shaped thousands of miles away from their home countries.[1] And tomorrow's marketing managers will face even more global competition than managers of the 1990s.

**IMPORT**
Foreign product purchased domestically.

**EXPORT**
Domestically produced product sold in foreign markets.

When thinking about marketing in our global economy, it is important to remember two key economic terms. **Imports** are foreign products purchased domestically. **Exports** are domestically produced products sold in foreign markets.

### EXHIBIT 3–1

Forces in Both the Domestic and the Foreign Environment Influence the Marketing Mix

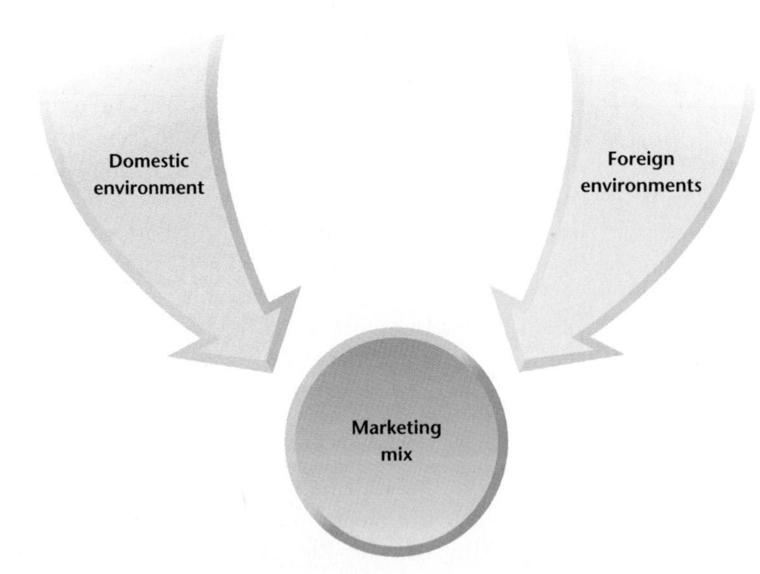


DISCUSSION CONSIDERATION
The United States imports many products, too. What kinds of products does the United States import? What does comparing the types of products imported by the United States with the products exported by the United States indicate about the American economy?

The United States is a major exporting country in terms of absolute dollar volume. Yet our international marketing efforts are somewhat low relative to those of other countries such as Germany and the United Kingdom. This is explained, in part, by the large and highly developed nature of the domestic market in the United States. Few countries have such an extensive, well-developed domestic marketplace. Therefore, marketers in many other nations have had to become involved in international marketing activities.

America's top export products are (1) agricultural products, (2) electrical machinery, such as circuit breakers, (3) data processing and office equipment, (4) aircraft, and (5) general industrial machinery, such as escalators. America's top export customers are (1) Canada, (2) Japan, (3) Mexico, (4) Britain, and (5) Germany.

## The Macroenvironment

**MACROENVIRONMENT**
The broad societal forces that shape every business and nonprofit marketer. The physical environment, sociocultural forces, demographic forces, economic forces, scientific knowledge and technology, and political and legal forces are components of the macroenvironment.

**MICROENVIRONMENT**
The environmental forces directly influencing a company, such as its customers and institutions that shape its marketing practice.

Whether we are discussing the domestic environment, a foreign environment, or the world environment, we can divide the environment into two categories: the macroenvironment and the microenvironment. The broad societal forces that influence every business and nonprofit marketer comprise the **macroenvironment.** Every company, however, is more directly influenced by a **microenvironment** consisting of its customers and the economic institutions that shape its marketing practices.

Our discussion in this chapter describes the macroenvironment. Chapter 4 deals with the more direct influences that comprise the microenvironment. The macroenvironment consists of the physical environment, sociocultural forces, demographic forces, economic forces, scientific and technical knowledge, and political and legal forces. (See Exhibit 3–2.)

## The Physical Environment

**PHYSICAL ENVIRONMENT**
The environment, domestic or foreign or both, consisting of natural resources and other aspects of the natural world.

The **physical environment** consists of natural resources, such as minerals and animal populations, and other aspects of the natural world, such as changes in ecological systems. The availability of natural resources may have a direct and far-reaching impact on marketing activities in a geographic region. Areas rich in petroleum, for example, may concentrate on the production and marketing of fuel oil, kerosene, benzene, naphtha, paraffin, and other products derived from this natural resource.

Marketing is influenced by many other aspects of the natural environment as well. Climate is one example.[2] It is not difficult to imagine that umbrella sales are greater in rainy Seattle than in desert-like Tucson or that more winter clothing is sold in Minneapolis than in Miami.

**EXHIBIT 3–2** Macroenvironmental Influences on the Marketing Mix

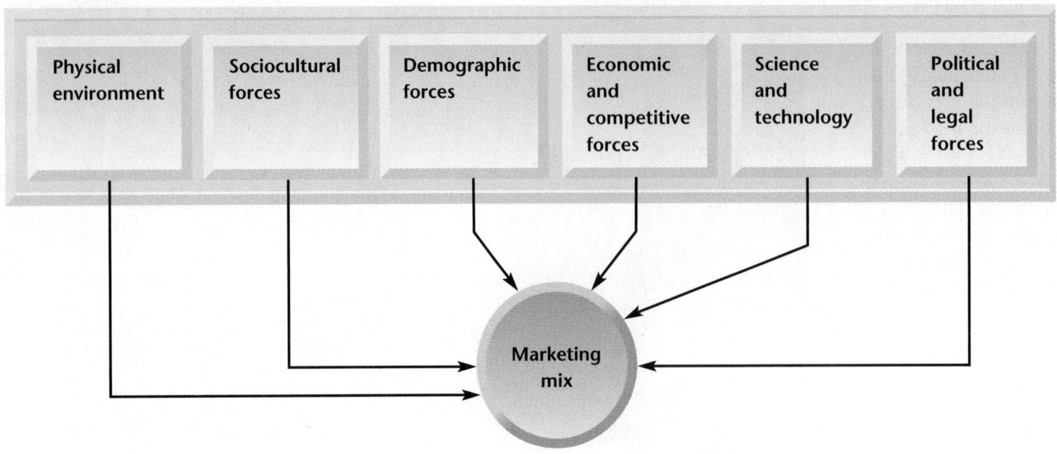


**POINT TO EMPHASIZE**
Another industry heavily affected by the physical environment is the tourism industry. Tourism has become a major source of revenue (often, revenue from foreign residents) in many nations of the world, including the United States. Another macroenvironmental factor that drives tourism is the monetary exchange rates. For example, when the American dollar is weak compared with a foreign currency, it makes the United States an inexpensive and therefore popular tourist destination.

Climate also greatly influences the timing of marketing activities. In India, more than 65 percent of all soft drinks are sold during the blazing hot months of June through September, for instance. Marketers adapt their strategies to such environmental differences. Kmart, for example, identifies every item stocked in its stores by climate. It knows that climate influences not only what is purchased but when. Grass seed, insect sprays, snow shovels, and many other goods must be in the right stores at the correct time of year.

Finally, the physical environment of marketing includes the presence or absence of substances harmful to the earth's ecology. Smog, acid rain, and pollution of the ocean are among the many conditions in this category. Such conditions are highly interrelated with aspects of the sociocultural environment.

Code Bleu Soda Pop Denim offers an example of how an ecological consideration can influence marketing strategy. Apparel makers had little success marketing organically grown, dye-free cottons. However, Soda Pop denim, which is a weave of 80 percent denim and 20 percent recycled, spun plastic (the equivalent of two 64-ounce bottles), was a big hit. Soda Pop denim looks like real denim, and teens and young adults like the "trash fashion" concept.[3] Code Bleu says, "Drink a bottle of soda, wear the bottle, save the planet." Lee's Ecojeans and Arizona Soda Pop jeans quickly followed in Code Bleu's footsteps. Marketing ecologically safe products and making efforts, as Code Bleu did, to help preserve or revitalize the physical environment is often called **green marketing.**

**GREEN MARKETING**
Marketing activities beneficial to the physical environment.

## Sociocultural Forces

Every society has a culture that guides its everyday life. In the environment of marketing, the word *culture* does not refer to classical music, art, and literature. Instead, **culture** refers to social institutions, values, beliefs, and behaviors. Culture includes everything we learn as members of society but does not include the basic drives with which we were born.

**CULTURE**
The institutions, values, beliefs, and behaviors of a society; everything we learn, as opposed to that with which we were born; that part of the environment, domestic or foreign or both, that is shaped by humankind.

Culture is shaped by humankind. It is learned rather than innate. For example, we are born with a need to eat; but what, when, and where we eat, and whether we season our food with ketchup or curdled goat's milk, we learn as part of our culture.

(Japanese eating habits are the subject of the accompanying Competitive Strategy feature.) That many U.S. women are free from traditional restraints, while few Saudi women are, is also a cultural phenomenon. Material artifacts and the symbolic meanings associated with these items also vary by culture.

## Values and Beliefs

**SOCIAL VALUE**
A value that embodies the goals a society views as important and expresses a culture's shared ideas of preferred ways of acting.

A **social value** embodies the goals a society views as important and expresses a culture's shared ideas of preferred ways of acting. Social values reflect abstract ideas about what is good, right, and desirable. For example, we learn from those around us that it is wrong to lie or steal. The following social values reflect the beliefs of most people in the United States:

**DISCUSSION CONSIDERATION**
While it is true that there are predominant beliefs across the United States, it is a mistake to assume all Americans share common beliefs. In fact, beliefs may differ from region to region in the United States. How do beliefs in your town, state, or region differ from those of the United States as a whole or from those of other regions?

*Freedom.* The freedom of the individual to act as he or she pleases is a fundamental aspect of the U.S. culture.
*Achievement and success.* The achievement of wealth and prestige through honest efforts is highly valued. Such achievement leads to a higher standard of living and improves the quality of life.
*Work ethic.* The importance of working on a regular basis is strongly emphasized. Those who are idle are considered lazy.
*Equality.* Most Americans profess a high regard for human equality, especially equal opportunity, and generally relate to one another as equals.
*Patriotism/nationalism.* Americans take pride in living in the "best country in the world." They are proud of their country's democratic heritage and its achievements.
*Individual responsibility and self-fulfillment.* Americans are oriented toward developing themselves as individuals. They value being responsible for their achievements. The U.S. Army's slogan "Be all that you can be" captures the essence of the desirability of personal growth.[4]

**BELIEF**
A conviction concerning the existence or the characteristics of something.

A **belief** is a conviction concerning the existence or the characteristics of physical and social phenomena. We may believe, for example, that a high-fat diet causes can-

Several new ice creams flavors from Ben & Jerry's—such as chocolate peanut butter cookie dough, peanut butter cup, and coconut almond fudge chip—are the result of the ice cream marketer's following a trend known as "pleasure revenge." Consumers who for years chose lowfat foods are doing so less often, opting instead for products that taste good. This movement by consumers toward good-tasting products is particularly noticeable in the dairy foods category. Cheese, sour cream, ice cream, and frozen novelties—with all the fat and flavor—are back in style.

COMPETITIVE STRATEGY: WHAT WENT RIGHT?

## *Japanese Like Seafood Really Fresh*

The latest in food rages in Japan is to eat fish live—flounder that flap around on the plate, finger-length eel swallowed raw. "The food moves around a lot—that's the whole idea," said Sunao Uehara, a chef at Chunagon, a well-known seafood restaurant in Ginza, one of Tokyo's most expensive entertainment districts.

Shrimp, flounder, and lobster are by no means the only energetic entrees on the trendy diners' menu. Other attractions include firefly squid, loaches, sea bream, and young yellowtail. Waiters bring the fish in wiggling, their eyes and mouths moving, then quickly slice open the midsection and gut it, so the fish is ready to eat. Like sushi or sashimi, the slices are dipped in a mixture of soy sauce and horseradish.

Lobster is served belly up, with an incision made along the length of the tail so diners can get at the meat. Small squid and eels are eaten whole. Shrimp are featured in a dish called "dance," and are expected to do just that.

Though some Japanese express misgivings about eating live food, it is a concept that fits in easily with the emphasis on freshness and au naturel presentation upon which Japanese gastronomy is based.

Toshio Fujii, an X-ray technician from a stretch of Japan's western coast where discerning seafood eaters are the rule, said he prefers to eat his fish live because "they don't come any fresher." "My 7-year-old daughter likes them, too," he said. "But eels are kind of gross. I had them in my beer one time. Too many little bones."

The recent resurgence in the popularity of eating live food in Japan—practiced for centuries by hungry Japanese fishermen—is part of a larger "gourmet boom" fueled by Japan's every-growing economy.

Japanese consumers, who have extra money to spend on meals outside the home, are looking for better-tasting, more unusual dishes. Live fish tend to be expensive. Lobster courses at Chunagon range from a basic $44 meal to the top-of-the-line $120 dinner. "The expense just makes it all the more appealing," said Fujii. "The more it costs, the better we expect it to taste."

A spokesman for the Japan Society for the Prevention of Cruelty to Animals said the group doesn't consider the practice to be cruel. In fact, many believe eating live fish is an unique aspect of Japan's culinary culture.

cer or that chocolate causes acne. Whether a belief is correct is not particularly important in terms of our actions. Even a totally foolish belief may affect how we behave and what we buy.

It is the marketer's job to "read" the social environment and reflect the surrounding culture's values and beliefs in a marketing strategy. For example, American women's values about the importance of careers may be changing. Research has shown that many women believe that the stress caused by their multiple roles—wife, mother, career woman, nurse, chauffeur—is too intense. Social values are changing to play down work and to focus on family and on emotional enhancement of personal life. (An associated trend toward casual living and relaxed dress codes has caused the sales of sheer pantyhose to decline.) In the 21st century, American women will continue to work, but they will be more interested in leisure and in spending more time with family. Such changing social values could result in more spending on products that offer fantasy, romance, humor, and fun.

Values and beliefs vary from culture to culture. Understanding why people in foreign countries behave and react as they do requires knowing how their values and beliefs affect the success of marketing efforts.[5] What seems like a normal idea, or even a great idea, to marketers in one country may be seen as unacceptable or even laughable to citizens of other lands. Campbell's offered its familiar, to us, red-and-white-labeled cans of soup in Brazil but found cultural values there too difficult for this product to overcome. Brazilian housewives apparently felt guilty using the prepared soups that Americans take for granted. They believed that they would not be fulfilling their roles as homemakers if they served their families a soup they could not call their own. Faced with this difficulty, Campbell's withdrew the product. However, the company discovered that Brazilian women felt comfortable using a dehydrated "soup starter" to which they could add their own special ingredients and flair. To market soup in Japan, the marketer must realize that soup is regarded there as a breakfast drink rather than a dish served for lunch or dinner.

**POINT TO EMPHASIZE**

Differences in cultural beliefs not only frustrate Americans but create ethical dilemmas. How does an American manager, whose company acknowledges that "gifts" are illegal and improper by American social values, deal with a demand for a "gift" if that practice is accepted in another country? Should the manager adopt the practice of the other country in order to complete the sale? Does it make a difference if the negotiation occurs in the United States or elsewhere? Should Americans try to export their social values to other countries?

Industrial buyers and government workers may also behave differently in different cultures. In some countries, business dealings are carried on so slowly that U.S. businesspeople are frustrated by what they perceive as delays. Yet this customary slowness may be seen by their hosts as contributing to a friendly atmosphere. Government officials in some countries openly demand "gifts" or "tips," without which nothing gets done. Of course, this practice is illegal in the United States because it conflicts with American social values.

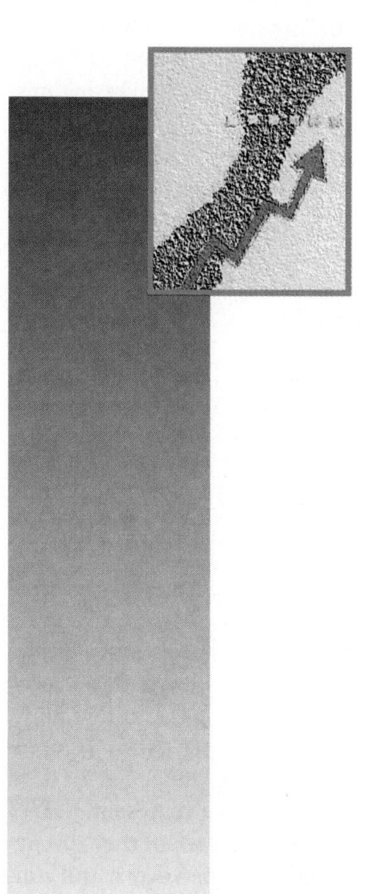

## FOCUS ON TRENDS

### *A New "Me Generation"*

On a Friday night in the heart of old Shanghai, the crowd at J. J.'s is working up a postsocialist sweat. Men in suits and ties gyrate with fashionably dressed young women; at small tables newly affluent entrepreneurs sip drinks between calls on cellular phones. The young people at J. J.'s revel in something unprecedented for China: personal and professional liberation. Those with the will and skill to take advantage of economic reform are freer than ever to seek their fortune, their mate and their own identity.

China's "Me generation" is less hostile to the Communist regime than indifferent to it. "The government is all around us, but we don't pay attention," says Nie Zheng, 23, a Beijing artist and photographer. That means forfeiting job security and welfare benefits that traditionally bound even artists to the socialist system. But Nie earns enough from free-lance work to pay for Japanese cameras, CDs and designer sunglasses. The parents of Pang Rui, 18, want him to have security as a teacher or a doctor. But the university-bound student from Xian demurs: "I want to be free to earn a lot of money from a job I like."

Zhao Li, 25, one of the many who choose to *xia hai* (plunge into the sea), quit her state-assigned job as an interpreter to work in a foreign-owned public relations firm. Her salary quintupled and she moved into her own two-room apartment. When her parents tell Zhao that her friends are all having children, she replies, "I have no time to be married." Chinese are marrying at a later age, casual premarital sex is more common, and the urban young increasingly choose their own spouses. "It used to be that Communist Party membership was important," said Wang Zhixiong, a Guangdong researcher. "Now peoples' tastes favor money, professional ranking and appearance." ■

After filming a commercial in Mexico, the advertising agency for Pace Foods left a truckload of salsa in the supermarket used in the commercial. The product sold out immediately. American-owned Pace investigated the situation and found an absence of processed salsa in the Mexican market. Pace learned that Mexican food processors, concerned about the Mexican cultural tradition of using only homemade salsa, had refrained from producing salsa to avoid insulting customers of their other products. However, increasingly time-pressed Mexican women were attracted to the American brand.

ALTERNATIVE EXAMPLE
Language is an important factor in marketing to minority cultures in the United States. In financial services, for example, Charles Schwab, a discount brokerage company, operates a telephone center in San Francisco that offers services in seven Chinese dialects and another center in Florida that offers services in Spanish and Portuguese. New York Life Insurance has an ethnic marketing unit whose agents represent 65 Asian, Hispanic, and black ethnicities. SOURCE: Leon E. Wynter, "Language Barriers As a Marketing Tool," *Wall Street Journal,* January 25, 1995, p. B1.

## Language

Language is an important part of culture, and the international marketer must be aware of its subtleties. For example, the French words *tu* and *vous* both mean "you." However, the former is used to address a social equal or an inferior and the latter to signify formality and social respect. In Japan, "yes" may often be meant as "yes, I understand what you said," not necessarily "yes, I agree." Numerous marketing mistakes have resulted from misinterpretations of language by unwary translators. The Chevrolet brand name *Nova* translates into Spanish as "no go." *Tomato paste* becomes "tomato glue" in Arabic. Translated into Spanish, Herculon carpet is "the carpeting with the big derriere."[6] The straightforward slogan "Come alive with Pepsi!" has been translated as "Come out of the grave with Pepsi!" and as "Pepsi brings your ancestors back from the grave." Gestures, too, can be misinterpreted, as illustrated in the accompanying Competitive Strategy feature.

DISCUSSION CONSIDERATION
Understanding the use of cultural symbols is also critical in the United States. Americans are as sensitive to the use and misuse of cultural symbols as citizens of any other nation. In the late 1960s, some young Americans sewed American flags into clothes. Is this something that is offensive today? Would it be offensive if a McDonald's restaurant in the United States used a religious symbol, such as a Christian cross or a Star of David, on its placemats?

## Cultural Symbols

Another aspect of culture involves cultural symbols. A cultural symbol stands for something else and expresses a common meaning to members of a society. Symbols may be verbal or nonverbal. The color white may represent purity, for example. A bull may represent strength. Such symbols may act as powerful unconscious forces, silently communicating to shape consumer attitudes and behavior. The use of cultural symbols can thus be of great importance in a marketing effort.

As with language, failure to fully understand cultural symbols can produce unpredictable results. According to myth, the site of the Aztec city of Tenochtitlan, now Mexico City, was revealed to its founders by an eagle bearing a snake in its talons. This image, now the official seal of Mexico, appears on the country's flag. To commemorate Mexico's Flag Day, two local McDonald's restaurants managed by U.S. citizens papered their serving trays with placemats embossed with a representation of the national emblem. Mexican government agents were infuriated when they discovered their beloved eagle splattered with ketchup. Authorities swooped down and confiscated the disrespectful placemats.[7]

**COMPETITIVE STRATEGY: WHAT WENT WRONG?**

## *Gestures Speak Louder Than Words*

"I knew I'd committed a monumental goof. But I just couldn't imagine how."

A young computer salesman from New Jersey is remembering his first overseas sales pitch. The scene was his company's offices in Rio, and it had gone like a Sunday preacher's favorite sermon. As he looked around the table, he knew he had clinched the sale. Triumphantly, he raised his hand to his Latin customers and flashed the classic American okay sign—thumb and forefinger forming a circle, other fingers pointing up.

The sunny Brazilian atmosphere suddenly felt like a deep freeze. Stony silence. Icy stares. Plus embarrassed smirks from his colleagues.

Calling for a break, they took him outside the conference room and explained. Our hero had just treated everyone to a gesture with roughly the same meaning over there as the notorious third-finger sign conveys so vividly here. Apologies saved the sale, but he still turns as pink as a Brazilian sunset when retelling the tale. It is only natural when you find yourself at sea in the local language to use gestures to bail yourself out. . . . Gestures pack the power to punctuate, to dramatize, to speak a more colorful language than mere words. Yet, like the computer salesman, you may discover that those innocent winks and well-meaning nods are anything but universal.

### Ethnocentrism

**ETHNOCENTRISM**
Belief in the superiority of one's own culture.

More often than not, as in the McDonald's example, failure to understand the market leads to unpleasant results. One reason that many managers fail to fully understand foreign cultures and marketing is that people tend to be ethnocentric. **Ethnocentricism** is the tendency to consider our own culture and way of life as the natural and normal ones.[8] We may mistakenly expect others to share these feelings. This unconscious use of our own cultural values as a reference point has been called the "self-reference criterion."[9] People doing business in a foreign country may be using the self-reference criterion, or may be ethnocentric, when they think their domestic strategy or reputation is better than that of any competitor in that country. But exporting our own biases into foreign markets results in mistakes—for example, when large U.S.-built cars with steering wheels on the left side are offered for use in overcrowded Japanese streets.

POINT TO EMPHASIZE
Ethnocentrism creates a myopic view of the world and may prevent business executives from seeing cultural differences. Pictures that elicit particular emotional responses in one country may not have the same meaning elsewhere, for example. Clearly, executives need to understand research options for learning about the cultures of global target markets.

Many Americans expect foreign businesspeople to conduct business the same way we do in the United States. However, often this is not the case. Assuming that, for example, it is appropriate to send a woman sales representative to Saudi Arabia, Yemen, or some other country in the Middle East shows a lack of understanding of cultural values. The women's movement has not had much impact in many Middle Eastern countries. Marketers must avoid such cultural nearsightedness by consciously recognizing its potentially biasing impact.

## Demographics

The terms *demography* and *demographics* comes from the Greek word *demos,* meaning "people," as does the word *democracy.* **Demography** may be defined as the study of the size, composition (for example, by age or racial group), and distribution of the

**DEMOGRAPHY**
The study of the size, composition, and distribution of the human population in relation to social factors such as geographic boundaries.

human population in relation to social factors such as geographic boundaries. The size, composition, and distribution of the population in any geographic market clearly influences marketing. Because demographic factors are of great concern to marketing managers, we discuss some basic demographic information and trends in this section. A wealth of demographic statistics for the United States can be found in the *Statistical Abstract of the United States* or on the Internet.[10]

## The U.S. Population

The population of the United States is constantly changing. If marketers are to satisfy the wants and needs of that population, they must be aware of the changes that are occurring and the directions in which these changes are moving the population.

In 1995, the Bureau of the Census estimated that there were 262 million people living in the United States. It has predicted that the population will reach 268 million in the year 2000. The birth rate is 15.2 per thousand, and the death rate is 8.7 per thousand. About 51.2 percent of the population is female, and about 48.8 percent is male.

In 1940, about 70 percent of the immigrants in the United States came from Europe. In 1992, only 15 percent came from Europe, while 37 percent came from Asia and 44 percent came from Latin America and the Caribbean. Today, the foreign-born population is approximately 20 million people, about 8 percent of the total U.S. population.

**Migration** Migration has always been an overwhelmingly important demographic factor in the United States. Much is heard about the effect of the Cuban and Haitian migrations into southern Florida and about the general migration into the Sunbelt states. However, migration into and around the country has been going on for hundreds of years.

The 1790 U.S. census showed the center of population to be 23 miles east of Baltimore, Maryland. The center of population represents the axis of two lines, one dividing the population into a northern and a southern half and the other, into an eastern and a western half. The 1790 population center was actually under the waters of the Atlantic Ocean because of the virtually absolute concentration of population along the East Coast and the curve of the coastline. The 1990 census moved the population center to Crawford County, Missouri, near Cherryville. Each census has moved the point farther south and west.

**Urbanization** The United States—and in fact, the entire world—has become increasingly urbanized since the 1800s. In the United States, the expansion of some metropolitan areas has brought neighboring cities and their suburbs so close together that they have, for all practical purposes, merged. Two examples of this phenomenon are the Northeast Corridor, which extends from Boston to Washington, D.C., and the string of communities stretching from north of Los Angeles to Tijuana, Mexico.

In fact, the 1990 census showed that more than half of the people in the United States live in the 39 metropolitan areas (that is, central cities and suburbs) with populations of more than a million. Approximately 76 percent live in the nation's 336 metropolitan areas—up from 56 percent in 1950.

Growth in U.S. metropolitan areas has not meant growth in the central cities. Crowded conditions, high crime rates, and other discomforts associated with city life, coupled with the great numbers of private cars owned by Americans, have encouraged the much-discussed "flight to the suburbs" of people seeking to enjoy a blend of country and city living. It is growth in suburban areas that has caused the populations of metropolitan areas to remain stable and even to rise. Indeed, the most dramatic growth of the past decade was in the suburbs. Suburbs like Mesa, Arizona, and Plano, Texas, actually became cities.

Although there has been some migration back to the central cities in recent years, the population cores of cities have continued to decline. In particular, many of the old manufacturing cities in the Northeast and Midwest have continued to lose people.

**GROSS DOMESTIC PRODUCT (GDP)**
The total value of all the goods and services produced by capital and workers in a country.

**GROSS NATIONAL PRODUCT (GNP)**
The total value of all the goods and services produced by a nation's residents or corporations, regardless of location.

**GDP and GNP** Two common measures of the health of a country's economy are **gross domestic product** (**GDP**) and **gross national product** (**GNP**). The GDP measures the value in all the goods and services produced by workers and capital *in the United States*. The GNP measures the value of all the goods and services produced by United States residents or corporations *regardless of location*. Thus, profits on overseas operations of American companies are included in GNP, but not in GDP. Profits that foreign companies make in the United States are included in GDP, but not in GNP. Both GDP and GNP provide economic yardsticks of business output. The difference between these two measures has to do with whether we wish to know what is produced inside our borders or what is produced by Americans around the world.[21]

In the United States per capita GDP was $24,696 and the inflation rate was in 3 percent in 1994. Exhibit 3–7 shows per capita GDP (in United States dollars) and inflation rates for several countries in 1993. Notice how different economic conditions are around the world.

**EXHIBIT 3–7** Per Capital GDP and Inflation Rates for Selected Countries

| COUNTRY | PER CAPITA GROSS DOMESTIC PRODUCT (U.S. DOLLARS) | ANNUAL CONSUMER PRICE INFLATION (PERCENT) |
|---|---|---|
| Argentina | $8,063 | 12.0% |
| Brazil | 3,034 | 2,200.0 |
| Chile | 2,924 | 12.0 |
| China | 387 | 9.0 |
| Colombia | 1,606 | 22.0 |
| Egypt | 643 | 17.1 |
| Greece | 5,916 | 12.5 |
| Hong Kong | 17,955 | 10.2 |
| Hungary | 3,495 | 20.2 |
| India | 298 | 7.5 |
| Indonesia | 762 | 9.3 |
| Israel | 12,613 | 10.3 |
| Jamaica | 1,530 | 14.0 |
| Malaysia | 3,347 | 5.0 |
| Mexico | 3,819 | 9.0 |
| Morocco | 1,085 | 4.0 |
| Nigeria | 1,085 | 50.5 |
| Pakistan | 418 | 10.7 |
| Peru | 1,703 | 40.0 |
| Philippines | 850 | 7.5 |
| Poland | 2,089 | 34.4 |
| Portugal | 7,524 | 6.8 |
| Sri Lanka | 508 | 3.5 |
| Taiwan | 10,620 | 4.2 |
| Thailand | 1,931 | 4.0 |
| Turkey | 2,721 | 58.0 |
| Venezuela | 2,670 | 33.0 |
| Zimbabwe | 376 | 114.0 |

Source: Excerpted from Jared Sandberg, "World Business (A Special Report): Rewards and Pitfalls—Country by Country: A Statistical Look at Emerging Markets," *Wall Street Journal*, September 24, 1993. Reprinted by permission of the *Wall Street Journal*, © 1993 Dow Jones & Company, Inc. All rights reserved worldwide.

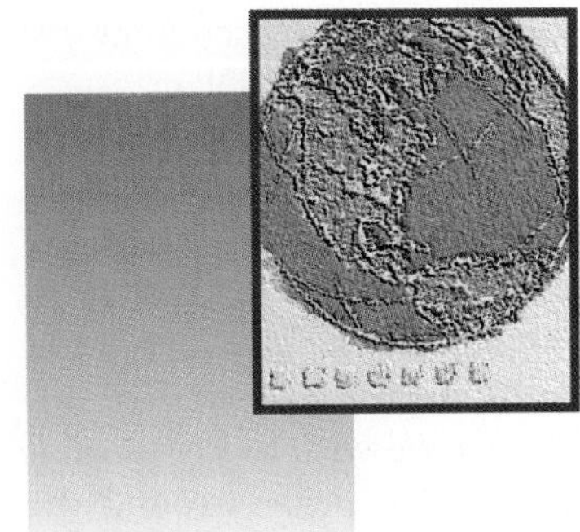

## FOCUS ON GLOBAL COMPETITION

### *Wu's Economic Barometer*

Gordon Wu is a Hong Kong billionaire who created an index that describes poor countries moving toward wealth. According to Wu's Economic Barometer, when per capita income starts coming up, the first thing people do is eat out. That's why American fast-food restaurants are rapidly growing in Asia. After that period, people in developing countries buy new clothes. The third thing they do is start accumulating new appliances. After that, they buy motorcycles, cars, and apartments. The fifth step—as the country moves toward greater affluence—is to travel overseas. ■

## Science and Technology

**SCIENCE**
The accumulation of knowledge about humans and the environment.

**TECHNOLOGY**
The application of science to practical purposes.

Although the two terms are sometimes used interchangeably, **science** is the accumulation of knowledge about human beings and the environment, while **technology** is the application of such knowledge to practical purposes. Thus, the discovery that certain diseases might be prevented by immunization is scientific, but how and when immunization is administered is technological.

Like other changes in the environment of marketing, scientific and technological advances can revolutionize an industry or destroy one.[22] Think of how advances in the development of virtual reality could change the electronics industry, for instance. Oat bran offers an example of how quickly such changes can occur. When the *New England Journal of Medicine* published a study downplaying oat bran's cholesterol-reducing potential, the market share of oat bran cereals fell by almost half within three months.[23]

ALTERNATIVE EXAMPLE
Consumer electronics and computers are industries in which the ability to develop a technological standard is a critical marketing advantage. Sony, whose Betamax format lost to the VHS format in videotapes, hopes that the video CD format it developed with Philips will become the industry standard. Its competitor is a format developed by Toshiba and Time-Warner, which has the support of Samsung, Matsushita, Hitachi, Pioneer, Mitsubishi, and Zenith. SOURCE: "Samsung Picks Format," *U.S.A. Today,* April 11, 1995, p. 1B.

Clearly, then, scientific and technological forces have a pervasive influence on the marketing of most goods and services. The discovery that sunburn can cause cancer certainly affected suntan-lotion marketers. Similarly, the knowledge that fish oil and aspirin may help reduce the risk of heart attack has led to the introduction of new diet supplements and changes in the advertising messages of existing products.

Space science and technology offer examples of advances that have been seized on by marketers. Besides Tang, freeze-dried ice cream, and some other food products, the space program has yielded solar calculators, liquid crystal wristwatches, and the microchips that are found in personal computer games and personal digital assistants. In addition, space technology has found industrial applications: A firefighter in a lightweight fire-fighting suit can now communicate with others through a built-in communication system. The nonfogging face protector the firefighter wears to improve visibility is also a product of space technology.

**INTERNET**
A worldwide network of computers linked by phone lines that gives users access to information and documents from distant sources.

Today, information technology has reshaped the way business is conducted around the world. The Internet has been of particular significance because it has influenced so many organizations. The **Internet** (discussed in the opening part of this chapter) is a worldwide network of computers that gives users access to information and documents from distant sources.[24] Using the Internet has become routine for millions of individuals and organizations. The Internet is described in more detail in Chapter 5.

The Internet, along with satellite communications systems, modems, fax machines, and other advances in information technology, have made communication with suppliers, distributors, and customers in other countries much more efficient and in many cases instantaneous.[25] Global information systems, which are discussed in Chapter 5, have been instrumental in the growth of global business. Indeed, many business analysts believe the key to success in the global economy lies in effective use of information technology.

Because of the global information systems, the location of a business enterprise has become less important than its ability to keep in touch with other company divisions or other companies via computers and telecommunications. A company in, say, Boise, Idaho, can keep in touch with world financial markets and global customers as easily as a company in Los Angeles or New York.

In the future, integration of computers, television, and telephones will further change the way business is conducted. In the not-too-distant future, for example, television viewers will be able to watch an automobile commercial and, with the press of a button, instantly summon up additional information to be delivered on screen or to a printer near the TV set.[26] Also with the press of a button, the viewer will be able to request a test-drive, and within an hour, a local dealer will telephone and schedule a convenient time to stop by with a car. Interactive television with programs on request, home shopping, and travel reservations is now being tested in selected areas.

**ALTERNATIVE EXAMPLE**

Newspapers have recognized the potential in electronic delivery of services. The *Chicago Tribune* allows customers to click into an electronic grocery store and order groceries through their computers. The *New York Times* is developing a system to allow purchases of theater and movie tickets. Gannett's *USA Weekend* plans on-line purchasing of travel and entertainment. SOURCE: Patrick M. Reilly, "Newspapers Expand On-Line Services to Grocery Shopping," *Wall Street Journal,* April 26, 1995, p. B8.

Marketers must not fail to adapt to such changes. Numerous examples of organizations that suffered because they did not adapt to changing technology can be found. For instance, Atari and several other marketers of video games fell victim to competitors such as Sega and Nintendo that switched to more technologically advanced, higher-performance microprocessors. (Sega's new Saturn game system

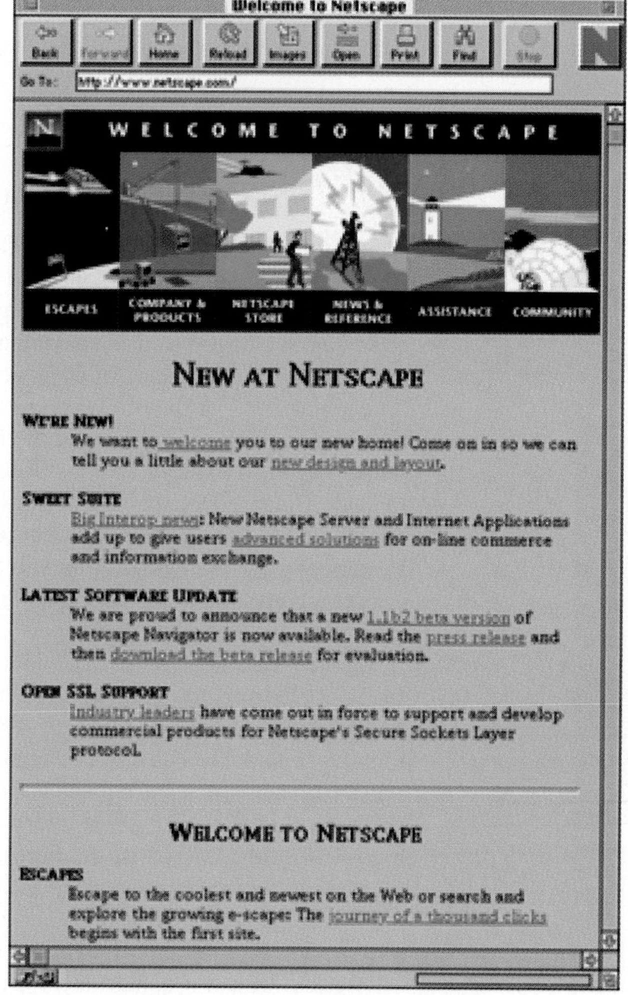


Over the course of history, the development of new technologies, such as the steam engine and the automobile, has determined the nature of civilization and profoundly changed the marketplace and workplace. Today, information technologies are the driving force changing the marketplace. The Internet, for example, is having an enormous impact on marketing.

For some consumers, interactive television is already available with Panasonic's interactive multiplayer equipment, called REAL for Realistic Entertainment and Active Learning. Marketing for the multimedia system, based on 3DO technology, is aimed at so-called videohead gamers. The first advertising campaign ran on MTV and other cable networks with youth appeal. The commercials take the form of updated side-by-side comparison tests. For example, in one commercial, the viewer first sees a dull, primitive video game featuring planes flying. "This is flying," the announcer says listlessly. Then the fun begins: Cut to a 3DO video game of planes bombing a building. The announcer enthuses: "This is REAL flying."

runs on a higher-performance processor than the original 1976 Cray supercomputer, accessible in its day only to distinguished physicists.[27]) Because changes related to science and technology can have a major impact, organizations of all types must monitor these changes and adjust their marketing mixes to meet them.

## FOCUS ON TRENDS

### *Morphing Down to the Showroom*

Today's computer technology can be characterized by the phrase "digital convergence." Almost all industries, professions, and trades are being pulled closer together by a common technological bond: the digitizing of the work product into the ones and zeros of computer language—in turn spawning revolutionary ways of executing that work.

Consider one sequence of events that show that new ways of doing business are "morphing out" of the old ways. In the mid-1970s, filmmaker George Lucas, while making *Star Wars,* formed a special-effects company called Industrial Light & Magic, which began to explore the possibilities of digital film editing. Soon after, in 1984, the U.S. Defense Department began funding research for its controversial Star Wars missile defense program, which never blossomed but helped push along several new makers of powerful workstations, including Sun Microsystems, now a $4-billion-a-year company, and a less successful but interesting company called Silicon Graphics, Inc., or SGI.

By the mid-1980s, Industrial Light & Magic was using 3-D computer graphics on SGI workstations to create a new generation of special effects for movies, probably best exemplified by the 1991 poly-alloy, liquid-metal character called T-1000 for the film *Terminator 2.* SGI was passing on some of these applications to other clients—Ford, for one, which started using the same technology in the liquid molding of auto parts. By 1993, ILM had created the ultimate (so far) in synthetic, photorealistic, high-resolution characters, the dinosaurs for Jurassic Park. In Dearborn, Michigan, meanwhile, Ford designers used exactly the same software to design the skin and interior features of their prototype vehicles, reducing the need for blueprints and cutaways. With computer-aided lasers, Ford can cut the prototype part cycle by up to 30 weeks. Now Ford marketers talk about virtual showrooms, where customers could drive cars that don't yet exist. ■

## Politics and Laws

**POLITICAL ENVIRONMENT**
The practices and policies of governments.

**LEGAL ENVIRONMENT**
Laws and regulations and their interpretation.

ALTERNATIVE EXAMPLE
The government has the power to set standards or grant exceptions to existing standards. The Food and Drug Administration, for example, permits 2 percent milk to be considered low in fat, despite one researcher's claim that three glasses of 2 percent milk contain as much fat as nine strips of bacon. SOURCE: "Pulse Points: In Focus," *U.S. News and World Report,* May 1, 1995, p. 20.

POINT TO EMPHASIZE
The political climate of other countries is a major factor in deciding which overseas markets are attractive. Evaluating this factor is particularly important when the risk of overseas marketing is high, such as when a firm plans to build production facilities overseas.

The **political environment**—the practices and policies of governments—and the **legal environment**—laws and regulations and their interpretation—affect marketing activity in several ways. First, they can limit the actions marketers are allowed to take—for example, by barring certain U.S. goods from leaving the country, as when Congress passed the Export Administration Act, which prohibited the export of strategic high-technology products to nations such as Iran and Libya. Second, some actions may be required, for example, cookies called "chocolate chip cookies" are required to contain chips made of real chocolate, and cigarette makers are required to print the surgeon general's warning on all cigarette packages. Last, certain actions can be prohibited, including the sale of products such as narcotic drugs and nuclear weapons, except under the strictest of controls.

Political processes in other countries may have dramatic impacts on international marketers. For example, the former Soviet Union's initiation of *perestroika* (economic restructuring) and *glasnost* (openness about public and political events) ultimately led to the dissolution of the union. These historic political actions opened new markets in Asia and Europe. Today, U.S. marketers in independent states, such as Russia, Lithuania, and Ukraine, find the business climate totally different from the climate that existed only five years ago.

The experience of Rwanda illustrates how uncertain political situations are and how swiftly they can change. After seeing the movie *Gorillas in the Mist,* thousands of international tourists traveled to Rwanda to pay $170 per hour to observe mountain gorillas in the Varunga volcanoes. However, soon after the 1994 civil war in Rwanda began, virtually all international tourism stopped.

Of course, not all political and legal influences involve dramatic changes like those in Rwanda. Laws, in particular, tend to have a stable long-term influence on marketing strategy. For example, almost all countries with commercial airlines have had long-standing bans on foreign ownership of these business.

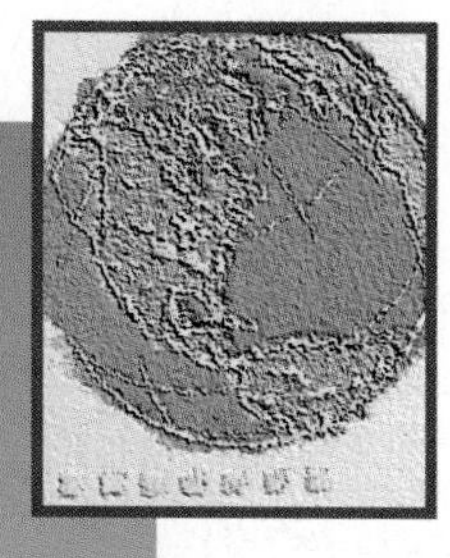

### FOCUS ON GLOBAL COMPETITION

### *Pepsi in India*

Political forces were clearly at play when Pepsi-Cola International was preparing for its introduction of Pepsi products into India. Just when Pepsi's cola, orange, and lemon soft drinks were a few weeks away from introduction to the Indian market, the new nationalist administration in India came up with a costly requisite in the name of patriotism. Pepsi had to change the name of its soft drinks from "Pepsi Era" to "Lehar Pepsi" (*Lehar* means "wave" in Hindi)—a move that cost the company a maharajah's ransom in design and packaging changes.

After years of political pressure, the name changing was just one final, expensive concession Pepsi was willing to make in order to boost its international market share. It was a struggle to enter this huge market, but Pepsi-Cola International kept fighting to get into the country, which had for many years locked out its chief rival, the Coca-Cola Co.

Pepsi's marketing efforts had been plagued by bad press and government inquiries, but the administration was not its only opponent. Parle Exports Ltd. of Bombay, which dominates India's soft-drink market with an estimated 80 percent share, threw up hurdles of another kind.

Parle played up patriotism in an aggressive campaign of propaganda, bad press, and image advertising. After elections in which a nationalistic government defeated the reform-minded Rajiv Gandhi, Parle managing director Ramesh Chauhan decided to launch a marketing war against Pepsi.

"The government should help Indian companies along," Chauhan said. "We are the ones in the fortress. Pepsi is the one trying to break in." Parle used every means at its disposal to keep Pepsi out of the market—including scheming with nationalist government forces and issuing threats.

Chauhan is well-connected politically and is part of a large and influential segment of Indian business that harbors a deep-seated fear of multinationals. Chauhan's bare-knuckle style works well in India, where knowing people in high places is key to business success.

When Pepsi began negotiations to set up operations in India several years earlier, no one anticipated it would become the center of one of the most publicized marketing struggles in India's history. However, after working for years to market soda and snacks in India, it now seems that Lehar Pepsi has overcome all the obstacles resulting from the political environment. ■

## Three Levels of U.S. Law

Legislation intended to maintain a competitive business environment, to protect consumers from dangerous products or unethical practices, and to preserve the natural environment can be found at the federal, state, and local levels. Because each of these levels has various departments, subdepartments, regulatory boards, and political subdivisions, such as counties and townships, it is possible that a single marketing organization could confront some 82,688 sets of laws and regulations.[28] When Disney explored the possibility of building a theme park in Virginia to celebrate America's heritage, the company learned that it would be reviewed by more than 30 state, local, and federal agencies and would have to obtain at least 72 permits.[29]

**The Federal Level** At the federal level of government, the U.S. Department of Justice, the Food and Drug Administration, the Federal Trade Commission, and many other agencies enforce a multitude of laws affecting business. The degree of specialization of some laws and agencies is suggested by the examples in Exhibit 3–8.

**ANTITRUST LEGISLATION**
Federal laws meant to promote competition in U.S. markets. The major antitrust laws are the Sherman Antitrust Act (1890), the Clayton Act (1914), and the Federal Trade Commission Act (1914).

Much federal control involves **antitrust legislation,** which prohibits acts such as restraint of trade and monopoly, price fixing, price discrimination, deceptive practices, misrepresentations in the labeling of products, and other behavior that tends to lessen competition. The Sherman Antitrust Act (1890), the Clayton Act (1914), and the Federal Trade Commission Act (1914) are the major antitrust laws.

**EXHIBIT 3–8** Sample of Specialized Federal Legislation Affecting Business

| LEGISLATION | MAJOR PROVISIONS |
|---|---|
| Federal Hazardous Substances Act (1960) | Requires warning labels on hazardous household chemicals |
| Kefauver-Harris Drug Amendment (1962) | Requires that manufacturers conduct tests to prove drug effectiveness and safety |
| Child Protection and Toy Safety Act (1969) | Prevents marketing of products so dangerous that adequate safety warnings cannot be given |
| Consumer Credit Protection Act (1968) | Requires that lenders fully disclose true interest rates and all other charges to credit customers for loans and installment purchases |
| Public Health Smoking Act (1970) | Prohibits cigarette advertising on TV and radio and revises the health hazard warning on cigarette packages |
| Poison Prevention Labeling Act (1970) | Requires safety packaging for products that may be harmful to children |
| Child Protection Act (1990) | Regulates the number of minutes of advertising on children's television |
| Cable Television Act (1992) | Regulates the price of cable television subscriptions |

**EXHIBIT 3–9** Key Federal Legislation Affecting Marketers

| ACT | PURPOSE |
|---|---|
| Sherman Act (1890) | Prohibits combinations, contracts, or conspiracies to restrain trade or monopolize |
| Clayton Act (1914) | Prohibits price discrimination, exclusive dealer arrangements, and inter locking directorates that lessen competition |
| Federal Trade Commission Act (1914) | Created the FTC and gave it investigatory powers |
| Robinson-Patman Act (1936) | Expands Clayton Act to prohibit sellers from offering different deals to different customers |
| Wheeler-Lea Act (1938) | Expands powers of FTC to prevent injuries to competition before they occur |
| Celler-Kefauver Act (1950) | Expands Clayton Act to prohibit acquisition of physical assets as well as capital stock in another corporation when the effect is to injure competition |
| Magnuson-Moss Act (1975) | Grants the FTC the power to determine rules concerning warranties and provides the means for class action suits and other forms of redress |
| Consumer Goods Pricing Act (1975) | Repealed "fair-trade" laws and prohibited price maintenance agreements among producers and resellers |
| Fair Debt Collection Act (1980) | Requires creditors to act responsibly in debt collection (e.g., bans false statements) and makes harassment of debtors illegal |
| FTC Improvement Act (1980) | Provides Congress with the power to veto the FTC industrywide Trade Regulation Rules (TRR); limits the power of the FTC |
| Federal Antitampering Act (1983) | Prohibits tampering with a product and threats to tamper with a product |
| Americans with Disabilities Act (1990) | Prohibits discrimination against consumers with disabilities (e.g., stores and hotels must be accessible to shoppers or guests who use wheel chairs) |
| North American Free Trade Agreement (1993) | Allows for free trade between U.S., Mexico, and Canada without tariffs and trade restrictions |
| Nutritional Labeling and Education Act | Requires that certain nutritional facts be printed on food product labels |
| Labeling Act (1994) | Requires that stickers be placed on all new vehicles stating the percentage of domestic and foreign parts used to make them |

**FEDERAL TRADE COMMISSION (FTC)**
Federal agency established in 1914 by the Federal Trade Commission Act to investigate and put an end to unfair methods of competition.

One major federal agency—the **Federal Trade Commission** (FTC), established in 1914—affects virtually all marketers on a regular basis. The FTC was given broad powers of investigation and jurisdiction over "unfair methods of competition." Initially, the FTC was to draft a fixed list of "unfair practices." It soon became clear that no list covering all situations could be developed. Thus, though the FTC publishes guidelines and uses past decisions as precedents for solving current problems, each situation investigated by the FTC is judged individually. Marketing managers, therefore, face considerable uncertainty in trying to develop programs that can withstand FTC scrutiny.

POINT TO EMPHASIZE
The political and legal system can operate to the benefit of marketers. The protection of trademarks and brand names and the protection afforded by patent and copyright laws are examples of how the political and legal system can aid a marketer.

Examples of political and legal constraints on marketing are easy to find. For example, the Food and Drug Administration has ordered cosmetic companies, such as Avon, Revlon, and Estee Lauder, to stop claiming that their so-called anti-aging skin creams can "reverse aging or make basic underlying changes in the skin." According to the FDA, wording such as "rejuvenate, repair or renew skin" and "retard or counteract aging" could subject anti-aging creams to the same regulations as drugs because it suggests that "a function or structure of the body will be affected by the product."[30]

It would be impossible to discuss all U.S. legislation dealing with marketing in this introductory treatment of the subject. Exhibit 3–9 summarizes selected federal legis-

In 1988, the U.S. Congress placed a luxury tax on boats; the 10 percent tax was applied to a new boat's value above $100,000. As a result, sales of 18-to-40-foot powerboats, sailboats, and yachts plummeted. From 1988 to 1993, sales of boats costing more than $100,000 declined by 70 percent. Hundreds of boat builders went out of business, and thousands of workers lost their jobs. When the luxury tax was repealed in 1994, the boating industry recorded its best year by satisfying pent-up demand.

lation that affects most marketers. Additional milestone legislation affecting major portions of the marketing mix are discussed throughout the book.[31]

**The State Level** Most states have created laws and agencies that parallel those at the federal level. State departments of agriculture, commerce, labor, and so on are commonly found, as are state-level consumer protection laws dealing with foods, manufactured goods, lending, real estate, banking, and insurance.

All states have laws that can affect organizations' marketing mixes. For example, in Oklahoma, distillers must sell their liquor brands to Oklahoma wholesalers at the lowest price in the country. Pennsylvania controls the sale of all hard liquors through a system of "state stores," while Ohio operates state stores and licenses independent stores, as well. Ohio does not tax take-out food but does tax food consumed in restaurants. Some farm states do not apply sales taxes if the seller is the actual producer of the goods sold. Michigan prohibits bars from serving free peanuts or potato chips, believing free food might encourage drinking, while New York requires that food be available where alcohol is served. California and Arizona prohibit the "importing" of certain fruits, plants, and vegetables. In addition, many states have laws mandating returnable beverage cans and bottles.

**The Local Level** Cities, townships, villages, and counties are all empowered to pass laws and ordinances and create regulatory agencies. In most areas, health department inspectors check restaurants and motels, weights and measures inspectors check for honest scales, and city and county prosecutors investigate misleading and unfair business practices. Local zoning laws affect where businesses such as meat processors, wholesalers, and retailers may be located. Local government units may tax some products but not others, require that certain stores be closed on Sunday, or, as in New York City, legislate that all bars must be closed for at least one hour a day and all customers removed from the premises.

A common local control on marketing is the issuing of vendors' or similar licenses. In most cases, the licenses are not sold to make money for local governments, although this can be a factor, especially in the case of liquor licenses. The major reason for licensing is so that licenses can be denied to organizations that violate laws or local custom.[32]

VIDEO CASE 3–1

## Union Camp Corporation

Union Camp Corporation is the result of the 1956 merger of Union Bag and Paper Corporation and Camp Manufacturing Company.

Union Bag and Paper Corporation was the outgrowth of several companies, the oldest of which was Union Paper Bag Machine Company. This was a patent-holding company formed in 1861 by Frances Wolle, a Moravian teacher and minister who, in 1852, invented the first paper bag machine.

Camp Manufacturing Company dates back to 1887 with the purchase of a lumber manufacturing operation that began production in Franklin, Virginia, in the 1850's. Camp entered paper manufacturing in 1938.

The two merged companies operated under the name of Union Bag–Camp Paper Manufacturing Corporation until 1966 when the company changed its name to Union Camp Corporation.

Union Camp Corporation, headquartered in Wayne, New Jersey, is a leading manufacturer of paper, packaging, chemicals and wood products.

The company ranks among the top 200 U.S. industrial companies in sales and employs about 20,000 people worldwide. Outside the United States, Union Camp has operations in 24 countries and Puerto Rico.

The paper manufacturing segment consists of four pulp and paper mills. Two produce white paper for business forms, printing, direct mail and other communications uses. The other two mills produce unbleached kraft paper and linerboard, primarily packaging materials.

Within a network of 46 packaging plants, Union Camp converts more than half of its unbleached kraft production into boxes and bags for consumer and industrial products. Three packaging plants produce plastic bags and films. Two others produce folding cartons. Three additional paper products plants manufacture school supplies and stationery.

The company's other domestic manufacturing plants include nine building products operators, four chemical plants and five flavors and fragrances facilities. Other domestic activities involve both residential and commercial land development.

Overseas, the company operates corrugated container plants, chemical plants and flavor and fragrance facilities.

Research and development are centralized at the company's Corporate Technology Center at Princeton, New Jersey. Chemical development laboratories are located at the company's Savannah, Georgia, manufacturing complex and Jacksonville, Florida, chemical plant. Flavor and fragrance development laboratories are in Montvale, New Jersey, the United Kingdom and Singapore. A woodlands research facility is in Rincon, Georgia.

Southeastern woodlands provide the raw material base for most of Union Camp's products. Union Camp's woodlands, which currently furnish 30 percent of the company's pulp mill and sawmill raw materials, total about 1.7 million acres in six states.

Compared with other major producers in the industry, Union Camp has relatively few pulp and paper mills, but they are all large-scale facilities. Two of them are the largest of their kind in the world. This concentration of high production capabilities at a few highly efficient sites is a major factor contributing to Union Camp's performance as one of the lowest-cost producers in the industry.

The company continually invests to upgrade and modernize its facilities to produce high quality products as efficiently as possible. For the five-year period of 1988–1992 alone, it spent about $2.5 billion on such programs.

### QUESTIONS

1. What economic factors in the environment influence Union Camp's business? Which have the greatest impact on its marketing mix?
2. The company markets fine paper, lightweight unbleached paper, heavy-duty liner board for corrugated containers, paper bags, folding cartons, and school supplies, such as notebooks, poster board, and index cards. What impact do social values about ecology have on these products? How does the technological environment relate to these social values?
3. As a marketer of packaging, such as bags for Scott's lawn care products and cardboard containers for Franzia wine, Union Camp works with many companies. What is the general nature of Union Camp's relationship with its customers?
4. Is it necessary, for a company like Union Camp to place a major emphasis on total quality management?

VIDEO CASE 3–2
FOCUS ON SMALL BUSINESS

## LION Coffee

James Delano, president of a Hawaiian firm that roasts coffee and sells it at wholesale and retail, unexpectedly was faced with regulatory action [in 1991] that could cripple the business.

The Woolson Spice Co.'s annual permit to import green coffee beans was expiring in two weeks. Now the state's Department of Agriculture notified Woolson, which does business as LION Coffee, of impending catastrophe: The permit might not be renewed because of a provision in an old state law that had not been applied to LION before.

Under the law, coffee beans may not be imported by roasters on Hawaiian islands where coffee is grown. Once, that affected only the state's biggest island, Hawaii, where coffee is grown on the Kona coast. But today, coffee is also grown on other islands, including Oahu, where Woolson is located.

LION produces blends almost exclusively. Without imported beans, its coffee roasting facility would have to shut down. It was the biggest challenge since Delano had brought a dormant Woolson Spice in 1979 and, with two employees, started roasting and packaging coffee in downtown Honolulu.

Action was required, and fast.

### QUESTIONS

1. How uncontrollable is the legal environment in the Hawaiian Islands? What actions should LION take to get the annual permit reissued?
2. What other environmental forces, other than legal action, might shape LION's marketing mix?

**Source:** Excerpted with permission from *Real-World Lessons for America's Small Business*, pp. 181–182, copyright 1992 by Connecticut Mutual Life Insurance Company.

CHAPTER

# 4 The Microenvironment in an Era of Global Competition

## LEARNING OBJECTIVES

After you have studied this chapter, you will be able to:

1. Understand how the microenvironment affects a company's marketing activity.
2. Identify the four Cs of marketing.
3. Recognize how marketing creates economic utility for customers.
4. Identify the various types of competitors and understand how marketers anticipate and react to competitors' strategies to gain competitive advantages.
5. Describe the value chain and explain why it must be managed.
6. Understand the importance of global competition in today's economy.
7. Apply the four Cs in a global business context.

petitors in some way. More specifically, it means to be superior in terms of price, quality, time, or location. A company may achieve superiority by operating a more efficient factory, by selling at a lower price, by designing better-quality products, by being the first on the market with an innovation, or by satisfying customers in other ways. In other words, market-oriented organizations can use many alternative strategies to outperform competitors in terms of price, quality, time, or location.

## Collaborators

**COLLABORATOR**
Person or company that works with a marketing company. Collaborators help the company run its business without actually being part of the company.

**SUPPLIER**
An organization that provides raw materials, component parts, equipment, services, or other resources to a marketing organization; also called a vendor.

Buying materials and supplies, hiring an advertising agency, or getting a loan from a bank requires that one company work with another company. These companies are collaborators. A **collaborator** is a person or a company that works with your company. Collaborators help the company run its business without actually being part of the company. They are often specialists who provide particular services or supply raw materials, component parts, or production equipment. Collaborators that provide materials, equipment, and the like are called **suppliers.**

The terms *alliances, networks,* and *informal partnerships,* as well as others, have been used to describe the kinds of relationships just mentioned. However, the term *collaborators* works well because it implies that a company and another party are engaged in an ongoing relationship. In today's business climate, companies must be flexible and able to change quickly. Working with collaborators helps companies enhance their flexibility, especially in global marketing activities.

The number of collaborative relationships has grown significantly in recent years, and organizational collaborations are expected to be increasingly important in the 21st century. Contemporary organizations no longer believe they have to perform all

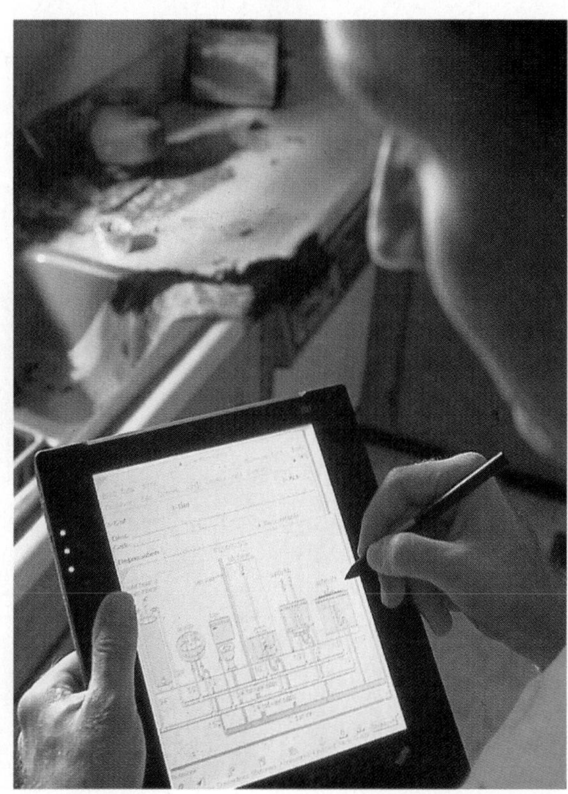

After a disaster, home owners don't want to wait long periods to be reimbursed by their insurance company. Time is important. State Farm Insurance's claims representatives once used ballpoint pens, paper and stacks of huge construction manuals in their offices to estimate damage from fires and other disasters. Today, they use IBM ThinkPad computers to review building data, calculate and print estimates at the loss site. Using modern information technology has reduced processing time for claims from weeks to hours. State Farm knows time is a competitive weapon in the marketing of its service.

**POINT TO EMPHASIZE**
Having outside collaborators is not a new idea in marketing. A classic example of outside collaboration is the use of advertising agencies. Many companies—even the largest—use advertising agencies to create advertising campaigns, purchase media space, and develop sales promotion strategies. Even companies that have advertising departments may use advertising agencies to perform some functions.

business activities internally. Managers recognize that organizational collaborators may have special competencies that allow them to excel at certain tasks. Companies today believe that there is value in making joint commitments and sharing resources.

Some companies' marketing strategies are highly dependent on collaborations. In fact, business thinkers have created a name for organizations that use collaboration extensively: *virtual corporations.* The name *virtual* is derived from terminology used in the early days of the computer industry. The term *virtual memory* described a way of making a computer act as if it had more storage capacity than it really possessed.[6] Thus, the so-called virtual corporation, which appears to be a single enterprise with vast capabilities, is the result of numerous collaborations whose resources are garnered only when they are needed.

## FOCUS ON QUALITY

### *Hyatt Hotel Corporation*

Hyatt Hotel Corporation's president, Darryl Hartley-Leonard, believes establishing long-term relationships with suppliers benefits both companies. Whether it's sheets and linen, emergency fire exit signs, or cheesecake, Hyatt buyers comb the globe looking for the highest-quality products. After Hyatt settles on a supplier, the company works hard at maintaining that relationship.

In the case of cheesecake, for example, Hyatt's team of talented chefs gave up their own efforts after tasting the wares produced by Ely's Cheesecake, a small bakery in Chicago. Hyatt's president says, "Big companies can make a mess of things like that. You end up with a cheesecake that doesn't look like a cheesecake." So, if Ely's makes "the best cheesecake in the world," as Hyatt's president proudly attests, why didn't Hyatt buy Ely out? Hyatt says "We run hotels and making cheesecake is not what we do best." The quality of Ely's cheesecake, which Hyatt now offers in its award-winning restaurants, is proof that collaboration between large and small companies can be a very sweet deal indeed. ■

**Source:** Adapted with permission from "Business 2000: The New World Order," (Special Advertising Section), *Inc.*, December 1993, p. 55. Copyright © 1993 by Goldhirsh Group Inc., 38 Commercial Wharf, Boston, MA 02110.

The notion of the virtual organization is based on collaborations. Automobile companies operate factories in which everything from carburetors to windshield wipers are outsourced. Suppliers design the parts, make them, and distribute the appropriate quantities to automakers' assembly plants exactly when they are needed. Collaboration with suppliers frees up automakers' resources so they can concentrate on what they do best. Having every organization in the value chain focus on core competencies results in lower-cost, better-designed products.

## The Value Chain

**VALUE CHAIN**
Chain of activities and relationships by which a company brings in materials, creates a good or service, markets it, and provides services after a sale is made. Each step creates more value for the consumer.

**DISCUSSION CONSIDERATION**
Ask students what they think the core competencies of the university or college that they attend are. This might lead into a discussion of the competitive advantages the university or college enjoys compared with competing institutions.

Exhibit 4–1 shows what we can call the **value chain.**[7] The activities portrayed in Exhibit 4–1 illustrate how operating a business involves a system of activities and relationships. Each part of the system—each link in the chain—adds value to the product customers ultimately buy.

The exhibit illustrates the relationships between a company and its customers and some of its collaborators by dividing activities into primary, upstream, and downstream activities. Notice that before the company engages in its *primary operations,* such as production, accounting, and pricing, it engages in *upstream activities,* such as purchasing equipment and materials from suppliers. *Downstream activities,* performed after the product has been produced, require dealing with other collaborators, such as transportation companies and retailers. These upstream and downstream activities are called *supportive activities.* They provide the support necessary for carrying out primary activities or for concluding the sale of goods or services to the final buyer.

Collaborators in the value chain create new value together.[8] These companies link themselves together to achieve a common purpose. Each company values the skills that its partners bring to the collaboration. By linking their companies' capabilities, the collaborators can increase the value that the ultimate customer obtains.

## Core Competencies

**CORE COMPETENCY**
A proficiency in a critical functional activity—such as technical know-how or a particular business specialization—that helps provide a company's unique competitive advantage.

Before an organization decides how much it will work with collaborators, its managers should ascertain the company's core competencies.[9] A **core competency** is a proficiency in a critical functional activity—such as technical know-how or a particular business specialization—that helps provide a company's unique competitive advantage. The company may be able to do something its competitors cannot do at

**EXHIBIT 4–1**
The Value Chain

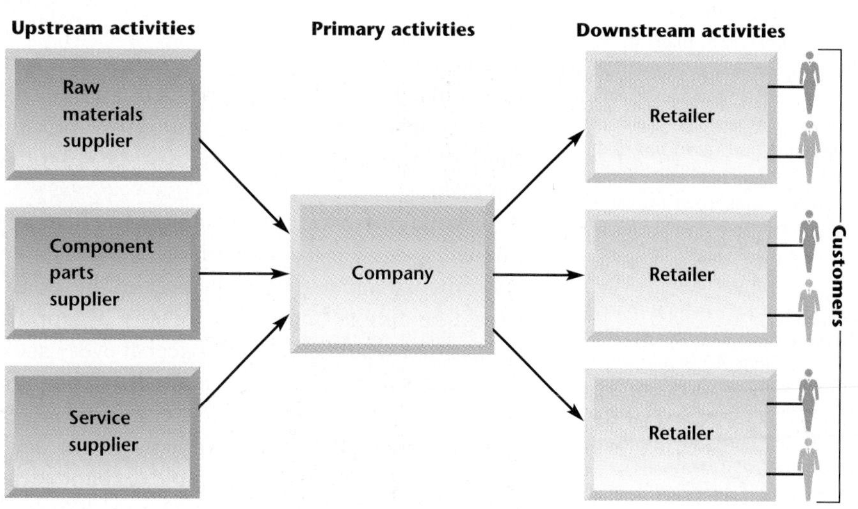

Each collaborator in the value chain values the skills that its partners bring to the collaboration. KFC and Mitsubishi collaborated to establish a KFC chain in Japan. KFC's capabilities included a well-known brand, a tested store format, and established operational skill. Mitsubishi had real estate and site-selection skill. The result of the collaboration was to increase the value that the Japanese customer obtains.

all or that they find difficult to do even poorly.[10] Simply put, core competencies are what the organization does best.

A company enhances its effectiveness by concentrating its resources on a set of core competencies that will allow it to achieve competitive superiority and provide unique or differentiated value for customers. For example, Nike manufactures only key technical components of its "Nike Air" system. All of its shoe production is performed by Asian collaborators. Research and development for product design and marketing are Nike's core competencies, not production.

**OUTSOURCING**
Buying or hiring from outside suppliers.

An understanding of core competencies helps managers determine what value-creating activities can be outsourced. **Outsourcing** means having these activities performed by collaborators—outside sources. Outsourced activities, such as the production of major parts or subassemblies by suppliers, may be integral to the company's operations. Consider that for Chrysler's Eagle Vision and its other LH series cars, there are ten distinct sections. Chrysler makes the engine, transmission, and metal exterior.[11] The remaining seven sections are made by contract manufacturers like Textron, which produces and delivers a fully assembled instrument panel containing a speedometer, radio, glove-box door, and air-conditioner louvers. For the 1998 models, Textron will also be responsible for detailed design and engineering tasks.

ALTERNATIVE EXAMPLE
Dell Computer Corp. plans to use Roadway Services, Inc., to handle all of its shipping. The outsourcing initiative will include both inbound raw materials and outbound finished products. Rather than add to its current staff to meet growth goals, Dell will rely on a single partner for all its shipping needs. Inbound logistics is a particularly important function, since Dell uses just-in-time manufacturing and keeps low raw material inventories. Since 40 percent of the cost of a Dell product can be attributed to logistics, cost savings could lead to higher company profits or the flexibility to lower prices.
SOURCE: Scott McCartney, "Dell Computer to Outsource All Shipping," *Wall Street Journal,* February 15, 1995, p. B6.

The major reason for outsourcing is that, simply put, few companies possess adequate resources and capabilities to perform all primary activities, upstream activities, and downstream activities themselves. In today's era of intense global competition, it would be almost impossible for any organization to have all the necessary competencies that would allow it to excel at every activity in its value chain. Companies that recognize this fact carefully plan their collaborations with other companies so they can combine complementary strengths to increase customer value.

Companies often have problems when they stray too far from their core competencies. Burger King, for example, expanded its menu with Snickers ice cream bars, chef salads, and Breakfast Buddy and bagel sandwiches. It offered a special dinner service, which included friend shrimp and trays brought to tables by staff.[12] After several years of broadening its offerings, the company realized it had veered too far group of economic partners may encompass most of the continent. Austria, Finland, and Sweden joined in 1992 and Iceland, Norway, and Switzerland approved a pact that over time will integrate these countries with the European Union. Three former Eastern bloc countries—the Czech Republic, Hungary, and Poland—are seeking associate status with the European Union, and they may become full members by the turn of the century. Some marketing analysts estimate that in the year 2000, the European Union's trading area will include 450 million people.

In North America, the stage has been set for the development of a single trading market of more than 350 million people. NAFTA, the North American Free Trade Agreement, was passed by the United States Congress in 1993. This agreement, which allows for increased trade between Mexico, Canada, and the United States, will have a major impact on production location, imports, exports, and unemployment in selected industries.

In 1994, NAFTA meant that the United States canceled tariffs on 60 percent of Mexican goods that had been subjected to taxes. **Tariffs** are taxes imposed by a nation on selected imported goods brought into that nation to make those goods more costly in the marketplace. Other tariffs are being phased out over a 15-year period. Exports from the United States grew by more than 20 percent in the first nine months NAFTA was in effect.[16] Mexican consumers bought U.S. products whose production requires technology that Mexico does not yet possess. U.S. consumers have increased purchases of Mexican agricultural products and other goods produced by operations that are labor-intensive.

We will continue to discuss global customers and their unique needs throughout this book.

POINT TO EMPHASIZE

Not just corporations but also small businesses engage in overseas marketing. One source estimates that 20 percent of companies with fewer than 500 employees exported goods in 1994. It is also estimated that small businesses will account for 50.8 percent of the manufactured goods that the United States will export in 1995. SOURCE: Amy Barrett, "It's a Small (Business) World," *Business Week,* April 17, 1995, pp. 96–101.

**TARIFF**

A tax imposed by a government on an imported product.

POINT TO EMPHASIZE

The decision by a corporation to engage in international or multinational marketing introduces other macroenvironmental factors that marketers need to understand. All the economic, cultural, and legal factors discussed in Chapter 3 need to be understood for each country in which the company operates. Furthermore, international currency exchange rates become a major factor. The strength or weakness of the American dollar compared with other currencies contributes to the ability of a company to sell in other countries.

## Competitors in a Worldwide Arena

We have already mentioned that marketers in the United States and throughout the world are confronted with global competition. Intensified global competition can stimulate and improve domestic competition in an industry. For example, consumers complained for years that American automobile manufacturers were unconcerned about quality and inattentive to market needs. When Japanese and European cars gained a large share of the U.S. auto market, American producers began to remedy these deficiencies. Such improvements in domestic competition spur improvements in living standards as well as general economic well-being.

International marketers hope they can compete on a "level playing field," one where no one has an "unfair" advantage. However, this is not the case for all products or all markets. Sometimes competitors headquartered in foreign countries enjoy government subsidies or benefit from legislation that grants them other economic advantages in their home markets.

The Japanese practice of *keiretsu* provides a good example of a fundamental difference in the way U.S. and Japanese companies conduct business in Japan. Keiretsu are groups of companies that form "corporate families." Bound together by mutual shareholdings or other financial ties, members of the keiretsu engage in cooperative business strategies. For example, because Toyota's keiretsu includes Koito Manufacturing, an automobile parts company, Koito has special privileges when supplying parts to Toyota. Outside companies find it difficult to market competitive products to Toyota in the same way as competitors who are members of Toyota's keiretsu.[17]

Governments often protect certain domestic industries by imposing tariffs to restrict the activity of foreign companies. Tariffs can have a dramatic impact on foreign competitors. Because the imported product is higher priced (as a result of the tariff), domestic production may be encouraged or consumption of the imported product may be discouraged. For example, at one time, the United States imposed a high tariff (50 percent) on imported motorcycles with engines larger than 700cc.

ALTERNATIVE EXAMPLE

In general, it is claimed that the Japanese market is extremely difficult to enter for non-Japanese marketers. Distribution systems effectively lock out non-Japanese products. Kodak, however, agreed to manufacture private-label film for a group of 2,500 retail stores. The film sells at about 38 percent less than Fuji (the industry leader) and Kodak. Through this move, Kodak gained a crucial channel of distribution in which it could also sell its branded film. Kodak's goals are modest: it seeks a 10 percent share of the market by the end of 1995. SOURCE: Wendy Bounds, "Kodak Pursues a Greater Market Share in Japan with New Private-Label Film," *Wall Street Journal,* p. B9.

Harley-Davidson, the only American-owned motorcycle manufacturer, made no motorcycles with engines smaller than 1000cc and did not care about small-engined motorcycles. Clearly, the existence of high restrictive tariffs in a country can discourage competitors of another nation from marketing in that country.

**IMPORT QUOTA**
A limit set by a government on how much of a certain type of product can be imported into a country.

**EMBARGO**
A government prohibition of trade, especially in a particular product.

**BOYCOTT**
An action in which some group refuses to buy certain products. A government may enforce a boycott of the products of some other country.

**Import quotas,** or government-imposed limits on a type of imported good, are another restrictive factor. Countries trying to promote domestic production or discourage domestic consumption may impose quotas on certain imported products. Some quotas set absolute limits, and goods can be imported only until the set level is reached. After that, no further imports are allowed. Other quotas are established with tariffs in such a way that an extremely high tariff is levied on goods imported beyond the quota limit. The ultimate forms of restriction are the **embargo** and the **boycott,** which may completely shut down trade with a particular country.

The automotive industry in the United States illustrates the use of quotas. Faced with increased competition from imported cars and increased pressure from automotive labor unions in the United States, the auto industry and the U.S. government have been trying to get Japan to agree to a limit on the number of cars Japanese companies export to the United States. Such a restriction would clearly be a form of import quota. Honda and Toyota, as well as Volkswagen and other foreign automobile markers, have established production facilities in the United States partly in response to these pressures.

DISCUSSION CONSIDERATION
Ask students whether there are any disadvantages to a national policy of restricting imports (using tariffs, quotas, or other means) in order to protect domestic industries. Two disadvantages that should be mentioned are the possibility that lower-priced competition will not be able to enter the market, so that consumers will have to pay high prices, and the possibility that consumers may not have a full range of brands and models from which to choose.

Governments may impose a variety of other restrictive controls to discourage foreign companies from doing business in their markets. Sometimes countries require that all trade with other nations be approved by some form of central ministry. This allows for the establishment of various types of quotas and controls over goods brought into the country. Still other nations establish boycotts or other barriers by using restrictive criteria set up to eliminate the importing of certain products. A local government may, for instance, establish buying criteria for food products so that food products may not be shipped in from certain countries.

Even when there is a level playing field without government restrictions, an exporter may face disadvantages relative to domestic competitors. Procter & Gamble's Pampers, for example, could not beat stiff competition in the Australian and New Zealand markets. Pampers were imported, rather than manufactured locally, and high transportation costs and currency fluctuations meant they had to be priced higher than the competition.[18]

Businesses in the United States have passed through a transition from a domestic economy to a global economy. Today, marketing managers conduct business around the globe. A trip to Asia is second nature to many executives in multinational corporations.

## FOCUS ON GLOBAL COMPETITION

### *John Deere*

Town council members in Greece, a suburb of Rochester, New York, were considering the purchase of a dirt-moving excavator to use for creek clearing. The choice was between John Deere and its only competitor, Komatsu.

During the deliberations, news media reported that a member of Japan's legislature had called American workers lazy. Council members, after receiving many phone calls from constituents urging them to "buy American," voted to buy the John Deere even though the Komatsu was $15,000 cheaper.

However, shortly after the decision had been made, the residents and the council learned that the Komatsu brand is made by Komatsu Dresser, an American-Japanese joint venture with headquarters in Lincolnshire, Illinois. Ninety-five percent of the company's dirt movers are made in the United States. The John Deere excavators are produced under a joint venture agreement between Deere and Hitachi. The engines for the John Deere machines are made in the United States, but the machines themselves are made in Japan.

This complicated buying situation reflects how business is conducted in our new global environment. "Who is us?" asks a Harvard professor, illustrating the point that, in today's world—where corporations owned and headquartered in the United States have foreign manufacturing facilities and foreign-owned corporations have assembly plants in the United States—the multinational corporation is truly a world enterprise rather than an organization rooted only in one country. Today's global manager competes in an environment in which the location of the headquarters is not a matter of great significance. "Us" is not necessarily a company, like John Deere, that is headquartered in the United States. ■

## The Company as an International Marketer

DISCUSSION CONSIDERATION
Ask students to list the advantages of NOT engaging in international marketing (besides cost savings—or avoiding stretching limited resources—as cited in the chapter text). Responses might include the ability to focus more narrowly on understanding one market and one set of competitors, to avoid the risks of marketing in unstable economies and countries, and perhaps to better control marketing operations.

In spite of the global nature of today's business environment, not all U.S.–based companies choose to market their products outside the United States. A bagel bakery may limit its marketing to New York City, for instance. The organization's resources or market demand may justify this strategy. Large corporations, of course, are more likely to find it advantageous to spend considerable time and effort marketing beyond their national boundaries. However, not all large corporations engage in international marketing. Southwest Airlines, for example, chooses to market its services only inside the United States.

The same fundamental marketing concepts that apply in domestic marketing apply in international marketing. Uncontrollable environmental factors must be analyzed, and target markets must be determined. Competitive market positions must be considered, and marketing mix strategies must be planned and executed to appeal to these target markets.

Political stability, tariffs, and exchange rates are some of the factors that a company must take into account when it is making the decision to market in another country. The factors that affect a company's decision to enter a certain market are discussed in Chapter 8, "Market Segmentation, Targeting, and Positioning Strategies."

After a company decides it will do business in a certain market, it must make decisions about what degree of ownership and management involvement it will pursue. Market potential, the organization's experience in international marketing, the organization's willingness to subject itself to risks, and host country policies often influence these decisions. These factors may cause a multinational marketer to be involved at different levels in different countries.

**EXHIBIT 4–3** Summary of International Involvement

| STRATEGY | LOCATION OF PRODUCTION FACILITY | FOREIGN COMPANY'S PRIMARY INVOLVEMENT | OWNERSHIP OF FOREIGN OPERATION | CAPITAL OUTLAY REQUIRED |
|---|---|---|---|---|
| | | ***Direct*** | | |
| *Direct Investment* | Foreign country | Native sales force may be used; sometimes foreign intermediaries used | Complete domestic ownership | High |
| *Direct Exporting* | Domestic | None | None | Low |
| | | ***Global Collaborators*** | | |
| *Indirect Exporting* | Domestic | Intermediary ensures foreign distribution and sales | Foreign ownership of intermediaries | Low |
| *Licensing/ Franchising* | Foreign country | Owns right to manufacture/ service and use product name; local marketing | Joint according to contract | Low |
| *Contract Manufacturing* | Foreign country | Production according to specifications | Foreign ownership of production facility | Low |
| *Joint Ownership* | Foreign country | Partner | Partner | Moderate to high |

The basic types of involvement are direct investment, exporting, and joint venturing. We examine direct investment and exporting next. With joint venturing, we move into the area of collaborations. Exhibit 4–3 outlines these strategies.

**DIRECT FOREIGN INVESTMENT**
Investment of capital in production and marketing operations located in a host foreign country.

If foreign market demand is great, a company may directly invest in manufacturing and marketing operations in a host foreign country. This is called **direct foreign investment.** Coca-Cola owns a bottling plant in Guangzhow (Canton) China, for example. Several Japanese automobile manufacturers have built automobile plants in the United States. This enables the automakers to minimize the shipping expenses and political pressures associated with selling foreign-made cars in the U.S. market. In other instances, an organization may directly invest in plant operations in developing countries to take advantage of low-cost labor. Whatever the reason, direct investment in manufacturing facilities and marketing operations reflects a long-term, high-level commitment to international marketing.

POINT TO EMPHASIZE
There is nothing that prohibits a company from mixing these strategies around the world. For example, a company may choose to use direct investment in the Japanese market, exporting in the Latin American market, and joint venturing in the European market.

Many risks are associated with a long-term direct investment strategy. For example, Iraq's invasion of Kuwait had a major impact on Exxon, Aramco, and other oil companies that had oil-exploration facilities destroyed or damaged during the Gulf War. In some countries, a change in governments may lead to nationalization of foreign companies' assets—that is, a transfer of the assets to the new government. If the risk of nationalization of a multinational's operations is high, direct investment becomes less attractive.

**EXPORTING**
Selling domestically produced products in foreign markets.

In contrast to direct investment, **exporting** is a relatively low-level commitment to international marketing. Exporters, manufacturing or harvesting in their home countries, sell some or all of their products in foreign markets. Such distribution may be accomplished either directly, through the company's sales force, or indirectly, through

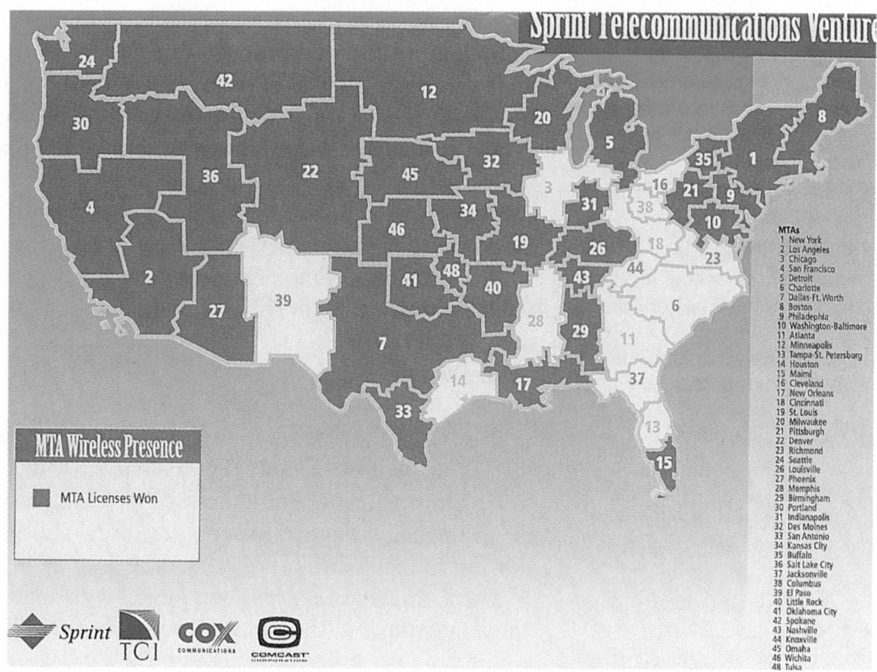


Sprint Corporation and three major cable television companies—Tele-Communications Inc., Comcast Corp., and Cox Enterprises Inc.—have formed a large-scale wireless and wired communications alliance in anticipation of information and telecommunication needs in the 21st century. Sprint and its collaborators will jointly pursue the technological development and marketing of personal communications services on the "information superhighway."

intermediaries. (Thus, exporting may or may not involve collaborators.) There is no investment in overseas plant or equipment in either case.

With indirect exporting, a domestic company does not deal directly with overseas customers. Instead, it sells a portion of its inventory to some intermediary that conducts business (usually buying) in the company's home country. The intermediary then distributes the product in foreign markets. The major strength of the intermediary is its accessibility to foreign customers. Some companies exporting indirectly do not routinely engage in this activity, viewing the international marketplace simply as a place to get rid of surplus inventory or unwanted products. Others choose to export on a more continuous and systematically planned basis. Whatever the degree of indirect exporting, the company uses its domestic sales force to sell its products to the intermediaries.

Direct exporting may be used when a firm wants greater control over the foreign sales of its product. Direct exporting can take several forms. Some companies use their own traveling salespeople, who make occasional visits to overseas markets to try to sell the product there. These salespeople may meet with limited success unless they can cultivate the right prospects and understand what is required to conduct business in another culture. Other companies establish a domestic-based export department or division. The scope of this unit is determined in part by the degree of commitment the company feels toward international marketing.

Because the perspective of these two approaches to direct exporting is often domestic-based, they do not always meet with success. Therefore, some companies choose to establish overseas sales offices, branches, or distributors to maintain a continued presence in the host country or overseas market. Such organizations can develop a better understanding of the differences in foreign markets than salespeople making occasional visits.

## Global Collaborations

Collaborations on a global scale have increased as a result of the globalization of the marketplace. Using export management companies, engaging in joint ventures, and outsourcing from companies operating outside the United States have allowed U.S. companies to marshal more resources for international marketing.

**EXPORT MANAGEMENT COMPANY**
A company that specializes in buying from sellers in one country and marketing the products in other countries. Such companies typically take title to the products.

In our discussion of exporting, we mentioned that indirect exporting requires the use of intermediaries. Companies often develop collaborative relationships with **export management companies,** intermediaries that specialize in buying from sellers in one country and marketing the products in other countries. Export management companies, which assume ownership of the goods, reduce the risk of multinational marketing for companies without a great deal of exporting experience. Like other wholesalers, export management companies perform many distribution functions for sellers. However, in most cases, selling and taking responsibility for foreign credit are their primary functions. Other intermediaries that represent companies in overseas selling activities include various types of export agents, who do not take title to the goods.

**JOINT VENTURING**
In international marketing, an arrangement between a domestic company and a foreign host company to set up production and marketing facilities in a foreign market.

In **joint venturing,** domestic and host companies join to set up production and marketing facilities in an overseas market. Unlike exporting, joint venturing involves some agreement for production of the product on foreign soil. The Whirlpool example at the beginning of this chapter discussed a joint-venturing agreement for operations in the Far East.

**LICENSING**
In international marketing, an agreement by which a company (the licensor) permits a foreign country (the licensee) to set up a business in the foreign market using the licensor's manufacturing processes, patents, trademarks, trade secrets, and so on in exchange for payment of a fee or royalty.

There are several forms of joint venturing. One simple method is **licensing,** in which a company (the *licensor)* wanting to do business in a particular overseas market enters into a licensing agreement with an overseas company (the *licensee)* that permits the licensee to use the licensor's manufacturing processes, patents, trademarks, trade secrets, and so on in exchange for payment of a fee or royalty.

Licensing provides a means to conduct business in a country whose laws discourage foreign ownership. One disadvantage of licensing is loss of managerial control. The foreign company makes key decisions without input from the licensor. On the positive side, a licensee may provide a greater understanding of the local culture, experience with the local distribution system, and the marketing skill required to succeed in the foreign market.

**INTERNATIONAL FRANCHISING**
A form of licensing in which a company establishes foreign franchises. Franchising involves a contractual agreement between a franchisor, often a manufacturer or wholesaler, and a franchisee, typically an independent retailer, by which the franchisee distributes the franchisor's product.

**International franchising** is a form of licensing in which a company establishes overseas franchises in much the same way it establishes franchises in its own country. Because many franchisors desire consistency, franchising agreements are most often found in markets where conditions are similar to those in the domestic market. A potential disadvantage of international franchising is the possibility that this type of operation will foster future competitors. Sometimes, after gaining enough training and experience, franchisees start their own rival companies.

**CONTRACT MANUFACTURING**
In international marketing, an agreement by which a company allows a foreign producer to manufacture its product according to its specifications; typically, the company then handles foreign sales of the product.

Some companies believe that the risks of licensing are too great and prefer to maintain greater marketing control. These companies use **contract manufacturing,** under which a company agrees to permit an overseas manufacturer to produce its product. The domestic company supplies the product specifications and the brand name, and the foreign company produces the product under that label for the domestic company. Overseas sales of the product are typically handled and controlled by the domestic company. In Mexico and Spain, for instance, Sears may establish its own stores; but rather than filling these stores with imported products, it often uses local manufacturers to produce Sears-label products to specifications. In many foreign markets, contract manufacturing also offers the opportunity to use labor that is less expensive, thus yielding lower product prices or greater savings to the company.

**JOINT OWNERSHIP VENTURE**
In international marketing, a joint venture in which domestic and foreign partners invest capital and share ownership and control.

A final form of joint venturing is the **joint ownership venture.** Under this arrangement, the domestic and foreign partners invest capital and share ownership and control of the partnership in some agreed-on proportion. Ownership is not always equal. AT&T has a joint venture agreement with PTT Telecom of the Netherlands and Ukraine's State Committee of Communications to modernize phone service in Ukraine, which currently routes long-distance calls through Moscow on poor-quality lines. The new venture, which will allow Ukrainians to direct-dial to foreign countries, is owned 39 percent by AT&T, 10 percent by PTT Telecom, and 51 percent by the government of Ukraine.

COMPETITIVE STRATEGY: WHAT WENT WRONG?

## *Pepsi Egypt*

Coca-Cola, which left all Arabic countries in the Middle East except Morocco and Tunisia in 1967, returned to Egypt in 1978. During Coca-Cola's absence, Pepsi-Cola became popular with Egyptian consumers.

But ask for a "Peps" in Egypt today and expect to be handed a Coke—a shocking phenomenon in a market where "Peps" had become a generic term for soft drink and the brand of choice for 48 years.

All that changed when the Egyptian government privatized its portion of the soft-drink bottling business. The government's decision to let private enterprise have its portion of the business led to the complete reversal of the two major soft drink brand's bottling organizations.

Two bottlers previously associated with Pepsi and former partners with the government, Shaher Adbel Hak and his brother Abdel Galil Abdel Hak, turned the Egyptian soft drink market upside down after they lost a bid for the government's portion of the Pepsi business to another company. When their bid was not accepted, they entered into a joint venture with Atlantic Industries (Coca-Cola Egypt).

Now Coke and Pepsi are battling it out for leadership in Egypt's $400 million market. Before the switch of bottlers, Pepsi brands held 47 percent of the market to Coca-Cola's 38 percent. Today, Coca-Cola has 22 bottling plants and Pepsi has 9. This has boosted Coca-Cola's market share above 60 percent.

**ALTERNATIVE EXAMPLE**
Euro Disney has lost nearly $2 billion since opening in 1992. This was a joint ownership project in which Disney's stake was 49 percent. Disney now has written off $625 million as its share of the losses. Joint ownership allowed Disney to have more control over the operation, including building the theme park to its exacting standards. However, greater involvement of Europeans might have helped Disney avoid mistakes like building too many expensive hotel rooms rather than fewer and more moderately priced hotel rooms. SOURCE: John Huey, "Eisner Explains Everything," *Fortune,* April 17, 1995, pp. 44–68.

A common reason for entering into a joint venture is that some countries that restrict foreign ownership of investments require such an arrangement. Mexico bars total foreign ownership of Mexican advertising agencies, for example. International agencies such as J. Walter Thompson, Inc., must therefore be involved in joint ventures if they wish to operate in Mexico. In other countries, the government may require that the local company maintain a majority interest in the venture, keeping foreign control in the company under 50 percent.

Another reason for joint ownership ventures is financial. A U.S. company may wish to set up European operations but may find it economically difficult. A joint ownership venture with a European firm may be the solution.

A key to the success of a joint ownership venture, as with any type of partnership, is finding and keeping the right mix of companies. Overseas and American firms do not always have the same views. Europeans tend to be engineering-oriented, for instance. The term *marketing* may simply mean "sales" to them. American companies, in contrast, often put marketing first. Management becomes difficult when the partners disagree on fundamental components of the business. Finding the right partner reduces these differences. Joint ventures are the topic of the accompanying Competitive Strategy feature.

Whatever form global collaborations take, technology plays a central role. Satellite communications systems, modems, fax machines, and other advances in information technology have made collaboration with companies in other countries much more efficient. In many cases, instantaneous communication is possible. Global information systems, which are discussed in Chapter 5, have been instrumental in the growth of global business and global collaborations. Many business analysts believe the key to success in the global economy lies in effective use of information technology.

## Summary

It is useful to organize all microenvironmental forces into four basic categories: company, customers, competitors, and collaborators. These are called the four Cs.

LEARNING OBJECTIVE **1** *Understand how the microenvironment affects a company's marketing activity.*

The microenvironment consists of the company, its customers, and other economic institutions that shape its marketing practices. Thus, the effect of the microenvironment is regular and direct.

LEARNING OBJECTIVE **2** *Identify the four Cs of marketing.*

The four Cs stand for company, customers, competitors, and collaborators. Each C represents a participant that performs essential business activities. The term *company* refers to the business or organization itself. Customers are the lifeblood of every company; a company that does not satisfy customers' needs will not stay in business in the long run. Competitors are rival companies engaged in the same business. Collaborators are persons or companies that work with your company.

LEARNING OBJECTIVE **3** *Recognize how marketing creates economic utility for customers.*

Marketing includes designing, distributing, storing, and scheduling the sale of products and informing buyers about them. It thus helps to create form utility and creates place, time, and possession utility. Together, these constitute economic utility. By creating economic utility, marketing delivers a standard of living to society.

LEARNING OBJECTIVE **4** *Identify the various types of competitors and understand how marketers anticipate and react to competitors' strategies to gain competitive advantages.*

Competitors are rival companies interested in selling their products and services to your company's customers and potential customers. There are four general types of competition: price, quality, time, and location. In general, a price that is lower than competitors' prices will attract customers to the lower-priced product. Many businesses choose to compete on the basis of quality rather than on the basis of price. Quality-based competition is more complex than price competition because consumers define quality in many different ways. Time-based competition is based on the idea that buyers prefer to take possession of their goods exactly when they need them, which is often as soon as possible. Location-based competition is based on providing more place utility than competitors. To establish and maintain a competitive advantage means to be superior to or different from competitors in terms of price, quality, time, or location. This may be accomplished by operating a more efficient factory, by selling at a lower price, by designing better-quality products, or by satisfying customers in other ways.

LEARNING OBJECTIVE **5** *Describe the value chain and explain why it must be managed.*

The value chain portrays the system of collaborative activities and relationships involved in operating a business. Each link in the chain adds value to the product customers ultimately buy. By managing these collaborations, companies free up their resources so they can concentrate on what they do best. Having every organization in the value chain focus on core competencies results in lower-cost, better-designed products.

LEARNING OBJECTIVE **6** *Understand the importance of global competition in today's economy.*

The United States—indeed, the world—has passed through a transition period from a domestic orientation to a global orientation. Today, with multinational organizations employing global marketing strategies, a domestic marketer must be aware of foreign competitors' influence not only in international markets but also in its own domestic market. Markets have been internationalized; competition is global; and the future of marketing is global.

LEARNING OBJECTIVE **7** *Apply the four Cs in a global business context.*

Because competition is global, companies must analyze microenvironments in various parts of the world. International companies must focus on satisfying customer needs by working with collaborators to gain competitive advantage. The four Cs often vary by country and culture.

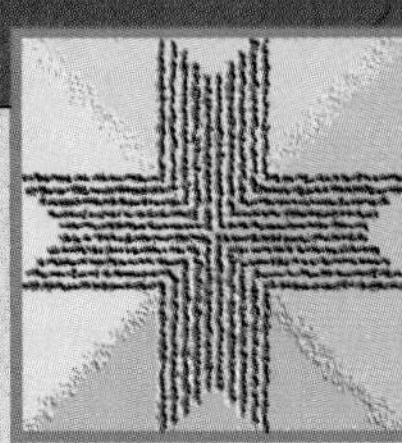

# Cross-Functional Insights

## PART ONE

Many theories and principles from other business disciplines can provide insights about the role marketing plays in an organization. The questions in this section are designed to help you think about integrating what you have learned about management, finance, production, and other functional areas taught in business courses with the marketing principles explained in this textbook.

### *Marketing Concept/Market-Driven Organizations*

The marketing concept stresses consumer orientation, long-run profitability, and integrating marketing functions with other corporate functions. Companies that have superior skill in understanding and satisfying customers are said to be market-driven.

What are the key revenue and expense items that influence an organization's long-run profitability?

Are entrepreneurs consumer-oriented? What characteristics of entrepreneurs would help them become successful marketers?

What traits should a person have to be a leader in a market-driven organization?

Does management contingency theory apply to marketing leadership positions?

### *Customer Satisfaction*

Market-oriented organizations embrace an organization-wide focus to learn their customers' needs so they can offer superior customer value—that is, so they can satisfy customer needs better than their competitors. Marketers should strive to increase customer satisfaction.

How important is a company's corporate culture in such efforts? What type of corporate culture would contribute most to the achievement of the goal of satisfying customers?

What type of performance appraisal system could be used to evaluate employees in terms of customer satisfaction?

### *Organizational Mission*

Top managers identify the organizational, or corporate, mission. This strategic decision influences all other marketing strategies. An organizational mission is a statement of company purpose. It explains why the organization exists and what it hopes to accomplish. It provides direction for the entire organization. When we discussed corporate mission statements, we looked at the mission from a marketing perspective.

What aspects of a mission statement would be important to a manager of human resources? A manager of engineering? A financial manager?

### *Total Quality Management*

A company that employs a total quality management strategy must evaluate quality through the eyes of the customer. Every aspect of the business must focus on quality—for example, management may institute a performance appraisal system to evaluate employees in terms of the service they provide to customers. Further, all participants must strive for continuous improvement.

Total quality management requires the cooperation of marketing, production, and many other functional areas of the business. How should this coordination be managed?

How important is knowledge of statistical analysis and statistical process control in analyzing a total quality management system?

What type of performance appraisal system could be used to evaluate employees in terms of the quality of goods and services produced?

Do companies need to solicit the opinions of as many employees as possible to be successful in a total quality effort?

### *Differentiation Strategy*

A differentiation strategy emphasizes offering a product that is unique in the industry, provides a distinct advantage, or is otherwise set apart from competitors' brands in some way other than price.

How do the laws of supply and demand apply to a marketer of branded goods or services that seeks to differentiate them from those of competitors? Would economists and marketers give the same answer to this question?

### *SWOT*

Situation analysis is the diagnostic activity of interpreting environmental conditions and changes in light of the organization's ability to capitalize on potential opportunities and to ward off problems. SWOT stands for external strengths and weaknesses and internal opportunities and threats.

How would a company's financial analysts look at internal opportunities and threats?

How would a top executive's chief concerns about internal opportunities and threats differ from marketers' concerns, if at all?

What is opportunity cost, and how does it relate to the strategic marketing process and SWOT analysis?

### *Competitive Advantage*

One of the most common goals of a business unit is to establish and maintain a competitive advantage—to be superior to or favorably different from competitors in a way that is important to the market.

Marketers think increasing customer satisfaction through product development is the key to competitive advantage. In what other ways might a top executive have the organization strive for competitive advantage?

Discuss marketing strategies for competitive advantage in the context of antitrust laws such as the Sherman Antitrust Act and the Federal Trade Commission Act.

### *Diversification*

Marketing new products to a new set of customers is called diversification.

What economic factors might bar a company from entering a market?

What organizational changes are necessary when a company diversifies?

### *Control*

To marketers, the purpose of managerial control is to ensure that planned activities are completely and properly executed.

What role does accounting play in the marketing control process?

Do organizational conflicts arise between marketers and accountants because of different perspectives on control activities?

### Four Cs

Working with collaborators is becoming increasingly important.

What organizational adjustments must be made when a company decides to form a strategic alliance or other collaboration with another company?

### Core Competencies

A core competency is a proficiency in a critical functional activity, such as technical know-how or a particular business specialization, that helps provide a company's unique competitive advantage.

At what level in the organization are core competencies determined? By what process?

### International Marketing

International marketing involves the adoption of a marketing strategy that views the world market rather than a domestic market as the basis for marketing operations.

What adjustments must a company make in its organizational structure when it becomes an international organization?

## Information Technology: Insights and Exercises

Information technologies are changing the way business is conducted around the world. The Internet is a new way of obtaining information and communicating with others. It is in its infancy right now, but it will become mature during the 21st century.

### Accessing the Internet[1]

Many colleges and universities have host computers with direct connections to the Internet, due in part to its history of use for research purposes. Faculty, staff, and students at these institutions may have individual "accounts" so that they can access the Internet through the school's host system. Other organizations also have host computers with direct access to the Internet and may provide their employees with access to some, if not all, of the Internet's features. Commercial on-line services, such as CompuServe, Prodigy, and America Online also provide access to the Internet to any of their customers who pay the required fee for that service.

The procedure for accessing the Internet through your computer is usually quite similar to accessing other network systems. When you are given an account, you are also given a **username** (also called a **user ID**) and an initial password (a password that you typically change to something else that you specify the first time you access the system). You need a password so that others who do not know your password cannot access your account. You access the host computer by whatever method has been set up for your system (many variations occur with different systems, but a menu option or screen picture or icon is usually involved). Once you gain initial access, you typically enter your username and a password at a system prompt. In some systems, the series of on-screen prompts and responses for your first use of the system is similar to this:

| System Prompt | Your Response |
|---|---|
| Login: | <USERNAME> |
| Password: | <INITIAL PASSWORD> |
| New Password: | <SECOND PASSWORD> |
| Verification: | <SECOND PASSWORD> |

In addition to a requirement that you change to a new password of your own design, many systems also require that you change your password at designated time intervals, such as monthly. You will see messages on the screen indicating that your password is expiring, at which time you will follow a similar procedure to indicate a new password. This procedure provides a little extra security for your account.

After these initial procedures of setting up an account are completed, you are ready to use whatever Internet resources are provided to you by your system. You can determine your options by looking at the menu choices that appear on your screen. For example, you may have an initial menu choice of accessing Internet that, when selected, provides you with a list of specific Internet features available to you as submenu options. Many of the Internet features are described in the sections below.

### Electronic Mail

*E-mail* is short for *electronic mail.* Because e-mail is transmitted almost instantaneously, it has many advantages over regular mail (which is often called "snail mail"). Internet provides electronic mail capabilities from any Internet user to anyone else who has access to Internet around the globe—the recipient's e-mail address is all that is needed to send a message or data. Typical e-mail capabilities are provided, such as replying to messages and forwarding them to others. You actually use your system's electronic mail capabilities for sending and receiving messages and use the Internet as a means of sending the message or data to any other address worldwide that is connected to the Internet.

You will need to determine the format for designating a recipient's Internet address at your location. A typical electronic mail address begins with the username followed by the "at" (@) symbol and other location identifiers that are separated by periods or "dots" (.), such as:

STUDENTA@SYSTEM1.UNIVERSITY1.EDU

This address provides the username, the name of the host computer system being used, the university name, and the general type of system (e.g., EDU = educational institution; COM = commercial business; GOV = government location). To specify the use of Internet to send a message when you are using your own system's e-mail facility, you may need to add an IN at the beginning of the address (depending on your system), such as:

IN:STUDENTA@SYSTEM1.UNIVERSITY1.EDU

Some systems require additional symbols in the address, such as:

IN%"STUDENTA@SYSTEM1.UNIVERSITY1.EDU"

Most schools with Internet access offer on-screen Help facilities, training sessions, or offices you can call for assistance if you have difficulty determining the appropriate format for a recipient's address.

Electronic mail is one of the most widely used features of Internet. In most businesses and schools, an electronic mail system has been provided as an internal network, and Internet is then used as a means of sending messages or data to addresses that would not be available within your own network.

### Usenet Newsgroups

Usenet began as a bulletin board system years ago and has expanded to thousands of computer sites and millions of participants. Its discussion areas, called **newsgroups,** are interactive computer discussions on a wide and continually expanding range of topics that you can simply read or can add information to. Usenet does not have a controlling person or group to determine what newsgroups can be included, but a Usenet computer site does have a news administrator who manages that site, cooperates with other news administrators, and exchanges articles. A news administrator can determine an expiration date for articles and remove them after the expiration date.

Data in a newsgroup are organized by topics or general areas of interest. A newsgroup name contains a designation of the main category, followed by other sections that provide more details about the type of newsgroup (each part of the name is separated by a dot).

### Menu Driven Searching—Gopher

***Gopher*** is an easy to use method of searching for information on the Internet. Named after the mascot at its inventor, the University of Minnesota (or as a slang term for Go-Fer), Gopher represents a menu-driven way to locate and display information on the Internet. Although text-based, Gopher is a very populat method that uses FTP (file transfer protocols). You can select information from a series of hierarchical menus. The Gopher software will automatically retrieve information with FTP as needed and will run Telnet sessions automatically. The individual user does not have to memorize addresses or obscure commands to use Gopher. Although gopher is a very useful searching tool, it has become less popular since the development of browsers on the World Wide Web.

### World Wide Web

**World Wide Web (WWW or "Web")** was designed in 1989 by Tim Berners-Lee, a computer scientist working in Switzerland, in an effort to help an international group use on-line technologies to collaborate in their research efforts. Between 1993 and 1995, it grew from about 100 Web "sites" to 10,000, with many businesses beginning to take advantage of its capabilities.

WWW provides a method of searching through databases using **hypertext** and **hypermedia.** Hypertext uses pointers or links from one item of text to another so that you can continue searching through multiple layers of related data. Hypermedia adds other forms to the text, such as sound, images, or animation. WWW is public domain software that is considered a global information system with access to a huge volume of information on Internet. For the Web user or "client," WWW uses a simple hypertext language called HTML (Hypertext Markup Language) that is based on ASCII code, making it easy to link applications written in many programming languages. Another component is a Web "server," a system that uses a process called HTTP (Hypertext Transfer Protocol), which is a simplified version of FTP for transfering files. The server is needed for distributing information through the WWW. The WWW includes all the Web servers on the Internet. Each server has a unique name, and each document or other resource on a Web server has a URL (Uniform Resource Locator) designation, which is similar to a file name, but including the type of resource (such as HTTP), the address of the resource, and a path name.

WWW contains thousands of documents or pages that can be displayed, with connections on one page to information on other pages that may be located elsewhere. To obtain information stored in the WWW, you need software called a **browser.** A browser retrieves HTML documents using the HTTP protocol and formats them for appropriate screen display. The browser is also capable of interpreting hyperlinks in a document and moving from one document to another, regardless of where the documents are actually stored. Two browsers currently available are **Mosaic** and **Netscape Navigator,** often referred to simply as Netscape. Mosaic was developed by the National Center for Supercomputing Applications (NCSA) at the University of Illinois and is sometimes referred to as NCSA Mosaic. Mosaic is a graphical user interface (GUI) browser that makes it easy to navigate the Internet by looking at pictorial screens and/or menus, clicking a mouse or keyboard to make selections. Highlighted or underlined items have links to data at other locations or on other pages, allowing easy touring through a "web" of information where the computer user defines the path. Access is provided to motion pictures and sound, as well as to still images.

Some enhancements or added capabilities based on Mosaic have been developed. For example, Netscape Communications was formed by some of the original team that developed Mosaic, who revised the browser as well as the HTTP server. Mosaic and Netscape are provided at no cost for noncommercial users, such as educational institutions. New browers and additional features continue to be developed. For example, Novell and Microsoft have developed browsers and related capabilities for use with their word processing software.

Web **home pages** are something like storefronts, where a potential customer can get an introduction to what is inside. Thousands of businesses of all types and sizes have developed Web pages. Many of these pages are designed to promote the businesses and/or to provide information quickly to potential customers. Web use has been increasing at an even greater rate than the overall growth rate for Internet. Web home pages are relatively easy to design and involve very little expense to get a few pages up and running. Because of the web concept of linking data, an introductory page can have multiple subsets of pages that can be viewed, with the pages that appear dependent upon selections made on the previous page. In addition, the contents can be updated regularly.

## *Exercises*

If one of the exercises or addresses given below does not seem to work, please check the West Publishing World Wide Web (WWW) address listed below. Updates and other information will be provided at this address as necessary. To reach the West Publishing WWW page with information about this book, use your Web browser to go to:

**http://www.westpub.com/Educate/Educ.Supp.htm**
Under **Business** and **Marketing,** choose the appropriate monthly update for **Zikmund/d'Amico, Marketing, Fifth Edition**

If you want to start at the West Publishing WWW home page and navigate to the page containing information for this book, use your Web browser to go to:

**http://www.westpub.com**
Choose **Fast or Slow Connection**
Select **Products and Services**
Select **College and School Division**
Choose **Educational Publishing: College and School**
Select **College Publications**
Select **Educational Supplements and Updates for College Products**
Under **Business** and **Marketing,** choose the appropriate monthly update for **Zikmund/d'Amico, Marketing, Fifth Edition**

## E-Mail Exercise

In Chapter 1, you learned that satisfying customer wants is a key aspect of the marketing concept. In order to satisfy customers, marketers listen to what the market has to say. Some marketers use simple techniques, like suggestion boxes, to listen to the market. Others use more sophisticated marketing research techniques, some of which you will read about in the next unit of this text.

Your marketing professor would like to listen to you, the customer, so that he or she can better satisfy future customers. Send an e-mail message to your marketing professor. Include at least two things in your message:

1. Tell the professor what you like about this class so far.
2. Tell the professor what you do not like about this class so far.

## Gopher Exercise

In order to compete successfully in global markets, marketers must understand how international marketing environments differ among countries. Use Gopher to go to:

**umslvma.umsl.edu**
Select **The Library**
Then select **Government Information**
Then select **International Business Practices Guide**
Now, select a region, such as **Asia and the Pacific Rim.**

You will see a list of countries. Choose two different countries and compare their business practices on such items as business organizations, exporting, commercial policies, foreign investment, taxation, intellectual property rights, and regulatory agencies. Of the two countries you selected, which one do you think would be the easiest one for a small U.S. export company to enter? Why? Which country would be best suited for a joint venture? Why? Which country would offer the best environment for a large multinational firm? Why?

## World Wide Web Exercise

Chapter 2 highlights the critical role of the organizational mission statement plays in the development and implementation of marketing strategy. Use your Web browser to go to the Gallup Organization's home page at:

**http://www.gallup.com/**

Select the **Mission Statement** option and read through the Gallup Organization's mission statement. On a sheet of paper, list five ways the Gallup Organization's mission statement differs from the mission statement of The Limited. (The mission statement for The Limited appears in Chapter 2 of this book.) On the same sheet of paper, list five similarities between the Gallup Organization's mission statement and the mission statement for The Limited. Bring your two lists to class for discussion.

## Listserv Exercise

Many people using the Internet appreciate mailing discussion lists, commonly referred to as lists or listservs. West Publishing has set up a special mailing discussion list just for students using this book. Once you are a member, you may send messages to the list. Everyone who has subscribed to the list will automatically receive your message. For example, you may post a question on the listserv, and another student may post a message as a response. In order to use this discussion list, you must subscribe to the list using the directions given below. When you decide you no longer want to be on the list, you must unsubscribe. In other words, you will continue to receive mail from the list until you unsubscribe.

If any address is unobtainable, check the West Publishing World Wide Web address for updates: **http://www.westpub.com/Educate/Educ.Supp.htm**

After you complete the instructions below for subscribing to the listserv, send a message to the listserv at:

**zikmund@westpub.com**

Include four things in your message:

1. List one store in your town or city that, in your opinion, definitely follows the marketing concept.
2. Explain why you think so or provide evidence for your opinion.
3. List one store in your town or city that, in your opinon, definitely does not follow the marketing concept.
4. Explain why you think so or provide evidence for your opinion.

**Subscribing to the Zikmund List Using the Subscription Address** To subscribe to the Zikmund listserv, use your e-mail utility to send a message to the following address:

**listserv@westpub.com**

The Subject line for the mail message should be left blank. The Body of the message needs to follow a specific syntax. In the Body, type the following:

**subscribe zikmund Firstname Lastname**
(If your name were Shawn Olson, the command would be:
subscribe zikmund Shawn Olson)

After some amount of time, depending on network load, you should receive an automatically generated message confirming your subscription to the list.

**Sending E-Mail Messages to the Zikmund List Using the List Address** To send messages, you use a different address from the one you used to subscribe to the list. The address you use to send e-mail messages is known as the list address. The list address for this book is:

**zikmund@westpub.com**

Anytime you want to send a message to other people on the list, use this address.

**Unsubscribing to the Zikmund List Using the Subscription Address** If you need to quit the list at any time, use your e-mail utility to send a message to the following address:

**listserv@westpub.com**

The Subject line for the mail message should be left blank. In the Body of the message, type the following:

**unsubscribe zikmund**

The listserv will be able to figure out whom to unsubscribe from your mail header. *Warning*: Make sure when you unsubscribe that you send your message to the subscription address, not the list address.

If any address is unobtainable, check the West Publishing World Wide Web address for updates: **http://www.westpub.com/Educate/Educ.Supp.htm**

### *Careers and the Internet*

Use your Web browser to go to the Career Magazine home page at:

**http://plaza.xor.com:80/careermag**

Select the **Job Openings** option and do a search for marketing-related jobs that have been posted on the Internet. Click on the **Click here to begin your Job Search** icon. Leave the Location field empty, enter **Marketing** in the Skills field and enter **Manager** in the Title field. Then submit your search by clicking on the **Submit Search** button. Browse through the jobs you find. Pick a job that looks interesting to you, write down the information, and bring it to class for discussion and to share with others in the class.

# PART TWO

# Analysis of Market and Buyer Behavior

GLOBAL INFORMATION SYSTEMS AND MARKETING RESEARCH

CONSUMER BEHAVIOR: DECISION-MAKING PROCESSES AND SOCIOCULTURAL FORCES

BUSINESS MARKETS AND ORGANIZATIONAL BUYING

MARKET SEGMENTATION, TARGETING, AND POSITIONING STRATEGIES

The secret of success is to be ready for opportunity when it comes.

BENJAMIN DISRAELI

CHAPTER

# 5

# Global Information Systems and Marketing Research

## LEARNING OBJECTIVES

After you have studied this chapter, you will be able to:

1. Explain why information is essential to effective marketing decision making.
2. Explain the importance of global information systems.
3. Describe a decision support system.
4. Explain the contribution of marketing research to effective decision making.
5. Describe the stages in the marketing research process.
6. Explain how exploratory research relates to specific marketing management problems.
7. Understand why secondary data are valuable sources of information.
8. Understand the uses of surveys, observation, and experiments.
9. Demonstrate your knowledge of the purposes of sales forecasting.
10. Evaluate the advantages and disadvantages of the various forecasting methods.

VIDEO CASE 5–1

## First Bank Systems of Minneapolis (A)

First Bank Systems (FBS) of Minneapolis engages in three core business areas: retail and community banking, commercial banking, and the trust and investment group. Retail and community banking includes consumer and corporate credit-card and payment-systems processing. Commercial banking provides lending, cash management, and other financial services to midsized and large corporate and mortgage banking companies. The trust and investment group includes corporate, personal, and institutional trust services; investment management services; and a full-service brokerage company. In March 1994, the company's assets exceeded $26 billion.

FBS's mission statement says, "We will be one of the top-performing banks, measured in terms of market share and long-term profitability." A major goal is to obtain the leading market share in the markets that FBS serves. This goal is pursued, in part, through acquisition.

FBS's growth strategy seeks to aggressively expand in a number of financial services. For example, Duluth-based St. Louis Bank for Savings—the fifth-largest thrift in the state—was acquired by FBS in 1994. The acquisition makes sense because it gives FBS a stronger presence in Duluth and falls in line with the company's strategy of trying to beef up its position in major cities and regional trade centers.

When FBS purchases a financial institution, it has determined many strategic, geographic, and logistic reasons why the institution is a good fit. One very important reason is the organization's customers. And retaining 100 percent of the acquired institution's customers is one of the most critical goals during acquisition and integration. Julie Cornelius, vice president of acquisitions integration, says, "We want customers of the acquired organization to be disrupted as little as possible. We want them to have confidence that with the new organization they'll receive more value for their banking relationships through new products and services. If we have to take something away, we hope we're adding benefits someplace else."

### QUESTIONS

1. Who are a bank's retail and community customers? What problems do these consumers have with banks? How can a marketing orientation improve the marketing of bank services?
2. When FBS makes an acquisition, what should it have as objectives to accomplish the integration of new customers?
3. In what way can the bank's information system be used to accomplish the integration of new customers?
4. How might a bank like FBS use marketing research in its retail and community banking operations?
5. What environmental factors are most likely to influence a bank's operations and its service to its customers? How can a bank obtain information about these factors?

CHAPTER

# 6

# Consumer Behavior: Decision-Making Processes and Sociocultural Forces

## LEARNING OBJECTIVES

After you have studied this chapter, you will be able to:

1. Understand the basic model of consumer behavior.
2. Describe the consumer decision-making process and understand factors, such as consumer involvement, that influence it.
3. Appreciate the importance of perceived risk, choice criteria, purchase satisfaction, and cognitive dissonance.
4. Recognize the influence of individual factors, such as motives, perception, learning, attitude, and personality, on consumer behavior.
5. Explain the nature of culture and subculture in terms of social values, norms, and roles.
6. Characterize social class in the United States.
7. Explain the influence of reference groups on individual buyers.
8. Examine the roles in the joint decision-making process.

Gabriella Sahlman dressed to the nines this past holiday season: a $250 red velvet dress, $15 white stockings, $55 patent leather flats. Her everyday wear was more casual: sweater, turtleneck, leggings, all told about $120 per outfit. She has six. Sahlman sleeps on a $750 antiqued wooden bed. Her wicker bureau ran to $2,000 at a Madison Avenue boutique.

No, Gabriella is no yuppie, not yet. On Feb. 6 she turned 21 months.

The consumer society neglects no potential markets, and so infant wear and other items for infants, toddlers and preschoolers, once the domain of hand-me-downs, is now a $23 billion business. While not entirely new, the idea of dressing little kids as if they were dolls has spawned a growth industry. The market is up by a third since 1987, according to the Port Washington, N.Y., NPD Group, which tracks consumer spending. That compares with 25% in women's wear.

"Babies are the BMWs of the Nineties," says Stanley Fridstein. That makes Fridstein happy. Sniffing the trend, he founded The Right Start catalog and retail operation, which specializes in children's products to make life easier for mom and dad.

Baby as status symbol. "It's 'Look at my child and see who this family is,'" explains James McNeal, a marketing professor at Texas A & M University who has been studying family spending habits for over 30 years. McNeal notes that as far back as the 1930s, parents tended to reach for status by spending money on soapflakes—to put clean clothes on the kids. It was okay if the fit was a bit loose and if a couple of generations of cousins had already used the stuff. It was enough that it was neat.

The baby business has demographics going for it as well as status. The U.S. population of kids under age 5 is at 23.6 million, up from 19.6 million in 1980. These babies are increasingly being born to dual-career couples who are waiting longer to have children and are thus able to spend more money on them once they arrive. The number of women who are 30 or older when their first child is born has more than quadrupled since 1970; the number of first children born to women over 40 more than doubled between 1984 and 1990, according to the National Center for Health Statistics.

And families have gotten smaller, making it easier to pamper the children, while working mom assuages some of her guilt by lavishing money on the child. "The girls' clothes just melt your heart. Since she's been born, I've hardly bought myself anything. I'd rather spend on her," says Texan Tracy Wolfe, a 34-year-old accountant and mother of 30-month-old Kelsey.

"I went nuts on layettes," says New Yorker Debra Kolitz, the mother of a 4-year-old and a 2-year-old. "Hundred-dollar blankets, $60 playsuits. My budget the first year? Not counting furniture? Between $5,000 and $10,000," says Kolitz.

In many ways Kolitz speaks for her generation of mothers: "It sounds sort of shocking, but it's true. You could probably do with a quarter of it, but it's so bloody appealing. I had my first child at 32. By the time they have that child, people like me are so caught up. These babies are so coveted that nothing is good enough."

Extravagant spending on babies' clothing, furniture, and accessories illustrates how consumers influence the marketing mix. It also shows how fascinating, yet baffling, consumer behavior can be. This chapter begins our explanation of why people buy. The chapter opens by developing a model that gives an overview of consumer behavior. It then explains the consumer decision-making process and the psychological factors that influence this process. Finally, it describes sociocultural factors in consumer behavior.

## What is Consumer Behavior?

Effective marketing must begin with careful evaluation of the problems faced by potential customers. This is because, according to the marketing concept, marketing efforts must focus on consumers' needs and provide answers to buyers' problems. A key to understanding consumers' needs and problems lies in the study of consumer behavior. A knowledge of consumer behavior gives the marketing manager information he or she can use to increase the chance of success in the marketplace.

**CONSUMER BEHAVIOR**
The activities people engage in when selecting, purchasing, and using products so as to satisfy needs and desires.

**Consumer behavior** consists of the activities people engage in when selecting, purchasing, and using products so as to satisfy needs and desires. Such activities involve mental and emotional processes, in addition to physical actions.[1] Consumer behavior includes both the behavior of ultimate consumers and the business behavior of organizational purchasers. However, many marketers prefer the term *buyer behavior* when discussing organizational purchasers.

## A Simple Start—Some Behavioral Fundamentals

**POINT TO EMPHASIZE**
The terms *consumer behavior* and *buyer behavior* are often used interchangeably. Both concern decision-making activities, but the former is used to refer to ultimate consumers and the latter to refer to organizational purchasers.

Our discussion of consumer behavior starts with a basic building block: Human behavior of any kind ($B$) is a function ($f$) of the interaction between the person ($P$) and the environment ($E$)—that is, $B = f(P,E)$. Simple though it is, this formula says it all.[2] Human behavior results when a person interacts with the environment. Whether behaviors are simple or complex, they flow from the person's interaction with environmental variables.

Exhibit 6–1 expands the basic formula for behavior, $B = f(P,E)$, into a more elaborate model of consumer decision making.[3] The model presents a decision-making process influenced by numerous interdependent forces rather than any single factor. Activities of marketers, such as television advertising, are environmental forces, as are social forces such as culture and family. The characteristics of the individual, such as attitudes and personality, may also influence the decision-making process at a particular moment in time.

## The Decision-Making Process

Marketers who study consumer behavior are ultimately interested in one central question: How are consumer choices made? One important determinant is the situation in which a decision is made. In regard to situation, there are three categories of consumer decision-making behavior: routinized response behavior, limited problem solving, and extensive problem solving.

**ROUTINIZED RESPONSE BEHAVIOR**
The least complex type of decision making, in which the consumer bases choices on past behavior and needs no other information.

**EXTENSIVE PROBLEM SOLVING**
In-depth search for and evaluation of alternative solutions to a problem.

**Routinized response behavior** is the least complex type of decision making. Here, the consumer has considerable experience in dealing with the situation at hand and thus needs no additional information to make a choice. To a cola drinker, purchasing a particular brand in a matter of seconds is a routine matter. The purchase of a new house by a consumer or a fleet of trucks by an organization, however, usually requires **extensive problem solving.** The process may take months to complete, with

EXHIBIT 6–1 A Consumer Behavior Model of How the Decision-Making Process Works and What Influences It

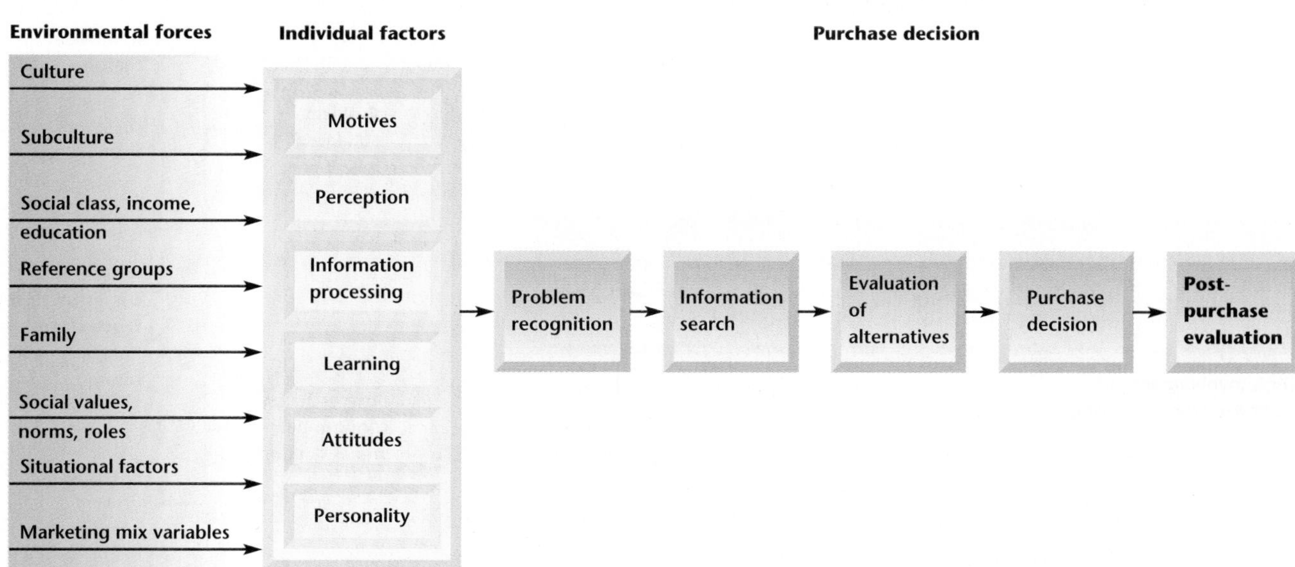


**LIMITED PROBLEM SOLVING**
An intermediate level of decision making between routinized and extensive problem solving in which the consumer has some purchasing experience but is unfamiliar with stores, brands, or price options.

**CONSUMER INVOLVEMENT**
The extent to which an individual attaches interest and importance to a product and is willing to expend energy in making a decision about purchasing the product.

ALTERNATIVE EXAMPLE
Women with concrete geese exhibit high consumer loyalty. They may buy as many as 50 outfits for their geese, sew the outfits, change them frequently, and wash and iron them. They may spray the clothes with Scotchgard to make them waterproof and weatherproof. All of this takes time and effort—primary aspects of consumer involvement. SOURCE: Gabriella Stern, "Pink Flamingos Are Out, but Here Come the Concrete Geese," *Wall Street Journal,* May 10, 1995, p. A1.

a series of identifiable decisions made at different points. **Limited problem solving** is an intermediate level of decision making in which the consumer has some previous purchasing experience but is unfamiliar with stores, brands, or price options.

The seeming "snap judgment" and the more extensive processes are more closely related than it may seem. The routine decision is likely to have been preceded by a series of trials and errors in which the consumer tested different brands of cola before becoming able to make a routine choice. Both the routine choice and the more extensive problem-solving procedures may involve the same series of steps completed at different speeds.

Related to these problem-solving situations is the consumer's involvement in the purchase. **Consumer involvement** has to do with the importance an individual attaches to a product and the level of energy he or she directs toward making a decision. High involvement occurs when the decision to be made relates to a high-interest product that is pertinent and relevant to the individual. The buying situation (buying a birthday gift, for example) and the product's price may also be factors in high involvement. A person who is highly involved with a product will exert more energy in decision making than a person whose involvement is low. Involvement may include both thoughts and feelings, so high involvement can mean thinking more strongly or feeling more strongly.[4] A new mother may be highly involved in the selection of a pediatrician but far less involved in the purchase of safety pins.

Exhibit 6–2 illustrates the steps in a high-involvement situation, a situation involving extensive problem solving. It also shows a low-involvement situation, which usually requires only a limited information search and no evaluation.

Let us look more closely at these steps, focusing primarily on situations in which extensive problem solving takes place. Remember, however, that (1) different consumers may pass through these steps at different rates of speed and (2) the five-step process need not be completed, even if it is begun. Many buyers take a long time to reach the purchase stage, if only because of a money shortage. Others do not reach the purchase stage at all because they evaluate alternatives and determine that no available alternatives are satisfactory.

EXHIBIT 6–2 Consumer Decision-Making Processses

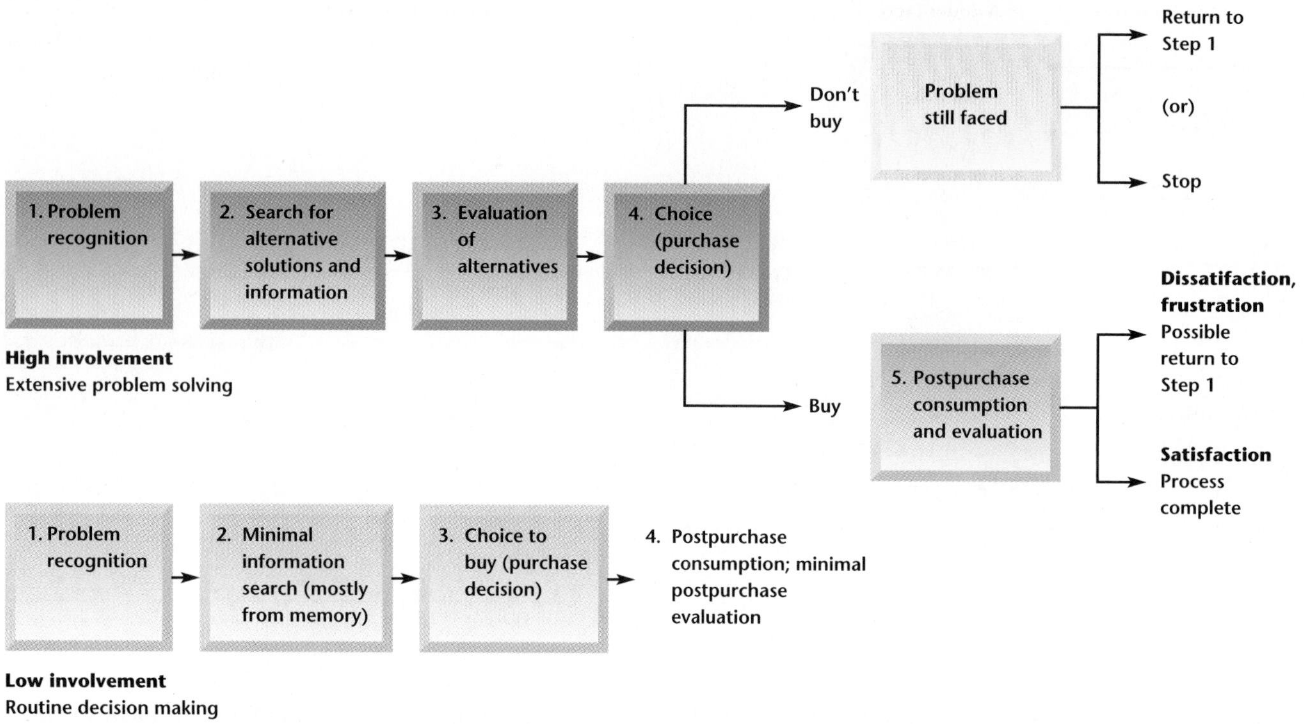

## Step 1: Problem Recognition

A tire blows out on a car being driven on an interstate highway. This is a case of instantaneous problem recognition. Alternatively, problem recognition can be a more complex, long-term process. A person whose car occasionally "dies" and isn't very shiny or attractive anymore may start to recognize a problem in the making. Perhaps when the new automobile models become available, she becomes aware that her needs are not completely satisfied. **Problem recognition** is this awareness that there is a discrepancy between an actual and a desired condition.

**PROBLEM RECOGNITION**
The awareness that there is a discrepancy between an actual and desired condition.

The person who has become aware that a new car is in order may take a bit of time getting one. However, a smoker who realizes that he is lighting his last cigarette is likely to make a purchase decision very rapidly, passing through Steps 2 and 3 of the decision-making process so quickly as to appear to have skipped them. For all practical purposes, these stages have been skipped, because the necessary information is stored in the consumer's memory. Marketers know that buyer behavior as routinized as this is difficult to alter. A buyer who devotes some time and consideration to decision making opens up more opportunities for effective marketers to appeal to him and to offer a product that may satisfy his need. Of course, marketers of the most popular brands of cigarettes, gum, and candy are happy that their regular customers have developed a routinized approach to solving problems.

ALTERNATIVE EXAMPLE
Many marketers use loyalty marketing, such as frequent-buyer plans, to encourage consumers to avoid steps in decision making. After making an initial purchase, consumers who use frequent-buyer plans can jump from problem recognition to purchase. To get consumers to engage in more "routinized purchasing," or brand loyalty, marketers are rewarding them with bonuses based on steady or frequent purchases of their products. SOURCE: Alice Z. Cuneo, "Savvy Frequent-Buyer Plans Build on a Loyal Base," *Advertising Age*, March 20, 1995, p. S10.

## Step 2: Search for Alternative Solutions and Information

Even the habitual buyer of Snickers candy bars is very likely to consider, however briefly, some other choices before selecting Snickers as usual. However, where highly involved buyers are purchasing a product for the first time or making a purchase that could have major financial, social, or other consequences, the search for alternatives and information about those alternatives is most easily observed.

**PERCEIVED RISK**
Consumers' uncertainty about the consequences of their future actions; the perception on the part of a consumer that a product may not do what it is expected to do.

That buyers in such positions behave as they do is explained by the theory of **perceived risk**—the perception that there is a chance the product may not do what it is expected to do. These consumers perceive that their actions may produce unpleasant consequences that cannot be anticipated with anything approaching certainty.[5]

Several types of risk are encountered when expensive clothing is purchased, for example: Is the clothing too expensive? Will it be durable? What will my friends say? Will I look good? Exhibit 6–3 identifies several types of risk that may concern potential buyers. The accompanying Competitive Strategy feature describes how one marketer solved a problem of perceived risk.

**INFORMATION SEARCH**
An internal or external search for information carried out by the consumer to reduce uncertainty and provide a basis for evaluating alternatives.

Buyers seek to reduce feelings of uncertainty by acquiring information. They may read advertisements. They may take family members or friends shopping with them. They may want the salesperson or some expert to tell them that the product is well made and a very popular item. In other words, consumers engage in **information search** to acquire information that will reduce uncertainty and provide the basis for evaluation of alternatives. Information search may be internal or external.

DISCUSSION CONSIDERATION
Ask students to describe the risk associated with the purchase of an auto airbag, toothpaste, and a birthday present for a girlfriend or boyfriend.

Internal search is the mental activity associated with retrieval of information from memory. After an individual has recognized a problem, the first step in solving it is to scan memory for pertinent information. Information stored in memory may have come from prior purchase behavior, advertising, conversations with friends, or other experiences. When the buying situation facing the consumer differs from past situations, internal search may not provide enough information.

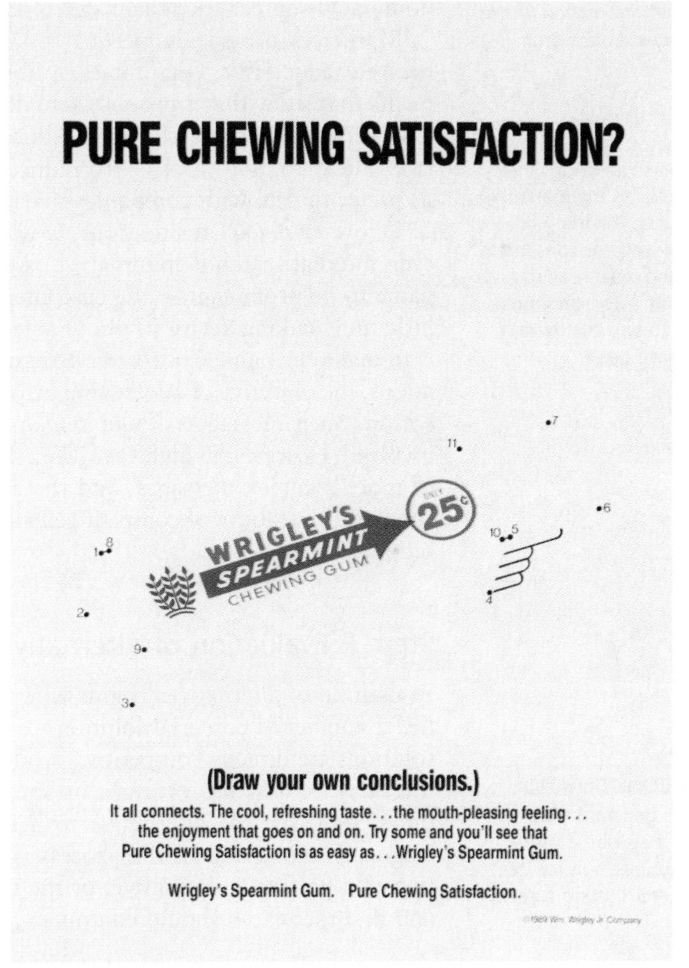
PURE CHEWING SATISFACTION?
WRIGLEY'S SPEARMINT CHEWING GUM
25¢
(Draw your own conclusions.)
It all connects. The cool, refreshing taste. . .the mouth-pleasing feeling. . .
the enjoyment that goes on and on. Try some and you'll see that
Pure Chewing Satisfaction is as easy as. . .Wrigley's Spearmint Gum.
Wrigley's Spearmint Gum. Pure Chewing Satisfaction.

The decision-making process is often shaped by the level of consumer involvement. For most people, chewing gum is a low-involvement product that is routinely purchased. This advertisement for Wrigley's Spearmint Gum attempts to get the reader to be more involved with the advertisement and to think more about the product.

ALTERNATIVE EXAMPLE
The goal of many investors is to avoid risk. A traditional rule of thumb is to buy gold in times of high inflation as a hedge. A recent study found that gold did perform well in periods of high inflation but was highly risky because of fluctuations in price. Surprisingly, gold was found to have a respectable return when inflation was low, with much less risk. How will seasoned and novice investors respond to this? Are they likely to begin buying gold in periods of low inflation? Sometimes it's hard to get people to change their risk-avoidance behaviors—even with new information. SOURCE: "Buy Gold When Inflation Is Low," *Business Week,* May 22, 1995, p. 34.

**EXHIBIT 6–3** The Types of Risk That Concern Potential Buyers

| TYPE OF RISK | TYPICAL CONCERN |
|---|---|
| Performance risk | The brand may not perform its function well; it may not work; it may break down. |
| Financial risk | The buyer may lose money; pay too much; miss buying something else. |
| Physical risk | The product may be harmful or unhealthy; it may cause injury. |
| Social risk | Friends, relatives, or significant others may not approve of the purchase. |
| Time-loss risk | Maintenance time or time required to return the product to the place of purchase may be excessive. |

DISCUSSION CONSIDERATION

Ask students to list everything they currently know about their top choice for a starting career position. Are they comfortable that they know enough now to perform well in an interview? What information would they seek in an external search process?

POINT TO EMPHASIZE

Providing numerous avenues by which consumers can obtain information is essential in the marketing of many products. Toll-free hotlines provide an easy way for consumers to learn anything from how to cook a turkey (even at 3 A.M. on a holiday) to where to find the nearest authorized service dealer.

External search—the gathering of information from sources other than memory—may require time, effort, and money. External search is most likely to occur in high-involvement situations and tends to be quite limited in low-involvement situations. Consumers gather external information from experience (such as shopping), personal sources (such as friends), public media (such as newspaper articles), and marketer-dominated sources (such as magazine advertisements).

Marketers provide numerous sources of information to satisfy the consumer's need to reduce risk. Guarantees, a liberal return policy, store displays or advertisements that show that a product actually delivers what is promised, and a pledge that "We service what we sell" may reduce the consumer's uncertainty about perceived risk. These are not "tricks." To reduce our chances of injury, damage, or loss, all of us prefer to deal with companies that give us such assurances.

In low-involvement situations, in which external search is almost nonexistent (and even internal search is minimal), it is extremely important for the company's brand name to be prominent in the customer's memory. Thus, assuming consumers spend little time making decisions about soft drink choices, an effective marketing strategy is to make the name Coca-Cola prominent in consumers' minds. Often, in such situations, the objective of advertising is to create awareness and familiarity through repetition. Such messages should remain simple, because the consumer is not highly involved. However, in high-involvement situations, consumers may be more receptive to more complex messages, and the advertising may emphasize information about comparative features of competitive brands, stressing unique benefits of the advertiser's brand.

## Step 3: Evaluation of Alternatives

DISCUSSION CONSIDERATION

Ask students to generate a list of the choice criteria they would use to choose (1) a business suit for job interviews or (2) a starting career position.

Evaluation of alternatives begins when an information search has clarified or identified a number of potential solutions to the consumer's problem. Often the alternative solutions are directly competitive products. An alternative to a Vermont skiing vacation may be a skiing vacation in Squaw Valley or St. Moritz, for example. Other times, however, the alternative to a skiing vacation in Vermont is a new station wagon. The outcome of the process is usually the ranking of alternatives, the selection of a preferred alternative, or the decision that there is no acceptable alternative and that the search should continue.

**COMPETITIVE STRATEGY: WHAT WENT RIGHT?**

## *You'll Be Brilliant*

Armstrong World Industries, a company that markets sheet-vinyl floor coverings to do-it-yourselfers, learned that women were the catalysts in the residential floor-covering purchase decision but men did the actual installation. Through its marketing research, Armstrong discovered that a high perceived risk—a fear of the first cut—was associated with the purchase. When interviewers asked people who examined but walked away from an in-store display why they did not buy the product, nearly 60 percent said they feared botching the job.

Trim Fit
Go on, cut. You'll be brilliant.
Armstrong guarantees it.
Install your new Armstrong sheet vinyl floor with a Trim and Fit kit, and if you goof while cutting or fitting, your Armstrong retailer will replace both the flooring and the kit.
Free. That's the Fail-Safe Guarantee. Just see your local home center or building supply retailer for details.
Armstrong


Armstrong developed a marketing strategy to combat this fear. A "Trim and Fit" kit was introduced and promoted with the message "Go on, cut. You'll be brilliant." When retailers were slow to push the kit because of its small retail markup, Armstrong added a sure-fire risk reducer—a "fail safe" guarantee. If the do-it-yourselfer made a mistake, the company would replace the floor covering at no cost. The biggest barrier to the purchase had been substantially removed. The strategy was a giant success.

**CHOICE CRITERIA**
The critical attributes a consumer uses to evaluate product alternatives.

In analyzing possible purchases, the prospective buyer considers the appropriate choice criteria. **Choice criteria** are the critical attributes the consumer uses to evaluate alternatives. For an automobile tire, product features (such as mileage, warranty, and brand name) and price might be typical choice criteria. Which choice criteria are used depends on the consumer and the situation. For example, some people who need automobile tires may buy them at the neighborhood service station even if prices there are higher than at other places. They may feel that the time saved is worth the extra dollars spent. They may know the local station owner and want to "give him some business." They may be trying to keep on the station owner's good side just in case they ever need emergency help. Or they may want to deal with a local seller so they can complain if something goes wrong.

DISCUSSION CONSIDERATION
Many buyers of computers don't know much about the technical aspects of these products, which means manufacturers can't focus on product attributes. So what do they put in their ads? Ask students to look for computer ads to determine the content. Many of those ads focus on what the computer can do. Ask students what else manufacturers might stress.

Many buyers appear not to want to evaluate too many factors when choosing among alternatives. The average person looking for a new car does not want (or cannot understand) the kinds of facts and figures mechanical engineers might be able to provide. The typical car buyer wants very simple facts: The car "looks good"; the car dealer is a "good guy." The buyer does not want an analysis of the car's aerodynamics or an art expert's opinion of its looks. In fact, Honda's "We make it simple" promotions were based on the finding that many consumers are confused about optional accessories and mechanical details. Offering only cars with "standard options" simplifies the choice criteria and the buying situation.

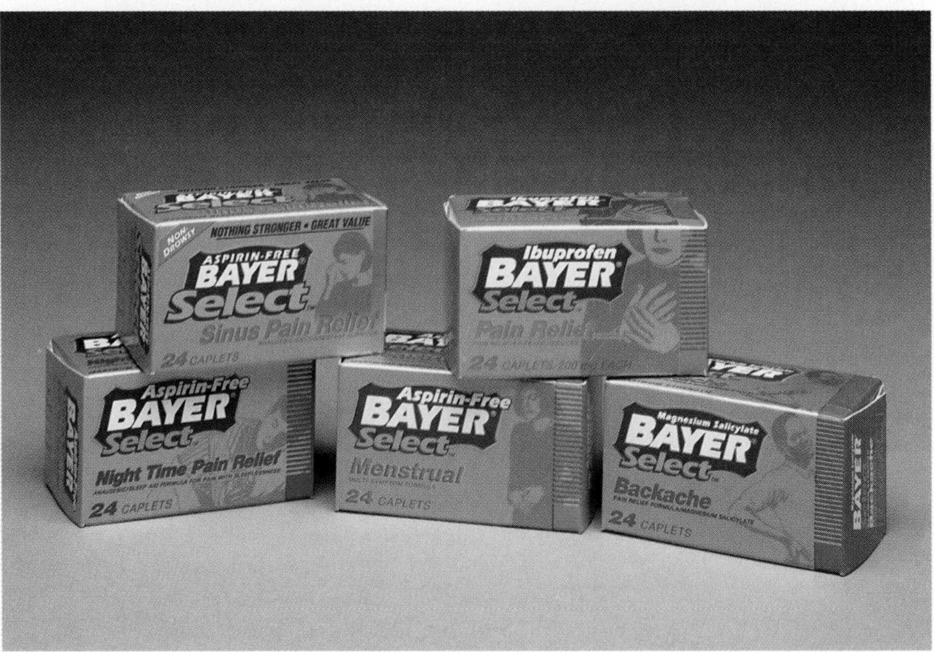


Bayer's consumer research indicated that consumers believed they had to be a chemist to figure out which product was right for them. Bayer used this knowledge about the consumer decision-making process when it developed Bayer Select pain relief products. The new Bayer products are symptom-specific, which simplifies the decision-making process for consumers. The product has been successful because consumers appreciate the fact that the company has made it simple for them to choose.

## Step 4: Choice—Purchase Decisions and the Act of Buying

Sooner or later the prospective buyer must make a purchase decision or choose not to buy any of the alternatives available. Assuming the decision maker has decided which brand to purchase and where it will be purchased, the mechanics of the purchase must be worked out. The actual purchase behavior may be simple, especially if the buyer has either a credit card or a checkbook with a sufficient balance. The decision to buy can bring with it a few other related decisions: Should the buyer get new valve stems too? How about a lifetime wheel-balancing agreement with the seller?

## Step 5: Postpurchase Consumption and Evaluation

**PURCHASE SATISFACTION**
The feeling on the part of the consumer that the decision to buy was appropriate.

Consumption, naturally, follows purchase. If the decision maker is also the user, the matter of **purchase satisfaction** (or dissatisfaction) remains. In some cases, satisfaction is immediate, as when the buyer chews the just-bought gum or feels pleased that the decision-making process is over. Frequently, after making a purchase, we think to ourselves or tell others, "Well, I bought a great set of tires today." Patting ourselves on the back in this way is an attempt to assure satisfaction. We are telling ourselves that we are pleased with the purchase because our expectations have been confirmed. In this case, marketing has achieved its goal of consumer satisfaction.[6]

However, the opposite can occur—we can feel uneasy over the purchase. Are the tires good on snow? Has someone acted surprised that we bought this brand instead of that one? Second thoughts can create an uneasy feeling, a sensation that the decision-making process may have yielded the wrong decision. These feelings of uncertainty can be analyzed in terms of the theory of cognitive dissonance.[7]

**COGNITIVE DISSONANCE**
In terms of consumer behavior, the negative feelings that may occur after a commitment to purchase has been made. It describes the tension that results from holding two conflicting ideas or beliefs at the same time.

In the context of consumer behavior, **cognitive dissonance** is a psychologically uncomfortable postpurchase feeling. More specifically, it refers to the negative feelings that can follow a commitment to purchase. It results from the fact that people do not like to hold two or more conflicting beliefs or ideas at the same time. Suppose the car owner has bought the tires and has left the shop; there's no money back now. Should he or she have bought Michelin tires instead, even though the price was a bit higher? Dissonance theory describes such feelings as a sense of psychic tension, a ten-

T, stamps, M, and E. Yet we read "TIME" because of our tendency to mentally "fill things in" or "finish things off." This aspect of perception is called **closure.** Many advertisements make use of this concept by not showing the product, showing only part of it, or showing only its shadow. The viewer supposedly becomes more involved with the advertisement through the process of closure. A person who can't perceive closure will be annoyed by the advertisement, so the closure idea is used only when the product is very well known and the advertiser is sure that the viewer can complete the picture.

**CLOSURE**
An element of perception by which an observer mentally completes an incomplete stimulus.

Selective perception may involve selective exposure, selective attention, or selective interpretation. **Selective exposure** exists because no individual is exposed to all stimuli. No one sees every advertisement. For example, many cable TV subscribers choose to block out the reception of certain channels. Thus, one way consumers avoid stimuli is simply to avoid exposure to them. This is selective exposure.

**SELECTIVE EXPOSURE**
The principle describing the fact that no individual is exposed to all stimuli.

Even if individuals are exposed to information, they may not want to receive certain messages, so they screen these stimuli out of their experience. They pay no attention—at least, no conscious attention—to the stimuli. This is **selective attention.** For example, a person who has just purchased a new Sony TV does not want to hear an advertisement announcing that Sony's prices have just been cut in half. The person may not pay attention to such advertisements.

**SELECTIVE ATTENTION**
A perceptual screening whereby a person does not attend to a particular stimulus.

Finally, even a person who pays attention may distort a newly encountered message that is incompatible with his or her established values or attitudes. This is **selective interpretation.** The owner of a Ford pickup truck is likely to distort information detailing why Dodge Rams are better trucks than Fords, for example. Looking carefully at perception teaches the truth of the old adage, "It's not what you (the marketer) say, it's what they (consumers) hear."

**SELECTIVE INTERPRETATION**
A perceptual screening device whereby a person distorts a stimulus that is incompatible with his or her values or attitudes.

There is not much the marketer can do to overcome selective exposure other than to carefully plan the placement of advertisements so that target customers will be reached. Selective attention may be overcome with attention-getting messages. The size of an advertisement, the colors used, the novelty of the pictures included, and many other **stimulus factors** have been shown to have considerable effects on the amount of attention a viewer will give an advertisement.

**STIMULUS FACTOR**
A characteristic of a stimulus—for example, the size, colors, or novelty of a print advertisement—that affects perception.

More subtly, an advertisement may gain increased attention by featuring aspects that speak to the viewer's needs, background, or hopes, because perception is also influenced by **individual factors.** Generally a full-page color advertisement will attract more attention than a quarter-page advertisement in black and white. However, a black-and-white advertisement offering the hope of "a better appearance" to balding men is likely to attract a lot of attention among its target group, balding men, because they are highly involved. Similarly, advertisements promising aid for losing weight will be noticed by people who need this help, even if others think the advertisements lack attention-getting features. Many rules of advertising (use color, don't be wordy) are profitably broken when the target consumers are willing to devote attention to a problem that means something to them. This illustrates a basic fact about the perception of advertising: Consumers pay attention to advertisements when the products featured interest them.

**INDIVIDUAL FACTOR**
With reference to perception, a characteristic of a person that affects how the person perceives a stimulus.

POINT TO EMPHASIZE
To ensure that students internalize the message, remind them that they are quite capable of "tuning out" an instructor to consider their weekend plans or an exam next period. Selective perception implies that we choose the stimuli that will receive our attention.

**Perception and Brand Image Marketing** Product distinctions often exist in the minds of consumers and not in the products themselves. The symbolic meaning associated with brand distinctions, developed as a result of selective perception, is known as brand image. A **brand image** is a complex of symbols and meanings associated with a brand. Over the years, for example, General Mills has established a strong image for its Betty Crocker brand. The image is one of dependability and honesty—valuable images for a food product. There never was a real Betty Crocker, but the General Mills products are good and reliable, just like Betty's image. Research has shown that brand image can be the key factor in a buying decision.

**BRAND IMAGE**
The complex of symbols and meanings associated with a brand.

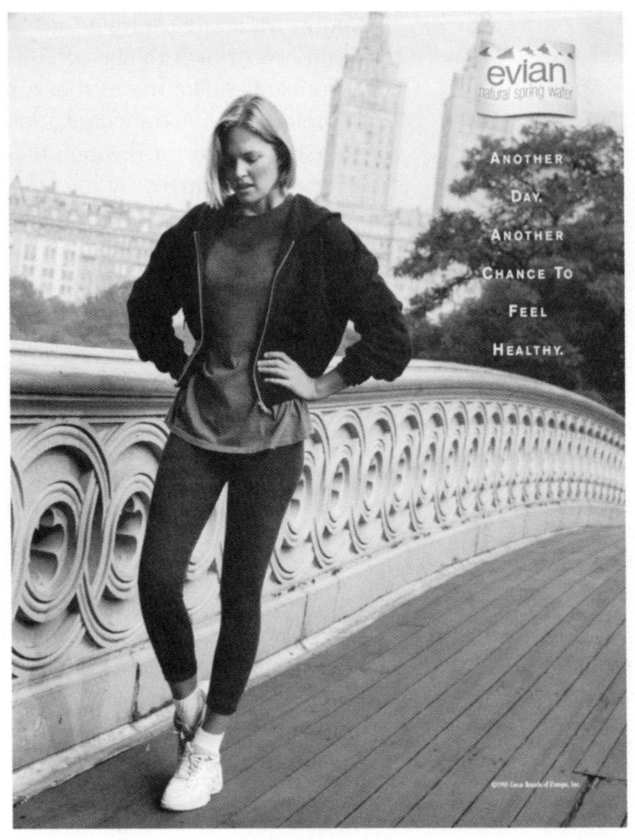


This Evian advertisement shows how stimulus factors—a colorful label on a black-and-white background—can be used to attract attention. Joggers are likely to pay even more attention to the advertisement because individual factors are also at play. The advertisement speaks to the needs of individuals who are concerned about a healthy lifestyle.

DISCUSSION CONSIDERATION

Personal need or arousal affects the vigilance of the selective perceptual processes. Marketers use such stimulus factors as color, contrast, novelty, movement, and intensity to increase the probability that their stimuli will be perceived. How might stimulus factors designed to attract the attention of 44- to 65-year-olds differ from those for the under-20 age group?

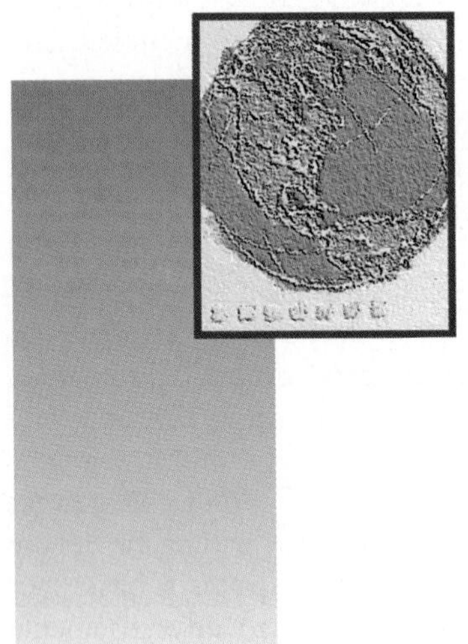

## FOCUS ON GLOBAL COMPETITION

### *Copying in Korea*

A package of gum sold in South Korea has a bright yellow wrapper, bold black lettering, and small red design at one end. It may look like Juicy Fruit gum, but it isn't. Most likely it's Juicy & Fresh gum from Lotte Confectionery Company. Or it could be Tong Yang, which has a very similar package. Then again, it could be Hearty Juicy, which mimics all three in hopes that consumers will perceive it to be similar to the other brands.

In South Korea, goods copying American brands are everywhere. Even some of the biggest companies imitate the world's best products in hope that consumers will perceive the copycat brands as similar to the originals. In supermarkets, Tie laundry detergent is packaged in orange boxes with a whirlpool design that differs little from Tide's. This brand is produced by Lucky Goldstar Group, one of South Korea's largest companies. Because of widespread copying like this, protecting intellectual property worldwide is a major problem for global marketers. ■

It has been shown in formal research that for a number of products—among them cola and beer—consumers cannot distinguish between brands once the labels have been removed. That *perception* of reality is extremely important in brand image marketing is demonstrated in various "taste test" ads we see on television. Diet 7Up, for example, humorously portrays a blindfolded man nervously awaiting a firing squad. After taking a "taste test" in which he, of course, cannot read the label, the blindfolded man indicates he prefers Diet 7Up to Diet Coke.[11]

**Subliminal Perception** Can advertisers send us messages of which we are not consciously aware? In the 1950s, there was considerable controversy about the possibility

POINT TO EMPHASIZE

Subliminal messages are not illegal in every state. Ethical concerns and the repercussions of disclosure if the practice were used prevent most firms from considering subliminal advertisements. However, firms do purchase subliminal tapes meant to deter shoplifting. The resulting reduction in loss is probably due to greater management vigilance (because of expenditures for the tapes) rather than effectiveness of the imbedded message.

of this so-called subliminal advertising. In a movie theater "experiment," the phrases "eat popcorn" and "drink Coca-Cola" were flashed on the screen so rapidly that people were unaware of them. Sales in the movie theater were reported to have increased 58 percent for popcorn and 18 percent for Coca-Cola. Psychologists, alarmed at this result, seriously studied the "experiment" and concluded that it had lacked scientific rigor. Subsequent investigations of *subliminal perception* (perception of stimuli at a subconscious level) suggested that advertisers trying to achieve "perception without awareness" would face technical problems so great that the public need not be apprehensive about the possibility. Subliminal stimuli are simply too weak to be effective. For example, only very short messages can be communicated, and the influence of selective perception tends to be stronger than the weak stimulus factors.[12]

It is interesting to note that the public frequently misuses the word *subliminal.* Symbolism is not subliminal, nor are embedded messages "hidden" in pictures. Neither symbolism nor embedded messages are perceived at an unconscious level—that is, without the individual's knowing of their existence. The picture shown in Exhibit 6–7 allegedly hides an embedded "subliminal" message. Can you see it? If you can, of course, you have not perceived it subliminally.

DISCUSSION CONSIDERATION

To which brands are you absolutely brand loyal—that is, for which brands will you accept no substitutes? Describe how you learned to like or trust this brand.

## Learning

If you were asked to identify a brand of light bulbs, what brand would you name? Would you say General Electric? If so, you'd be agreeing with 86 percent of consumers asked this question. Furthermore, 55 percent of consumers said they would

Guess Jeans are purchased not only for their high-quality construction but also because of the brand's sexy image.

**EXHIBIT 6–7**

Is There a "Subliminal" Message Embedded in This Ad?

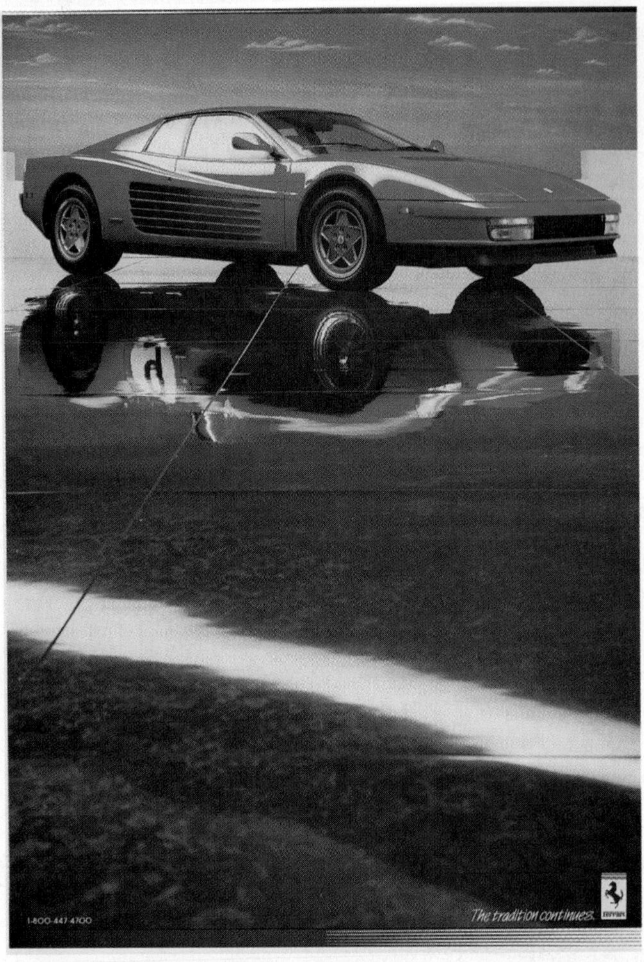


**POINT TO EMPHASIZE**

Cognitive learning results from the decision-making process whereby consumers actively acquire information to solve a problem. Behavioral learning concerns the pairing of a stimulus and a response or the use of reinforcement in operant conditioning to alter the probability of future behavior.

**LEARNING**

Any change in behavior or cognition that results from experience or interpretation of experience.

**MEMORY**

The information-processing function involving the storage and retrieval of information.

pick GE the next time they bought a light bulb. Most consumers have learned to be brand-loyal to GE light bulbs. How does such learning take place?

**How Learning Occurs** Learning occurs as a result of experience or of mental activity associated with experience. Thus, the expression "older and wiser" is not far from the mark, because older people have had the opportunity to learn from many experiences. Experiences related to product usage, shopping, and exposure to advertisements and other aspects of marketing add to consumers' banks of knowledge and influence their habits.

**Learning** is defined as any change in behavior or cognition resulting from experience or interpretation of experience. Suppose a package or display—say, for a crayon that can be cleaned away with soap and water—attracts the attention of a shopper, and the shopper gives the product a try. If the crayon works to the customer's satisfaction, she learns through experience that the new product is acceptable. If it does not, she learns that fact instead. This knowledge becomes information in the consumer's memory. **Memory** is the information-processing function that allows people to store and retrieve information.

A type of learning called *social learning* can occur by observation of the consequences of others' behavior. For example, a younger child observes an older sibling's punishment and learns to avoid that punishment by avoiding the situation that brought it about. Similarly, buyers often purchase products that were recommended by other people who have used these products. Much television advertising is based on the idea that social learning occurs when we watch others and model their behavior. We observe the satisfaction that others, perhaps role models like Michael Jordan, derive from a product; as we do, we learn by interpreting their experiences.

**OPERANT CONDITIONING**
The process by which reinforcement of a behavior results in repetition of that behavior.

**REINFORCEMENT**
Reward; reinforcement strengthens a stimulus-response relationship.

Many theories attempt to explain exactly how learning occurs. All of the widely accepted theories acknowledge the great importance of experience. One important viewpoint focuses on **operant conditioning,** a form of learning believed to occur when a response, such as a purchase, is followed by a **reinforcement,** or reward. Exhibit 6–8 illustrates the consumer learning process according to this theory. Here, some aspect of the product provides the stimulus, and the purchase is the consumer's response to the stimulus. If the product proves to be satisfactory, the consumer receives a reward—a reinforcement. The fact is that the purchase is made in the hope that satisfaction will follow. When it does, the effect is to strengthen (reinforce) the stimulus-response relationship. Learning takes place as this phenomenon occurs over and over.

**DISCUSSION CONSIDERATION**
Marketers often use stimulus-response approaches to pair music with products. What advertisements can you recall that use themes you like or dislike? Does the like or dislike carry over to the product in the ad?

Some theories of learning stress the importance of repetition in the development of habits. For example, the more you are exposed to a television message such as Duracell's claim "You can't top the copper top," the more likely it is that you will learn the content of the sales message. Repeatedly rewarding a behavior strengthens the stimulus-response relationship. More simply, repeated satisfaction creates buying habits and loyal customers. (See Exhibit 6–8.)

**Learning Theories and Marketing** Most learning theories are compatible with marketing activities and marketing's key philosophy, the marketing concept. The theories tell us that positive rewards or experiences lead to repeated behaviors. The marketing concept stresses consumer satisfaction, which leads to repeat purchases and long-term profitability for the organization.

## Attitudes

**ATTITUDE**
An individual's general affective, cognitive, and intentional responses toward a given object, issue, or person.

An **attitude** comprises an individual's general affective, cognitive, and intentional responses toward a given object, issue, or person.[13] People learn attitudes. In terms of marketing, they learn to respond in a consistently favorable or unfavorable man-

**EXHIBIT 6–8**

Effects of Reinforcement on Consumer Behavior: First Trial and Repeat Purchase Situations

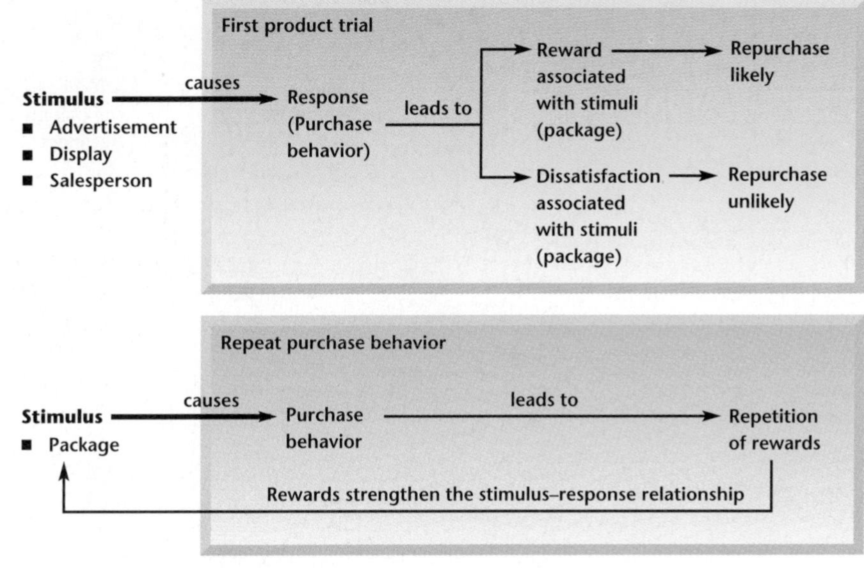

ner with respect to products, stores, advertising, and people.[14] Notice that because attitudes are learned it is possible to change them. This is a goal of much promotional activity.

DISCUSSION CONSIDERATION
Consider the last impulse purchase you made. What emotion were you feeling at the moment you decided to purchase the product?

DISCUSSION CONSIDERATION
Are there products toward which you have a negative attitude? Why?

ALTERNATIVE EXAMPLE
Sales of "attitude wear" are growing—especially among young people. Also known as verbiage wear, attitude wear adds in-your-face verbiage to slogans on T-shirts (for example, "Slap it like you hate it/Roller Hockey and Starter—It's about team.") Large companies like Nike, Reebok, and Starter are planning to produce attitude wear of their own. Small companies like No Fear can also enter this market. So what are you gonna put on your shirt? SOURCE: Jack Neff, "In-Your-Face to On-Your-Body," *Advertising Age,* March 13, 1995, p. 28.

**The ABC Model: A Three-Part Theory of Attitudes** The ABC model is the traditional way to view attitudes. In this view, an attitude has three parts. The A component is the affective, or emotional, component. It reflects a person's feelings toward the object. Is the brand good or bad? Is it desirable? Likable? The B component is the behavioral component, which reflects intended and actual behaviors toward the object. This component is a predisposition to action. The C component is the cognitive component. It involves all the consumer's beliefs, knowledge, and thoughts about the object—the consumer's perception of the product's attributes or characteristics. Is it durable? Expensive? Suitable as a gift for Aunt Mary? This model is graphically portrayed at the top of Exhibit 6–9.

**Modern Attitude Theory Stresses Affect** In recent years, attitude theory has changed. The current practice is to define attitude as affect. Attitude is thus seen as comprising feelings about products or brands. The shift in view does not discount the importance of cognitive or behavioral components but simply does not define them as components of attitude. Indeed, as Exhibit 6–9 shows, in this view attitudes are based on cognitive beliefs. Behavioral intentions are in turn influenced by both cognitions and attitude (affect).[15]

**How Do Attitudes Influence Buying Behavior?** Let's examine a consumer's attitude toward Kodak cameras? The consumer may hold several cognitive beliefs about the product: that it takes clear pictures and that its features make it easy to use, for example. She may have certain feelings about the camera as well—for example, she may feel that Kodak is a good brand or that the Kodak is desirable because it is the "official camera" of the Olympics. In the current view, these feelings make up her attitude—which may create a predisposition to buy the product.

EXHIBIT 6–9
Two Views about the Nature of Attitudes

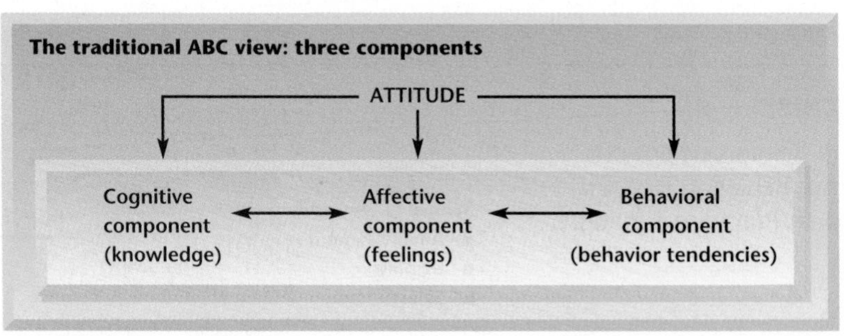


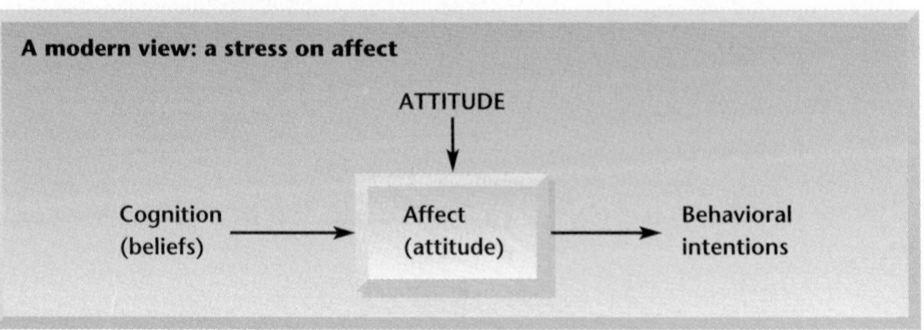

Note that the consumer's attitude serves as a general indicator of behavior toward the attitudinal object. That is, the consumer will consider buying the product—she will not necessarily buy it. A favorable attitude toward a particular brand may not result in purchase of that brand. After all, consumers have attitudes toward competing brands as well. Furthermore, attitudes are not the sole determinant of behavior. Situational, financial, and motivational forces, as well as attitudes, influence behavior.

Because attitudes are situational, their effects are controlled by circumstances. Most Americans have very favorable attitudes toward Rolls Royce and Mercedes automobiles, yet not many own one of these cars. Many people admire—that is, have attitudes that favor—mansions surrounded by well-tended formal gardens. Few people live in such places, however. Attitudes may also be affected by other attitudes. People who don't like winter weather will probably not like snow skiing, or buy a snowmobile, or plan to live out their days in Minnesota.

Thus, it is difficult to predict a specific behavior from an attitude toward a single object. Nevertheless, in many situations, there is consistency between attitudes and behavior. For example, we may think that the personnel are friendly in a certain department store. We may also think that the store is clean and the prices are reasonable. These beliefs may lead us to have a positive attitude toward the store. In turn, our purchasing behavior may be consistent with our attitude. Much managerial strategy is based on the assumption that, all other things being equal, a positive attitude toward a store or brand will predispose the consumer to shop at the store or use the brand.

POINT TO EMPHASIZE

Although personality theories are intuitively appealing, it is difficult to clearly differentiate consumer behavior for many products based on this variable alone. Introverts and extroverts may both purchase Crest toothpaste or a Ford automobile, for example. Personality is best used to supplement other segmentation variables.

## Personality and Self-Concept

We have been discussing several individual differences in consumer behavior. Where do such differences come from? Many individual differences in human behavior are related to personality and self-concept.

**PERSONALITY**

The fundamental disposition of an individual; the distinctive patterns of thought, emotion, and behavior that characterize an individual's response to the situations of his or her life.

**What Is Personality?** Like many psychological terms, the word *personality* is used in nontechnical ways in our everyday vocabularies. When Bill says, "Mike gets along well with others because he has a pleasing personality," the word is not used technically. In consumer behavior theory, **personality** is the fundamental disposition of an individual and the distinctive patterns of thought, emotion, and behavior that characterize that individual's response to the situations of his or her life. Personality especially refers to the most dominant characteristics, or traits, of a person, such as introversion and extroversion. Many personality traits—such as dominance, gregariousness, self-confidence, masculinity, prestige-consciousness, conservativeness, and independence—have been identified. We might expect such traits to affect behavior. Introverts and extroverts might be expected to purchase different types of automobiles, for example.

**SELF-CONCEPT**

The individual's perception and appraisal of himself or herself.

**Self-Concept: How We See Ourselves** The term **self-concept** refers to an individual's perception and appraisal of himself or herself. Of course, the appraisal of others plays a part in this. Ultimately, though, the self-concept is the person's own picture of who he or she is (the real self) and whom he or she would like to be or is in the process of becoming (the ideal self). According to self-concept theory, consumers shop at stores and purchase goods and services that reflect and enhance their self-concepts.

DISCUSSION CONSIDERATION

The sports and fitness industry emphasizes themes of improving self-concept. What messages do you recall that focus on an aspirational self-concept, like the army's "Be all that you can be."

**Personality Theory Evaluated** The hypothesized relationship of personality (including self-concept) to buying and other aspects of consumer behavior has been extensively studied. The results indicate that the predictive power of personality to explain why one brand is chosen over another is inconsequential and that marketing managers can make only scant use of personality in formulating their marketing strategies. That is, investigating personality in isolation from other factors, such as demographic characteristics, is not an effective method of predicting specific consumer behavior.[16] Nevertheless, the intuitive appeal of a relationship between personality and consumer behavior leads some marketing practitioners to base strategy on notions associated with personality theory.

Problems with the practical application of personality research led to the development of psychographic profiles of consumers, discussed in Chapter 8. The focus of personality theory in psychology is on the person as a person, whereas consumer behavior theory focuses on the person as a consumer, emphasizing traits related closely to day-to-day consumer activities. This seems to be a more appropriate way for marketing managers to implement ideas about individual differences in consumers.

## Interpersonal Influences on the Decision-Making Process

ALTERNATIVE EXAMPLE

The eighties emphasized materialism and acquisition, but the nineties appear to be a return to the sacred. "It's a reaction to the '80s . . . and feeling the world is spinning out of control, the feeling of 'does anyone have any values anymore.'" Sales of religious items are up. Does all this marketing activity relate to a "real" change in values or a "return" to values? Have our values changed? Are we becoming more religious? SOURCE: Cyndee Miller, "'People Want to Believe in Something,'" *Marketing News,* December 5, 1994, p. 1.

We have examined many individual factors that influence the decision-making process. But, as Exhibit 6–1 showed, environmental influences also exert an effect. In this section, we focus on sociocultural aspects of the environment. The lives of consumers are subject to countless sociocultural forces, including those created by the culture, the subculture, and various groups. Sociologists refer to these forces as *interpersonal influences.*

### Social Values, Norms, and Roles

People hold certain social values, follow certain norms, and fill certain roles. As we will see, values, norms, and roles have various sources, from the overall culture to much smaller social groups.

**Social Values** Chapter 3 defined social values as the goals that a society views as important. As such, they reflect the moral order of a society and give meaning to social life. For example, winning is a value considered important by our sports-oriented society.

ALTERNATIVE EXAMPLE

Sales of home hair coloring kits are up as marketers such as L'Oreal try to convince females aged 12–25 to change their hair color frequently. But a surprising boom is occurring in sales of hair coloring to men—traditional holdouts. In 1994, sales of hair dye to men grew by 30 percent to over $63 million. Is the norm that men don't dye their hair about to disappear? SOURCE: Pat Sloan, "Hair Coloring Tints Sales a Green $1B," *Advertising Age,* February 20, 1995, p. 10.

**Norms** Norms are rules of conduct to be followed in particular circumstances. Behavior appropriate to one situation may be inappropriate to another; thus, norms are "situation specific." In the United States, the general norm is for pedestrians to avoid touching each other. Jostling and crowding together are to be avoided in most circumstances, and persons not following this norm are rewarded with angry stares or comments. At a parade, however, crowding and pushing are more acceptable. The norm changes with the situation.

Norms, like values, strongly affect our lifestyles and our day-to-day behavior patterns, including consumer behavior. The increasingly commonplace norm of not smoking in certain public places influences the planning of service providers such as restaurants, airports, and shopping malls. Another example of a norm is the custom of buying a diamond engagement ring. Many couples would not even consider choosing between, for example, a ruby ring and an emerald ring.

Norms vary among cultures. The Japanese attending the Tokyo Disneyland are far more restrained than Americans attending Disneyland in this country. For example, passengers on the rides in Japan do not raise their hands in the air and scream as do their American counterparts. It is not the accepted norm.

**Roles** Any social institution, from the smallest group to the largest organization, creates and defines roles for its members. These, like norms, are customary ways of doing things. **Roles** define appropriate behavior patterns in reference to other roles. Thus, the role of son or daughter includes expected behavior patterns that differ from but correspond with the behavior patterns expected of someone in a parental role. The

**ROLE**

A cluster of behavior patterns considered appropriate for a position in a social setting.

ALTERNATIVE EXAMPLE

For years, mom—the all-American purchasing agent—bought most goods used in the household except for some big-ticket items such as cars and life insurance. But today, the average American family has two wage earners, and neither reigns supreme in deciding which brands to buy, no matter how expensive the item. As a result, more men are in the grocery store and more women are shopping for cars. The role of shopper has lost some of its gender orientation. SOURCE: John Steere, "How Asian-Americans Make Purchase Decisions," *Marketing News,* March 13, 1995, p. 9.

role of a wage earner and that of a student also require different behaviors. Furthermore, some students may dress in jeans and T-shirts to demonstrate their status as students. However, during a job interview, students of business administration may dress more formally and carry attaché cases to act out their roles as business students.

Roles obviously carry over into purchasing situations. There are consumer and seller roles. The shopper expects to have certain rights and expects the store employee to fulfill certain obligations. An employee in an expensive fur salon is expected to behave differently from a check-out clerk at Kmart.

## Culture

Many of our values, norms, and roles come from our overall culture. The term *culture,* though frequently used, is difficult to define clearly because it encompasses so much about the way a society lives. Recall that a culture consists of values, beliefs, and customary behaviors learned and shred by the members of a particular society. Essential to the concept of culture is the notion that culture is learned rather than innate. Thus, that children are born is "natural," but how the mating process is conducted and how the children are treated is "cultural."

It is important for marketers to understand the many aspects of culture. Culture obviously varies from place to place around the globe and affects the success of marketing worldwide.

DISCUSSION CONSIDERATION

Brainstorm examples of products marketed to specific subcultural groups. For example, retirement communities target the elderly, and Goya foods targets Hispanics.

**SUBCULTURE**

A group within a dominant culture that is distinct from the culture. A subculture will typically display some values or norms that differ from those of the overall culture.

## Subcultures: Cultures within Cultures

Within a society there is a dominant culture. However, there are also cultural differences. Language differences are an example. Some countries have two (Canada and Belgium) or more (Switzerland has four) official languages. In China, five major and many minor languages are spoken. In the United States, several language groups can be identified. Spanish is now spoken by almost 20 percent of the U.S. population.

A **subculture** is a group within a dominant culture that is distinct because it differs from the dominant culture in one or more of a number of important ways—language, demographic variables such as ethnic or racial background, or geographical

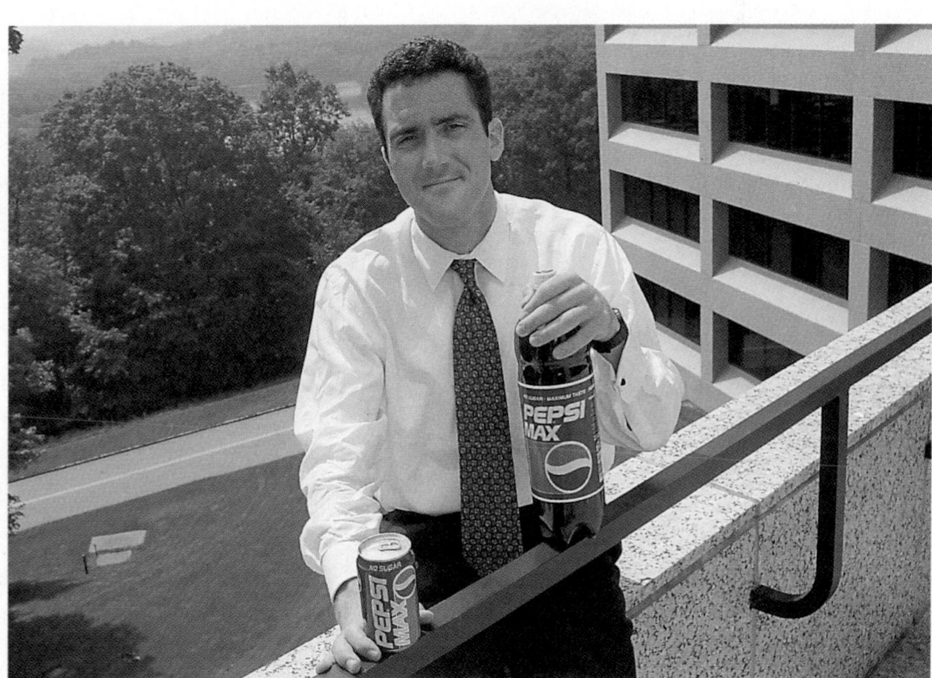


Pepsi recently introduced Pepsi Max in Europe on a country-by-country basis, calling the product a cola with zero calories and "the same great taste of a regular." In Europe, where men felt diet soft drinks were wimpy, Pepsi Max was given a masculine image. When it left test markets, it obtained 4 percent of the market in its national introduction in the United Kingdom. Commercialization in Germany has also been a success.

region, for example. The subculture will also differ from the overall culture in some values, norms, and beliefs.

Within the U.S. culture, there are many subcultures. Subcultures made up of particular racial or ethnic groups, such as the African American, Hispanic, and Jewish subcultures, are easiest to identify, but the marketer must recognize the many other subcultural differences. These may be as simple as regional differences in food preferences.[17] In the Northeastern states, people often eat lamb chops, for example, but in West Texas, beef is the staple, and lamb chops are hard to find. Subcultural differences provide marketers with challenges and with segmentation possibilities that are rich in potential.

## Social Classes

**SOCIAL CLASS**
A group of people with similar levels of prestige, power, and wealth who also share a set of related beliefs, attitudes, and values in their thinking and behavior.

Within every culture there are social classes. A **social class** is a group of people with similar levels of prestige, power, and wealth who also share a set of related beliefs, attitudes, and values in their thinking and behavior.[18] Exhibit 6–10, which summarizes one view of U.S. social classes, shows five discrete groups. Class structure is actually more like an escalator, however, because it runs from bottom to top without any major plateaus.

Social class explains many differences in behavior patterns and lifestyles. Social class may have a major impact on shopping patterns or products purchased. An advertisement for Lucchese boots, which are exquisitely tooled and made from the finest leathers, states that the boots are "available only at finer stores." This simple phrase may stop some readers from further consideration of these boots. Why? One of the classic studies in consumer behavior explains that the lower-status woman believes that if she goes into a high-status department store, the clerks will snub or insult her in various subtle ways, making it clear that she does not "belong." Members of different social classes know which stores and products are for people of their class.

POINT TO EMPHASIZE
Status crystallization is low in the United States, which means that people can vary widely on individual measures while retaining membership in a social class. For example, people with little education have made fortunes, and some people with fairly high incomes have working-class occupations.

The impact of social class on consumer behavior is often indirect. For example, most people prefer to live in neighborhoods made up of people from their own class.[19] Thus, small-membership groups within the neighborhoods that may directly affect purchases have been touched by the influence of social class.

In our diverse society, there are many subcultures based on color, language, religion, and geography. Consumption of foods, preferences for music, and forms of socializing can be strongly influenced by values, norms, and roles prescribed by the subculture.

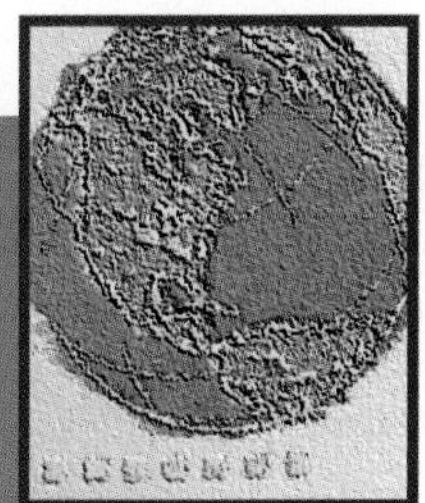

## FOCUS ON GLOBAL COMPETITION

### *Conspicuous Consumption in Asia*

Young and erect, outfitted in designer eyeglasses and a fashionable button-down shirt, diamond scion Jatin Mehta glides to his office in a chauffeured gray Mercedes-Benz. He weaves slowly through Bombay's urban phantasmagoria—the zippy motor rickshaws spewing diesel smoke, the swarms of pedestrians, the water-streaked office towers packed like pickets against the Arabian Sea.

Some might see poverty through Mehta's tinted windows. It's out there, of course. But Mehta sees something else: the glint of working women's jewelry. And in that glint, he sees the impending arrival of a glittering new diamond age in India—the world's second most populous nation, now opening fully to global trade for the first time in half a century. The challenge facing Mehta's Suraj Diamond (India) Ltd. and his backers at the De Beers international diamond cartel is to persuade 400 million–plus Indian women, many of them trapped by lonely, arranged marriages and feudal family values, that diamonds are their best friend. "When you work so hard for your money, family life changes—let's face it," Mehta explained as he rose through his office skyscraper in an elevator packed with smartly dressed, youthful working women. "With exports growing, with income growing, these ladies are going to look for themselves—to buy what they want. . . . "It's the beginning of the takeoff," he declared. "We see a great future. We see us reaching a $1 billion turnover. Everything is opening up."

The story of how the world's diamond cartel is pushing its wares into Asia illustrates a wider change in the global economy. As Third World and ex-communist countries abandon self-sufficient development strategies, tear down import barriers and join global trading regimes, not only are their exports rising, but in many cases they are buying bundles of new goods from abroad—especially consumer goods associated with Western images of success. Nowhere is this change more striking or more important to the global economy than in Asia.

Here the region's two behemoths, India and China, are racing to rejoin the global trading economy after decades of ideologically inspired isolation. China is already well down the path; India is gaining as its socialist leaders enact free market reforms. Around these giants stand roughly half a dozen smaller Southeast Asian nations whose streaking economic growth has become the envy of the West and of poor countries wishing to become rich.

Now Asia's boom is producing a critical mass of conspicuous consumption. In heavily populated India, China and Indonesia, sizable and socially ambitious middle classes with disposable income are forming for the first time in history. Their spending power and sheer numbers beckon as an El Dorado to Western and Japanese corporations selling everything from baubles to refrigerators to cellular telephones.

In Thailand, Malaysia, Hong Kong, Singapore, Taiwan and South Korea—much wealthier countries, although less populous—surging middle classes are buying Western consumer goods as if possessed by a virulent shopping fever. Per capita purchasing power in the wealthier Asian countries ranged in 1993 from an estimated $5,200 in Thailand to $18,500 in Hong Kong—higher than in Australia.

The Asian acquisitive classes buoyed by this growth seek above all Western brand names, famous designer labels—anything with cachet. Nike tennis shoes, Tiffany and Cartier stores, and Gucci luggage predominate in the region's newly constructed indoor shopping malls. Even Asian franchises of American fast-food chains have a prestigious and polished atmosphere unfamiliar at many McDonald's restaurants in the United States. Asia's Western-imitative consumer spurt is comparable to "what happened in the U.S., France and Europe in the 19th century," said jewelry industry consultant Samuel Beizer. "They will spend money on those things which they think are important to middle-class status. In the U.S. in the 19th century, it was French silks. Now [in Asia] it is Mercedes, jewelry . . . a certain kind of value—Tiffany, Cartier, Gialatti, Van Cleef." ■

**EXHIBIT 6–10** The American Class System in the 20th Century—an Estimate

| CLASS (AND PERCENTAGE OF POPULATION) | INCOME (1994 DOLLARS) | PROPERTY | OCCUPATION | EDUCATION |
|---|---|---|---|---|
| Upper class (1–3%) | Very high income (over $675,000) | Great wealth, old wealth | Investors, heirs, capitalists, corporate executives, high civil and military leaders | Liberal Arts education at elite schools |
| Upper middle class (10–15%) | High income ($65,000 or more) | Accumulation of property through savings | Upper managers, professionals, successful small business owners | College, often with graduate training |
| Middle class (30–34%) | Moderate income (average almost $40,000) | Some savings | Small business people, lower managers, farmers, semiprofessionals, nonretail sales and clerical workers | Some college, high school |
| Working class (40–45%) | Low income (about $25,000) | Some savings | Skilled labor, unskilled labor, retail sales operatives | Some high school, grade school |
| Lower class (20–25%) | Poverty income (below $18,750) | No savings | Working poor, unemployed, welfare recipients | Grade school or illiterate |

Source: Adapted from Dennis Gilbert and Joseph Kahl, *The American Class Structure* (Homewood, Ill.: Dorsey Press, 1982); and from Daniel W. Rossides, *Social Stratification: the American Class System in Comparative Perspective,* © 1990, pp. 406–408, reprinted by permission of Prentice Hall, Inc., Englewood Cliffs, NJ.

In the upper middle class, the nouveaux riches are most likely to purchase furs or yachts because these products signify achievement. The expensive car, the bigger house, private college for the kids, a summer home, a boat, and frequent vacations are all symbolic expressions of success. This kind of buying behavior was well described by the turn-of-the-century American economist Thornstein Veblen, who coined the term **conspicuous consumption.** Veblen, in criticizing persons who buy products simply to visibly consume or openly display them, hit on a fact of human nature. Consumption of certain items is a means to express one's social-class status. Even if we snicker with Veblen at this behavior, the desire to express one's feelings (or show off) may be real and quite important to an individual who aspires to or has achieved membership in a higher social class. Marketers should not ignore this.

**CONSPICUOUS CONSUMPTION**
Consumption for the sake of enhancing social prestige.

## Reference Groups

Each individual belongs to many groups. From a marketing perspective, the most important are reference groups. A **reference group** is a group that influences an individual because that individual is a member of the group or aspires to be a member of it. The reference group is used as a point of comparison for self-evaluation.[20]

**REFERENCE GROUP**
A group that influences an individual because that individual is a member of the group or aspires to be a member.

The **membership group** is a group of which the individual is actually a part. Examples include clubs, the freshman class, and UCLA alumni. Such groups strongly influence members' behavior—including consumer behavior—by exerting pressure to conform, or *peer pressure.* In a **voluntary membership group,** such as a group of college peers or a political party, the individual is free to join or withdraw. Sometimes, however, the individual has little or no choice as to group membership. People approaching middle age may not like that fact, but they nevertheless make changes in their lives as a result of the influence of their middle-aged peers.

**MEMBERSHIP GROUP**
In reference to an individual, a group to which the individual belongs. If the individual has chosen to belong to the group, it is a voluntary membership group.

A second major type of reference group is the **aspirational group.** Individuals may try to behave or look like the people whose group they hope to join. Thus, a little brother may try to act like a big brother and his buddies, or a little sister may try to act like a big sister's teenage friends. Similarly, the young business manager may

**ASPIRATIONAL GROUP**
In reference to an individual, a group to which the individual would like to belong.

ALTERNATIVE EXAMPLE

Thanks to media such as MTV, teens around the world may be the first truly global consumers. They all wear Levis, eat Big Macs, and use Clearasil. Teens across Europe think of themselves as European rather than Spanish, Italian, or the like. Thus, some reference group memberships along national lines may be declining in favor of one large global reference group. SOURCE: Cyndee Miller, "Teens Seen as the First Truly Global Consumers," *Marketing News,* March 27, 1995, p. 9.

choose to "dress for success." This usually means dressing like the women or men the manager hopes to join one day in the organization's higher ranks.

**Reference Groups Influence Some Products More Than Others** The use of some products is highly subject to group influence. Examples include clothing, cars, and beer consumed publicly. The use of other products is subject to almost no group pressure. These products are so mundane or so lacking in visibility that no one uses them to express self-concept. The risks of using the "wrong" brand in private are small. One rarely hears comments about someone's eating Libby's canned peaches instead of Del Monte's. Note that some product categories can be subject to reference group influences without regard to brand name or design: "Why don't you break down and get an air conditioner, Harry?" "You mean you use instant coffee? No, thank you." Reference groups, then, may influence the type of product consumer, the brand purchased, or both.

## FOCUS ON RELATIONSHIPS

### *Harley-Davidson*

Owners of Harley-Davidson motorcycles strongly identify with the membership group of Harley owners. They often fancy Harley riders as cowboys, desperadoes, or knights in shining armor. Marketers at Harley-Davidson exert considerable effort to make Harley owners feel special and part of the Harley-Davidson tradition. The company endorses a club—Harley Owners Group, or HOG—a newsletter—*Hog Tales*—and many special events. For example, ZZ Top has played at HOG-members-only shows sponsored by Harley-Davidson. ■

**OPINION LEADER**

A group member who, because of some quality or characteristic, is likely to lead other group members in particular matters.

ALTERNATIVE EXAMPLE

When Marta Limbaugh, a rabid football fan, tried the strips used by pro football players to keep their nasal passages open, she was wowed by their performance. So she told her husband, Rush, who told the 20 million people who listen to his talk show. Overnight, sales of Breathe Right Nasal Strips increased by 46 percent. So unexpected was the demand that many drugstores were out of the strips for weeks. SOURCE: Michael Oneal, "Everybody's Talkin' at Us," *Business Week,* May 22, 1995, p. 104.

**Opinion Leaders** Groups frequently include individuals known as **opinion leaders.** Opinion leaders might be friends who are looked up to because of their intelligence, athletic abilities, appearance, or special abilities, such as skill in cooking, mechanics, or languages.[21] In any group, with respect to buying behavior, the role of opinion leader moves from member to member, depending on the product involved. If someone is planning to buy a car, that person may seek the opinion of a friend or family member who is thought to know about cars. The same person might seek a different "expert" when he or she is buying stereo equipment, or good wines, or investment plans.

In certain situations, the most powerful determinant of buying behavior is the attitude of those people the individual respects. Thus, word-of-mouth recommendations may be an important buying influence. One reason that marketers try to satisfy their customers is their hope that the customers will recommend the product or organization to members of their social groups. The best thing a homeowner can hear when hiring a house painter, for example, is that the painter did a good job on a neighbor's or friend's house.

## The Family

**FAMILY**

A group of two or more persons related by birth, marriage, or adoption and residing together.

The United States Census Bureau defines a **family** as a group of two or more persons related by birth, marriage, or adoption and residing together. An individual's family is an important reference group. The family is characterized by frequent face-to-face interaction among family members, who respond to each other on the basis of their total personalities rather than on the basis of particular roles. It is not surprising that values, self-concepts, and the products we buy are influenced by our families. That influence may continue to be strong throughout our lives.

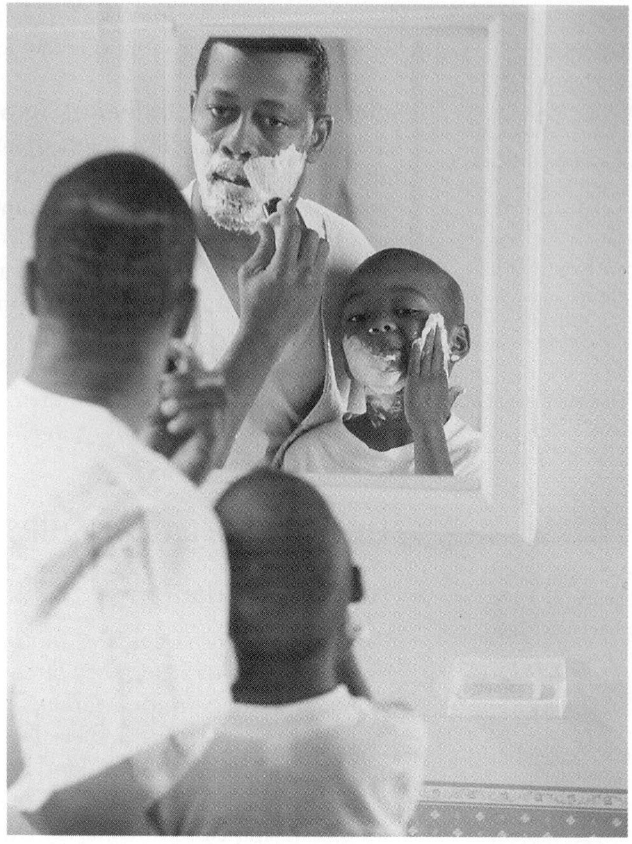

The family is the group primarily responsible for the socialization process. Socialization is the passing down of cultural values, norms, and roles—including buying behavior. As a part of their socialization, children observe how their parents use, evaluate, and choose products.

**SOCIALIZATION PROCESS**
The process by which a society transmits its values, norms, and roles to its members.

**POINT TO EMPHASIZE**
Because of increasing divorce and remarriage rates, the average American family is changing. Today, households are likely to be headed by single parents. This changes the demand for products. For example, single parents need more convenience goods because they are frequently short of time.

The family is the group primarily responsible for the **socialization process**—that is, the passing down of social values, norms, and roles. Socialization includes the learning of buying behavior. Children observe how their parents evaluate and select products in stores.[22] They see how the exchange process takes place at the cash register and quickly learn that money or a credit card changes hands there. That is how children learn the buying role. When children receive money as gifts or allowances and are permitted to spend it, they act out the buying role, thus learning an activity they will perform throughout their lives.

### Social Situations

Another environmental influence on the decision-making process is the social situation. Consider the gasoline-buying consumer who is late for an appointment and notices the tank is nearly empty. The situational pressure may increase the importance of convenient location as a choice criterion and decrease the importance of other attributes. It would be impossible to list all the social situational influences on buying behavior. However, it is important to appreciate that one brand may be purchased in one social situation and another in a different social situation.

## Joint Decision Making

**JOINT DECISION MAKING**
Decision making shared by all or some members of a group. Often, one decision maker dominates the process.

Some consumer choices are made not by individuals but by groups of two or more people. This is referred to as **joint decision making** (or household decision making). Families may, for example, choose a car or a house together. Or parents may sit down together to talk over insurance purchases, furniture purchases, or retirement plans.

Despite this image of togetherness, most purchases are dominated by one group member. In the case of the family group, the parents dominate rather than the grade-school kids. Older children may have greater influence—as when the teenage son, who "knows all about cars," advises his parents on the selection of a new auto. The dominant role in group decision making is commonly taken by different group members for different purchases. Even though changing sex roles are influencing traditional roles in family decision making, in most households the husband usually dominates decisions relating to purchases of insurance, while decisions regarding clothing for the children, food, and household furnishings are most often wife-dominated.[23] This reflects our society's norms and traditional role expectations. Decisions made by husband and wife together are common when entertainment, housing, and vacation choices are being made. It should be noted that changes taking place in our society are making the process of identifying the major decision-influencer more difficult.

**ALTERNATIVE EXAMPLE**

Marketing to Asian-Americans is difficult because of the number of nationalities included under that name and the differences in buying roles among nationalities. Among Vietnamese, for example, men are likely to make large purchases and women to buy for the home, whereas neither gender is more likely than the other to make large purchases among Indian Americans. Chinese American households vary greatly, depending in part on how many generations the family has been in the United States. SOURCE: John Steere, "How Asian-Americans Make Purchase Decisions," *Marketing News*, March 13, 1995, p. 9.

To simplify the discussion, we have not mentioned the distinctions among consumers' roles during the buying effort. However, there are several roles to be played in any buying decision. These roles are (1) the *buyer*, who, narrowly defined, is the person who goes to the store and actually purchases the product; (2) the *user*, who, narrowly viewed, is the person who actually consumes or uses the product; and (3) the *decision maker*, who decides which product or brand to buy. Think about it for a while. Each role could be played by a different person, or all could be played by the same person, or the roles could be played by any combination of people.

The purchase of baby food is the classic example of a situation in which different people play the roles. The baby eats the food but is denied any comment on it. The buyer could be an older child sent to the store by Mom. Mom is the decision maker who, by means of experience, the influence of advertisements, or her own mother's suggestions, has determined which brand of baby food to buy. The purchase of gum or a haircut, however, may involve only one person performing all three roles.

In more complex buying decisions, such as the purchase of a new home or a family automobile, a family member may also play the role of influencer or gatekeeper. The **influencer** expresses an opinion about the product or service to persuade the decision maker. ("Dad, we need to sell the station wagon and buy a car that won't embarrass me.") The **gatekeeper** controls the flow of information ("I won't tell Bob about the house on Rockwood Drive because I liked the one on Hazel Boulevard better.")

**INFLUENCER**

A group member who attempts to persuade the decision maker.

**GATEKEEPER**

A group member who controls the flow of information to the decision maker.

The focus of marketing changes with the role structure of the buying decision. When only one person is involved, marketing can be more concentrated than when several people in different roles are involved. In the baby food example, whom should the marketer attempt to reach? The decision maker—the person with the real "say" in the matter—should be the target. Thus, baby food advertisements appear in publications read by mothers as well as on TV and radio programs that reach mothers. These advertisements stress the concerns of mothers, such as nutrition. These are matters that neither the baby nor the older sibling sent to the store really cares about.

## Summary

Understanding consumer behavior helps the marketer bring about satisfying exchanges in the marketplace. Consumer behavior is affected by a variety of individual and interpersonal (sociocultural) factors, which influence the decision-making process. They must be taken into account by marketers.

LEARNING OBJECTIVE **1** *Understand the basic model of consumer behavior.*

Consumer behavior results from the interaction of person and environment, $B = f(P,E)$. Consumer behavior theorists have expanded and explained this basic model with many theories.

LEARNING OBJECTIVE **2** *Describe the consumer decision-making process and understand factors, such as consumer involvement, that influence it.*

The decision-making process varies depending on how routine the consumer perceives the situation to be. For decisions involving extensive problem solving, consumers follow a multistep process: (1) recognizing the problem, (2) searching for alternative solutions, (3) evaluating those alternatives, (4) deciding whether to buy, and (5) if a purchase is made, evaluating the product purchased. Many internal and environmental factors affect this process, including consumer involvement as well as situational influences such as physical settings, social circumstances, and economic conditions.

LEARNING OBJECTIVE **3** *Appreciate the importance of perceived risk, choice criteria, purchase satisfaction, and cognitive dissonance.*

Perceived risk is the consumer's uncertainty about whether a product will do what it is intended to do. Choice criteria are those critical attributes the consumer uses to evaluate a product alternative. Purchase satisfaction on the consumer's part means that marketing has achieved its goal. However, the consumer may instead experience cognitive dissonance—a sense of tension and uncertainty—after deciding to make a purchase. Marketers must address all these issues if satisfactory exchanges are to take place.

LEARNING OBJECTIVE **4** *Recognize the influence of individual factors, such as motives, perception, learning, attitude, and personality, on consumer behavior.*

Motivation theory attempts to explain the causes of goal-directed behavior in terms of needs, motives, incentives, and drives. Needs can be classified in many ways. Maslow's needs hierarchy ranks human needs from the most basic (physiological) to the highest (self-actualization). As the lower needs are satisfied, the higher needs become more important. Perception is the process of interpreting sensations and stimuli. Each person's perceptions differ at least slightly from everyone else's. Selective perception is the process of screening out or interpreting stimuli—including marketing stimuli. Learning is important to marketing because consumers learn to favor certain products and brands and to dislike others. Consumers also learn to have certain attitudes. Personality reflects the individual's consistent ways of responding to his or her environment. It is generally agreed that the influence of personality on consumer behavior should be studied only along with other factors, such as attitudes and demographic characteristics, to predict specific behaviors.

LEARNING OBJECTIVE **5** *Explain the nature of culture and subculture in terms of social values, norms, and roles.*

Marketers look at culture as the values, beliefs, and customary behaviors learned and shared by the members of a society. Insofar as consumers in a society share a culture, they think and act in similar ways. A subculture is a group within a dominant culture that has values and distinctive characteristics not shared with the larger culture. Cultures and subcultures prescribe certain values, norms, and roles for the members.

LEARNING OBJECTIVE **6** *Characterize social class in the United States.*

A social class is a group of people with similar levels of prestige, power, and wealth. According to one view, U.S. society may be roughly divided into five social classes determined by wealth, education, occupation, and other measures of prestige. Social classes differ in lifestyle, purchase preferences, and shopping and consumption patterns.

LEARNING OBJECTIVE **7** *Explain the influence of reference groups on individual buyers.*

Groups strongly influence individuals' behavior. Reference groups, including membership and aspirational groups, provide points of comparison by which the individual evaluates himself or herself. These groups have many direct and indirect influences on purchasing behaviors.

LEARNING OBJECTIVE **8** *Examine the roles in the joint decision-making process.*

The joint decision-making process includes the roles of buyer, user, and decision maker, as well as influencer and gatekeeper in more complex decisions. In general, the decision maker should be the focus of marketing efforts.

Five years ago, Exchange Resources opened a center in Minneapolis where financial traders could go if their workplaces were hit by a fire, flood or other disaster. The center had 440 seats, complete with desktop computers, Reuters and Quotron machines—tools of the trader's trade.

"It was the field of dreams, except we built it and nobody came," recalled Kenneth Israel, the company's founder.

Then Israel got a little celestial help: Hurricane Andrew in Florida, an earthquake in San Francisco, a Con Edison failure in New York, all . . . [put into perspective] . . . the specter of millions of sales dollars going down the drain with flood waters or ashes.

Now, client subscriptions to seats at the Minneapolis center and at a larger one Exchange Resources has opened at Telehouse in Staten Island, N.Y., are bringing in $35 million a year. In 1994, Israel . . . opened two more centers, one in New York and another in Rutherford, N.J.

Organizations' attitudes toward disaster-recovery services have changed dramatically in recent years. Highly publicized disasters such as the World Trade Center bombing have highlighted the fact that companies, which increasingly rely on computers and telecommunications for everyday transactions, need to keep their systems up and running. Organizational buyers now see the need to deal with companies offering places where they can do business in emergencies. The disaster-recovery industry is expanding its services to satisfy the needs of organizational buyers.

The chapter begins by defining business-to-business marketing and organizational buying behavior. Then it explains the various types of organizational buying decisions and the role of the buying center. Finally, it discusses the nature of industrial demand and the characteristics of business markets.

**ALTERNATIVE EXAMPLE**

VF Corp. uses a computerized market response system to keep tabs on what shoppers buy and reorder automatically so that VF's Wrangler jeans can be on a retailer's shelf three days after an order is placed. One of VF's customers, Wal-Mart, sells millions of pairs of Wranglers through 2,100 outlets by ordering every night after checking sales on the outlets' scanner data for that day. VF wants to expand its system to find sales patterns that can help retailers forecast ideal supply levels. SOURCE: Joseph Weber, "Just Get It to the Stores on Time," *Business Week,* March 6, 1995, pp. 66–67.

**POINT TO EMPHASIZE**

Business-to-business marketing offers numerous professional job opportunities in sales, in distribution, and in product management. New college graduates who don't consider these jobs may be ignoring lucrative positions.

# Organizational Buying Behavior

**BUSINESS-TO-BUSINESS MARKETING**
Marketing aimed at bringing about an exchange in which a product or service is sold for any use other than personal consumption. The buyer may be a manufacturer, a reseller, a government body, a nonprofit institution, or any organization other than an ultimate consumer. The transaction occurs so an organization may conduct its business.

**ORGANIZATIONAL BUYING BEHAVIOR**
The decision-making activities of organizational buyers that lead to purchase of products.

A business marketing transaction takes place whenever a good or service is sold for any use other than personal consumption. In other words, any sale to an industrial user, wholesaler, retailer, or organization other than the ultimate consumer is sold in the business market. This marketing process takes place between businesses. Hence, the marketing activity necessary to bring about an exchange among organizations is often called **business-to-business marketing.**

All products sold in the business market are called organizational products because they are used to help operate an organization's business. The term *organizational* is broader and more inclusive than the term *business* or *industrial,* but both of the latter terms remain in common use. In fact, the term *business market,* which narrowly defined would refer only to manufacturers, service marketers, wholesalers, and retailers, is broadly used by most marketing writers to include organizational buyers such as governments, churches, and other nonprofit entities.

When faced with indecision as to whether a product is a consumer product or an organizational product, ask these two questions.

1. Who bought it?
2. Why did they buy it?

Notice that it is not necessary to ask the question "What did they buy?" For example, an airline ticket may be a consumer or an organizational product, depending on who bought it and why it was purchased. The fact that it is an airline ticket is not relevant to its classification in this regard.

What, then, do organizations buy? Manufacturers require raw materials, equipment, component parts, supplies, and services. Producers of nonmanufactured goods require many of these same products. Wholesalers and retailers purchase products for resale, as well as equipment such as trucks, shelving, and computers. Hospitals, zoos, and other nonprofit organizations use many goods and services to facilitate the performance of their business functions, as do federal, state, and local governments. In fact, the federal government is the largest single buyer of organizational products. In participating in business-to-business exchanges, all these organizations display **organizational buying behavior.** Exhibit 7–1 illustrates some of these behaviors.

Buying is a necessary activity for all business and not-for-profit organizations. In organizational buying situations, the purchase of goods and services, such as semiconductors and accounting services, may involve a complex process. Purchasing agents and other organizational members determine the need to purchase goods and services, engage in information-seeking activities, evaluate alternative purchasing actions, and negotiate the necessary arrangements with suppliers.[1]

The clothing and equipment used by firefighters and smokejumpers who put out wildland fires are organizational goods. The term *organizational product* is broader than *industrial product* or *business product.* Organizational buyers include governments, nonprofit entities, manufacturers, wholesalers, retailers, farms, construction companies, and many others.

Placing an order with a supplier is generally not a simple act. Organizational buying takes place over time, involves communications among several organizational members, and entails financial relationships with suppliers. The organizational buying process is performed by informed individuals attempting to be rational in their selection of alternative suppliers, brands, and quantities. The steps to be followed in making purchasing decisions, as well as specific purchasing standards, may be spelled out in organizational manuals.

Service is an important organizational buying motive. IBM recognizes that service must go beyond servicing IBM equipment. Customer companies need service for entire systems.

pliers that do not adopt TQM programs of their own. Thus, not only must product quality conform to customer requirements, but it may also have to exceed the buyer's expectations. High quality, as the customer defines it, is a major reason for buying in the 1990s.

## Related Services

Service is an important variable in organizational purchasing. Before the sale is consummated, the marketer may have to demonstrate the ability to provide rapid delivery, repair service, or technical support. After the sale, the supplier had better be able to deliver the promised services, because "downtime" costs money and may be a great source of frustration for the buyer of, for example, an office photocopier, a computer, or an assembly line conveyor system.

In business-to-business situations, relationship marketing often means effectively being part of a collaborator's organization. Red Star Speciality Products, a Universal Foods Company, is the largest North American producer of yeast-based flavor enhancers. It offers clients applications support, technical seminars, prototype products, and a technically trained staff of sales representatives.[12] Maintaining and enhancing relationships with its customers by providing "extra services" is a vital aspect of the company's marketing efforts. Marketing strategies to achieve high service quality are discussed in Chapter 11.

**ALTERNATIVE EXAMPLE**

Many companies have hired outside computer firms to handle routine tasks. To date, the results have been mixed. An example is Southern Pacific Rail's experience with IBM: Computer breakdowns delayed accounting statements, and connections failed at a major California railyard, leaving a technician to direct 1,200 cars a day by hand. Worse yet, companies are paying through the nose for these services. As a result, more companies may decide to use their own computer departments. SOURCE: Louise Lee, "Hiring Outside Firms to Run Computers Isn't Always a Bargain," *Wall Street Journal,* May 18, 1995, p. A1.

**ALTERNATIVE EXAMPLE**

A factor in the price of imported goods is tariffs. As the Clinton administration considered imposing 100 percent tariffs on luxury cars from Japan, Japanese auto makers rushed to get boatloads of cars to the U.S. before the tariff deadline. Meanwhile, dealers contemplated laying off employees because of lost sales due to higher prices. The tariff was being used as a weapon to force the Japanese to open their markets to U.S. auto companies, so this price change had nothing to do with costs, operations, or shipping.

## Prices

Price is the single most important determining factor in many organizational buying decisions. There is an old adage that says: "Farmers are price takers, not price makers." It suggests that farmers (who are organizational marketers) face keen competition in a marketplace where the products sold are more or less the same. Not all organizational marketers are quite so much at the mercy of market forces as farmers, but many organizational goods and services face strong competition from products that are close substitutes. In such situations, price is likely to be the key to completing a

ALTERNATIVE EXAMPLE

UPS is advertising its new management services as "moving at the speed of business". To improve its delivery services, it has added an information system to track the goods that it will warehouse and ship for customers. It has even purchased SonicAir to fly goods to clients the day they are needed. UPS hopes to lead the industry in distribution of business goods. SOURCE: Alan Salomon, "UPS Rewraps Image as Problem Solver," *Advertising Age,* February 6, 1995, p. 4.

sale. Organizational buyers often gather competitive bids from suppliers, further heightening the effects of competition on price.

Organizational buyers can be expected to analyze price carefully, examining not just the list price but also any discounts, terms of sale, and credit opportunities that accompany a purchase agreement. Further, some buyers make a distinction between first cost (initial price) and operating cost (price over a specific time period). Coupled with a thorough knowledge of the product, such cost analysis allows buyers to make detailed comparisons of value, increasing the potency of price as a buying criterion.

## Reliable Delivery and Inventory Management

For many organizations, the assurance of reliable delivery of purchases is essential. A related concern, inventory management, may also be an important buying criterion. As business becomes more global and as information technology advances, organi-

Advertising addressed to organizational buyers often deals with these buyers' concerns with operating costs. This Learjet advertisement suggests that, even though the Learjet's initial price is higher than the prices of some competitors, the Learjet is a better value in the long run.

Imagine Buying A Learjet
To Save Money.
The Learjet 31A is the most cost-efficient jet on the market today, boasting an operating cost-per-mile that beats the economy jet from Cessna — guaranteed. So, while many firms purchased Learjets to save time, more and more are buying them to save money, too — every mile, every trip, every day.
It's hard to imagine why anyone would invest in any other jet.
To discuss the contribution a Learjet 31A can make to your business and your bottom line, contact Ted Farid, Vice President Marketing at (316) 946-2450.

Learjet

zational buyers are increasingly concerned with collaborative efforts and with building strategic alliances with other organizations. Strategic alliances related to inventory management take the form of single-sourcing.

**SINGLE-SOURCING**
Purchasing a product on a regular basis from a single vendor.

**Single-sourcing** occurs when an organization buys from a single vendor. The degree of cooperation may be so great that the supplier is highly involved in the design of products or subassembly components. Usually in such situations the organizational marketer works closely with the buyer to coordinate delivery of inventory items just as the buyer's inventory is being depleted. Buyer and seller share a common data base reflecting the customer's current inventory. Single-sourcing such as this almost always involves electronic data interchanges between companies. Inventory management is discussed more fully in Chapter 14, which deals with physical distribution management.

POINT TO EMPHASIZE
Increased use of total quality management and just-in-time production have increased the emphasis on single-sourcing as buyers and suppliers foster closer ties. As inventory levels decrease and delivery frequency increases, business professionals work to develop trust, open communication, and shared responsibilities in developing cost-efficient methods.

## The Bottom Line

The relative importance of each of the major organizational buying criteria—product quality, service, price, and delivery—may vary with the buyer, the situation, or the product. For example, at Copperweld Robotics, a producer of industrial robots, research showed that customers wanted answers to three questions in the following order: (1) Will it do the job? (2) What service is available? (3) What is the price? Copperweld's director of marketing says that, for the industrial robot industry, "Service is absolutely the number one part of the marketing function because if one portion of the robot doesn't work, the whole line shuts down."[13]

In general, in an organizational buying decision, the criteria interact. Each contributes to the final decision, and each affects the importance of the others. Yet they often boil down to one overriding factor: the need to operate an organization. General Motors' truck and coach division emphasizes issues like corrosion resistance and low fuel consumption in its organizational advertising. The strategy is based on the belief that GM organizational customers buy vehicles because they need them to make money.

## FOCUS ON QUALITY

### *Corning Incorporated*

Marketers at Corning Incorporated know the importance organizational customers place on on-time delivery and high-quality products. The company's quality strategy is aimed at making it a leader in delivering error-free products and on-time service that meet customer requirements 100 percent of the time. At Corning, quality is "knowing what needs to be done, having the tools to do it right, then doing it right the first time." According to the Corning Incorporated Quality Statement:

> It is the policy of Corning Incorporated to achieve Total Quality performance in meeting the requirements of external and internal customers. Total Quality performance means understanding who the customer is, what the requirements are, and meeting those requirements, without error, on time, every time. . . .
>
> It is intended that every employee be taught what Total Quality is and why it is necessary to attain it. Each employee will be trained in how to achieve Total Quality in his or her job and given the tools to do the job right the first time. Management will provide the resources, structure and atmosphere that will allow and encourage individuals and groups to meet the Total Quality goal and policy. While responsibility for achieving the goal must ultimately rest with management, the actions required to realize Total Quality rest with each employee of the company. ■

# The Nature of Organizational Demand

**ALTERNATIVE EXAMPLE**
Otis Elevator is gambling that the Russian economy will grow in the next decade. It opened a plant in St. Petersburg in 1993 which today makes about 300 elevators annually—8 percent of capacity. This venture is typical of Otis, which usually partners with a local firm in hopes of reaping benefits when the market takes off. Otis believes that being there first is extremely important. SOURCE: Lawrence Ingrassia, Amal Kumar Naj, and Claudia Rosett, "Overseas, Otis and Its Parent Get In on the Ground Floor," *Wall Street Journal*, April 21, 1995, p. A6.

The nature of the demand for goods and services in the multifaceted organizational marketplace differs greatly from the demand for most consumer goods. Some generalizations can be made about organizational demand and in particular about demand in the business segment of the organizational market. It is: (1) derived, (2) inelastic, and (3) fluctuating.

## Derived Demand

**DERIVED DEMAND**
Demand for a product that depends on demand for another product.

A reduction in consumer demand for housing has a tremendous and obvious impact on the building supply products industry. The demand for aluminum depends on the demand for products such as airplanes and trucks as well as products packaged in aluminum. Downturns in the economy may cause people to cut back on their use of airlines, which in turn reduces the need for airplane fuel and the parts and tools used in airplane maintenance. Ultimately, even the demand for such mundane items as the brooms used to sweep out airplane hangars will decline as airline usage declines. All of these examples demonstrate a basic truth—all organizational demand depends ultimately on consumer demand. It is **derived demand**—that is, derived from consumer demand.

Exhibit 7–5 demonstrates the power of derived demand in the business marketplace. Notice that derived demand ultimately depends on consumer demand even in purchasing situations far removed from consumers.

No retailer would buy so much as a can of soup for resale unless management thought that the soup could be sold to a customer. It may be less obvious that no manufacturer of cardboard-box-making machines would buy even a pencil for use at the factory unless management believed that box makers would buy box-making machines, that packers would buy boxes, that wholesalers and retailers would buy boxed items, and that retailers would be able to sell those items to ultimate consumers.

**ACCELERATION PRINCIPLE**
A principle describing the situation in which demand for a product that derives its demand from another product may either increase or decrease at a much higher rate than demand for the product from which demand is derived.

Economists have coined the phrase **acceleration principle** to describe the dramatic effects of derived demand. According to this principle, demand for a product that derives its demand from another product may greatly accelerate if there is a small

**EXHIBIT 7–5** An Example of Derived Demand at Work in the Marketplace

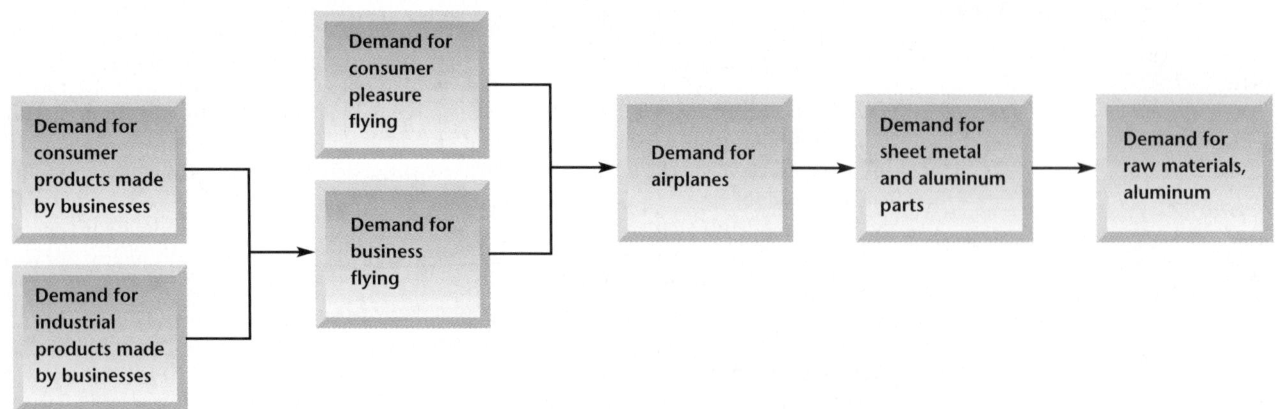

DISCUSSION CONSIDERATION
Have students discuss derived demand, the acceleration principle, and their anticipated effects as they relate to Otis elevators. Pratt and Whitney (makers of aircraft engines), Sikorsky helicopters, and United Technologies' automotive parts all have the same philosophy as Otis (all are United Technologies companies). How could derived demand affect demand for these companies' products in Russia?

increase in demand for the product from which demand is derived. For example, VGA graphics cards derive demand from color monitors. When demand for color monitors increases, makers of color monitors will buy more VGA graphics cards. Furthermore, the increase in demand for the graphics cards will be disproportionally higher than the percentage increase in sales for color monitors, because manufacturers will want to protect against the possibility of running out as demand grows. Similarly, when demand for a consumer product declines, the demand for component parts may decline faster.

The effects of derived demand on marketing efforts is important to organizational marketers, and not just because those effects are potentially devastating. Derived demand also presents certain opportunities. Under some circumstances, the organizational marketer can stimulate demand for the consumer product on which demand for the organizational product depends. This draws demand through the channel until it reaches the seller. For example, advertisements suggesting that milk is better in unbreakable plastic jugs may be sponsored by the producers of plastic jugs or the manufacturers of machines that make plastic jugs. Recognizing a trend of declining per capita beef consumption, the Beef Industry Council targeted consumers with advertisements in an attempt to reverse the trend. Pork producers and lamb producers have done much the same thing, even though all these organizations represent farmers and ranchers who are several steps removed from the consumer in channels of distribution.

The Beef Industry Council experience suggests another advantage of understanding derived demand. Alert marketers, keeping an eye on the ultimate demand on which they depend, can foresee developments that may soon affect their businesses. In some cases, such marketers can take steps to influence these developments or to make adjustments that offset their effects. Responding to trends in the marketplace is an important part of the job of all marketers, of course, but organizational marketers must pay special attention. Unfortunately, their distance from the consumers on whom they ultimately depend may make it more difficult for them to focus attention on developments that may affect their sales.

This advertisement shows Olympic champion Kristi Yamaguchi with a "milk mustache" and explains that milk has nine essential nutrients. The advertisement is sponsored by the Milk Industry Foundation. Trade associations often engage in marketing activity to stimulate consumer demand. If the demand for milk increases, then all members of the milk processing and dairy farming industries will derive the benefits resulting from an expanded market.

## Price Inelasticity

Compared with the demand for consumer goods, the rises and falls in organizational demand based on price are modest. Industry demand is relatively inelastic in the short run because it is not likely to significantly change as a result of price fluctuations. There are two very good reasons for this price inelasticity. First, organizational buyers are in a position to "pass along" price increases to their customers. If the price of the sheet metal used to make Jeep fenders goes up, Chrysler, maker of Jeep, can raise the price of its products to cover the increased cost of the metal because the demand for Jeeps is strong. The second, less obvious, reason for price inelasticity is the tendency for the price of any one product to be an almost insignificant part of the total price of the final product of which it is a part. When the price of sheet metal goes up, raising the cost of a fender by a few dollars, it has comparatively little effect on the total price of a finished Jeep. Note, however, that although organizational prices tend to be inelastic in general, buyers are not insensitive to them—especially if there are several competing sellers. Therefore, marketers must consider price in view of each customer's special situation.

**DISCUSSION CONSIDERATION**
Ask students to estimate the cost of seat covers, aircraft engines, and auto parts in terms of the selling price of airplanes and automobiles. How would a 10 percent increase in the price of these items affect the selling price of airplanes and automobiles?

**POINT TO EMPHASIZE**
As the slow economic recovery of 1992 showed, companies are reluctant to add new employees until they are sure demand is rising. Generally, they start by paying present employees a bit more for working longer hours rather than adding new full-time employees. As the economy cycles from prosperity toward a downturn, organizations tend to cut back much more quickly.

### Fluctuating Demand

Most organizations prefer steady operating schedules. Thus, it might be expected that organizational demand would be more or less constant. Actually, compared with the demand for consumer goods, the industry demand for organizational goods is characterized by wide fluctuations in demand. There are three logical reasons for this.

First, organizational purchases can usually be closely linked to the state of the economy. As the economy moves through its up-and-down cycles, demand for many organizational products goes through cycles as well. During prosperous times, firms tend to maintain large inventories. When the economy slows or enters a downturn, retailers, wholesalers, manufacturers, and most other business customers tend to sell off or use up their existing inventories. They also tend to postpone purchases of new supplies, equipment, and other products. If the direction of the economy is uncertain, purchases are again postponed. This is especially true for machine tools, pumps, materials handling equipment, and other products that can be repaired and made to last until better economic times seem imminent. Hence, demand in this part of the organizational market, influenced by environmental dynamics, can fluctuate widely.

Second, many organizational purchasers have a tendency to "stock up" on the products they buy. They then do not need to make further purchases until their stock is somewhat depleted. And finally, many organizational products have long lives, as in the case of buildings and major equipment.

## The SIC System—Classifying Business Markets

A wide variety of profit and not-for-profit institutions make up the business market. Knowing how many of each kind of organization are in operation, where they are located, their size, and so on can help marketers to implement research activities and plan marketing strategies. Fortunately, there is a great deal of data available on business markets. Although much of it is gathered by private companies, governmental agencies are also important sources of this information.

**STANDARD INDUSTRIAL CLASSIFICATION (SIC) SYSTEM**
A numerical coding system developed by the U.S. government and widely employed by organizational marketers to classify organizations in terms of the economic activities in which they are engaged.

A major tool for use in researching the organizational marketplace is the **Standard Industrial Classification (SIC) system.** The SIC system is a numerical coding system developed by the federal government and used to classify a broad range of organizations in terms of the type of economic activity in which they are engaged. The major divisions used in the system are shown in Exhibit 7–6. The two-digit codes shown in

**EXHIBIT 7–6** Primary SIC Divisions

| PRIMARY DIVISION | TWO-DIGIT SIC CODE |
|---|---|
| Agriculture, forestry, and fishing | 01 to 09 |
| Mining | 10 to 14 |
| Construction | 15 to 17 |
| Manufacturing | 20 to 39 |
| Transportation and public utilities | 40 to 49 |
| Wholesale trade | 50 to 51 |
| Retail trade | 52 to 59 |
| Finance, insurance, and real estate | 60 to 67 |
| Services (including agricultural services) | 70 to 89 |
| Public administration/government | 90 to 97 |

EXHIBIT 7–7

Selected SIC Codes for Major Group 26—Paper and Allied Products

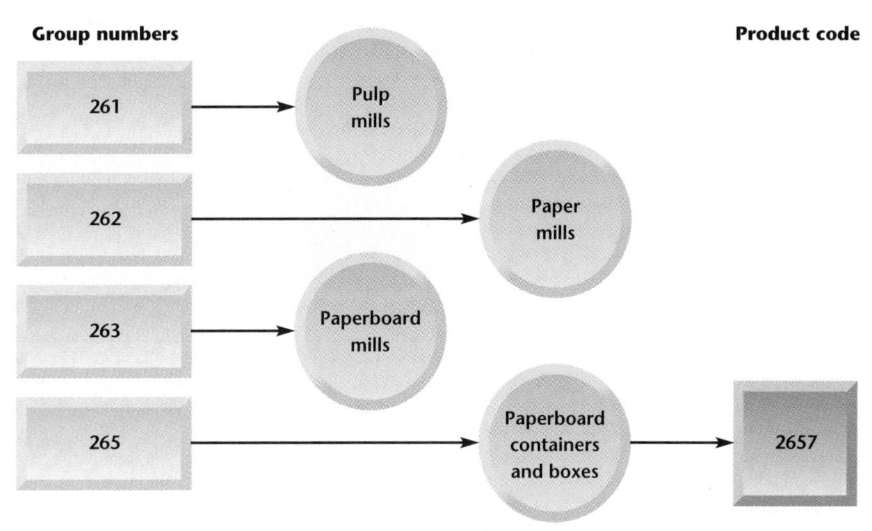


the exhibit can be lengthened to identify finer and finer gradations of differences within any particular area.

Consider, for example, the industry that manufactures paper and allied products. This broad category, or major group, is represented with the code number 26. As shown in Exhibit 7–7, adding a third digit creates a group number, which identifies a specific manufacturing function in the paper and allied products industry, such as paperboard container and box manufacturing. A fourth digit more exactly identifies a particular product category—in the exhibit, folding paperboard boxes—with a product code. A fifth digit identifies a still narrower product category with an item code, and additional digits define individual manufacturers and products. When people familiar with the SIC system use the word *industry,* they are referring, in effect, to a four-digit grouping in the SIC. For example, the code number 2657 is used to identify the folding paperboard box industry.

The SIC code system is important to marketers because it is a guide to vast amounts of information published by the federal government. The *Census of Retail Trade,* the *Census of Manufacturing, County Business Patterns,* and many other useful government publications are based on the SIC system. Furthermore, because the system is so heavily employed in government statistics, it is also used by most private companies that generate marketing research data.

Government statistics reported by SIC codes are often used to calculate geographical market potential. For example, suppose a manufacturer of industrial lubricants wishes to estimate the market potential in each sales territory. To do this, the company establishes the following procedure:[14]

1. The company determines that industrial lubricant sales are concentrated in three industries: apparel products manufacturing (SIC 23), chemicals (SIC 28), and fabricated metals (SIC 34).
2. A survey of purchasing agents in each of these SIC industries is conducted. Purchasing agents indicate their average annual rate of purchase (in pounds) and the number of employees in their plants. On the basis of the survey, the company estimates the current rate of purchase in pounds per employee for each type of industry.

**EXHIBIT 7–8** Market Potential for Cook County, Illinois, for Industrial Lubricants

| SIC CODE | INDUSTRY | NUMBER OF EMPLOYERS | POUNDS PER EMPLOYEE | ESTIMATED POTENTIAL (POUNDS) |
|---|---|---|---|---|
| 23 | Apparel | 10,087 | 30 | 302,610 |
| 28 | Chemicals | 19,822 | 50 | 991,100 |
| 34 | Fabricated metals | 61,660 | 65 | 4,007,900 |
| | | | | 5,301,610 |

Source: Updated from U.S. Department of Commerce, *Measuring Markets: A Guide to the Use of Federal and State Statistical Data* (Washington, D.C.: Government Printing Office, August 1974), p. 51; *County Business Patterns* (Washington, D.C., Government Printing Office, 1992).

3. Employment data for each industry are obtained on a county-by-county basis from *County Business Patterns.*
4. Market-potential estimates for each county are then derived as indicated in Exhibit 7–8 for Cook County, Illinois.

## Summary

The behavior of organizational buyers often differs significantly from that of ultimate consumers. Marketing managers must understand the special characteristics of this unique market.

LEARNING OBJECTIVE **1** *Identify the types of organizations that make up the business, or organizational, market.*

The business, or organizational, market is composed of businesses, nonprofit groups, charitable and religious organizations, governmental units, and other nonconsumers. Thus, a marketer's organizational customers may include manufacturers, farmers, churches, schools, and a host of others.

LEARNING OBJECTIVE **2** *Outline the steps involved in an organizational buying decision.*

Organizational buying takes place over time, involves communications among several organizational members, and demands financial relationships with suppliers. An organizational buying decision is the result of a multistage process that includes: (1) anticipating or recognizing a problem, (2) determining the characteristics and quantity of the product needed, (3) describing product specifications and critical needs, (4) searching for and qualifying potential sources, (5) acquiring and analyzing proposals, (6) evaluating proposals and selecting suppliers, (7) selecting an order routine, and (8) using feedback to evaluate performance.

LEARNING OBJECTIVE **3** *Characterize the three basic organizational buying situations: the straight rebuy, the modified rebuy, and the new task purchase.*

The straight rebuy requires no review of products or suppliers; materials are reordered automatically when the need arises. The modified rebuy occurs when buyers are discontented with present products or supplier performance and investigate alternative sources. The new task purchase involves evaluating product specifications and reviewing possible vendors in a purchase situation new to the organization.

LEARNING OBJECTIVE **4** *Explain why the buying center concept is important in business-to-business marketing.*

The buying center is an informal network of persons who have various roles in the purchasing decision process. The people and their roles vary over time. Roles include users, gatekeepers, influencers, deciders, and buyers. Marketers must identify members of the buying center and evaluate their importance to various stages of the process.

LEARNING OBJECTIVE **5** *Appreciate the needs of organizational buyers and explain how marketers can react to those needs.*

Needs of organizational buyers include product quality, related services, low price, and reliable delivery (perhaps including enhanced inventory management). The relative importance of these factors may vary with the buyer, the situation, or the product. The marketer must first determine these needs and then react to them through appropriate adjustments in the marketing mix.

LEARNING OBJECTIVE **6** *Describe the nature of organizational demand.*

Consumer buying decisions affect many organizations because demand for products in the organizational marketplace ultimately depends on consumer demand, even where purchasing decisions are far removed from consumers. Organizational demand is price inelastic in that the amounts of products demanded by buyers are not likely to change significantly as the prices for the products rise and fall. Finally, for a number of reasons, the demand for industrial goods fluctuates widely.

LEARNING OBJECTIVE **7** *Describe the SIC system and analyze its usefulness to marketers.*

The SIC system, a coding method used to classify organizations, can be used to identify products, individual manufacturers, purchasers of various products, and other useful facts. Governments, trade associations, and other sources use these codes to categorize information. Marketers who understand the system have access to vast amounts of published data and can use the codes to determine market potentials and gain other insights into the structure of markets.

## Key Terms

business-to-business marketing (p. 206)
organizational buying behavior (p. 206)
strategic alliance (p. 208)
buy phase (p. 209)
straight rebuy (p. 210)
modified rebuy (p. 210)
new task buying (p. 210)
buying center (p. 212)
user (p. 214)
buyer (p. 214)
gatekeeper (p. 214)
decider (p. 214)
influencer (p. 214)
single-sourcing (p. 219)
derived demand (p. 220)
acceleration principle (p. 220)
Standard Industrial Classification (SIC) system (p. 222)

## Questions for Discussion

1. In what ways does business-to-business marketing differ from consumer marketing?
2. Compare and contrast the consumer's decision-making process and the organization's decision-making process.
3. For the following products, indicate whether the organization's buying task will be a straight rebuy, modified rebuy, or new buying task. Briefly explain your answers.
   a. Lawn maintenance for the Mercedes-Benz regional headquarters building in suburban New Jersey
   b. Roller bearings as a component part for Snapper lawn mowers
   c. An industrial robot to perform a function currently done manually
   d. Personal computers for top-level managers
4. What difficulties for sellers are suggested by the buying center concept?
5. What variables might be used to estimate demand for the following products?
   a. Paper clips
   b. Staplers
   c. Lubricants for industrial-quality drill presses
   d. Forklift trucks
6. Define *derived demand* and give an example of its effect on the sale of packaging materials.
7. Explain in your own words why the demand for organizational products is generally inelastic with respect to price.
8. Is a business-to-business marketer more likely to stress personal selling or advertising in promoting a product? Why?
9. Form small groups as directed by your instructor. Pick a local business organization and identify at least four job titles held by the owner and employees. Discuss who will influence the company's buying decisions for straight rebuys, modified rebuys, and new task buying.

ETHICS IN PRACTICE

## Ethics Exercise 7

A woman wrote the following:

Working women in the U.S. had better start thinking seriously about what the increasing affluence of the Japanese means to us. A friend of mine, an elegant man of middle years who works in the same financial circuit where I earn my living, recently told me with some bemusement about an evening reception he had attended. A major New York bank was playing host to an equally formidable Japanese institution. The wine flowed, the canapés circulated, the flowers nodded in the waft of conversation among several hundred polite and expensively clad people—almost all of them men.

Now, my pal can dish the manly bonhomie with the best of them. But this was no locker room; this was a party, for heaven's sake. Where were the women? His polite probing produced one inescapable conclusion: It was deemed important that the Japanese visitors be put at ease, that they feel at home. And at home is where the women in their lives traditionally stay. So their ever-so-tactful New York hosts apparently decided that their women—wives and executives—should stay home, too.

## Questions

1. If you were in charge of a social function for Japanese businessmen, would you invite women?
2. Should women be part of an international sales team?
3. Is there a conflict between equal opportunity law and foreign business customs?

## Take a Stand

1. A purchasing agent likes to work with Company A, whose prices are rarely the lowest. The purchasing agent solicits competitive bids from Company A and two other companies that are known for exceedingly high quality and extremely high prices. Two other companies whose quality meets the organization's specifications and whose prices are generally the lowest in the industry are not invited to submit bids. Company A, whose product meets minimum quality specifications, wins the contract. Is this ethical?
2. A purchasing agent attends a lewd party sponsored by a company that wants to do business with the agent's company. Should the purchasing agent have attended?
3. A company gives preferential treatment to minority-owned raw materials suppliers. Is this a good policy?

VIDEO CASE 7–1

## Nypro

Nypro of Clinton, Massachusetts, is a privately owned company engaged in the manufacture of injection-molded plastics, a business that some consider a commodity business.

Started 40 years ago with one machine in a garage in Clinton, Nypro today is 70 percent owned by President Gordon B. Lankton. About 100 employees own the remaining 30 percent. The company has a long-standing profit-sharing policy that covers all employees. Under this plan, $20 million has been distributed since 1964.

Nypro makes mostly penny items, with many ranging from 3 cents to 5 cents, for its customers. These products vary from simple plastic items such as toothbrush handles to intricate plastic structures like diagnostic units, which Nypro makes for practically all the major health care products companies. Nypro also churns out small containers and wire fasteners, women's shavers (30 million in 1993), cellular telephone components, computer parts, three-color ink jet printer cartridges, and components for pagers.

Nypro is a major producer of floppy disks for computers. Another low-cost, large-volume item is contact lens molds. Nypro makes toothbrushes for Johnson & Johnson, fasteners for Avery Dennison, and cellular phone components for Motorola.

The health care market is Nypro's most important, accounting for more than 50 percent of its sales. It used to represent two-thirds of Nypro's overall business; but while the health care products business grew in 1994, the segment's overall share of revenues was reduced by design, because Nypro did not want to become wholly dependent on one market segment.

Nypro used to be the fifth-largest injection molder but dropped to ninth place after a number of large molders in Detroit merged and surpassed it. These companies are mostly geared to the automotive industry. Nypro also does some work for that market, but it is not a major business.

Nypro's marketing strategy involves seeking to do business only with the best customers. The strategy stems from the belief that having too many customers may cause quality problems if each customer has its own quality system, its own way of communicating specifications, and so on.

Nypro wants to build relationships with customers that will be desirable partners. Nypro is proud of its high standards for customers. If a customer can't meet its criteria, it might as well go elsewhere, because Nypro won't do business. Nypro hasn't pursued many contracts with automakers, for instance, because they're driven by unit price and cronyism rather than quality and supplier partnerships.

Nypro's criteria for doing business relate directly to the customer's purchasing philosophy and strategy. "If they like to play hardball by dividing up the business and playing one supplier against the other in terms of price, we're not interested," says Brian Jones, vice president of quality. "If they're used to short-term commitments, if their supplier relationships are driven by fear and intimidation rather than improvement and collaboration, or if the only way they know how to evaluate a supplier's performance is on price and delivery, we don't want them."

Nypro prefers customers that are open to a certain amount of training on how to source. They also most be interested in a close involvement with their suppliers.

"We have engineers who are living full-time in our customers' operations and are helping in yield and manufacturing improvements," Jones says. "We want to share technologies and help our customers set more vigorous standards than their market requires."

Nypro customers must be interested in a collaborative, not autocratic, arrangement.

"Most purchasers like to tell their suppliers what their latest market-driven requirements are—whether it be JIT, EDI, or TQM—and then turn on the heat to make them comply," Jones says. "We prefer a shared movement forward, where the purchaser listens as well as speaks."

Nypro's commitment to quality is illustrated by its 1989 decision to "shoot for the moon." The industry standard at the time was 10,000 defects per million, yet Nypro chose to adopt the so-called six sigma standard (3.4 defects per million). That meant firing, in effect, about 90 percent of the company's 800 customers and focusing on about 30 (such as Baxter International and Gillette) sophisticated enough to appreciate Nypro's extreme quality commitment.

### QUESTIONS FOR DISCUSSION

1. How important is strategic planning to Nypro? Overall, how would you characterize Nypro's marketing strategy?
2. Is reducing the number of customers a wise marketing strategy? Why would Nypro want fewer rather than more customers?
3. How important is technology to a company like Nypro?
4. Identify what type of organizational buying situations face most of Nypro's customers.
5. Is Nypro following the marketing concept?

**VIDEO CASE 7–2 FOCUS ON SMALL BUSINESS**

## National Customer Engineering

Any company that relies primarily on one customer has nightmares about the thought of losing that customer. Such a nightmare became reality for National Customer Engineering, a computer maintenance company headquartered in San Diego, California.

Three quarters of NCE's revenues came from servicing hardware produced by a single computer manufacturer. The manufacturer had contracted with NCE to provide maintenance on warranties for its line of multi-user computer systems throughout the country. NCE also had service contracts with dealers who offered extended warranties in selling the manufacturer's products.

Suddenly the manufacturer announced it would go into computer maintenance itself. It refused to supply NCE with parts for new products and began competing for other NCE customers who dealt in its computers. Some left NCE. Revenue fell dramatically. Employee morale plummeted.

**Source:** Excerpted with permission from *Real-World Lessons for America's Small Business*, pp. 134–135, copyright 1992 by Connecticut Mutual Life Insurance Company.

### QUESTIONS

1. How unusual is it for an organizational marketer to rely on a single customer or a few organizational buyers? In this situation, what is the nature of the buying task?
2. What direction should National Customer Engineering take to obtain new organizational customers?
3. How can it prevent a similar situation from occurring in the future?

CHAPTER

# 8

# Market Segmentation, Targeting, and Positioning Strategies

## LEARNING OBJECTIVES

After you have studied this chapter, you will be able to:

1. Define the term *market.*
2. Explain the concept of market segmentation.
3. Relate the identification of meaningful target markets to the development of effective marketing mixes.
4. Distinguish among undifferentiated, concentrated, differentiated, and custom marketing strategies.
5. Demonstrate the effect of the 80/20 rule and the majority fallacy on marketing strategy.
6. List the market segmentation variables available to marketing managers and explain how marketers identify which ones are appropriate.
7. Explain the purpose of a positioning strategy.

ヒトを彩るサイエンス
SHISEIDO
食事、おしゃべり、キス、着がえ。
落ちない、つかない、パーフェクトルージュ
Perfect Rouge
Perfect Rouge
レシェンテ
Perfect Rouge
パーフェクトルージュN 10色各3,000円
新発売


Japanese marketers are racing to keep pace with a progressive new cultural evolution involving women.

While some marketers still picture the stereotypical housewife in ads for cleaning products and the like, a new breed of working woman is being addressed in advertisements for products as diverse as frozen vegetables, cigarettes, and no-smear lipstick.

More than half of Japan's married women now hold full- or part-time jobs, according to the government's Management & Coordination Agency, and women comprise 40.5 percent of Japan's 64.5 million workers. The agency said that even during the height of the recession in 1993, there were 26.1 million working women in Japan, up from 23.7 million in 1985.

The change in attitude toward working women was a slow process. Unlike the United States, which was swept by women's liberation in the 1970s, Japan experienced the women's rights movement as an evolutionary, not a revolutionary, process.

And much progress still needs to be made. A survey by the Labor Ministry, for example, reported that 60.1 percent of young women on a career track felt they were "treated unfairly in hiring, promotions, and job responsibility." And a private survey showed that women have become presidents of only 5 percent of Japan's one million companies.

But while Japanese women haven't become as liberated as Western women, they have become as busy. Working women are increasingly looking for products that are convenient and time-saving. Because of their unique needs, they are an attractive target market.

For example, the rise of working women in Japan has given birth to a fad one can't kiss off easily: long-lasting, no-smear lipstick. Targeted at fast-moving Japanese businesswomen, the products, which didn't even exist three years ago, are now a booming $45 million business monthly.

The long-lasting lipsticks give women the power to pucker up without compunction. The country's largest cosmetic marketer, Shiseido, touts this in commercials for Reciente Perfect Rouge long-lasting lipstick brand, telling women they can "dine, chat, kiss, and change [their] dress without leaving smudges." The commercials feature Ryo, a popular 21-year-old model, racing through her day wearing no-smear lipstick.

This freedom doesn't come cheaply. The lipsticks come in a variety of colors and are priced at $30 for a 3.6 gram tube. A cleansing agent to remove the lipstick costs $10.

The popularity of no-smear lipstick is attributed to the 50 percent of Japanese women who work outside the home and prefer brands that eliminate time-consuming applications. No-smear lipstick also solves a sticky yet common problem in crowded Japan. A Shiseido survey found that 40 percent of all male commuters have been smeared by lipstick in Tokyo's infamous jam-packed trains and subways. Lipstick smudges, of course, have caused more than one of these men to have problems at home.

Reciente Perfect Rouge sold 2.3 million units in the first two months of introduction, more than double the company's normal lipstick sales of one million units during an average two-month period in the Japanese market.

**ALTERNATIVE EXAMPLE**

Companies with loyal buyers tend top serve homogeneous groups. MBNA, a highly profitable bank that issues MasterCard and Visa credit cards, loses customers at half the industry rate. One reason: MBNA is the biggest issuer of "affinity cards," used by members of organizations ranging from the American Dental Association to Ducks Unlimited, a wildlife conservation group. The group's logo is imprinted on the card.

This chapter considers in greater depth the definitions of the terms *market* and *market segmentation.* It discusses how marketers determine which target marketing strategy will best serve their objectives. Then it examines the many variables used to segment consumer and organizational markets. Finally, it considers how marketers develop positioning strategies.

## What Is a Market? What Is Market Segmentation?

DISCUSSION CONSIDERATION
Have students generate examples of products (perhaps clothing and cosmetics) that they would not purchase if the prices were "too low" and examples of products (such as medicine and water) whose prices would not be a factor.

We have already defined *market,* but let us look again at that definition. A market is a group of actual or potential customers for a particular product. More precisely, a market is a group of individuals or organizations that may want the good or service being offered for sale and that meet these three additional criteria:

1. The purchasing power to be able to buy the product being offered.
2. The willingness to spend money or exchange other resources to obtain the product.
3. The authority to make such expenditures.

Economics textbooks often give the impression that all consumers are alike. As long as there exists a willingness and an ability to buy, economists frequently draw no distinctions among different types of buyers. Young and old buyers, men and women, people who drink 12 beers a day and those who drink one beer on New Year's Eve are all lumped together. Experience tells us, however, that in many cases, buyers differ from one another even though they may be buying the same products. Marketers try to identify groups and subgroups within total markets—that is, they try to segment markets.

Recall that market segmentation consists of dividing a heterogeneous market into a number of smaller, more homogeneous submarkets. Almost any variable—age, sex, product usage, lifestyle, expected benefit—may be used as a segmenting variable, but the logic of the strategy is always the same.

POINT TO EMPHASIZE
As markets become increasingly fragmented, it becomes harder to identify a homogeneous market for any product. Salt may once have been undifferentiated; but current meaningful submarkets for this product include low-salt, no-salt, and salt-substitute products.

- Not all buyers are alike.
- Subgroups of people with similar behavior, values, and/or backgrounds may be identified.
- The subgroups will be smaller and more homogeneous than the market as a whole.
- It should be easier to satisfy smaller groups of similar customers than large groups of dissimilar customers.

Usually, marketers are able to cluster similar customers into specific market segments with different, and sometimes unique, demands. For example, the computer software market can be divided into two segments: the domestic market and the foreign market. The domestic market can be segmented further into business users and at-home users. And the at-home user segment can be further subdivided into sophisticated personal computer users, people who hate but use personal computers, people who use computers only for games, and so on. The number of market segments within the total market depends largely on the strategist's ingenuity and creativity in identifying those segments.

Needless to say, a single company is unlikely to pursue all possible market segments. In fact, the idea behind market segmentation is for an organization to choose one or a few meaningful segments and concentrate its efforts on satisfying those selected parts of the market. Focusing its efforts on these *targeted market segments*—that is, *targeting*—enables the organization to allocate its marketing resources effectively. Concentrating efforts on a given market segment should result in a more precise marketing program satisfying specific market needs.

Delta knows that the needs of experienced business flyers and frequent flyers are different from those of the occasional flyer. Its Medallion sky miles program promotes upgrades to first class for those who are regular Delta customers. The smaller and more specialized a market segment, the easier it is to identify its particular interests and special needs.

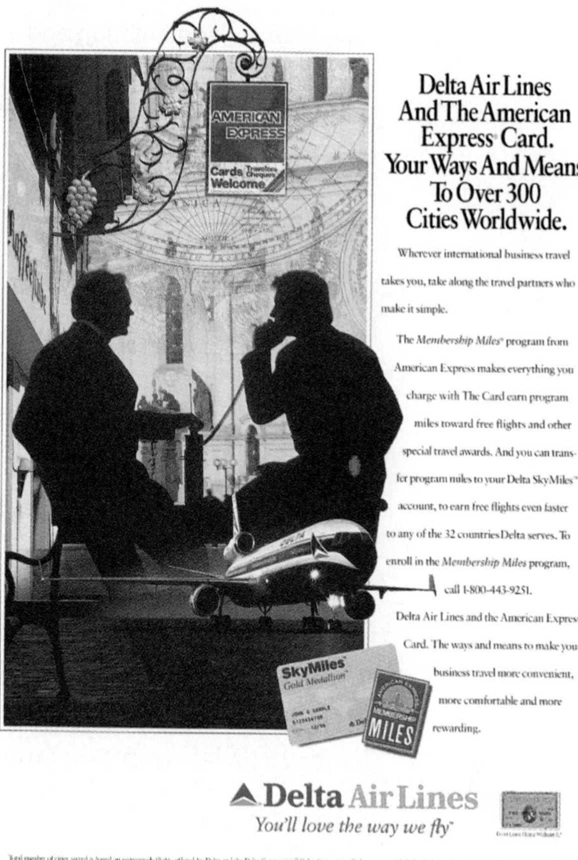


As mentioned in Chapter 2, the market segment, or group of buyers, toward which the organization decides to direct its marketing plan is called the *target market.* The target market for Shower Shaver, for example, is that subgroup of women who shave their legs in the shower.

ALTERNATIVE EXAMPLE

Hearth Song is a cataloger selling items inspired by Native American cultures. It sells dream-catcher kits, tepees, multicultural crocheted dolls, and other crafts. It sends out more than 5 million catalogs annually and has six stores in the San Francisco Bay area. Together, the catalog and stores generate over $20 million dollars a year in sales. SOURCE: Michael Wilke, "Toy Companies Take Up Diversity Banner," *Advertising Age,* February 27, 1995, pp. 1, 8.

Because it is possible to segment markets in so many ways, target marketing opportunities abound. For example, there are "left-hander" shops specializing in products for left-handed people, tobacco shops catering to wealthy pipe smokers, and dress shops like the 5-7-9 Shops that target women who wear certain clothing sizes. In addition, numerous products bear the names of symbols of sports teams, such as the NFL's San Francisco 49ers and NBA's Chicago Bulls, and are marketed to team fans. Some companies even sell items to people who hate particular teams—a once popular sports-related item was the "I Hate the Yankees Hanky." As you can see, the process of segmentation provides hints on how to market to the targeted segments identified.

Selection of the target market or markets (in some cases, more than one may be selected) is a three-step process, as shown in Exhibit 8–1. First, the total market, consisting of many different customers, is studied and broken down (or disaggregated) into its component parts—that is, individual customers, families, organizations, or other units. The customers are then regrouped by the marketing strategist into market segments on the basis of one or several characteristics that segment members have in common. Then the strategist must target segments to which the organization will appeal. When that is done, the strategist has answered the question "What are our target markets?"

EXHIBIT 8–1 The Major Steps in Market Segmentation and Selection of Target Markets

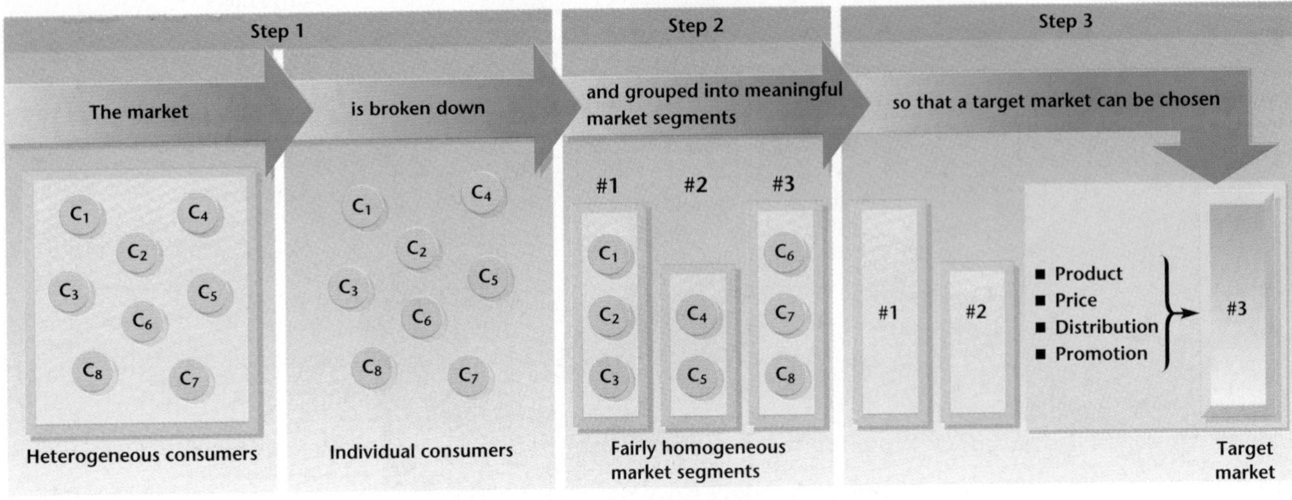


## Choosing Meaningful Market Segments

Target marketing rests on the assumption that differences among buyers are related to meaningful differences in market behavior. The identification of market segments that are not meaningful has little value. The following five criteria make a segment meaningful:

1. The market segment has a characteristic or characteristics that distinguish it from the overall market. This characteristic should be stable over time.
2. The market segment has a market potential of significant size—that is, large enough to be profitable.
3. The market segment is accessible through distribution efforts or reachable through promotional efforts.
4. The market segment is responsive. The market segment has a unique market need, and the likelihood that the segment will favorably respond to a marketing mix tailored to this need is high.
5. The segment's market potential should be measurable. Ease of measurement facilitates effective target marketing by helping to identify and quantify group purchasing power and to indicate the differences among market segments. Although ease of measurement is desirable, it is not mandatory.

Exhibit 8–2 outlines these criteria. The general goal of profitability can depend on how well marketers use the criteria to identify target markets. Selecting a group that is not easily distinguishable or accessible, or appealing to a segment that is too small to generate adequate sales volume, or selecting a group that the company is unable to attract is not effective market segmentation.

Consider an example. Cuban citizens born on October 1 form a possible market segment. This is undoubtedly a large group. But even assuming it has unique market demands (which is probably not the case), this segment is not meaningful. The U.S. government has placed an embargo on exports to Cuba, and these restrictions completely shut down trade with this island. The market segment consisting of Cubans born on October 1 does not meet the criterion of accessibility. The accompanying Competitive Strategy feature describes a vivid example of unsuccessful targeting.

DISCUSSION CONSIDERATION

Saturn automobiles are sold according to a one-price policy, with no haggling over price. Obviously, GM thinks that some car buyers want to avoid haggling and may be price-insensitive. Ford has adopted the one-price policy for its Escorts at some dealerships. Does the one-price policy effectively target some consumers? Is this a meaningful basis on which to develop a marketing strategy?

## EXHIBIT 8–12 Consumption Patterns of Families in Several Life-Cycle Stages

| STAGE | CONSUMPTION PATTERNS |
|---|---|
| Young single | Outdoor sporting goods, sports cars, fashion clothing, entertainment and recreation services |
| Young married without children | Recreation and relaxation products, home furnishings, travel, home appliances<br>High purchase rate of durables |
| Young married with children | Baby food, clothing, and furniture; starter housing; insurance; washers and dryers; medical services and supplies for children; toys for children |
| Young single parent | Money-saving products, frozen foods, rental housing, child care, time-saving appliances and foods |
| Middle-aged married with children at home | Children's lessons (piano, dance, etc.); large food purchases (respond to bulk-buying deals); dental care; higher-priced furniture, autos, and housing; fast-food restaurant meals |
| Middle-aged married without children at home | Luxury products, travel, restaurants, condominiums, recreation<br>Make gifts and contributions, have high discretionary incomes and solid financial position |
| Older (married or single) | Health care, home security, specialized housing, specialized food products, recreation geared to the retired |

Source: Adapted with the permission of Prentice Hall, Inc. from *Consumer Behavior,* third edition, by John C. Mowen. Copyright © 1993 by Macmillan College Publishing Company.

arrived—perhaps golf, tennis, and partying. Another father in the same stage of the family life cycle may drop his sports and social activities to devote more time to the children. The two demographically similar men differ in terms of lifestyle or psychographic variables.

As you can imagine, there are many different lifestyles, and there is no agreement about a standard set of lifestyle categories or psychographic measures. The accompanying Competitive Strategy feature illustrates how Porsche uses psychographics to supplement its knowledge about its demographic market segments.

DISCUSSION CONSIDERATION

Describe various lifestyles of the college student population. As common characteristics emerge, students may generate names for the segments and estimate the size of each. (For example, Studious Samsons study and exercise, Partying Preps attend all the social functions, Working Waifs divide time between jobs and class.)

Chrysler targets each of its three LH sedans at a specific segment of the baby boomer market. The Concorde is intended for older, professional boomers who accept mainstream social values. The Vision is aimed at consumers who are intensely interested in technology. These people are attracted to European and Japanese cars because of their styling, performance, and technological advances. The Intrepid targets the biggest boomer market—people with families who want stylish, dependable transportation.

COMPETITIVE STRATEGY: WHAT WENT WRONG?

## *Porsche*

After having sold a record 30,000 automobiles in the United States in 1986, Porsche sold only 4,000 or so in 1993. Price was partly responsible. During the 1980s, the price of a Porsche 911 Carrera coupe was less than the average U.S. household's annual income. In 1993, the price was about 25 percent higher because of the strength of the Deutsche mark and a luxury tax passed by Congress. However, after conducting marketing research to learn what market segments were prime customers, Porsche Cars North America found out increased price wasn't the only thing that had gone wrong.

The research showed that the demographics of Porsche owners were utterly predictable: a 40-something male college graduate earning over $200,000 per year. The psychographics, however, were of more interest. Porsche owners were placed into the following rather unusual—and not necessarily flattering—lifestyle categories as shown below.

Porsche's vice president of sales and marketing found the results astonishing. He said, "We were selling to people whose profiles were diametrically opposed. You wouldn't want to tell an elitist how good he looks in the car or how fast he could go."

As a result of its new insights about its target markets, Porsche has cut its prices, launched a new advertising campaign, and introduced a redesign of its classic rear-engine car, the 911.

| Type | Percent of All Owners | Description |
|---|---|---|
| Top Guns | 27% | Driven, ambitious types. Power and control matter. They expect to be noticed. |
| Elitists | 24% | Old-money blue bloods. A car is just a car; no matter how expensive. It is not an extension of personality. |
| Proud Patrons | 23% | Ownership is an end in itself. The car is a trophy earned for hard work, and who cares if anyone sees them in it? |
| Bon Vivants | 17% | Worldly jet setters and thrill seekers. The car heightens the excitement in their already passionate lives. |
| Fantasists | 9% | Walter Mitty types. The car is an escape. Not only are they uninterested in impressing others with it, they also feel a little guilty about owning one. |

Numerous products bear the names, mascots, and symbols of sports teams, such as the NFL's Vikings and the NBA's Suns, and are marketed to team fans. Fans who strongly identify with a particular team reflect a sports-oriented lifestyle. Fans serve as a target market not only for the team's services but also for products ranging from T-shirts to coffee mugs to conventions.

POINT TO EMPHASIZE
Since psychographic data are less readily available than demographic data, many firms may miss the guidance such data provide for promotion, pricing, product design, and development of channel options. Many journal articles profile psychographic segments, and these may supply students with ideas as their careers progress.

Whatever the classification scheme, lifestyles and psychographics are often used to segment markets. *Outdoor Life, Flying, Travel and Leisure,* and many other magazines define their target markets by lifestyle, for example. By reaching certain lifestyle segments, they provide advertising media for other marketers who wish to appeal to those segments.

Psychographic variables are more difficult to deal with than demographic and socioeconomic variables. Library research can tell the marketer approximately how many male Hispanic Americans there are in California, for instance, but there are no statistics on the number of carefree people or good family men. This is one reason marketers typically use psychographic variables in combination with other variables. For example, marketers might decide that the psychographic lifestyle of a Porsche sports car buyer can be tied to more concrete demographic and economic descriptions.[5]

## Geographic Segmentation

DISCUSSION CONSIDERATION
Ask students to geographically segment their town for (1) a Salvation Army outlet or (2) a designer clothing store. Can they derive segmentation "rules" (for example, placing Salvation Army outlets in lower-class neighborhoods with subsistence lifestyles) for locating sites nationwide? Internationally?

Simple geography can be an important basis for market segmentation. The demand for suntan lotion is far greater in Florida, for example, than in Saskatchewan. In some cases, a geographic variable might indicate to a marketer that there is absolutely no demand for a certain product in a certain area, such as snow shovels in Puerto Rico.

Most marketers use geography as a basis to segment markets. Virtually all marketers decide if they will engage in international business or market only in their home country. International marketers recognize that people in Mexico, Egypt, and Malaysia have different needs and customs. In Argentina, for instance, most Coca-Cola is consumed with food, but in many Asian countries, it is consumed primarily as a refreshment and rarely served with meals.

Not all U.S–based firms choose to market their products outside the United States, of course. However, geographical differences are also important in the United States. Domestic marketers should recognize that for many products, such as mass transportation, people in New York City have different needs from people in Wyoming.

ALTERNATIVE EXAMPLE

The *Los Angeles Times* publishes a news and entertainment paper, *Nuestro Tiempo,* written by a Latino staff. Three-fourths of *Nuestro Tiempo's* issues are distributed on postal carrier routes where more than 50 percent of the households are Hispanic. *Nuestro Tiempo* is distributed separately from the *Times* because the publishers are aiming at the 73 percent of the Hispanic market that read only Spanish. SOURCE: Kelly Shermach, "Spanish-Language Press Is Catching On Slowly," *Marketing News,* March 13, 1995, p. 10.

**Some Geographic Bases of Segmentation** Geographic segmentation includes distinctions based on continents, cultural regions, and climate. Another basis for segmentation is political boundaries, such as state and city lines and the like. However, populations are not always adequately described by political boundaries. Marketers are most often concerned with the population map—where the people are—rather than with such matters as the "line" that "separates" Billings Heights, Montana, from Billings, Montana. Various expressions are used to reflect this fact—"Greater New York," "the Dallas–Fort Worth Metro-Plex," "the Bay Area," "the Twin Cities." These phrases, and others like them, indicate that for certain market segments, there is no distinct political boundary line.

**Geodemographic and Zip Code Segmentation** Direct marketers, especially those who sell through catalogs sent my mail, often use zip codes as a basis for market segmentation. The phrase "birds of a feather flock together" is quite appropriate here. People and households in the same zip code area are often similar in demographic characteristics.

**GEODEMOGRAPHIC SEGMENTATION**

A type of market segmentation by which consumers are grouped according to demographic variables, such as income and age, as identified by a geographic variable, such as zip code.

**Geodemographic segmentation** refers to use of a geographic variable, such as zip codes, to characterize clusters of demographically similar individuals. Claritas Corporation's PRIZM system has analyzed each of the 36,000 zip codes in the United States and, based on demographic similarities, classified them into 40 market segments. Each has a colorful name like Shotguns and Pickups (large rural families with modest means) and Gray Power (active retirement communities).

**Geographical Considerations for Global Marketers** Global marketers who segment markets based on geography must recognize that certain factors may discourage international marketing in certain countries. As explained in Chapter 4, sometimes countries require that all trade with other nations be approved by some form of central ministry. Governments may also impose tariffs, import quotas, or other restrictive controls to discourage foreign companies from doing business in their markets. For example, in 1995, because of widespread and blatant production and sale

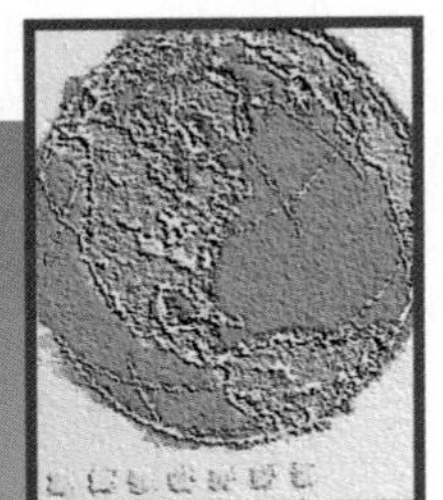

## FOCUS ON GLOBAL COMPETITION

### *Children in China*

Xiang Yinchao, a 10-year-old boy, waits quietly in a crowded Shanghai department store while his mother asks a saleswoman a barrage of questions about the VTech alphabet desk, a $70 computer keyboard that helps teach Mandarin-speaking children English. Yinchao's mother knows it's expensive, but she says, "Chinese parents want their kids to speak English. It's the international language."

Limited to one child by government regulations and determined to see their kids get ahead, Chinese parents—along with grandparents, great-grandparents, aunts, and uncles—are spoiling, fussing over, and doting on their children as never before.

Known in China as Little Emperors, Chinese kids are being showered with everything from candy to computer games. With at least 300 million people in China under the age of 15, according to government statistics, a huge market is emerging that caters to China's kiddie dynasty.

Business is driven by the "six-pocket syndrome," a phrase referring to the fact that as many as six adults may be indulging the whims of each child. The president of Walt Disney's Asian-Pacific consumer products division says, "When you look at the combined spending power of those grown-ups, the Chinese child probably has more spent on him than a child in the West." ■

ALTERNATIVE EXAMPLE
Cosmetics manufacturers often vary their products. P&G adds brighter colors to Max Factor makeup for the Latin American market and more conditioners to Vidal Sassoon shampoo for the Far Eastern market. In the Far East, Maybelline offers a high-humidity face makeup. Its Shades of You, sold to African American women in the United States, is also marketed in South Africa, and it sells bolder lip colors in Argentina and Peru. SOURCE: Paulette Thomas, "Cosmetics Makers Offer World's Women An All-American Look with Local Twists," *Wall Street Journal,* May 8, 1995, p. B1.

of pirated compact discs, laser discs, CD-ROM discs, and other American intellectual property, the United States threatened to impose trade sanctions against an array of Chinese products, ranging from toys to athletic shoes. China threatened to retaliate with its own sanctions against the United States.

Such restrictive factors may strongly influence decisions to target certain market segments. At the same time, the changing political climate, away from Communism and toward market economies, provides many opportunities.

## Behavior Pattern Segmentation

Individual consumers exhibit different behavior patterns and habits worthy of marketers' attention. Some individuals purchase apparel only at specialty men's or women's shops, for example, while others buy their clothing at department stores, in discount shops, or from catalogs. Shopping habits and other behavioral differences may be used as bases for segmentation. Seven-Up increased efforts to have its products sold in fast-food outlets and in vending machines. Why? Because marketing analysts found that these two types of outlets, which are aimed at people who behave in certain ways, accounted for 40 percent of industry sales but only 20 percent of 7-Up's sales volume.

## Consumption Pattern Segmentation

DISCUSSION CONSIDERATION
To emphasize the relationship of the text to their behavior, ask students where they would take their boss for a working lunch and where they would take an old friend on the day before pay day.

Buyers can vary their consumption from heavy use to nonuse. Therefore, in many cases, consumption patterns provide a good basis for market segmentation. Both the New York Mets and the New York Metropolitan Opera offer season tickets to heavy users of their products. Banks are aware that many of their customers are long-term clients who loyally deal with only one institution—thus slogans like "a full-service bank" and "the only bank you'll ever need." Light users or nonusers of the same bank's services require a different marketing mix, perhaps one stressing convenient

Markets for services may be segmented by the benefits customers receive. In London, a new type of motorcycle taxi called TaxiBike offers a precious benefit to many airplane travelers—time. The price for a trip from central London to Heathrow airport on a TaxiBike is $50, about the same as that for an automotive taxi; but when traffic is heavy, the customer arrives in about 30 minutes instead of an hour and a half. The motorcycle has heated leather seats, and the passenger is provided with waterproof coveralls and a helmet with a built-in headset for a cellular phone. Of course, the passenger in a regular taxi benefits by having a little more room for luggage.

**CROSS-SELLING**
Marketing activities used to sell new services to customers of an existing service.

locations or free merchandise for new depositors. Banks and many other marketers of services target some existing customers by using a technique known as **cross-selling.** Cross-selling refers to marketing activities used to sell new, "extra" services to customers for an existing service. Thus, a bank may make it easy for a customer with a home mortgage loan to obtain a low-cost safety deposit box and a checking account with a credit line.

Just a few years back, while the giants of the personal computer industry were still focusing their energy on selling machines by the hundreds to the lucrative corporate market, Packard Bell Electronics Inc. was quietly selling low-priced computers one at a time at Wal-Mart Stores Inc. and other discount and department stores. It was this consumer-market retailing strategy that helped Packard Bell rise from obscurity to the top ranks of the computer industry.

The privately held company recently unseated IBM to become the nation's third-largest seller of personal computers, and it now sells more computers to the consumer and home-office market than any other company.

Consumption patterns may also differ with circumstances. The purchase occasion may prove to be the underlying force creating consumption patterns and thus be useful in distinguishing among buyer groups. A holiday drinking glass decorated with a Christmas tree or Santa Claus is obviously geared to buyers planning seasonal entertaining rather than to people looking for everyday glassware. Lava soap and other hand cleaners are sold for use on the dirty, messy, or greasy occasion.

Of course, some buying patterns are strongly linked to other buying patterns. Ownership of one product may encourage the purchase of additional products. For example, owners of computers that use Windows-based operating systems are likely to buy additional Windows-based software. In contrast, marketers of custom sheepskin van seat covers can expect to sell very few products to people who don't own vans, and storm windows are seldom bought by people who don't own houses. In many instances, consumption patterns can be the major clue in identifying meaningful marketing segments.

## Consumer Predisposition Segmentation

Consumers generally vary widely with respect to product knowledge, beliefs about products and brands, and reasons for purchase. The sophisticated, knowledgeable buyer of stereo equipment is, for marketing purposes, almost totally different from the novice buyer. The veteran buyer knows what to look for, what questions to ask, where to buy, where to get service, and even what the price should be. The novice knows almost nothing of these things and so looks to salespeople for guidance. The novice seeks a store with a good reputation and trustworthy salespeople. The veteran buyer trusts his or her own knowledge and judgment.

**BENEFIT SEGMENTATION**
A type of market segmentation by which consumers are grouped according to the specific benefits they seek from a product.

Furthermore, the major benefits sought by consumers are likely to vary considerably. Seeking to identify groups of customers by the benefits they seek is called **benefit segmentation.** Even when two or more buyers are purchasing exactly the same product, the expected benefits may vary. Just as in the commercial, some people buy Miller Lite because it tastes great, others because it's less filling. A mouthwash might be bought because it kills germs or because it tastes "mediciney" and therefore must really freshen breath.

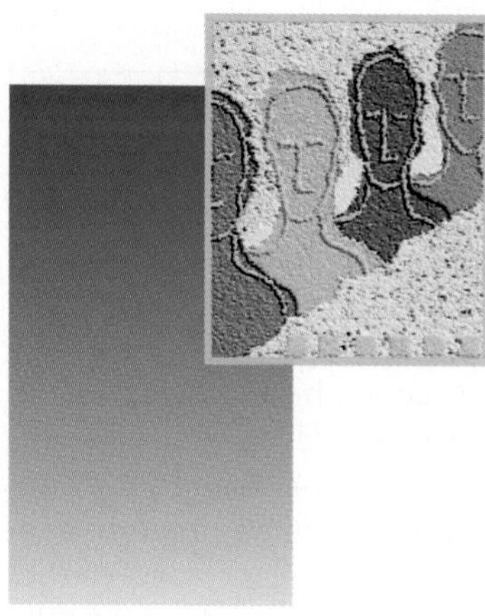

## FOCUS ON RELATIONSHIPS

### *USSA*

A customer who is brand-loyal to a service—a customer who repeatedly purchases from the same company—is an especially important segment of the market. Thus, marketers such as American Airlines and Avis put special efforts into establishing enduring relationships with these customers.

USSA, an insurance and financial service company, loses customers at a rate far below the industry rate. USSA retains 98 percent of its auto insurance customers yearly, versus about 85 percent for the industry as a whole, even though the military officers it specializes in covering are constantly on the move. Having designed its service around its customers' needs, USSA deals almost exclusively by phone and mail and operates a data base in San Antonio that allows clients to relocate anywhere without switching agents. ■

# Segmenting Business Markets

To a great extent, business markets may be segmented by use of variables similar to the ones just discussed. The difference, of course, is that, instead of using characteristics and behavior of the individual consumer, the segmenter uses characteristics and behavior of the organization. For example, marketers of electrical resistors decided to investigate their market on the basis of benefit segmentation. A study of the benefits sought from electrical resistors uncovered two major benefit segments. Military engineers purchasing for the government and engineers purchasing for consumer electronic companies both sought performance stability and reliability. But military buyers were concerned with failure rate and promptness in review of specifications, while low price was the major benefit sought by the consumer products engineers.

Exhibit 8–13 shows that business markets may be segmented on the basis of geography, organizational characteristics, purchase behavior and usage patterns, and organizational predispositions.

**EXHIBIT 8–13**

Selected Bases for Segmentation of Business Markets

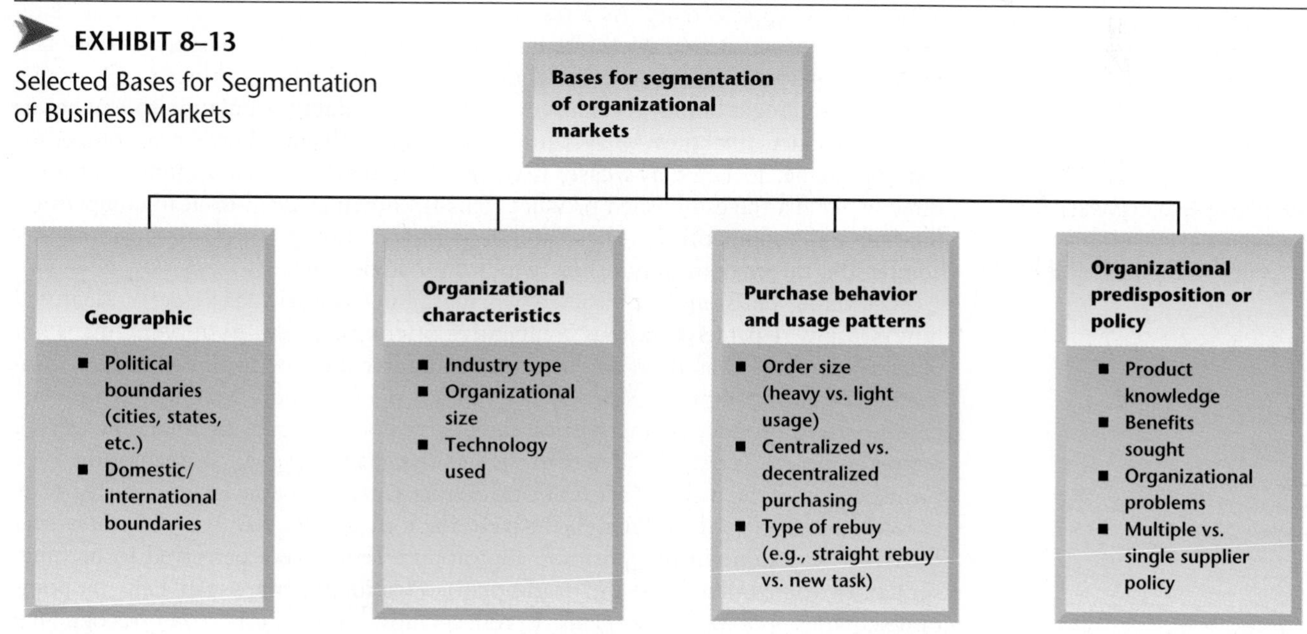

## Finding the "Best" Segmentation Variable

POINT TO EMPHASIZE

The "best" segmentation variables may change in dynamic environments as consumers seek novelty, as the family life cycle evolves, and as culture dynamically alters values and norms.

As already suggested, the "best" segmentation variable is the one that leads the marketer to the identification of a meaningful target market segment. Some experts have argued that the benefits customers seek from products are the basis for all market segments. This may be so. After all, that idea supports the view that consumer orientation is the foundation of the marketing concept.

But contributing to differences in benefits sought are geographical differences and buyers' characteristics. Thus, many segmentation variables may be found to be working together, complementing one another. The heavy user of Coors Light, for example, is age 21–34, is in the middle or upper income group, lives in an urban or suburban area, belongs to a health club, buys rock music, travels by plane, gives parties and cookouts, rents videos, and is a heavy television sports viewer.[6] Because variables often complement each other, it is in the marketer's interest to target the best bundle of segmenting variables—two to five or more—so that the most advantageous match of market and marketing mix can be achieved. The marketer's goal is to segment the market in a way that helps it select market opportunities compatible with its ability to provide the right marketing mix.

## Positioning: The Basic Focus for the Marketing Mix

POINT TO EMPHASIZE

As more firms allow employees to wear casual clothes to work, apparel items are repositioned. What was once intended only for play or leisure can now be used for work, creating a major change in how consumers think about casual slacks and knit shirts. This repositioning reflects a change in lifestyles (we're becoming more casual) and should result in an increase in sales of casual clothing. Ask students whether they think consumers will wear the same jeans or Dockers to work as they wear for play.

After a target market has been selected, marketing managers choose the position they hope the brand will occupy in that market. Recall that market position, or competitive position, represents the way consumers perceive the brand relative to its competition. The thrust of a typical positioning strategy is to identify a product's or brand's competitive advantage and to stress salient product characteristics or consumer benefits that differentiate the product or brand from those of competitors.

For example, Ben-Gay was for years positioned as a pain relief product for arthritis and backache sufferers. However, unsolicited letters from athletes indicated that the product could also be positioned to a younger, more athletic market segment as a "warm-up" sports cream. As a result, Ben-Gay was positioned "away from" pain relief competitors such as Metholatum Deep Heating Rub. Of course, as mentioned in the discussion of market segmentation, a brand cannot be all things to all people. Thus, positioning a brand—perhaps even altering product formulation to emphasize certain product attributes—may cause long-term problems. Further, a competitor (Sports Creme, in Ben-Gay's case) may enter the market and position its product directly against the established product. This is known as **head-to-head competition** (or "me too" competition). The objective here is to occupy the same position as a competitor, rather than to position away from competitors.

**HEAD-TO-HEAD COMPETITION**
Positioning a product to occupy the same market position as a competitor.

Positioning decisions are easier when marketing research has clearly identified how consumers perceive various competitive offerings. Often, positioning maps are drawn, sometimes based on sophisticated computer models, to illustrate how consumers see each competitor's product. Exhibit 8–14 shows positioning maps for tea based on two product characteristics: flavor (traditional versus unique) and serving temperature (iced versus hot). A map such as this reflects benefit segmentation.

Inspection of the map in Part A illustrates that when Luzianne entered the tea market, it was positioned as being exclusively for iced tea. Part A also illustrates that Luzianne was alone in this position. Lipton and Tetley were perceived to be quite similar to each other (hot and traditional). Positioning maps can help pinpoint opportunities and problems. Part B reflects how competitors, after recognizing

# Cross-Functional Insights

## PART TWO

Many theories and principles from other business disciplines can provide insights about the role marketing plays in an organization. The questions in this section are designed to help you think about integrating what you have learned in other business courses with the marketing principles explained in this textbook.

### Decision Support Systems for Marketing

Decision support systems serve specific business units in a company. The decision support system is a computer system designed to store data and transform the data into accessible information. Its purpose is to allow decision makers to answer questions through direct interaction with data bases.

What data-base software might be used by marketing research managers?
What spreadsheet software might be used by marketing research managers?
What statistical software might be used by marketing research managers?
In what ways must a marketer's decision support system be coordinated with the organization's information system?

### Research Is Systematic and Objective

Marketing research allows managers to make decisions based on objective, systematically gathered data rather than intuition.

How can a knowledge of statistical hypothesis testing help a marketing researcher?
What steps might a marketing researcher take in testing a statistical hypothesis about a mean?

### Simple Random Sampling

A sample is simply a portion, or subset, of a larger population. It makes sense that a sample can provide a good representation of the whole. A simple random sample consists of individuals' names drawn according to chance selection procedures from a complete list of all people in a population.

Discuss what type of statistical errors are associated with simple random sampling.
How likely is the occurrence of random sampling error? How much control does a statistician have over the probability that an error will occur?
A mail questionnaire has a question with *excellent, good, fair,* and *poor* as the responses. If simple random sampling is utilized, what statistical test will be used to determine if the observed distribution is different from the expected uniform distribution?

### Sales Forecasting

Sales forecasting is the process of predicting sales totals over some specific future period. An accurate sales forecast is one of the most useful pieces of information a marketing manager can have because the forecast influences so many plans and activities. Identifying trends and extrapolating past performance into the future is a relatively uncomplicated quantitative forecasting technique. Time series data are identified and even plotted on a graph, and the historical pattern is projected for the upcoming period. The market factor method of forecasting may be used when there is an association between sales and another variable, or factor.

How could correlation analysis be used to identify market factors?
How could regression analysis be used to forecast sales?
How might the moving averages method be used in the projection of sales trends?

## Consumer Behavior

Consumer behavior consists of the activities people engage in when selecting, purchasing, and using products so as to satisfy needs and desires. Such activities involve mental and emotional processes in addition to physical actions.

Explain economists' theories about consumer behavior and how they differ from marketers' theories.
The concept *caveat emptor* ("let the buyer beware") was introduced in the 16th century. What is the history of this concept in the 20th century? Is it an important aspect of consumer behavior?

## Buying Center

The buying center in any organization is an informal, cross-departmental decision unit whose primary objective is the acquisition, dissemination, and processing of relevant purchasing-related information.

What impact do the management concepts of job description, authority, and responsibility have on the activities of a buying center?
How important is a company's corporate culture in the establishment of buying centers? What type of corporate culture would contribute most to the establishment of effective buying centers?
Suppose an organizational structure identifies profit centers. What impact might this have on organizational buying?
How might purchasing agents with different levels of need for achievement, need for power, and need for affiliation (as explained by McClelland's need theory) differ in their organizational buying behavior?

## Gatekeeper Role

The role of collecting and passing on information—or withholding it—is known as the gatekeeper function.

What theories of communication within organizations help explain this function?

# Information Technology: Insights and Exercises

If one of the following exercises of addresses does not seem to work, please check the West Publishing World Wide Webb (WWW) address listed below. Updates and other information will be provided at this address as necessary. To reach the West Publishing WWW page with information about this book, use your Web browser to go to:

**http://www.westpub.com/Educate/Educ.Supp.htm**
Under **Business** and **Marketing**, choose the appropriate monthly update for **Zikmund/d'Amico, Marketing, Fifth Edition**

If you want to start at West Publishing WWW home page and navigate to the page containing information for this book, use your Web browser to go to:

**http://www.westpub.com**
Choose **Fast or Slow Connection**
Select **Products and Services**
Select **College and School Division**
Choose **Educational Publishing: College and School**
Select **College Publications**
Select **Educational Supplements** and **Updates for College Products**
Under **Business** and **Marketing**, choose the appropriate monthly update for **Zikmund/d'Amico, Marketing, Fifth Edition**

## E-Mail Exercise

Send an e-mail message to another student in your marketing class. In your message, answer the following questions:

1. How does organizational buying behavior differ from consumer buying behavior? List at least five ways.
2. How are organizational buying behavior and consumer buying behavior similar? List at least five ways.

You may need to refer back to Chapter 6 and 7 to answer these questions. Send a copy of your message to your instructor.

## Gopher Exercise

The company you started five years ago is doing so well in the United States that you are considering exporting your product to other countries. Before making a decision, you need to do some marketing research, and you wonder how international marketing research might differ from domestic marketing research. You also wonder what sources of information might be available to someone who wants to export products. You remember that Gopher gives you access to information stored all over the world, including articles and books. Use Gopher to go to:

**umslvma.umsl.edu**
Select **The Library**
Then select **Government Information**
Then select **Basic Guide to Exporting**
Then select **Chapter 3—Market Research**

If any address is unobtainable, check the West Publishing World Wide Web address for updates: **http://www.westpub.com/Educate/Educ.Supp.htm**

You are now looking at Chapter 3 of the book *Basic Guide to Exporting*. Read Chapter 3 and answer the following questions:

1. What helpful hints for collecting secondary data did you discover?
2. Read the section "A Step by Step Approach to Market Research." How does marketing research for exporting seem to differ from marketing research for domestic markets?
3. List ten sources of market research information recommended in the book *Basic Guide to Exporting.*

## World Wide Web Exercise

Marketers scan the environment for changes in social values and beliefs. Go to the Gallup Organization's home page at:

**http://www.gallup.com/**

Select the option **Gallup Poll Monthly Newsletter Archives**. Read the results of a recent survey. What are the implications for marketers of the societal attitudes the survey reports? Make a list of five businesses that would be affected by the results of the survey you looked at. Go back and select the option **Take a Gallup Poll**. Complete one of the Gallup Polls before you exit.

Use your Web browser and go to:

**http://www.asiresearch.com/surveys/survey.htm**

You will see a list of surveys that are offered on the Web. Complete one of the questionnaires listed at that site. Pay special attention to the design of the interactive survey. Do you think this is an appropriate way to administer surveys? What are the advantages? What are the limitations? To see what the future holds for interactive communication, you may want to check out:

**http://www.kaworlds.com**

Use your Web browser to go to the SRI International home page at:

**http://future.sri.com**

Select the **Values and Lifestyles (VALS) program** option and read some of the background information on the VALS system. Select **Discover Your iVALS Type** or another available option to complete a VALS survey on-line. When you have completed your questionnaire, select the **Submit** button to submit your completed questionnaire. Wait for the analysis (your answers will be analyzed in less than a minute).

What is your primary VALS type? What is your secondary VALS type? Read the descriptions provided so that you understand the VALS data. (Refer to Case 8–2 in this book for related information about VALS.) Explore the information provided on media, music, packaged goods, and so on used heavily by your VALS type. What are the top geographical locations for your VALS type? Check out the **VALS Questionnaire FAQ** to get answers to frequently asked questions about VALS.

## Listserv Exercise

The Internet is a powerful tool for conducting marketing research. For example, online focus groups provide a very inexpensive way to gather rich information, and groups can include members from all parts of the world. Use your Web browser and go to Chiat Day's home page at:

**http://www.chiatday.com/factory/**

Next, go to ASI Research at:

If any address is unobtainable, check the West Publishing World Wide Web address for updates: **http://www.westpub.com/Educate/Educ.Supp.htm**

**http://www.asiresearch.com/**

These are just two examples of organizations that provide on-line focus groups. Check to see if any focus groups are currently scheduled; you may be able to participate in one.

Listservs and discussion lists are other inexpensive ways to collect valuable information. For example, a firm may choose to set up a listserv as an alternative to organizing focus group interviews.

Think of a product that is currently used by most college students. Develop an exploratory research question for the product. The question may deal with how people feel about the product, how people feel about a particular advertisement for the product, or the like. You may find it helpful to review the marketing research process discussed in Chapter 5.

Send your research question to the West Publishing listserv at:

**zikmund@westpub.com**

(*Note*: If you are not already a member of the listserv, see page 136 for instructions on how to subscribe, send messages, and unsubscribe to the listserv.) Monitor the answers to your question that are posted on the listserv for one week. Write a one-page report that summarizes what you found out. Include a brief discussion of the limitations of your findings.

### *Careers and the Internet*

Use your Web browser to go to the NPD Group, Inc., home page at:

**http://www.npd.com**

Choose the **Career Opportunities** option to find out what a career in marketing research might look like. Look at the **Getting Started at NPD** in the **Building a Career at NPD** section. In what areas does the company hire new recruits? What qualifications is it looking for? What tasks is a research analyst expected to perform? What types of training does the company offer?

If any address is unobtainable, check the West Publishing World Wide Web address for updates: **http://www.westpub.com/Educate/Educ.Supp.htm**

# PART THREE

# Product Strategy for Global Competition

BASIC CONCEPTS ABOUT GOODS AND SERVICES

STRATEGIES FOR NEW PRODUCTS AND THE PRODUCT LIFE CYCLE

THE MARKETING OF HIGH QUALITY SERVICES

Quality is never an accident; it is always the result of intelligent effort.

JOHN RUSKIN

CHAPTER

# 9

# Basic Concepts about Goods and Services

## LEARNING OBJECTIVES

After you have studied this chapter, you will be able to:

1. Define *product*, and explain why the concept of the total product is important to effective marketing.
2. Differentiate among convenience products, shopping products, and specialty products.
3. Categorize organizational products.
4. Explain the difference between product lines and product mixes.
5. Understand brand-related terminology, including *brand, brand name, brand mark, trademark, manufacturer brand, distributor brand,* and *family brand.*
6. Discuss the characteristics of effective brand names.
7. Analyze the importance of packaging in the development of an effective product strategy.
8. Discuss the role of customer service in product strategy.

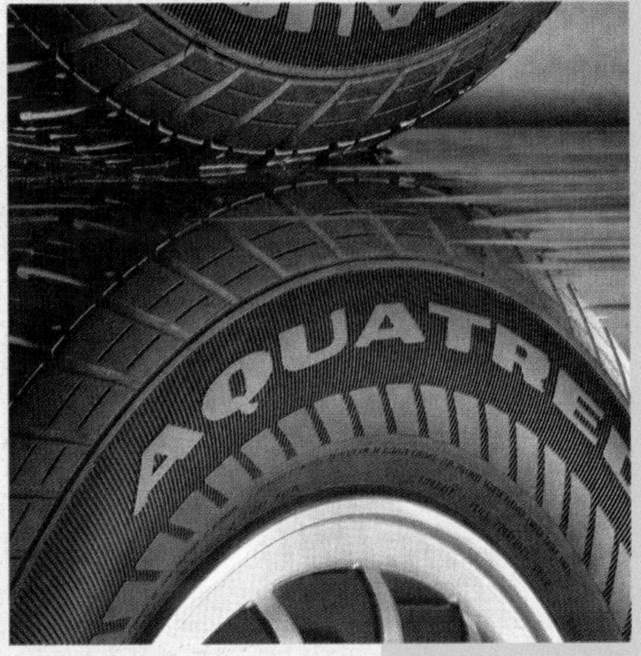


The Goodyear Aquatred, an all-season radial tire, works like most tires, with one major difference. Goodyear designed Aquatred to be the best wet-weather radial tire that has ever been put on a car. The basic idea was to solve drivers' problems in stopping, starting, turning corners, and steering in wet weather without sacrificing any performance on dry roads.

To improve traction, Goodyear developed a deep Aqua-Channel that evacuates water—a product feature that makes Aquatred visibly different from other tires. A chemical ingredient, SIBR, also enhances traction. The wet traction benefit gives the Aquatred a unique competitive advantage in the marketplace.

Of course, to reach the market, many marketing functions other than product development must be performed. But let's stick with the product itself. Its brand name, Aquatred, is easy to say and remember. It is descriptive; it tells consumers that this is more than an ordinary tire. Most consumers know that *aqua* means water. Using *aqua* as part of the brand name reinforces the basic product benefit.

There is no package for a tire, but there is a warranty. Aquatred is made and designed so well that it comes with a 60,000-mile tread warranty. This reduces the consumer's perceived risk as to the tire's durability.

Aside from the tangible things, the buyer of an Aquatred purchases intangible things, such as the Goodyear name and reputation. The name Goodyear is associated with the best tires in the world. Consumers associate Goodyear's quality with safety.

A Goodyear Aquatred is more than a tire; it is a bundle of satisfactions. As a bundle of benefits, it is an organization's product.

This is the first of three chapters dealing with product issues. It begins by explaining how marketers view products and product strategy. It then categorizes products using several different classification schemes and goes on to discuss the nature of product lines and product mixes. Next, it discusses the nature of branding, packaging, warranties, and customer service.

**ALTERNATIVE EXAMPLE**

The Coca-Cola company's soft drink with the brand name OK was targeted at 12–25 year old males. It was a fruity cola, a citrusy, pepper-brown cola, that was supposed to speak to Generation Xs with different attitude. The cans, designed by a comic book artist, were stark gray and black. They carried messages, such as "What's the point of OK? Well, what's the point of anything?" An auxiliary dimension of the product was an 800 telephone number that young consumers could use to talk about the product. Coca-Cola abandoned OK after a 17 month test period. SOURCE: Melanie Wells, "Coca-Cola Drops OK Brand," *USA Today*, September 13, 1995, p. 4b.

# What Is a Product?

DISCUSSION CONSIDERATION
Ask students what the total product is for McDonald's or another fast food restaurant, a personal computer, and a college education.

The product an organization offers to its market is not simply a bar of soap, a rental car, or a charitable cause. As with so many other marketing elements, there is more to the product than meets the eye. A product may be a thing, in the nuts-and-bolts sense, but it does not have to be something tangible. It can be a reward offered to those willing to pay for it: a mowed lawn is the payoff for someone who buys a lawn mower. To an organization, a product is a bundle of benefits. This customer-oriented definition stresses what the buyer gets, not what the seller is selling. For example, a DisneyWorld resort hotel provides more than a place to stay. It offers sun and fun, relaxation and entertainment, and a sense of being a good parent.

Defining the product in terms of benefits allows anything from tangible items to services to ideas to be identified as products. Whether an organization's offering is largely tangible (a ship), intangible (financial counseling), or even more intangible (the idea of world peace), its offering is a product.

## The Total Product

**TOTAL PRODUCT**
The wide range of tangible and intangible benefits that a buyer might gain from a product after purchasing it.

**PRIMARY CHARACTERISTIC**
A basic feature or essential aspect of a product.

**AUXILIARY DIMENSION**
An aspect of a product that provides supplementary benefits, such as special features, aesthetics, package, warranty, repair service contract, reputation, brand name, or instructions.

Because a product can have so many aspects and benefits, marketers think in terms of the **total product**—the broad spectrum of tangible and intangible benefits that a buyer might gain from a product once it has been purchased. Marketers view total products as having characteristics and benefits at two levels. **Primary characteristics** are basic features and aspects of the core product. These characteristics provide the essential benefits common to most competitive offerings. Here, consumers expect a basic level of performance. A quarter-inch drill, for example, is expected to provide quarter-inch holes. **Auxiliary dimensions** of a product provide supplementary benefits and include special features, aesthetics, package, warranty, instructions for use, repair service contract, reputation, brand name, and so on. Each auxiliary dimension is part of the *augmented product*. Together, these two groups of features fulfill the buyer's needs. Any one of many benefits may be important to a particular buyer. Effective marketers build strategies emphasizing those benefits that are most meaningful to the target markets.

The smell of a leather interior is an important auxiliary dimension of the total luxury automobile. People who pay for expensive leather automobile seats want their cars to have a leather aroma. However, tanning, processing, and coloring leather neutralize its natural smell. So automobile manufacturers inject fragrant industrial oils to create an aroma of leather for consumers to perceive. Because the smell of leather is subjective, the marketers must determine what the leather should smell like. A leading leather supplier says "For some people, it will be a saddle. For others, it's an old baseball glove." Some automobile makers use different scents in different models to give the impression that higher-priced models have richer leather.

**EXHIBIT 9–1**

The Core Product and the Augmented Product

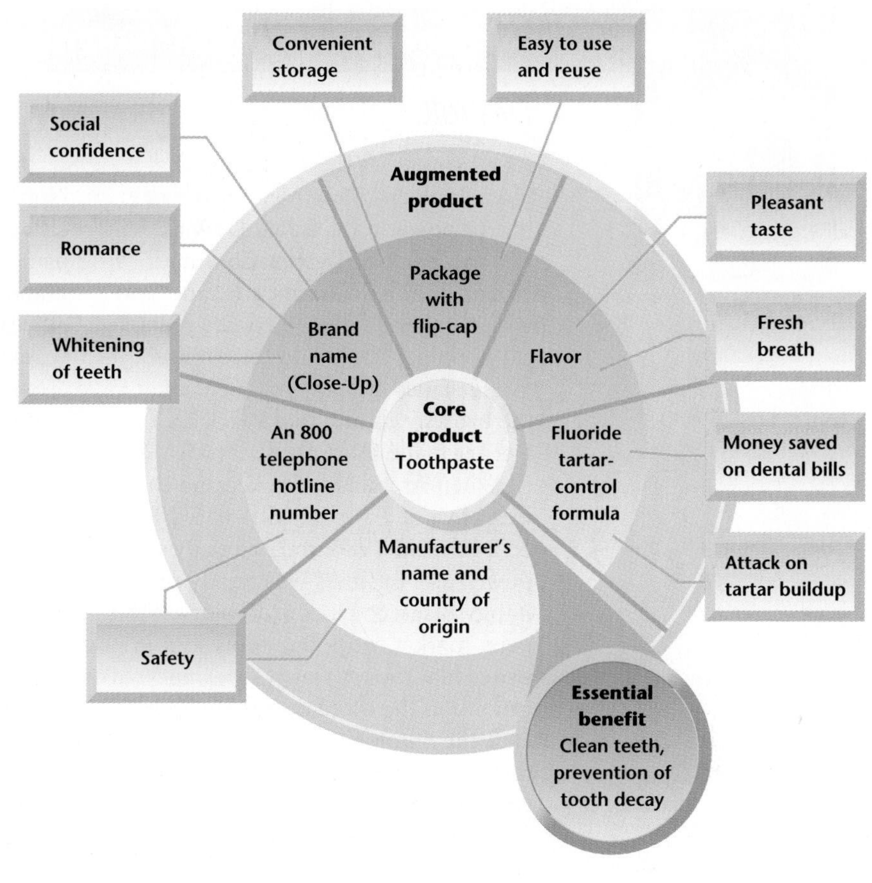


**POINT TO EMPHASIZE**

Remind students that particular benefits are more important to some customers than others. That means that while certain customers emphasize a certain set of benefits, other customers emphasize a different set of benefits. This is one of the core ideas behind segmentation: that different groups of customers want different things from the product.

Exhibit 9–1 uses Close-Up toothpaste to illustrate the nature of a core product and the associated auxiliary dimensions. The essential benefits of any toothpaste are cleaning teeth and preventing tooth decay. Close-Up's package (a tube with a flip-cap) also benefits the consumer by making the product convenient to store, easy to use, and easy to reuse. The brand name Close-Up suggests social confidence and romance. The manufacturer's name, country of origin, and telephone hotline number printed on the package provide a safety benefit. Each auxiliary dimension adds a benefit that may be important to a buyer.

## Product Strategy and the Product Concept

**PRODUCT STRATEGY**

The planning and development of a mix of the primary and auxiliary dimensions of a product's attributes.

**PRODUCT CONCEPT**

The marketing strategist's selection and blending of a product's primary and auxiliary dimensions into a basic idea emphasizing a particular set of consumer benefits. Also called the *product positioning concept.*

**Product strategy** involves planning the product concept and developing a unified mix of product attributes. As the earlier discussion of the Goodyear Aquatred tire shows, successful product strategy requires that all aspects of the product be analyzed and managed in light of competitive offerings. Deciding on which product features and which consumer benefits to stress is the creative dimension of product strategy.

The **product concept** (also called the *product positioning concept)* defines the essence or core idea underlying the product features and benefits that appeal to the target market. The product concept reflects the marketing strategist's selection and blending of a product's primary characteristics and auxiliary dimensions into a basic idea or unifying concept. In short, it provides a reason for buying the product. The

COMPETITIVE STRATEGY: WHAT WENT RIGHT?

## DeWalt

As a browser at the 1992 National Homebuilders Show examined a new line of power tools called DeWalt, he noticed Black & Decker Chairman Nolan Archibald's name tag, and said with a smirk, "These guys are going to eat you up." Archibald just smiled.

He smiled because he knew what the browser didn't: that Black & Decker made those DeWalt tools.

When Archibald, 51, became chief executive of Towson, Md.–based Black & Decker in 1986, the company's power-tool business was barely profitable. Black & Decker dominated the mass market for power tools sold in stores like Kmart, but was losing ground at the more profitable high end, the durable tools that cost two to three times as much. At residential construction sites, a key market, Black & Decker had been losing ground for a decade. By 1991 Japan's Makita had 53% of that market, Black & Decker just 8%. It's tough to sell a $130, 3/8-inch cordless drill to professionals when the same nameplate appears on a $30 drill sold to amateurs.

Joseph Galli, current head of the North American power-tool division, came up with a solution. A new brand name. He resurrected a nearly defunct brand that Black & Decker had acquired 32 years earlier, DeWalt. DeWalt was for years the manufacturer of a rugged radial arm saw. Black & Decker had abandoned this line of business by 1989, but the name still connoted solidity and quality to older tradesmen.

Galli selected 30 of the drills, saws and sanders in the Black & Decker professional and industrial power-tool lines, colored them the yellow of construction hardhats rather than the black of the regular lines and slapped on only a hint of DeWalt's ownership: a note on the flap of the packaging saying, "serviced by the Industrial Tool Division of Black & Decker."

"Anything we made yellow was viewed as a new tool in the marketplace," remarks Galli. In some cases the DeWalt tools are a little bit new. DeWalt models feature keyless chucks and big knobs the user can adjust while wearing gloves. In the case of

**DISCUSSION CONSIDERATION**

Ask students about the product concept of other brands with which they might be familiar. Using the same industries as in the previous discussion consideration, other brands might include McDonald's, IBM (for personal computers), and the college or university attended by the students.

product concept often is described in the same terms used to characterize the competitive market position that the product is expected to occupy in consumers' minds. For example, Vaseline Intensive Care Lotion's product concept stresses that it is a thick and rich cream that penetrates the skin quickly to make dry skin feel soft and smooth.[1] Some widely used product concepts are:

"Our product has the most advanced technology."
"We build the highest-quality product."
"Our product is made in the U.S.A."
"Ours is a basic, no-frills product; it's the best value."

## Product Differentiation

**PRODUCT DIFFERENTIATION**
A strategy that calls buyers' attention to aspects of a product that set it apart from its competitors.

Calling buyers' attention to aspects of a product that set it apart from its competitors is called **product differentiation.** To do this, marketers may make some adjustment in the product to vary it from the norm or may promote one or more of the product's the circular saw—where Emerson Electric's tough-to-beat Skilsaw has almost become a generic name for the tool category—the DeWalt model was the first to come with a clip to keep the cord out of the blade's path.

DeWalt's new features were quickly copied into Black & Decker's industrial tools. Now nothing but the color distinguishes a DeWalt tool from a Black & Decker industrial tool. Like the Mercury Sable and Ford Taurus, the machinery is the same but the packaging changes to appeal to different customers. DeWalt, aimed at the residential construction trade, is sold through retailers such as Home Depot and Lowe's, while the larger industrial line is sold through distributors such as W. W. Grainger. To establish a premium image, Galli kept DeWalt off mass marketers' shelves.

Galli understands well the psychology of pricing. He priced DeWalt tools 10% higher than Makita products. "Price denotes quality," says Galli. Previously, Black & Decker had been underpricing Makita.

Galli also notices a paradox of marketing: "If you target the do-it-yourselfer, you lose the tradesman," he says, but it doesn't necessarily follow that if you target the tradesman you lose the serious do-it-yourselfer. Black & Decker estimates that about half of DeWalt sales go to the do-it-yourselfers.

To reach the contractors, Galli emblazoned a fleet of 26 yellow vans and trucks with the new DeWalt logo and filled them with pitchmen who visit construction sites and hardware stores to demonstrate DeWalt tools. He established an 800 telephone number for the fictitious DeWalt Industrial Power Tool Co. that logs 2,000 calls a week.

The image makeover is working. Only two years old, the DeWalt line is expected to top $300 million in sales for 1994. Black & Decker, meanwhile, still sells $150 million a year worth of high-end construction and industrial tools using its own name.

ALTERNATIVE EXAMPLE

A company, having established a product concept, can modify it. For example, McDonald's has recently returned to a familiar theme in its advertising. The firm's advertising in the early 1990s emphasized price and value as the primary product concept. Realizing that customers associated the word "break" with McDonald's, the firm recently adopted a new slogan—"Have you had your break today?"—that hearkens back to the "You deserve a break today" product concept of the 1980s. SOURCE: Kevin Goldman, "McDonald's Mixes Past with New Slogan," *Wall Street Journal*, February 17, 1995, p. B4.

tangible or intangible attributes. For example, an automobile battery with a selector dial that switches on a supplemental booster battery when the primary battery fails to hold a charge will be more competitive than an ordinary battery. This product feature is a tangible difference that provides a functional benefit.

What differentiates one product from others need not be a scientifically demonstrable improvement. Stylistic and aesthetic differences accomplished through changes in color, design, and shape, as well as technological differences, can play a role in product differentiation. For example, recipes for dishes such as Salad Niçoise are printed on Viva Cuisine paper towels. This sets the brand apart visually from competitors marketing plain paper towels or paper towels decorated with floral patterns. Dreamland Nursery dolls come with telephone calling cards that allow children to call the company at no charge to "register" their dolls' names. The children later receive birth certificates and other personalized accessories. If consumers see such variations as important, then the variations differentiate the product from its competitors. The accompanying Competitive Strategy feature describes a successful attempt to differentiate a product.

## Classifying Products by the Nature of the Market

POINT TO EMPHASIZE

The aspects of a product chosen to set it apart from competitors in order to differentiate it must be aspects valued by customers. Nothing will be gained by using attributes that customers do not value. Since different segments of customers might value different product attributes, the marketer might need to establish several points of differentiation in order to serve the needs of many customers.

Many factors influence the buyer's decision-making process. One of the strongest is the product itself, because the product includes so many physical, psychological, and purchase-behavior dimensions. For this reason, marketing managers have developed some widely-accepted product classifications that describe both products and, more important, buyers' perception of them. We begin by discussing consumer products and then consider organizational products.

### Classifying Consumer Products

Furniture, appliances, groceries, hardware, and many other categories of consumer products can be identified. The great number and diverse nature of products offered for sale make consumer product classification a complex task. Products may be classified on the basis of many criteria. We will discuss two widely accepted systems: classification by tangibility and durability and classification by consumers' buying behavior.[2] (See Exhibit 9–2.)

**DURABLE GOOD**

A physical, tangible item that functions over an extended period.

**NONDURABLE GOOD**

A physical, tangible item that is quickly consumed, worn out, or outdated.

**SERVICE**

A task or activity performed for a buyer; an intangible that cannot be handled or examined before purchase.

**Tangibility and Durability** Products may be classified according to tangibility and durability: whether they are durable goods, nondurable goods, or services. Goods have a tangible form. **Durable goods** function over an extended period. Consumers use durable goods, such as automobiles and refrigerators, many times. **Nondurable goods**—which are quickly consumed, worn out, or outdated—are consumed in a single use or a few uses.[3] Chewing gum, paper towels, and hand soap are examples of nondurable goods. **Services** are tasks, activities, and other intangibles.

The distinction between goods and services is meaningful, but remember that services, like the physical, tangible items we call goods, should be referred to as products. This is especially important because the service industry now accounts for more

The core product for a hotel is a room to sleep in. However, there are many auxiliary dimensions to this service product that help customers differentiate competitive offerings. Hotel personnel who provide speedy, friendly personal service and who go out of their way for hotel guests are product characteristics that provide competitive advantage.

**ALTERNATIVE EXAMPLE**

Coca-Cola introduced packaging for its 20-ounce soft drinks shaped like the old contoured Coca-Cola bottles. The company sees the shape of the bottle as a point of instant identification and differentiation. Advertising is expected to reinforce this theme, building further recognition for the "contour bottle" shape as a symbol for the Coca-Cola brand. SOURCE: Kevin Goldman, "Coke Fits New Ads to Contour of Bottle," *Wall Street Journal*, February 14, 1995, p. B12.

Packages perform many functions. They contain a product and protect that product until it is ready for use. Beyond this, packages facilitate the storage and use of products. (Think again about the Glue Stic container.) Thus, packages should be designed for ease of handling.

Consumers often identify products by their packages. Because distinctive packages on a shelf can attract attention, they can play a major part in promotional strategy. For example, the Good Stuff company markets oval pieces of cedar that help keep moths away from woolen clothing in closets and drawers. The wood chunks are called Sweater Eggs and are packaged in egg cartons. The packaging lends charm to the product and reinforces the brand name. A package on the retailer's shelf may be surrounded by 10 or more other packages competing for consumers' attention. In these days of self-service, every package design must attract attention and convey an easily identifiable image. The package must have shelf impact. It must tell consumers what the product is and why they should buy it.

Today, environmental considerations may also strongly influence packaging decisions. Packaging waste is piling up, and many industries, such as the fast-food industry, try to make all packaging biodegradable or easy to recycle.[9]

**PACKAGING**

An auxiliary product dimension that includes labels, inserts, instructions, graphic design, shipping cartons, and sizes and types of containers.

In summary, **packaging** provides a containment function, a protection-in-transit function, a storage function, a usage facilitation function, a promotion function, and an ecological function. Packaging thus involves making many decisions, including decision about labels, inserts, instructions for use, graphic design, and shipping cartons, as well as decisions about the sizes and types of physical containers for individual product items within the outer package.

Pepsi occasionally changes its cans for seasonal promotions. These cans were packaged in four designs. When cans with two of the designs were stacked one on top of the other, the word *sex* appeared. Pepsi spokespersons said the computer-generated designs were supposed to be randomly ordered letters from the word *Pepsi* and that the spelling of any other word was unintentional.

## FOCUS ON TRENDS

### *High-Tech Packaging*

Rarely since the advent of cellophane in 1923 has the packaging industry come up with so many new materials and designs. Today's high-tech packages can look better than traditional bottles, boxes, and cans. And when the packaging's work is done and the stuff goes the way of all wrappers, it takes up less space in the local landfill. Some high-tech packages even act on the products they contain.

Printpack of Atlanta used film coated with metal strips, called susceptors, to line the pouch it created for Rudolph's Bacon Snaps pork rind nuggets. When the package is placed in a microwave, some of the susceptors heat up to make the nuggets brown and crispy, while others deflect energy from the nuggets to promote more even cooking. Other packaging manufacturers such as Cryovac . . . and Evert-Fresh . . . make films that keep fruits and vegetables fresh by reducing the concentration of gases like oxygen and ethylene that aid ripening.

The packages of the future will be even more versatile. Temperature-sensitive labels will indicate whether products have gotten too hot or too cold during shipping. Microwave films for TV dinners will deep-fry some parts of the meal, like chicken, while keeping others, such as applesauce, cool. Some day, when peaches are covered with protein film and peas come in a bag that dissolves as they cook, we may even be able to eat the packages themselves.

## Labeling—Telling About the Product

**LABEL**
The paper or plastic sticker attached to a container to carry product information. As packaging technology improves, labels become incorporated into the protective aspects of the package rather than simply being affixed to the package.

The paper or plastic sticker attached to a can of peas or a mustard jar is technically called a **label.** But as packaging technology improves and cans and bottles become less prominent, labels become incorporated into the protective aspects of the package. In the case of a box of frozen broccoli, for example, a good portion of the vegetable's protection comes from the label, which is more properly called, in this case, the wrapper.

Whether the label is a separate entity affixed to a package or is, in effect, the package itself, it must perform certain tasks. It carries the brand name and information concerning the contents of the package, such as cooking instructions and information relating to safe and proper use of the product. A label may also carry instructions on the proper disposal of the product and its package, or at least the plea that littering be avoided. The label must contain any specific nutritional information, warnings, or legal restrictions required by law. Some labels, such as those of Procter & Gamble, also give an 800 telephone number for customers' ideas and complaints. Consumers' calls are a major source of Procter & Gamble's product improvement ideas.

**UNIVERSAL PRODUCT CODE (UPC)**
The array of black bars, readable by optical scanners, found on many products. The UPC permits computerization of tasks such as checkout and compilation of sales volume information.

Most consumer package goods are labeled with an appropriate **Universal Product Code (UPC)**, an array of black bars readable by optical scanners. The advantages of the UPC—including computerized checkouts and computer-generated sales volume information—have become clear to distributors, retailers, and consumers in recent years.

## Global Implications and Legal Guidelines for Packaging

Package designers are relatively free to develop package designs. However, when the package will be used in several countries, marketers must determine whether to use a single package with one language, a single package with two or more languages, or multiple packages tailored to the separate countries. Decisions about use of colors and symbols, protection in transit over long distances, and other aspects of package design should be made only after local culture and usage patterns have been considered.

Anyone who has had a routine physical knows getting a blood test is a pain—and not just because of the needle. First you pray that the technician finds your vein quickly. You watch (or look away squeamishly) as he fills two or three entire test tubes with your precious bodily fluid. Next you wait at least a day for results from the lab.

All that may change with the advent of the Piccolo Point-of-Care Whole Blood Analyzer, a desktop machine that provides blood test results in about 12 minutes. This innovative new product from Abaxis Corporation requires only a finger prick's worth of blood.

The Piccolo uses standard test chemicals that Abaxis freeze-dries in tiny beads. It seals these in chambers along the rim of a molded plastic disk, or rotor. The technician deposits the blood sample in a well at the rotor's center and pops the disk into the Piccolo, which spins it at about 4,000 rpm. Centrifugal force separates plasma from blood cells and forces precise quantities of it through thin tubes to the chambers. As the plasma and chemicals react, a spectrophotometer reads changes in color and the machine prints out results. Getting data right away lets the doctor prescribe medicine with no need for a follow-up visit or call to discuss the test.

The Federal Drug Administration has approved the Piccolo and a version of the rotor containing five tests. Abaxis plans to offer combinations of about 50 tests; it will charge $8,000 for the analyzer and $8 to $20 for each disposable rotor, making Piccolo testing about as expensive as that done by a large lab.

Piccolo is based on U.S. space program efforts to design a blood analyzer for astronauts to use in space. Funding ran out after the Challenger disaster in 1986, and Abaxis founders Gary Stroy and Vladimir Ostoich snapped up exclusive rights in 1988.

The Piccolo weighs just 15 pounds, takes up as much room as an oversize toaster, and can operate on a 12-volt battery, making blood tests possible in ambulances, field hospitals, and primitive countries. Nor has Abaxis forgotten space: France's space agency hopes to test the analyzer on a NASA shuttle flight in the near future.

ALTERNATIVE EXAMPLE

In the mid-1990s researchers at Pepsi tried to identify the cola preferences of Generation X. They learned that many twentysomethings dislike the taste of diet cola, but don't want all the calories of regular colas. So they developed Pepsi XL which falls in between its diet and regular colas for those who grew up drinking cola but who have become more conscious of food additives and health. Pepsi XL ('X' for excellent and 'L' for less sugar) has a mix of 50% sugar and 50% artificial sweetener (aspartame). A 12-ounce can of Pepsi XL will have 70 calories instead of 150 calories for full-sugar Pepsi. Diet Pepsi has no calories. Pepsi XL is not Pepsi's first attempt to market a mid-calorie category: Pepsi Light, also a 70-calorie soda, was introduced in 1978 but was phased out during the mid-1980s; Jake's Cola, with 15 calories, never made it out of the test market in 1986. Pepsi Light and Jake's had been marketed as an alternative to diet colas, a strategy that won't be followed with Pepsi XL. This time, Pepsi thinks targeting regular Pepsi fans is the formula for success. SOURCE: Paul Abercrombie, "A new drink for a new Pepsi generation; The soft-drinkmaker targets Generation X with "XL", *St. Petersburg Times*, March 23, 1995.

This chapter begins by addressing the nature of new products and the characteristics associated with new product successes. It goes on to depict the new product development process and address the fact that most new products fail. Then the focus shifts to the product life cycle, an extremely influential concept in the planning of products from their births to their deaths. The adoption and diffusion processes, discussed next, help explain products' acceptance over the course of product life cycles. The chapter then addresses issues related to the marketing of products that have been on the market for some time and discusses strategies for expanding product lines and withdrawing or eliminating goods or services that no longer enjoy adequate market demand. Finally, it addresses ethical issues associated with the marketing of products.

## What Is a New Product?

**NEW PRODUCT**
A product new to a company. The meaning of this relative term is influenced by the perceptions of marketers and consumers; in general, it refers to any recently introduced product that offers some benefit that other products do not.

The Piccolo Point-of-Care Whole Blood Analyzer just described certainly appears to be a new product. Before reading further, however, pause for a second to decide in your own mind what a **new product** is. Think of an example or two, and try to identify what makes them new. Is the video game "Sonic: The Hedgehog 3," with two-player competition mode, really a new product? Is a computer workstation that can be linked to other computers with invisible infrared light signals truly different from the first microcomputers? Does the ingenious, and highly practical, pocket-sized electronic language translator qualify as really new?

To some marketers, a new product may be a major technological innovation. For example, the first electronic computers were introduced in the 1940s. Though primitive by today's standards, they were at that time altogether new to the market. At one time or other, so were microwave ovens, radial tires, adjustable rate mortgages, and automatic teller machines. To other marketers, new products might be simple additions to an otherwise unchanged product line, such as new shades of lipstick or hair coloring introduced by Revlon or Clairol. Even a "me, too" item, developed in imitation of a competitor's successful product, is a new product to the imitating company. Furthermore, a product may be new because it offers some benefit that similar product offerings do not. For example, Velcro tabs on paper diapers, which allow parents to run wetness checks and reseal the diapers with a sure fit, makes a product different from the one that was merely resealable with ordinary adhesive tape. The marketing concept, after all, tells us to consider the product as a bundle of tangible and intangible benefits. If the bundle of benefits offered by a product differs from the bundle already available, then the product can be said to be new.

**DISCUSSION CONSIDERATION**
Ask students whether they would consider this textbook a new product if it were available through an electronic bulletin board. Ask students whether they would consider this textbook a new product if it were available on a computer floppy disk or a CD-ROM disk.

From the buyer's point of view, a product may be new if it is something never before purchased, even if it has been on the market for years. In international marketing, old products may become "new" again, especially when a manufacturer's established product is being offered to people in a less developed country. There are, for example, places in the world where videocassette recorders, and even color television, are new to most people.

It is clear, then, that the term *new* and the related term *novel* are used in a relative sense. They are influenced by our perceptions, whether we are marketing managers or consumers. Let's begin by taking the manager's perspective.

## Management's Perspective on New Products

**ALTERNATIVE EXAMPLE**
The pioneering research behind Tagamet won the Nobel Prize for Medicine. Tagamet was a prescription medicine from 1977 to 1995 when it became an over-the-counter drug that reduces the production of stomach acid. When Tagamet was introduced it was a new-to-the-world product.

Managers may classify new products as new to the market or simply new to the company.[1] Here, we discuss new-to-the world products, product category extensions, product line extensions, and product modifications. Companies have considerable experience marketing product modifications but far less with the first three categories.

- *New-to-the-world products* are inventions that create an entirely new market. These are the highest-risk products, because they are new both to the company and to the market. The technology for producing these innovative products, which is itself new to the company, is often the result of a large investment in research and development.[2]
- *Product category extensions* are new products that, for the first time, allow a company to diversify and enter an established market for an existing product category. These products are not entirely new to the market, but the company has had no previous technological or marketing experience with them. If these products imitate competitive products with identical features, the term "me, too" products provides a good description.

## EXHIBIT 10–2

The General Stages in the Development of New Products

Source: Adapted from Roger A. Bengston, "Nine New Product Strategies: Each Requires Different Resources, Talent, Research Methods," *Marketing News,* March 19, 1982, p. 7. Reprinted by permission of the American Marketing Association.

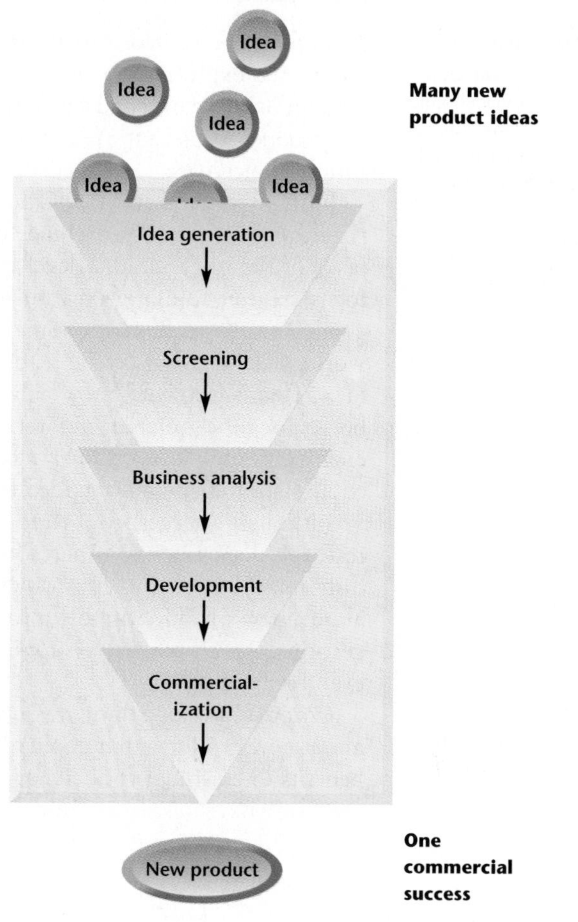


ALTERNATIVE EXAMPLE

The Advanced Care Cholesterol test is the perfect new product for a society in which heart disease is the leading cause of death. The test allows consumers to measure their total cholesterol level at home. Administering the test involves using a device that pricks the finger to draw a drop of blood. The drops are placed in a test well, and a color indicator informs the consumer when the process is completed. The product is still in development, but it is easy to see that trialability may be difficult (especially if the product is high priced) and that using the product is somewhat complex. SOURCE: "Chrysler, Johnson & Johnson Are New Product Marketers of the Year," *Marketing News*, May 8, 1995, pp. E2, E11.

St. Louis who ran out of paper cups and rolled pancakes into serving cones—the first ice cream cones.

On occasion, the amateur inventor working in a basement comes up with an innovation that goes on to great success. However, these days, when innovations require sizable financial investments and other resources for support and commercialization, most innovations come from serious research and development efforts undertaken with the support of formal organizations.[5] For example, the Piccolo Point-of-Care Whole Blood Analyzer mentioned at the beginning of this chapter required years of research and development at NASA and later at Abaxis Corporation.

The new product development process can be quick, the result of a sudden flash of insight. But in many cases, such as in the development of space satellites, telecommunication systems, and other highly technical products, the process can take years. The development process may be lengthy not so much because of technical problems but because it takes time to research and understand potential market resistance to a new product. Even when a new product has a technological advantage, customers may not accept it.

Exhibit 10–2 shows the five general stages in the development process of new products: idea generation, screening, business analysis, development, and commercialization. Products pass through these stages at varying rates. A product may stall for a time in one, for example, and pass through another so quickly that it appears to have skipped it entirely.[6]

## Idea Generation

**IDEA GENERATION STAGE**
The stage in new product development in which the marketer engages in a continuing search for product ideas consistent with target market needs and the organization's objectives.

In marketing-oriented organizations operating in dynamic environments, **idea generation**—the exploration stage of new product development—is less a period of time than an ongoing process. Thus, the idea generation stage involves a continuing search for product ideas that are consistent with target market needs and with the organization's objectives.

In many organizations, particularly those in industries with complex technology, generating ideas and searching for technological breakthroughs are likely to be the tasks of the research and development (R & D) department. R & D personnel may focus creative thinking on transferring a technology from an existing product category to a new product, on miniaturization, or on basic research to create new-to-the-world products. For example, Sony's DataDiskman came from a technology-driven idea. This "electronic book" allows a person to carry around an encyclopedia, law books, or other reference materials in a Walkman-sized computer. R & D engineers creatively applied consumer electronics technology from Sony's video and audio equipment to generate the idea for this product.

DISCUSSION CONSIDERATION
Ask students to visualize every step involved in recycling paper, glass, aluminum, and plastic from the consumer back to the original manufacturer or the recycled products manufacturer. Then ask students to generate new product ideas for households, distribution centers, or packages that would improve the current approach.

Although a large proportion of new product ideas flow from technology-driven research departments, other sources should not be ignored. New product suggestions may come from customers. Sales representatives may uncover, or be told about, new product opportunities. Marketing research can yield new product suggestions. An employee, a supplier, or a distributor may come up with a good—or even brilliant—idea.

Companies can stimulate idea generation by encouraging employees to think about new products that could address consumer complaints, make a task easier, add benefits to existing products, or provide new uses for existing products. Many organizations have instituted reward systems to encourage employee suggestions. The focus at this stage is on encouraging creativity rather than on evaluating suggestions. The organization wishes to generate ideas, not kill them.

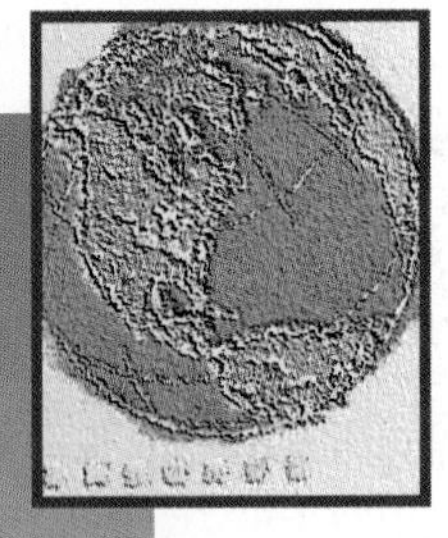

### FOCUS ON GLOBAL COMPETITION

### *Yamaha*

Insights into possibilities for new products that are fundamentally different—that is, new-to-the-world products—may be garnered in ways that go beyond traditional modes of marketing research.

Toshiba has a Lifestyle Research Institute; Sony explores "human science" with the same passion with which it pursues the leading edge of audiovisual technology. The insights gained allow these firms to answer two crucial questions: What range of benefits will customers value in tomorrow's products, and how might we, through innovation, preempt competitors in delivering those benefits to the marketplace?

Yamaha gained insights into the unarticulated needs of musicians when it established a "listening post" in London, chock-full of the latest gee-whiz music technology. The facility offered some of Europe's most talented musicians a chance to experiment with the future of music making. The feedback helped Yamaha continually push out the boundaries of the competitive space it had staked out in the music business.

Yamaha's experience illustrates an important point: To push out the boundaries of current product concepts, it is necessary to put the most advanced technology possible directly into the hands of the world's most sophisticated and demanding customers. Thus arose Yamaha's London market laboratory: Japan is still not the center of the world's pop music industry. ■

## Screening

**SCREENING STAGE**
The stage in new product development in which the marketer analyzes ideas to determine their appropriateness and reasonableness in relation to the organization's goals and objectives.

The **screening stage** of the product development process involves analyzing new ideas to determine which are reasonable, pertinent to the organization's goals, and appropriate to the organization's target markets. This step is extremely important, because the underlying assumption of the entire product development process is that risky alternatives—possibilities that do not offer as much promise for success as others—should be eliminated from consideration. Resources can then be concentrated on the best prospects so that market failures can be avoided.

The screening stage is also important because it is the first stage at which alternative ideas are sorted. New ideas may now be rejected. From time to time, of course, any management team is likely to reject some ideas that they later wish they had accepted. Since mistakes will be made, managers must conduct screening with caution. In fact, because an idea rejected at this stage is eliminated from further consideration, some companies prefer to allow a marginal idea to progress further rather than risk rejecting it too early in the process. However, at later stages, the costs of analysis and evaluation are substantially increased. Balancing the costs of additional investigation against the loss of a viable product idea is one of management's most delicate tasks.

At Procter & Gamble, three basic questions are carefully answered before new product projects are approved. The questions are general enough to be used by almost any organization in its own product screenings. These deceptively simple questions demand hard answers on which more than a few managers' careers may depend:

**POINT TO EMPHASIZE**
The closer a product is to a "new-to-the-world" product, the more difficult it may be for consumers to assess. When the product is completely different from their prior experience, consumers may have difficulty imaging how they could use the product or how it could meet their needs. For example, early research indicated to Chrysler that consumers were ambivalent toward minivans. Thus, some caution must be exercised in evaluating the results of marketing research.

1. Is there a real customer need for the product?
2. Does the organization have the scientific and technological ability to develop the product?
3. Is the potential for such a product large enough to offer some promise of making a profit?

Extensive marketing research is associated with later stages in the development process, but some marketing research and discussions with salespeople, executives, and knowledgeable consumers can be used to help screen new product ideas. The discussion on exploratory research in Chapter 5 suggested forms of research appropriate to this stage.

## Business Analysis

**BUSINESS ANALYSIS STAGE**
The stage in new product development in which the new product is reviewed from all organizational perspectives to determine performance criteria and likely profitability.

A product idea that survives the screening process enters the **business analysis stage,** where it is expanded into a concrete business recommendation. This recommendation includes both qualitative and quantitative means of evaluation. Creativity and analysis come together at this stage.

The qualitative evaluation seeks such specifics as a listing of product features, information on resources needed to produce the product, and a basic marketing plan. Although qualitative evaluations of the product and its likely success are important, business analysis requires quantitative facts and figures. The new product idea is evaluated with increasingly detailed quantitative data on market demand, cost projections, investment requirements, and competitive activity. Formal buyer research studies, sales and market forecasts, break-even analyses, and similar research efforts are undertaken. In short, the business analysis is a review of the new product from all significant organizational perspectives. It emphasizes performance criteria and chances for success in the marketplace.

## Development

**DEVELOPMENT STAGE**
The stage in new product development in which a new product concept is transformed into a prototype. The basic marketing strategy also develops at this time.

A new product idea that survives the preliminary evaluative stages is ready for the fourth stage, **development.** In the development stage, the proposed new product idea is transformed from a product concept to a product prototype. The basic marketing strategy is developed and includes decisions about the product's physical characteristics, package design, and brand name, as well as the company's market segmentation and positioning strategies for the product. Specific tactics within the product strategy are also researched during this stage.

In the development stage, paper-and-pencil concepts become demonstrable products. Research and development or production engineers give marketers a product that can be tested in customer usage studies, sold in test markets, or investigated in other limited ways. This is not to say that the product is in final form. For example, soft drink marketers may taste-test a new formulation on a panel of consumers. If the product is not well accepted, it may be reformulated or its package changed. The product can be retested until the proper set of characteristics has been discovered. We discuss two popular forms of testing here.

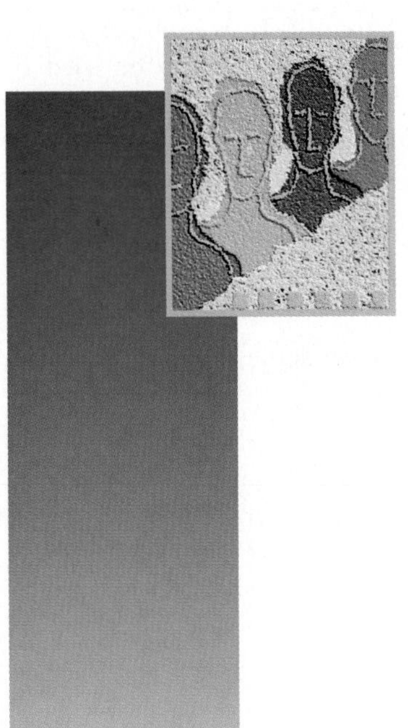

### FOCUS ON RELATIONSHIPS

*3M*

When relationship marketing is successful, marketers and customers reach a level of mutual trust that can lead to the development of new products. 3M's medical and surgical products division in Brookings, South Dakota, has a low-tech program to help build the supplier-customer relationship.

All 750 employees, from production-line workers to senior executives, meet face to face with customers, mostly doctors and nurses, at three area hospitals. Employees don scrubs and go into the operating rooms to watch their surgical tapes, drapes, and prep solutions in action. Says a 3M executive, "We get to feel the pulse of our customers. We see their problems and frustrations up close."

The work teams observed that some products' packaging was difficult to open, and the packaging of other products, designed for reuse, could not be easily closed. They suggested to 3M's product development people that a Ziplock-type opening and closure would make their customers' jobs easier. The suggestion became reality within a few months. Says Valerie Smidt, staff education coordinator for the operating room of Sioux Valley Hospital in Sioux Falls, South Dakota: "The 3M people give us pointers on how to better utilize some items, and we in turn suggest how to make some of their products more user-friendly."

The hospital staffs have also been giving the company an unsolicited wish list of future products, which 3M has been evaluating. ■

**CONCEPT TESTING**
Research procedures used to learn consumers' reactions to new product ideas. Consumers presented with an idea are asked if they like it, would use it, would buy it, and so on.

**Concept Testing** **Concept testing** is a general term for many different research procedures used to learn consumers' reactions to a new product idea. Typically, consumers are presented with the idea—shown a pictorial or written description—and asked if they would use it, if they like it, if they would buy it, and so on.

Concept testing helps to ensure that product concepts are developed with the needs of the consumer or user in mind. For example, General Electric's design engineers are sent out to talk with dealers and customers about new product concepts to ensure that market feedback goes where it can do the most good—to the engineers who design the products. GE describes the process in this way: "Engineers working at the drawing board are getting their directions from customers. The whole business is oriented toward bringing the technology and the consumer demand together."[7]

## COMPETITIVE STRATEGY: WHAT WENT WRONG?

### *Oven Lovin' Dough Falls Flat*

When Pillsbury rolled out Oven Lovin' cookie dough in a resealable tub, it looked like another sweet success. Consumers' renewed focus on the home as the center of family life had helped keep cookie dough sales rising. And in preliminary, exploratory research, consumers raved about Oven Lovin', which was loaded with Hershey's chocolate chips, Reese's Pieces, and Brach's candies. Within months of its launch, the product was available in 90 percent of supermarkets, and sales were climbing. But less than two years later, even Pillsbury had to concede that the Oven Lovin' brand had crumbled.

What went wrong in Pillsbury's test kitchens? The company had plenty of reason to believe it was on the right track. It has been marketing refrigerated cookie dough since 1957 and still dominates the $114-million-a-year business. An earlier effort to make its traditional cookie dough seem more homemade had been a hit. And Pillsbury had previously tested dough in plastic tubs in Britain and declared it a success.

Even early testing in the United States indicated Oven Lovin' was a hot concept. But in its eagerness to bring Oven Lovin' to market, Pillsbury cut corners on marketing research. After gathering information on the concept by interviewing panels of consumers, the company skipped test marketing and launched the product nationally, a cost-saving strategy pursued by more and more marketers.

The result illustrates the uncertainty of marketing research that does not test new products under actual market conditions. Consumers often find it difficult to evaluate products based on limited experience. Marketing consultants say consumers who respond to surveys are also inclined to give positive feedback and tend to be especially generous about new foods, unless the products taste truly wretched. But while consumers may give a test product high marks in a controlled environment, that doesn't necessarily mean they would drop the same product into their shopping carts if they had to pay for it themselves.

"People try to be helpful and typically don't like to criticize the product they're testing," says Richard Reiser, chairman of BAI, a marketing research firm in Tarrytown, New York.

Indeed, consumers said they liked the Oven Lovin' resealable tubs. At home, however, many shoppers found they ended up baking the entire package at once—or gobbling up leftover dough raw instead of saving it—eliminating the need for the pricier packaging. "The package provided a benefit consumers didn't really need," says Robert McMath, director of the New Products Showcase and Learning Center in Ithaca, New York. "They should have asked how many cookies people usually make at one time."

And although Oven Lovin' may fill a need for small families and single consumers, those shoppers don't bake cookies very often. Most cookie dough buyers are families with young children, a group of consumers that are often on tight budgets. What's more, a tub of Oven Lovin' contains only 18 ounces of dough, compared with 20 ounces in a tube of Pillsbury Best dough.

"We'd like to believe we know a lot about the cookie-dough category," says Craig Evanich, vice president of Pillsbury Brands. "But it turned out that Oven Lovin' was a very big deal to a very small number of consumers."

**TEST MARKETING**
A controlled experimental procedure in which a new product is tested under realistic market conditions in a limited geographical area.

**Test Marketing** **Test marketing** is an experimental procedure in which marketers test a new product under realistic market conditions in order to obtain a measure of its potential sales in national distribution. Test markets are cities or other small geographical areas in which the new product is distributed and sold in typical marketplace settings to actual consumers. No other form of research can beat the real world when it comes to testing actual purchasing behavior and consumer acceptance of a product.

Note that test marketing involves scientific testing and controlled experimentation, not just trying something out in the marketplace. Simply introducing a product in a small geographical area before introducing it nationally is not test marketing.

POINT TO EMPHASIZE
There are other forms of test marketing besides that described in the text. Controlled test marketing involves only a few stores in which the manufacturer buys shelf space. Simulated test marketing involves bringing consumers into a test facility to determine whether they will purchase a new product from a simulated store. One advantage of these alternatives is that they cost less than standard test marketing.

Test marketing serves two important functions for management. First, it provides an opportunity to estimate the outcomes of alternative courses of action. Managers can estimate the sales effect of a specific marketing variable—such as package design, price, or coupons—and then select the best alternative action with regard to that variable. Second, test market experimentation allows management to identify and correct any weaknesses in either the product or its marketing plan before making the commitment to a national sales launch, by which time it is normally too late to make changes.

In selecting test markets, the marketer must choose cities that are representative of the population—of all cities and towns—throughout the United States. Test market cities should be representative in terms of competitive situation, media usage patterns, product usage, and other relevant factors. Of course, no one ideal test market is a perfect miniature of the entire United States. Nevertheless, it is important to avoid selecting areas with atypical climates, unusual ethnic compositions, or uncommon lifestyles, any of which may dramatically affect the acceptance of a new product. Some of the most popular test markets are mid-sized cities where costs won't be prohibitive, such as Tulsa, Charlotte, Evansville, Green Bay, Little Rock, Nashville, Omaha, and Spokane.

DISCUSSION CONSIDERATION
Ask students to identify the kinds of products that should be test-marketed. To initiate the discussion, mention a few examples, such as a new sandwich at a fast-food restaurant chain, a new line of salt-free canned vegetables, a dishwashing detergent that is unchanged except for its color, and a new line of cookies sweetened with an artificial sweetener. The focus should be on showing students that the riskiness of the new product is a major determinant in whether it should be tested.

Test marketing is expensive. Developing local distribution, arranging media coverage, and monitoring sales results take considerable effort. The cost of test marketing a consumer product can be several million dollars. However, if a firm must commit a substantial amount of money to investments in plant and equipment to manufacture a new product, the cost of test marketing may appear minimal compared with the cost of a possible product failure. The marketer, then, must balance the cost of test marketing against the risk of not test marketing.

## Commercialization

**COMMERCIALIZATION**
The stage in new product development in which the decision is made to launch a new product's full-scale production and distribution.

After passing through the filtering stages in the development process, the new product is ready for the final stage. It is **commercialization,** the decision to launch full-scale production and distribution. The decision entails risking a great deal of money, because this stage involves a serious commitment of resources and managerial effort. It is the last chance to stop the project if managers think the risks are too high. Many successful marketing firms, such as Procter & Gamble, remain willing to stop a project right up to the last moment. Although a lot of money may have been spent in reaching the commercialization stage, any amount is small compared with the sums that full commercialization will demand.

Even when great caution is employed, product failures still occur. It is not difficult to find products that should have been killed before commercialization. For example, the Dow Chemical Company developed a compound of resins and methanol to be sprayed on car tires to increase their ability to maintain traction on ice. The product, Liquid Tire Chain, truly did work, as proved by in-use testing. Not surprisingly, however, buyers stored the pressurized cans of the product in their cars' trunks. When the aerosol containers froze in winter weather, the material within them solidified, making the product useless. The in-use tests Dow had undertaken somehow missed this factor. The product failed, unfortunately for Dow, after commercialization. Had testing been more complete, this could have been avoided.

## Why Do New Products Fail?

New product failures and near-failures occur with some regularity. As we pointed out earlier, it is estimated that there is a one-in-three failure rate among new product introductions. Earlier, a Competitive Strategy feature explained how Oven Lovin' failed after millions of dollars had been spent in the new product development process. Cajun Cola tried to compete regionally against Pepsi and Coke at a time when the two cola giants were engaged in an intensive cola war, with reduced prices and increased advertising. Cajun Cola didn't have the resources to compete. General Mills introduced Benefit, a high-soluble-fiber cereal made with psyllium, and stressed its ability to reduce cholesterol levels. When sales did not meet expectations, the company learned that although consumers understood the role of oat bran in reducing cholesterol levels, they were confused about the term *soluble fiber.* The death knell for the product rang when a barrage of publicity questioned whether Benefit with psyllium was a drug or a cereal.[8]

DISCUSSION CONSIDERATION

In the fall of 1996 Ralph Lauren will introduce Polo brand jeans. The denim designer jeans will be sold in department and specialty stores. Ask your students why or why not they think this product will fail.

What are the most common reasons for product failures? Here, briefly stated, are several:

- *Inadequate product superiority or uniqueness.* If a "me, too" product is merely an imitation of products that are already on the market—if it does not offer the consumer a relative advantage—the product may be doomed from the start. While the Everlast brand has been around boxing for years, Everlast sports drink was not much different from Gatorade. It took only a short time for the product to fail.
- *Inadequate or inferior planning.* Many product failures stem from failure to conduct proper marketing research about consumers' needs and failure to develop realistic forecasts of market demand and accurate estimates of the acceptance of new products.[9] Overly optimistic managers may underestimate the strength of existing competition and fail to anticipate future competitive reactions and the need for sizable promotional budgets. Too often, the enthusiastic developer of a new product is surprised to find that it takes more time and effort than expected to launch a new product successfully. Fab 1 Shot, a single-packet washer-to-dryer detergent with fabric softener, provides a perfect example. Procter & Gamble and Clorox were test-marketing similar products when Colgate-Palmolive, anxious to beat its rivals to market, commercialized Fab 1 Shot. Initially, the product, which was supported with coupons and rebates, sold well. But when the company began pricing to make a profit, it quickly learned that although people found the product convenient, it was not cost-effective for large families. The lesson Colgate-Palmolive learned in the marketplace was learned in test markets by its competitors, who spent more time planning.
- *Poor execution.* No matter how good the plans, adequate resources must be allocated so that strategies can be properly executed. Many new products fail because managers who think the product is so good it will sell itself do not provide adequate resources for tactical execution. For example, Pillsbury failed with Appleeasy because at the last minute it reduced the amount of apples in its recipe in response to increasing apple prices. In addition, sometimes a new product requires production or marketing activities for which the organization lacks expertise, and the product fails for that reason.
- *Technical problems.* Problems may stem from the product itself—failures in production or design. Hot Scoops, a microwavable hot fudge sundae, caused consumers problems. If the microwave timer wasn't set exactly right, the consumer ended up with a mess rather than a sundae.

ALTERNATIVE EXAMPLE

IBM's mistakes in logistics and supply cost it $1 billion in ThinkPad sales. The 1992 product introduction was a hit with consumers, but the hottest models were constantly in short supply. IBM's 1995 product introduction, the "subnotebook" Butterfly, seems to be plagued by the same poor planning. Even before the first models hit the store, advance orders guarantee that a short supply situation will exist for months. SOURCE: Bart Ziegler, "Can Butterfly Help IBM Fly Higher?" *Wall Street Journal*, pp. B1, B10.

**POINT TO EMPHASIZE**
Empirical research shows that the "classic" product life cycle shape occurs more often at the level of a product category (toothpaste) than at the level of an individual brand within the product category (Crest).

- *Poor timing.* The market may have changed before the new product was introduced, or the company may have entered the market too early or too late in the product life cycle. For instance, if a new luxury product is introduced just as a downturn in the economy occurs, the product's chances for success are substantially reduced.

All managers planning new product introductions have one thing in common: They must attempt to predict the future. The product designed in 1995 but commercialized in 1997 may meet an environment somewhat different from the one that existed when the product was being designed. Hence, marketing plans may not work as well as expected. New product marketing deals with forecasting. As the wry old adage goes, "Forecasts are dangerous, particularly those about the future."

## The Product Life Cycle

**PRODUCT LIFE CYCLE**
A marketing management concept providing a graphic description of a product's sales history. The cycle is depicted as having four stages: introduction, growth, maturity, and decline.

The **product life cycle** is a graphic depiction of a product's sales history from its "birth," or marketing beginning, to its "death," or withdrawal from the market. Generally, a product begins its life with its first sale, rises to some peak level of sales, and then declines until its sales volume and contribution to profits are insufficient to justify its presence in the market. This general pattern does vary from product to product, however. Products such as salt and mustard have been used for thousands of years. Arm & Hammer baking soda has been used for over 150 years. Cellular phones and fax machines are mere youngsters by comparison. Some products, such as Topp's Talking Baseball Cards, fail at the very start of their lives. But whether a product has a very short, short, long, or very long life, the pattern of that life may be portrayed by a charting of sales volume.

Traditionally, the product life cycle has been thought of as reflecting the life of a product class or product category as a whole—for example, the life cycle of handheld video games as a group, without regard to model or brand. However, marketing managers also use the product life cycle idea in evaluating specific brands of products, because most brands, as well as most products, have limited market lives.

The product life cycle is portrayed in Exhibit 10–3. A product's life, as suggested earlier, typically flows through several distinct stages as sales volume is plotted over time. These stages are introduction, growth, maturity, and decline. Both sales volume and industry profit change over the course of the life cycle, as shown in Exhibit 10–4. This exhibit also shows the period of product development, which precedes the introductory stage. During this period, no sales are being made, but investments are being made in the belief that later profitable sales will justify them.

**EXHIBIT 10–3**
General Pattern of the Product Life Cycle

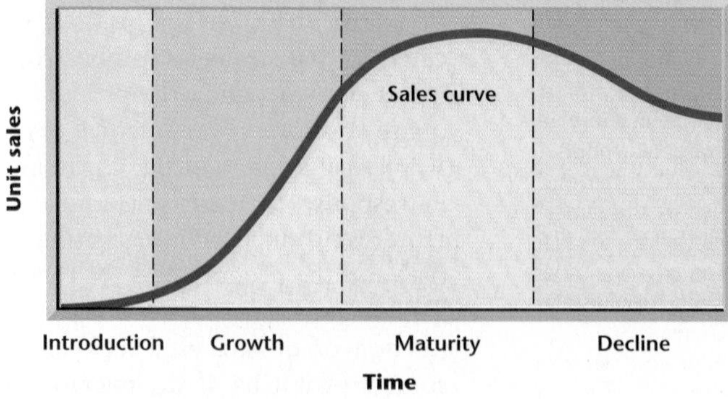

nonadopter (p. 329)
product modification (p. 330)
cost reduction strategy (p. 330)
total quality management strategy (p. 332)
product enhancement (p. 332)
cross-functional team (p. 333)
product design (p. 334)
style (p. 334)
fashion (p. 335)
fad (p. 335)
product line strategy (p. 337)
full-line, or deep-line, strategy (p. 337)
limited-line strategy (p. 337)
single-product strategy (p. 337)
product line extension (p. 337)
product category extension (p. 337)
brand extension (p. 337)
cannibalization (p. 338)
flanker brand (p. 338)
enhanced model (p. 338)
globalization strategy (p. 340)
customization strategy (p. 340)
right to safety (p. 341)
right to be informed (p. 341)
quality of life (p. 342)
product obsolescence (p. 342)
physical obsolescence (p. 343)
planned obsolescence (p. 343)
right to choose (p. 343)

## Questions for Discussion

1. What is your definition of a new product?
2. Classify the type of innovation used in each of the following products.
   a. A personal communications device that combines a cellular phone, a pager, keys, and credit cards
   b. An identity checker that verifies, in seconds, people's identity for banks and classified areas by use of magnetically coded cards and electronic sensors to check hand geometry
   c. A new Mercedes sports utility vehicle priced around $30,000 that will ride and handle like a car.
3. For the products in Question 2, identify salient product features that might speed acceptance.
4. Identify the steps in the new product development process. What takes place in each?
5. What are the main reasons why new products fail?
6. What are the benefits and limitations of test marketing?
7. At what stage of the product life cycle would you place each of the following products?
   a. Cigars
   b. Coffee
   c. Pen-based (stylus-activated) personal computers (digital personal assistants)
   d. Theme amusement parks
   e. Tennis balls
   f. Slide rules
8. Try to trace the product life cycle for a particular brand, such as the Sony compact disc player.
9. Identify some typical marketing mix strategies used during each stage of the product life cycle.
10. Does marketing grow in importance as a product matures and moves from the introductory stage through the growth stage and into the maturity stage? Explain.
11. What are the most prominent characteristics of each adopter group in the diffusion process?
12. What guidelines would you suggest for rejuvenating old brands in the mature stage of the product life cycle?
13. How important is product quality to being competitive around the world?
14. What companies have recently implemented cost reduction strategies? Are such strategies always incompatible with product quality strategies?
15. How important is brand equity to a line extension strategy?
16. What are the pitfalls of a brand extension strategy that, for example, extends a name from a hair spray product to a facial cream?
17. Some homes are now being marketed with cable setups so that computer terminals may be installed. What product strategy does this reflect?
18. SNOT (Super Nauseating Obnoxious Treat), Wurmnz n Dirt, and Bubble Tongue are names of some recently introduced novelty candy items. Form groups as directed by your instructor.
    *Step 1:* You have 10 minutes after the instructions "Begin brainstorming" to generate new product ideas for novelty candies. Do not evaluate the ideas, just generate as many as you can.
    *Step 2:* In the next 10-minute period, evaluate the ideas and decide which products should be considered for business analysis.
    *Step 3:* Discuss as a class how each group's ideas emerged and how the group did or did not come to a consensus about which products were best.

ETHICS IN PRACTICE

## Ethics Exercise 10

Coffee is a product in the mature stage of its life cycle. It has been served for hundreds of years.

McDonald's franchisees are required to prepare coffee at very high temperatures because McDonald's coffee consultants say hot temperatures are necessary to fully extract the flavor during brewing. McDonald's operations and training manual says coffee must be brewed at 195 to 205 degrees and held at 180 to 190 degrees for optimal taste. Coffee made at home is normally 135 to 140 degrees.

Not long ago, an Albuquerque woman bought a 49-cent cup of coffee at the drive-in window of a McDonald's and, while removing the lid to add cream and sugar, spilled it, causing third-degree burns of the groin, inner thighs and buttocks. She was in the hospital for over a week. Later, she sued McDonald's. Her lawsuit claimed the coffee was "defective" because it was so hot. A jury awarded the woman $2.9 million.

## Questions

1. If this case were being appealed, what stand would you take?
2. If you owned a fast-food franchise other than McDonald's, at what temperature would you serve your coffee?

## Take a Stand

1. What arguments are given by critics who say that it is inappropriate for marketers to strive to make perfectly good products obsolete?
2. Pet owners complain that a new flea and tick spray is making their dogs sick. Should the marketer take the product off the market?
3. A pajama manufacturer develops a new fire-resistant chemical that will not wash out of children's pajamas until they have been washed more than 100 times. Should this product be marketed as fire resistant?
4. In the United States, packaged goods meant to be ingested by consumers must be approved by the Food and Drug Administration before they can be marketed. A multinational company, which has conducted its own laboratory test on a new over-the-counter drug, has not received approval from the FDA to market the drug in the United States. It plans to market the drug in several Asian countries where there are no requirements for government approval. Is this socially responsible?
5. Marketers introduce more than 10,000 new consumer package goods every year. One year, 31 baby foods, 123 breakfast cereals, and 1,143 beverages were introduced. Does society need all these new products?
6. Is it ethical to initiate a cost reduction strategy that requires closing a U.S. factory and opening a factory in a third-world nation?
7. Are flanker brands and line extensions really needed by consumers?

CASE 10–1

## Motorola

Motorola is a large manufacturing organization that supplies electronic equipment, system components, and services to markets worldwide. The company is headquartered near Chicago and has operating locations throughout the United States and the world. Motorola takes pride in its long history of creating world-class products.

Motorola's goals include building a corporation that is continually moving forward while strengthening its foundation of uncompromising integrity. Motorola plans to grow rapidly around the world and gain global market share by providing customers with exciting, high-quality products and services when they need them.

In 1988, Motorola's excellence was recognized when it won the first Malcolm Baldridge Award. The company did not view the award as an end in itself but rather as a symbol of its long-term drive for competitive excellence through product and service quality. Although the company learned many lessons along the way to this award, top management was above all seeking to challenge employees to be more creative and innovative, especially in achieving customer satisfaction.

To achieve this lofty goal, Motorola's management created the Customer Satisfaction Team Competition. The competition, now in its third year, has unleashed the creative spark of employee teams by empowering and encouraging them to develop high-quality products and provide excellent service. The event challenges employees to use their team problem-solving skills to look at concerns from the customer's point of view.

Teams from around the world are entered in the competition. They present their ideas to a panel of Motorola managers and customers, who judge and rank the teams. The teams are evaluated on (1) teamwork, (2) problem selection, (3) analysis, (4) remedies, (5) results, (6) institutionalization of remedies, and (7) team presentation. The competition focuses attention on a significant cultural change at Motorola and shows employees' ability to work together to drive initiative and provide the best products and service to customers.

The Customer Satisfaction Team Competition is one way Motorola challenges and rewards employees for being creative and innovative. At Motorola, total customer satisfaction is more than a vision.

### QUESTIONS

1. Discuss ways in which Motorola encourages its employees to be creative.
2. How are the criteria for evaluating the competition related to the total quality management process?
3. If you were an employee at Motorola, how would you view the Customer Satisfaction Team Competition?

VIDEO CASE 10–2
FOCUS ON SMALL BUSINESS

## Sashco Sealants, Inc.

The following account by Les Burch, president of Sashco Sealants, Inc., explains how the company decided to develop unique products and to avoid distribution through discount home-building-materials outlets:

> We introduced a new product to our line in 1987, and before long we knew we had a winner. Sales of the new item, a clear sealant that comes in a clear cartridge, took off. During the next three years, our company, Sashco Sealants, Inc., located near Denver, watched revenues triple, reaching $6 million. The product lines that had previously driven the company, meanwhile, accounted for less than 10 percent of those sales.
>
> We had bet the firm on the new product, buying $600,000 in equipment and more than tripling our production and warehouse space. The clear sealant, called Lexel, succeeded because it was different, almost in a category of its own. It doesn't mar the appearance of the gutters, windows, and doors being treated. And unlike silicone sealants, Lexel can be painted.
>
> When I compared it with the rest of the product line, it was obvious that most of our other goods were "me-too" items—made because the competition had them first, not because we had something better.
>
> Only two of our products—Lexel and a sealant called Big Stretch—were "really us". We eventually developed another product —an adhesive called Glue Buddy—and jettisoned eight longtime products.
>
> At first, members of our sales and management teams were not eager to do this. They feared that big customers—the ones buying all our products—would leave if Sashco eliminated 80 percent of its line. To be honest, we had no idea how those accounts would react. But fear usually means you are focusing on what you have to lose, not on what you stand to gain. In our case, we lost nothing. While a few customers complained about the loss of our other products, no one left us. In fact, revenues and profits grew the year the product line was cut.
>
> Narrowing our focus didn't stop with products. Lexel's success drew the attention of discount stores like Kmart and Home Depot. Up to that point, Sashco's customers included only independent dealers and smaller home center chains and co-ops, like Ace and True-Value.
>
> Some sales team members were excited about selling to discounters, if only because five chains—Kmart, Home Depot, Wal-Mart, Builders Square, and Home Base—account for 20 to 25 percent of the hardware market. At the same time, we feared that by selling to discounters, our reputation for quality would suffer and our products would take on the "me-too" image we had worked so hard to avoid.
>
> While a lot of companies like the exposure of building traffic for a national chain, we feared having products sold at or below cost. It is no great honor to be a loss leader when you sell a specialty item—especially when it endangers the enthusiasm of long-standing customers.
>
> One morning, in 1991, our management team discussed Sashco's identity and how we were inclined to introduce more-expensive specialty items for people who are truly concerned about how the products work. Our head engineer, Dan Lewis, was at the table that day. He is the quiet type who soaks up information without much comment, but he has a knack for boiling an hour's conversation down to a single, clear-cut principle. After much discussion, he had this credo for our products: "You can't buy them at Kmart."
>
> That summarized the entire meeting and became the cornerstone of the company's next strategic move. We not only decided not to sell to discounters but also announced our policy to the industry, with full-page ads pledging to independent dealers that our products cannot be purchased at the Big Five chains.

### QUESTIONS

1. Characterize the stages of the product life cycle for Sashco's product lines.
2. Evaluate Sashco's new product strategy.
3. Do you agree with Sashco's efforts to reduce its product line?
4. How intertwined are new product and distribution strategies? Is the Sashco case typical in this regard?

VIDEO CASE 10–3

## Spanier & Bourne Sailmakers

A pleasure sail from New Zealand to the New Hebrides Islands in 1978 came to an abrupt end for young Geoff Bourne and Barry Spanier. Their boat, a 38-foot one-master that Spanier had built, was destroyed in a violent storm, and they were shipwrecked on a small island in New Zealand waters occupied only by two caretakers. It took 22 days to get transport off the island. In a way, the misfortune made the fortunes of two men who, after getting out of college in California, had wandered from job to job—most connected with sailing—while taking lots of time off.

Today they own a Hawaii firm that has successfully applied new technology to an old craft, sailmaking. Spanier & Bourne Sailmakers, Inc., located in Kahului on the island of Maui and known widely as Maui Sails, has earned international recognition and growing revenues, primarily from designing windsurfing sails and equipment for a Hong Kong manufacturer. The firm also does custom manufacturing—of sails for boats as well as sailboards—and runs a wholesale/retail business.

Barry Spanier and Geoff Bourne had been enjoying a vagabond existence in 1978, but the shipwreck left Spanier broke and Bourne with no plans. It seemed a time to reenter the world of employment.

From a visit to Maui, Spanier knew there were many charter sailboats there, but no sailmakers. With $10,000 of starting capital—Bourne's savings—the friends rented a loft and went into business. They had sailmaking experience and talent, and they soon had numerous customers in Maui's charter fleet.

In 1980 a monster storm hit Maui, wrecking many boats. Maui Sails' customer base was wiped out. For some time to come, the charter skippers wouldn't be sailing or buying sails, just salvaging what they could.

Luckily, some California windsurfers, sailing in Maui's Hookipa area, brought in sails for repairs. "We had tons of high grade material for yacht sails and suggested that we could improve on the design and construction of their rigs," Spanier says. The firm became so popular with windsurfers that international sailboard brands asked for its services as a designer.

Two years later it became the exclusive research and development facility for Neil Pryde, owner of Neil Pryde Ltd., of Hong Kong, a major manufacturer of sailboards and other windsurfing equipment. Maui Sails, which had two employees, hired more—it has 11 now—and invested in tools and material.

Things went swimmingly until, in 1986, Pryde lost his largest customer to bankruptcy. As one step to save his business, he cut Maui Sails' royalties. Unsure of the future, the firm concentrated on increasing its custom sail output—and on something new.

Spanier and Bourne applied the computer to sailmaking. With the aid of a skilled programmer, Sandy Warrick, and financial backing from Pryde, who worked his company back to profitability, they developed a computerized system of designing windsurfing sails. The system cut costs and spurred sales by speeding design changes.

In the past few years defense spending cutbacks have propelled talented people into work for competitors of Maui Sails. There has been a technological explosion as light but strong aerospace materials have been used in sailing.

But storm survivors Spanier and Bourne, who began using aerospace materials in 1983, believe they have the answer to sophisticated competition. Maui Sails, which now has $1.2 million in annual revenues, will be taking the next steps first, they say. Their competitors will have to run just to keep up.

**Source:** Excerpted by permission from *Real-World Lessons for America's Small Business: Insights from the Blue-Chip Enterprise Initiative 1994*, pp. 91–92, 

### QUESTIONS

1. Discuss the general nature of the product life cycle for sails.
2. Spanier & Bourne is a small business. How does its new product development process differ from that of a large corporation?
3. How important are technology and the production process in the development of Spanier & Bourne's products?
4. What steps would be necessary for Spanier & Bourne to implement a total quality management program?

CHAPTER

# 11

# The Marketing of High-Quality Services

## LEARNING OBJECTIVES

After you have studied this chapter, you will be able to:

1. Define *service* in its technical, specific sense.
2. Explain the four basic characteristics of services.
3. Understand demand management strategies.
4. Describe the strategies of standardization and customization.
5. Name some of the variables used to classify services.
6. Discuss the need for marketing in the not-for-profit area.

Does the Occupational Safety and Health Act (OSHA) have any influence on product strategy?

### Product Portfolio Analysis

Evaluation of a company's or strategic business unit's product mix is called *product portfolio analysis.* Product portfolio analysis uses a matrix. The horizontal scale of the matrix depicts relative market share as high and low. On the vertical scale, the same words refer to market growth rate. The combinations of these variables yield four quadrants: high-market-share product in a high-growth market, high-market-share product in a low-growth market, low-market-share product in a high-growth market, and low-market-share product in a low-growth market.

How are cash flow and product portfolio analysis related?

### Services

Like other products, services are defined as bundles of satisfactions. However, to be more specific, a service is an instrumental activity performed for a consumer or a consummatory activity involving consumer participation in but not ownership of an organization's products or facilities.

Many services are delivered by people. In what ways might a service worker be negligent?

In what ways might a service worker's job (perhaps the job of a hotel clerk) be enriched?

What type of on-the-job training might restaurant service workers require?

Design a facilities layout (process layout) for a small pizza restaurant.

## *Information Technology: Insights and Exercises*

If one of the following exercises or addresses does not seem to work, please check the West Publishing World Wide Web (WWW) address listed below. Updates and other information will be provided at this address as necessary. To reach the West Publishing WWW page with information about this book, use your Web browser to go to:

**http://www.westpub.com./Educate/Educ.Supp. htm**
Under **Business** and **Marketing**, choose the appropriate monthly update for **Zikmund/d'Amico, Marketing, Fifth Edition**

If you want to start at the West Publishing WWW home page and navigate to the page containing information for this book, use your Web browser to go to:

**http://www.westpub.com**
Choose **Fast or Slow Connection**
Select **Products and Services**
Select **College and School Division**
Choose **Educational Publishing: College and School**
Select **College Publications**
Select **Educational Supplements and Updates for College Products**
Under **Business** and **Marketing**, choose the appropriate monthly update for **Zikmund/d'Amico, Marketing, Fifth Edition**

## E-Mail Exercise

Send an e-mail message to another student in your marketing class. In your e-mail message, answer the following questions:

1. What is the worst product you have ever purchased?
2. What was wrong with the product? Was the problem related to quality, price, warranty, service, packaging, unrealistic expectations, or some other factor?
3. Using Copeland's consumer product classification scheme, would you classify the product as a convenience, shopping, or specialty product?
4. Was the product a manufacturer brand, distributor brand, or generic brand?
5. Reread the section "Why Do New Products Fail?" in Chapter 10. Which, if any, of these reasons for product failure appear to be related to your dissatisfaction with the product?

Send a copy of your message to your instructor.

## Gopher Exercise

Use Gopher to go to:

**wiretap.spies.com**
Then select **Wiretap Online Library**
Then select **Music**
Then select **Various Top 100 Lists**
Then select **MTV Top 100 Videos of 1985**

Look over the list of MTV's top 100 videos from 1985. You might be surprised to find the names of brands or artists who are still popular today. You might also be surprised to find bands or artists who have not been heard from for many years. After looking through the list, answer the following questions. Bring your answers to class for discussion.

1. Does the product life cycle concept apply to bands, musical artists, and performers?
2. What bands or artists on the list were in the introduction stage in 1985? Growth stage? Maturity date? Decline stage? (You may have to guess a little.)
3. How does the shape of the product life cycle differ for different bands or artists? For example, are some artists really novelty products?
4. What strategies have bands and artists used to reverse the downward trend of their products?
5. Give an example of a band or artist whose life cycle was extended because of nostalgia, new marketing strategy, reformulated product, product modification, or repositioning.
6. How insignificant is the adoption and diffusion process for bands or musical artists?

## World Wide Web Exercise

Is this unit, you learned that the term *product* represents a bundle of benefits or satisfactions, not just a good, service, idea, or person. Go to the White House home page at:

**http://www.whitehouse.gov/**

If any address is unobtainable, check the West Publishing World Wide Web address for updates: **http://www.westpub.com/Educate/Educ.Supp.htm**

1. What bundle of benefits or satisfactions is offered by the White House?
2. Does the information provided by the White House on the Web page help differentiate the president from competitors?

3. Do you think the home page is consistent with the president's positioning strategy?
4. In what stage of the product life cycle is the current president of the United States?
5. Should presidential candidates go through new product development stages? Should they use concept testing and test marketing?
6. What is your overall opinion of the White House home page?

## *Listserv Exercise*

Reread the section titled "The Adoption and Diffusion Processes" in Chapter 10. Think of a product for which you would be classified as an innovator. Next think of products for which you would be classified as an early adopter, as a member of the early majority, as a member of the late majority, as a laggard, and as a nonadopter?

After you answer the questions above, send a message to the Zikmund listserv at:

**zikmund@westpub.com**

(Note: If you are not already a member of the listserv, see page 136 for instructions on how to subscribe, send messages, and unsubscribe to the listserv.) In your message, list the product for which you classified yourself as an innovator. Do the same for early adopter, early majority, late majority, laggard, and nonadopter. Make sure you list your adoption category next to each product so it is clear to anyone reading the message. Monitor the messages on the list for one week. Then bring your answers to the following questions to class.

1. Do you see any patterns in the adoption profiles of other individuals on the list?
2. Do you see any implications for market segmentation? What other information do you need in order to use these data?
3. Are you surprised by any of the answers? Are you shocked to find that some people have not adopted certain products? What products surprise you most?

## *Careers and the Internet*

The Internet's Online Career Center (OCC) is a wonderful resource for people seeking jobs, as well as companies seeking new employees. Check out the Online Career Center home page at:

**http://www.occ.com/occ/**

Once at the Online Career Center home page, choose **Jobs.** Then choose **OCC Member Jobs** for a listing of jobs posted by OCC members. You will find a wide range of companies, including AT&T, CNA Insurance, DowElanco, Du Pont, Procter & Gamble, and SmithKline Beecham Pharmaceutical. Choose several companies and look at what jobs they have posted on the OCC. Keep looking at different companies until you find some marketing-related positions. Why are there so many technology-related positions on the OCC? Is this good target marketing? Why? Check out the other options at the OCC. You will find information under **Résumés, Career Assistance, Recruiter's Office,** and others that may help you find a job or internship.

If any address is unobtainable, check the West Publishing World Wide Web address for updates:
**http://www.westpub.com/Educate/Educ.Supp.htm**

# PART FOUR

# Distribution Strategy

You seldom accomplish much by yourself. You must get the assistance of others.

HENRY J. KAISER

CHAPTER

# 12 The Nature of Distribution

LEARNING OBJECTIVES

After you have studied this chapter, you will be able to:

1. Explain the general purpose of distribution in the marketing system.
2. Show how distribution contributes to an effective marketing mix.
3. Understand why all marketers—even not-for-profit and service organizations—engage in distribution.
4. Characterize the functions of channel intermediaries.
5. Identify the major channels of distribution used by marketers of consumer and organizational products.
6. Describe the major vertical marketing systems.
7. Differentiate among channel cooperation, channel conflict, and channel power.
8. Describe some of the ethical and legal concerns associated with the development and management of channels of distribution.

Greens and fairways at the nation's 14,000 golf courses take a daily beating from golf carts and divot diggers. Keeping the grounds up to par can be tough for maintenance crews, so for help many rely on Lesco's "store on wheels." The company's fleet of 59 tractor-trailers deliver a full stock of Lesco fertilizers, pesticides, and equipment—just about any landscaping product a greenskeeper might need. They bring the store to the clubhouse door at nearly half the courses in the United States, including such gems as Grand Cypress and Augusta National.

The manufacturing company, in Rocky River, Ohio, has three plants, where it makes more than 17,000 lawn care products for the professional landscaping market. It sells such tools of the trade as mowers and seed spreaders and their replacement parts. Lesco's other main products are fertilizers and turf-protection mixes, many of which it makes specifically for different regions of the country. In Florida, for example, it markets a special fertilizer to replenish the nutrients in sandy soil.

Although the stores on wheels have traveled to golf courses since 1976, the majority of Lesco's sales today occur at its 121 service centers, scattered mainly through the South, Northeast, and Midwest. The company plans to open more service centers, where most of the sales staff are trained as agronomists and able to consult with customers on the latest products.

In 1993, Lesco entered the consumer market, and now it distributes its products through 103 Home Depot stores. Lesco executives see an opportunity for growth in the consumer products category, but the company is cautious because it doesn't want to risk losing focus on its efforts in the professional market.

ALTERNATIVE EXAMPLE

Rental car companies find that about 70% of their business occurs at airports. Doing business beyond airports in local markets is strongly influenced by their distribution strategies. In Arizona and New Mexico Budget Rent A Car distributes their services in supermarkets. Since rental booths entered Smith's Food & Drug Center stores, their rental bookings have been 25 percent more than stand-a-lone rental locations in Phoenix and Albuquerque. Enterprise Rent-A-Car also emphasizes the distribution element with its "Pick Enterprise. We'll pick you up" campaign which picks up customers at auto repair shops or at home. SOURCE: "Rental Service Bounds into Front Seat," *Advertising Age*, September 27, 1995, p. 4.

Of course, Lesco products set the company apart from most others, but Lesco relies on a distribution strategy that utilizes a number of channels of distribution. Much of Lesco's success can be traced to its effective performance of the distribution function.

This chapter provides an overview of the purpose of the distribution element of the marketing mix. It defines *channels of distribution* and explores the functions intermediaries perform. It then explains the advantages and disadvantages of the many alternative channels of distribution. Next, it addresses the major decisions managers make in planning a distribution strategy. It discusses how the implementation of a distribution strategy may create channel conflict and, finally, describes some legal and ethical issues related to channels of distribution.

## Distribution Delivers a Standard of Living to Society

ALTERNATIVE EXAMPLE
Dell Computer is an example of the importance of distribution decisions. Dell markets its computers directly to customers and holds no inventories. As a result, its operating costs are 5.4 percent of revenues, compared with 13 percent for Compaq. Furthermore, Dell's prices do not reflect the normal 4–10 percent margins earned by retailers. However, logistics remains 40 percent of the cost of a Dell computer. SOURCE: Peter Burrows, "The Computer Is in the Mail," *Business Week,* January 23, 1995, pp. 76–77; Scott McCartney, "Dell Computer to Outsource All Shipping," *Wall Street Journal,* February 15, 1995, p. B6.

POINT TO EMPHASIZE
Distribution is important even for services, where the problem of inseparability often means that the customer and provider must meet. Although transporting the product over long distances is not the issue, distribution strategies cannot be ignored.

The major purpose of marketing is to satisfy human needs by delivering products of various types to buyers when and where they want them and at a reasonable cost. A key element in this statement of marketing's mission is delivery. In many ways, all marketing effort comes to nothing unless products are placed in the hands of those who need them. Thus, distribution is of overwhelming importance in any discussion of marketing functions. Distribution is estimated to account for about one-quarter of the price of the consumer goods we buy. Most would agree that this is a cost well worth bearing. Distribution creates time utility and place utility.

Distribution of products among the members of a society becomes necessary with the development of the idea that efficiency can be gained, even in a primitive economy, if one person specializes in a certain activity, such as hunting, and another person specializes in a different activity, such as fishing or farming. In a primitive economy, distribution is straightforward; but in today's global economy, it is far more complex. For example, products shipped into Denver may ultimately be sold in Oregon, and Washington state apples may be consumed in Florida. The basic function of distribution, however, remains the same. One way or another, the distance between the grower or producer of a product and the final user of that product must be bridged. The distance to be covered can be quite long, as when Mexican oil ends up in Australia. It can also be quite short, as when a farmer at a roadside stand sells the watermelon that grew just a few yards away. Whatever the distance required to move a good from a producer to a buyer or consumer, society relies on the marketing function of distribution to do the job—to provide products in the right place at the right time.

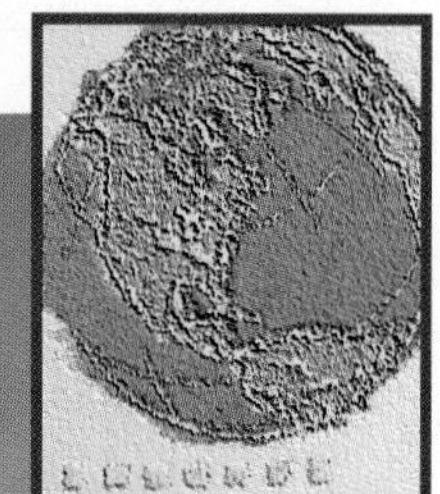

### FOCUS ON GLOBAL COMPETITION

### *The Former Soviet Union*

As you probably know, August 1991 marked a historic event—the collapse of the Communist government in the U.S.S.R. and the beginning of the end of the union itself. The desire to move away from a centrally planned economy toward capitalism and a market economy was a major underlying reason for this political upheaval. The seeds of economic change had been planted.

In fact, before August 1991, the Soviet Union had made modest strides toward changing its failing economic system. Several circumstances had made it clear to many in the U.S.S.R. that things had to change. Communism provided too few goods and a meager living for most citizens. The productivity of factories was low by Western standards, and goods were often of poor quality.

Equally trying for Soviet consumers was the fact that they couldn't get their hands on even the shoddy goods being produced. Farm produce often rotted because trucks to deliver it to state-owned stores in the cities didn't work and repair parts were impossible to find. Goods often went to Communist party bosses and labor leaders rather than to the stores. Bureaucratic corruption was prevalent. Many goods were sold on the "black market" at ten times the official price. In state-owned stores, shelves were often bare. When food and other goods were available in stores, customers often faced long waiting lines for everyday items. In other words, the distribution system did not deliver an adequate standard of living. One result was the one the world saw in August 1991. ■

The main business of the Hollywood movie studios once was simply making films—that is, production. Today, the crucial factor determining a studio's profitability is film distribution. Major U.S. film studios produce only about half the movies they distribute. They purchase many films from independent studios. The large studios concentrate on distribution and other marketing functions and are compensated for these efforts through a fee system, usually 25 to 30 percent of a film's rentals. Film distribution itself has also changed in recent years. Supplying films to theaters is no longer enough. Home Box Office, Showtime, and other cable systems, as well as TV networks, independent stations, and videocassette marketers, are now critical in the film marketing process. Distribution is the name of the game in Hollywood.

## Distribution in the Marketing Mix—A Key to Success

ALTERNATIVE EXAMPLE
Fox Broadcasting Co. provides another example of the importance of distribution. In 1994, Fox lured a number of strong affiliate stations away from CBS, NBC, and ABC, replacing smaller affiliate stations in key cities. This gives Fox a substantial competitive advantage because affiliate stations, which serve to distribute programming, typically distribute programming for one network only. The linchpin in this gain was the $1.6 billion bid that gained Fox the right to telecast National Football League games. SOURCE: Ronald Henkoff, "Smartest and Dumbest Managerial Moves of 1994," *Fortune*, January 16, 1995, pp. 84–97.

Increasing levels of competition, cost-consciousness brought on by world and national economic developments, and consumer concerns with efficiency in marketing are among the main reasons why distribution has become increasingly important to organizations in recent years.

Some organizations compete successfully against much larger competitors by basing their market appeal almost entirely on distribution. Mary Kay Cosmetics, although it has grown to be a large firm in its own right, competes against such giants as Procter & Gamble by employing a distribution system much different from Procter & Gamble's. Mary Kay's products go right to the consumer's door.

Even activities not usually thought of as involving much in the way of distribution may rely heavily on this aspect of the marketing mix. Not-for-profit and social-service organizations such as the American Heart Association have used distribution effectively to better perform their functions. The American Heart Association makes blood pressure checks available in many locations, including schools, libraries, and fire stations, for example.

## What Is a Channel of Distribution?

We briefly discussed channels of distribution in Chapter 1. The channel of distribution may be referred to by other names, and terms vary from industry to industry. But whether the term *channel, trade channel,* or some other variant is used, the functions performed remain the same.

The term *channel of distribution* has its origins in the French word for canal. This suggests a path that goods take as they flow from producers to consumers. In this sense, the channel of distribution is defined by the organizations or individuals along the route from producer to consumer. Because the beginning and ending points of the route must be included, both producer and consumer are always members of the channel of distribution. However, there may be intermediate stops along the way. Several marketing institutions have developed to facilitate the flow of the physical product or title to the product from the producer to the consumer. Organizations that serve as marketing intermediaries (middlemen) specializing in distribution rather than production are external to the producing organization. When these intermediaries join with a manufacturer in a loose coalition to engage in exploiting joint opportunities, a channel of distribution is formed.[1]

**CHANNEL OF DISTRIBUTION**
The complete sequence of marketing organizations involved in bringing a product from the producer to the ultimate consumer or organizational user.

A **channel of distribution,** then, consists of producer, consumer, and any intermediary organizations that are aligned to provide a vehicle that makes possible the passage of title or possession of the product from producer to consumer. The channel of distribution can also be seen as a system of interdependency within a set of organizations—a system that facilitates the exchange process.

All discussions of distribution channels concern a product that has taken on its final form. The channel of distribution for an automobile begins after the product has become a finished automobile. It does not include the paths of raw materials (such as steel) or component parts (such as tires) to the automobile manufacturer, which is an industrial user in these other channels. It should be emphasized that the channel's purpose in moving products to people is more than a simple matter of transportation. The channel of distribution must accomplish the task of transferring the title to the product as well as facilitating the physical movement of the goods to their ultimate destination. Although title transfer and the exchange of physical possession (transportation) generally follow the same channel of distribution, they do not necessarily need to follow the same path.

**MERCHANT INTERMEDIARY**
A channel intermediary, such as a wholesaler or a retailer, that takes title to the product.

**AGENT INTERMEDIARY**
A channel intermediary that does not take title to the product. Agent intermediaries bring buyers and sellers together or otherwise help to consummate a transaction.

All but the shortest of channels include one or more intermediaries—individuals or organizations specializing in distribution rather than production. (In the past, intermediaries were called middlemen.) A distinction may be made between **merchant intermediaries,** which take title to the product, and **agent intermediaries,** which do not take title to the product. Although agent intermediaries never own the goods, they perform a number of marketing functions, such as selling, that facilitate further transactions in the exchange process.

Distribution is as important to service marketers as it is to the marketers of goods. The American Heart Association offers blood pressure checks, cholesterol checks, and other services in shopping centers and other high-traffic locations because people are more likely to have their health checked in convenient locations.

POINT TO EMPHASIZE
The agreements between channel members may be formal, written agreements but are most often informal, implicit agreements.

Most intermediaries are independent organizations tied to the producers they deal with only by mutual agreement; they are not owned by the producers. Some intermediaries *are* owned by producers, such as the company-owned sales branches and sales offices that sell NCR office equipment. However, these company-owned sales offices and branches are easily identified as being separate from the production facilities operated by the company.

In service marketing, it sometimes appears that there is no channel of distribution. When a beautician delivers a product, such as a haircut or make-up advice, he or she deals directly with the customer. But even in these shortest of distribution channels, where no intermediaries are involved, marketing functions are being performed. The required activities are simply performed by the provider of the service (or, in a self-service environment, by the ultimate consumer).[2]

When identifiable intermediaries are present, the channel members form a coalition intended to act on joint opportunities in the marketplace. Each channel member, from producer to retailer, must be rewarded or see some opportunity for continued participation in the channel. Ultimately, for the channel to work properly, the consumer, who is not an institutional member of the channel but is the final link in the process, must also perceive a likely reward. Thus, the large merchandise selection and low retail prices offered by a Venture or Target store must be seen as compensation for driving an extra mile or two to the store.

CONVENTIONAL CHANNEL OF DISTRIBUTION
A channel of distribution characterized by loosely aligned, relatively autonomous marketing organizations that carry out a trade relationship.

VERTICAL MARKETING SYSTEM
A vertical network of marketing establishments operating as a centrally coordinated distribution system. They may be linked by ownership, contractual agreement, or strategic alliance.

The coalition between channel members may be a loose one resulting from negotiation or a formal set of contractual arrangements identifying each party's role in the distribution process. The **conventional channel** is characterized by loosely aligned, relatively autonomous marketing organizations that have developed a system to carry out a trade relationship. In contrast, formal **vertical marketing systems** are more tightly organized systems in which the channel members are either owned by a manufacturer or a distributor, linked by contracts or other legal agreements such as franchises, or informally managed and coordinated as an integrated system through strategic alliances. Vertical marketing systems are discussed in greater detail later in this chapter.

Not included in the channel of distribution are transportation companies, financial institutions, and other functional specialists that sell services that assist the flow of products. They are collaborators, playing a specialized role by providing a limited facilitating service useful to channel members.

## Marketing Functions Performed by Intermediaries

Perhaps the most neglected, most misunderstood, and most maligned segment of the economy is the distribution segment. Retailers are seen by some as the principal cause of high consumer prices simply because retailers are the marketers with whom consumers most frequently come into contact. Retailers collect money from consumers, so even though much of that money is passed to other distributors or manufacturers, retailers often bear the brunt of customers' complaints. Wholesalers are also seen as causing high prices, perhaps because much of what they do is done outside the view of consumers.

POINT TO EMPHASIZE
Cutting out channel intermediaries can benefit remaining members, who can then share the profits that would have been earned by the intermediary. However, the remaining channel intermediaries also must assume the lost intermediary's functions. If the remaining channel members cannot perform these functions as efficiently as the lost intermediary, the increased costs may more than offset the gains.

In either case, "cutting out the middleman" is suggested by many as a means to lower the prices of consumer goods. This sentiment goes back thousands of years. The activities of those who perform the distribution function have long been misunderstood, and so it continues today. Students of marketing should understand that an efficient distribution system must somehow be financed. Most of the time, "eliminating the middleman" will not reduce prices, because the dollars that go to intermediaries compensate them for the performance of tasks that must be accomplished regardless of the economic system in effect. In other words, a company can eliminate intermediaries, but it cannot eliminate the functions they perform.

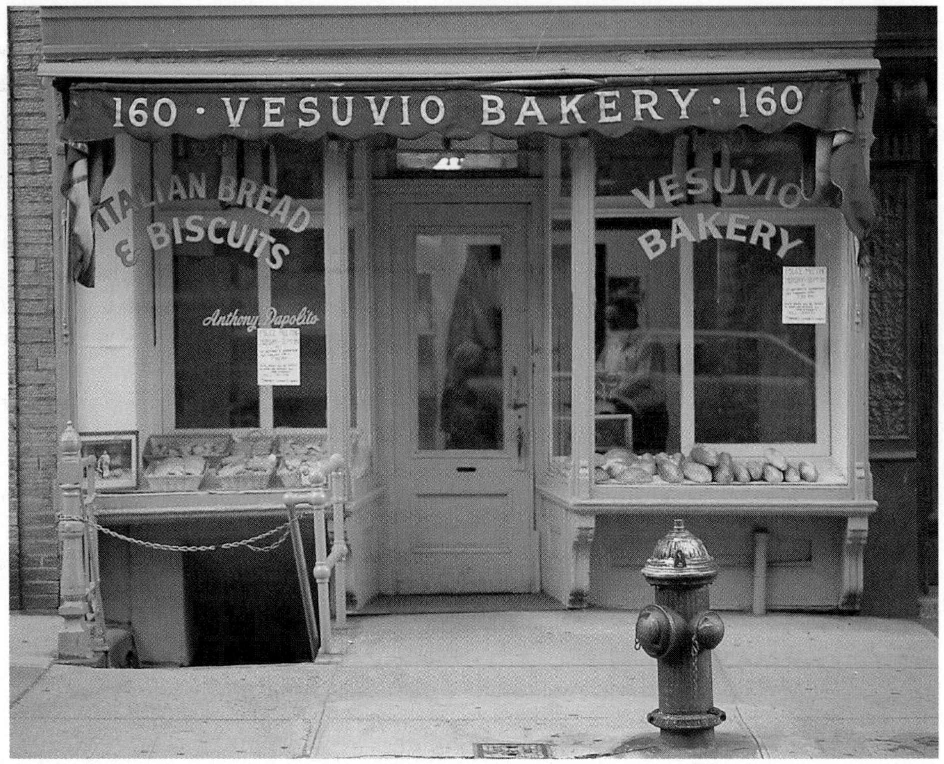


A neighborhood bakery is a direct channel of distribution. The product passes directly from the bakery to the consumer.

## How Intermediaries Fit in Channels

In Chapter 1, we outlined a conventional channel of distribution consisting of a manufacturer, a wholesaler, a retailer, and the ultimate consumer. Not all channels include all of these marketing institutions. In some cases, a unit of product may pass directly from manufacturer to consumer. In others, it may be handled by not just one but two or more wholesalers. To see why these many variations exist, let us examine the role of intermediaries in marketing channels.

Consider this conventional channel of distribution:

Manufacturer → Retailer → Ultimate consumer

It is possible, as we show here, to have a channel of distribution that does not include a separate wholesaler. A manufacturer can choose to sell directly to retailers, in effect eliminating the wholesaler. However, the marketing functions performed by wholesalers must then be shifted to one of the other parties in the channel—the retailer or the manufacturer. If the manufacturer assumes some or all of these functions, they are said to have been shifted backward in the channel. If the retailer assumes them, they are said to have been shifted forward in the channel. For example, the manufacturer may decide to perform the function of breaking bulk—sending comparatively small orders to individual retail customers. With the wholesaler out of the picture, the manufacturer may have to create a sales force to call on the numerous retailers. On the other hand, the retailer may be willing to accept truckload lots of the product, store large quantities of it, and perform the activity of breaking down these larger quantities into smaller quantities.

In any case, the functions performed by the eliminated wholesaler do not disappear; they are simply shifted to another channel member. The channel member that assumes these functions expects to be compensated in some way. The retailer may expect lower prices and higher margins for the "extra" work performed. The manufacturer may expect larger purchase orders, more aggressive retail promotion, or more control over the distribution process.

**EXHIBIT 12–3** What a Channel Intermediary Does for Its Suppliers and Its Customers

| MARKETING FUNCTION | PERFORMED FOR SUPPLIERS | PERFORMED FOR CUSTOMERS |
|---|---|---|
| **Physical Distribution Functions** | Breaking bulk<br>Accumulating bulk<br>Creating assortments<br>Transportation<br>Storage | Sorting into desired quantities<br><br>Assorting items into desired variety<br>Delivery (transportation)<br>Storage |
| **Communication Functions** | Promotion, especially selling and communication of product information<br>Gathering customer information | Buying based on interpretation of customer needs<br>Dissemination of information |
| **Facilitating Functions** | Financing customer purchases<br>Providing management services<br>Risk taking | Credit financing<br>Repair service<br>Management assistance |

ALTERNATIVE EXAMPLE

Although retailers take possession of CDs in the music business, it is the manufacturers that bear the risk. In this industry, returns are paid in full by the manufacturers. The risk is even greater for manufacturers because, in many cases, it is more economical to dispose of returned CDs than to place them back in the inventory at the warehouse. SOURCE: Glenn Rifkin, "EMI: Technology Brings the Music Giant a Whole New Spin," *Forbes ASAP*, February 27, 1995, pp. 32–38.

favor with the buying public because of fashion shifts or quickly dying fads. It is also possible for the product to spoil while in storage or be lost through fire or some other disaster. Intermediaries bear these risks in addition to market risk.

Intermediaries run obvious risks in offering credit to the individuals and organizations to which they sell. They take legal risks in that intermediaries, not just manufacturers, can be held responsible for problems caused by faulty products or misleading claims.

When intermediaries, for whatever reason, seek to avoid the service of risk taking, the distribution system loses effectiveness. In hard economic times, for example, retailers and wholesalers are tempted to engage in "hand-to-mouth" buying, ordering small quantities of products and attempting to sell them before placing yet another small order. Such behavior defeats the whole purpose of the marketing channel by eliminating the "buy in large quantities—sell in smaller quantities" premise on which most channels are based.

Exhibit 12–3 summarizes the basic functions that channel intermediaries perform.

## Typical Channels of Distribution

We have already suggested that not all channels of distribution are alike. In fact, the variety of distribution channels is extensive indeed. That is because marketers are constantly seeking new ways to perform the distribution function. Both manufacturers and intermediaries have contributed to this effort and have developed all sorts of variations on the basic theme of distribution. Each variation was developed in an effort to better perform the distribution function and thereby attract business.

Channels may be distinguished by the number of intermediaries they include; the more intermediaries, the longer the channel. Some organizations choose to sell their products directly to the consumer or organizational user; others use long channels that include several wholesalers, agents, and retailers to reach buyers.[3] Our discussion focuses on the most common of the numerous channels of distribution available. Exhibit 12–4 shows the primary channels for consumer and organizational products.

EXHIBIT 12–4 Alternative Channels of Distribution

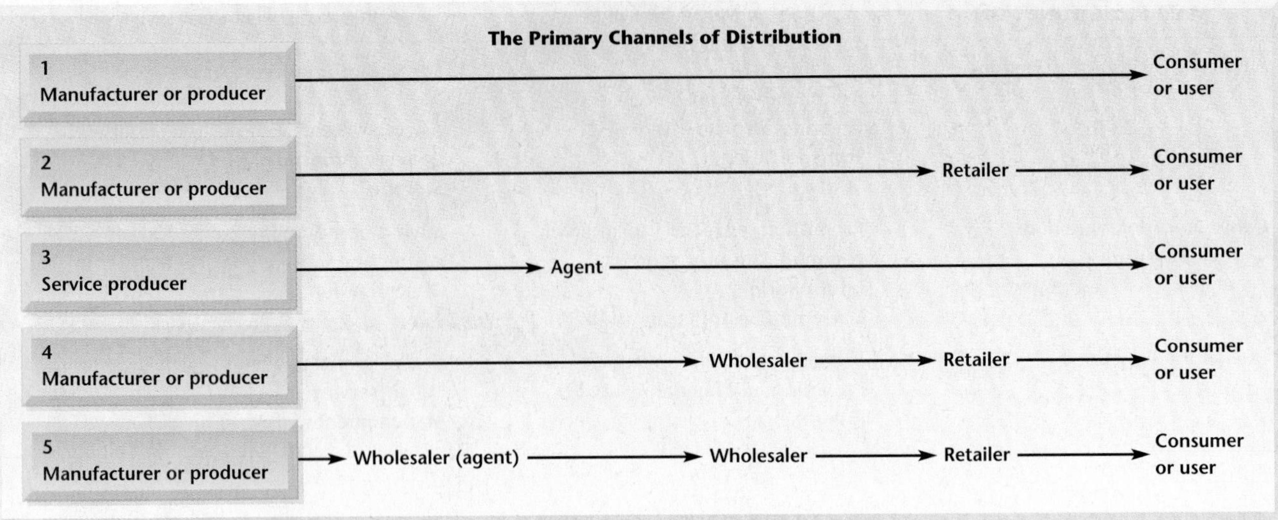
The Primary Channels of Distribution
1
Manufacturer or producer
Consumer or user
2
Manufacturer or producer
Retailer
Consumer or user
3
Service producer
Agent
Consumer or user
4
Manufacturer or producer
Wholesaler
Retailer
Consumer or user
5
Manufacturer or producer
Wholesaler (agent)
Wholesaler
Retailer
Consumer or user

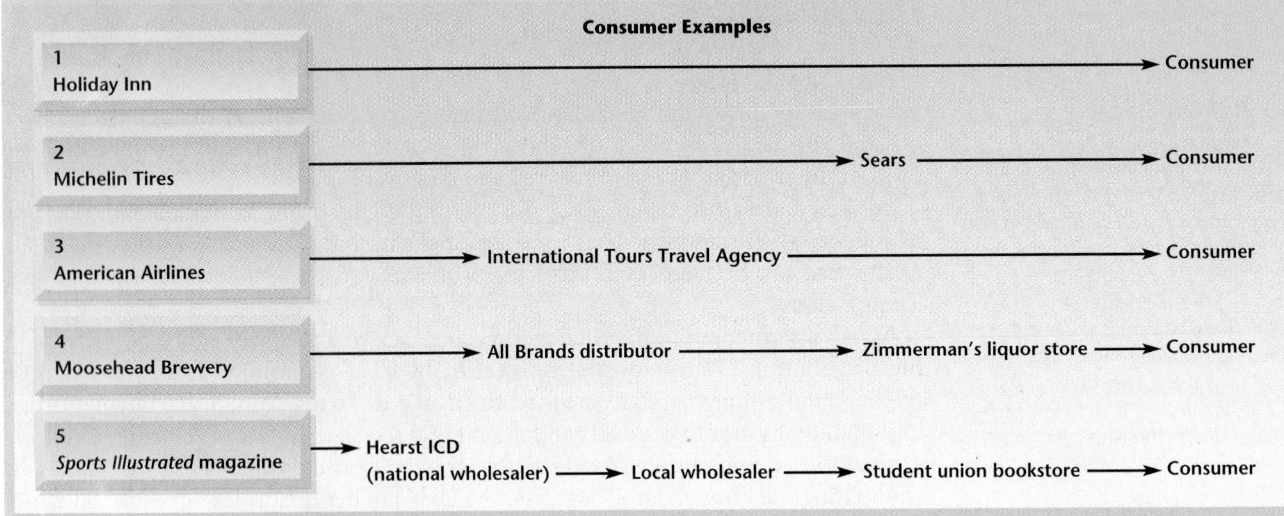
Consumer Examples
1
Holiday Inn
Consumer
2
Michelin Tires
Sears
Consumer
3
American Airlines
International Tours Travel Agency
Consumer
4
Moosehead Brewery
All Brands distributor
Zimmerman's liquor store
Consumer
5
Sports Illustrated magazine
Hearst ICD (national wholesaler)
Local wholesaler
Student union bookstore
Consumer

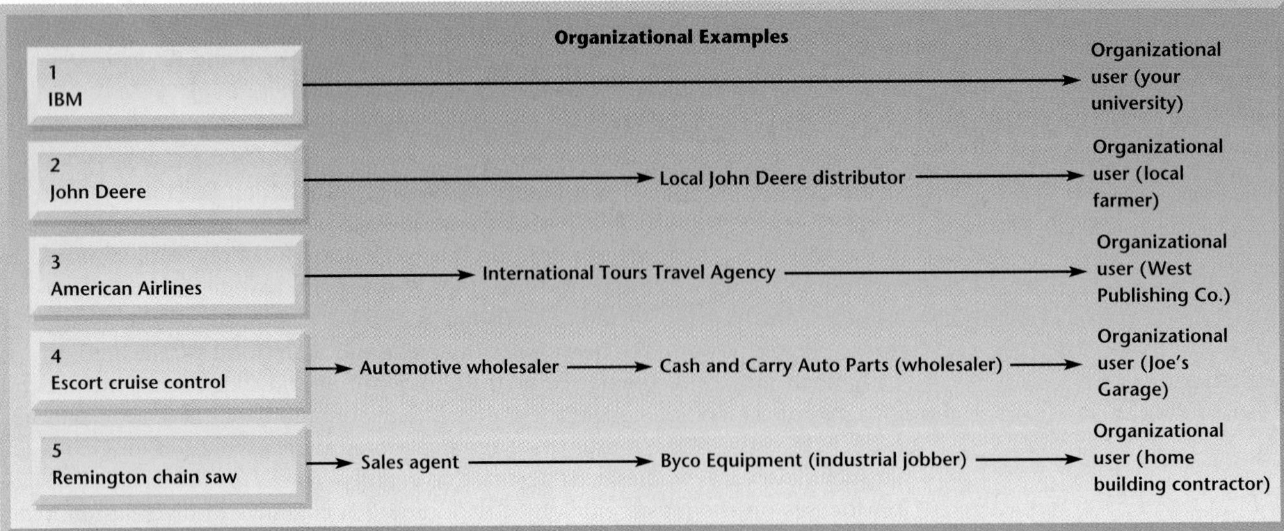
Organizational Examples
1
IBM
Organizational user (your university)
2
John Deere
Local John Deere distributor
Organizational user (local farmer)
3
American Airlines
International Tours Travel Agency
Organizational user (West Publishing Co.)
4
Escort cruise control
Automotive wholesaler
Cash and Carry Auto Parts (wholesaler)
Organizational user (Joe's Garage)
5
Remington chain saw
Sales agent
Byco Equipment (industrial jobber)
Organizational user (home building contractor)

## Channels of Distribution for Consumer Goods and Services

The middle panel of Exhibit 12–4 gives examples of typical channels for the distribution of consumer goods and services.

**The Direct Channel for Consumer Goods and Services** A good example of the direct channel is the neighborhood bakery, which converts flour, water, and other raw materials into a product and then retails the product, providing any other functions that might be necessary to complete the transaction. The direct channel is also familiar as the distribution method used by many marketers of services and not-for-profit groups that solicit donations.

DISCUSSION CONSIDERATION
Ask students what other products they, as consumers, buy directly from the manufacturer.

POINT TO EMPHASIZE
According to research, the average American family receives 100 catalogs a year. In the direct-mail business, economies of scale in costs for 800 phone numbers and postage give larger firms an advantage. SOURCE: Howard Rudnitsky, "Growing Pains," *Forbes,* February 27, 1995, pp. 58–60.

Marketers of consumer goods and services that promote their products through mail-order catalogs, telemarketing (telephone sales), and 800 numbers listed in advertisements and that distribute directly to consumers through the mail or a delivery service are also classified as using direct channels. The strategies of these direct marketers, which do not use retail outlets or contact customers in person, rely largely on data-based management and certain direct-response promotional strategies. We discuss direct marketing further in later chapters.

DISCUSSION CONSIDERATION
In addition to Wal-Mart, what other retailers seem large enough to warrant the manufacturer-retailer-consumer channel of distribution?

**The Manufacturer (Producer)-Retailer-Consumer Channel** The manufacturer-retailer-consumer channel is commonly employed when the retailer involved is a sizable organization, such as a discount chain like Wal-Mart. This type of retail marketing organization may prefer to deal directly with manufacturers to be able to order specially made merchandise or obtain discounts or other benefits. Generally, the benefits must be important enough to make the retailer willing to perform many wholesaling functions. However, in an effort to please large retailer customers, the manufacturer may agree to perform wholesaler functions. Efficiencies that accrue to a manufacturer because of the large orders placed by Sears or Wal-Mart can more than offset the wholesaling costs the manufacturer may have to absorb.

Service producers also use this channel of distribution. Home Box Office is test-marketing its HBO Visitor Information Network (VIN) in 20 Atlanta hotels. This tourism channel provides continuous programming for hotel rooms, highlighting Atlanta attractions, dining, and shopping. Marketing research will also be conducted in eight other major cities. If successful, VIN will be available in 40 U.S. markets nationwide in its first year of national distribution and in international markets the following year.[4] The channel of distribution for this service is VIN-hotel-guest, which represents a producer-retailer-consumer channel.

Many other service marketers use a producer-retailer-consumer channel when consumers can benefit from the location, product information, or other services a retailer offers. For example, many retail dry cleaners have their customers' suede clothing dry-cleaned by companies specializing in the dry-cleaning process rather than in retailing.

POINT TO EMPHASIZE
As discussed later in this chapter, the nature of the product itself influences the structure of distribution channels. For example, gum, which has a long shelf life and can withstand a lot of handling, can have a long distribution channel. Fresh flowers cannot bear a long distribution channel.

**The Manufacturer-Wholesaler-Retailer-Consumer Channel** The manufacturer-wholesaler-retailer-consumer channel of distribution is the most commonly used channel structure for consumer goods. This is because most consumer goods are so widely used. It would be virtually impossible for the Wrigley Company, for example, to deal individually with every retailer stocking chewing gum, let alone every consumer of gum. Thus, a long channel, using at least two intermediaries, is needed to distribute the product. Wholesalers can also be used in the distribution of services. The use of information services by libraries is an example.

**Channels That Include Agents** Some channels include agents. A familiar type of agent is the real estate agent. Consumers marketing their homes (or other used goods) often lack time and marketing skills, so they hire agents.

Manufacturers, especially those lacking expertise in marketing a particular product line, may choose to permit *manufacturers' agents* or *selling agents* to handle the marketing of their products. Such agents do not take title to the goods they sell and usually earn commissions rather than a salary.

In marketing channels for consumer goods, agents may, depending on circumstances and the products they offer, sell to retailers or wholesalers. The manufacturer-agent-wholesaler-retailer-consumer channel is widely used in the marketing of consumer products, especially convenience goods.

It might seem that travel agents used by airlines function as retailers. Technically, however, this is a channel using an agent. The service producer–agent–consumer channel is common in the marketing of consumer services. Ticketmaster provides a selling and capacity-management service for sports teams like the Chicago Bulls and Chicago Cubs.

## Channels of Distribution for Business-to-Business Marketing

**ALTERNATIVE EXAMPLE**
Dell and Gateway 200 are personal computer companies that operate as business-to-business marketers. They sell directly to businesses, especially businesses that are knowledgeable enough to need very little assistance in choosing models and placing orders. The low investment in "hand-holding" sales personnel is one difference between these organizations and other business-to-business marketers discussed in the text. SOURCE: Peter Burrows, "The Computer Is in the Mail," *Business Week*, January 23, 1995, pp. 76–77.

Business-to-business marketers use channels that are similar to those used by the marketers of consumer products. The primary channels are illustrated in the bottom panel of Exhibit 12–4.

**The Direct Channel in Business-to-Business Marketing** The name *business-to-business* suggests the importance of the direct channel in the marketing of organizational products. Indeed, the direct channel is the one most commonly found in the marketing of organizational goods. Direct organizational sales of industrial machinery such as escalators, power-generating machinery such as turbine engines, metals such as titanium, and many other products require well-informed salespersons, and perhaps engineers, who can help the buyer fit the product into the organizational facility or manufacturing process. Otis Elevator, for example, is a business-to-business marketer that uses a direct channel.

**The Manufacturer–Wholesaler–Organizational User Channel** Because, by definition, retailers deal with consumers, there is no distribution channel for organizational goods that directly parallels the manufacturer-retailer channel. However, there is a trade channel for organizational goods that relies on just one wholesale intermediary, which performs a function much like that of a retailer. This is the manufacturer–industrial distributor–organizational user channel. The names for this type of wholesaler vary from industry to industry; among the most common terms used is **jobber.**

**JOBBER**
A wholesale intermediary in a channel of distribution for an organizational good.

Snap-On Tools, maker of socket wrenches and other hand tools, uses industrial distributors who, working out of well-stocked vans, call directly on Snap-On's customers, professional mechanics. Industrial distributors may also operate store-like facilities that buyers, such as electricians or plumbers, may patronize. In either format, industrial distributors perform storage and communications functions. They may, as in the Snap-On example, provide delivery and may also supply credit or other functions. The industrial distributor is classified as a merchant intermediary, because this distributor takes title to the goods.

Channels of distribution for organizational goods sometimes include more than one merchant wholesaler. This is most common in international marketing.

**Business-to-Business Marketers Also Use Agents** The manufacturer–agent–organizational user channel is commonly used in business-to-business marketing by small manufacturers that market only one product to many users. The wide range of customers to which agents sell suggests their main attraction to manufacturers—flexibility. One type of agent intermediary, the broker, can be used on an occasional basis as needed. No continuing relationship—and therefore no continuing financial remuneration or other obligation—is necessary. Similarly, manufacturers' agents operate on a commission basis within fixed geographic territories. Therefore, they appeal to small organizations with limited financial resources that have difficulty funding their own sales forces. Manufacturers' agents are also attractive because they can be employed in "thin" market areas or in foreign countries where potential sales do not seem to justify a manufacturer's employment of its own sales force.

## Are Channels of Distribution What Textbooks Say They Are?

ALTERNATIVE EXAMPLE

An emerging trend is for manufacturers to open their own flagship stores, even if they compete with traditional retailers of their products. Manufacturers are opening stores in part because they have seen many department stores close and many retailers pushing higher-margin private label brands over manufacturer brands. The stores also boost consumer awareness of brands. Examples of manufacturer-owned stores include Speedo Authentic Fitness Stores (48 stores), Original Levi's Stores and Dockers Shops (16), Nike Town (4), Oshkosh B'Gosh (3), and Reebok Concept Stores (3).
SOURCE: Mary Kuntz, "These Ads Have Windows and Walls," *Business Week,* February 27, 1995, p. 74.

As we have seen, many alternative channels of distribution are available to marketing managers. Decisions concerning the selection of a channel or the determination of how many wholesalers or retailers or other intermediaries are needed to achieve the desired degree of market exposure are extremely important and difficult to make. Our discussion has focused on channel members as institutions. In actual practice, the determination of a channel may be complicated by less-than-perfect institutions.

A famous marketing management article asked: "Are Channels of Distribution What Textbooks Say They Are?"[5] The point made was that orderly presentations such as the one in Exhibit 12–4 are somewhat misleading. The baker who sells his or her own products may also be a retailer of other producers' candy or specialty items, for example.

Consider this complicated situation. In most of its business transactions, Sam's Wholesale Club is a retailer. If Sam's sells you a tire for your family car, it is engaging in a retail transaction. However, if it sells a business a tire for the company car, Sam's is a wholesaler. If Sam's arranges for its own private branded products to be manufactured, which it does, it is both a manufacturer and a retailer. That is, unless a business buys the product. Then it is both a manufacturer and a wholesaler. As you can see, what an institution is in a channel of distribution depends on the perspective from which we view the channel.

A sports store selling tennis balls may buy from a different type of wholesaler or be involved in a different type of channel of distribution than a department store selling tennis balls. The manufacturer that wishes to satisfy the consumer's desire to have the product available in a variety of outlets will implement a multiple channel strategy.

Another reason channels are not always what textbooks suggest they are is that many areas of the country are not served by the types of intermediaries a given manufacturer may wish to employ. So different geographical areas may be served by different channels of distribution. Furthermore, many manufacturers routinely use multiple channels, distributing different products or even a single product in several different ways, depending on the desires of particular customers. Sometimes a manufacturer uses multiple channels of distribution because the product is sold in a variety of retail outlets, such as grocery stores and drugstores. (Scrambled merchandising occurs when a product traditionally sold in one type of retail outlet is sold in many different types of retail stores.[6]) Textbook descriptions, while accurate for many situations, generally do not describe such complexities.

## Vertical Marketing Systems

In many industries, such as the fast-food restaurant industry, the dominant distribution structure is the vertical marketing system. The concept of a vertical marketing system emerged along with the need to manage or administer the functions performed by intermediaries at two or more levels of the channel of distribution.

Vertical marketing systems, or vertically integrated marketing systems, consist of networks of vertically aligned establishments that are professionally managed as centrally administered distribution systems. Central administration is intended to provide technological, managerial, and promotional economies of scale through the integration, coordination, and synchronization of transactions and marketing activities necessary to the distribution function. There are three types of vertical marketing systems: corporate systems, contractual systems, and administered strategic alliances.

### Corporate Systems—Total Ownership

**CORPORATE VERTICAL MARKETING SYSTEM**
A vertical marketing system in which two or more channel members are connected through ownership.

The **corporate vertical marketing system** connects two or more channel members through ownership. It is exemplified by a retailer, such as Sears, that integrates backward into manufacturing to assure quality control over production and corporate control over the distribution system. A manufacturer may obtain complete control of the successive stages of distribution by vertically integrating through ownership. Sherwin-Williams administers a corporate vertical marketing system by owning more than 2,000 retail paint outlets.

### Contractual Systems—Legal Relationships

**CONTRACTUAL VERTICAL MARKETING SYSTEM**
A vertical marketing system in which channel coordination and leadership are laid out in a contractual agreement.

In a **contractual vertical marketing system,** channel leadership is assigned not by ownership but by agreement in contractual form. In such a channel, relationships are spelled out so that there is no question about distribution coordination. The relationship between McDonald's franchise holders and McDonald's headquarters is a contractual one wherein the rights and responsibilities of both parties are clearly identified. The idea behind such an approach to distribution is that if all parties live up to their sides of the agreement, the system will work smoothly and well. In the main, this has certainly been the case for McDonald's, although the "secret" of McDonald's success is not merely the employment of a contractual vertical marketing system but also the hard work required to make it succeed.

**RETAILER COOPERATIVE ORGANIZATION**
A group of independent retailers that combine resources and expertise to control their wholesaling needs, as through a centralized wholesale buying center.

There are three subtypes of contractual systems: retailer cooperative organizations, wholesaler-sponsored voluntary chains, and franchises. A **retailer cooperative organization** is a group of independent retailers, such as Certified Grocers, that maintains a centralized buying center to perform a wholesaling function. These retailers have combined their financial resources and their expertise to more effectively con-

LEARNING OBJECTIVE **3** *Understand why all marketers—even not-for-profit and service organizations—engage in distribution.*

All marketers, including not-for-profit, service, and for-profit concerns, engage in some form of distribution because there is always some gap between the marketer and the customer that must be bridged.

LEARNING OBJECTIVE **4** *Characterize the functions of channel intermediaries.*

Channel intermediaries perform a variety of functions, including breaking bulk, accumulating bulk, sorting, creating assortments, reducing transactions, transportation, storage, communication, financing, management services, and other facilitating functions.

LEARNING OBJECTIVE **5** *Identify the major channels of distribution used by marketers of consumer and organizational products.*

The major distribution channels for consumer goods are: (1) producer to consumer; (2) producer to retailer to consumer; (3) service producer to agent to consumer; (4) producer to wholesaler to retailer to consumer (the most commonly used consumer goods channel); and (5) producer to wholesaler (agent) to wholesaler to retailer to consumer. The major organizational products channels are: (1) producer to user; (2) producer to wholesaler to user; and (3) producer to agent (wholesaler) to user. There are many variations on these basic channel models, many of which involve specialized intermediaries.

LEARNING OBJECTIVE **6** *Describe the major vertical marketing systems.*

In the corporate vertical marketing system, the members are owned outright by the controlling organization to ensure cooperation and increase effectiveness. In a contractual vertical marketing system, the members are linked to the channel leader by formal contract. An administered strategic alliance is made up of organizations that follow the lead of the dominant member of the system or engage in a collaborative effort. In all cases, the purpose of the vertical marketing system is to ensure cooperation among channel members, and the goal is increased effectiveness of the channel.

LEARNING OBJECTIVE **7** *Differentiate among channel cooperation, channel conflict, and channel power.*

Channel cooperation occurs when channel members share harmonious marketing objectives and strategies. Channel conflict characterizes channels of distribution in which there is some disharmony. Conflict should not go unmanaged. Channel power is the ability of one organization in a channel of distribution to exert influence over other channel members. The most powerful organization is the channel leader.

LEARNING OBJECTIVE **8** *Describe some of the ethical and legal concerns associated with the development and management of channels of distribution.*

Several ethical issues arise concerning the macromarketing role of distribution. Many of these issues have been addressed by laws. Exclusive dealing arrangements can be seen as stopping the distribution of competitors' goods and are thus sometimes illegal. So are territorial arrangements, which may restrict free trade. Tying agreements, which tie purchase of one product to purchase of another, are in almost all cases illegal.

## Key Terms

channel of distribution (p. 384)
merchant intermediary (p. 384)
agent intermediary (p. 384)
conventional channel of distribution (p. 385)
vertical marketing system (p. 385)
bulk-breaking function (p. 387)
bulk-accumulating function (p. 388)
assembler (p. 388)
sorting function (p. 388)
assorting function (p. 388)
selling function (p. 390)
buying function (p. 391)
service function (p. 391)
credit function (p. 392)
risk-taking function (p. 392)
jobber (p. 396)
corporate vertical marketing system (p. 398)
contractual vertical marketing system (p. 398)
retailer cooperative organization (p. 398)
wholesaler-sponsored voluntary chain (p. 399)
franchise (p. 399)
administered strategic alliance (p. 399)
intensive distribution (p. 402)
selective distribution (p. 403)
exclusive distribution (p. 403)
channel cooperation (p. 405)
channel conflict (p. 405)
channel power (p. 407)
channel leader, or channel captain (p. 407)
backward channel (p. 408)
exclusive dealing (p. 409)
exclusive territory (p. 409)
tying contract (p. 410)

## Questions for Discussion

1. What might happen if we eliminated wholesaler intermediaries for the following brands?
   a. Izod Lacoste shirts
   b. Cutty Sark Scotch whiskey
   c. Weyerhauser lumber
2. Outline the macromarketing functions performed by wholesalers and retailers.
3. At a national bottlers' meeting, the vice president of marketing for the Dr Pepper Company said: "No matter how good a job we do, [consumers] can't get Dr Pepper unless you [bottlers] have made the sale to retailers." Why would the vice president say this?
4. Several years ago, Airwick professional products division, which sells a variety of disinfectants, cleaning agents, insecticides, and environmental sanitation products, sold its products through a network of 65 distributors and 10 branch sales offices. The company decided to drop its sales branches. What circumstances might lead to such a change in channel strategy?
5. Only recently have medical professionals started to realize that they, like manufacturers, must give thought to their distribution systems. What distribution decisions might hospitals, dentists, and pediatricians have to make?
6. How will the decision of Sam's Wholesale Club, Price Club, Costco, and similar stores to sell food affect Procter & Gamble's distribution system?
7. If you were the manufacturer of the following products, what channels of distribution would you select?
   a. Fax machines
   b. Automobile mufflers
   c. Personal computers
   d. Telephones
   e. Toy dolls
8. Outline the channel of distribution for the following.
   a. An airline
   b. A bakery
   c. A pizza restaurant
9. What advantages do vertical marketing systems have over conventional marketing systems?
10. Would you use exclusive, selective, or intensive distribution for the following products? Why?
    a. Dr Pepper
    b. Lexus automobiles
    c. Panasonic videocassette recorders
    d. Ethan Allen furniture
    e. Fieldcrest Mills towels
    f. Michelin tires
11. What environmental forces might shape international distribution strategies?
12. Identify the possible sources of conflict in a channel of distribution.
13. What macromarketing functions do intermediaries perform for society at large?
14. Under what conditions is exclusive dealing legal?
15. Under what conditions are exclusive territories legal?
16.  Form groups of six people with two students representing a supermarket retailer, two students representing a grocery wholesaler, and two students representing a manufacturer of packaged foods. Identify at least three issues over which channel conflicts might arise. Each channel member team should state its position on these issues.

ETHICS IN PRACTICE

## Ethics Exercise 12

A manufacturer of construction equipment historically has marketed its product only in the eastern United States, where it uses wholesalers to sell to construction contractors. It plans to expand into the western United States, using agents to sell to wholesalers until the volume of its business is large enough to make hiring its own sales force in the new market feasible. Arrangements are made with several agents to sell the product. The company, however, does not mention its plans to hire its own sales force after the agents have established a wholesale distribution system. Is this ethical?

## Take a Stand

1. A liquor wholesaler wishes to purchase five cases of a small California winery's vintage cabernet sauvignon (a red wine), which has received favorable reviews. The winery says this wine is in short supply and it ships five-case orders only to wholesalers that also purchase five cases of its chablis (a white wine). The chablis is rated as a very ordinary wine, and the wholesaler sells many comparable brands. What should the wholesaler do?
2. A supermarket sells many products packaged in aluminum cans and glass bottles. It does not offer any recycling facility or service. Is this responsible?
3. Wal-Mart notifies manufacturers that it no longer will deal with intermediaries. Its intentions are to deal directly with manufacturers. The move squeezes independent wholesalers and brokers out of the picture. Is this right?

VIDEO CASE 12–1
FOCUS ON
SMALL BUSINESS

## Aquathin Corporation

"Be humble." "It's not what happens during the day—it's how you handle it." "The customer is always right—within reason." "Profit is not a dirty word—if you earn it."

Those maxims are on a list of 23 "Aquathin axioms" disseminated by Aquathin Corp., a Pompano Beach, Florida, maker of water purification systems. It calls them principles under which the company operates. If Aquathin's founders have difficulty observing the first one, it is understandable. Alfred Lipshultz and his father, Mitchell, have every right to take great pride in their company's success.

The company began operations in 1980, with the Lipshultzes and a partner putting up $14,000 as start-up capital for making a sink-top purifier. The partner was to handle manufacturing and the Lipshultzes marketing. But things didn't go well.

Revenues, $70,000 the first year, fell to $30,000 the next. There were problems with assembling the product and financial disagreements with physicians' clinics that were selling it. The Lipshultzes bought out their partner and shifted sales from the clinics to a dealer network.

Now Aquathin's revenues top that second-year figure every three days. It has 57 water purification products and three patents, including one for a reverse osmosis/deionization system that cleanses tap water of salts, heavy metals, disease-causing microorganisms, industrial pollutants, and pesticides.

Aquathin's purifiers are used in homes, businesses, and laboratories. When the company realized that problems existed abroad with drinking water supplies and inferior filters, the company saw opportunities for international marketing.

### QUESTIONS

1. What is the nature of Aquathin's markets?
2. In your opinion, what type of distribution system would work best for Aquathin?
3. What tactics would be necessary to implement the distribution system you suggested?
4. In your opinion, what type of distribution would be necessary for international marketing?

**Source:** Excerpted by permission from *Real World Lessons for America's Small Business,* pp. 52–53, copyright 1992 by Connecticut Mutual Life Insurance Company.

VIDEO CASE 12–2

## Lanier (B)

Lanier is engaged in five main business areas under one umbrella: copying systems, facsimile systems, information management systems, dictation systems, and presentation systems. Lanier—Part A discussed the company's business mission. The company's SWOT analysis (strength and weaknesses, opportunities and threats) identified two core competencies—sourcing and distribution. Although Lanier manufactures central dictation equipment and configures imaging equipment, it sources products for copying, facsimile, and presentation systems. Selection of manufacturing sources for products that Lanier will distribute is based on answers to the following three questions:

1. Does the company make a quality product?
2. Does the company have technological and manufacturing strengths?
3. Is there a conflict of interest with the company in terms of distribution?

Lanier's distribution system has 84 branches in 113 locations and 44 dealers in 110 locations for a total of more than 200 outlets. According to Lanier, with this dual-distribution system, it can cover every parish and county in the United States. Having only branches cannot provide coverage outside the major metropolitan areas. Having only dealers does not allow a coordinated national account program. However, in Lanier's case, its dealers have been with them for 30 to 40 years, are well supported by Lanier, and are almost like branches despite being independent entities. Having both branches and dealers can provide both national coverage and major account coordination. Moreover, relying more heavily on branches, as Lanier does, allows the company to have more control and to serve the customer better. Lanier reports that, in terms of revenue, its major account business is growing faster than other portions of its business.

### QUESTIONS

1. How important is distribution to Lanier's marketing mix?
2. How would you characterize Lanier's intensity of distribution?
3. Evaluate Lanier's distribution system.

**Source:** Adapted from "Dataquest Perspective: Document Management, Copiers North America;" Product code: copy-NA-D-9311, December 27, 1993.

**VIDEO CASE 12–3 FOCUS ON SMALL BUSINESS**

## StockPot Soups

StockPot Soups is a manufacturer of fresh, homemade-style soup concentrates. The Fortun brothers founded StockPot Soups after 20 years in the food business. The company has 100 employees. The company's product line includes homemade-style soups, such as lobster bisque, chicken-flavored vegetable gumbo, cream of broccoli, and clam chowder. Production of the fresh soup product is labor-intensive, which drives up the cost of production.

Grocery wholesalers and retailers often stock five or six competing brands. Most competitors offer national brands. Like many small start-up companies in their early years, StockPot faces the daunting challenge of convincing distributors to carry its products. Wholesalers that supply grocers simply do not want to carry another soup. This is also true of wholesalers that supply food services and institutional customers.

**Source:** Adapted by permission from *Strengthening America's Competitiveness*, p. 56, copyright 1991 by Connecticut Mutual Life Insurance Company.

### QUESTIONS

1. Describe StockPot's channel or channels of distribution.
2. What strategy can StockPot use to gain distribution?
3. Are there any innovative channels of distribution that StockPot can tap?

CHAPTER

# 13 Retailing and Wholesaling

LEARNING OBJECTIVES

After you have studied this chapter, you will be able to:

1. Describe the nature of retailing and wholesaling in the distribution system.
2. Categorize the various types of retailers by ownership and prominent strategy.
3. Analyze the historical patterns in American retailing and evaluate the theories proposed to explain them.
4. Understand the nature of retailers' marketing mixes.
5. Distinguish between merchant wholesalers and agents and describe their function in the distribution system.
6. Show how full-service and limited-service merchant wholesalers contribute to the marketing system.
7. Identify the marketing contributions of agent intermediaries such as brokers, auction companies, and selling agents.
8. Understand the key elements of wholesalers' strategies.

**CATEGORY DISCOUNTER**
A specialty mass merchandiser offering extensive assortment and depth in a specific product category; also called a *category killer.*

and sporting goods. A mass merchandise discounter specializing in a certain product category is called a **category discounter**, or *category killer.* Sportsmart, which sells 100,000 different items, provides an example. It is radically different from the typical independent sports store because it stocks virtually all competitive offerings of soccer balls, baseball gloves, sports team jackets, and the like rather than carrying a single brand, as most sports stores do. Category discounters apply a deep discount strategy, with prices even lower than those of general mass merchandisers, and offer the most extensive assortment and greatest depth in the product lines they carry. This retailing strategy is expected to attract most of the local business for the product category and eliminate ("kill") the competition.

*Other Discount Retailers* More traditional specialty store retailers and others may also use variations of the discounting strategies just discussed. Crown Books, a specialty retailer, is a bookstore chain that discounts every book on the *New York Times* best-seller list by 35 percent. It focuses on best sellers and ignores low-volume books.

**DIRECT MARKETING**
Marketing that uses advertising, telephone sales, or other communications to elicit a direct response from consumers.

**Direct Marketing** **Direct marketing** involves the use of advertising, telephone sales, or other communications to elicit a direct response from consumers. Manufacturers, wholesalers, retailers, and nonprofit organizations may engage in direct marketing. Retailers who offer the buying public a retail marketing mix that does not include a store at all are direct marketers. Direct marketing in a retailing context has also been called *nonstore retailing* and *direct-response retailing.* The many means of retailing via direct marketing include mail-order, door-to-door selling, home television shopping, in-home computer retailing, and vending machines.

Whether direct marketing uses catalogs, letters, pamphlets, television, the Internet, or telephone to reach consumers, it always calls for a direct response, generally an order by traditional mail, e-mail, telephone, or fax. Consumers find direct marketing appealing for a number of reasons. In particular, they like the ability to shop when it is convenient for them (for example, late at night or on weekends), the depth of product line selections (for example, more colors and unusual sizes of garments), and the ability to purchase unique items not elsewhere available (for example, replicas of museum jewelry).

2Market, a new company formed by America Online, Apple Computer, and Medior, offers a catalog on CD-ROM. The CD-ROM features a guide who complains in a five-minute opening spiel about the hassle of retail shopping and then walks users through a menu screen that allows them to choose among several shopping methods. Individual items may be selected by brand, price range, or various item groups. Shown here is a screen from the personal shopper.

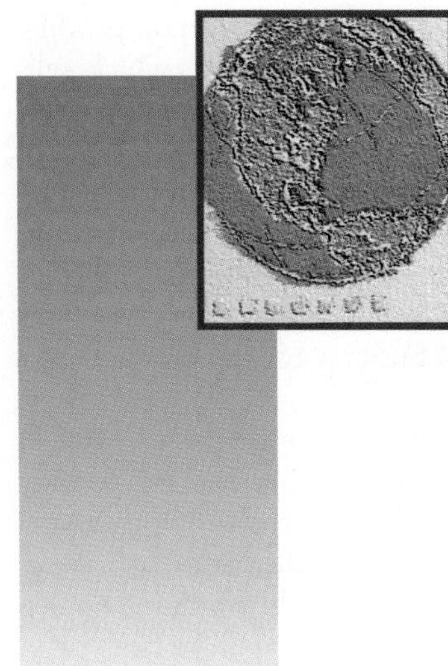

## FOCUS ON GLOBAL COMPETITION

### *European Direct Marketing*

Figures from the European Direct Marketing Association show that the average Belgian gets 78 pieces of direct mail a year. To most Americans, that would be a relief, because they get that many pieces of direct mail every month. But the average Belgian gets more mail than other Europeans. The typical German gets 61 pieces of direct mail a year; the typical French person, 55; and the typical English person, 42. In Spain, the average person gets only 24 pieces; and in Ireland, the average is 11, less than one catalog or letter every month.

The direct mail industry has developed much more slowly in Europe than in the United States because the various countries have vastly different privacy laws, postal rates, and postal delivery systems. For example, an automotive dealer in the United States can buy automobile registration information from state motor vehicle bureaus. However, the United Kingdom's Driving and Vehicle Licensing Center does not sell its data for commercial purposes. ■

**DISCUSSION CONSIDERATION**
Ask students what mail-order retailers they patronize. Ask whether there are mail-order retailers they would not patronize, and why. Can students guess where specific mail-order retailers might have obtained their (the students') names?

*Mail-Order Catalogs* Mail-order retailing through catalogs is one of the oldest forms of direct marketing. Sears, Roebuck and Company began in the mail-order business and moved on to other types of marketing. Today, the famous Sears *Wishbook* catalog no longer exists. However, companies such as Banana Republic and Sharper Image still combine catalog advertising with both mail-order and in-store retailing. Others, like Sundance, are exclusively committed to direct marketing operations.[3]

Catalog retailers and some other mail-order marketers make extensive use of *data-based marketing,* discussed in earlier chapters. They buy computer-generated mailing lists from companies that specialize in developing them. The lists can be narrowly focused on selected interest groups, such as gardeners or cyclists, or on specific individuals whose buying patterns are recorded in the data base.

*Direct-Response Advertising* Advertising in magazines and other print media may call for a direct response and thus may constitute direct marketing. Certain target customers may be effectively reached by such marketing efforts. Purveyors of vitamins and other health aids for senior citizens, for example, conduct a brisk business through advertisements placed in such magazines as *Modern Maturity,* the publication of the American Association of Retired Persons.

Direct marketers who advertise on television and fill orders via the mail or express delivery service have proliferated by hawking everything from cutlery to Elvis Presley memorabilia. The familiar television campaigns that urge viewers to write or call an 800 number are good illustrations of this approach to retailing.

**POINT TO EMPHASIZE**
There is growing resistance to both telemarketing and door-to-door marketing among consumers, who feel these techniques are an invasion of privacy.

*Television Home Shopping* *Television home shopping* is a direct marketing innovation developed with the advent of cable TV. Here, viewers tuning in the cable shopping channel see a "show" where products are demonstrated by a "host." Consumers call the host while the show is on the air to ask questions about the product or purchase it.

*Telemarketing* *Telemarketing,* the selling of retail merchandise by telephone, is a growing aspect of direct marketing. It involves both data-based management and direct personal selling. We discuss personal selling in Chapter 17.

**COMPUTER-INTERACTIVE RETAILING**
A retailing method through which consumers shop at home using personal computers and interactive computer services.

*In-Home Retailing with Computers* Among the newer developments in nonstore retailing is **computer-interactive retailing,** through which consumers can shop at viding nutritional information, making deliveries within a half-hour window (for an additional $4.95) rather than the usual 90-minute window, accepting detailed requests (such as three ripe and three unripe tomatoes), and delivering alcoholic beverages.

Peapod views delivery as another opportunity to learn about customers' preferences. It asks its deliverers to find out where customers would like the groceries left when they're not at home and anything else that will enhance the relationship. They fill out an "interaction record" for every delivery to track those preferences (as well as entering basic service metrics, such as the time of the delivery).

Even with the rates it charges, Peapod has to be efficient and effective to make money in what is a low-margin business. That is why it mass-customizes all shopping and delivery processes. Each order is filled by a generalist, who shops the aisles of the store, and as-needed specialists, who provide the produce, meats, deli, seafood, and bakery items to the generalist. The generalist pays for the groceries, often at special Peapod counters in the back of the store. The order is then taken to a holding area in the supermarket or in a trailer, where the appropriate items are kept cold or frozen until the deliverer picks up a set of orders and takes them to the customers. At each stage—ordering, shopping, holding, and delivery—the processes are modularized to provide personalized service at a relatively low cost.

If a customer has a problem, he or she can call Membership Services, and a service representative will try to resolve the matter. Peapod treats each call as yet another opportunity to learn (and remember) each customer's preferences and to figure out what the company can do to improve service for customers as a whole. For example, service representatives found that some customers were receiving five bags of grapefruits when they really wanted only five grapefruits. In response, Peapod now routinely asks customers to confirm orders in which quantities might be confused.

Peapod's results stand as a testament to the power of learning relationships. The four-year-old service, which has 7,500 customers and revenues of about $15 million, has a customer-retention rate of more than 80%. And the service accounts for an average of 15% of the sales volume of the 12 Jewel and Safeway stores where Peapod shops for its customers.

**Source:** Reprinted by permission of *Harvard Business Review.* From "How Peapod Is Customizing the Virtual Supermarket," in "Do You Want to Keep Your Customers Forever?" by B. Joseph Pine II, Don Peppers, and Martha Rogers (March–April 1995), p. 109. 

## QUESTIONS

1. Outline Peapod's marketing mix.
2. What marketing elements provide the primary reasons for Peapod's success?
3. What other types of retailers would benefit by imitating Peapod's marketing strategy? Briefly explain.

CHAPTER

# 14 Physical Distribution Management

LEARNING OBJECTIVES

After you have studied this chapter, you will be able to:

1. Evaluate the role of logistics and physical distribution in the marketing mix.
2. Show how distribution managers can make physical distribution provide maximum satisfaction to buyers while reducing costs.
3. Explain the total cost approach to physical distribution.
4. Compare the advantages and disadvantages of the modes of transportation available to shippers.
5. Identify the purposes of warehousing, order processing, materials handling, and inventory control.
6. Understand materials management activities and their influence on many marketing decisions.

VIDEO CASE 14–2

## EkkWill WaterLife Resources

It's tough to make a living in aquaculture. Success stories are rare; failures are common.

Tim, Sherry, and Mike Hennessy had experienced one of the failures, in a shrimp-farming venture. Nevertheless, they wanted to try again, focusing this time on tropical fish.

The Hennessys—Tim and Mike are brothers; Sherry is Tim's wife—had no cash. But that didn't stop them.

A Gibsonton, Florida, fish farm was for sale 12 years ago; the owner wanted to retire and would finance 80 percent of the purchase price. Developing a detailed business plan, the Hennessys persuaded financial institutions to lend them the other 20 percent plus working capital. The debts were secured by multiple mortgages on the property, subordinated to the seller.

Successful in buying a business although they had no money, the Hennessys tackled problems in marketing and production.

They changed the business' name from Ekk-Will Tropical Fish Farm to EkkWill WaterLife Resources, to better represent what they wanted it to be about: selling not only tropical fish for the aquarium market, but also amphibians, reptiles, and aquatic plants. (EkkWill sells these wares to wholesalers. To other acquaculturists, it sells the Pacu, an Amazon River foodfish.) An eye-catching logo was developed. The firm began angling for sales in Europe, Latin America, and the Far East and got some—a first for Florida fish farming.

Source: Excerpted with permission from *Real-World Lessons for America's Small Business*, pp. 1–2, copyright 1992 by Connecticut Mutual Life Insurance Company.

### QUESTIONS

1. How do uncontrollable environmental factors influence a business like EkkWill?
2. How important are distribution and logistics to a company like EkkWill?
3. In your opinion, what is the nature of materials management and physical distribution in a company like EkkWill?

VIDEO COHESION CASE

## Minnesota Twins

This section includes seven cases dealing with various marketing issues facing the Minnesota Twins. The cases are interrelated, but each can stand alone. The cases are supplemented with several videos that help tie the issues and concepts together to portray a cohesive picture of how an organization deals with planning, implementing, and controlling all aspects of marketing strategy.

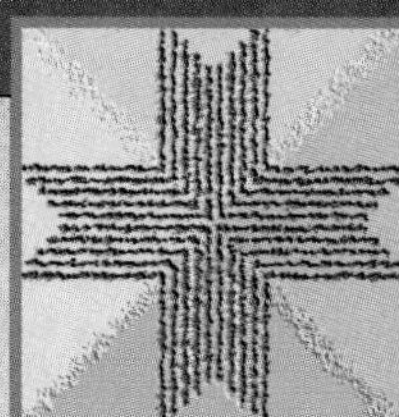

# Cross-Functional Insights

**PART FOUR**

Many theories and principles from other business disciplines can provide insights about the role marketing plays in an organization. The questions in this section are designed to help you think about integrating what you have learned in other business courses with the marketing principles explained in this textbook.

## *Distribution Delivers a Standard of Living to Society*

The major purpose of marketing is to satisfy human needs by delivering products of various types to buyers when and where they want them and at a reasonable cost.

How does the economic concept of scarcity relate to the distribution of a standard of living?

## *Channel Conflict*

Channel conflict refers to a situation in which channel members disagree and their relationship is antagonistic. Disagreements may relate to the channel's common purpose or the responsibility of certain activities. The behavior of one channel member may be seen as inhibiting the attainment of another channel member's goals.

How are conflicts between channel members similar to conflicts that an organization's cross-functional teams experience? Can similar techniques be used to reduce these conflicts?

## *Retailers*

Retailing consists of all business activities involving the sale of goods and services to ultimate consumers.

Are most retailers entrepreneurs? What characteristics of entrepreneurs would help them become successful retailers?

What stages of company growth would be typical for a successful retail business started by an entrepreneur?

If an entrepreneur were starting a retail business, what form of ownership would be best: a sole proprietorship, a partnership, or a corporation?

What would the typical small retailer's balance sheet look like?

What should a retailer know about teamwork? What types of teams might a retailer utilize?

What type of inventory cost system should a retailer have?

## *Merchant Wholesalers and Agent Wholesalers*

Channel members may be merchant wholesalers, who take title to the goods, or agent wholesalers, who do not take title to goods.

Who may be a legal agent?

How is agency authority in a channel of distribution created?

How is an agency relationship in a channel of distribution ended?

How does the Uniform Commercial Code apply to the relationship between manufacturers and merchant wholesalers?

### Logistics

Logistics describes the entire process of moving raw materials and component parts into the firm, in-process inventory through the firm, and finished goods out of the firm. Logistics management thus involves planning, implementing, and controlling the efficient flow of both inbound materials and outbound finished products.

What factors should a company consider when determining locations for factories and company-owned warehouses? How important are logistics and physical distribution in this decision?

How do labor unions influence logistics management and physical distribution functions?

## Information Technology: Insights and Exercises

If one of the following exercises or addresses given below does not seem to work, please check the West Publishing World Wide Web (WWW) address listed below. Updates and other information will be provided at this address as necessary. To reach the West Publishing WWW page with information about this book, use your Web browser to go to:

> **http://www.westpub.com/Educate/Educ.Supp.htm**
> Under **Business** and **Marketing,** choose the appropriate monthly update for **Zikmund/d'Amico, Marketing, Fifth Edition**

If you want to start at the West Publishing WWW home page and navigate to the page containing information for this book, use your Web browser to go to:

> **http://www.westpub.com**
> Choose **Fast or Slow Connection**
> Select **Products and Services**
> Select **College and School Division**
> Choose **Educational Publishing: College and School**
> Select **College Publications**
> Select **Educational Supplements and Updates for College Products**
> Under **Business** and **Marketing,** choose the appropriate monthly update for **Zikmund/d'Amico, Marketing, Fifth Edition**

### E-Mail Exercise

Tim Schweizer, a marketing professor at Luther College, is known for his nontraditional approach to teaching the principles of marketing. With the help of Professor Carolyn Tripp at the University of Tennessee–Martin and Professor Carolyn Siegel at Eastern Kentucky University, Professor Schweizer is developing a new model of marketing principles. According to Professor Schweizer and his colleagues, a true marketing principle is an idea or concept that is generalizable to other situations, across industries, across time, and so on. In other words, "Wal-Mart is one of the leading retailers in the United States" is a statement of fact, but it is not a marketing principle. On the other hand, "One can eliminate intermediaries, but one cannot eliminate the functions they perform" is a marketing principle. It should be relatively easy for

If any address is unobtainable, check the West Publishing World Wide Web address for updates: **http://www.westpub.com/Educate/Educ.Supp.htm**

you to think of an example of a principle, as well as develop practical applications of the principle.

Send Professor Schweizer an e-mail message at:

**schweizt@luther.edu**

Include three things in your message:

1. Identify what you believe to be a true principle of marketing.
2. Give one example of the principle.
3. Give an application of the principle.

Don't be surprised if you hear from Professor Schweizer. Send a copy of your message to your professor.

### *Gopher Exercise*

Traditionally, travel agents have played a key role in the distribution system for travel services. As use of the Internet continues to expand, however, radical changes are taking place in the travel services distribution system. Use Gopher to go to:

**cscns.com**
Then select **Internet Express Gopher by Subject**
Then select **Airlines—Reservation Systems Available Through Internet**

Read the document for information about using the Internet to purchase airline tickets. Then answer the following questions on a sheet of paper. Bring your answers to class for discussion.

1. What are the best ways to make airline reservations using the Internet?
2. Who is most likely to use the Internet as the distribution system for airline tickets?
3. Who will be unserved by this distribution system? What alternative channel will best reach the unserved group?
4. Is there potential for channel conflict? Explain your answer.
5. What is the future of this distribution system for airline tickets? For other travel services? Why?

### *World Wide Web Exercise*

Distribution is a bigger business than most people realize. One of the large companies that facilitates the distribution process is the A. C. Nielsen Company. Use your Web browser and go to:

**http://nielsen.com/**

Read through the information on the Nielsen WWW page that gives an overview of the BrokerNet, Nielsen, and Nielsen Select services. Then select **BrokerNet** and go to the BrokerNet page. Next, select **Get more information about BrokerNet** or select the **Overview** button. What services does Nielsen offer to those in the distribution channels. Who uses BrokerNet? What different types of reports do subscribers receive?

Return to the first Nielsen page and select **Nielsen** this time. Select **Browse The Nielsen Virtual Store.** Once in the store, select a product category to determine what types of products Nielsen tracks. Return once more to the original Nielsen page and select **Nielsen Select.** Select one of the categories to see what the report is about. How much does the report cost? Are you surprised? Select another category to see what other reports are available.

To learn what's hot in international retail, go to the Imagine If. . . home page at:

**http://www.imagine-if.be/retail/**

Spend some time looking at the various options. What did you learn about international retailing? Do you think it would be difficult to understand international retail markets? Why?

If any address is unobtainable, check the West Publishing World Wide Web address for updates: **http://www.westpub.com/Educate/Educ.Supp.htm**

## *Listserv Exercise*

Send a message to the West Publishing listserv at:

**zikmund@westpub.com**

(Note: If you are not already a member of the listserv, see page 136 for instructions on how to subscribe, send messages, and unsubscribe to the listserv.) In your message, include your answer to the following questions:

1. What is your favorite clothing retailer? Why?
2. Is your favorite clothing retailer a special store, a department store, a mail-order retailer; or some other type of retailer?
3. What services does this retailer provide for customers? *Hint:* You may want to reread Chapter 12 to help you answer this question.
4. What is your favorite retailer of prepared food? (Include restaurants, fast food chains, and so on.) Why?
5. What services does this retailer provide for customers?
6. Compare your two lists of services. Are the services provided by the clothing retailer any different from those provided by the prepared-food retailer? Why would the services differ?

## *Careers and the Internet*

Use your Web browser to go to the JobNet home page at the following address:

**http://www.westga.edu/~coop/**

Read through the information on the JobNet home page to learn about the services available at JobNet. Select **Employment Trends** to find out more about the current condition of the job market. Select **Employment Cost Index, Text Only** to find out how quickly wages and benefits are rising in the current job market. Then go back and select **Employment-Unemployment Statistics by State (text)** to find out which states have the highest unemployment.

Return to the JobNet home page, and select **subject** to see a listing of jobs by subject. Select the **Corporate and Technology** option. Then select **IntelliMatch.** This should take you to the IntelliMatch Online Career Services home page. If this connection does not work, use the direct WWW address **http://www.intellimatch.com/intellimatch/** to go the IntelliMatch Online Career Services home page. Select the **Online Job Center** option to look at current **job listings.** You can also choose other **job-related sites** to see other career resources available on the Internet. If you feel daring, return to the IntelliMatch Online Career Services home page and select **Watson** to fill out the Watson Online Résumé form. Next, select **Online Watson.** There should be no charge to use this resource. It may, however, take a few minutes to complete the forms on-line. There are specific sections for accounting and finance, sales and marketing, and so on. Be careful—you might end up with a job!

If any address is unobtainable, check the West Publishing World Wide Web address for updates: **http://www.westpub.com/Educate/Educ.Supp.htm**

# PART FIVE

# Integrated Marketing Communications

It is a luxury to be understood.

RALPH WALDO EMERSON

CHAPTER

# 15 Integrated Marketing Communications

## LEARNING OBJECTIVES

After you have studied this chapter, you will be able to:

1. Discuss the three basic purposes of promotion.
2. Define the four major elements of promotion.
3. Describe the basic model for all communication processes, including promotion.
4. Explain the hierarchy of communication effects.
5. Explain how the elements of promotion can be used to support one another in a promotional campaign.
6. Identify the general promotional strategies known as push and pull strategies.
7. Classify the major approaches used by marketing managers to set promotional budgets.
8. Discuss promotional campaigns and provide examples.
9. Take a stand about the ethics of persuasion in society.

**ALTERNATIVE EXAMPLE**
Freixenet USA, maker of champagne, is actively entering the wedding market. In its print ads, it gives a toll-free number to call for a free Freixenet wedding beverage guide. The booklet also includes special wedding offers, such as a book of toasts and graces. Freixenet offers a coupon for a $1 refund for each 760-milliliter bottle of champagne purchased. Thus, the advertising is heavily supported with sales promotion devices. SOURCE: Cyndee Miller, "'Til Death Do They Part," *Marketing News,* March 27, 1995, p. 1.

ness in a specific time period. Sales promotions add value to the product offering or provide an incentive for certain behavior. Thus, special offers of free goods, coupon deals, display items for store use, training programs, in-store demonstrations, and trips to attractive vacation spots for top salespeople are sales promotions. With a few exceptions, these are not routine events but special, out-of-the-ordinary occurrences. Although they typically involve programs paid for by an identified sponsor, they are distinguished from advertising because they are temporary offers of a material reward to customers, salespeople, or sales prospects.

Sales promotion programs amplify or bolster the advertising and personal selling messages offered by the organization. More often than not, these effects occur at the point of purchase. For instance, advertising may create an awareness of a new product like KFC Colonel Rotisserie Gold, but the cents-off coupon is the enticement that gets the consumer to try the broasted chicken for the first time. Sales promotion is not a "poor cousin" of the other elements of promotion, however. American marketers spend billions of dollars on sales promotion, just as they do on advertising and personal selling.

The main purpose of sales promotion is to achieve short-term objectives. Free samples or cents-off coupons encourage a first-time trial of a product. The use of a premium offer or sweepstakes may stimulate interest in a product and be used to encourage off-season sales. A contest may require that individuals visit the store or showroom to see if they have won. Whether the sales promotion takes the form of a trade show, a consumer rebate, a point-of-purchase display for retailers, or pens and calendars for wholesalers to give away, the best sales promotions support and are coordinated with other promotional activities. Sales promotion is discussed further in Chapter 18. The characteristics of the four elements of promotion are summarized in Exhibit 15–1.

## Integrated Marketing Communications—The Promotional Mix

**PROMOTIONAL MIX**
An organization's combination of promotional elements. The promotional mix attempts to attain integrated marketing communications.

The effective marketer recognizes that each of the four elements of promotion—advertising, publicity/public relations, personal selling, and sales promotion—has certain strengths.[1] The combination of elements a marketer chooses is the marketer's **promotional mix.** Some organizations, like the San Diego Zoo, emphasize advertis-

**EXHIBIT 15–1** Characteristics of the Four Elements of Promotion

| | PERSONAL SELLING | ADVERTISING | PUBLICITY[a] | SALES PROMOTION |
|---|---|---|---|---|
| *Mode of communication* | Direct and personal | Indirect and nonpersonal | Indirect and nonpersonal | Indirect and nonpersonal |
| *Regular and recurrent activity?* | Yes | Yes | No—only for newsworthy activity | No—short-term stimulation |
| *Message flexibility* | Personalized and tailored to prospect | Uniform and unvarying | Beyond marketer's direct control | Uniform and unvarying |
| *Direct feedback* | Yes | No | No | No |
| *Marketer control over message content?* | Yes | Yes | No | Yes |
| *Sponsor identified?* | Yes | Yes | No | Yes |
| *Cost per contact* | High | Low to moderate | No direct costs | Varies |

[a] Public relations firms and departments work to mange publicity. In other words, a primary function of public relations is the management of publicity.

The 1995 America's Cup sailing championships featured an all-female team, America3. The team was supported by more than a dozen corporate sponsors, including Chevrolet, whose logo appears on the spinnaker sail of America3 and on crew members' uniforms. Public interest in the women was so high that the news media generated a barrage of publicity. Chevrolet, pleased with the team's performance, created an integrated communications effort that included advertising, direct marketing, racing results posted on Prodigy, and sales promotions such as shopping mall displays, boat show exhibits, and dealer showroom materials.

ing and public relations efforts in their promotional mixes. Others, especially those engaged in business-to-business marketing, make personal selling the main ingredient. No matter what promotional elements are involved, marketers should strive to blend those elements to create communications that are cohesive from the consumer's point of view. Marketers must seek to integrate and unite the appropriate elements to accomplish their promotional objectives. The term **integrated marketing communications** is used to remind managers that all elements of the promotional mix should be coordinated and systematically planned to be in harmony with each other.

**INTEGRATED MARKETING COMMUNICATIONS**
Marketing communications in which all elements of the promotional mix are coordinated and systematically planned to be harmonious.

Marketers should organize all promotional elements so they work together to achieve unified promotional objectives. Personal selling efforts should reinforce advertising messages. Public relations undertakings should not be disjointed efforts unrelated to the company's basic promotional goals. Sales promotion should be coordinated so that it reflects the unified message conveyed in other media. Publicity, speeches, letters, point-of-purchase materials, and brochures as well as advertising and personal selling must be integrated in a unified communications effort that reiterates the same message or creates the same image or position.

In many cases, the task of integrated marketing communications involves a process that starts and ends with a data base. First, information about customers and prospects is collected. The customer base is segmented; communications objectives are set and a promotional program is tailored to each segment; and results from the marketing effort are fed back into the data base for the next round.[2]

Later in this chapter, we will discuss what specific factors marketers consider when choosing a promotional mix. Before we do, however, we consider how communication occurs.

## The Communication Process

**COMMUNICATION**
The process of exchanging information with and conveying meaning to others.

**Communication** is the process of exchanging information with and conveying meaning to others. But communication of even a single, apparently simple, idea is not easy. Effective promotional strategists need to understand this fact so they can carefully construct methods to get sales messages to customers and sales-related information to other organizations with which they must deal.

**RECEIVER**
In communication theory, the one at whom a message is aimed.

**SOURCE**
In communication theory, the one who sends a message.

ALTERNATIVE EXAMPLE
For communication to occur, we have to speak the same language, which is why Spanish-language media are so important to marketers. Studies show that individuals who speak Spanish are more confident consumers and are better able to locate the American producer of the good or service they want *if* they have seen or read ads in their native language. Obviously, ads in English aimed at the Hispanic market have the potential to do a poor job of communication! SOURCE: Kathy Shermach, "Spanish-Language Press Is Catching On Slowly," *Marketing News,* March 13, 1995, p.10.

**ENCODING**
In communication theory, the process by which the sender translates the idea to be communicated into a symbolic message, consisting of words, pictures, numbers, gestures, or the like, so that it can be transmitted to the receiver.

The goal of communication is a common understanding of the meaning of the information being transmitted. That is, the goal is to have the **receiver** of the information understand as closely as possible the meaning intended by the sender, or **source,** of the message. It is, for the most part, the sender's responsibility to see that this goal is accomplished. In marketing, after all, the sender of an advertisement or other promotional message wants the intended receiver to be able to grasp the information offered and act upon it. In order for this goal to be accomplished, the sender must understand the characteristics of the target audience, thus enabling the sender to tailor the message and choose the appropriate medium to reach that audience. If necessary, the audience must have opportunities to supply the proper feedback.

One communication theorist described communication as "*who* says *what* to *whom* through *which channels* with *what effect*.."[3] In slightly different terms, he was saying that to achieve the desired effect, the marketer considers the *source*, the *message*, the *channel*, and the *receiver.* Exhibit 15–2 summarizes in visual form each of these basic components of the communication process. In considering the exhibit, remember that it describes all types of communication—words, gestures, pictures, and so on. The model may be used to describe an advertisement, a telephone sales call, a point-of-purchase display, or any promotional communication.

## Encoding the Message

Evaluate the Sony Handycam advertisement shown in Exhibit 15–3 in terms of the model in Exhibit 15–2. Who says what to whom? The communication source (the advertiser) wishes to communicate the notion that the camera is a high-tech, high-quality product that helps families capture those special, often unanticipated moments in life that they wish to remember. This idea—not an easy one to get across—is the message of the advertisement. The advertisement uses few words. The message is communicated primarily in a visual and symbolic way, through the intriguing image of a cat capturing a mouse's image through a Sony Handycam. The sender's idea has been encoded by means of this picture. **Encoding** is the process of translating the idea to be communicated into a symbolic message consisting of words,

 **EXHIBIT 15–2** A Basic Model of the Communication Process

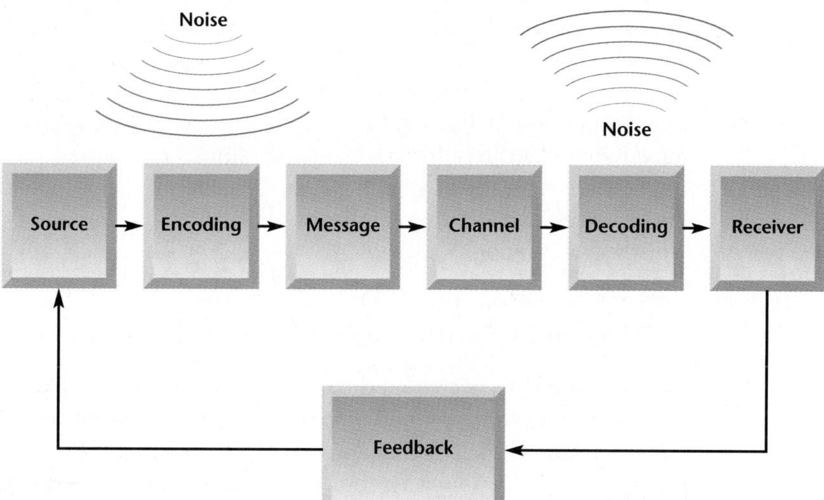

**EXHIBIT 15–3** What Is Communicated in This Advertisement?

SONY
CAPTURE THE ONES YOU LOVE.
Don't let the little things get away.
Cherish them forever with Sony Handycam.®
America's most popular camcorder.
SONY
8x
Hi-Fi Stereo
video Hi8
Handycam
Which Sony Handycam® camcorder is right for you? For a free brochure call 1-800-421-SONY.

pictures, numbers, gestures, or the like. This is a necessary step, because there is no way to send an idea from one person to another in its pure form.

As in the Sony advertisement, nonverbal messages and nonrational symbolism are essential to the encoding process, because words can be hopelessly inadequate to express emotions. "There are just no words to express the various nuances of sensation and feeling, to express such things as mood and aesthetic impression. Try to describe to a child how a strawberry tastes compared to a raspberry, how a carnation smells, why it is pleasurable to dance, what a pretty girl looks like."[4] The emotional definition of a situation or the precise meaning of human feelings may be determined almost entirely from facial expressions; from movements of the body, such as the gestures of a traffic officer; from the general state of excitement, such as weeping, blushing, or laughter; or from involuntary exclamations and sounds, such as whistling or singing.

ALTERNATIVE EXAMPLE

Outdoor advertising, is getting a makeover. Outdoor billboards now carry upscale brands such as Calvin Klein, Donna Karan, Tommy Hilfiger, and Ralph Lauren. And advertisers are discovering new vehicles for outdoor advertising. Little Me babywear is shown on the *tops* of buses in the hopes that office workers will be gazing out of windows. Donna Karan's DKNY line was featured on trains that ran under Bloomingdale's, where a DKNY "superstore" had just opened. SOURCE: Cyndee Miller, "Outdoor Gets a Makeover," *Marketing News,* April 10, 1995, p. 1.

## Transmitting the Message through a Channel

Once the sender has created the message by encoding it into a transmittable form, it must somehow be conveyed to the receiver: It must be sent through a *channel of communication,* such as a magazine or other medium. Even our own casual conversations are sent in this way, though the medium is the less obvious one of vibrating vocal cords and movements of sound through air.

POINT TO EMPHASIZE
A challenge in communicating with older adults is portraying them positively. Ads that show someone who has fallen and can't get up, for example, seem insulting to the vast majority of older consumers.

The message arrives at the receiver via the channel of communication. But some receivers are more receptive than others. For example, some receivers of the communication about the Sony Handycam will be elderly people who for one reason or another have little interest in high-technology products. It is thus the sender's job to pick the medium that will reach the maximum number of target receivers and the minimum number of nontarget receivers.

## Decoding the Message

**DECODING**
In communication theory, the process by which the receiver of a message interprets the message's meaning.

The message arrives and is viewed, heard, or otherwise sensed by the receiver. But in order for communication to occur, the receiver must decode it. **Decoding** is the mental process by which the receiver interprets the meaning of the message. A difficulty encountered at this stage of the communication process is that receivers may interpret the message in different ways, given their particular biases, backgrounds, and other characteristics. That is, selective perception operates as the message is decoded. We color or interpret promotional messages with meaning drawn from our personal experiences and backgrounds (as explained in Chapter 6). An advertisement for cigarettes may be viewed differently by different people, for example. Nonsmokers may pass over the message entirely; antismokers may be angered by it; smokers satisfied with another brand may note the advertisement only causally. Some who see the advertisement may not "get it" at all; for whatever reason, the intended imagery may escape them completely.

## Feedback

**FEEDBACK**
Communication of the receiver's reaction to a message back to the source.

Often, the communication process includes **feedback**—communication of the receiver's reaction back to the source of the message. In a personal selling situation, the feedback may be direct and immediate, as when the customer raises questions about the product or states why no purchase will be made. Indeed, as mentioned, the great attraction of personal selling is that there can be a two-way conversation that will ensure greater understanding between the people involved.

Feedback from advertising, sales promotion, and publicity/public relations is in most cases slower and less direct. For instance, advertisers may conduct surveys, count coupon redemptions, or evaluate letters and telephone calls from consumers to learn the audience's reactions. Although advertisers can get delayed feedback about an advertisement's effectiveness, the feedback rarely provides all the desired information about the receivers' responses to the message.

POINT TO EMPHASIZE
Organizations must carefully encode messages to avoid potential harm due to misunderstandings. When SunLight dishwashing liquid was first introduced, the label featured pictures of lemons. Several consumers perceived the product to be lemon juice and became ill after drinking it in their tea. They later filed suit against the company for transmitting a misleading message.

## Perfect Communication

Ideally, if perfect communication is to take place, the message that is decoded and enters the mind of the receiver is exactly the same as the one the sender had in mind, encoded, and transmitted. Communication is facilitated when the sender and the receiver have some commonality in their psychological fields of experience. In other words, if the sender and receiver share a common social background and have similar needs, it is more likely that they will similarly interpret the meaning of the words and symbols in the message. This perfect transmission is never possible, although in many cases—such as advertising featuring the Energizer Bunny who "keeps going and going and going"—the sender is able to develop a message that is decoded by the target audience in ways approximating what the sender had in mind.

**NOISE**
In communication theory, any interference or distraction that disrupts the communication process.

It is likely—perhaps even inevitable—that any communication process will be interrupted or distorted by factors that communication experts term "noise." **Noise** is interference or distraction, and it may disrupt any stage of the communication process. Noise may come in the form of conflicting messages, misunderstood terminology, inadequacies in the channel of communication, and so on. A radio advertisement might not be heard because of loud traffic noises outside the car. In a cigarette advertisement, the Surgeon General's warning is noise. The sources of noise may be external to the individual, such as traffic noises, or internal, such as daydreaming that interrupts concentration on a sales presentation. Many advertising messages cause people to think of a competing product. Brand loyalties and past learning are internal distractions that may interfere with the decoding process.

DISCUSSION CONSIDERATION
Collect examples of or describe organizational communications you feel are potentially misleading.

All of this points to the importance of the marketer's understanding of how communication takes place. Message content is not the only important factor in promotion. The model in Exhibit 15–2 shows the steps in the communication process. Each step is another spot where something can go wrong. If the source is wrong, if the intended message is encoded poorly, if an inappropriate transmission medium is chosen, if the decoding process does not work properly because of distractions, if the receiver lacks experience with the product or has a poor vocabulary, the message transmittal system cannot work well. The marketer's problem is to perform each step carefully while trying to reduce the chance of ineffectiveness.

In short, effective communication comes from the right *who* saying the right *what* to the right *whom* through the right *channel*. The accompanying Competitive Strategy feature illustrates a communication that was not effective.

## The Hierarchy of Communication Effects

United has extolled the virtues of its "friendly skies" thousands of times. McDonald's has made hundreds of different advertisements for its burgers. Why are there so many commercials for the same products? Creativity aside, the main reason is that a single communication, no matter how cleverly designed and implemented, may not be enough to persuade a customer to change an attitude or make a purchase. Promotion, as a rule, becomes more effective with repetition. Promotion usually seeks to change people, and people tend to change very slowly. The habits and beliefs developed over long periods of time will not be altered quickly by just a few messages. The presentation of a message may be varied, as in the McDonald's example, because the effectiveness of a promotion may wear out as the repetitive presentation becomes boring.

Marketers have come to expect various responses to their communications. To understand the various effects that promotion may bring about, we next discuss the promotion process as a "staircase," or a series of hierarchial steps.

ALTERNATIVE EXAMPLE
Lamborghini is not as well known as it would like to be. It sells relatively few cars—just 33 in 1993 and 89 in 1994. To create more awareness, it has had a Lamborghini (the Diablo VT) designated as a pace car for the 1995 Indy Car World Series. To add credibility and increase consumer knowledge, it is making a Diablo VT available to auto journalists for test drives. To increase liking for the car, it is making demonstrators available to dealers. To increase the probability of purchase, it is introducing a lease program. You can lease a Diablo VT for $2,999 a month with only $52,000 down. SOURCE: Raymond Serafin, "Even Lamborghini Must Think Marketing," *Advertising Age,* May 1, 1995, p. 4.

### The Promotion "Staircase"

We can conceive of promotion as a force that moves people up a series of steps called the hierarchy of communication effects.[5] This promotion "staircase" is shown in Exhibit 15–4.

1. Near the bottom of the steps stand potential purchasers who are completely unaware of the existence of the product in question.
2. Closer to purchasing, but still a long way from the cash register, are those who are merely aware of its existence.
3. Up one step are prospects who know what the product has to offer.
4. Still closer to purchasing are those who have favorable attitudes toward the product—those who like the product.
5. Those whose favorable attitudes have developed to the point of preference over all other possibilities are up still another step.

with television, personal computers, and laser storage technologies. Potential buyers are to be found at all steps of the hierarchy staircase.

Let's consider how the promotional mix can work to move a consumer through several steps of the hierarchy. Suppose you want to purchase a personal computer. You have probably advanced beyond total brand ignorance and are increasingly aware of the different brands and their advertised benefits. Your interest in the product has led you to pay more attention to computer advertising and to magazine stories about computers. Newspaper columnists may be writing about their own personal computers, thus providing publicity for these brands. Your friend the computer expert may regularly read these columns and may talk to you about recent improvements in personal computers. Sales promotions, such as the offer of a free software package or lessons in computer use, may ultimately bring you into a computer store, where personal selling communicates to you the benefits associated with a particular brand of computer. You may then decide to buy a particular brand, be it Macintosh, IBM, or Gateway 2000.

Which aspect of the promotional mix brought you to the decision to buy the brand of computer you chose? Perhaps one factor, such as the expertise of the salesperson, was a major influence, but the fact is that all elements of the mix did their parts in bringing about the sale. Each had a role to play and a function to perform. In this case, advertising proved effective in generating awareness and, perhaps, positive attitudes toward the brand. The sales promotion offer of software led to the decision to visit the store. Personal selling proved, as it usually does, most effective in consummating the sale.

**DISCUSSION CONSIDERATION**

Describe promotional mix elements that influenced a purchasing decision you have made. Did a brochure or advertisement prompt you to search for more information? Did a salesperson assist you with a purchase?

Commonly, as here, there is a strong interaction among the variables within the promotional mix. While consumers are strongly influenced by the advertising for cold remedies, for example, in-store displays, packaging, sales promotions aimed at retailers, and the activities of a personal sales force may all play some role in the ultimate purchase of a given medicine. The interaction of promotional mix variables is even more obvious in the business market. Here, advertising alone is unlikely to sell many products, yet it performs an important function in supplementing and supporting the personal sales force. The salesperson will get nowhere at all with a tough organizational buyer unless the buyer is at least familiar with the salesperson's company or line of goods. In other words, companies dealing with organizational buyers had better advertise and use personal selling because these promotional elements support each other.

While each promotional element has its relative strengths, any promotional element may be called upon to accomplish a communication objective. Marketers select and combine the various promotional mix elements available to them as best as they can. Some organizations have considerable flexibility in developing a promotional mix. Others, usually small companies without vast resources, are primarily limited to personal selling by employees whose chief responsibility is running the business.

## Push and Pull Strategies

The prime target of a promotional strategy may be either the ultimate consumer or a member of the distribution channel. Using this as a basis for classification, we can identify the basic strategies of push and pull. There is no single strategy of either type; but in general, they can be described as follows and illustrated as in Exhibit 15–7.

**PUSH STRATEGY**

A promotional strategy whereby a supplier promotes a product to marketing intermediaries with the aim of pushing the product through the channel of distribution.

A **push strategy** emphasizes personal selling, advertising, and other promotional efforts aimed at members of the channel of distribution. Thus, the manufacturer of a product heavily promotes that product to wholesalers and other dealers. The wholesalers then promote the product heavily to retailers, who in turn direct their selling efforts to consumers. Not infrequently, the wholesalers and retailers are offered

EXHIBIT 15–7 Flow of Promotional Dollars and Effort in Push and Pull Strategies

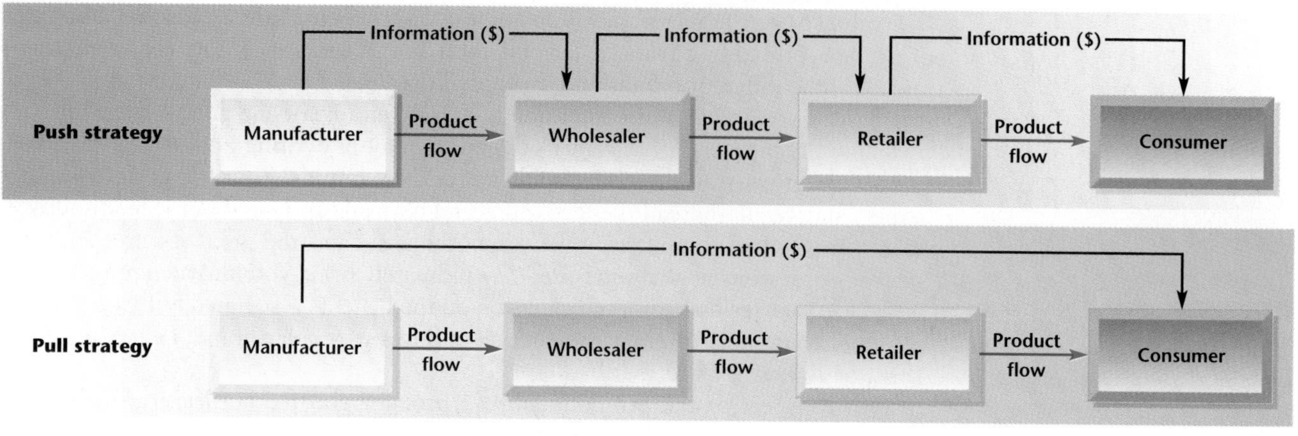


strong price incentives or discounts as part of this process. The term *push* comes from the fact that the manufacturer, with the help of other channel members, pushes the product through each level in the channel of distribution. The push strategy may be thought of as a step-by-step approach to promotion, with each channel member organizing the promotional efforts necessary to reach the channel member next in line.

**PULL STRATEGY**
A promotional strategy whereby a supplier promotes a product to the ultimate consumer with the aim of stimulating demand and thus pulling the product through the channel of distribution.

In contrast, the manufacturer implementing a **pull strategy** attempts to stimulate demand for the product through promotional efforts aimed at the ultimate consumer or organizational buyer. The goal is to generate demand at the retail level in the belief that such demand will encourage retailers and wholesalers to stock the product. If the customer is pulled into the store, each channel member will "pass back" the demand. In other words, the demand at the buyer end of the channel pulls the product through the channels of distribution.

POINT TO EMPHASIZE
Clothing marketers use both push and pull strategies. While some brands such as Bugle Boy pants and Armani suits, are heavily advertised (and thus use a pull strategy), other brands, such as Austin Hill and Cricketeer are not heavily advertised—which means there is no "right" strategy to use.

In sum, the push strategy suggests a step-by-step promotional effort, while the pull strategy attempts to develop ultimate buyer demand and a smooth flow of products from the manufacturer to the buyer via cooperative intermediaries. Consumers are most familiar with the pull strategy because they often encounter promotional messages that say, in effect, "go to the store and ask for this." However, a moment's thought suggests products sold by the push approach. An imported watch or an expensive perfume might be purchased even though the brand name is totally unfamiliar because the salesperson mentions that this product is "the best."

Marketing organizations do not limit themselves to using only a push or only a pull strategy. Effective marketing plans generally make use of both push and pull. Consider these remarks by Dr Pepper executives:[6]

> "We are a sales company."
> "The Dr Pepper bottler is the key to our success."
> "No matter how good a job we do, [consumers] can't get Dr Pepper unless [bottlers] have made the sale to the retailers."

These comments indicate that a push strategy is being used to motivate local salespeople. Yet Dr Pepper commercials are frequently seen on television and in magazines and newspapers and heard on radio. These commercials are obviously aimed at pulling the product through the channels of distribution. Here, the combination strategy employed acknowledges that the makers of Dr Pepper have more than one type of customer. Thus, a portion of the promotional campaign is geared toward channel members and has the promotional objective of encouraging aggressive promotion by local bottlers. Another portion is intended to generate purchase by development of favorable consumer attitudes toward the product.

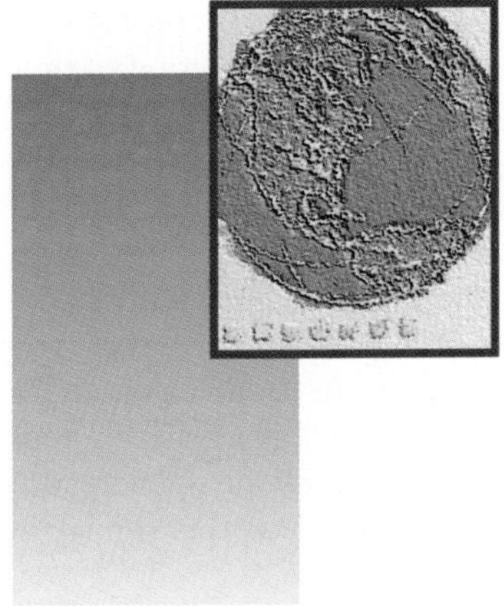

## FOCUS ON GLOBAL COMPETITION

### *Coca-Cola*

Most of us probably envision a pull strategy when we think about the promotion of Coca-Cola. However, if we think about how Coke expanded into international markets, we realize access to international markets was by no means certain from day one; consumer preference was not inevitable. The company had to build up fairly complete local distribution systems and use a push strategy to establish local demand. In Japan, for example, the long-established preference was for carbonated lemon beverages know as *saida*. Consumer demand did not pull Coke into this market; the company had to persuade the bottlers to push it. Today, because the company properly executed its expansion, Coke is a universally desired brand in many countries. But it got there by recognizing the need for both push and pull strategies. ■

# Determining the Promotional Budget

After managers have planned the promotional mix, they must determine if the organization can afford it. This is a matter of budgeting. Marketers attempting to determine the size of their promotional budgets are often reminded of the adage "If you can't make a splash, don't make a ripple." This old bromide seems to suggest that marketers using a very small amount of promotion may not effectively transmit their messages to buyers. Giant organizations that can place promotional messages in many media and use other promotional tools as well are thus in an enviable position indeed. However, even smaller organizations can mount successful promotional campaigns by carefully setting advertising budgets and selecting those themes, media, and schedules that most effectively transmit the desired messages. These matters are dealt with more fully in later chapters because they specifically concern advertising and personal selling rather than promotion in general. Regardless of the promotional tools employed, the marketer must determine how much money will be available in the promotional fund before focusing on these other matters. Next we consider some methods used to determine the size of a promotional budget.

## The Objective and Task Method

**OBJECTIVE AND TASK METHOD**
A method of setting a promotional budget whereby the marketer decides the objective to be accomplished, determines the tasks necessary to achieve the objective, and budgets amounts sufficient to accomplish the tasks.

The **objective and task method** of setting a promotional budget, also called the *task approach*, is probably the most logical of the budget-setting techniques. It calls for first identifying the objective to be accomplished and then determining the costs and efforts required to carry out the tasks necessary to attain the objective. An appropriate objective for a retail marketer budgeting for 1998 might be to double 1996 furniture sales, for example. Assuming that this objective is reasonable, the retailer would then budget the promotional resources necessary to achieve it. The logical appeal of such an approach is greater than that of entrusting these important decisions to some mathematical formula based on strictly quantitative data. Here, the job to be done, rather than sales figures or industry tradition, determines the size of the budget. Despite the clear logic underlying the objective and task approach, it is not the most commonly used method of setting a promotional budget. Using this approach is seldom easy, and it may require a great deal of time, mainly because it is difficult for the planner to develop obtainable objectives and then calculate what it would take to achieve these goals.

DISCUSSION CONSIDERATION
State some objectives for promotion, based on the hierarchy of effects, and describe the tasks that may be required to implement these objectives.

## The Percent of Sales Method

**PERCENT OF SALES METHOD**
A method of setting a promotional budget in which the amount budgeted is some set percentage of sales, often a standard percentage for a given industry.

The **percent of sales method** is probably the most commonly applied means of setting advertising budgets. The planner using the percent of sales method need only know a sales figure, take a percentage of that amount, and use that percentage as the promotional budget. For example, in the men's clothing business, 7 percent is considered a "reasonable" percentage of sales to spend on promotion. If sales for a period of time are $100,000, then the promotional budget "should" be $7,000. The percentage used varies from industry to industry; for example, the food marketing industry typically uses 1 percent of sales for promotion, and movie theaters generally spend about 14 percent for promotion.

A clear advantage of this method is the fact that the marketer need only know sales totals to be able to easily calculate the budget. Moreover, the appropriate percentage for a given industry—that is, the industry average or standard—can be obtained from trade associations or other sources. The user of this method is thus spared having to determine what percent of sales figures to use. He or she may also feel comfortable knowing that the budget developed is reasonable and is similar to that of other companies.

Although the percent of sales method is simple to use, it has many disadvantages. First, there is the logical problem of deriving a promotional budget from a sales figure. Supposedly, sales result from promotion. This method makes promotion a result of sales. In fact, the percent of sales method implies that the sales would have occurred with or without promotional expenditures. There is also the problem that such a method cannot cover all circumstances. For example, if sales are declining, it might be better to increase promotional expenditures, rather than reduce them as the formula would have us do.

Two defenses of the percent of sales method have been offered. First, given that promotion is tied to sales, it is reasonable to assume that the sales have generated sufficient money to pay for the promotion. The logical flaws of the method, however, make this defense quite unsatisfying. Second, it is possible to defend the method for use in certain circumstances. Some industries—for example, electric power companies—are mature and face predictable market changes. A mathematical formula is more appropriate here than in more dynamic marketing environments.

## The Comparative Parity Method

**COMPARATIVE PARITY METHOD**
A method of setting a promotional budget whereby the marketer tries to match competitors' expenditures.

The **comparative parity method** for determining a promotional budget boils down to doing what the competitors do. Brewers compare their dollars-per-barrel promotional expenditures with those of competitors in an effort to assure that they are not falling behind. Supermarkets operating in a given city commonly spend almost precisely what their competitors in that city spend. In a two-department-store town, it is common to see both stores represented in the Sunday newspaper in nearly identical forms—similar in size, placement, and cost.

The comparative parity method for determining promotional budgets is based on the notion that the moves made by competitors or industry leaders somehow must be matched. Like the percent of sales method, this technique takes little note of changes in the marketplace or of opportunities that may suddenly arise. In fact, the method makes one firm's promotion a near mirror image of another's. The competitor is thus determining the promotional budget of the other firm. As suggested, this method has problems similar to those of the percent of sales method.

**MARGINAL APPROACH**
A method of setting a promotional budget whereby the marketer attempts to spend resources until additional expenditures would not be justified by the additional sales and profits they would generate.

## The Marginal Approach

Theoretically, the **marginal approach** to almost anything in business is "the best." When applied to the setting of promotional budgets, such a method would have the organization spend promotional dollars until the payoff from the last dollar spent indicates that it is no longer worthwhile to continue to raise the budget. Unfortunately, the dynamic nature of markets, the actions of competitors, and the difficulty of determining exactly how much benefit was purchased with the "last promotional dollar spent" make this method difficult to implement.

### The All-You-Can-Afford Method

The name of the all-you-can-afford method is self-explanatory. Using this method, the marketer spends whatever is available to be spent on promotion. Organizations using this method typically do not have enough cash flow to justify using other methods. A new business, just starting out and facing the frightening statistics on new business failures, for example, would be well advised to spend, in effect, as much as is available for promotion. This method further implies that the promotional dollars are not borrowed but represent the "cash on hand" that remains available.

### The Combination Approach

Solutions to real-world problems are seldom left to one formula or one method of analysis. Even a planner who can use the objective and task approach effectively might employ a percent of sales formulation to generate some ball-park figures to be considered as the planning process progresses. A planner relying on the comparative parity method may be brought back to reality by the all-you-can-afford method when calculations yield a budget figure that is unreasonable given the organization's assets.

### Cooperative Promotional Programs

Many marketers at all levels in the distribution process employ a cooperative approach to advertising and other promotion. For example, a manufacturer of videocassette recorders may offer to pay for a portion of a retailer's advertising with the understanding that the advertisements will feature that manufacturer's brand of recorder.

The attractiveness of these programs is clear. Every channel member gets some of the benefits of the others' promotional efforts, and no individual channel member must bear the full cost. All concerned parties realize savings. In some situations, the rates charged by advertising media may also be reduced, because some newspapers and broadcasting stations charge lower rates to local businesses than to national advertisers. If a manufacturer paying part of the cost of the advertisement has the local retailer actually place the advertisement, this lower rate may be realized. Cooperative advertising as a sales promotion incentive is discussed further in Chapter 18.

## Promotional Campaigns

Throughout this chapter, we have considered the individual aspects of promotion while emphasizing that the parts of the promotional effort must fit together and complement each other. A trade magazine mailed to owners of automobile muffler shops promotes itself to potential buyers of advertising space as the place to advertise to reach target customers. The magazine's management may sponsor race cars or make awards to outstanding people in the muffler business to build the magazine's image as a major force in the trade. All of these activities fit together into a *unity of presentation* so that the magazine publisher's total promotional effort is an integrated marketing communication.

**PROMOTIONAL CAMPAIGN**
A series of promotional activities aimed at achieving a specific objective or set of objectives.

As mentioned in an earlier chapter, military terminology is commonly used in football and business. We see this once again in the term **promotional campaign.** A promotional campaign is a part of a firm's promotional mix, just as a military campaign

**IMAGE BUILDING**
A promotional approach intended to communicate an image and generate consumer preference for a brand or product on the basis of symbolic value.

is a portion of a total war effort. Thus, a promotional campaign is a series of promotional activities with a particular objective or set of objectives.

The phrase *particular objective* is important here, because it is this objective that indicates the goal to be reached. The campaign must be constructed to achieve that goal. The task of introducing a new product requires a promotional campaign considerably different from one intended to increase the sales of an established or widely recognized product. Comparing advertisements for Gillette's Sensor Shaving System used in the product-launch stage with advertisements used in the product's mature stage shows just how different these campaigns may be.

Because most products are in the mature stage of their product life cycles, this section focuses primarily on promotional campaigns for mature products. However, aspects of these strategies can also be applied to product introductions and to products in the growth stage of the life cycle. There are four major approaches to developing a promotional campaign for a mature product. They are image building, product differentiation, positioning, and direct response.

Outback Steakhouse's promotional objective is to convey the image of a casual, Australian-themed restaurant where customers can feel comfortable and away from it all, while enjoying good food. The advertising conveys the image of a relaxed place: "No rules. Just right." Some of the advertising features Rachel Hunter along with several Down Under characters. When one character "dying" in the desert hallucinates and thinks he sees his "sweetheart," Rachel Hunter says, "Sweetheart? You're not dying, you're dreaming." The image portrayed is relaxed, casual, and not too serious (customers don't even have to use the right fork).

## Image Building

The product or brand image is an individual's net impression of what the product or brand is all about. It is the symbolic value associated with the brand. Buyers frequently prefer one product or brand over another because of its image. Brands or products are thus often purchased or avoided not because of what they cost or how they work but because of what they say about the buyer-user—how they symbolize the user's personality or lifestyle. Marketers are properly concerned with this symbolic value or image. Thus, many promotional campaigns are aimed at **image building.**

Over the years, for example, the Girl Scouts of America established a strong image for the organization. The image of a Girl Scout was one of dependability, trustworthiness, and honesty. However, in the MTV era, many young girls saw this positive image as being too squeaky-clean.[7]

Girl Scout membership had been dropping, especially in the 8–11 age group. Focus group research showed that these preteens perceived Girl Scouts as childish. So the organization's marketers decided that the Girl Scouts had to move away from the uniformed, goody-goody image and show that Girl Scout meetings were a fun, mature, cool place to be.

The not-for-profit organization developed an image-building campaign that portrayed a hipper, more active organization. Past campaigns had tried to appeal to both girls and their parents. According to the Girl Scouts' advertising agency, "They were too soft, warm and fuzzy." That approach didn't work in the 1990s with girls who wanted independence at an even younger age.

To overcome its image as an organization "locked in time," the Girl Scouts used a promotional campaign aimed at making the organization more relevant to the older age group while emphasizing the activities available to all girls who join. The new image portrayed Girl Scouts as more action-oriented. For example, cookie packages showed Girl Scouts engaged in outdoor games such as volleyball.

Using MTV-style graphics, the TV advertising incorporated rap music, a TV teen sex symbol and fantasy images such as windsurfing, skiing, and parachuting, to suggest that the Scouts could offer girls a lot of fulfilling activities. One television ad closed with the line, "The Girl Scouts. As great as you want to make it."

DISCUSSION CONSIDERATION

What is your perception of the environmental image of Dow Corning, Ben & Jerry's ice cream, and Union Carbide? Identify a few other companies and describe your perception of their images.

In general, image-building promotional campaigns do not focus on product features but emphasize creating impressions. These may be impressions of status, sexuality, masculinity, femininity, reliability, or some other aspect of the brand's character thought to be alluring to target customers. The Marlboro campaign is a classic example. Similarly, most advertisements for perfumes (such as Chanel No. 5 and Obsession) and jeans (Calvin Klein and Guess) concentrate almost entirely on creating impressions.

## Product Differentiation

**PRODUCT DIFFERENTIATION**

A promotional approach in which the marketer calls buyers' attention to those aspects of a product or brand that set it apart from its competitors.

A promotional campaign aimed at developing **product differentiation** focuses on some dimension of the product that competing brands or competing products do not offer or accents some way in which using the product provides the solution to a consumer problem. During the years when gasoline prices rose to their highest levels, some automobile manufacturers began to stress their products' mileage benefits in terms of miles per gallon (mpg). Promotional campaigns emphasized mgp. Other manufacturers noted that buyers feared running out of gas in a remote spot where no gas stations were open. They advertised cars with larger gas tanks. Their promotional campaigns emphasized the number of miles per tankful rather than miles per gallon. In both cases, the focus of the promotional campaigns was on attributes of the product, not its image or price. Salespeople and dealer promotions stressed mileage. Booklets were produced showing customers the benefits of higher mpg and suggesting ways to achieve that goal through better driving habits and auto upkeep after the car was purchased. All portions of the promotional campaign focused on the brand's differential advantage.

**UNIQUE SELLING PROPOSITION (USP)**

A unique characteristic of a product or brand identified by the marketer as the one on which to base a promotional campaign; often used in a product differentiation approach to promotion.

Product differentiation and related promotional efforts often take the form of the **unique selling proposition (USP)**. As the name suggests, the basic idea of the USP is to identify and promote an aspect of the product that the competition does not offer or, because of patents or other reasons, cannot easily offer. Visine eyedrops were the

Both the Mylanta and Pepto-Bismol lines contain tablet and liquid versions of the same product.

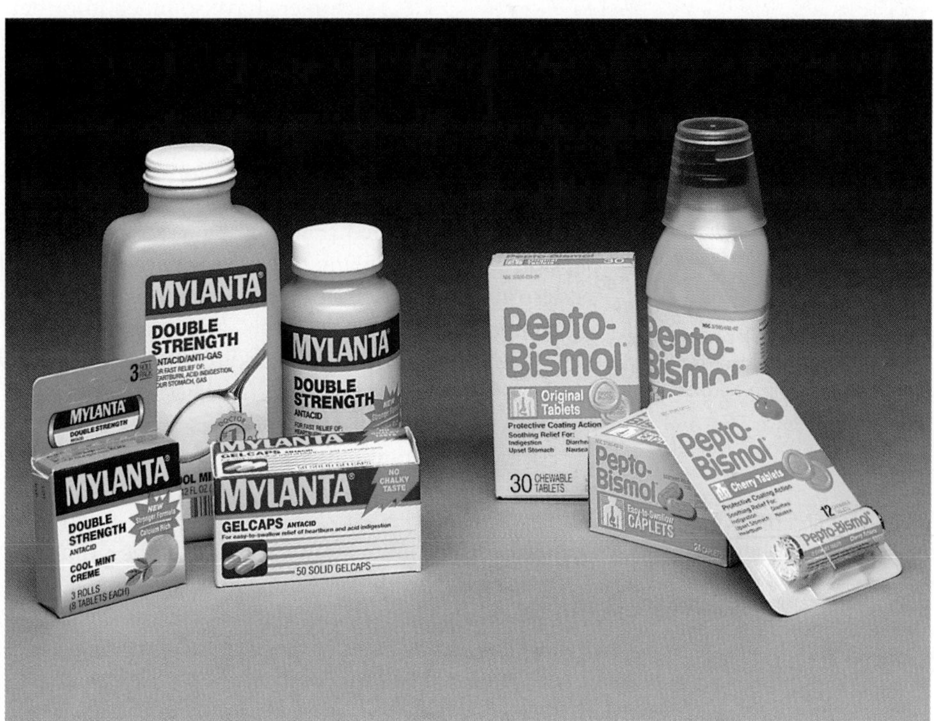


ALTERNATIVE EXAMPLE

Golden Books has replaced its abstract logo with Poky the puppy. The abstract logo was supposed to be a child looking at an open book, but consumers did not interpret it correctly. After testing various logos, the company chose Poky because it was perceived more positively than other symbols.

DISCUSSION CONSIDERATION

Evaluate the unique selling propositions these firms stress: Mercedes Benz (engineered like no other car in the world), Coors (the silver bullet), AT&T (true rewards), Nike (just do it) and Travelers (umbrella production).

first to "get the red out" using tetrahydrozoline. Initially, Murine, the market leader, had no such ingredient and no such benefit. Although Murine eventually did offer its own similar product, Visine had successfully exploited the unique aspect of its product and made it a successfully promoted market offering. Today, Opcon-A promotes itself as the only eyedrop that relieves both redness and itching. Similarly, Crayola Washable Crayons brand is portrayed as a unique product that offers advantages other crayon brands do not match. The product's patented formula provides a unique selling proposition around which a promotional campaign has been built. The USP tells buyers that if they buy a product, they will receive a specific, exclusive benefit.

Generally, mature products are not truly unique, especially from the point of view of performance. Yet *parity products*—ones with ingredients nearly identical to competitors' brands, such as Tylenol brand of acetaminophen—are often promoted as if they were special. This can be done because products have aspects other than the strictly functional ones. The auxiliary features can be promoted as effectively as functional features. Elmer Wheeler illustrated this fact in the classic statement "Don't sell the steak, sell the sizzle."[8] Keep in mind, though, that the point stressed in the unique selling proposition, whatever it is, must be meaningful to the potential buyer. It is possible to "sell the sizzle" only if the sizzle means something to the buyer—that is, if it satisfies a need. If buyers do not care about the USP, it does not influence the purchasing decision.

It's not just a letter. It's a way to get work done.
The letter is X. The company is Xerox. And the story is all about change.
Change is something we're comfortable with at Xerox. It's what we've been doing since the day we created the first copier, and changed forever the way people work with documents.
Indeed, we've built our business by following the document wherever it takes us. Today, few things in business change as fast as the document. It begins on a computer screen. It moves around the world on interactive, electronic networks. It exists in multimedia environments. It can be scanned, stored, retrieved, revised, distributed, printed and published where, when and how you want it.
In short, the document is constantly moving from digital form to paper, and back again. Which is why now, more than ever, our mission as The Document Company is clear: to put together the innovative document services you need—the systems, solutions, products and people—to make your business more productive.
It is also why this new "digitized" X is more than a letter to us. It is a symbol of change and vitality in the newly emerging digital world. It represents everything we do to help you get your work done, and make your life at work a little more satisfying and rewarding.
We'll be using this new symbol in many different ways, so keep your eyes open for it.
For us, it signals the next step in a long Xerox tradition of taking the first step into the future. And in a world that won't stop changing, that's still the most productive step anyone can take.
THE DOCUMENT COMPANY
XEROX


Xerox, long thought of as "the copier company," now positions itself as "the documents company." Its offerings include products that translate text and pictures into digital data that can be stored, revised, retrieved, printed, or sent on interactive electronic networks to computers thousands of miles away. The digitized X in this advertisement is meant to symbolize Xerox's changing capabilities.

## Positioning

You may recall that a brand's competitive position is the way consumers perceive it relative to its competition. The positioning approach, which promotes a brand's competitive position, is often the focal point of promotional campaigns. The campaign objective is to get consumers to view the brand from a particular perspective.

In launching such a campaign, the marketer assumes that consumers have so much information about other brands and similar products that it must create a distinct position for the brand in prospects' minds. The Avis campaign advertising "We're only number two" is a classic example of this strategy. By positioning itself as the second-largest automobile rental company, Avis dramatically increased market share. Business was taken away from the smaller rent-a-car companies, rather than Hertz, because consumers remembered both the Avis and Hertz positions. Customers remembered that, while Hertz was number one, Avis was in the number-two slot, where a company has to "try harder." Today, Hertz, having learned a marketing lesson from Avis, positions its service against competitive services by emphasizing that competitors are "not exactly" like industry leader Hertz's.

How do marketers go about positioning their brands? Exhibit 15–8 shows that there are many positioning strategies. It also suggests that brand image campaigns and product differentiation campaigns can be thought of as ways to position the product. Positioning strategies often communicate what the product does and identify whom the product is for. Positioning strategies may promote a single product attribute—"the car dealer with the lowest prices in town"—or multiple attributes—"the high-performance luxury car." Sometimes the promotional campaign positions a brand by its users—"for the working woman." In general, the important point about positioning is not what "selling point" is used as the basis of positioning but the idea that promotion can be used to position a brand relative to the competition. Note, too, that promotional campaigns that stress positioning are highly interrelated with the market

POINT TO EMPHASIZE

Aquatred, the high-traction tire for wet weather, uses a unique selling proposition campaign. Advertising stresses the tire's wide, water-expelling groove—a unique product feature that can be visually promoted.

The message began on the bottle. When Coors Brewing Co. printed the Internet address "zima.com" on the labels of its clear malt beverage, it figured that Zima's computer-literate quaffers would search it out. And when Zima's home page on the World Wide Web went up in November [1994], it marked one of the first attempts by a packaged-goods company to explore the fastest-growing part of the Internet.

Zima drinkers—primarily college kids and young women—"don't all have the same habits and choose to watch the same media, so we go after them in ways that are relevant to them," says Zima brand manager Mark Lee. "And if the Internet or commercial on-line services are one of the ways they choose to communicate, then that's an avenue we've made available with our interactive program."

**ALTERNATIVE EXAMPLE**

On May 11, 1995, Sega began a media blitz of ads for its Saturn video-game player on the Fox and MTV channels. The ad seemed ordinary enough; but viewers who hit the "separate audio program" button on the TV remote control were assaulted with bathroom babble, such as "Belly button lint is nutritious." This kind of gag is perfectly designed for Sega's audience, which is mostly male and responds to off-the-wall, in-your-face tactics. SOURCE: Kate Fitzgerald, "Sega 'Screams' Its Way to the Top," *Advertising Age,* March 20, 1995, p. S2.

Everyone who accesses the Zima home page first sees in white type "ZIMA.COM" superimposed over a dude-friendly visual, which, like many elements in the Web site, changes every two weeks. Clicking on the third icon below the primary visual leads "interacters" into areas where they can write to Zima, join a special Internet-only club called Tribe Z and learn facts about the brand. (One recent factoid sought to dispel the notion that Zima does not show up on a breathalyzer test.)

The content of the Zima pages flows loosely around an unseen character named Duncan, who, not surprisingly, is a Gen X net surfer. Chapters in Duncan's virtual life are hashed out in "episode meetings" attended by the account team, creatives and the client. They typically plot six to eight installments in the Duncan saga, with Zima-focused copy points kept in mind. "We are using Duncan as almost a cursor or a navigational device to get the consumer to understand some critical things about the brand," explains Jim Davis, creative director at Modern Media. "We're trying to get Zima to have equanimity to beer within their minds."

In each Zima "episode," various sound bites and icons can be downloaded. One purpose is to help a benign Zima virus grow; consumers can use the Zima icons—in effect, small product billboards—to replace the icons on their computer screens. The domain is also cross-referenced with other sites via hypertext links and hot buttons. (When someone clicks on a word specially coded in hypertext, it zips the computer user elsewhere in the Web.) For example, when Duncan was looking for a Christmas present for his girlfriend, users could click on the word "gift" and zima.com would send them to the Internet Shopping Network, an on-line shopping mall. "We're actually helping the consumer surf the net," explains Coors' Lee. "We're trying to add some value by saying, 'Hey, let Zima show you some things we think are pretty cool.'" Other recent links include the London Surf Club, a game called "Find the Spam", and the *Babylon 5* site.

The "fridge" which sits, waiting to be opened, at the bottom of the Zima home page, is a virtual storage device. By clicking on a hypertext link, which emits a creaking sound as it opens the refrigerator, visitors can forage for earwacks (sound bites) and "holusions" and go into the graffiti bin, where they

ALTERNATIVE EXAMPLE

Gatorade introduced a new tagline in 1995: "Life is a sport, drink it up." Ads feature Michael Jordon again, and Gatorade may even bring back the "Be like Mike" ads. Gatorade is reeling from loss of market share and increased competition from Pepsi and Coca-Cola. Its new tagline seems to be aimed at increasing consumption. Gatorade marketers hope Jordon will be more successful in selling Gatorade than Ken Griffey, Jr., will be in selling All Sport. Jordan's image is crucial in positioning Gatorade. SOURCE: Andrew Wallenstein, "Gatorade Rivals Will Heat Up Summer," *Advertising Age,* May 1, 1995, p. 29.

can post observations about Zima. (In one, a consumer hoped aloud that he or she would never talk like the people who populate Zima commercials.)

Still under construction is the freezer, an area within the fridge that will hold more multimedia surprises. But there's a catch. It will open only to Tribe Zers. . . . In fact, when non-members try to get in, they will be told they're "not cool enough yet" and will be referred to the area within the Zima site where they can join the tribe.

By capturing such data, Coors realizes that consumer research is a natural extension of the Web site. "I think what we're going to find when we start doing some of this, that it's probably going to be tremendously higher [in terms of significance] than some other forms of media we've done," says Lee. "Especially when we talk about the depth of relationship that we're getting through the e-mail and on-line content, because that relationship is a lot more genuine."

Those who doubt the "genuiness" of a corporate sponsored Internet site can always find refuge in the free-form, non-hierarchical newsgroup alt.zima.

As this story about Zima's advertising on the Internet illustrates, advertising is quick to reflect trends in society. For a marketer that can creatively take advantage of these trends, the power of advertising can be amazing. This chapter explores the captivating world of advertising.

The chapter begins with a general discussion of the purpose of advertising. Next, it outlines the stages in an advertising campaign and describes each stage. It examines communication goals and advertising objectives, creative strategy, media strategy, and the use of research to evaluate these strategies. Finally, the chapter closes with a consideration of ethics.

## The Nature of Advertising

Chapter 15 defined advertising as a persuasive message carried by a nonpersonal medium and paid for by an identified sponsor. This definition indicates two basic parts of advertising: the message and the medium. Both work together to communicate the right ideas to the right audience.

Advertising promotes goods, services, and ideas in mass media, such as television, radio, newspapers, and magazines, to reach a large number of people at once. It serves as a substitute for a salesperson talking to an individual prospect. Advertising is a one-way communication and, unlike a salesperson, cannot receive direct feedback and immediately handle objections.

Advertisers, who must pay the mass media to "run" their advertisements, or commercials, control the exact nature of the one-way message that will be communicated to the target audience. The impersonal nature of advertising also allows marketers to control the timing and degree of repetition that is necessary. These features often provide benefits that far outweigh disadvantages associated with lack of feedback.

ALTERNATIVE EXAMPLE

To reach a broader audience, in 1995 Pepsi changed its ads. Rather than using a heavy lineup of celebrities, Pepsi will use humor and warmth in ads that tell stories. One spot features an elderly gentleman reminiscing to his preteen granddaughter about this first Pepsi. He gets carried away, remembering the next 2,000 Pepsis he's had, but at the end gets his granddaughter's name wrong. Pepsi hopes that the audience will watch these ads to the end, anticipating a humorous twist. SOURCE: Kevin Goldman, "Pepsi Ads Dazzle with Humor, Not Stars," *Wall Street Journal,* January 20, 1995, p. B2.

Marketers of soft drinks, cosmetics, soaps, and many other products that do not require direct and immediate feedback often rely heavily on advertising. For these marketers, the challenge is to effectively present messages to an audience that may not be interested in seeing or hearing them. They must contend with readers who quickly turn the magazine page. They must deal with viewers who tape-record programs and then fast-forward through commercials. They must cope with competitors who use advertising to compare brands. Because of these demands, advertising is often highly creative and innovative.

We all recognize and appreciate creative advertising. You probably remember a humorous Nike commercial or lively Diet Pepsi commercial that grabbed your attention. You may even have talked to your friends about some advertising you liked. Creative advertising can stimulate people to talk to other people about products, services, and ideas. This word-of-mouth communication may be one of the most effec-

DISCUSSION CONSIDERATION

Find print advertisements or describe television advertisements, for both products and institutions, that use direct appeals and indirect appeals.

ALTERNATIVE EXAMPLE

From November 24, 1994, to January 22, 1995, Apple ran an infomercial in 20 major markets promoting family use of the Macintosh Performa line. The infomercial generated over 100,000 phone calls—three to four times what Apple expected. By the end of January, Apple was so impressed by the results that it planned to run the infomercial again in February and began to adjust it slightly to show in Europe. SOURCE: J. McIntyre, "Apple Performa Infomercial Bags 100,000 Calls," *Advertising Age,* January 30, 1995, p. 6.

tive means of communicating a message to prospective customers. The ability to use advertising's power to influence word-of-mouth communication can be a great asset to a marketer.

Advertising supports other promotional efforts. It may communicate information about a sales promotion or announce a public relations event. Advertising helps the salesperson "get a foot in the door" by preselling prospects. A salesperson's job can be made much easier if advertising informs the prospect about unique product benefits or encourages prospects to contact a salesperson. Without advertising, the salesperson's efforts may be hindered because the prospect does not know about the company or its products.

Advertising can be subdivided into many different sorts of categories. A very basic scheme classifies advertising as product advertising or institutional advertising.

## Product Advertising

**PRODUCT ADVERTISEMENT**
An advertisement promoting a specific product.

Advertisements for Pert Plus shampoo/conditioner, Garth Brooks concerts, Hilton hotels, Lego building blocks, and many other brands are clearly intended to persuade consumers to purchase a particular product—indeed, a particular brand. These are **product advertisements.** An advertisement for Ford trucks that declares "Ford trucks—the best never rests" and suggests that viewers go down to the local Ford dealership is a product advertisement because it features a specific product.

**DIRECT-ACTION ADVERTISEMENT**
An advertisement designed to stimulate immediate purchase or encourage some other direct response. Also called direct-response advertisement.

If the Ford advertisement goes on to recommend that viewers go to the showroom for a test drive during an inventory reduction sale—that is, suggests an immediate purchase—it is also a **direct-action advertisement,** or **direct-response advertisement.** Many television advertisements and many direct-mail efforts are of this type. An increasing number of these involve direct marketing, which includes both direct-action advertising and a direct channel of distribution. For example, record companies frequently urge consumers to order special albums by calling a toll-free 800 number and using Visa or Mastercard. The Book-of-the-Month Club mails announcements of its latest offering to club members' homes and includes a return envelope so that the latest selections can be ordered. Direct-action advertisements, in general, utilize coupons, toll-free telephone numbers, or invitations to call collect in order to facilitate action and encourage people to "buy now." Much retail advertising emphasizes direct action.

**INDIRECT-ACTION ADVERTISEMENT**
An advertisement designed to stimulate sales over the longer run.

Less assertive advertisements, designed to build brand image or position a brand for an eventual sale rather than to sell merchandise right this minute, are also forms of product advertising. For example, consider an advertisement portraying the romance and adventure of Jamaica. The advertiser knows the consumer is not going to run directly to a travel agency after seeing such an advertisement. The objective is to provide information so that the next time the family is considering a vacation, Jamaica will be among the spots considered. This so-called **indirect-action advertisement** makes use of a soft-sell approach calculated to stimulate sales over the longer run.

### FOCUS ON QUALITY

### *Phillips*

For some years, Phillips Petroleum has been running institutional advertising to call attention to its involvement in worthwhile community projects and to tell consumers about its lesser-known activities, those beyond oil exploration and refining. The company's intention is to demonstrate that it is socially responsible and productive. It hopes to promote goodwill and increase investment in the company. These and similar advertisements are aimed at the roles we all play as citizens, investors, and voters, rather than our roles as buyers. ■

THE YOUNG CHEFS NUMBER FIVE IN A SERIES.
"Butter Adds A Burst Of Flavor To Almost Everything."
Chef George Morrone, Aqua, San Francisco
"That's why I use it here and at home.
Citrus and mint flavored butter turns grilled swordfish into something incredibly delicious. Here's what I do. I simply blend grated lemon and orange peel with mint and softened butter. I put a pat or two on the swordfish to baste it and keep it moist. Delicious! Try it yourself. You'll enjoy your own sauce creation."
NOTHING BRINGS OUT THE TASTE LIKE
BUTTER


The American Dairy Farmers association uses institutional advertising to remind consumers that butter adds a burst of flavor to food. The advertisement benefits all brands of butter and all dairy farmers.

ALTERNATIVE EXAMPLE
Faced with falling demand for jets, Boeing is trying to stimulate air travel with commercials aimed at final consumers. In the ads, travelers are shown in desirable foreign locations. For example, one ad shows Michael Morgan, conductor of the Seattle Symphony, cradling a huge double bass in Tokyo as two curious girls look on. The tagline is "The Magic of Flight." Ask your class whether they think ads like these will stimulate air travel. If not, does Boeing accomplish anything with these ads? SOURCE: Douglas Gantenbein, "Boeing Banks on 'Magic'," *Advertising Age,* March 6, 1995, p. 33.

### Institutional Advertising

**INSTITUTIONAL ADVERTISEMENT**
An advertisement designed to promote an organizational image, stimulate generic demand for a product, or build goodwill for an industry.

**Institutional advertisements** aim to promote an organizational image, to stimulate generic demand for a product category, or to build goodwill for an industry. "Baseball fever . . . catch it" is an institutional advertising slogan. So is DuPont's "Better things for better living" and United Artists' "Escape . . . to the movies." These institutional advertising slogans do not stress a particular ball team, brand, or movie. Instead, they accent the sponsoring institutions. The baseball advertisement, for example, attempts to build demand for the sport as a whole. The advertisements paid for by DuPont and United Artists stress how wonderful, responsible, or efficient those companies, taken as wholes, actually are. Contrasting the "baseball fever" slogan with such team slogans as "Royals baseball. You've got a hit on your hands" or "Wrigley Field—there's no place like it" makes the difference between institutional advertising and product advertising quite clear. Institutional advertising is often part of a larger public relations effort. (See Chapter 18.)

## Planning and Developing Advertising Campaigns

Developing an effective advertising campaign requires a stream of interconnected decisions on such matters as budgeting and media, as well as a strong creative strategy. The process followed in planning and developing an advertising program is shown in Exhibit 16–1. The activities involved in the process are discussed in the following sections.

As we have seen throughout this book, goals and objectives must be established before work on specific plans and actions is begun. This relationship between objectives and plans holds true where advertising is involved. Before developing a single advertisement, management must ask what the advertising is expected to do.

Of course, advertising is supposed to sell the product. That statement, however, is too broad to be truly useful to marketing planners. Advertising is, after all, only one element of the marketing mix. It affects and is affected by the product, the price, the packaging, the distribution, and the other elements of promotion. All these elements combine to sell the product; advertising does not do the job alone. Regardless of the appeal and longevity of advertising campaigns, such as those of De Beers diamonds, BMW, or United Airlines, successful advertisements do not stand by themselves. Effective advertising campaigns are developed as part of an overall marketing strategy and are tightly coordinated with the other facets of the promotional mix.

## Communication Goals for Advertising

**COMMUNICATION GOALS**
In the context of marketing, what the marketer wants the promotional message to accomplish: to gain attention, to be understood, to be believed, and to be remembered.

What are appropriate goals for advertising? Because advertising is a method of communication, objectives directly related to advertising should be **communication goals.** In general, advertisers expect to accomplish four broad communication goals: Advertisements are expected to *generate attention*, to be *understood*, to be *believed*, and to be *remembered*. These goals relate to selling the product, but they are primarily matters of communication.

If these broad communication objectives are not considered and met, more specific objectives will not be met either. For example, if no one pays attention to an advertisement, the advertisement cannot achieve its more specific objective of, say, enhancing a romantic brand image. Likewise, an advertisement must be understood and believed if it is to reinforce or change perceptions and attitudes about a brand's characteristics. And if it is not remembered, it will have little effect on buyer behavior. With these broad objectives in mind, marketers developing advertising campaigns can set more specific objectives.

**EXHIBIT 16–1** Advertising Planning and Development

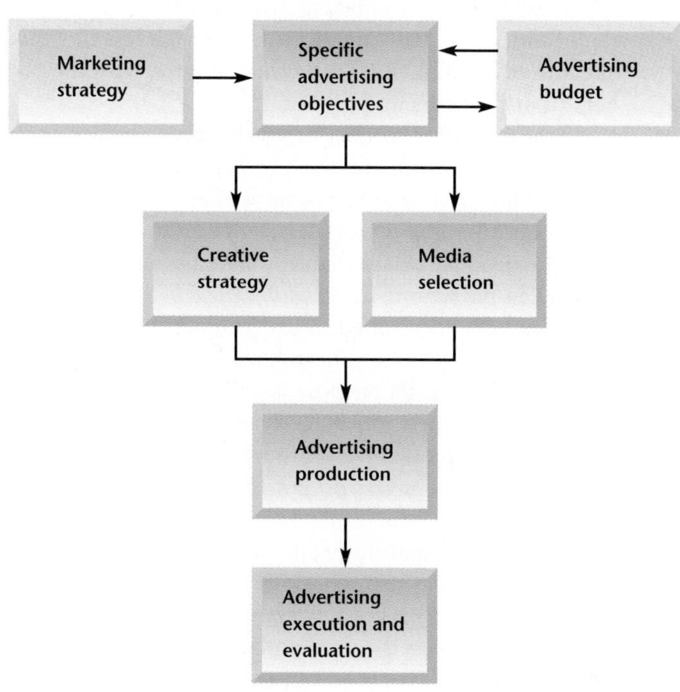

## Specific Advertising Objectives

POINT TO EMPHASIZE
Many enjoyable ads don't relate to the product or its attributes. The armadillo doesn't have anything to do with beer. The Miller Lite commercials that were entertaining and effective drove home Lite's major benefits—tastes great and (is) less filling.

Encouraging increased consumption of a product by current users, generating more sales leads, increasing brand awareness, increasing repeat purchases, and supporting the personal selling effort are typical specific objectives for advertisements. As Exhibit 16–1 illustrates, these objectives are developed from the marketing strategy and provide the framework for creative strategy and media selection.

Many advertisements have disappeared from the media, even though "everybody liked them," because they did not contribute to accomplishment of specific objectives. For example, almost everyone enjoyed a unique advertising campaign featuring a fictitious (off-screen) giant armadillo that rambled across the Lone Star State terrorizing Texans in its quest to satisfy its unquenchable thirst for Lone Star beer. Texans loved to talk to friends about the state's favorite animal's exploits. However, the advertisements, while humorous and attention-getting, did not sell the product. Because the ultimate objective is to sell the product, the advertisements were changed. When a "great advertisement" does not contribute to success in increasing market share, introducing a new product, or the like, it is only great in the creative sense. In the business sense, it is far from great.

DISCUSSION CONSIDERATION
Describe a television commercial and identify your perception of its primary objective.

Opportunities in the marketplace, competitive advertising campaigns, and prior marketing strategy decisions, such as selection of a target market segment, all influence the development of specific advertising objectives. An important influence is the product's stage in the life cycle.

ALTERNATIVE EXAMPLE
The first endorsement contract Michael Jordan signed after returning to the NBA was with Renewal batteries, made by Rayovac. Why did Rayovac want Jordan? "Because Michael has renewed a basketball career," according to Thomas Pyle, CEO of Rayovac. While that has nothing to do with batteries, Rayovac hopes that Jordan's popularity will keep Renewal batteries the best seller among rechargeable batteries. SOURCE: Bruce Horovitz, "Jordan Charges Up Battery Wars," *USA Today*, April 11, 1995, p. 4B.

## Advertising Objectives and the Product Life Cycle

Advertising objectives change with environmental conditions, as do all other aspects of marketing. Marketing is dynamic; advertising, as one of its most visible components, must be especially reflective of change.

The concept of the product life cycle usefully illustrates the notion of change. As Exhibit 16–2 shows, advertising objectives change over the course of a product's life. During the introductory stage of the cycle, developing consumer brand awareness and getting customers to try the product are normal advertising objectives. Trade advertising, which is aimed at attracting distributors and interesting them in carrying the product, is equally important, although less obvious, during this stage. Additional trade advertising may be developed later, with the objective of increasing the numbers of distributors and retail outlets.

**GENERIC DEMAND, OR PRIMARY DEMAND**
Demand for a product class as a whole, without regard to brand.

**PRIMARY DEMAND ADVERTISING**
Advertising aimed at stimulating primary demand.

At the start of a product life cycle, it may be necessary to develop **generic demand,** or **primary demand,** for the product—that is, demand for the product class as a whole. This kind of advertising, which often must be so basic as to explain what a product is and how it works, is called **primary demand advertising.** It seeks to introduce the product rather than to make brand comparisons. Advertising of this sort is also called *pioneering advertising.*

As we have mentioned, most products are in the maturity stage of the life cycle. Advertising for a mature brand, such as French's mustard, may be aimed at regular, brand-loyal users. Its purpose is substantially different from that of advertising used to introduce a new product. Promotion to loyal customers requires a campaign designed to remind them of the product's image and of their satisfaction with the product. Regular buyers do not need detailed information about the product and its contents.

In the case of mature products, then, advertisers give relatively little emphasis to explaining product features. Messages that are increasingly symbolic accompany the product's "aging process." Partly, this reflects the fact that mature products have found their niche in the marketplace. They have been positioned, either by marketers or by the competitive forces of the market itself, to appeal to smaller and more specialized market segments than when they were new and lacked intense competition.

**EXHIBIT 16–2** Objectives Change over the Product Life Cycle

| Sales | Preintroduction | Introduction | Growth | Maturity | Decline |
|---|---|---|---|---|---|
| General promotional objective | Define objectives and plan promotional campaign | Develop product awareness, stimulate generic demand, and attract distributors | Create product acceptance and brand preference if there are competitive products | Maintain and enhance brand loyalty; convert buyers and distributors of competitive brands | Phase product out |
| Advertising strategy | Screen concepts, create advertisements, and plan media selection | Primary demand advertising to get potential purchasers to try product; trade advertising to introduce product | Extensive advertising expeditures emphasizing advantages of product and brand | Reminder and emotional advertising and promotions to promote repeat purchases and differentiate brands | Minimal advertising expenditures emphasizing low price to reduce inventory |
| Primary objective of message | | Inform | Persuade | Remind | |

Time

POINT TO EMPHASIZE

Wrigley's Spearmint gum is a mature product. Its basic theme, "pure chewing satisfaction," was enhanced when its advertising took advantage of the passage of no-smoking laws. The gum was positioned as an alternative to smoking for smokers who were in no-smoking situations.

**SELECTIVE DEMAND ADVERTISING**

Advertising aimed at stimulating demand for a particular brand.

DISCUSSION CONSIDERATION

Ask students how a marketer of soup could appeal to new market segments in advertising. Answers might be: by advertising in different magazines or on TV shows that appeal to different audiences or by showing a variety of different people eating the soup in a wide variety of situations.

The Oshkosh B' Gosh advertisement in Exhibit 16–3 is a good example of an advertising campaign for a product in the maturity stage of the product life cycle. The advertisement does not explain anything about the characteristics of the product. Rather, it reflects the psychological or emotional dimensions of the brand and the situations in which it is consumed. Because most products on the market are in their maturity stages, much advertising emphasizes psychological benefits to differentiate brands. Such advertisements stress the reasons a brand is better than its competitors instead of emphasizing the newness or uniqueness of the generic product, as is done at the start of the product life cycle. Advertising of this kind is called **selective demand advertising.**

The most commonly encountered advertising objectives for mature products may be summarized as follows:

1. Increase the number of buyers.
   - Convert buyers of competitive brands.
   - Appeal to new market segments.
   - Reposition the brand.
2. Increase the rate of usage among current users.
   - Remind customers to use the brand.
   - Inform regular consumers of new uses.
   - Enhance brand loyalty and reduce brand switching among current customers.

After determining the advertising campaign's objective, marketing managers begin to develop a creative strategy and to select advertising media. These activities are

EXHIBIT 16–3

Often, Advertising for a Mature Product Emphasizes the Emotional Aspects of the Brand

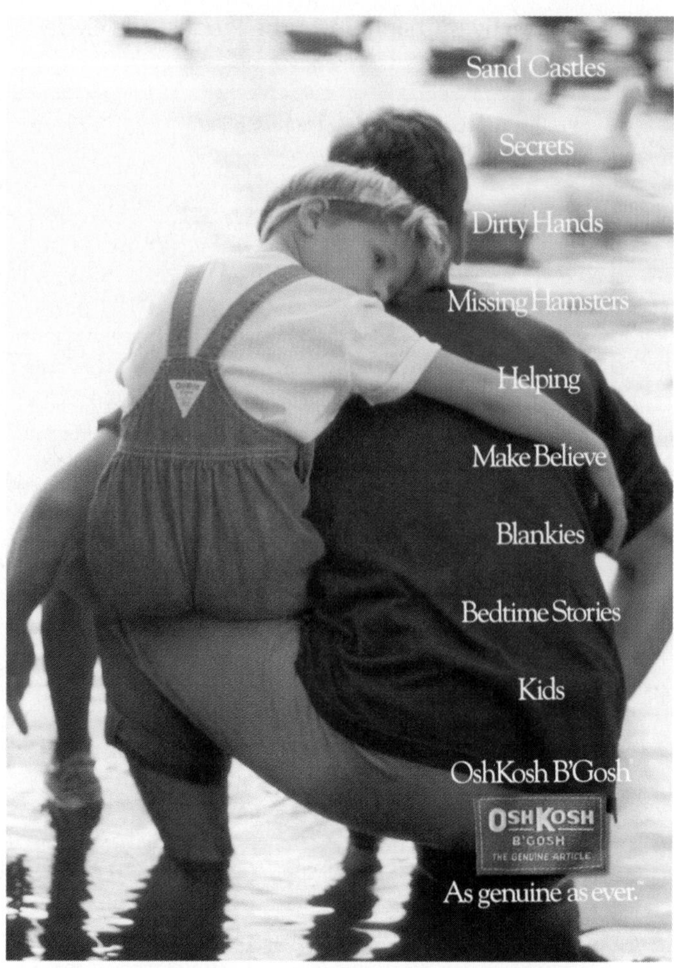


interrelated. In fact, the interrelationship between advertisement and medium is so strong that it is often impossible to tell whether the selection of the medium or the development of the advertisement comes first. For the purposes of our discussion, we will first examine how marketers create and produce advertisements and commercials.

## Creative Strategy

**CREATIVE PROCESS**
In the context of advertising, the generation of ideas and the development of the advertising message or concept.

In advertising, the generation of ideas and the development of the advertising message or concept make up the **creative process.** Actually, creativity is necessary to all aspects of the marketing mix, but the term has come to be particularly associated with the people who actually develop and construct advertisements. Whether creative activity is based on information gathered by marketing research or on analysis by management, the basic thrust of an advertising message is developed primarily by the creative departments of advertising agencies.

Discussing creativity is a difficult task. It is possible to outline schematically the steps involved in the creative process, as illustrated in Exhibit 16–4. The role played by that elusive something called creativity, however, can only be shown as the occurrence of a "creative spark." Advertising objectives provide a framework for creative efforts, but the creative spark is probably what supplies the persuasion to the advertisement.

Advertising copy writers, art directors, and other creative people are responsible for the task of answering two questions: What to say and how to say it. These questions reflect the two basic parts of the creative strategy.

## What to Say—The Appeal

**ADVERTISING APPEAL**
The central theme or idea of an advertising message.

The central idea of an advertising message is referred to as the **advertising appeal.** The purpose of the appeal, and of the advertisement, is to tell potential buyers what the product offers and why the product is or should be appealing to them. Thinking about advertisements we have seen brings to mind the many kinds of appeals advertisers employ. It may be that the product offered has sex appeal, is compatible with the target customer's lifestyle (or desired lifestyle), or solves some particular problem such as "morning mouth," "medicine breath," or the need for healthy gums. Commercial messages making firm promises, like "Never again will you have to weed your lawn, thanks to Jiffy Kill," are frequently heard. Many advertisers believe an approach that specifically describes the answer to a problem in this manner is the most effective. Other advertisements are built around appeals that are less straightforward, such as cosmetic, beer, and hotel advertisements that stress brand image.

**ADVERTISING THEME**
An advertising appeal used in several different advertisements to give continuity to an advertising campaign.

When the same advertising appeal is used in several different advertisements to provide continuity in an advertising campaign, it is referred to as an **advertising theme.** The Army, for example, uses the theme "Be all that you can be" in its advertising to both high school dropouts and college graduates.

To get a feel for how creative advertising appeals vary across an industry, it is useful to consider several brands of the same product and the advertisements developed for each.

ALTERNATIVE EXAMPLE
Porsche had a problem. Thanks to previous advertising campaigns, it had an arrogant image based on speed and power. To soften that image, Porsche's ad agency, Goodby, Silverstein & Partners, pictured Porsches driving down winding roads with the aim of making the car and the road one. The pictures were highly effective in attracting readers; the Porsche ads were one of the eleven most heavily read ads in Starch's annual ad survey. SOURCE: Phillip Sawyer, "The Ultimate Judges—Consumers—Speak," *Advertising Age,* May 15, 1995, p. K4.

The Visa credit card is positioned and advertised as the most widely accepted card. Advertising communicates the message that because Visa is accepted at more places, it is "Everywhere you want to be." Mastercard takes a different approach by advertising itself as a smart payment service. For instance, one advertisement explains that if a MasterCard is stolen, the cardholder has to pay only for what he or she has bought—not what the thief has charged. Other advertisements discuss using MasterCard in nontraditional ways such as in doctor's offices or supermarkets. MasterCard says, "It's more than a credit card. It's smart money." The Discover card's appeal is different in that it stresses the fact that there is no annual fee for using Discover and that cardholders receive cash-back bonuses on purchases. Discover advertises, "People who really know money use the Discover Card. It pays to Discover." Diners Club International's card uses the appeal "Rich in Rewards" as its basic message. Its advertising points out that customers earn extra frequent flyer miles or other rewards each time they use the Diners Club International card to make a purchase. American Express's advertising reminds viewers that its card does not have spending limits. One advertisement illustrates that a holder of the American Express card, unlike the

EXHIBIT 16–4
Creativity Is an Important Aspect of the Advertising Process

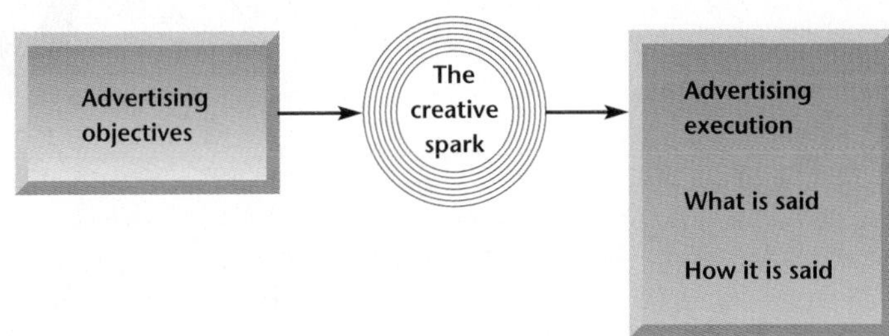

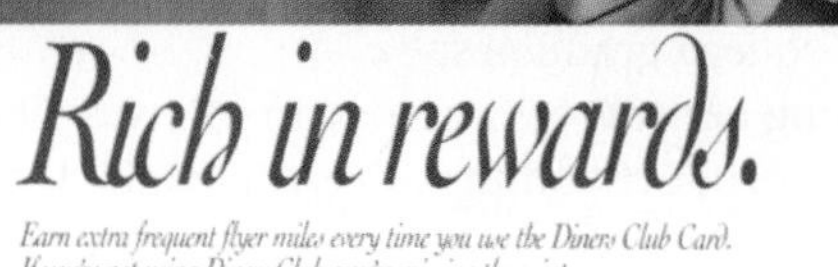

Rich in rewards.
Earn extra frequent flyer miles every time you use the Diners Club Card.
If you're not using Diners Club, you're missing the points.
Diners Club International


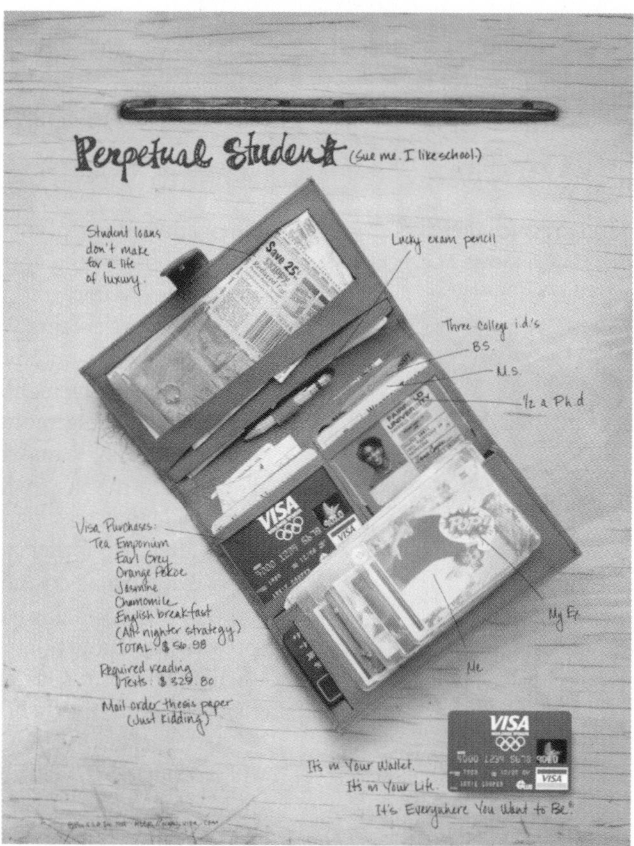


Although the basic service they market is almost identical, these 3 credit card marketers use 3 different advertising appeals.

It's One Of The Most Useful Credit Cards On The Planet. *Unless You've Stolen It.* Your MasterCard is stolen. You panic, get angry, panic some more. Then you call and cancel it. Now

the thief is in possession of, oh, about seven cents worth of stolen plastic. (Maybe he can use it as a coaster when he entertains at the hideout.) So relax. You only have to pay for stuff *you* bought, and you can even get a new card the next day. It'll be accepted at millions of places, one of which must sell wallets.

*MasterCard. It's more than a credit card. It's smart money.*

ALTERNATIVE EXAMPLE

Miller is trying to create a different image with its virtual taproom on the Internet. The taproom has a feature, called "Ask the Brew Master," that provides e-mail interaction with the brewer. The site also carries offbeat regional news stories and items on sports that Miller sponsors, such as race-car driving. SOURCE: "Burma Shave Signs on the I-Way," *Business Week,* April 17, 1995, p. 102.

users of its competitors, will never be embarrassed by a waiter, saying that the card's credit limit has been reached.

The important thing to note here is that the advertisements for these products, as well as those for many others, feature different appeals. If every credit card company simply said, "Our credit card is more convenient than paying with cash," no brand's advertising would be unique or memorable. Creativity is responsible for this uniqueness.

But there's more to creativity than that. Many advertising appeals, such as the appeals for credit cards just described, are part of positioning promotional campaigns. Advertisers create these appeals so that consumers will perceive their brands as holding distinctive competitive positions. This strategy may be so successful that claims—perfectly true claims—that the producer of one brand wants to make are not believable because of the competitive positions other brands hold in consumers' minds. Creativity, then, is more than an advertising tool. It is a competitive tool.

## FOCUS ON TRENDS

### *Sex Appeal*

Be young. Have fun. Be sexy. Politically incorrect? Unabashedly. But, after several years of drab dress and neutered ads, consumers are craving a little levity.

Bare asceticism in fashion is giving way to glamour: Vibrant colors, coquettish skirts, corsets and bustiers that are bold enough to make Victoria's Secret blush.

Advertising, too, is loosening up. After a period when even fragrance marketers sublimated a sexy sell for one of self-affirmation, sex is creeping back into the lexicon. A model lip-synchs to the music of "I'm Too Sexy" in ads for the new Head Over Heels fragrance; Brut Actif models are miming sex in a pool; and designer Gianni Versace depicts woman as both dominatrix and mistress of her domain.

"We are dealing with a post-feminist moment in fashion, fragrance and a lot of areas," said Richard Martin, curator of the Metropolitan Museum of Art's Costume Institution.

Observes psychologist and advertising consultant Carol Moog: "We've gone through this terribly serious period of time talking about sexuality, protesting it to the point where you have to deal with the existence of all levels of sexuality and all the pain that comes with it. To deal with the trauma you need to go through stages of healing. One helpful stage is playfulness."

A recent University of Chicago study on sexuality presents a culture more monogamous and less experimental than previously thought. "The majority of Americans approve of sex outside of marriage but in a relational context with love," said Edward Laumann, the University of Chicago sociologist who headed the research team. "That's why sex sells. It's appealing to everybody. But it's a turnoff if an ad emphasizes the casualness of sex and the promiscuity implied in it."

From an advertiser's perspective, the trick is to keep the mood of the advertisements playful. For example, a TV commercial for apparel marketer Jordache reprises Diet Coke's office voyeurs ogling Lucky Vanous that shows four women having a grand time peering through their camcorder at actor/model Jeff Bowles.

"The wave of the future is if you have to use sex in advertising, it will be the men who are the sex objects," predicts Jordache Director of Advertising Kaaryn Denig, who created the commercial. "Woman are comfortable with and allowed to show appreciation for a man's body without being stereotyped in a negative sense. But there's a sense of humor." ■

## How to Say It—Execution of the Appeal

Even when a copy writer or artist has an important and meaningful message to relate, its effect can be lost if it is not presented in the right way and in the right context. Marketing research can help in this regard. For example, an advertising agency's research indicated that many women who buy frozen dinners lead hectic lives and, because of time constraints, have trouble coping with everyday problems. So far so good. On this basis, advertising was developed for Swanson frozen dinners showing a rundown woman flopping into a chair just before her family is to arrive home demanding dinner. Suddenly realizing that she has a problem, the woman gets the bright idea of cooking a frozen dinner.

The problem was real enough, but the appeal was wrong. The last thing harried women want is to be reminded of how tired they are. Television viewers are fond of pointing out that married women in commercials are almost always peppy and well groomed even when they are doing the laundry or washing the floor. Advertisers use such images to bring the solution to a problem to the target customer's attention without making her feel like cursing the laundry or the dirty floor. Realizing this, Swanson changed its advertising appeal.

**DISCUSSION CONSIDERATION**
The text suggests that appeals should be stated in a positive way. Remember the old Whisk commercials featuring "ring around the collar"? These ads usually featured a wife who was embarrassed because she hadn't gotten her husband's collar clean. The ads sold a lot of Whisk. Ask students why they think these ads worked when the Swanson commercials didn't.

**ALTERNATIVE EXAMPLE**
Norwegian Cruise Lines had one of the most effective still-life ads of 1994. The ad's black background made brightly colored images pictured in cut-outs "pop out" at the reader. The colors and contrast in the pictures reinforced the theme of the headline, "It's different out here." By being visually appealing, the ad attracted enough readers to be one of the most heavily read ads of 1994. SOURCE: Phillip Sawyer, "The Ultimate Judges—Consumers—Speak," *Advertising Age,* May 15, 1995, p. K4.

**ALTERNATIVE EXAMPLE**
One successful storyline commercial was an infomercial for fitness equipment maker SLM. It featured a real motocross race and sexual tension between a female personal trainer and her client, Jack, a race competitor. Viewers would naturally want to see who won the race and what happened between the woman and the man. SOURCE: Jo McIntyre, "Tyee Takes Fast track with infomercials." *Advertising Age,* March 13, 1995, p. 4.

How to say something is as important as—and sometimes more important than—what to say. This is perhaps doubly true in advertising. The person delivering the message, the emotional tone, and the situation in which the action takes place all influence the effectiveness of the advertisement. Although some advertisements are simple, straightforward statements about the characteristics of a product, creating advertisements that grab the intended audience's attention often requires some embellishment. Advertisements should effectively say things to people, both with and without words, and the creative spark clearly is vital here. The Suzuki motorcycle slogan "Suzuki—The ride you've been waiting for" tells the target customer something about the excitement of Suzuki motorcycles. "I'm stuck on Band-Aid, and Band-Aid's stuck on me" is a catchy phrase. The Hathaway man's eye patch is a symbol rich in meaning. So is the Marlboro man's cowboy hat and horse. One mark of the talent and success of creative individuals is that much of their work is so powerful that it can be used effectively in advertisements for decades. Many slogans, pictures, and other components of advertisements can be immediately identified with particular products by generations of consumers. These successes depend on the creative person's ability to capture a feeling or fact with just the right phrase and the right symbols. Compare, for example, these common advertising phrases with the way they might have been written:

"Are you a saltaholic?"
"Is it possible that you ingest undesirable levels of salt?"

"Michelin—because so much is riding on your tires."
"Michelin tires are safe."

**EXECUTION FORMAT**
The style in which the advertising message is delivered.

How an advertisement says something is its **execution format.** The execution format is influenced by the medium that is used to convey the message. Obviously, a newspaper advertisement cannot duplicate the sound of a railroad train, but that sound might be effectively used in a radio advertisement. Determining how to communicate the message, then, is interrelated with selecting advertising media. Nevertheless, advertisers can present or creatively implement a basic appeal in a number of ways.

Whitney Houston in an AT&T commercial uses a singing format to present the sales message. A Prudential Insurance company commercial tells a short story about a fellow who actually dies and goes to heaven. These execution formats are quite different. What execution formats are selected by the people assembling the advertisements, and how they use those formats, are matters of creativity.

Looking at some of the major execution formats used in advertisements, especially TV commercials, helps put the creative strategies behind advertisements into perspective. The major formats include: storyline, product uses and problem solutions, slice of life, demonstration, testimonial and spokesperson, lifestyle, still life, association, montage, and jingle.

**STORYLINE FORMAT**
An advertising format that gives a history or tells a story about the product.

**SLICE-OF-LIFE FORMAT**
An advertising format that dramatizes a "typical" setting wherein people use the product.

**DEMONSTRATION FORMAT**
An advertising format in which a clear-cut example of product superiority or consumer benefits is given.

**Storyline** The **storyline format** gives a history or tells a story about the product. For example, initial advertising for the Saturn automobile told the story of how a town, a company, and its employees were changed when General Motors made the decision to build a new kind of automobile. Similarly, certain European vacation spots are shown in all their historical glory from the Middle Ages to the present.

In television commercials using the storyline format, unseen announcers (in a technique called a *voiceover*) often narrate stories with recognizable beginnings, middles, and ends. Some copy writers attempt to make the product the "hero" of the story.

**Product Uses and Problem Solutions** A straightforward discussion of a product's uses, attributes, benefits, or availability is a frequently utilized advertising format. A unique selling proposition, discussed in Chapter 15, is the central focus of such an advertisement. Comparatively simple advertisements for products ranging from Crest toothpaste to Texaco gasoline explain uses of the product and how the product can solve a problem. Crest fights tooth decay. Texaco stops your car from "pinging." The makers of exercise equipment may point out that being fat and out of shape is a problem ("your chest doesn't belong on your stomach") and may show that their product is a solution to the problem.

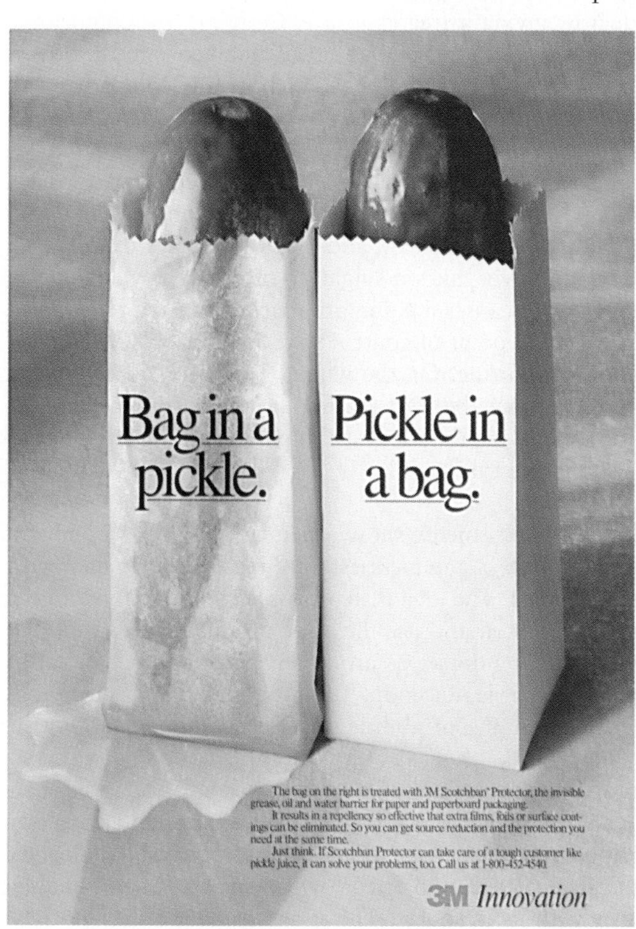

Bag in a pickle.
Pickle in a bag.
The bag on the right is treated with 3M Scotchban™ Protector, the invisible grease, oil and water barrier for paper and paperboard packaging.
It results in a repellency so effective that extra films, foils or surface coatings can be eliminated. So you can get source reduction and the protection you need at the same time.
Just think. If Scotchban Protector can take care of a tough customer like pickle juice, it can solve your problems, too. Call us at 1-800-452-4540.
3M Innovation


Problem-solution advertisements straightforwardly describe how to solve a problem. The 3M trade advertisement shown here tells how packaging made with 3M Scotchban Protector resists ruin from leaking liquids. The product's benefit is clearly seen as the solution to the problem.

**Slice of Life** The **slice-of-life format** dramatizes a "typical" setting wherein people use the product being advertised. Most of these commercials center on some personal, household, or business situation. An older editor reluctant to use e-mail at Grammercy Press, an attractive neighbor's visit next door to borrow some Taster's Choice coffee, and two homemakers talking about a laundry problem are examples of slice-of-life advertisements.

The slice-of-life commercial often begins just before a character discovers an answer to a problem. Whether the trouble is dandruff, bad breath, or not being home for a holiday, emotions are running high. The protagonist may know of the problem or may be told about it by another character. The product is then introduced, recommended, and tried by the needy person. Just before the end of the commercial, we are told—and, indeed, can see for ourselves—that the new user of the product is now satisfied, a happier person.

This advertising format is most common in TV commercials, but similar real-life stories can be developed in print media through the use of a series of pictures and in radio advertisements through the use of character voices. The slice-of-life format is essentially a dramatized variation on the product-solution format.

**Demonstration** Certain products lend themselves to a **demonstration format.** For example, the Master Lock advertisement in which bullets are repeatedly fired into a lock that does not open is suspenseful and self-explanatory. The demonstration format makes its sales pitch by showing a clear-cut example of how the product can be used to benefit the consumer. It does this by either dramatically illustrating product features or proving some advertised claim. The Master Lock advertisement certainly seems to prove that product's claim to toughness.

Unusual situations, although occasionally bordering on the fantastic, can draw attention to product benefits. When Bic throw-away ballpoint pens were new to the market, advertisements "proved" their high quality by showing rifle champions shooting Bic pens through blocks of wood. The pens still wrote. The novel situation drew viewers' attention and illustrated Bic's quality.

**INFOMERCIAL**
A television commercial, usually 30 minutes long, that has the appearance of a television program.

**COMPARATIVE ADVERTISING**
A type of demonstration advertising in which the brand being advertised is directly compared with a competing brand.

Many demonstrations occur in infomercials. **Infomercials** are commercials, usually 30 minutes long, that have the appearance of programs, such as cooking shows or talk shows. The product is repeatedly demonstrated on the infomercial. Often, telephone numbers are flashed on the screen so the viewer can order the item.

**Comparative advertising,** which directly contrasts one brand of a product with another, is a form of demonstration advertising. In a comparative advertisement, the sponsor's product is shown to be superior to other brands or to Brand X in a taste test, laundry whiteness test, toughness test, or other appropriate contest. This format is somewhat controversial on two counts.

First, some advertisers believe that calling attention to another company's brand helps that competitive product by giving it free exposure. Certainly, the competitive brand receives some attention, but this fact itself can be advantageous to the advertiser. Brands that do not have a high market share are intentionally compared with the best-known products to suggest that the two brands are equal. Pepsi, the challenger, thus urges comparisons with market leader Coke. For example, in one television commercial, delivery-truck drivers for both Coca-Cola and Pepsi-Cola order a meal at a diner. The Coca-Cola driver offers his competitor a sip from his Coke can. The Pepsi driver takes a sip, returns the Coke can, and then offers the Coke driver a sip from his Pepsi. After the Coke driver takes a single sip of Pepsi, he wants more. He refuses to return the Pepsi, which causes a commotion at the diner.

DISCUSSION CONSIDERATION
One of the best-known comparative advertising campaigns features the Energizer bunny. Everyone recognizes these ads and enjoys them, but do they work? An early study by the *Wall Street Journal* showed that many consumers associated the bunny with Duracell rather than Energizer. Test this in class by asking students who sponsors the bunny, and then discuss why consumers experience this confusion. Some critics say that the top brands in a category have more top-of-the-mind awareness, and that's why we think of them first.

This commercial suggests a second point of controversy: Some people do not feel that such comparisons are fair or sporting. On the whole, however, advertisements using the direct comparison format have been increasing in number in recent years. The Federal Trade Commission, believing that honest comparisons will help the consumer to make choices, has supported this trend.

**TESTIMONIAL**
A type of advertising in which a person, usually a well-known person, states that he or she owns, uses, or supports the product being advertised.

**Testimonial** **Testimonials** and **endorsements** show a person, usually a prominent show business or sports figure, making a statement establishing that he or she owns, uses, or supports the brand advertised. The idea is that people who identify with the celebrity will want to be like that person and use the same product. Alternatively, it is hoped that consumers will see the endorser as an honest person who would not lend his or her name to a product that is not good. Testimonials may use celebrities or others who, by virtue of their training or abilities, are seen as "experts" on the products being advertised.

**SPOKESPERSON**
A person who, representing the advertiser, directly addresses the audience and urges them to buy the advertiser's product.

A variation on the testimonial appeal is the use of a **spokesperson**. The spokesperson represents the company and directly addresses the audience, urging them to buy the company's product. Shaquille O' Neal is a spokesperson for Reebok. Reebok hopes that people who admire and trust "the Shaq" will associate his personable, warm, and humorous manner with its products. The spokesperson, often the commercial's central character, need not be a real person. The Poppin' Fresh Dough Boy for Pillsbury and the Keebler elves are well-known animated spokespersons.[1]

**LIFESTYLE FORMAT**
An advertisement that reflects a target market's lifestyle or hoped-for lifestyle.

**Lifestyle** The **lifestyle format** combines scenes or sequences of situations intended to reflect a particular target market's lifestyle. Soft-drink and fast-food advertisements, as well as those of many other consumer goods, frequently show product users in a sequence of daily activities. Young people might be shown enjoying some weekend activity and topping off a perfect day with a Mountain Dew or a visit to Burger King.

This still-life format is combined with interesting copy which makes for an effective advertisement.

Thus, the enjoyable aspects of teenage life are shown in association with product usage. Important to such advertisements are the sorts of people actors portray.

**STILL-LIFE FORMAT**
An advertisement that makes the product or package its focal point, emphasizing a visually attractive presentation and the product's brand name.

**ASSOCIATION FORMAT**
An advertising format that uses an analogy or other relationship to stimulate interest and convey information.

**Still Life** The **still life format** portrays the product in a visually attractive setting. The product or package is the focal point of the advertisement. Reminder advertising often uses still-life formats because the most important purpose of the message is to reinforce the brand name. Absolut vodka has used this format with great success.

**Association** The **association format** concentrates on an analogy or other relationship to convey its message. This creative strategy often "borrows interest" from another, more exciting product or situation. Thrilling activities, such as skydiving or windsurfing, and scenes of beautiful places, such as the coast of Maine or a mountain wilderness, are used in this way. The purpose of such analogies, which are often accompanied by music, is to create an emotional mood. The psychological benefits of the product are communicated through the associations drawn by the viewer. More prosaic analogies are also used to make the product and its benefits easier for the consumer to understand. For example, Lysol uses an analogy when it says, "It's like having a brush in a bottle."

**FANTASY FORMAT**
In the context of advertising, a type of association format in which the intention is to link the product with the target buyer's wildest dreams and hopes.

**Fantasy** is a special associative format. The long-lived series of advertisements for Chanel perfume is a perfect example of the fantasy approach. The fantasy appeal seeks to associate the product not merely with a glamorous setting but with the target buyer's wildest dreams and hopes.

**MONTAGE FORMAT**
An advertising format that blends a number of situations, demonstrations, and other visual effects into one commercial to emphasize the array of possibilities associated with product usage.

**Montage** The **montage format** blends a number of situations, demonstrations, and other visual effects into one commercial. The effect may be one of a swirl of colors or an exciting array of possibilities associated with product usage. Typical of such a format are travel advertisements for places like Jamaica. In these TV spots, the varied sights and sounds of an island paradise are strung together not only to show the many activities that are to be found there but also to suggest the excitement of the place and the sense that there is so much to do that the trip will surely be worth the investment.

Volvo uses an analogy to convey a message about the safe construction of its cars.

**JINGLE**
A song or other short verse used in an advertisement as a memory aid.

**Jingle** "My bologna has a first name...it's O-S-C-A-R." Can you remember the rest of this jingle? What restaurant do you think of when you hear "For the seafood lover in you"? What does one have to do if one wants to "Reach out, reach out and touch someone"? Commercial **jingles,** many of them written by well-known composers, have what could be termed "memory value." You literally cannot get them out of your head. We find ourselves thinking of them—or, at least, able to remember them almost word for word once our memories have been jarred—even after they have been withdrawn from the market. Product names, phone numbers, and addresses, in jingle form, are remembered. Thus, jingles serve best as a memory aid; they can have a significant effect on product recall.

**Other Formats** This short list of advertising formats is far from exhaustive. Animation and special effects, for example, have not been mentioned. However, this discussion should help you to think of other advertising formats and of the ways they work in an effective marketing program.

## Producing an Effective Advertisement

ALTERNATIVE EXAMPLE
The interaction of the announcer and the product sponsor is especially pronounced in radio. Many attribute the success of Snapple to Rush Limbaugh's reading of Snapple ads and his personal endorsements. SOURCE: Kelly Shermach, "Talk Radio Attracts Ads As Well As Listeners," *Marketing News,* January 30, 1995, p. 8.

Advertisements consist of verbal elements, visual elements, and auditory elements.[2] The exact combination of these elements depends on the people who design the advertisement. As suggested, their choices are strongly influenced by the advertising medium to be used. However, the ultimate consideration is that an advertisement must reflect advertising objectives. The promotional mix should be a unified whole, employing all appropriate means of delivering a message. Thus, many TV, radio, and print advertisements for a product advance virtually the same message or appeal, even though each is constructed to fit the appropriate medium.

### Copy—The Verbal Appeal

**COPY**
In the context of advertising, any words contained in an advertisement.

The term **copy** refers to the words in an advertisement. The words may be printed or verbalized by a character in a commercial or by an announcer. In certain advertisements, such as radio advertisements, the copy makes the biggest contribution to the advertisement's effectiveness. Even in a visual medium, such as television, copy is likely to retain its supremacy, because many of the claims an advertiser makes must be supported by the comments of the announcers or the characters. For example, advertisements for laundry detergents may show two piles of wash. It is the copy that assures viewers that the pile washed in Cheer is the whitest. The fact that a man is relaxing in a hammock drinking lemonade does not, of itself, tell the viewer that he can relax because he has a Lawnboy mower. The man in the advertisement, or an unseen announcer, tells us that is the case.

Some advertisements are loaded with copy and have few illustrations. For that type of advertisement to succeed, many members of the target market must be so interested in a product's possible benefits that they are willing to read long paragraphs of information.

## Art—The Visual Appeal

**ART**
In the context of advertising, any aspect of an advertisement other than copy, including pictures, layout, and white space.

The term **art** is broadly used to mean all aspects of an advertisement other than its verbal portions. Thus, pictures, graphs and charts, layout (the arrangement of the visual elements), and even white space (places where neither pictures nor words appear) fall under the heading of art.

The function of pictures in an advertisement is to illustrate a fact or idea or to attract attention. White space and layout are more subtle in their purposes. Layout can be effectively used to focus the viewer's attention on the picture of the product. It can also be used to draw attention to the brand name, the price, the place of sale, or the written portion of the ad. White space can be used in similar ways but it is more commonly used to suggest high quality. Notice that many newspaper and magazine advertisements employ considerable white space to accent the product. A great deal of white space says that the pictured item is special, probably expensive, and certainly high quality. It implies that the product deserves the spotlight given it by a plain field that accents its appeal. Thus, many advertisements for expensive jewelry picture the item on a plain-colored velvet cloth; only a few words are included so consumers are not distracted from the beauty and perfection of the jewelry. In contrast, a busy advertisement featuring a jumble of words and pictures and a small amount of white space may suggest low price and low quality. Look closely at the advertisements in your newspaper or favorite magazines and notice how layout is used in ways such as these. Art often involves camera work. The accompanying Competitive Strategy feature describes some camera work that caused an advertiser considerable embarrassment.

ALTERNATIVE EXAMPLE
Ameritech Cellular Services put art students in charge of its advertising in Chicago's United Center. One ad entitled "Bubbular Communications," features a large tank in which two porcelain fish converse. Computer-controlled bubbles attract the attention of passersby and are translated on an LED display. The "bubble, bubble, bubble" dialogue is occasionally interrupted with more meaningful words, such as "air time." This ad really focuses on the art aspect of advertising. SOURCE: Kelly Shermach, "Art of Communication," *Marketing News,* May 8, 1995, p. 2.

**COMPETITIVE STRATEGY: WHAT WENT WRONG?**

### *Sandstorm at Qantas*

There's a lot of talk in these austere times about how advertising agencies have had to give up trips to faraway places on shoots for ads and commercials. However, D'Arcy Masius Benton & Bowls learned that such frugality isn't always appreciated.

A D'Arcy film crew in Hawaii, instead of traveling on to Australia for client Qantas Airways, used a shot of a beach in Hawaii in a Qantas ad touting the beaches and other pleasures of Australia. It was one of those cutesie pictures—a man in an airplane seat placed at the water's edge under the headline, "You'll feel like you're in Australia as soon as you're on Qantas."

Sand is sand, right? But the gaffe became public, and Qantas fired the advertising agency (bid D'Arcy g'day). The lesson here? Not more trips but more computers.

With today's computer technology, you can shoot the actors on a Long Island or Los Angeles sound stage and then "magically" place them in Fiji, Paris, or wherever stock footage has been shot. Substitutes for real places are not necessary. Computer technology can save money—and the account.

Your body's a temple
and judging from your clothing,
it's a cheap little joint on the outskirts of town.

HAGGAR
Stuff
you can wear.
Pictured here is a 100% wool City Casuals jacket, about $125, with a pair of 100% cotton Wrinkle-Free khakis, about $45, and a 100% cotton shirt, around $38. Your mother would be proud. Shocked, but proud.


An effective advertisement draws attention immediately. In the advertisement shown here the headline copy and the art work together to gain the reader's attention.

**AIDA**
An acronym for attention, interest, desire, and action. The AIDA formula is a hierarchy of communication effects model used as a guideline in creating advertisements.

ALTERNATIVE EXAMPLE
An iguana that likes cinnamon-raisin bagels with bananas and a little brother who wants potato chips on his bagel are images from two ads for Manhattan Bagel Company shown on the East Coast. These ads, which always feature unusual participants and situations, have been so successful that Manhattan Bagel is thinking of using them when it engages in a national roll-out. SOURCE: Fara Warner, "Two Outsiders' Bagel Ads Raise Eyebrows," *Wall Street Journal*, May 12, 1995, p. B5.

## Copy and Art Working Together—The AIDA Formula

Most advertisements, with the exception of radio advertisements, feature both copy and art. The two elements must work together and complement each other to accomplish the communication objectives set by management. To do this, most advertisers follow a hierarchy of effects model known as the AIDA formula. **AIDA** stands for attention, interest, desire, and action.

**Attention** An effective advertisement must draw attention from the very first glance or hearing. Whatever follows will prove of little use if the target viewer has not first been influenced to pay attention to the message. Copy can be used to accomplish this, as when radio advertisements start out sounding like soap operas or mystery stories to draw attention. The copy can be enhanced by illustration. Often a person, representing the target customer, is shown in situations that make the viewer think, "What's going on here?" or "What happened to these people?" For example, to attract the attention of luggage users, Samsonite luggage company has for years run advertisements showing such things as suitcases falling out of airplanes and suitcases supporting automobiles that have flipped over on top of them. Humor is another attention-getting device, as the accompanying Competitive Strategy feature illustrates.

**Interest** After attention has been attracted, the arousal of interest is next. If the attention-getter is powerful enough, interest should follow fairly automatically. However, it may be necessary to focus the viewers or listeners on how the product or service being advertised actually pertains to them.

**Desire** Immediately following the arousal of interest is the attempt to create a desire for the product. A TV commercial for ChemLawn demonstrates this. The

COMPETITIVE STRATEGY: WHAT WENT RIGHT?

## *Translating British Humor for Americans*

While most Americans say they dislike advertising, polls show that the British seem to enjoy it. One reason, advertising people say, is the higher portion of humor and the softer sell in British ads.

Among the most popular figures in British advertising is a comic actor well-known to Americans: John Cleese, who is the spokesman for Schweppes soft drinks in the United States and Britian. Neither campaign bears any resemblance to the ads featuring the dignified, bushy-bearded Commander Whitehead; they were developed by David Ogilvy in the United States in the 50s and ran for 18 years.

The new, self-deprecating campaigns accept the notion that advertising is inherently silly. The British ads, which Mr. Cleese co-wrote, begin with a voice-over in which he talks about the haggling that went on over his contract. He then appears on a beach flexing his biceps, in a parody of typically exuberant soft-drink commercials.

One of Schweppes's American ads mocks British and American sterotypes. Mr. Cleese plays a stuffy British aristocrat who sips Schwepps by his fireplace and pontificates indecipherably. Then, dressed in shorts and a Hawaiian shirt, he takes on the Americans. He bursts through a Schweppes poster at a beach and lip-syncs to an ebullient voice-over that exhorts the viewer to "Buy a truckload today!"

This final version is more hyperactive than the original, Mr. Cleese says; in testing, American audiences did not recognize the parody.

"In England," Mr. Cleese said, "having someone scream out to buy something would be considered rude, and a bit vulgar." Advertising, he said, has its limits: "You can't sell in an advertisement. You can interest someone in a product by giving them a favorable association."

viewer sees one homeowner carrying tools and bags of lawn chemicals. One of the bags breaks, and the exhausted do-it-yourselfer looks on helplessly. The viewer at home sees, however, that the unfortunate fellow's neighbor has a very nice-looking lawn but does not look harried or sweaty. Certainly he has no piles of spilled lawn-care products around his property. The viewer is interested in this story: Why is one fellow miserable while his neighbor smilingly pities him? The contented homeowner is a subscriber to the ChemLawn service, of course. The viewer is treated to some scenes of the ChemLawn man applying liquid lawn chemicals in one easy step. The ChemLawn people know what and when to spray—another load off the homeowner's mind. Thus, interest in and desire for the product are established in nearly simultaneous steps.

ALTERNATIVE EXAMPLE

Ford builds campaigns around slogans that have been used for a long time: "Built Ford Tough," first used in 1975; "Have you driven a Ford lately?" first used in 1982; and "Quality is Job 1," first used in 1981. By repeating these slogans in a variety of ads, Ford has greatly improved its market share. SOURCE: Fara Warner, "Ford Bests Calvin Klein in '94 Ad Rankings," *Wall Street Journal,* May 9, 1995, p. B5.

**Action** Action is the last part of the AIDA formula. In the ChemLawn example, the commercial ends with a call to action. In effect, the advertisement urges viewers to phone the local ChemLawn dealer for an estimate of what it will take to make them as happy as the man who has a nice lawn with no effort. Thus, the means to act is provided. Usually, the advertiser makes the action seem as effortless as possible by giving a phone number or closing with a note that credit cards are accepted.

**How the AIDA Formula Works** The AIDA formula is based on a consumer behavior theory that closely parallels the hierarchy of communication effects model discussed in Chapter 15. The formula describes consumers' behavior and serves as a guideline for creating advertising. AIDA makes good sense as an advertising tool and is widely known and followed.

It must be understood that it may not be possible for every advertisement to move the reader or viewer through the four stages to action with a single exposure. Repetition is usually necessary so that the advertisement's message can "sink in." Repetition also increases the chance that the target customer will see or hear the message at a time when there are no distractions. Finally, repetition recognizes the buyer's changing environment. The target buyer who has just been paid or has received a tax return may perceive an already-seen advertisement in a different light. Eventually, if the advertisement is an effective one aimed at the proper people, buyers are likely to move psychologically through the AIDA stages and then act.

As we have already indicated, developing a creative strategy and developing a media selection strategy are interrelated processes, and the planning of these activities occurs simultaneously. We now turn our attention to the selection of media.

## Media Selection

Suppose you have decided to open a retail store. You have already decided to have a Yellow Pages advertisement but are undecided about whether to use radio, television, or newspaper advertising as well. This choice is a matter of selecting a communication channel for your message. In making the choice, you are determining a **media selection strategy,** which must take account of the message you wish to transmit, the audience you want to reach, the effect you want to have, and the budget you have to support this effort.

**MEDIA SELECTION STRATEGY**
Strategy involving the determination of which media are most appropriate for an advertising campaign.

DISCUSSION CONSIDERATION
Which media would you suggest be used to promote a concert by (a) the Grateful Dead, (b) Frank Sinatra, and (c) The London Philharmonic.

Developing a media strategy requires answers to two questions: (1) Which media will efficiently get the message to the desired audience? (2) What scheduling of these media will neither bore people with too-frequent repetition of the message nor let too many people forget the message? Before we address these questions, let's look briefly at what the term *media* includes.

### Mass Media and Direct-Marketing Media

**MASS MEDIA**
Advertising media, such as radio and television, that reach a broad audience that includes many market segments.

**DIRECT-MARKETING MEDIA**
Advertising media that are directed to selective audience members. Many direct-marketing media use computers to access data bases and customize the advertising message to a household or an individual.

When we think of advertising, we normally think of **mass media,** such as radio and television. However, we must remember **direct-marketing media** as well. Exhibit 16–5 shows the individual advertising media in each of these classifications.

Advances in technology have changed the nature of direct-marketing media in recent years. Direct mail has been in existence for more than a century, for example, but modern computer technology has improved the selectivity of this medium. Now computers can access data bases to customize what materials will be sent and to personalize the direct-response advertising message to a household or an individual.

ALTERNATIVE EXAMPLE
To increase tourism, Beverly Hills is using a direct-mail campaign. If you are one of the select, you may receive a letter from the city's mayor pointing out what Beverly Hills has to offer such as fine shopping, dining, and year-round sunshine. If interested, you can ask for a video which takes you on a tour of the city. SOURCE: Laura Loro, "Beverly Hills' Inviting Idea," *Advertising Age,* March 20, 1995, p. 24.

There are three important points to mention about strategies stressing direct-marketing media. First, new products and services, such as fax machines and computer voice-recognition systems, are used much as direct mail has always been used. That is, a list containing many individuals' names is used to directly contact potential buyers. A new technology, perhaps with sound or movement, replaces the postal service, but the process is essentially the same.

Second, as mentioned, computers are used to develop data bases that can customize the message any individual consumer or household receives. For example, a personalized greeting may appear on a letter that, in addition to conveying an advertising message, indicates the name of a local retailer that sells the brand being advertised. If the data base records the ages of the children in households, an advertiser using direct marketing can send coupons only to those households with, say, children in diapers. Furthermore, if the data base also indicates the brand of diapers a con-

**EXHIBIT 16–5**

Mass Media and Direct-Marketing Media

| **Mass media** | **Direct media** |
|---|---|
| Broadcast media | Printed |
| ■ Network television | ■ Letters and pamphlets |
| ■ Cable television | ■ Catalogs |
| ■ Radio | ■ Bill inserts |
| Print media | ■ Flyers |
| ■ Newspapers | Phone/Fax |
| ■ Magazines | ■ Computerized calls |
| ■ Directory/Yellow Pages | ■ Fax advertisements |
| Outdoor | Electronic/Interactive |
| ■ Billboards | ■ Internet |
| ■ Posters | ■ Commercial interactive services |
| In-Store | ■ Electronic mail |
| ■ Point-of-purchase displays | |
| ■ Video presentations | |
| Other | |
| ■ Movie theater | |
| ■ Transit | |

ALTERNATIVE EXAMPLE

Talbots, a retailer of conservative women's clothing, conducts most of its promotion through catalogs and direct mail. Customers are encouraged to order items not available in the store from the catalog through the use of in-store telephones. Selling through the catalog has enabled Talbots to build a data base of 7 million women. By using the data base, Talbots can communicate with customers about new styles and sales and can determine where to locate stores. SOURCE: Jeanne Whalen, "Talbots Sidesteps Fad Frenzy with Style," *Advertising Age,* May 8, 1995, p. 4.

sumer regularly purchases, then an advertiser like Huggies can limit the mailing list to consumers who are loyal to Pampers or other competitive brands.

Third, today's direct-marketing media can be interactive. An individual using an **interactive medium** can electronically converse via computer with an advertiser or information service. The story that opened this chapter explained how Zima advertises on the Internet. This new interactive medium is expected to have almost a billion users within the next ten years. Commercial interactive media include CD-ROM materials and on-line information services. For example, the MTV discussion group on America Online—the most popular attraction of this information service—is interactive.

**INTERACTIVE MEDIA**

Media that allow consumers to interact with a database to search for information and/or order products via computers or other electronic technologies.

## Which Media?

Certain media lend themselves to certain tasks. If we assume, for the moment, that budget considerations can be set aside, certain factors become dominant in choosing the medium to carry a sales message. If demonstration or visual comparison of one brand with another is the goal, television becomes the most logical contender. If a lengthy explanation of sales points is required, print advertisements (magazines and newspapers) come to mind. If consumers require a message to remind them of package identification or a short sales idea, outdoor advertising (billboards) makes sense. Thus, before a marketing planner starts thinking about what medium to use, he or she must know what is to be said. Once what is to be said has been decided, the marketer's attention can turn to which media can best say it. Ultimately, several different media may be selected to communicate the multiple messages the marketer wishes to communicate.

POINT TO EMPHASIZE

Different media might be used at different phases of the AIDA process. Television and outdoor ads might be effective in generating awareness. To create interest, the marketer might use print ads. Desire and action could be generated through ads offering trial samples or direct-mail letters offering consumers an opportunity to try the product. An infomercial might also be used to generate interest, desire, and action.

Several media may appear to be able to do a particular job. When this is so, the marketing planner can narrow the choice by considering which media will hit the all-important target market. At this point, the media expert becomes a market expert. Knowing the target market—who are the heaviest buyers, what are their demographic and psychographic characteristics—leads to a determination of which media

ALTERNATIVE EXAMPLE

Kaleidoscope is a new cable channel aimed at persons with disabilities. The 24-hour-a-day channel reaches 15 million homes. One feature is a shopping program on which manufacturers can demonstrate products for free. Profits are split between the manufacturer and the channel. Other features are news, information, sports, movies, and children's shows. According to the government, there are 49 million disabled Americans, which is a large target audience. SOURCE: Jamie Goldman, "Channel for Disabled Adds 'Shopping!'" *Advertising Age,* May 15, 1995, p. 12.

will deliver these prospects. For example, the media planner in the insurance industry may be trying to target young males between the ages of 18 and 34; a European airline may be targeting well-educated, high-income men and women between the ages of 25 and 49; the primary customers for a sun-block cream may be youthful, fashion-conscious woman. What media will reach each of these targets most effectively?

Most products can be related to a demographic profile. The data gathered pertaining to media are geared to that same profile information. Thus, if the target audience includes men and woman, and it has been decided that television will do the best job and that the media budget permits such an expensive choice, the media planner may go for prime-time television—from 8 P.M. to 11 P.M. The next task is to determine which television vehicles (shows) have audiences whose profiles match those of the target customers.

Careful analysis of any organization's marketing communication efforts might show that what appears to be the most appropriate advertising medium is, in fact, quite inappropriate. Where should one advertise a product like children's crayons? Saturday morning television shows, with their ability to show happy children drawing and coloring and with their excellent demographics, would seem to be an obvious choice. But when Crayola's marketing managers discovered that mothers were the prime factors in the purchase of crayons, they shifted a large portion of their advertising budget out of children's TV and into women's magazines. The copy theme they developed—"Give them a fresh box of crayons and see how they grow"—reflected the shift in audience and the new media strategy. TV advertisements were still useful, but TV advertisements coupled with woman's magazine advertisements were better.

Each advertising medium has its strengths and weaknesses. Magazines allow advertisers to target specific market segments. For example, almost all of the *Men's Journal* readership consists of college educated men between 25 and 49 with incomes above $60,000 per year.

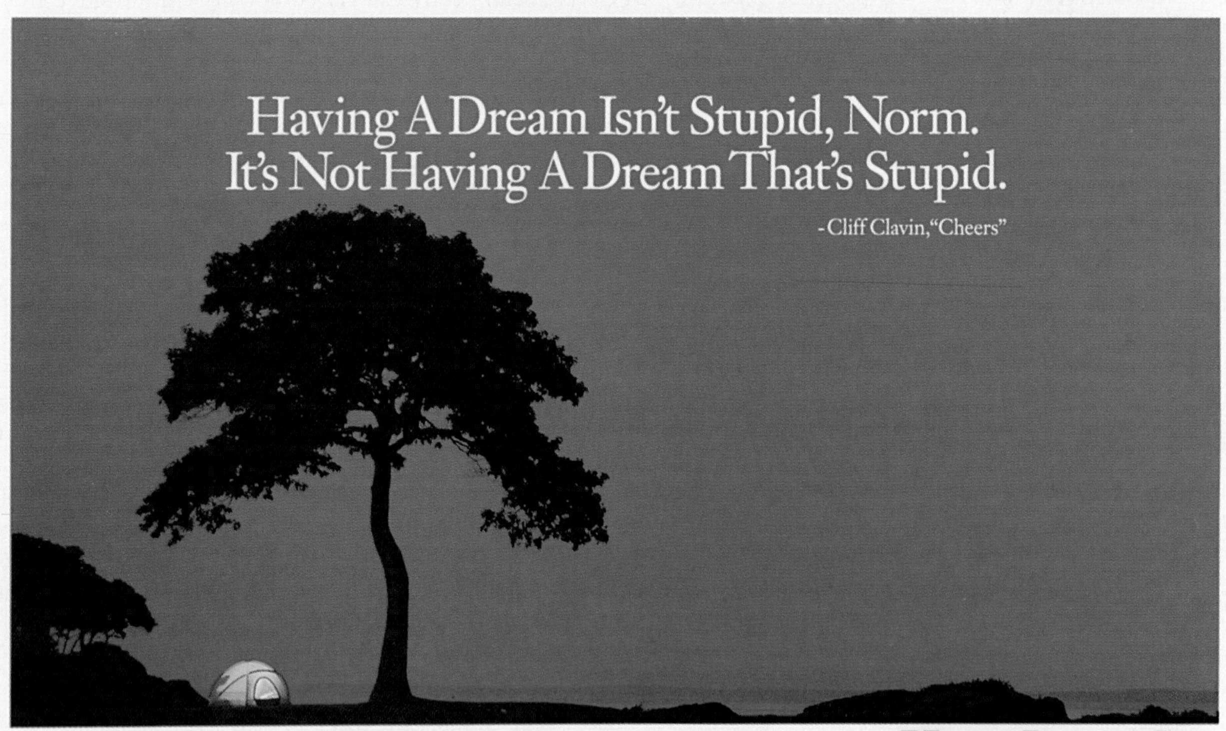

Having A Dream Isn't Stupid, Norm.
It's Not Having A Dream That's Stupid.
-Cliff Clavin, "Cheers"
Men's Journal
Men 25-49, Med. HHI $61,800, College Educ. 88.3%.
It's not an invitation to escape life, it's a way to dive in.

VIDEO CASE 16–1

## Fallon McElligott

Fallon McElligott is an advertising agency known for its creativity. It is also known as something of an outsider because its headquarters is in Minneapolis-St. Paul. Although it is not located on Madison Avenue in New York City, is clients include some of the world's major advertisers. Lee Apparel Company, Porsche, Timex, and Continental Bank are among its major accounts.

An example of the agency's creativity is its perception/reality advertising campaign for *Rolling Stone* magazine—considered an advertising classic. *Rolling Stone's* customers, advertising agency media buyers, thought its audience was made up of old hippies from the 1960s without much money or much interest in purchasing anything, let alone upscale items. The advertising campaign (see Case Exhibit 16–1) juxtaposed old hippie images with actual characteristics and buying patterns of *Rolling Stone's* readership. This advertising was not only creative, it served a marketing objective extremely well. And Fallon McElligott's creativity works in the marketplace. For example, its advertising for Lee Jeans helped increase market share from 14.6 percent to 22.1 percent during the back-to-school selling season.

Fallon McElligott's mission statement comes up every day on its Macintosh computer system. The computer screen indicates that the mission is "To be the premier,

**CASE EXHIBIT 16–1** Fallon McElligott's Advertisement for *Rolling Stone*

Perception.

Reality.

If your idea of a Rolling Stone reader looks like a holdout from the 60's, welcome to the 80's. Rolling Stone ranks number one in reaching concentrations of 18-34 readers with household incomes exceeding $25,000. When you buy Rolling Stone, you buy an audience that sets the trends and shapes the buying patterns for the most affluent consumers in America. That's the kind of reality you can take to the bank.

award-winning agency in America that produces extraordinary, effective work for a short list of blue chip clients." The focus is on doing good creative work as well as on the agency's entrepreneurial nature.

Fallon McElligott has 211 full-time employees. The agency does not have an organizational structure with multiple levels of management. There are no vice presidents in an industry where the title of vice president is commonplace. Titles, such as management supervisor, account supervisor, and account executive, reflect functional activity. The agency focuses on creating great advertising rather than on chain-of-command decisions and power struggles for senior positions. At Fallon McElligott, cultivating a star system and giving recognition for authorship are important.

Like account personnel in most advertising agencies, account personnel at Fallon McElligott deal with clients. At Fallon McElligott, however, the focus is on creating a partnership with the client. It is the job of account personnel to be involved in clients' business and to be problem solvers. With research personnel, they analyze available research to help them understand clients' marketing communication tasks. Account personnel are responsible for communicating clients' needs to creative personnel and media personnel.

Fallon McElligott's media strategists and planners develop media strategies to match clients' objectives. Media personnel buy media time or space from media representatives. The job entails sharing target market information with media representatives, finding the best match, and negotiating the best deals.

### QUESTIONS

1. Is a Minneapolis location a disadvantage in the advertising agency business?
2. Evaluate Fallon McElligott's mission statement.
3. What is the nature of the relationship between an agency and a client?
4. What steps are necessary for an advertisement to be created by an advertising agency? What role does the agency play in making creative decisions and selecting media?
5. What special considerations might an agency take into account in managing creative personnel?

## VIDEO CASE 16–2 Lee Jeans

During the 1980s, as the baby boom generation aged into thirtysomething and fortysomething groups, marketers of denim jeans saw a steady decline. From a demographic perspective, the number of teenagers, the heavy user segment, had declined. Many denim jeans marketers concentrated on marketing high fashion jeans.

Lee's business hadn't been built on one key market segment. Its sales volume reflected market sales in general. Consequently, as the product category declined, so did Lee's business. Furthermore, the market segment with the strongest brand loyalty to Lee, women aged 25–54 years, was not perceived as a desirable group for a denim company in a fashion-driven market. Thus, in the 1980s, Lee began to target younger consumers with fashion jeans in an attempt to restore brand loyalty with retailers and consumers. This fashion focus resulted in production and delivery problems, which alienated retailers. As a result, retailers began to carry only one or two styles. Many used the Lee jeans as a loss leader. Many stopped carrying the brand altogether. Market share declined as consumers could no longer identify with the brand or find it at retail outlets.

The company faced several problems: how to stop sales volume and market share from declining, how to restore the power of the Lee brand, and how to impact retail distribution.

Marketing research was conducted with woman aged 24-54. It found that these women were still very loyal to the Lee brand. The research uncovered that this loyalty was based on the belief that Lee offered a superior-fitting, well-made, high-quality product. It also showed that Lee had failed to establish an emotional relationship with female consumers. There was a rational reason to buy Lee, but no emotional reason. However, no other brand had built an emotional bond with female consumers, either. When given a choice, these consumers picked Lee as the brand they would most like to associate with.

The research also showed that women saw jeans in several ways, as work jeans, those worn for work in the house or out in the yard; casual jeans, for shopping, school, and other regular activity; and dress-up jeans, for social occasions. Lee concluded that it was the only brand that could function for all three purposes.

The company also knew that there was a great deal of discomfort associated with wearing many brands of jeans. Lee was the brand that fit the best. Lee jeans provided working women with a sense of relaxation as well as a sense of energy. Women believed that coming home to their jeans after a day at work in a uniform or office attire was a pleasurable experience.

## QUESTIONS

1. What overall marketing mix objectives would you set for Lee jeans?
2. What creative strategy for advertising would you recommend?
3. What media strategy would you recommend?

CHAPTER

# 17

# Personal Selling and Sales Management

LEARNING OBJECTIVES

After you have studied this chapter, you will be able to:

1. Describe the role of personal selling and relationship management.
2. Identify marketing situations in which personal selling would be the most effective means of reaching and influencing target buyers.
3. Show how the professional salesperson contributes to a modern marketing firm.
4. Outline the steps involved in making a sale.
5. Explain why the marketing process does not stop when the sale is made.
6. Characterize the major aspects of the sales manager's job.
7. Classify the various forms of sales compensation.
8. Identify some of the ethical issues facing sales personnel.

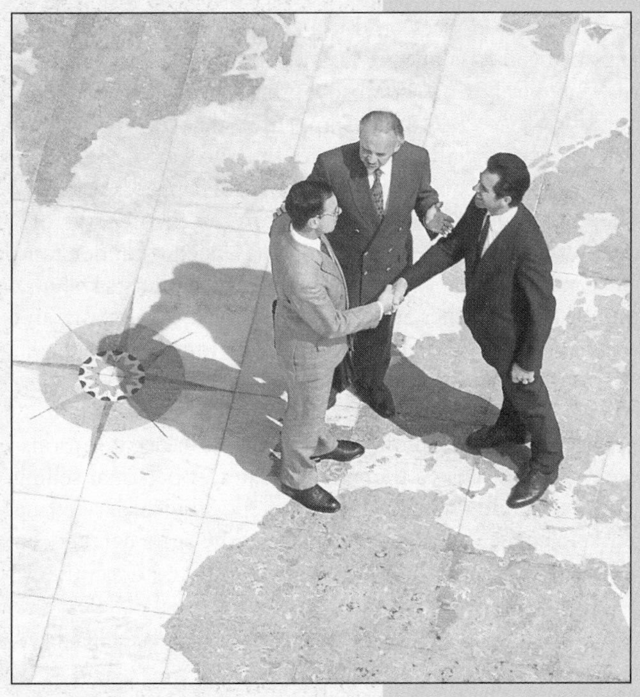

"I see them everywhere, and I have come to understand that they are among the bravest of us. They face on a daily basis what we all dread the most: flat, cold rejection. Even the best of them hears 'No' more than he hears 'Yes' . . . Yet all of them get up each morning and go out to do it again." So says Bob Greene, describing salespeople in his book *American Beat.* Probably many of us share Greene's image of what salespeople's lives are like.

But salespeople don't just make sales. For many, if not most, salespeople, servicing accounts—working with existing customers—is a big part of the job. That means they hear questions like "Can you help me solve this?" as often as simple "Yes" and "No" answers. To prosper, most salespeople need to know more than the customer about some aspects of the customer's own business. Today's salesperson is often a cross between a consultant and a vendor.

ALTERNATIVE EXAMPLE

Unfortunately, selling has a negative image among many people. To overcome this, Sales and Marketing Executives International gives salespeople the opportunity to become SMEI Certified Sales Persons (SCPS). To qualify, salespeople must meet a number of requirements, including passing a four-hour exam. One company that sent its sales force through the SMEI testing was Cutler-Hammer, a Pittsburgh seller of electrical distribution equipment. According to Bruce Broussard, a district sales manager for Cutler-Hammer, "Certification is a professionalism and credibility issue." SOURCE: Andy Cohen, "Should Your Salespeople Be Certified?' *Sales and Marketing Management,* April 1995, p. 138.

Also, many of today's salespeople are women—28 percent of sales jobs are held by women, according to a recent survey of sales forces. More than 80 percent of salespeople have at least some college education. On average, salespeople (including sales managers) work 49 hours a week and earn almost $50,000 a year.

Christine Sanders, a top sales representative for Eastman Kodak copiers, typifies today's successful salesperson. Selling and leasing machines that cost from $18,000 to $105,000, Sanders may spend up to six months to close a sale. Her commission ranges from a few hundred to a few thousand dollars. The sales she feels best about are the ones "you earn because you really understood a customer's applications or because you worked hard or were persistent in the face of a lot of competition," she says.

At Northwestern University, Sanders earned a bachelor's degree in a special program that combined economics and communications. She didn't plan on a sales career, but she effectively trained for one through extracurricular activities that often involved fund raising.

After recruiting her in a campus interview, Kodak sent Sanders through a 10-week training program that included classroom work, real and simulated sales calls, and many sessions probing the innards of the copiers she would eventually sell. The training was "intense," she recalls, "good preparation for the real world."

Sanders shone in the suburban Chicago territory she was given and quickly advanced, eventually to a territory that includes a handful of major accounts in downtown Chicago.

Forty-hour workweeks are uncommon for Sanders; the job typically demands 50 to 60. "Whatever it takes to satisfy the customer," she says.

Companies that buy or lease Kodak copiers get a package of services along with their hardware. Training is one of these services, and if a customer with 24-hour administrative operations needs to conduct late-night training sessions, a Kodak sales representative may oblige. For one such session, Sanders got up at 4 A.M. and drove to the customer's office. No trainees appeared that morning. "But I was there," she says, "and the customer will never forget that."

Her advice to newcomers in the sales profession is to know their product, their competitors' products, and their customers. That way, they can sell the benefits of their product without slamming a rival firm. A salesperson may need to understand what bothers a prospective customer about a competing product, Sanders says, "but you don't need to harp on that. I'd rather sell the benefits of my company and myself than ever bad-mouth the competition, because I think it's unprofessional and it doesn't really buy you anything—and it could come back to haunt you."

This chapter begins by explaining the nature of personal selling in organizations and its importance in our economy. It discusses the various types of personal selling jobs and then describes the creative selling process and the tactics that order-getting salespeople use in each stage of this process. Next, it explains how sales careers can provide entry into managerial positions and why many managerial and executive jobs require personal selling skills. After describing the basic principles of sales management, the chapter ends with a discussion of some ethical issues facing both salespeople and sales managers.

## Personal Selling Defined

Personal selling, as noted in Chapter 15, is a person-to-person dialogue between the prospective buyer and the seller. Thus, it consists of human contact and direct communication rather than impersonal mass communication. Personal selling involves developing customer relationships, discovering and communicating customer needs, matching the appropriate products with these needs, and communicating benefits.[1]

The salesperson's job may be to remind, to inform, or to persuade. In general, the salesperson's responsibility is to keep existing customers abreast of information about the company's products and services and to persuasively convey a sales message to potential customers. Salespeople are also expected to be aware of changes in the markets they serve and to report important information to their home offices. Professional sales personnel are vitally important as a direct link to the company's customers. Salespeople communicate the company's offer and show prospective buyers how their problems can be solved by the product. They finalize the sale by writing orders.

**RETAIL SELLING**
Selling to ultimate consumers.

**FIELD SELLING**
Nonretail selling that takes place outside the employer's place of business, usually in the prospective customer's place of business.

**TELEMARKETING**
Using the telephone as the primary means of communicating with prospective customers. Telemarketers usually use computers for order taking.

**INSIDE SELLING**
Nonretail selling from the employer's place of business.

Many different businesses—farms, factories, retailers, banks, transportation companies, hotels, and many other enterprises—use personal selling. Each faces personal selling tasks that are unique. Various methods of personal selling may be used to accomplish these tasks.

We are all familiar with **retail selling**—selling to ultimate consumers. Field selling, telemarketing, and inside selling are the three basic methods for personal selling in business-to-business transactions. **Field selling** is performed by an "outside" salesperson, who usually travels to the prospective account's place of business. **Telemarketing** involves using the telephone as the primary means of communicating with prospective customers. **Inside selling** is similar to retail selling by store clerks; here, salespeople sell in the employer's place of business. They deal with customers on a face-to-face basis. For example, the typical plumbing wholesaler employs inside sales personnel to assist customers—plumbers—who travel to the wholesaler's place of business to obtain fixtures, tools, or parts.

Telemarketing is becoming a major activity of many sales representatives.

## The Importance of Personal Selling

**DISCUSSION CONSIDERATION**

Ask students what their majors are. Chances are, some of them are not marketing majors. Discuss the likely career paths in their fields. For example, science majors may wind up as salespeople for companies that produce dyes, drugs, agricultural products, or food products. Finance majors may become stockbrokers, which will involve selling. This exercise is designed to emphasize that many students will wind up selling even though they aren't marketing majors.

Personal selling is the most widely used means by which organizations communicate with their customers. In other words, it is the most commonly used promotional tool. It is possible to find profit or nonprofit organizations that make no use whatsoever of advertising. For decades, the Hershey company did not advertise. Certainly, there are companies so obscure that they get no publicity at all. It is, however, difficult to imagine any organization making no personal contact with its clients. Even the one-person machine shop deals with clients through some kind of personal contact and sales effort. And although you may not have thought of it in this way, accountants, stockbrokers, dentists, lawyers, and other professionals are personal salespeople in that they deal with clients and sell a service. For example, many hard-working accountants (who generally were not marketing majors) promoted to a partnership in an accounting firm find that they spend more time trying to generate new business than they spend working out accounting problems. Robert Louis Stevenson was not far from the mark when he said, "Everyone lives by selling something."

In terms of dollars spent, personal selling is again the foremost promotional tool. Money spent on personal selling far exceeds money spent on advertising, despite advertising's costs and visibility. This becomes clear when one considers the number of people engaged in selling and the cost of training, compensation, and deployment of sales forces.

Personal selling is also the most significant promotional tool in terms of the number of people employed. It is estimated that at least 12 million people, or 10 percent of the U.S. work force, are engaged in sales. In contrast, fewer than 200,000 people work in advertising. As impressive as these statistics are, they underestimate the importance of personal selling in our economy and in other aspects of our social life. Professional selling is an activity of many individuals whose job titles may obscure this fact. Company presidents, advertising executives, and marketing researchers are frequently engaged in personal selling, for example.

Why is personal selling so important in our economy? The answer is that the salesperson is the catalyst that makes our economy function. The adage "nothing happens until a sale is made" reflects the importance of personal selling in all aspects of business. Few of us have ever purchased a car from a plant engineer or a financial manager; we buy cars from salespeople. Salespeople build and maintain relationships that stimulate economic activity and produce revenue for the organization. They keep the economy going.

## The Characteristics of Personal Selling

Two basic characteristics that contribute to the importance of personal selling are its flexibility and its value in building relationships. We will look more closely at these characteristics, then discuss the disadvantages of personal selling.

### Personal Selling Is Flexible

POINT TO EMPHASIZE
Students may not have considered the variety of sales positions available because of stereotypical images of the field. Ask students to think of products that might be fun, challenging, or rewarding to sell. For example, consider selling supplies to bungee-jumping services, physicians, or retailers of roller blades, college annuals, or golf clubs.

Perhaps the key word to describe personal selling's advantages over other means of promotion is *flexibility*. Flexibility means that the salesperson can adapt a sales presentation to a specific situation. When a sales prospect has a particular problem or series of problems to solve, the professional salesperson can adjust the presentation to show how the product or service offered can solve these problems and satisfy the individual needs of the potential customer. Similarly, the salesperson can answer questions and overcome objections that may arise. The salesperson can even "read" the customer. Sensing that the client agrees with a certain aspect of the presentation or is not interested in a given point, for example, the salesperson can shift gears and move to another benefit or adjust in some other way the manner in which the sales talk is presented.

All this is possible because personal selling entails a two-way flow of communication. Direct and immediate feedback is elicited. Consider the following examples of how feedback allows the salesperson to gather as well as impart information.

- The salesperson discovers in casual conversation that potential buyers have problems that no products on the market can solve.
- A customer suggests how existing products can be modified to better suit customer needs.
- A customer provides the salesperson with new sales leads by mentioning other firms that could use the salesperson's merchandise.
- The salesperson elicits a customer's view of the competition's sales message and uses it to good advantage.

Forget the mythic lone-wolf sales ace; today's trend-setting salespeople tend to work in teams. The traditional sample case? It's more likely to hold spreadsheets than widgets, and the person hauling it around probably regards herself as a problem solver, not a vendor. These days you don't "sell to" people, you "partner with" them. At the rhetorical frontier of the new sales force, even the word "salesman" is frowned upon; the preferred title is "relationship manager."

ALTERNATIVE EXAMPLE
Relationship building is a broad term for many skills frequently attributed to women: listening, following through, and conveying genuine concern. According to Brian Tracy, sales training expert, building trust replaces closing and getting the sale. The tactics used to "get the sale" by men in the past don't work nowadays. Women, who are used to listening and paying attention to customer needs, tend to excel at building trust. SOURCE: Nancy Arnott, "It's a Woman's World," *Sales and Marketing Management,* January 1995, p. 54.

Personal selling is also flexible because it allows the carrier of an organization's message to discover new sales prospects and concentrate on the best ones. In contrast, a television advertisement might be seen by just about anyone, including many people who will never be interested in the product offered for sale. This "waste circulation," as marketers call it, can be reduced or even eliminated by effective personal sellers. With personal selling, large-volume buyers can be visited or called frequently. Personal selling allows efforts to be concentrated on the profitable accounts because it is a selective medium.

## Personal Selling Builds Relationships

Throughout this book, we have emphasized that the relationship between marketer and buyer does not end when the sale is made. Long-term success often depends on the sales force's ability to build a lasting relationship with the buyer. This is especially true in business-to-business marketing. For many business-to-business marketers, the relationship intensifies after the sale is made. How well the marketer manages the relationship becomes the critical factor in what buying decision is made the next time around.[2]

**RELATIONSHIP MANAGEMENT**
The sales function of managing the account relationship and ensuring that buyers receive appropriate services.

In the context of personal selling, the term **relationship management** refers to managing the account relationship and ensuring that buyers receive the appropriate services. The goal of relationship management is to help a salesperson's customers to expand their own organizational resources and capacities through the relationship. The salesperson is the key in relationship management, for it is the salesperson who makes sure the product solves the customer's problems and contributes to the success of the customer's organization. When a salesperson understands and solves a customer's business problems, the relationship will deepen.

ALTERNATIVE EXAMPLE
Kodak is reorganizing its sales force by type of retailer. Kodak marketers believe that grocery stores and photo specialty shops sell photographic supplies for different reasons. Salespeople should specialize by type of retailer so they can offer customized solutions for retailers. SOURCE: Michael Wilke, "Kodak Customizes Sales Force for Retailers," *Advertising Age,* January 30, 1995, p. 8.

## Some Limitations of Personal Selling

Our emphasis on the advantages of personal selling as an effective communication tool should not overshadow its major limitations. Personal selling cannot economically reach a mass audience and therefore cannot be used efficiently in all marketing situations. Face soaps, such as Ivory and Dove, may be used by tens of millions of people; millions more are potential users. Reaching these target customers by personal selling would be too expensive. Advertising via mass media is the appropriate

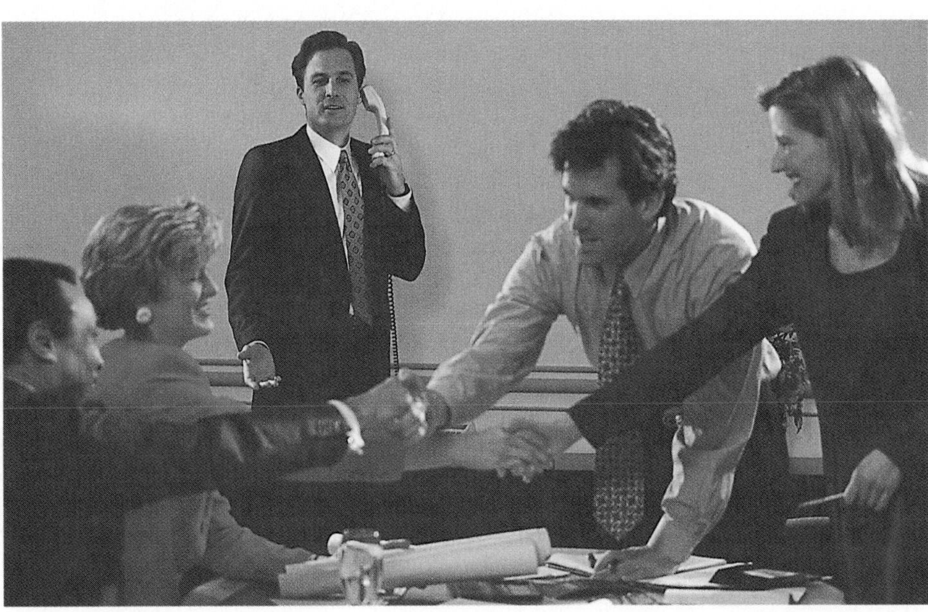

Building and managing relationships with customers is a major selling objective. A good track record and a loyal relationship are often critical factors in buying decisions.

ALTERNATIVE EXAMPLE
Gary Moore of Moore Industries, Inc. has built a direct-selling business that sells nearly $5 billion worth of goods annually. He has built this business through a network of salespeople who call on customers door-to-door selling Filter Queen vacuum cleaners. Much of his success may be attributed to staying close to customers. Moore's salespeople don't disappear after the sale. SOURCE: William Keenan, "Direct Results," *Sales and Marketing Management*, January 1995, p. 78.

tool in cases like these because it can reach a mass audience economically. (Personal selling does, however, play a role in marketing these products when sales representatives call on the major retailers and wholesalers that distribute them.)

Personal selling is expensive because it involves one-on-one communication. The cost per thousand viewers and cost per sale for a high-priced TV advertisement are quite small because the ad is seen by a vast audience. In contrast, the average cost per call for personal selling exceeds $300 for many organizational products. The high cost results from the fact that recruiting, training, and paying salespeople costs the marketer a great deal. Each salesperson, because of the nature of the job, only talks to one or a few people at a time. Furthermore, a great deal of time may be spent just driving to and from appointments and waiting in reception rooms. When we also realize that many sales calls may be needed to generate a single sale, we can see that the cost per sale can be tremendously large. The many advantages of personal selling, however, often offset the high cost per sale. In some cases, as in selling machinery custom-made for the buyer, personal selling is the only way a sale can be made. Fortunately, fax machines, e-mail, and other advances in information technology are helping to counter the cost of in-person sales calls.

## The Types of Personal Selling Tasks

The importance of personal selling varies considerably across organizations. Some organizations rely almost entirely on their sales forces to generate sales, while others use them to support a pulling strategy based on advertising. Some organizations employ salespeople who do little professional selling, such as store clerks at Target and Kmart, while others employ engineers and scientists as technical sales representatives. Clearly, these two types of sales representatives are not comparable.

Because of this diversity, it is useful to differentiate among selling tasks. The marketing manager must do this, for example, in deciding which selling skills and job descriptions are appropriate to the sales objectives to be accomplished. To assign a highly skilled salesperson to a task that could be accomplished as efficiently by a less skilled individual is a waste of an important resource. Here, we discuss the categories of order taking, order getting, and sales support.

### Order Taking

**ORDER TAKER**
A salesperson who is primarily responsible for writing up orders, checking invoices, and assuring prompt order processing.

**SUGGESTIVE SELLING**
Suggesting to a customer who is making a purchase that an additional item or service be purchased.

Millions of people are employed in sales jobs of a routine nature. These people, who do very little creative selling, are called **order takers.** They write up orders, check invoices for accuracy, and assure timely order processing. The term *order taking* is appropriate here because the customer decides on the appropriate products and then tells the salesperson what the order is to be. The order taker's job is to be pleasant and helpful and to ensure that the order truly satisfies the customer's needs. The order taker may engage in **suggestive selling** by suggesting that the customer purchase an additional item ("Would you like French fries with your hamburger?") Suggestive selling is important. However, the typical order taker's primary task is to keep selling existing products to well-established accounts.

In general, order-taking salespeople are divided into the "inside" sales group and the "outside," or field, sales group. Inside order takers are exemplified by auto parts salespeople. Here, the customer has come to the shop seeking the part; the salesperson has not sought out the customer. The inside salesperson may provide some advice on product quality or installation and may even suggest that additional parts or tools would make the job easier or that the customer might as well change the oil filter while handling the other repairs. However, the order taker typically does not extensively modify the basic order presented by the customer.

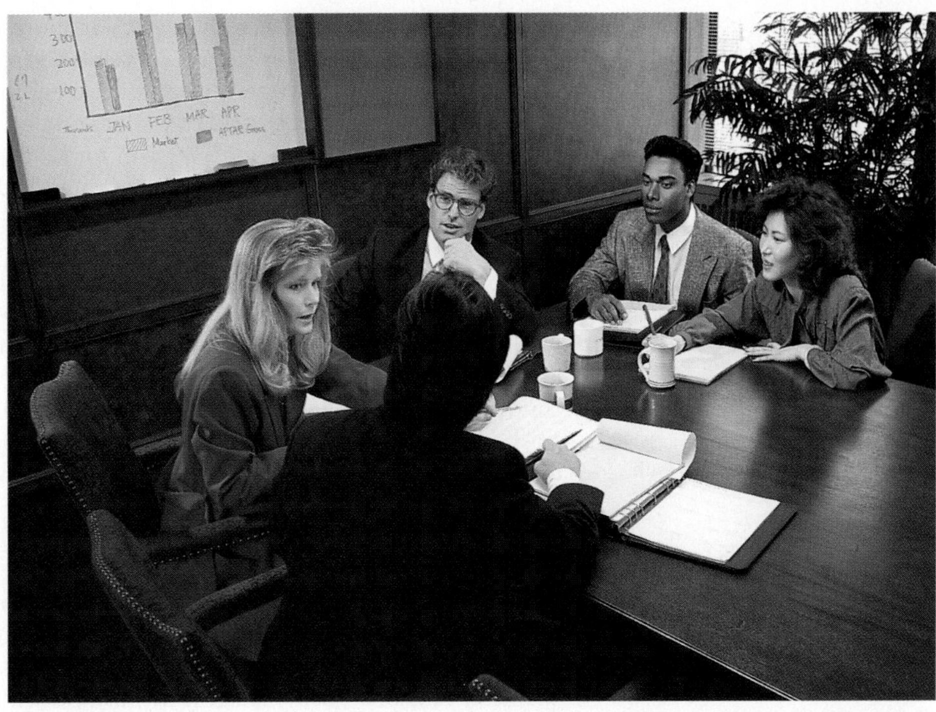


The salesperson may be supported by a sales team. Technical specialists, account service representatives, and sales managers often work in tandem with the salesperson.

ALTERNATIVE EXAMPLE

Continental Insurance is offering a menu-driven service that lets CompuServe subscribers use their keyboards to shop for insurance, make policy changes, file claims, educate themselves on the basics of insurance, and confer with Continental customer service representatives. This can change order getting into order taking done by machine. SOURCE: David C. Jones, "Continental Taps Major Market via CompuServe," *National Underwriter,* July 25, 1994, p. 8.

Telemarketing is becoming a major activity of many inside order-taking sales representatives. Telemarketing involves the use of telephone selling in conjunction with computer technology, which is used for order taking. Of course, all salespeople telephone prospects and customers, and telephone selling is an important part of many order-getting sales jobs. However, here we use the term *telemarketing* to mean using the telephone as the primary means of communication.

Outside, or field, salespeople may also be order takers. Manufacturer or wholesaler representatives selling such well-known products as Campbell's soups find themselves in this position. The question they ask their customers is essentially "How much do you want?" Because nearly every grocery store stocks Campbell's soups, there is little need for aggressive selling. Some sales representatives holding sales positions of this sort do a better job than others in enlarging order size, tying the product to special promotional opportunities, and so on. Such efforts are likely to be rewarded with a promotion or a bonus.

Overall, however, taking orders requires less persuasive skill than selling expensive computer systems to corporate executives or new airplanes to the transportation industry. Thus, order takers in general make less money than order getters.

## Order Getting

**ORDER GETTING, OR CREATIVE SELLING**

An adaptive selling process that tailors sales efforts and product offerings to specific customer needs. An order getter is primarily responsible for developing business for the firm. Order getters seek out customers and creatively make sales.

In **order getting**—also called **creative selling**—the sales job is not routine. Order getters must seek out customers, analyze their problems, discover how the products for sale might solve those problems, and then bring these solutions to the customers' attention.

Creative selling calls for the ability to explain the product and its auxiliary dimensions in terms of benefits and advantages to the prospective buyer and to persuade and motivate the prospect to purchase the product in the appropriate quality and volume. Whereas the order taker's job is to keep the sale, the order getter's job is to make the sale. Put another way, the primary function of the creative salesperson is to generate a sale that might not occur without his or her efforts.

Creative salespeople generally invest far more time and effort in making a sale than do order takers. And while it is possible to engage in creative selling in either an inside or a field environment, it is far more common for creative salespeople to go to the customer's place of business to evaluate the needs to be addressed. This process can take a very long time. A salesperson for Boeing, attempting to demonstrate that a particular airplane is the best available to meet the needs of an airline, can literally spend years preparing to make a sale.

**PIONEERING**
In sales, concentrating on selling to new prospects or on selling new products.

**ACCOUNT MANAGEMENT**
In sales, concentrating on maintaining an ongoing relationship with existing customers.

ALTERNATIVE EXAMPLE
Linda Draves is a sales representative for Roberts-Hamilton, a plumbing and supply company in Minneapolis. When she learned at a trade show that a particular lubricant was changing the corrugating industry, she saw huge sales potential. At the library, she found a publication listing every company in the corrugating industry. She shifted her focus to corrugators, opening a new market for her employer and greatly enhancing her own earnings. SOURCE: Nancy Arnott, "It's a Woman's World," *Sales and Marketing Management*, January 1995, p. 54.

Order getters may specialize in certain types of selling. For example, some organizations have sales personnel, often called **pioneers,** who concentrate their efforts on selling to new prospects or selling new products. Selling an established product or service for the first time to a new customer or selling an innovative product new to the market to an existing customer generates new business for the organization. In contrast, **account managers** concentrate on maintaining an ongoing relationship with existing customers and actively seek additional business for reorders or for other items in the product line. Although pioneering and account management activities may be specialized in some organizations, in many instances the creative salesperson may be involved in both.

Organizations that segment their markets based on account size often make a distinction between major accounts and smaller accounts. For major accounts, a field salesperson may spend a considerable amount of time at the client's headquarters. In contrast, telemarketing is often the primary means of selling to small accounts. For example, Cincinnati Bell manages any business with fewer than 10 lines through telemarketing. The sales representatives never see customers. They use a data base that shows sales and telephone activity levels to monitor customers' usage of their product. Based on this information, they telephone clients with suggestions: "Here's a better way to do it; here's a less expensive way to do it. We've noticed you're making a lot more long-distance calls; how about an 800 number?"[3]

An order-getting salesperson's primary responsibility is, of course, selling. However, order getters, especially account managers, may spend a great deal of time engaged in other activities. Exhibit 17–1 classifies the job activities of order getters.

**EXHIBIT 17–1** Activities of Order-Getting Salespeople

| ACTIVITY NAME | SELECTED ACTIVITIES |
|---|---|
| Selling function | Prospect for and qualify leads; prepare sales presentations; make sales calls; overcome objections |
| Working with orders | Enter orders; expedite orders; handle shipping problems |
| Servicing the product | Test equipment; teach safety instructions; supervise installations, minor maintenance |
| Information management | Receive feedback from clients; provide feedback to superiors |
| Servicing the account | Perform inventory; set up point-of-purchase displays; stock shelves |
| Conferences/meetings | Attend sales conferences; set up exhibitions, trade shows |
| Training/recruiting | Recruit new sales representatives; train new sales representatives |
| Entertaining | Take clients to lunch, sporting events, golfing, tennis, etc. |
| Out-of-town traveling | Traveling; spend night on road; travel out of town |
| Working with distributors | Establish relations with distributors; extend credit; collect past-due accounts |

Source: Adapted from William C. Moncrief, "Selling Activity and Sales Position Taxonomies for Industrial Salesforces," *Journal of Marketing Research*, August 1986, pp. 261–270. Reprinted by permission of the American Marketing Association.

## FOCUS ON QUALITY

### *Hallmark Cards, James River Corp.*

Building durable customer relationships is one thing when you're hawking mainframes, cars, or organs; it's a rather different story when you're pushing a product as short-lived as a greeting card. That's why the sales force at Hallmark Cards, the world's largest greeting card company, concentrates on pleasing retailers. Says Al Summy, a vice president of sales and service for cards sold through large merchandisers like Target, Kmart, and A&P: "We're not selling to the retailer, we're selling *through* the retailer. We look at the retailer as a pipeline to the hands of consumers."

Anything his salespeople can do to make Hallmark products more profitable for retailers, he figures, will ultimately benefit Hallmark.

As a result, Hallmark is reorganizing its entire sales and marketing operation into specialized teams designed to work effectively with product managers at major retailers. In the old days—less than 24 months ago—Hallmark sold pretty much the same mix of cards to every store. Now, using data derived from bar codes at the checkout counter and laptops that supply merchandising information from Hallmark headquarters, salespeople can tailor displays and promotions to a retailer's demographics.

James River Corp., which sells toilet tissue, napkins, Dixie cups, and the like, also understands that when it puts its head together with its retailers', both sides benefit. Specifically, James River shares proprietary marketing information with its customers that enables them to sell more paper products. For instance, it told its West Coast client, Lucky Stores, how often shoppers generally buy paper goods and which items they tend to buy together. Lucky has since reshelved all its paper products and managed to win market share in the category from competing stores.

James River has reorganized the way it calls on customers. Previously, three or more salespeople would approach a company like Lucky Stores: one with plates, one with cups, and one with toilet paper. If all three secured orders, Lucky was obliged to buy three full truckloads, one for each product, to get the lowest price from James River. Today, a unified team from James River will sell Lucky Stores one truckload with a mix of paper products at the lowest price. ■

## Sales Support and Cross-Functional Teams

**MISSIONARY SALES PERSONNEL**
Salespersons who visit prospective customers, distribute information to them, and handle questions and complaints but do not routinely take orders. Missionaries really serve as customer relations representatives.

Many salespeople hold jobs whose titles suggest that they are involved in special selling situations. One commonly encountered salesperson of this sort is the so-called **missionary.** Pharmaceutical manufacturers, for example, employ missionaries, called *detailers,* to call on doctors and provide them with information on the latest prescription and nonprescription products. Detailers do not take orders; sales occur only when the doctor prescribes medication for patients. Missionary sales personnel in fact rarely take or actively seek orders; their primary responsibility is to build goodwill by distributing information to customers and prospective customers and by "checking in" to be sure that buyers are being satisfactorily serviced by company representatives and other relevant channel members such as wholesalers. Even missionary salespeople working for consumer goods companies and calling on retailers do not directly sell anything. If a retailer insisted on placing an order, the missionary would not refuse to accept it but would simply pass it on to the salesperson who regularly handles the retailer's account. Missionaries are, in effect, employed by the manufacturer to perform a public relations function.

DISCUSSION CONSIDERATION
Assume you are the missionary sales representative for this text, an employee of West Publishing. What benefits of the text would you emphasize to university professors? What questions would you ask to identify their needs?

Other specialized sales support people are found in industries in which scientists and engineers serve as technical specialists to support the regular field sales force. The credentials and expertise of these sales engineers, applications programmers, and other technical support personnel are often helpful in concluding sales of complicated products such as nuclear reactors, computer installations, and advanced jet engines.

COMPETITIVE STRATEGY: WHAT WENT RIGHT?

## *Client Teams at IBM*

For IBM a sales force remake was simply a matter of survival. The company has cut its cost of selling by close to $1.5 billion in the past two years. Its worldwide sales and marketing team, now 70,000 strong, is close to half the size it was in 1990.

Those who survived are part of a new operation that is a *cross between a consulting business and a conventional sales operation.* Big Blue now encourages buyers to shop for salesmen before they shop for products. [John] Gorney, [head of information systems at Cleveland's] National City Corp., a superregional bank (assets: $30 billion), handpicked Don Parker as the bank's sales representative after interviewing a half dozen IBM candidates. Says Gorney: "I wanted this person to be a member of my team." An engineer by training, Parker maintains an office at National City, and Gorney has sought his help to drive down the bank's costs of delivering services within the bank and to retail customers in the branches.

Consultants obviously need a more sophisticated set of skills than metal pushers, and IBM has not stinted on their training. For the 300 people like Parker who head client teams, the company has developed a voluntary yearlong certification program. The classroom component consists of a three-week stint at Harvard: one week devoted to general business knowledge, one to consulting, and one to the industry they specialize in serving. For the rest of the year, enrollees work on case studies and then write a thesis on their particular customer. Harvard professors grade the papers. So far, 28 IBM employees have received the certification, along with a raise. (Parker is in the midst of writing his thesis on National City.) Those who fail can keep trying.

In their new role as purveyors of solutions rather than products, IBM's sales teams don't always recommend Big Blue's merchandise. About a third of the equipment IBM installs is made by DEC and other competitors. Says senior vice president Robert LaBant: "In the Eighties we never would have recommended another company's product because all we were paid to do was install Blue boxes."

ALTERNATIVE EXAMPLE

Dendrite International, a sales-automation pharmaceutical software company, uses cross-functional teams. Dendrite's salespeople are allied with specialists from areas such as communications, customer service, and high-tech development. The salesperson's job is to open the door and plan the coordination of specialists. In a 12-month period, as many as 50 Dendrite employees may talk to a customer before the sale is consummated. SOURCE: Nancy Arnott, "Selling a Relationship," *Sales and Marketing Management,* January 1995, p. 14.

Some firms, especially those whose customers may require a little extra push at some point in the selling process, have master salespeople or sales experts on their selling staffs. These salespeople are held in reserve until less senior or less capable salespeople need help. Real estate sellers frequently find a sales expert helpful when, for example, a customer on the verge of buying a new house gets cold feet because of financing worries. At such a point, the salesperson may call on the owner of the agency to "clinch" the sale by working through contacts at the bank or simply by lending an expert helping hand in moving the customer to the purchase point. Dealers in automobiles and major appliances also use this approach at the consumer level. Suppliers of organizational goods adapt the technique to their selling situations.

In many organizations, the salesperson in contact with the customer is supported by a **cross-functional sales team.** If a creative salesperson successfully closes a deal, he or she has perhaps called upon a technical specialist in engineering or logistics or a master salesperson for aid. Perhaps the path to a successful selling experience was made easier by a missionary sales person. After the sale, the missionary may play a further role in keeping the buyer content and certain that the best choice was made. Order takers, whether in the field or at the home office, may see to it that orders are

**CROSS-FUNCTIONAL SALES TEAM**
The sales representative and those who support his or her efforts in making sales and servicing accounts. Support personnel may include technical specialists, missionary salespeople, and others.

**ACCOUNT SERVICE REPRESENTATIVE**
A sales employee at company headquarters or at a branch office who corresponds with clients and provides customer service to established accounts. Sometimes called a *sales correspondent.*

handled with dispatch and without error. The customer may be provided with the name and phone number of an **account service representative,** someone at company headquarters who can answer questions about delivery, post-sale service, installation, and repair parts when the salesperson is away from the home office. A toll-free 800 number may also be provided.

The effective cross-functional sales team is a good illustration of the marketing concept in action. It reflects an effort to satisfy customers, not just sell products. Many people in the organization, from accountants to engineers, engage in a unified effort to build relationships. The accompanying Competitive Strategy feature on page 564 describes effective sales teams at IBM.

## The Creative Selling Process

As we have seen, in some selling jobs the salesperson does little true selling. Perhaps the least creative selling situation involves the "canned presentation." Here, the salesperson memorizes a descriptive or persuasive speech and is directed to give that speech to any and all potential customers without variation. Such an approach is common in many door-to-door and telephone selling situations. Although such a strategy may have little appeal for most people, it should be mentioned that encyclopedia companies and other door-to-door sales organizations frequently devote much time and effort to developing what is thought to be the "best" sales talk. These organizations obviously believe that the method's likelihood of success justifies the lack of individual selling creativity.

**CREATIVE SELLING PROCESS**
The six-step process by which creative selling is carried out: (1) identifying and qualifying prospects, (2) approaching the prospect, (3) making the sales presentation, (4) handling objections, (5) closing the sale, and (6) following up.

Except perhaps for the canned-sales-talk deliverer, all salespeople can benefit from knowledge of the **creative selling process.** This series of steps provides guidelines for the salesperson. It suggests that professional selling is an adaptive process that begins with the identification of specific potential customers and tailors the sales dialogue and product offering to each prospect's needs. The salesperson sells a solution to the customer's problem. The ultimate goal is customer satisfaction.

The creative selling process includes the following steps: (1) identifying and qualifying prospects, (2) approaching the prospect, (3) making the sales presentation, (4) handling objections, (5) closing the sale, and (6) following up. These steps are portrayed in Exhibit 17–2. Again, the steps represent guidelines to help salespeople think about the tasks that face them. Unlike the canned sales presentation, they are not to be slavishly followed.

**EXHIBIT 17–2**
The Creative Selling Process

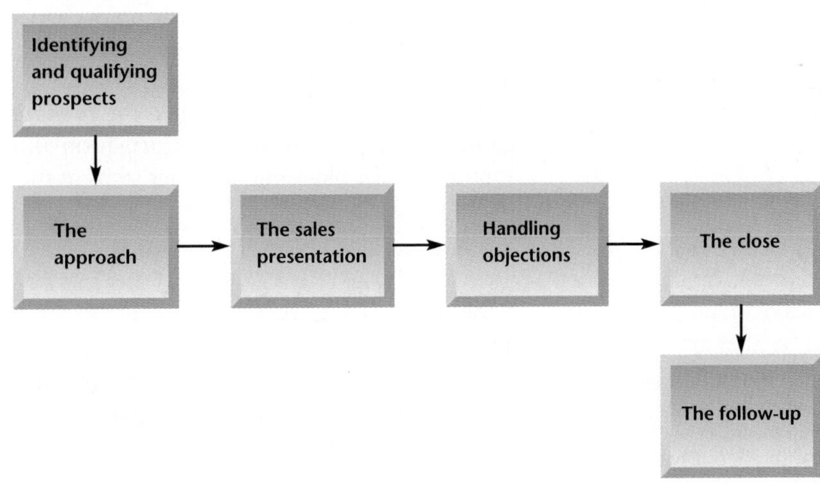

ALTERNATIVE EXAMPLE

Moore Industries sells an insulin injection device. The company uses telemarketing, direct mail, and other forms of targeted marketing, as well as radio. Ron Santo, a former all-star third baseman for the Chicago Cubs has diabetes and is featured in radio ads. After Santo's first ad, the telephone lines were clogged. SOURCE: William Keenan, "Direct Results," *Sales and Marketing Management*, Jan. 1995, p. 78.

## Step One: Identifying and Qualifying Prospects

An established sales representative may rely on regular customers for most of their business, but a successful salesperson is not content to service only existing accounts. Sales calls to regular customers are only part of the sales job. New customers, or new accounts, must be sought. However, making a sales presentation to someone who has no need for the product, who cannot pay for it, or who is not empowered to purchase it is not an efficient use of time unless the person being addressed may become a customer sometime in the future. The salesperson must thus identify likely customers, or prospects.

PROSPECTING

In sales, identifying likely customers. In prospecting, the salesperson may search lists of previous customers, trade association lists, government publications, and many other sources.

**Identifying Prospects** Identifying prospects is called **prospecting.** Lists of previous customers, referrals, trade lists, advertising inquiries (such as postcards or coupons returned to the sales office by interested parties), and other sources may provide the names of prospects. While each industry or line of business has its traditional means of generating "leads," such as membership lists published by trade associations, good salespeople are prepared to dig harder for prospects. Government publications providing breakdowns of business patterns in particular states and counties can be used, and perhaps even cross-referenced with other sources, to develop lists of likely buyers. Some salespeople spend considerable time on the telephone screening possible clients. Others talk with organizations that supply or buy from firms that seem like possible customers. The number of prospecting tools is nearly unlimited.

**Qualifying Prospects** Identifying prospects is only the beginning. Prospects must be shown to need the product, to be able to pay for it, and to be in a position to make, or at least contribute to, the buying decision. Determining that conditions such as these are met is called **qualifying** the prospect. Another part of the qualifying process is determining whether the prospective buyer's order will be of sufficient size—that is, whether the account has an adequate sales potential.

QUALIFYING

In sales, evaluating a prospect's potential. Key questions are whether the prospect needs the product, can pay for it, and has the authority to make, or at least contribute to, a decision to buy.

On the basis of the qualification process, a potential customer may be assigned to a qualified group, a nonqualified group, or a group falling somewhere in between. Thus, careful consideration of a prospect may lead to the conclusion that the prospect represents insufficient potential and should be eliminated from further attention, or that the prospect is worthy of close attention and a series of sales calls and presentations, or that the prospect is worth a phone call or two but not a full presentation. Care must be taken to assure that a highly qualified prospect is not relegated to the wrong category because of inadequate investigation.

Another important fact to be learned through qualifying is what member of an organization should be contacted. Who has the authority to make the purchase decision? Who else strongly influences the purchase decision? A plant superintendent may be a "boss," but calling only on the superintendent is the wrong tactic if the vice president makes all the buying decisions. The process of qualifying is difficult and may require considerable tact and effort.

DISCUSSION CONSIDERATION

Salespeople tend to wear dark-colored suits—navy, black, or gray. Recalling that we typically form initial impressions within the first three minutes of meeting a person, generate a list of items that should create favorable impressions during a sales call (for example, laptop computer, briefcase).

Qualifying is sometimes called the *preapproach*. That is because the information gained in this step, especially information about the prospect's requirements, lays the foundation for planning the other steps in the selling process, including the next step, the approach itself.

## Step Two: The Approach

APPROACH

The step in the creative selling process wherein the salesperson makes initial contact and establishes rapport with the prospect.

The **approach** involves making an initial contact and establishing rapport with the prospect. If the prospect is already familiar with the salesperson and the company, the approach may be as simple as making a telephone call to request an appointment or knocking on the prospect's door with a friendly greeting. In other situations, the salesperson may have to be more creative in obtaining an appointment with the prospect or getting past the prospect's secretary.

ALTERNATIVE EXAMPLE
Maria Bayne is a senior consultant at Johnson & Higgins, an insurance broker and risk management consulting firm. Before each sales call, she explores the client's business—not only its insurance needs but also its management style and culture. "If they're involved in TQM, I read up on it; if they follow Stephen Covey's recommendations, I brush up on his writings. Then I use key words and expressions in my presentation. This really pays off." SOURCE: Nancy Arnott, "It's a Woman's World," *Sales and Marketing Management,* January 1995, p. 54.

The salesperson may approach the prospect by mentioning an offer that can benefit the prospect. What better way to persuade a prospect to grant time for a sales presentation than to offer a benefit that will save money for the customer, make products offered by the company more attractive to buyers, or add prestige to the customer's good name?

The approach is intended to make a good impression and to solidify the prospect's willingness to listen to the sales presentation. Effective sales personnel recognize that making a good impression during the first few seconds of the approach is important. Experience is a great helper in this matter, but research and caution can serve the seller well, too. For example, smoking a cigar or cigarette in a nonsmoker's office may lose a sale before the presentation has even begun. Not wearing a hard hat in a location where protective gear is required may make the salesperson appear too unfamiliar with a situation in which he or she is supposedly going to solve a client's problem. The importance of making a "good impression" should not be underestimated.

The best way for a salesperson to build a creative sales approach is to do some homework on the prospect, gathering specific information about the prospect's needs for the products being offered. Once these needs are identified, they can provide the basis for effective personal communication by phone, letter, or direct personal contact.

## FOCUS ON TRENDS

### *F. D. Titus & Son*

To deliver service anywhere, anytime, companies are turning to instant-access machines such as the personal communicator—a hand-held, mobile device that is a combination pen-based computer, cellular phone, fax machine, pager, electronic agenda, and e-mail box. This everything machine bridges distances of space and time and enables users to stay in touch with customers in distant locations at any hour of the day or night.

F. D. Titus & Son, a distributor of medical supplies, has equipped its entire 144-member sales staff with AT&T's EO 880 personal communicator. With the tap of their fingertips, sales reps have ready access to information about the 14,000 products in the company catalogue, and they can send a fax to a customer when stalled in freeway traffic. Says sales representative Don Durben: "Having everything you need to service customers in one place is a whole new way of working. Before, I had to carry around a book with the customer's history, our thick catalogue, and my agenda. Now I have everything in one place, and I can answer a customer's questions on the spot." ■

## Step Three: The Sales Presentation

**SALES PRESENTATION**
The step in the creative selling process wherein the salesperson attempts to persuasively communicate the product's benefits and to explain appropriate courses of action.

The **sales presentation** is the salesperson's attempt to persuasively communicate the product's benefits and to explain appropriate courses of action to the potential buyer. Typically, effective presentations tell the product "story."

The presentation begins by focusing the prospect's attention on the story. Some salespeople do this by producing a physical object, such as the product itself (if it is both portable and eye-catching), a model of the product, or something that relates to the product in an interesting or even humorous way. It is more common, however, to have an opening statement designed to attract attention. Thus, opening lines such as "I'm here to show you how we can save $5,000 a week in your factory" and "I've got a computer networking system that everyone in your organization will consider user-friendly" are frequently encountered.

After focusing the prospect's attention, the salesperson must generate interest in the product being offered. An opening comment that the salesperson can save the client a great deal of money in income taxes may gain attention, but it must be fol-

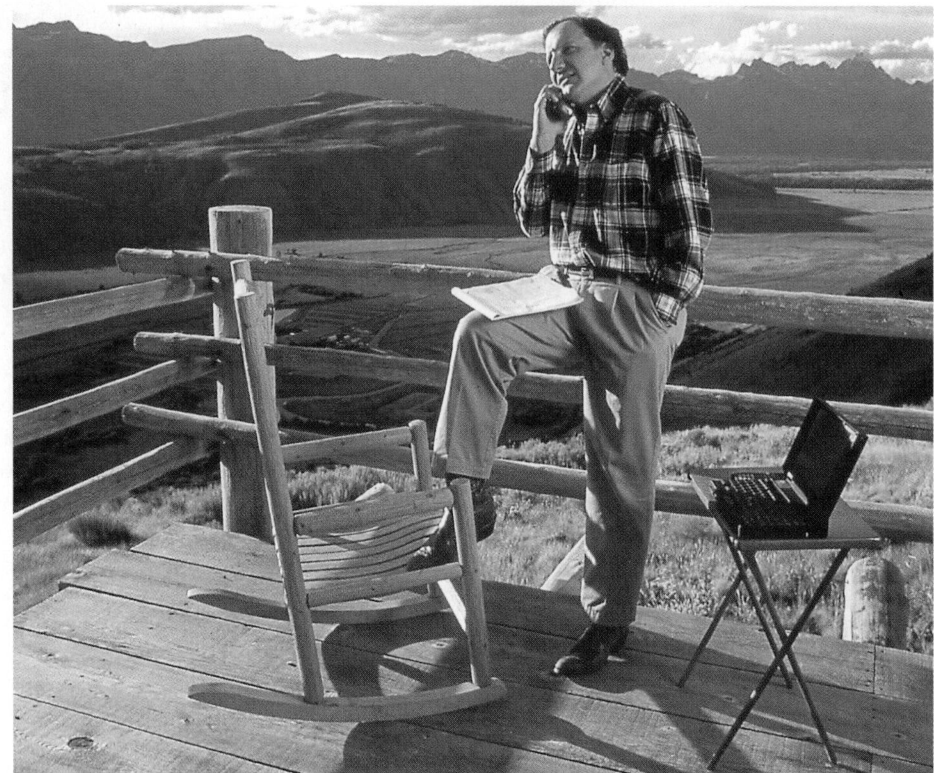

The communication revolution has freed sales representatives from the office. Computers have enormously increased the amount of information a salesperson can gather about his or her customers. With cellular phones, fax machines, portable computers, and information systems, a sales representative can tap into company data bases and transmit information from any remote location.

ALTERNATIVE EXAMPLE

Sales representatives for Toshiba American Medical Systems would find it difficult to fit CT and MRI scanners in their sample case. To solve this problem, Toshiba developed laptop-based interactive presentation featuring elaborate 3-D animations, high-resolution scans, and video clips of the products in operation, as well as testimonials from satisfied customers and architectural schematics showing the exact space requirements of the machines. SOURCE: Robert Lindstrom, "Training Hits the Road," *Sales and Marketing Management*, June 1995, p. 10.

lowed by the development of interest in the product being sold as the means to save the money. Describing the product's benefits in an interesting way, explaining how it works, or demonstrating its use can all be part of an effective presentation.

Arousing interest in the product itself is still not enough to make a sale. A desire to purchase the product must also be generated. A scale model of an executive jet plane may be interesting, but it is of little use if it does not help bring about a desire to own the plane itself.

In assembling effective sales presentations, the salesperson may find the inclusion of visual aids such as flip charts, slide presentations, and sound and video recordings an effective way to illustrate a product's benefits. In recent years, some salespeople have come to rely on computers in their presentations. They either operate portable, laptop units at the place of presentation or offer computer-generated data that answer the customer's "what if" questions. For example, representatives of an industrial robotics firm may bring a laptop computer into the prospect's office, ask for information such as production schedules, delivery requirements, and so on, and enter that information into the computer. Within minutes, the computer can yield output that shows exactly how the salesperson's product will affect the prospect's business operations.

It should be noted that some of the communication in the sales presentation may not be verbal. Many successful salespeople use body language, seating arrangements, and clothing colors to communicate important nonverbal messages to their clients.

DISCUSSION CONSIDERATION

Generate a list of nonverbal communication signals that indicate a negative response. Consider a mother trying to keep a child from harm, a manager providing feedback to an employee, a police officer controlling a crowd, and a customer rejecting an offer.

## Step Four: Handling Objections

In most sales presentations, the salesperson does not make a one-way presentation while the customer passively listens. The customer, no matter how friendly or interested in the product, may have reservations about committing money or other

COMPETITIVE STRATEGY: WHAT WENT RIGHT?

## SOQ NOP

The senior regional sales manager from John Deere was wearing an odd tie tack. It was in the shape of a cross. The vertical letters spelled out DEERE, the horizontal SOQ NOP. When asked what the letters stood for, his reply was "Sell on quality, not on price." He added, "It's my toughest job, in down markets, to make my own people realize that the objective is to sell the benefits, not just resort to price. I tell them a story. I was going after a sale some years ago. It came down to two final contenders. The fellow making the buy called me in to give me one last chance. His message in a nutshell: 'You're just too high on the price side. No hard feelings, and we hope we can do business with you again in the future.' I was about to walk out the door, unhappy to say the least. Then I had an inspiration. I turned and said, 'Those are nice-looking boots you've got on.' He was a bit surprised, but said, 'Thanks,' and he went on to talk for a minute or so about those fine boots, what was unique about the leather, why they were practical as well as fine. I said to him, at the end of this description. 'How come you buy those boots and not just a pair off the shelf in an Army-Navy store?' It must have taken twenty seconds for the grin to spread all the way across his face. 'The sale is yours,' he said, and he got up and came around his desk and gave me a hearty handshake."

resources in a purchase agreement. Questions or strong objections are likely to arise. Because objections explain reasons for resisting or postponing purchase, the salesperson should listen and learn from them.

Indeed, the sales call should be a dialogue or conversation in which objections may frequently arise. It is undesirable to have the prospect sit quietly until the end of the talk and then say "No" without any explanation. Effective salespeople encourage prospects to voice reasons why they are resisting the purchase. Even though the well-prepared sales presentation covers such topics as the quality of the product, the reputation of the seller, postsale services, and the like, the objection or question tells the salesperson which point is most important to the customer.

Occasionally, such points are almost a surprise to the salesperson. For example, a representative of a pest-control company may launch into a lengthy discourse on company reputation and demonstrate the product by poisoning a bug right before the prospect's eyes. It may take an objection to discover that the prospect is quite willing to buy the exterminator's service but is concerned that neighbors will see the pest-killer's truck parked in front of the house or place of business. In such a case, the salesperson might respond by promising to have a nonuniformed exterminator drive to the client's location in an unmarked truck. Such a response is a means of **handling objections.**

**HANDLING OBJECTIONS**
The steop in the creative selling process wherein the salesperson responds to questions or reservations expressed by the prospect.

There are many ways to handle objections. When an objection indicates that the prospect has failed to fully understand some point that was made, the salesperson can explain the area of uncertainty. A question about a product characteristic may mean that the prospect has not grasped how the product works or seen the benefits it can provide. A salesperson who encounters an objection of this type can provide additional persuasive information, clarify the sales presentation, or offer the basic argument for the product in a different manner.

Objections can also be turned into counterarguments by experienced sales representatives. A stockbroker might say, "You are right, Dr. Williams. The price of this stock has dropped 50 percent in the last six months. That is exactly why I am recommending it to you. At this low price, it is now underpriced and is an excellent buy in the opinion of our analysts."[4]

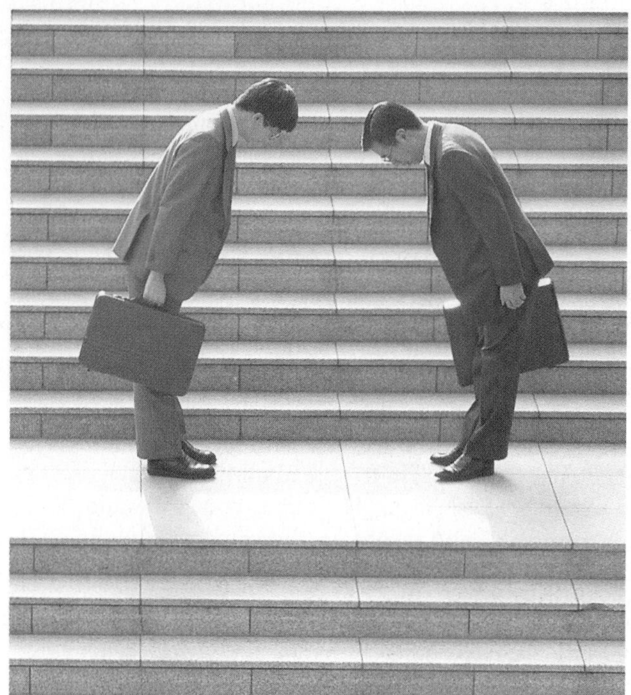

Salespeople should be aware of nonverbal communication. This is especially true in international sales, where nonverbal communication can take on unfamiliar meanings because of cultural differences. A navy blue suit is inappropriate for sales presentations in Hong Kong, for example, because it signifies mourning.

One tactic for handling objections, then, is to agree with the prospect, as did the stockbroker mentioned above, accepting the objection with reservation. This is consistent with the marketing concept's prescription to sell the product from the customer's point of view. The salesperson's counterargument is intended to refute the objection: "Yes, that is true, but this is also the case." The purpose of this method of dealing with objections is to avoid getting into an argument with the prospect. If the customer says the price is high and the salesperson says it is low, the discussion goes nowhere fast. But if the salesperson responds, "Yes, it is priced higher than many, but our product's quality is higher than the competitor's, so you get more for your money," the salesperson has agreed and counterargued at the same time. More importantly, the seller has given a reason for the higher price. Another approach to a price objection is described in the accompanying Competitive Strategy feature.

The prospect's questions, objections, and other comments may reveal how close the prospect is to making a purchase decision. Good salespeople use such clues to determine whether they should attempt to enter the closing stages of the sales presentation.

## Step Five: Closing the Sale

Ultimately, salespeople must make the sale. In selling, the term **closing** indicates that the sale is being brought to a finish. The main advantage of personal selling over other forms of promotion is that the salesperson is in a position to conclude negotiations by actually asking for an order.

**CLOSING**
The step in the creative selling process wherein the salesperson attempts to obtain a commitment to buy from the prospect.

Unfortunately, many salespeople are knowledgeable and convincing when making sales presentations, but they never get around to asking for the order. Sometimes this is due to the presenter's genuine belief in the product being offered—a belief so strong that he or she can barely stop talking about it. In other cases, worry about receiving a negative answer or misreading the client's willingness to deal may be the cause.[5] In any case, there comes a point when the presentation must be drawn to its logical conclusion.

Because closing the sale is so vital, experienced sales personnel constantly try to read prospects' reactions to the presentation for signs that a conclusion is in order. Signs revealing that prospects are ready to buy are called **closing signals.** For example, a comment such as "These new machines should reduce the number of breakdowns we've been having" may indicate a readiness to purchase. Should a signal like this occur, the sales representative should quickly respond and ask for the prospect's signature on the order.

**CLOSING SIGNAL**
A sign from the prospect revealing that he or she is ready to buy.

When the prospect's willingness to close is not clearly revealed, the salesperson may utilize what is called the **trial close.** A trial close is a tactic intended to draw from the prospect information that will signal whether a sale is imminent. For example, the salesperson may attempt to focus the conversation on closing the sale by asking which model the customer prefers. If the customer indicates a preference in a positive way, the sale may almost be made. If the customer is unable to decide, or if he or she

**TRIAL CLOSE**
A personal selling tactic intended to elicit from a prospect a signal indicating whether he or she is ready to buy.

outlook; earnings; related occupations; and sources of additional information. On a sheet of paper, write down five things that you were surprised to find out. On the same sheet of paper, write down five things that were about what you expected. Bring your lists to class for discussion.

# PART SIX

# Pricing Strategy

Everything is worth what its purchasers will pay for it.

SYRUS

CHAPTER

# 19 Introduction to Pricing Concepts

## LEARNING OBJECTIVES

After you have studied this chapter, you will be able to:

1. Define *price* and discuss it.
2. Tell how price interacts with the rest of the marketing mix.
3. Analyze price's place in our economy.
4. Outline the fundamentals of pricing strategy.
5. Characterize the relationship between price and organizational objectives.
6. Relate the demand in a target market to the prices charged.
7. Understand that demand and cost considerations influence pricing.
8. Differentiate among price elasticity, price inelasticity, and price cross-elasticity.

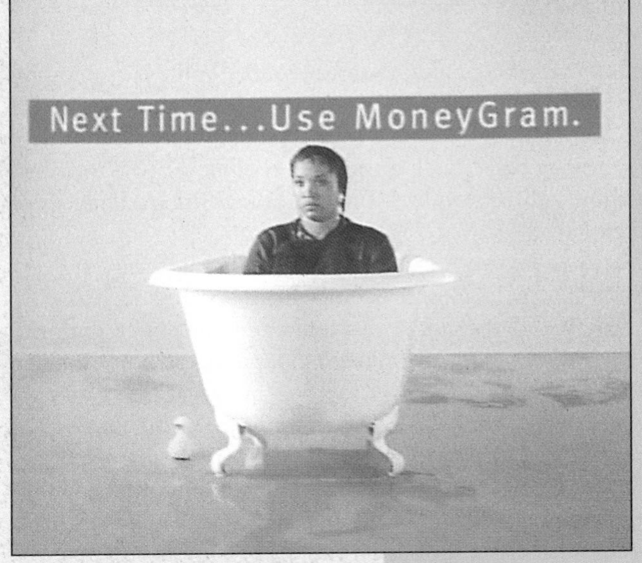
Next Time...Use MoneyGram.

Long before there was an information superhighway, long before the emergence of the Internet, long before a sojourn in cyberspace, there was Western Union.

The financial services company, which pioneered mass telegram service and has long been synonymous with wiring money, is one of the oldest and remains one of the strongest brand names in the world despite recent financial woes. Now, its power is about to be put to the test in the opening salvo of what could become a money-transfer price war.

A brash competitor, the MoneyGram money wiring service, began a major television and radio advertising campaign in November 1994, proclaiming that sending money through its service is significantly cheaper. The MoneyGram ads attacked Western Union with sarcastic humor. In one ad, a fully dressed woman was sitting in a bathtub. As she was doused with gallons of water, the voiceover said, "Still using Western Union to wire money? Next time, go to MoneyGram and save up to 19 bucks. Because taking one bath a day is enough."

Using a competitive promotional pricing strategy, the MoneyGram service charged customers $10 to wire as much as $300, instead of its usual $18 rate; Western Union charged $29. This price effort is the most aggressive since the MoneyGram service was created in 1988.

MoneyGram is currently owned by American Express and managed by First Data, a New Jersey company. Ownership will pass to First Data in April 1997.

First Data is not just any rival. It is the most pesky of adversaries, a spurned suitor. In September 1994, First Data was one of three companies bidding for Western Union, which had filed for protection against creditors in U.S. Bankruptcy Court in Newark, New Jersey. First Data bid $1.13 billion, but First Financial Management emerged as the winner.

"We felt our businesses would have been a good fit," says Rob Ayers, First Data's senior vice president of marketing. "But since we couldn't come to an agreement, we felt a price-comparison campaign was the best way to get our message across."

The money-transfer business may not be glamorous—many who use it live in low-income urban areas and don't have bank accounts—but it does generate an impressive amount of business. Each year, $6 billion to $8 billion is wired, and that represents $500 million to $600 million in combined revenues for Western Union and the MoneyGram service.

**ALTERNATIVE EXAMPLE**

An advertisement for GM's Electro-Motive division in a railroad trade magazine shows a locomotive (engine car) upside-down. The headline reads: "You could lose $40,000 a year waiting for an old locomotive to die a natural death." The message explains that, although the price of a new locomotive is high, older locomotives built before 1980 are not as fuel efficient as today's models. In addition to the fact that new models will outperform the old models, GM offers a great trade-in allowance. GM says the new locomotive will pay for itself. This pricing strategy recognizes what the demand is for locomotives and the role that costs play in pricing and buying decisions.

Price, as the story about the money-transfer business illustrates, plays a major role in the marketing mix. A lower price can be a means to enter a market or to gain a competitive advantage. A proper price can make the difference between success and failure.

This chapter focuses on the nature of price as a marketing mix variable and the role of price in our economy. The chapter provides a framework by examining the fundamental concepts underlying pricing strategy. It shows the interrelationship between overall organizational and marketing objectives and the organization's pricing objectives. In doing this, it addresses target market considerations, supply and demand, price elasticity, and the nature of costs.

## What Is Price?

**VALUE**
The power of one product to attract another product in an exchange.

**BARTER**
The exchange of products without the use of money.

As we have seen, marketing involves exchanging things of value. **Value** is a quantitative measure of the power one good or service has to attract another good or service in an exchange. An auto mechanic could exchange four tuneups for two months of coffee and doughnuts from a nearby diner. Such a trade is possible because the tune-ups, the coffee, and the doughnuts all have value. When products are exchanged for one another, the trade is called **barter.**[1]

While it would be possible to value every product in the world in terms of every other product, such a system would be complicated and unwieldy. It is far easier to express these many values in terms of the single variable of money. Price is thus a statement of value, because it is the amount of money or other consideration given in exchange for a product.

Price has many names. These names vary according to tradition or the interests of the seller. For example, *rent, fee,* and *donation* are terms used in specific exchange situations to describe price. Some sellers avoid using the word *price* in order to make what is offered for sale appear to be of a quality that price cannot fully describe. Thus, the student pays tuition, not a price, for education. The commuter pays a toll. The professor who gives an off-campus speech "accepts an honorarium." The physician charges a fee for professional services. Universities, governments, professors, and doctors all sell their services for a price, no matter what that price is called.

In brief, marketing involves exchanges of things that have value. The name most commonly used to describe this value is *price.* In the United States, it is most commonly expressed in dollars and cents.

## Price As a Marketing Mix Variable

**POINT TO EMPHASIZE**
Competitors can meet price changes quickly, too. Thus, price is a weak competitive weapon, at least in the short term, when competitors can meet it. In the long term, a price advantage built on a cost structure lower than the competition's may lead to a sustainable competitive advantage.

**LIST PRICE**
The basic price quote, before adjustment.

Price has a special significance in that it ultimately "pays" for all of the firm's activities. Because sales revenue equals price times unit sales volume, the price of a product is one of the prime determinants of sales revenues. If a price can be increased while unit volume and costs remain the same, revenues and profits will be increased. For this reason alone, pricing decisions are important. But price is important for another reason. It, like other marketing mix variables, influences unit sales volume. Thus, proper pricing of a product is expected to increase the quantity demanded. Price is perhaps the most flexible element of the marketing mix because it can be changed rapidly in response to changes in the environment.[2]

In setting prices, many marketers start with a basic price quote called a **list price.** Price adjustments can be made when the season changes, when a buyer makes a large-quantity purchase, or for another reason. Many marketers adjust list price with discounts or rebates. For example, retailers often mark down, or reduce, the list price when merchandise is out of season or moving slowly.

A list price functions as a communications tool by adding symbolic value to a good or service and by helping to position the brand in relation to competitors. A high price may suggest a high-status good, a low price may suggest a bargain, and a discount coupon or rebate may be used to encourage purchases by people who would otherwise not buy the product. Entire positioning strategies may revolve around price. For example, Tiffany's, a chain of exclusive jewelry stores maintains an image of the highest quality by stocking reliable products and providing special services and also by charging comparatively high prices. Wal-Mart and Price Club stress bargains and must therefore keep prices at the lowest levels.

**DISCUSSION CONSIDERATION**
Ask students whether they believe that a higher price is indicative of a higher-quality product. Have students cite examples of products for which they believe this relationship true and examples of products for which they do not believe it true.

Price is closely related to other marketing variables and cannot be discussed without simultaneous consideration of product, place, and promotion. Pricing strategies must be consistent with the firm's other marketing mix decisions and must support

CASE 19–1

## Pearl Jam

Pearl Jam is the intense Seattle-based band that has become the top rock act in the country.

Ticketmaster is the colossus of American ticket brokers, a tough, aggressive computerized service that sells more than $1 billion in sports and entertainment tickets annually.

A bitter fight between the band and the ticket service has now landed in the U.S. Department of Justice and the outcome could change the way tickets to major events are priced and sold.

Pearl Jam believes rock concert tickets are often too expensive, priced so high that many of the youngsters who most ardently support the music can't afford to buy them. Top prices for rock concerts have broken the $100 barrier in some venues, and it is common for concertgoers across the country to shell out $25 to $50 per ticket. The price includes the face value of the ticket and a service charge for the ticketing agency that issues it.

Pearl Jam, which has a strong teenage following, has wanted to keep the total cost of its tickets below $20. The band members, fabulously rich now, remember what it was like just a few years ago when they were broke. They empathize with the 50 percent or so of their fans who earn less than $12,000 a year. They don't think those fans should be frozen out of Pearl Jam concerts. So the band proposed that its concert ticket sell for $18 plus a 10 percent service charge.

That was a problem. A $1.80 service charge is well below the average for concert tickets. Such charges often run $6 to $10 each, and sometimes higher. The service charge for a $350 Barbra Streisand ticket was $18.

Ticketmaster, to put it delicately, did not find Pearl Jam's proposal congenial.

Pearl Jam tried to find other ways to distribute its tickets but that is not so easy. In 1991 the Justice Department scrutinized and then gave the green light to a deal in which Ticketmaster purchased the contracts of its only viable competitor, Ticketron. Since then, according to Steven Holley, a lawyer for Pearl Jam, Ticketmaster has dominated the field, becoming the only national distribution service that handles rock concerts.

The fight between Pearl Jam and Ticketmaster escalated. Pearl Jam argued that greed is what keeps service charges high. The group noted that promoters and concert halls get a portion of the service-charge revenues, and thus there is no incentive to lower the charges. Ticketmaster has said it wants to compromise, but Pearl Jam won't negotiate its demands.

Then Pearl Jam dropped a bomb. It charged in a memorandum filed with the Antitrust Division of the Justice Department that it had to cancel its summer tour because of a group boycott organized by Ticketmaster. According to Pearl Jam's complaint, members of a national association of top concert promoters, prompted by Ticketmaster, refused to deal with Pearl Jam as long as the band stuck to its demand for a $1.80 service charge.

The memorandum also charged that Ticketmaster, because of its lack of competition and its exclusive contracts with nearly all of the major promoters, has a virtual monopoly on the national distribution of tickets to rock concerts. According to Pearl Jam, there is no reasonable alternative to doing business with Ticketmaster.

[In March 1994,] Ben Liss, executive director of the North American Concert Promoters Association, told his members in a memo that Fredric D. Rosen, president and chief executive officer of Ticketmaster, "intends to take a very strong stand on this issue." Mr. Liss urged his members "to be very careful about entering into a conflicting agreement which could expose you to a lawsuit."

A spokeswoman for the Justice Department said, "We are investigating possible anti-competitive practices in the ticket distribution industry." She did not specifically name Ticketmaster and would give no details of the investigation.

Ticketmaster has vigorously denied all of Pearl Jam's allegations. "Our perspective is that we are being victimized by the band," said Ned Goldstein, the company's general counsel. He especially denied that Ticketmaster had engaged in any monopolistic practices.

When asked if there were any other nationwide ticket distribution services that handled rock concerts, Mr. Goldstein replied, "I don't know that that's the point."

## QUESTIONS

1. How important is price in a person's decision to attend a Pearl Jam concert?
2. How do the forces of supply and demand operate when the product is a rock concert?
3. In your opinion, is Ticketmaster violating antitrust laws?

CHAPTER

# 20 Pricing Strategies and Tactics

## LEARNING OBJECTIVES

After you have studied this chapter, you will be able to:

1. Identify the various pricing strategies.
2. Discuss the nature of differential pricing strategies.
3. Describe skimming and penetration pricing.
4. Show how competition affects pricing activity.
5. Discuss the effects of inflation on pricing.
6. Discuss the nature of product-line pricing strategies.
7. Explain some of the psychological aspects of price.
8. Show how geography influences pricing decisions.
9. Discuss such pricing tools as list price and cash, trade, quantity, and other discounts.
10. Describe the major legal restrictions on pricing freedom.
11. Identify major ethical issues related to price.

# Information Technology: Insights and Exercises

If one of the following exercises or addresses does not seem to work, please check the West Publishing World Wide Web (WWW) address listed below. Updates and other information will be provided at this address as necessary. To reach the West Publishing WWW page with information about this book, use your Web browser to go to:

**http://www.westpub.com/Educate/Educ.Supp.htm**
Under **Business** and **Marketing,** choose the appropriate monthly update for **Zikmund/d'Amico, Marketing, Fifth Edition**

If you want to start at the West Publishing WWW home page and navigate to the page containing information for this book, use your Web browser to go to:

**http://www.westpub.com**
Choose **Fast or Slow Connection**
Select **Products and Services**
Select **College and School Division**
Choose **Educational Publishing: College and School**
Select **College Publications**
Select **Educational Supplements and Updates for College Products**
Under **Business** and **Marketing,** choose the appropriate monthly update for **Zikmund/d'Amico, Marketing, Fifth Edition**

## E-Mail Exercise

Send an e-mail message to your marketing professor. In that message, explain why you think everybody at your school should be required to take at least one marketing class. (It's OK to be creative.)

## Gopher Exercise

Catalog shopping has become even easier with the use of the Internet. Consumers like on-line catalogs because they can compare prices among many resellers or vendors. Companies like on-line catalogs because they can adjust their prices quickly at a very low cost. To see a sample of catalog shopping on the Internet, use Gopher to go to:

**pccatalog.peed.com**
Select the heading **What is PC Catalog?** and read about this Internet service
Go back and select **Browse PC Catalog's Product Listings**
Then select **PC Software**
Next select **Word Processing**

Compare prices on the word-processing products listed, and answer the following questions. Bring your answers to class for discussion

1. What is the lowest price listed for the latest version of MS Word for Windows? Who is the vendor?
2. What is the highest price listed for the same software? Who is the vendor?
3. What is the lowest price listed for the latest version of WordPerfect for Windows? Who is the vendor?
4. What is the highest price listed for the same software? Who is the vendor?

If any address is unobtainable, check the West Publishing World Wide Web address for updates: **http://www.westpub.com/Educate/Educ.Supp.htm**

5. Is the low-price vendor the same for both products? Are you surprised?
6. Are you surprised at the price differences among vendors? What possible reasons are there for the price differences you found?
7. Do you think that catalog marketers are more apt to use price competition or nonprice competition?
8. What evidence do you see of competitive pricing strategies? Product-line pricing strategies? Psychological and image pricing strategies? Distribution-based pricing strategies?
9. If you searched through the other product categories in the PC Catalog every week, would you expect to find any cases of cross-elasticity of demand? Explain.

## World Wide Web Exercise

In this unit, you learned a lot about pricing. You might be surprised to find out that even bands like Pearl Jam need to know a lot about pricing. Using your Web browser, do a Web search for information about Pearl Jam. When you find information about the band, search the Pearl Jam pages for articles that mention Ticketmaster. *Hint:* You may find the information under headings like "statement before Congress" or "article on Ticketmaster." What was the problem that Pearl Jam ran into? What did the group learn about pricing? Given what you have learned about pricing in this book, how would you respond to their complaints?

## Listserv Exercise

Now that you know more about pricing, are you curious whether you paid too much for this book? Send a message to the West Publishing listserv at:

**zikmund@westpub.com**

(Note: If you are not already a member of the listserv, see page 136 for instructions on how to subscribe, send messages, and unsubscribe to the listserv.) Include three things in your message:

1. The price you paid for this book.
2. Whether you bought the book new or used.
3. Where you purchased the book (from a friend, at the campus bookstore, at an off-campus bookstore, or the like).

Monitor other people's messages (listserv messages are often called postings) for one week. Write a one-page report that summarizes what you found out. Include a brief discussion of whether or not you paid a "fair" price for the book. Also include an estimate of the worth of your book now. *Hint:* Look back at the Syrus quotation at the beginning of Part VI of this book. "Everything is worth what its purchasers will pay for it." Also reread the section "What Is Price?" in Chapter 19.

## Careers and the Internet

Use your Web browser to go to the CareerMosaic home page at the following address:

**http://www.careermosaic.com/cm/**

Read through the information on the home page to see what is going on at CareerMosaic this month. Then select **College Connection** to get information on co-op opportunities, entry-level jobs, résumés, and the like. Select one of the companies on the list and find out what marketing-related employment opportunities are listed. If the company doesn't have any marketing jobs listed, select another company.

If any address is unobtainable, check the West Publishing World Wide Web address for updates: **http://www.westpub.com/Educate/Educ.Supp.htm**

1. What marketing jobs did you find available?
2. What advice did the company post to potential employees?

Go back to the CareerMosaic home page and select **Jobs Offered.** Read the directions for entering a job search. Then enter a search on something like **sales and marketing.** Submit your search and let the computer do the work. Read through some of the many job postings to see if any look interesting to you?

# Epilogue: A Closing Note

In the preface to this book, we said that marketing is a fascinating subject. Now that you are about to finish your first course in marketing, we hope you agree. Before we end this book, however, we must add some final comments.

As a marketing plan is being executed, and afterward, it is referred to as the *marketing program,* a term that embraces all of the activities associated with marketing research as well as implementation and control of the individual elements of the marketing mix. All of the elements of the marketing program must come together as a synchronized, integrated whole. The parts of the program are so tightly interrelated that any change in one area almost certainly affects all others. The goal is a unified program made up of pieces solidly put together.

An effective marketing program requires the proper implementation of new strategies and the effective execution of continuing strategies. As we mentioned in Chapter 2, execution requires organizing and coordinating people, resources, and activities. Staffing, directing, developing, and leading subordinates are major activities used in implementing plans. Properly executing these activities—that is, "doing things right"—can make the difference between success and failure. A marketing program has the greatest chance for success if the appropriate strategy is chosen and then is effectively executed. But the marketer is in for trouble if the proper strategy is selected and then is not properly executed. Clearly, even the best of marketing plans, if not well implemented, is likely to result in disappointment, if not failure.

Now that you have read this entire book it is important that you keep in mind that marketing success depends on the interaction of strategy and implementation. At this point it is also important for you to think about what you have learned from this textbook. We would like you to think about the big picture and try to put the many aspects of marketing all together. Listed below are just some of the important marketing themes and trends that you should remember if you are to be an effective marketer:

The primary emphasis of marketing involves an exchange process.

Marketing in our global economy requires understanding consumers and knowing how to satisfy them.

Listening to consumers and buyers, whether through marketing research or other means, is the way to discover opportunities.

Not all groups of customers are alike. Selecting target markets and positioning brands remains central to marketing management.

Marketers focus on building relationships with customers, suppliers, and distributors.

Satisfying customers while being socially responsible is possible.

Marketing organizations are increasingly focusing on core competencies to achieve competitive advantages.

A worldwide trend toward working with collaborators in strategic alliances has created many "virtual corporations."

Around the globe, new markets and new opportunities are constantly emerging. Marketers should use marketing research to keep abreast of these changes.

Rapid changes in information technology are transforming the nature of marketing. Data-based marketing and mass customization illustrate the magnitude of this trend.

A market position represents the way consumers perceive a brand relative to its competition.

The total product includes a broad spectrum of tangible and intangible benefits. Brand image is important.

The product life cycle influences most aspects of the marketing mix. It is an important planning tool.

Product innovation, product differentiation, and continuous quality improvement are vital to marketing success.

Product quality and value are defined by the customer.

Distribution is a means for delivering a standard of living to society.

Channels of distribution, especially retail institutions, are constantly evolving.

Distribution, especially logistics, should not be overlooked as a means to gain competitive advantage in our global economy.

Marketing communications are in the eye of the beholder.

Marketers should strive for integrated marketing communications within all media. New media are developing. The Internet is changing the way marketers communicate with customers.

Personal selling remains the most common form of promotion, but wireless communication of digital information has changed its face. Teamwork, especially cross-functional teamwork, is becoming increasingly important.

Prices have names like *fee, rent,* and *donation,* but they are always an expression of value.

Price and value are determined by many factors. Increasingly, the ability to produce around the globe has a dramatic impact on the nature of pricing.

We could go on and on. However, we hope we have communicated the notion that marketing involves a company and its ever-changing relationship with customers, collaborators, and competitors. Marketing is dynamic because it must change in response to activities operating within our society and the global economy.

We hope we have answered many of your questions about the nature of marketing. We know we have not answered them all. You now know that marketing is not a black-and-white area in which there is always one best strategy. There are many gray areas that require analysis, considerable experience and skill, and a touch of creativity. And because marketing is dynamic, yesterday's answers will not be suitable as our world changes.

If our book has instilled in you the desire to continue to ask questions about marketing, we have done our job. We sincerely hope you are a satisfied customer.

APPENDIX

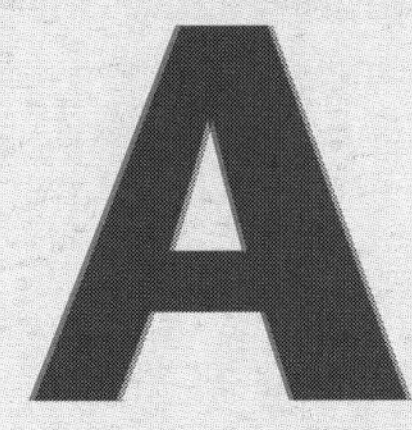

# Career Opportunities in Marketing

Marketing is a fascinating field. Students interested in a challenging career will find that it offers many opportunities that are hard to equal elsewhere. College students who have studied marketing provide a fresh source of talent for major corporations as well as smaller organizations. This appendix briefly discusses a variety of marketing careers and job opportunities and portrays some of the excitement of marketing. Of course, we cannot give a detailed portrait of marketing positions here. When you have read about the opportunities described in this appendix, you might begin to think about other marketing courses that will help you decide which marketing career most appeals to you.

## The Executive Level

We look first at the executive level. Consider Beth Culligan, a corporate executive. As a vice president at Sterling Drug, Inc.—one of only three women vice presidents in the company—Beth Culligan is leaping up the ladder of corporate America. But she'd rather not dwell on her experiences on the bottom rungs or what she expects at the top. To her, the only thing that matters is the task at hand.

Culligan joined Sterling to help analyze and set the company's worldwide strategy for all its over-the-counter products, from aspirin to acne creams. Sterling lured her away from Bristol-Myers, where she had been rising through the marketing ranks for 15 years.

It was her extensive experience with products like analgesics, as well as her ability to earn people's trust and respect, that made Culligan attractive to Sterling, says her boss, Robin Mills, vice president of strategic resources for over-the-counter medicines. "The world is becoming a smaller place, and global strategies are becoming more important," he says. "We knew that Beth would be good at getting each country, which sees itself as its own empire, to join onto a single team."

Helping to lead the over-the-counter division of the company in formulating strategy around the globe includes evaluating which countries Sterling's products should be sold in, what new drugs should be developed to fill open niches, and how the company can position itself to best advantage—clearly a big job. But Culligan says she thrives on challenge. For as long as she can remember, she says, she's had a can-do attitude.

Culligan's can-do approach helped her find career success at Bristol-Myers, which she joined as an entry-level marketing assistant straight out of St. Mary's College at Notre Dame, Indiana. "I discovered the challenge of marketing in my business courses there. When I graduated I knew that I wanted a marketing job at a large consumer-products company, and that I would get one." Six promotions later, she broke through the ranks to become vice president of marketing for new products.

When Sterling called, she says, she found the position too enticing to refuse. It was a chance for her to go beyond marketing and into the business at large—and international business at that.

Although there aren't yet many women at her level—at Sterling or elsewhere—Culligan is certain that she won't be the last. "There aren't a lot of women in senior management because they don't have enough experience," she says. While she believes that it's incumbent on corporations to offer women that experience, she also believes that it's within a woman's own power to put herself in an environment that recognizes and rewards good people, whatever their gender.[1]

Beth Culligan's profile illustrates that it takes experience to get to the executive level. Let's look at some jobs that provide marketing experience.

## Product and Brand Management

Often, top marketing executives in large companies are responsible for many brands. They frequently supervise other managers who are responsible for marketing activities associated with a single brand or a small family of products. The *brand managers,* sometimes called *product managers,* are typically middle-level managers. Such a manager may be viewed as the president of a "small company" operating within a larger organization. Philip Morris has a brand manager for Miller Genuine Draft Beer and another for Lite; Procter & Gamble has separate brand managers for Tide, Cheer, and Ivory Snow. The brand manager is a coordinator who orchestrates the activities of marketing research, packaging design, production scheduling, distribution and sales activities, and advertising. Assisting the brand manager may be an *assistant brand manager* or a *brand assistant.* To work within a brand group, a manager needs a sound knowledge of marketing management and good human relations skills.

## Retail Management

In recent years, retail competition has become increasingly vibrant. Effective marketing—that is, analyzing and filling customer needs—is necessary for retailers' survival and success.

A retailing career offers many opportunities. A hard-working college graduate willing to put in the time and effort necessary is virtually guaranteed advancement into such management positions as *buyer, department manager, branch manager,* and *store manager.*

A career in this field typically involves some sales training and sales work at the start. Retailing has traditionally had a reputation for low wages; however, although salaries of those in retail management training position may be less than salaries found in industrial sales or other fields, the salaries of managers can be quite high. One reason for this pattern is that, at the sales level, personnel turnover is high. Thus,

APPENDIX

# B The Marketing Audit

A **marketing audit** is a comprehensive appraisal of the organization's marketing activities. It involves a systematic assessment of marketing plans, objectives, strategies, programs, activities, organizational structure, and personnel. Such a thorough study of a marketing operation requires an objective attitude. Thinking about bank auditors, whose cautious care makes them hard to fool, provides good insight into the marketing audit process. A good marketing audit, therefore, is:

*Systematic* It follows a logical, predetermined framework—an orderly sequence of diagnostic steps.

*Comprehensive* It considers all factors affecting marketing performance, not just obvious trouble spots. Marketers can be fooled into addressing symptoms rather than underlying problems. A comprehensive audit can identify the real problems.

*Independent* To ensure objectivity, outside consultants may prepare the marketing audit. Using outsiders may not be necessary, but having an objective auditor is essential.

*Periodic* Many organizations schedule regular marketing audits, because marketing operates in a dynamic environment.

Managers often describe the audit process as costly, complex, and upsetting to organizations and individuals. This is because the audit emphasizes not only what is being done but why it is being done; it evaluates both current tactics and past strategies. Ideally, the audit should stress correcting procedures rather than assigning blame to individuals. Organizations that conduct regularly scheduled marketing audits can avoid problems by pointing out that the process is scheduled from time to time and is not aimed at criticizing an individual or a part of the organization.

Marketing audits typically begin with a meeting between the organization's officers and the people who are to conduct the audit. They decide on the audit's objectives, report format, timing, and other matters. A typical audit consists of numerous sections, as shown in Exhibit B–1.

**EXHIBIT B–1** Sample of Items from a Marketing Audit

*Environment*
How are environmental trends monitored?
What population trends are expected to affect existing and planned strategy?
What social and psychological patterns (attitudes, lifestyle, etc.) are expected to affect buyer behavior patterns?
How are present and pending legal developments affecting your operation?
What are the effects of competitors (their products, services, technologies) on your operation?
What other environmental opportunities and threats seem likely?

*Objectives*
Are the marketing objectives of your department consistent with overall company objectives?
Should these objectives be altered to fit changing environmental variables?
Are objectives consistent with one another?
How do objectives relate to marketing strengths and market opportunities?

*Strategy*
What is the relationship between objectives and strategies?
Are resources sufficient to implement the strategies?
What are the company's strengths?
What are the company's weaknesses?
How do you compare your strategies with those of competitors?

*Product Decisions*
How are new products developed within your business unit?
How are existing products evaluated?
How are products phased out of the line?

*Pricing Decisions*
How are pricing decisions made?
How do pricing decisions reflect the influences of competitors and the concerns of channel members?

*Distribution Decisions*
How are channel members selected, evaluated, and dropped if necessary?
How are channel members motivated?
How are decisions to modify channel structures reached?

*Promotion Decisions*
How are promotion mix decisions made?
How are salespeople selected, monitored, and evaluated?
How are payoffs associated with promotional efforts estimated?

*Market Information*
How is marketing research information transmitted to, and used within, the business unit?
Is a global information system in place?

*Activities and Tasks*
How are tasks scheduled, described, and planned? How are the responsibilities of individuals determined?
What spans of supervision, reporting relationships, and communication patterns exist? How are they evaluated?

*Personnel*
What level of competence has been attained by personnel in each position?
Are remedies to problems being planned in case they are needed? What are they?
What is the state of morale? Motivation? What are present plans in these areas?
Describe the career development paths. Are replacements for personnel in key positions being groomed?

Note: This list of items is intended to represent matters typically treated in a marketing audit. It is not intended to be a complete checklist.

APPENDIX

C

# Organizing the Marketing Function

Organizing the marketing function consists of assigning tasks, grouping tasks into organizational units, and allocating resources to organizational units. This activity determines the structure of the marketing organization and assigns responsibilities for the implementation of marketing activities.

Organizational design emphasizes the efficient allocation of marketing personnel and other resources. Each organizational structure has advantages and difficulties, but all provide ways to assign authority and responsibility for marketing activities to individuals and divisions within the total organization.

## The Marketing Era Organization

The marketing concept mandates two major features of the marketing organization. One is that the entire organization or the strategic business unit (if SBUs are identified) should clearly identify some person responsible for managing all marketing activities. This manager holds a title such as vice president of marketing. The second feature is the concentration of all marketing subfunctions under the direction of the primary marketing officer.

All firms can make use of the marketing concept's organizational prescription: assigning marketing responsibilities to a single executive and placing all marketing subfunctions under the control of that person. Yet each organization, especially if it is diversified, will be faced with the problem of refining its organizational structure to fit individual circumstances. Experience has shown that many types of organizational structures are well suited to marketing operations. We discuss some of them here.

### The Functional Organization

Marketing is divisible into many specific functions, or areas of specialization. It makes sense to consider organizing marketing activities around such functions or activities as sales, advertising, marketing research, and so on. The type of organization that results is the functional organization.

A functional organization is considered appropriate for small companies with centralized operations and for some larger firms, if their marketing operations are not complex. However, for firms, especially large ones, serving multiple market segments with many products and brands, this form of organization can lead to coordination problems.

### Organization by Product Type

Organizations that produce a wide variety of products often find it best to organize marketing activities around those products. The major rubber producers, for example, typically focus one set of managers and efforts on the sale of standard automobile tires and another on the sale of off-the-road tires—the huge tires used for construction vehicles, tractors, and the like. Still another group of managers works with specialty tires for racing, motorcycles, and other specific uses. Belts, gaskets, and other products are handled by yet another part of the firm. The product-based organization allows product or brand managers to concern themselves with a relatively small number of products or brands. This is especially efficient when managers must have extensive knowledge of technical, industrial products.

### Organization by Market

Another form of organization involves a market manager who is responsible for administering all marketing activities (forecasting, product planning, pricing, and so on) that relate to a particular market. In this context, *market* is typically defined as a customer group (industry) or product application. A manufacturer of forklift trucks might sell to grocery wholesalers, but also to steel mills, and perhaps even to firms engaged in pulpwood logging. Because these types of customers clearly differ in what they expect from the forklift manufacturer, an organizational structure built around varying customer needs may be appropriate. Differences in the marketing mix required for each customer group may be so great that it is most efficient to have separate market managers, each with considerable knowledge about customer needs in a specific industry. Organization by market, or customer type, is most efficient when the strategic business unit has a single or dominant product line and divergent customer types that are readily identifiable.

### Geography-Based and Combination Organizations

In more complex marketing operations—those active in numerous markets, those marketing numerous and varied products, or both—marketing activity may become decentralized and may be divided by geographic region. This is often the case with sales territories. In addition, entire strategic business units may be based on geographical decentralization. Geography-based organizations are used by companies that market to customer groups whose needs vary significantly from one geographic area to another. For example, Ford Motor Company has a North American division, a European division, a Latin American division, and so on.

There often is a certain amount of overlap among functional, product-based, market-based, and geography-based organizations. Usually, all factors—product mixes, customer needs, geography, marketing functions—are considered. Thus, the organizational model followed by many companies is that of the combination organization.

## Organizing for New Product Development

New product development is a key to long-term success in the marketplace. Therefore, the organization must be structured to permit and encourage innovation. However, many organizations are constructed around the day-to-day chores needed to keep operations moving smoothly and successfully in existing marketing areas.

In many cases, product managers or market managers are responsible for new product development. Product managers, for example, may be considered by their organizations to be extremely knowledgeable individuals who are well placed to detect market opportunities, to identify or conceptualize appropriate additions to product lines, and to evaluate the chances of success or failure for new product offerings. It is easy to see the disadvantages in this arrangement, however. Product managers, as specialists, may be unlikely to develop product ideas outside their limited areas of specialization. They may be concerned that new products will undermine their established products. Product managers may be so busy safeguarding current success that they have no time for new product development. It can also be argued that the abilities needed to manage an existing product or brand are not necessarily those appropriate for developing new product ideas. Furthermore, although individual product managers are responsible for the product's or brand's success, they rarely have authority over many of the individuals with whom they must work. Managers of sales and other marketing functions do not report directly to the brand or product category manager. Thus, brand managers must rely on the cooperation of the sales manager and sales force, because they do not have direct authority over these individuals or their activities.

Managers in each functional area understandably concentrate on meeting immediate objectives and solving current problems. Despite the fact that everyone knows forecasting the future is important, current problems can easily blot the future from view. Individual managers may defend this situation with the observation that if today's problems are not solved, there will not be any future. Although there is an element of truth in this statement, long-range survival of an organization requires that long-range problems be solved. The organizations that enjoy the most success in new product introductions are the ones that have given the greatest care to organizing for developing those products. Many organizational forms have been designed in an effort to encourage the smooth development and introduction of new products.

## The Venture Team

The venture team is a group of specialists in the various functional areas of the organization who are intended to operate in an entrepreneurial environment. Team members are freed from their daily organizational responsibilities. The team is supposed to develop a new business—a new venture—without operating as a closely controlled part of the whole organization. The team plays an independent role, therefore, in developing a new product, as well as in testing and commercialization. If the new product, or new business, is brought into full commercialization, the team members may be assigned to manage it. This assignment, as well as financial bonuses tied to the venture's success, may serve as a significant reward for team members.

## The New Products Department

A new products department, unlike a venture team, is a permanent department within an organization, headed by a director or even a vice president. Under this system, a high-ranking organizational official has clear-cut responsibility for new products and, by virtue of the position, can deal with other important executives as an equal. Furthermore, because the new product manager or director is a high-level officer dealing directly with the chief executive officer, he or she can expedite matters related to product development.

The new product manager is most likely to be found in a consumer goods company confronting a market in which marketing issues (rather than production or technical problems) predominate. New product managers are expected to be creative people who understand the unique problems of introducing new products to the market. The new product manager is a specialist in activities such as concept testing and test marketing.

In general, new products departments work in one of two ways. The department may be fairly large and have its own research staff and other experts, or it may be small and call on people from other areas of the corporation as needed. Once a new product has reached the commercialization stage, in either type of organization, responsibility for the new product is turned over to the regular departments of the firm, perhaps with the new products department maintaining some coordinating role. Another difference from the venture team approach is evident here: the venture team often maintains full responsibility for the new product or business.

## The New Products Committee

A new products committee is a group similar to any other committee. Usually, the heads of the organization's functional departments constitute the committee membership, and the chair is the chief executive officer. The committee also includes the new products director or other officer directly involved in such matters. New products committees create and review new product policies, assign priorities to various new product options, evaluate progress, and ultimately decide whether to commercialize new products. In fact, new products committees are frequently used in connection with other new product management formats, such as new products departments. The committee can help new products departments or new products managers with its input into the decision-making process. Most important, however, the new products committee puts the weight of its high-ranking, executive membership behind new product plans.

## The Task Force

Task forces are used in new product development situations much as they are used in government. A group whose membership spans numerous groups within the organization, typically the functional departments, is created. This task force ensures that a specific new project gets the support and resources that the various departments are able to offer. Unlike the new products committee, which is a continuing group, the task force is disbanded at project completion. Task force members also differ from the venture group because they handle task force duties in addition to their usual assignments. However, a few members are sometimes given leaves of absence from their regular jobs to devote their full attention to the task until it is completed.

APPENDIX

# Marketing Arithmetic for Business Analysis

The marketing concept stresses profitability as well as consumer orientation. To achieve this aim and to accomplish other marketing objectives, which are often stated in financial terms, marketing managers need to know how to evaluate an organization's financial success. To do this, they must understand the operating statement and certain performance ratios from a marketing perspective.

## The Profit and Loss Statement

Every manager needs to be able to interpret whether the organization or an organizational segment (strategic business unit, department, product line, or the like) is making a profit or contributing to profits. The basic equation for profit is:

Profit = Sales − Costs

The **profit and loss statement,** or **operating statement,** identifies an organization's sales revenues and costs over a given period—typically a year, quarter, or month. This statement allows a marketer to determine which elements are most strongly associated with profits or losses.

Exhibit D–1 shows a profit and loss statement for a retailer. The first item, **gross sales,** represents all sales revenues—that is, the total dollar amount the organization receives for the sale of its products. Retailers often refund money for returned goods or make allowances for damaged goods or for other reasons. These **returns** and **allowances** are subtracted to yield **net sales.**

Once net sales have been determined, costs are subtracted. In Exhibit D–1, the basic equation of profit = sales − costs is presented in greater detail:

| | |
|---|---|
| Net sales | $707,500 |
| Less cost of goods sold | 340,000 |
| Gross margin (gross profit) | 367,500 |
| Less operating expenses | 325,500 |
| Net profit | $42,000 |

**EXHIBIT D–1** Profit and Loss Statement for a Retailer

| PROFIT AND LOSS STATEMENT | | | |
|---|---|---|---|
| Gross sales | | | $730,500 |
| Less returns | $15,200 | | |
| Less allowances | 7,800 | | |
| Total | | $23,000 | |
| Net sales | | | $707,500 |
| Less cost of goods sold | | 340,000 | |
| Gross margin (gross profit) | | | $367,500 |
| Less operating expenses: | | | |
| Marketing expenses | | | |
| Advertising | $53,000 | | |
| Sales salaries | 89,000 | | |
| Delivery | 18,000 | | |
| Total | | $160,000 | |
| Administrative Expenses | | | |
| Office salaries | $102,000 | | |
| Office supplies | 9,600 | | |
| Miscellaneous | 4,500 | | |
| Total | | $116,100 | |
| General expenses | | | |
| Rent | $43,000 | | |
| Miscellaneous | 6,400 | | |
| Total | | 49,400 | |
| Total operating expenses | | $325,500 | |
| Net profit before taxes | | | $42,000 |

The **cost of goods sold** is the dollar amount the organization spends to purchase (or, if the organization is a manufacturer, to produce) the merchandise it sells. The **gross margin** is the difference between net sales and cost of goods sold. It represents the gross profit available to cover operating expenses. The **operating expenses** include salaries, rent, and all other costs associated with operating the business. Subtracting these from gross margin gives **net profit.** Net profit is often referred to as the "bottom line," because all costs have been deducted from net sales and no more calculations are necessary to determine profit or loss.

Many items in the profit and loss statement can be presented in greater detail. For example, our statement has only a single line representing costs of goods sold. However, if the retailer wishes to show the relationship between the beginning and ending inventory for the time period represented in the statement, the entry may appear as follows:

| | |
|---|---|
| Beginning inventory | $100,000 |
| New purchases | 400,000 |
| Total goods handled | 500,000 |
| Ending inventory | 160,000 |
| Total cost of goods sold | $340,000 |

Here, new purchases are added to the beginning inventory to derive total goods handled. Subtracting ending inventory from total goods handled indicates the total cost of goods sold as it appears on the profit and loss statement in Exhibit D–1.

## Marketing Analysis and Performance Ratios

Managers often use profit and loss statements from previous periods as benchmarks for evaluating marketing performance. In this process, they scrutinize differences between periods to identify actions that may improve performance. Many organizations forecast future profit and loss in statements called **pro forma profit and loss statements.** Actual performance may later be compared with these forecasted (or budgeted) amounts.

Changes in profit and loss statements and other aspects of an organization's operations are often evaluated by use of performance ratios. These analytical ratios depict items on the profit and loss statement as percentages of net sales, profits, or some other line item. Many organizations compare their performance ratios with their industry's ratios or with another company's ratios to supplement comparisons with their own past performance.

Performance ratios that use information from the profit and loss statement include the gross margin percentage, net profit percentage, operating expense ratio, returns and allowances percentage, and stock turnover ratio. We calculate each of these below with figures from Exhibit D–1.

The **gross margin percentage** is the percentage of revenues available to cover expenses and provide a profit after the cost of goods sold has been paid.

$$\text{Gross margin percentage} = \frac{\text{Gross margin}}{\text{Net sales}}$$

$$= \frac{\$367{,}500}{\$707{,}500}$$

$$= .52 \text{ or } 52 \text{ percent}$$

The **net profit percentage,** also called the **net income ratio,** identifies the percentage of profit from each sales dollar.

$$\text{Net profit percentage} = \frac{\text{Net profit}}{\text{Net sales}}$$

$$= \frac{\$42{,}000}{\$707{,}500}$$

$$= .06 \text{ or } 6 \text{ percent}$$

The **operating expenses ratio** is the percentage of operating expenses needed from each sales dollar.

$$\text{Operating expense ratio} = \frac{\text{Total operating expenses}}{\text{Net sales}}$$

$$= \frac{\$325{,}500}{\$707{,}500}$$

$$= .46 \text{ or } 46 \text{ percent}$$

Other cost-to-sales ratios, such as advertising expense to net sales and sales expense to net sales, can be calculated if greater detail is required.

The **returns and allowances percentage** indicates whether the percentage of sales volume being returned is large or small or if many allowances are being given.

$$\text{Returns and allowances percentage} = \frac{\text{Returns and allowances}}{\text{Net sales}}$$

$$= \frac{\$23{,}000}{\$707{,}500}$$

$$= .03 = 3\%$$

The **stock turnover ratio,** or **inventory turnover ratio,** indicates the number of times inventory (or, in our example, a retailer's stock) turns over (is sold) during the period specified in the profit and loss statement. Calculation of the stock turnover ratio requires two steps. The first is to determine the average inventory for the period.

$$\text{Average inventory} = \frac{\text{Beginning inventory} + \text{Ending inventory}}{2}$$

$$= \frac{\$100{,}000 + \$160{,}000}{2}$$

$$= \$130{,}000$$

Stock turnover is then determined in one of two ways: either by dividing sales by average inventory or by dividing cost of goods sold by average inventory.

$$\text{Stock turnover ratio at retail} = \frac{\text{Net sales}}{\text{Average inventory}}$$

$$= \frac{\$707{,}500}{\$130{,}000}$$

$$= 5.44 \text{ times per period}$$

$$\text{Stock turnover at cost} = \frac{\text{Cost of goods sold}}{\text{Average inventory}}$$

$$= \frac{\$340{,}000}{\$130{,}000}$$

$$= 2.62 \text{ times per period}$$

Turnover has an important influence on the return on investment (ROI) of many organizations, especially retailers and wholesalers. Grocery store pricing strategies, for example, recognize that a rapid turnover may generate a higher return on investment. Thus, a grocery store may have a profit margin of less than 2 percent, but if its stock turnover is high, it may still have a high return on investment.

## Return on Investment

*Return on investment* is the ratio of net profit to assets (or net worth) of an organizational segment (company, division, or the like), product line, or brand. It is a measure of financial efficiency that is often used to set marketing objectives. Calculating this ratio requires that net profit information be obtained from the profit and loss statement and that information about assets be obtained from the balance sheet. (An organization's **balance sheet** is a financial statement that reports, assets, liabilities, and net worth.) Suppose we looked at our retailer's balance sheet for the period of the profit and loss statement and found that it showed total assets of $425,000. The ROI percentage would be as follows:

$$\text{Return on investment} = \frac{\text{Net profit}}{\text{Total assets}}$$

$$= \frac{\$42{,}000}{\$425{,}000}$$

$$= .0988 \text{ or } 9.88 \text{ percent}$$

## Break-Even Calculations

Chapter 20 discusses the *break-even point,* the point at which costs and revenues meet, and shows a graphic means for deriving the break-even point. A computational formula is as follows.

$$\text{Break-even point} = \frac{\text{Fixed cost}}{\text{Selling price} - \text{Variable cost}}$$

Suppose a marketing manager faced the following situation.

| | |
|---|---|
| Selling price | \$10 |
| Variable cost | \$5 |
| Fixed cost | \$50,000 |

The break-even point would be calculated as follows.

$$\text{Break-even point} = \frac{\$50{,}000}{\$10 - \$5}$$

$$= \frac{\$50{,}000}{\$5}$$

$$= 10{,}000 \text{ units}$$

## Price Elasticity

In Chapter 19, *price elasticity* is defined as the effect of a change in price on the quantity of product demanded. To determine this quantity mathematically, we must calculate the ratio of the percentage change in quantity to the percentage change in price. Price elasticity is usually stated without regard to algebraic sign.

$$E = \frac{(Q_1 - Q_2)/Q_1}{(P_1 - P_2)/P_1}$$

Where:

$E$ = Elasticity
$Q_1$ = Initial quantity demanded
$Q_2$ = New quantity demanded
$P_1$ = Initial price
$P_2$ = New price

Suppose the initial price was \$5 and the initial quantity demanded was 100 units. If the price was raised to \$6 and the quantity demanded declined to 90 units, the elasticity would be as follows:

$$E = \frac{(100 - 90)/100}{(5 - 6)/5}$$

$$= \frac{10/100}{-1/5}$$

$$= \frac{.1}{-.2}$$

$$= -.5\text{, or simply } .5$$

Unitary elastic demand occurs when elasticity equals 1. If demand is elastic, *E* will be greater than 1. In our example, elasticity is .5, which is less than 1, indicating that demand is inelastic.

## Economic Order Quantity (E.O.Q.)

An organization considers several factors in deciding the order size at which total costs can be minimized. Annual demand in units, unit cost of placing an order, annual holding costs as a percentage of the cost of one unit, and cost of one unit in dollars can be weighed mathematically to determine the purchase order size yielding the lowest total cost of order processing and inventory holding. This is the economic order quantity, or E.O.Q.

To illustrate, assume the following:

| | |
|---|---|
| Buyer's annual demand | 5,000 units |
| Unit cost of the merchandise | $1.50 |
| Pre-unit holding costs (warehousing, insurance, etc.) | $1.30, or 20 percent of the unit cost |
| Cost of placing an order | $5.00 |

The E.O.Q. can be calculated with the following formula.

$$\text{E.O.Q.} = \sqrt{\frac{2 \times (\text{Annual demand in units} \times \text{Unit cost of placing an order})}{\text{Annual holding costs as percent of cost of one unit} \times \text{Cost of one unit in dollars}}}$$

In our example, this becomes:

$$\text{E.O.Q.} = \sqrt{\frac{2\ (5000 \times \$5)}{.20 \times \$1.50}} = \sqrt{\frac{2 \times \$25{,}0000}{\$.30}} = \sqrt{\frac{\$50{,}000}{\$.30}}$$

$$= \sqrt{166{,}666.66} = 408.25 \text{ units per order}$$

Showing the problem in tabular form requires some additional computations, as shown in Exhibit D–2.

## EXHIBIT D–2 Economic Ordering Quantity

| ORDER SIZE | AVERAGE INVENTORY[a] | HOLDING COSTS[b] | ORDERING COSTS[c] | TOTAL COSTS[d] |
|---|---|---|---|---|
| 50 | 25 | $ 7.50 | $500.00 | $507.50 |
| 150 | 75 | 22.50 | 166.66 | 189.16 |
| 250 | 125 | 37.50 | 100.00 | 137.50 |
| 300 | 150 | 45.00 | 83.33 | 128.33 |
| 350 | 175 | 52.50 | 71.43 | 123.93 |
| 400 | 200 | 60.00 | 62.50 | 122.50 |
| 407 | 203.5 | 61.05 | 61.43 | 122.48 |
| **408** | **204** | **61.20** | **61.27** | **122.47** |
| 409 | 204.5 | 61.36 | 61.13 | 122.49 |
| 420 | 210 | 63.00 | 59.52 | 122.52 |

NOTE: The figures shown in the table may also be shown on a graph. Such a portrayal would show clearly that as order size increases holding costs increase and that as order size increases the total cost of placing orders decreases. A graph would also show, of course, that the data combine to indicate an E.O.Q. of 408 (actually, 408.25) units.

[a]Average inventory $= \frac{\text{Beginning inventory (order size)} - \text{Ending inventory (O)}}{2} = 50\%$ order size

For example, with an order size of 50:

Average inventory $= \frac{50 - 0}{2} = 25$

[b]Holding costs = Average inventory × Cost per unit × Holding cost per unit (%)

For example, for an average inventory of 25, given the per unit costs in the text:

Holding costs = 25 × $1.50 × .20 = $7.50

[c]Ordering costs = Number of orders necessary × Cost of placing an order

For example, to obtain 5,000 units per year with an order size of 50 (requiring 100 orders), given the cost of placing an order as stated in text:

Ordering costs = 100 × $5 = $500

[d]Total cost = Holding costs + Ordering cost

For example, using the results in the preceding notes:

Total cost = $7.50 + $500.00 = $507.50

APPENDIX

# E Evaluating Marketing Performance

Effective marketing requires managerial control to ensure that planned activities are completed and properly executed. Thus, the first aspect of control is to establish acceptable performance standards. Control also requires investigation and evaluation of marketing performance. Investigation involves determining whether the activities necessary for the execution of the marketing plan are in fact being performed. Actual performance must then undergo analysis.

Analysis is the application of logic to data to determine consistent patterns and to summarize details. Analysis of marketing performance requires a careful comparison of preestablished performance standards, or results planned for a specific period of time, with the results actually achieved.

Even when planned results are achieved, analysis of marketing performance may indicate an opportunity to refine and adjust the marketing effort to attain greater success and cost efficiency in the future. For example, analysis may indicate that a company has too many customers for its resources. Most marketers would rather spend their resources on profitable, high-volume customers or on the customers whose purchases yield the highest profit margins. Analysis of sales and cost figures will permit managers to identify these attractive customers.

Marketing managers prefer that sales, accounting, and other performance information be subdivided into small segments under the control of one individual or organizational administration. Thus, the analysis of marketing performance often looks at a particular functional area or segment of marketing operations. This type of analysis might include singling out profitable territories and determining which accounts are the fastest growing, which accounts buy the newest products, how various means of transportation might improve service or lower costs, which sales districts have the greatest potential, and which advertising media deliver the most "bang for the buck."

whereby a firm's efforts are specialized and expended according to the business functions involved.

**Gap Analysis** The type of analysis marketers use to identify the sources of the expected service–perceived service gap.

**Gatekeeper** A group member who controls the flow of information to the decision maker; the buying-center role played by the organizational member who controls the flow of information related to the purchase.

**General Agreements on Tariffs and Trade (GATT)** A series of agreements reached by a number of trading nations around the world and intended to encourage international trade.

**General Line Wholesaler** Full-service merchant wholesaler that sells a large number of different product lines.

**General Mass Merchandiser** A retailer that sells a wide variety of products at discount prices.

**General Merchandise Wholesaler** Full-service merchant wholesaler that sells a large number of different product lines.

**General-specific-general Theory** Theory describing the development of retailing as a cyclic process in which general merchandisers are replaced by specialty merchandisers, which in turn are replaced by general merchandisers, and so on.

**Generic Brand** See *generic product.*

**Generic Demand** Demand for a product class as a whole, without regard to brand. Also called *primary demand.*

**Generic Name** A brand name so commonly used that it is part of the language and is used to describe a product class rather than a particular manufacturer's product.

**Generic Product** A product that carries neither a manufacturer nor a distributor brand. The goods are plainly packaged with stark lettering that simply lists the contents. Also called a *generic brand.*

**Geodemographic Segmentation** A type of market segmentation by which consumers are grouped according to demographic variables, such as income and age, as identified by a geographic variable, such as zip code.

**Geography-based Organization** An organizational structure in which the market area is divided into territories, and marketing efforts are specialized and expended by geographic area.

**Global Information System** An organized collection of telecommunications equipment, computer hardware, software, data, and personnel designed to capture, store, update, manipulate, analyze, and immediately display information about worldwide business activity.

**Globalization Strategy** A plan by which a marketer standardizes its marketing strategy around the world. Also called a standardization strategy.

**Green Marketing** Marketing products beneficial to the physical environment.

**Gross Domestic Product (GDP)** The total value of all the goods and services produced by capital and workers in a country.

**Gross Margin** Net sales minus cost of goods sold over a specified period. Also called *gross profit.*

**Gross Margin Percentage** The percentage of revenues available to cover expenses and provide a profit: gross margin/net sales.

**Gross National Product (GNP)** The total value of all the goods and services produced by a nation's citizens or corporations, regardless of location.

**Gross Profit** See gross margin.

**Gross Rating Point (GRP)** A unit of measure combining reach and frequency. GRP equals reach (in percentage points) times frequency.

**Gross Sales** Total sales over a specified period, before deduction of returns and allowances.

**Growth Stage** The stage in the product life cycle when sales increase at an accelerating rate.

**Handling Objections** The step in the creative selling process wherein the salesperson responds to questions or reservations expressed by the prospect.

**Head-to-head Competition** Positioning a product to occupy the same market position as a competitor.

**Horizontal Cooperative Promotion** An approach whereby channel members at the same level jointly sponsor particular promotions.

**Host** A computer through which smaller computers connected to it can access network services.

**Human Resources** The number and quality of an organization's employees.

**Hypermarket** A mass merchandise outlet featuring an especially large variety of products and an especially large size. Also called a superstore.

**Hypothesis** An unproven proposition that can be supported or refuted by marketing research. Research objectives are often stated as hypothesis.

**Idea Generation Stage** The stage in new product development that involves a continuing search for product ideas consistent with target market needs and the organization's objectives.

**Image Building** A promotional approach intended to communicate an image and generate consumer preference for a brand or product on the basis of symbolic value.

**Import** Foreign product purchased domestically.

**Import Quota** A limit set by a government on how much of a certain type of product can be imported into a country.

**Incentive** Something believed capable of satisfying a particular motive.

**Independent Retailer** A retail establishment that is not owned or controlled by any other organization.

**Indirect-action Advertisement** An advertisement designed to stimulate sales over the longer run.

**Indirect Cost** A cost that is not directly traceable to a particular segment of operation. Also called a *common cost.*

**Indirect Exporting** Exporting through an intermediary.

**Individual Brand** A brand assigned to a product within a product line that is not shared by other products in that line.

**Individual Factor** With reference to perception, a characteristic of a person that affects how the person perceives a stimulus.

**Industrial Buyer** An organization that purchases a product to use in the production of another good or service or in the operation of its business.

**Influencer** A group member who attempts to persuade the decision maker; the buying-center role played by organizational members (or outsiders) who affect the purchase decision by supplying advice or information.

**Infomercial** A television commercial, usually 30 minutes long, that has the appearance of a program.

**Information** Data in a format useful to decision makers.

**Information Search** An internal or external search for information carried out by the consumer to reduce uncertainty and provide a basis for evaluating alternatives.

**Innovator** A member of the first group of customers to buy a new product.

**Inseparability** A characteristic of services that reflects the fact that production often is not distinct from the consumption of a service.

**Inside Selling** Nonretail selling from the employer's place of business.

**Institutional Advertisement** An advertisement designed to promote an organizational image, stimulate generic demand for a product, or build goodwill for an industry.

**Intangibility** A characteristic of services referring to the customer's inability to see, hear, smell, feel, or taste the service product.

**Integrated Marketing Communications** Marketing communications in which all elements of the promotion mix are coordinated and systematically planned to be in harmony with each other.

**Intermodal Service** Service by which loaded truck trailers or other sealed containers are carried by rail, ships, or airplanes to destinations from which they can be moved by truck.

**Intensive Distribution** A distribution strategy aimed at obtaining maximum exposure for the product at the retail level or wholesale level.

**Internal Marketing** Marketing efforts aimed at a company's own employees.

**Internal Records and Reports System** System for collecting data inside an organization, such as shipping and accounting records; part of the organization's data collection system.

**International Department** An organizational unit that manages the firm's international marketing operations.

**International Franchising** A form of licensing in which a company establishes foreign franchises. Franchising involves a contractual agreement between a franchisor, often a manufacturer or wholesaler, and a franchisee, typically an independent retailer, by which the franchisee distributes the franchisor's product.

**International Marketing** See *multinational marketing*.

**Internet** A worldwide network of computers linked by phone lines that gives users access to information and documents from distant sources.

**Intrapreneurial Organization** An organization that encourages individuals to take risks and gives them the autonomy to develop new products as they see fit.

**Introduction Stage** The stage in the product life cycle when the new product is attempting to gain a foothold in the market.

**Inventory Control** The activities involved in decisions relating to inventory size, placement, and delivery.

**Inventory Turnover Ratio** See *stock turnover ratio*.

**Isolation Effect** An effect by which a product appears more attractive next to a higher-priced alternative than in isolation.

**Jingle** A song or other short verse used in an advertisement as a memory aid.

**Jobber** A wholesale intermediary in a channel of distribution for an organizational good.

**Joint Decision Making** Decision making shared by all or some members of a group. Often, one decision maker dominates the process. Decisions truly made jointly are syncratic decisions.

**Joint Ownership Venture** In international marketing, a joint venture in which domestic and foreign partners invest capital and share ownership and control.

**Joint Venturing** In international marketing, an arrangement between a domestic company and a foreign host company to set up production and marketing facilities in a foreign market.

**Judgment Sample** A nonprobability sample chosen according to the judgment and experience of the selector.

**Just-in-time (JIT) Inventory System** A materials management system in which inventory arrives just in time for use.

**Keystoning** Retailers' practice of doubling the wholesale price of an item and making this the regular retail price.

**Label** The paper or plastic sticker attached to a product that carries product information.

**Laboratory Experiment** An experiment in a highly controlled environment.

**Laggard** A member of the group of final adopters in the diffusion process.

**Lanham Act** A U.S. law declaring that brand names cannot be confusingly similar to registered trademarks.

**Late Majority** In the diffusion process, a group of consumers who purchase a product after the early majority, when it is no longer perceived as risky.

**Learning** Any change in behavior or cognition that results from experience or an interpretation of experience.

**Leased Department Retailer** An independent retailer that owns the merchandise stocked but leases floor space from another retailer and usually operates under that retailer's name.

**Legal Environment** Laws and regulations and their interpretation.

**Legitimate Power** Power based on legal agreement.

**Less-developed Country** A country in which small, low-technology companies may be developing but in which marketing mechanisms typically do not exist.

**License** A contractual arrangement by which a firm may use another firm's trademark.

**Licensing** In international marketing, an agreement by which a company (the licensor) permits a foreign company (the licensee) to set up a business in the foreign market using the licensor's manufacturing processes, patents, trademarks, trade secrets, and so on in exchange for payment of a fee or royalty.

**Lifestyle** An individual's activities, interests, opinions, and values as they affect his or her mode of living.

**Lifestyle Format** An advertising format that reflects a target market's lifestyle or hoped-for lifestyle.

**Limited-function Wholesaler** See *limited-service merchant wholesaler.*

**Limited-line Strategy** Product line strategy that entails offering a smaller number of variations than the full-line strategy.

**Limited Problem Solving** A level of decision making intermediate between routinized and extensive problem solving in which the consumer has some purchasing experience but is unfamiliar with stores, brands, or price options.

**Limited-service Merchant Wholesaler** Merchant wholesaler that offers less than full service and charges lower prices than a full-service merchant wholesaler. Also called a *limited-function wholesaler.*

**Line Extension** See *product line extension.*

**List Price** The basic price quote, before adjustment.

**Location-based Competition** Competition based on providing place utility by delivering the product where the consumer wants it.

**Logistics** The activities involved in moving raw materials and parts into the firm, in-process inventory through the firm, and finished goods out of the firm.

**Logo** A brand name or company name written in a distinctive way; short for logotype.

**Loss Leader** A product priced below cost to attract consumers, who may then make additional purchases.

**Macroenvironment** The broad societal forces that shape every business and nonprofit marketer. The physical environment, sociocultural forces, demographic forces, economic forces, scientific knowledge and technology, and political and legal forces are components of the macroenvironment.

**Macromarketing** The aggregate of marketing activities in an economy or the marketing system of a society, rather than the marketing activities in a single firm (micromarketing).

**Magnuson-Moss Warranty Act** Federal law requiring that guarantees provided by sellers be made available to buyers before purchase and that they specify who the warrantor is, what products or parts of products are covered, what the warrantor must do if the product is defective, how long the warranty applies, and the obligations of the buyer.

**Mail-order Wholesaler** A limited-service merchant wholesaler that uses catalogs, mail or telephone ordering, and mail delivery.

**Majority Fallacy** The error embodied by a marketing effort that blindly pursues the largest, or most easily identified, or most accessible market segment. The error lies in the fact that other marketers will be pursuing these same segments.

**Manufacturer Brand** A brand owned by the maker of the product. Also called a national brand.

**Manufacturers' Agent** Independent agent intermediary that represents a limited number of noncompeting suppliers in a limited geographical area. Also called a manufacturers' representative.

**Marginal Analysis** A method for determining the costs and revenues associated with the production and sale of each additional unit of a product.

**Marginal Approach** A method of setting a promotional budget whereby the marketer attempts to spend resources until additional expenditures would not be justified by the additional sales and profits they would generate.

**Marginal Cost** The net addition to a firm's total costs that results from the production of one additional unit of product.

**Marginal Revenue** The net addition to a firm's total revenue that results from the sale of one additional unit of product.

**Market** A group of potential customers that may want the product offered and that have the resources, the willingness, and the authority to purchase it.

**Market Development** The strategy by which an organization attempts to draw new customers to an existing product, most commonly by introducing the product in a new geographical area.

**Market-Driven Organization** See *market orientation.*

**Market Factor** A variable associated with sales that is analyzed in forecasting sales.

**Market Factor Index** A sales forecasting tool used in analyzing the association between sales and a number of other variables. Also called the market index.

**Marketing** The process of planning and executing the conception, pricing, promotion, and distribution of ideas, goods, and services to create exchanges that will satisfy individual and organizational objectives.

**Marketing Audit** A comprehensive review and appraisal of the total marketing operation; often performed by outside consultants or other unbiased personnel.

**Marketing Concept** The idea that organizations should focus on satisfying consumers' wants and needs. The marketing concept stresses consumer orientation, long-range profitability, and the integration of marketing and other organizational functions.

**Marketing Ethics** The principles that guide an organization's conduct and the values it expects to express in certain situations.

**Marketing Information System (MIS)** An organized set of procedures and methods by which pertinent, timely, and accurate information is continually gathered, sorted, analyzed, evaluated, stored, and distributed for use by marketing decision makers. Most such systems are computerized and consist of a data collection system and a decision support system.

**Marketing Intelligence System** A network of diverse sources that provide data about the marketing environment; part of an organization's data collection system.

**Marketing Management** The process of planning, executing, and controlling marketing activities to attain marketing goals and objectives effectively and efficiently.

**Marketing Mix** The specific combination of interrelated and interdependent marketing activities in which an organization engages to meet its objectives.

**Marketing Myopia** Failure to define organizational purpose from a broad consumer orientation.

**Marketing Objective** A statement about the level of performance the organization, SBU, or operating unit intends to achieve. Objectives define results in measurable terms.

**Marketing Opportunity Analysis** The interpretation of environmental attributes and change in light of the organization's ability to capitalize on potential opportunities.

**Marketing Organization** The part of an organization to which marketing responsibilities are assigned.

**Marketing Orientation** Organizational philosophy focused on learning consumers' needs and offering superior value.

**Marketing Plan** A written statement of the marketing objectives and strategies to be followed and the specific courses of action to be taken when (or if) certain events occur.

**Marketing Program** All of the activities associated with marketing research and the implementation and control of the individual elements of the marketing mix.

**Marketing Research** The systematic and objective process of generating information for use in marketing decision making.

**Marketing Research System** System for gathering new data to solve specific problems; part of an organization's data collection system.

**Marketing Strategy** A plan identifying what marketing goals and objectives will be pursued and how they will be achieved in the time available.

**Market Manager** An individual responsible for administering all marketing activities that relate to a particular market, including forecasting, product planning, and pricing.

**Market Orientation** Organizational philosophy that focuses on consumers' wants and needs.

**Market Penetration** The strategy by which sales of an established product grow because of increased use of the product by existing customers in existing markets.

**Market Position** The way consumers perceive a product relative to its competition. Also called competitive position.

**Market Potential** The upper limit of industry demand. That is, the expected sales volume for all brands of a particular product during a given period.

**Market/Product Matrix** A matrix containing the four possible combinations of old and new products with old and new markets. The purpose of the matrix is to broadly categorize alternative SBU opportunities in terms of basic strategies for growth.

**Market Segment** A portion of a larger market, identified according to some shared characteristic or characteristics. Dividing a heterogeneous market into segments is *market segmentation*.

**Market Segmentation** Dividing a heterogeneous market into segments.

**Market Share** The percentage of total industry sales accounted for by a particular firm, or the percentage of sales of a given product accounted for by a particular brand.

**Markup on Cost** A markup expressed as a percentage of the cost of an item.

**Markup on Selling Price** A markup expressed as a percentage of the selling price of an item.

**Mass Customization** A strategy that combines mass production with computers to produce customized products for small market segments.

**Mass Medium** An advertising medium, such as television, that reaches a broad audience that includes many market segments.

**Materials Handling** The physical handling and moving about of inventory.

**Materials Management** The activities involved in bringing raw materials and supplies to the point of production and moving in-process inventory through the firm.

**Maturity Stage** The stage in the product life cycle when sales increase at a decreasing rate.

**Media Schedule** A schedule identifying the exact media to be used and the dates on which advertisements are to appear. Also called a media plan.

**Media Selection Strategy** Strategy involving the determination of which media are most appropriate for an advertising campaign.

**Meeting-the-competition Strategy** A pricing strategy whereby an organization sets prices at levels equal to those of competitors.

**Membership Group** In reference to an individual, a group to which the individual belongs. If the individual has chosen to belong to the group, it is a voluntary membership group.

**Memory** The information-processing function involving the storage and retrieval of information.

**Merchant Intermediary** A channel intermediary such as a wholesaler or a retailer, that takes title to the product.

**Merchant Wholesaler** An independently owned wholesaling concern that takes title to the goods it distributes.

**Microenvironment** The environmental forces directly influencing a company, such as its customers and the economic institutions that shape the organization's marketing practices.

**Micromarketing** The marketing activities in a single firm, as opposed to macromarketing.

**Misleading Advertising** Advertising that, although not strictly untrue, leads consumers to less-than-accurate conclusions. Also called *deceptive advertising*. Intentionally misleading consumers is an extreme form of this type of

Martin, "Machine Dreams," *Brandweek*, April 26, 1993, pp. 17–22.

Focus on Trends box, p. 430: Information from Erin Flynn, "American Greeting Cards Creates a New Card Pitch," *Brandweek*, November 14, 1994, p. 24.

Competitive Strategy box, p. 434: Adapted with permission of Progressive Grocer from Stephen Bennett, "Natural Foods: A Fad No More," *Progressive Grocer*, May 1, 1994.

Competitive Strategy box, p. 436: Adapted with permission from Patricia Sellers, "Look Who Learned about Value," *Fortune*, October 18, 1993, pp. 75, 78; with updates from Andrew Serwer, "McDonald's Conquers the World," *Fortune*, October 17, 1994, pp. 103–117. © 1993, 1994 Time Inc. All rights reserved.

Focus on Quality box, p. 439: Adapted from "The New K-Mart Has the Last Laugh," *Adweek's Marketing Week*, February 24, 1992, p. 26. © ASM Communications, Inc. Used with permission from *Adweek*.

Focus on Quality box, p. 441: Excerpts reprinted with permission from Denise Grady, "The Sears, Roebuck of Science," *Discover*, September 1982, pp. 71–72. Denise Grady/ © 1982 Discover Magazine.

Video Case 13–1, p. 451: Adapted with permission from (1) James Fallon, "Getting Clubby with Costco in Britain," *Daily News Record*, December 3, 1993. Copyright Capital Cities Media Inc., 1993. (2) Arthur Markowitz, "Vote Set for Price/Costco Merger; Deal Will Fuel Expansion in U.S., Abroad," *Discount Store News*, October 18, 1993. Discount Store News, Food Merchandising, Copyright Lebhar-Friedman, Inc., 425 Park Avenue, New York, NY 10022.

## Chapter 14

Opening vignette, pp. 455–456: Adapted with permission from Ronald Henkoff, "Delivering the Goods: Logistics Has Become a Hot Competitive Advantage as the Companies Struggle to Get the Right Stuff to the Right Place at the Right Time," *Fortune*, November 11, 1994, pp. 64, 75, 76. © 1994 Time Inc. All rights reserved.

Focus on Relationships box, p. 461: Adapted with permission from Rahul Jacob, "Why Some Customers Are More Equal than Others," *Fortune*, September 19, 1994, p. 220. ©1994 Time Inc. All rights reserved.

Focus on Global Competition box, p. 463: Adapted with permission from Ronald Henkoff, "Delivering the Goods: Logistics Has Become a Hot Competitive Advantage as the Companies Struggle to Get the Right Stuff to the Right Place at the Right Time," *Fortune*, November 11, 1994, pp. 64, 75, 76. © 1994 Time Inc. All rights reserved.

Focus on Quality box, p. 464: Information from Barnaby J. Feder, "Formica: When a Household Name Becomes an Also-Ran," *New York Times*, August 12, 1990, p. F12.

Photo caption, p. 467: Adapted with permission from Rahul Jacob, "Why Some Customers Are More Equal than Others," *Fortune*, September 19, 1994, pp. 218. © 1994 Time Inc. All rights reserved.

Competitive Strategy box, p. 470: Adapted with permission from Martin Keller, "A Pet Project," *Express Magazine*, a publication of Federal Express Corporation, Winter 1990, pp. 6–7.

Case 14–1, p. 474: Reprinted by permission from Julie Candler, "Tracking All Trucks," *Nation's Business*, December 1994, pp. 60–61. Copyright 1994 U.S. Chamber of Commerce.

## Chapter 15

Opening vignette, pp. 483–484: Adapted with permission of Sales & Marketing Management magazine from Nancy Arnott, "Heating Up Sales," *Sales & Marketing Management*, June 1, 1994. Copyright 1994 Bill Communications.

Focus on Quality box, p. 486: Adapted from Kevin Goldman, "Coke Contours New Ads to Fit Cultural Icon of Shapely Bottle," *Wall Street Journal*, February 14, 1995, p. B6. Reprinted by permission of the *Wall Street Journal*, © 1995 Dow Jones & Company, Inc. All rights reserved worldwide.

Focus on Relationships box, p. 488: Adapted with permission from Mark D. Fefer, "Taking the Pain Out of Holding Patterns," *Fortune*, January 10, 1994, p. 20. © 1994 Time Inc. All rights reserved.

Competitive Strategy box, p. 495: Adapted with permission from Geoffrey Lee Martin, "Aussie Ad Probe Comes to a Boil over Dorf Ads," *Advertising Age*, February 20, 1995, p. I6. Copyright Crain Communications, Inc. All rights reserved.

Focus on Global Competition box, p. 501: Adapted from *The Borderless World* by Kenichi Ohmae, p. 26. © 1990 by McKinsey & Company, Inc. Reprinted by permission of HarperCollins Publishers Inc.

Photo caption, p. 504: Information from "Outback Steakhouse," *Advertising Age*, July 4, 1994, p. S19.

Competitive Strategy box, p. 508: Adapted with permission of Sales & Marketing magazine from Nancy Arnott, "The Grand Design," *Sales & Marketing Management*, June 1, 1994. Copyright 1994 Bill Communications.

Ethics Exercise 15, pp. 511–512: All but the questions at the end excerpted from Bruce Horovitz, "Statue of Liberty Tobacco Ad Ignites Firestorm," *USA Today*, April 27, 1995, p. B1.2. Copyright 1995, *USA Today*. Reprinted with permission.

## Chapter 16

Opening vignette, pp. 517–518: Reprinted with permission from Cathy Taylor, "Z Factor," *Brandweek*, February 6, 1994, IQ pp. 14–18. © ASM Communications, Inc.

Focus on Trends box, p. 527: Adapted with permission from Pat Sloan, "Fashion Gives Sex Another Try," *Advertising Age*, October 31, 1994, pp. 1, 8. Copyright Crain Communications, Inc. All rights reserved.

Competitive Strategy box, p. 533: Adapted with permission from "Sandstorm at Qantas," *Advertising Age*, November 8, 1993, p. 30. Copyright Crain Communications, Inc. All rights reserved.

Competitive Strategy box, p. 535: Excerpted from Craig Bloom, "Madison Avenue, Where Humor Can Get Some Respect: Translating Quintessential British Humor for Americans," *New York Times*, August 19, 1990, p. F5. © 1990 by The New York Times Company. Reprinted by permission.

Focus on Trends box, p. 539: First paragraph adapted with permission from Patricia Sellers, "The Best Way to Reach Your Buyers," *Fortune*, Autumn–Winter 1993, pp. 14, 16. © 1993 Time Inc. All rights reserved. Second paragraph adapted from Nicholas Negroponte, *Being Digital* (New York: Knopf, 1995), pp. 168–169.

Ethics Exercise 16, p. 549: Excerpted with permission of the author from Debbie Seaman, "Carpe Dyin'," *Advertising Age*, Special Creativity Insert, January or February 1991, pp. 8–9.

Video Case 16–1, pp. 551–552: We greatly appreciate the help of the professionals at Fallon McElligott, especially Mary Ann O'Brien, in the preparation of this case and the accompanying video. Some information in the case is from David M. Steward, "Twin Piques," *Advertising Age*, June 3, 1991, pp. 20C–25C; and some information and the quotation are from Joyce Rutter Kaye, "Group Therapy," *Advertising Age*, July 2, 1990, pp. S16–S17.

## Chapter 17

Opening vignette, pp. 555–556: Adapted from Kevin McManus, "Selling," pp. 48–56. Reprinted by permission from the October 1990 issue of *Changing Times Magazine*. Copyright © 1990 The Kiplinger Washington Editors, Inc.

Focus on Quality box, p. 563: Excerpted with permission from Jaclyn Fierman, "The Death and Rebirth of the Salesman," *Fortune*, July 25, 1994, pp. 86, 88. © 1994 Time Inc. All rights reserved.

Competitive Strategy box, p. 564: Excerpted with permission from Jaclyn Fierman, "The Death and Rebirth of the Salesman," *Fortune*, July 25, 1994, p. 86. © 1994 Time Inc. All rights reserved.

Focus on Trends box, p. 567: Excerpted with permission from Faye Rice, "The New Rules of Superlative Service," *Fortune*, September 22, 1993. © 1993 Time Inc. All rights reserved.

Photo caption, p. 568: Adapted with permission from Thomas A. Stewart, "Welcome to the Revolution," *Fortune*, December 13, 1993, pp. 66–67. © 1993 Time Inc. All rights reserved. (This material did not appear as a caption in the article.)

Competitive Strategy box, p. 569: Reprinted from Tom Peters and Nancy Austin, *A Passion for Excellence* (New York: Random House, 1985), p. 51.

Focus on Global Competition box, p. 571: Adapted from Franklin R. Root, *Entry Strategies for International Markets* (Lexington, Mass.: Lexington Books, 1987), pp. 252–255. See also John L. Graham, "The Influence of Culture on the Process of Business Negotiations: An Exploratory Study," *Journal of International Business Studies*, Spring 1985, pp. 81–96.

Competitive Strategy box, p. 573: Adapted from *The Borderless World* by Kenichi Ohmae, pp. 17–18. Copyright © 1990 by McKinsey & Company, Inc. Reprinted by permission of HarperCollins Publishers Inc.

## *Chapter 18*

Opening vignette, p. 589: Adapted with permission from Elaine Underwood, "U.S. Vintners Are Bearing Fruit with a Cultural, Culinary Approach," *Brandweek*, September 5, 1994, pp. 28–29. © ASM Communications, Inc.

Photo caption, p. 593: Adapted with permission from "Periodontist's Mail Order Smiles," ©*American Demographics*, February 1987. For subscription information, please call 800/828-1133.

Focus on Quality box, p. 597: Adapted with permission from Rayna Skolnik, "Portraits of the 'Most Admired' Companies: How Public Relations Helps Build Corporate Relationships," *Public Relations Journal*, May 1994. Copyright Public Relations Society of America 1994.

Competitive Strategy box, p. 601: Reprinted with permission from Chuck Stogel, "Chemical Bank Corporate Challenge," *Brandweek*, September 19, 1994, p. 43. © ASM Communications, Inc.

Competitive Strategy box, p. 603: Information from Michael Himowitz, "Pentium Flaw May Be More Important than Intel Says," *Tulsa World*, December 11, 1994, p. B10; Kevin Maney, "IBM Won't Sell PCs with Flawed Intel Chip," *USA Today*, December 13, 1994, p. 1A; "IBM Stops Pentium PC Shipments," Prodigy Interactive Personal Service, December 12, 1994; James G. Kimball, "Can Intel Repair Pentium PR?" *Advertising Age*, December 19, 1994, p. 36; James Kim, "Intel Puts Chips on the Table," *USA Today*, December 21, 1994, pp. B1–B2.

Photo caption, p. 604: Adapted with permission from Gerry Khermouch, "It's Miller Time around the World: NBA's International Expansion Should Boost Genuine Draft Beer," *Adweek Eastern Edition*, July 11, 1994. © ASM Communications, Inc. Used with permission from *Adweek*.

Focus on Trends box, p. 605: Excerpted with permission from Rahul Jacob, "Why Some Customers Are More Equal than Others," *Fortune*, September 19, 1994, p. 224. © 1994 Time Inc. All rights reserved.

Focus on Trends box, p. 606: Adapted with permission from Sam Whitmore, "Is Your Spin Doctor Ailing? Here's One Way to Find Out," *PC Week*, April 4, 1994. Copyright © 1994 Ziff-Davis Publishing Company.

Case 18–1, pp. 609–610: Excerpted with permission of the National Association of Criminal Defense Lawyers from Robert Shapiro, "Using the Media to Your Advantage," *The Champion*, January–February 1993, pp. 7+; as it appeared in "Robert Shapiro: O.J.'s Lawyer Tells How to Use Media," *USA Today*, August 1, 1994, p. 11A. Permission needed from the National Association of Criminal Defense Lawyers.

## *Chapter 19*

Opening vignette, p. 621: Adapted from Kevin Goldman, "A Telegram for Western Union: MoneyGram Wants Market Share," *Wall Street Journal*, November 25, 1994. Reprinted by permission of the *Wall Street Journal*, © 1994 Dow Jones & Company, Inc. All rights reserved worldwide.

Focus on Global Competition box, p. 636: Adapted with permission from Joel M. Ostrow, "Prices Soar at McDs," *Advertising Age*, November 12, 1990, p. 16. Copyright Crain Communications, Inc. All rights reserved.

Ethics Exercise 19, p. 640: Information from Jennifer Steinhauer, "Scholarships for the Genuinely Special," *New York Times*, October 30, 1994, p. E2.

Case 19–1, pp. 641–642: Reprinted from Bob Herbert, "Ticket Trust Busters," *New York Times*, June 5, 1994, p. E17. © 1994 by The New York Times Company. Reprinted by permission.

## *Chapter 20*

Opening vignette, pp. 645–646: Reprinted from Nina Munk, "'I'm Here to Sell!'" *Forbes*, June 19, 1995, pp. 48, 50. Reprinted by permission of *Forbes* magazine. © Forbes Inc., 1995.

Focus on Global Competition box, p. 649: Information from "Kodak Alleges Fuji Photo Is Dumping Color Photographic Paper in the U.S.," *Wall Street Journal*, September 1, 1993; Joan E. Rigdon, "Marketing and Media: Kodak Quietly Offers Film Discounts of 10% to 20% to Some Big Customers," *Wall Street Journal*, August 17, 1993; Gerry Khermouch, "Kodak Breaks with Past for Value Film Line," *Brandweek*, January 17, 1994, p. 1.

Focus on Quality box, p. 651: Adapted from Martha T. Moore, "Extra Value Pays Off," *USA Today*, November 24, 1993, p. 2B. Copyright 1993, *USA Today*. Reprinted with permission.

Focus on Relationships box, p. 655: Excerpted from R. Lee Sullivan, "School for Cheerleaders," *Forbes*, October 25, 1993, p. 118. Reprinted by permission of Forbes Magazine. © Forbes Inc., 1993.

Competitive Strategy box, p. 656: Excerpted from Steve Lohr, "Microsoft Raises the Ante in 'Suite Wars,'" *Austin American-Statesman*, October 18, 1993, p. D2. © 1993 by The New York Times Company. Reprinted by permission.

Case 20–1, p. 672: Excerpted from Joshua Levin and Seth Lubove, "Cash and Bury," *Forbes*, May 11, 1992, pp. 162–163. Reprinted by permission of Forbes magazine. © Forbes Inc., 1992.

Case 20–2, pp. 673–674: By Jon M. Hawes, University of Akron; and Cynthia Santucci, Ohio Edison. © copyright 1992 by Jon M. Hawes. Used with permission.

## *Video Cohesion Case*

Minnesota Twins (F)—The Strike, pp. 688–692: All but the last five paragraphs of this case are excerpted by permission of *The Sporting*

*News* from Steven P. Gietschier, "Baseball's Darkest Days," *Sporting News*, April 10, 1995, p. 31. The information about the aftermath of the strike is from Bob Klapisch, "Labor Pains? Thorny Issues Result from Unsettling end to the Strike," *Sporting News*, April 10, 1995, p. 30.

Minnesota Twins (G)—Pricing, pp. 692–694: The information and the quotation in the opening paragraph are from Ray Waddell, "Attendance Strong for American League, Blue Jays Post Record-Setting 4 Mil+," *Amusement Business*, November 29, 1993, p. 15. The information in the first paragraph under "Salary Costs" and the information about economic constraints near the end of the case is from Pete Williams, "Free Agents Abound, but Many Teams Looking to Cut Losses," *Baseball Weekly,* April 5, 1995, p. 3. The section about the Montreal Expos is excerpted from Deron Snyder, "Expos, Pirates Singing Small-Market Blues," *Baseball Weekly*, May 3, 1995; copyright 1995, *USA Today*; reprinted with permission. The quotations from Kirby Puckett are from "Frugality Could Cost Twins," *Baseball Weekly*, April 12, 1995, p. 13. The information and quotations in the section on promotions are from Ray Waddell, "Major, Minor Leagues Stretching to Give Fans More for the Money," *Amusement Business*, May 10, 1993, p. 5.

# Photo Credits

**3** Raoul Duffy, "Billboards at Trouville, 1906," Paris, Musee national d'Art moderne; **5** All photos by Advertising Age; **6** Photos courtesy of MTV, Hallmark, Keebler, The American Cancer Society, United Technologies, A. Schulman, Inc., and Rockwell; **8** Courtesy of Bandai America, Inc.; **9** Courtesy of Arizona Office of Tourism; **10** © Tony Stone Images/Don Smetzer; **11** Courtesy of Federal Express; **13** © Gary Malerba/LGI Photo Agency; **15** Courtesy of 1-800-FLOWERS; **20** Courtesy of Dutch Boy Paints; **35** © Ted Hardin; **37** © Ann Limongello; **39** Courtesy of Gerber; **41** Travelpix/FPG with the cooperation of Walt Disney Company; **43** Courtesy of General Electric; **46** Courtesy of Morton and Samsonite Italia; **52** © Visa U.S.A. Inc. 1996. All rights reserved. Reproduced with the permission of VISA U.S.A. Inc.; **54** © Carmine Filloramo; **69** Bob Kalmbach, Photo courtesy of the University of Michigan; **71** © Steve Elmore/The Stock Market; **73** Courtesy of Ben & Jerry's; **76** Courtesy of Pace Salsa; **78** © Tony Stone Images/Ed Honowitz; **81** © Telegraph Colour Library/FPG International Corp.; **82** © Jose L. Pelaez '93/The Stock Market; **84** Courtesy of Circle Ten Council, Boy Scouts of America; **86** © 1995/Comstock; **89** Courtesy of Netscape Corporation; **90** Courtesy of Panasonic; **94** © Tony Stone Worldwide; **96** © '93 Russell Munson/The Stock Market; **103** © Tony Stone Images/Don Smetzer; **107** © James Robinson; **108** © Tony Stone Images/ Andy Sacks; **110** Courtesy of Kentucky Fried Chicken Corporation (KFC); **112** Courtesy of American Honda Motor Co., Inc., Photo: Carl Furuda; **116** © Dewitt Jones/Allstock; **119** Courtesy of Sprint Corporation; **139** Erich Lessing/Art Resource, NY. Klimt, Gustav. Mrs. Adele Bloch-Bauer, 1907. Oesterreichische Galerie, Vienna, Austria; **141** Courtesy of the Southland Corporation; **145** © Tony Stone Images/Christopher Bissell; **153** Courtesy of Focus Suites; **171** © 1995 Alexander Mares-Manton; **175** Reprinted courtesy of the Wm. Wrigley Jr. Company; **177** Courtesy of Armstrong World Industries; **181** Matthew Lindroth/Courtesy of Giro Sport Design, Inc.; **182** © 1991 The Time Inc. Magazine Co.; **184** Courtesy of Evian; **185** Art Director: Paul Marciano, photographer: Dewey Nicks, Guess © 1995; **186** Courtesy of Ferrari; **191** Advertising Age/© Doug Goodman; **192** © Tom Wilson/FPG International Corp.; **196** ©Tony Stone Images/Andy Sacks; **205** © Tony Stone Images/Brian Blauser; **206** © Gary Moss; **210** Courtesy of AtoHaas North America; **213** Bruce Ayres/© Tony Stone Worldwide; **217** Courtesy of IBM Corporation; **218** Courtesy of Lear-jet; **221** Kristi Yamaguchi © 1995 National Fluid Milk Processor Promotion Board; **231** Reciente Perfect Rouge, Art Director: Masao Ota, Photographer: Noriaki Yokosuka, Designer: Naomi Yamamoto, Copyrighter: Tetsuro Kanegae; **233** Courtesy of Delta Airlines, Inc.; **235** Courtesy of Quaker State; **247** Courtesy of Levi Strauss & Co.; **249** Reprinted with permission of Nike, Inc.; **251** Courtesy of the Chrysler Corporation; **253** Courtesy of Gary Winter; **255** © 1994 Barry Lewis—Network/Matrix; **256** © Andy Freeberg; **260** DiGiorno is a registered trademark of Kraft General Foods, Inc., Reproduced with permission; **273** Henry Spencer Moore, *Large Interior Form.* On long-term loan to the Nelson-Atkins Museum of Art, Kansas City, Missouri, from the Hall Family Foundations; **275** Courtesy of Goodyear Tire & Rubber Co.; **276** © 1994/Comstock; **280** © 1990 Ed Wheeler/The Stock Market; **284** © Guy Aroch; **287** © Gilles Mingasson/The Gamma Liaison Network; **292** Courtesy of Xerox Corporation; **294** Courtesy of Minnesota Moose Hockey, created by Valentine Design & Marketing, Edina, MN; **297** Mary Herlehy, Advertising Age photographer; **307** © Alan Levenson '94; **310** Courtesy of 3M; **322** Courtesy of Sony; **323** Burton Team Rider Aleksi Vanninen, photograph by Jeff Curtes; **334** Courtesy of the Gillette Company; **335** Courtesy of Samsung; **339** Courtesy of PepsiCo Foods International; **351** Courtesy of Progressive Corporation; **353** Courtesy of Transamerica Corporation; **359** Courtesy of Samsung; **362** Courtesy of SKF Company; **365** © FPG International Corp.; **366** The Bettmann Archive; **367** Courtesy of Walter Thompson Co.-Chicago/Brookfield Zoo; **379** Tate Gallery, London/Art Resource, NY. Derain, Andre. The Pool of London (1906). (Copyright ARS, NY) Tate Gallery, London, Great Britain; **381** Dave Cannon/© Tony Stone Worldwide; **383** Archive Photos/Fotos International; **384** © 1991 L. Steinmark/Custom Medical Stock Photo; **386** © Richard Laird 1991/FPG International Corp.; **387** Courtesy of Wm. Atwood Lobster Company; **397** © Tony Stone Worldwide/Don Smetzer; **405** Courtesy of Samsung; **417** Courtesy of the Bombay Company; **418** © Valrie Massey 1995/Photo 20-20; **423** Courtesy of Rand McNally Map & Travel Stores; **427** Courtesy of 2Market; **429** Courtesy of the Internet Shopping Network; **430** Courtesy of COINSTAR, Inc.; **433** © David J. Sams/Texas Inprint; **437** Courtesy of Sears Roebuck and Co. 1993; **438** © Art Streiber/Time; **455** © Stephen Marks/Image Bank; **459** © Jeff Zaruba/The Stock Market; **463** © H. P. Merten 1994/The Stock Market; **467** Courtesy of 3M; **468** © '93 Jon Feingersh/The Stock Market; **481** Tate Gallery, London/Art Resource, NY. Lewis, Percy Wyndham. Workshop © copyright must be cleared. Tate Gallery, London, Great Britain; **483** Courtesy of Schott Glaswerke, Mainz, Germany; **484** Courtesy of Rollerblade, Inc.; **490** © 1995 Duomo/Rick Rickman; **492** © Sony; **497** Nautica International Inc.; **504** Courtesy of Outback Steakhouse; **506** Courtesy of Xerox; **509** Courtesy of Sietsema, Engel & Partners Advertising Agency; **517** Courtesy of Zima Beverage Company; **520** Courtesy of America's Dairy Farmers, Dairy Management Inc.; **524** Courtesy of Oshkosh B'Gosh; **526** Courtesy of Diner's Card International, Visa U.S.A., and MasterCard; **529** Courtesy of 3M Specialty Chemicals Division—Paper in Packaging Products, Ad agency; Kerker & Associates; **531** Courtesy of Steel Packaging Council. American Iron and Steel Institute; **532** Courtesy of Volvo Car UK Limited; **534** © 1994 Haggar Apparel Company; **538** Courtesy of *Men's Journal*; **551** Courtesy of Fallon McElligott and *Rolling Stone;* **555** © Tony Stone Images/Greg Pease; **557** © 1991 Don Mason/The Stock Market; **558** © Rob Lewine/ The Stock Market; **559** © 1995/Comstock; **561** © 1991 Tom Stewart/The Stock Market; **568** Ted Wood/Time Magzine; **570** © Tony Stone Images/Will & Deni McIntyre; **574** © 1992 Chuck Savage/The Stock Market; **588** Courtesy of Cakebread Cellars, Photographer: Terrence McCarthy; **593** © Tony Stone/Andrew Sacks; **594** Courtesy of Odor-Eaters; **596** S.S./Shooting Star; **598** © Mark Reinstein 1995/FPG International Corp.; **599** © Everett Collection; **600** © Archive Photos/Lawrence Siskind; **604** '87 Roy Morsch/The Stock Market; **611** Courtesy of Cascia Hall Preparatory School; **619** © Kevin Macpherson/The Image Bank; **621** Courtesy of Jerrold E. DeWitt/MoneyGram; **623** Courtesy of Samsung; **626** © Ken Biggs/ The Stock Market; **629** © 1994/Focus on Sports; **630** © Dean Siracusa/FPG International Corp.; **645** © Tony Stone Images/Bruce Ayres; **648** © Lee Kuhn 1992/The Stock Market; **657** © Tony Stone Images/Jess Stock; **661** © Cathy Blaivas; **664** Courtesy of Southwest Airlines.

# Name Index

# Company Index

## D

# E

# J



# K



# L

# T



# U

## V



## W



## X



## Z

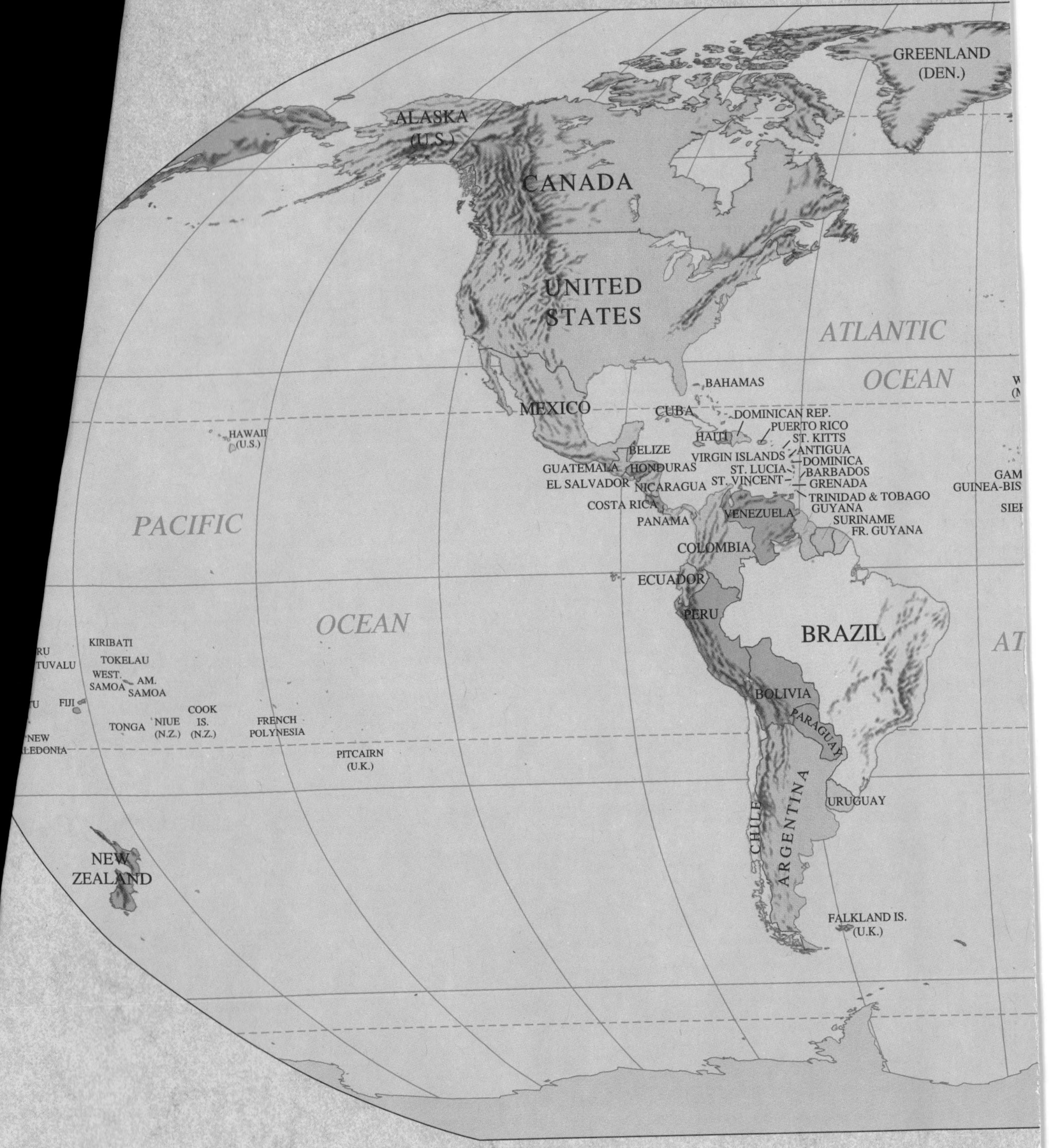

GREENLAND
(DEN.)
ALASKA
(U.S.)
CANADA
UNITED
STATES
ATLANTIC
OCEAN
BAHAMAS
MEXICO
CUBA
DOMINICAN REP.
PUERTO RICO
ST. KITTS
ANTIGUA
DOMINICA
BARBADOS
GRENADA
TRINIDAD & TOBAGO
GUYANA
SURINAME
FR. GUYANA
HAITI
VIRGIN ISLANDS
ST. LUCIA
ST. VINCENT
BELIZE
GUATEMALA
HONDURAS
EL SALVADOR
NICARAGUA
COSTA RICA
PANAMA
VENEZUELA
COLOMBIA
ECUADOR
PERU
BRAZIL
BOLIVIA
PARAGUAY
URUGUAY
CHILE
ARGENTINA
FALKLAND IS.
(U.K.)
HAWAII
(U.S.)
PACIFIC
OCEAN
KIRIBATI
TUVALU
TOKELAU
WEST.
SAMOA
AM.
SAMOA
FIJI
TONGA
NIUE
(N.Z.)
COOK
IS.
(N.Z.)
FRENCH
POLYNESIA
PITCAIRN
(U.K.)
NEW
ZEALAND
GUINEA-BIS

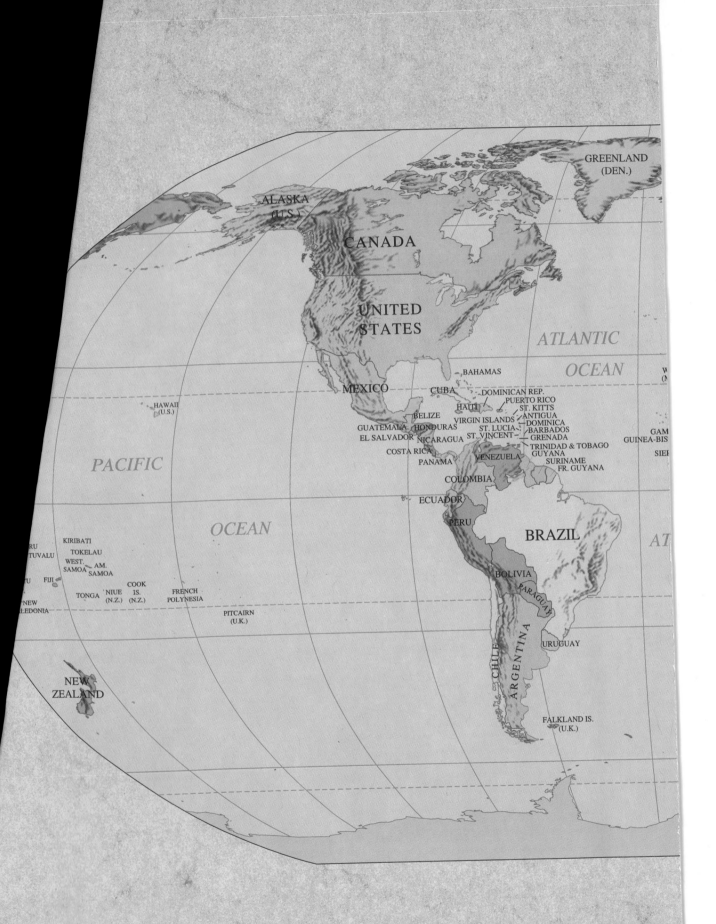

SOLOMON
ISLANDS